The Politics of Bureaucracy

On the fourth edition:

"This is a wonderful, encyclopaedic work of considerable merit and utility.... As the mostly widely used book in this area, it remains peerless."

Nicholas Lovrich, *Washington State University*

"Professor Peters' *The Politics of Bureaucracy* is one of the major contributions to the study and understanding of public management."

Professor Akira Nakamura, *Meiji University*

B. Guy Peters' comprehensive exploration of the political and policy-making roles of public bureaucracies is newly available in a fully revised and updated fifth edition. Written by a leading authority in the field it offers an extensive, well-documented, comparative analysis stressing the effects of politics and organized interests on bureaucracy. It continues to provide students of public administration with an excellent insight into bureaucracies of nations around the world.

New to the fifth edition:

* a chapter on administrative reform
* more material on administration in developing countries
* more coverage of the European Union countries and more discussion of international bureaucracies
* extensive revision and updating to take into account the wealth of new literature that has emerged in recent years.

B. Guy Peters is Maurice Falk Professor of American Government and chair of the Department of Political Science, University of Pittsburgh, Pennsylvania.

The Politics of Bureaucracy

Fifth edition

B. Guy Peters

London and New York

Fourth edition published 1995 by Longman

Fifth edition published 2001
by Routledge
2 Park Square, Milton Park, Abingdon, Oxon,
OX14 4RN

Simultaneously published in the USA and
Canada by Routledge
270 Madison Ave, New York NY 10016

*Routledge is an imprint of the Taylor & Francis
Group*

Transferred to Digital Printing 2006

Typeset in Century Old Style by Wearset,
Boldon, Tyne and Wear

British Library Cataloguing in Publication Data
A catalogue record for this book is available
from the British Library

*Library of Congress Cataloging in Publication
Data*
Peters, B. Guy.
  The politics of bureaucracy / B. Guy Peters.
  – 5th ed.
    p. cm.
  Includes bibliographical references and
index.
  1. Public administration. 2. Bureaucracy.
  3. Comparative government. I. Title.

JF1501 .P43 2000
351–dc21   00-055335

ISBN 0–415–19476–8 (hbk)
ISBN 0–415–19477–6 (pbk)

Contents

CONTENTS

CONTENTS

Figures

Tables

TABLES

Chapter 1

The persistence, growth and change of government and administration

I began my introduction to this book with the statement that government has become a pervasive fact of everyday life and that, in addition, public administration has become an especially pervasive aspect of government. This statement remains true despite the long terms in office of a number of Conservative governments in many industrialized nations (Ronald Reagan and George Bush in the United States, Margaret Thatcher and then John Major in the United Kingdom, Helmut Kohl in West Germany). These governments were joined later by right-of-center governments in unlikely places such as Sweden.

More recently, governments on the political left have returned to power in most industrialized democracies, but they are not the same types of social democrats as in the past.[1] Most of these governments have accepted many of the same premises about the need to reduce the size of government, and have made concerted attempts to reduce the role of government in the lives of their citizens. Bill Clinton in the United States and Tony Blair in the United Kingdom have both pledged to keep government small while, at the same time, using government as a positive instrument to improve the lives of their citizens. Social Democratic governments all over Europe, with the possible exception of France, have adopted some of the same rhetoric of the "Third Way," albeit in varying degrees. Government is not the enemy that it once was, but neither is there much acceptance of the "tax and spend" behavior of left governments in the past.[2]

What is true for the industrialized democracies is especially true for countries of the former communist bloc, and for many countries of the Third World. These political systems have undergone almost total transformations of their governmental structures, and, particularly in the former communist systems, there is often a need felt to reduce the intrusiveness of government and to permit greater personal freedom – economically as well as politically. These changes in values have been accompanied by radical transformations of the public sector. The changes have included numerous public enterprises being privatized and public employment being downsized.

Despite the best efforts of political leaders, however, an enhanced role for the public sector appears to persist in many countries, and in some cases that role even continues to increase. Leaders of governments have usually found government more difficult to control than they had believed before taking office. This chapter will attempt to document briefly the generalization – if indeed any documentation is required – that the public sector is difficult to control and even more difficult to "roll back." Indeed, as the state is rolled back in some ways it almost inevitably must "roll forward" in others. Privatizing industries – especially public utilities – will mean that those industries will have to be regulated in some way to ensure that the public is treated fairly.[3] The large-scale privatization occurring in Eastern Europe has meant that legal principles like property rights and contracts, as well as regulatory mechanisms, must be created by government. In other countries, where the central government has assumed a smaller role in society, lower tiers of government have accepted enhanced roles, and in some cases whole new tiers of government have been created.[4] In all of these cases, governments remain involved in the economy and society, just in less obvious ways.

The growth and contraction of government have become objects of scholarly research. Attempts to change the size of government have also become a rallying cry for political activity, whether the attempt is to expand or to contract the public sector. Any number of explanations have been offered for the growth and persistence of the public sector. Likewise, the expansion of the public bureaucracy has been conceptualized as either a by-product of the general growth in the public sector or as a root cause of that growth. Further, if government is not able to decrease its size and its influence in a society, the blame is often placed on an entrenched public bureaucracy. For example, the expanding role of the European Community in the daily lives of the citizens of the 12 member countries is often phrased in terms of expansionary ideas of the "Eurocrats." The arguments concerning the expansion and blocking power of public bureaucracy are, however, too numerous to discuss effectively here.[5]

On the other hand it is important to place contemporary public administration in its political and intellectual context, and the increased concern about the magnitude and impact of government remains an important factor in shaping the current debate about the public sector and public administration. At home, governments seeking to provide better and more equitable services to the public must also be conscious of the resistance of the public to taxation. Internationally the international financial community is skeptical of a large public sector and exerts an influence through the bond and currency markets.

The modern public sector

The above paragraph was written as if the "size of government" could be clearly and unambiguously measured.[6] In fact, it is a fundamental feature of contemporary government, especially in industrialized societies, that the boundaries between government and society – between what is public and what is private – are increasingly vague. As a consequence of that imprecision, any attempt to say unambiguously that government is growing or shrinking is subject to a great deal of error and misinterpretation. For example, by some measures the government in Russia would be larger in 2000 than it was prior to the collapse of the former system because taxes are now higher as a proportion of Gross Domestic Product than under communism.[7]

Further, the imprecision in measuring the size of the public sector can be utilized politically to make arguments about the successes or failures of incumbent governments to exercise proper control over the public sector. In an era of skepticism about the public sector and resistance to taxation, the issue of controlling the public sector is often important politically.[8] Opposition politicians find it very convenient to argue that their opponents have let the public sector "run amok" and can usually muster some evidence to support that assertion. Likewise, incumbent politicians can gather their own evidence to demonstrate that they have indeed been good stewards of the public purse.

Several examples of the difficulties in measuring the size of the public sector may help to clarify this discussion. One obvious example is the role of the tax system in defining the impact of government on the economy and society – an impact that is not adequately assessed by most measures of the size of government. In the United States, for example, subsidies for housing through the tax system (primarily through the deductibility of mortgage interest and local property taxes) exceed direct government expenditures for public housing by more than 150 percent; this continues to be true even after the "tax reform" bill of 1986.[9] Likewise, although the United Kingdom has had a large (albeit declining sharply) program of council (public) housing, tax relief for owner-occupied housing exceeds £1 billion.[10] Similar tax concessions are available to citizens of the majority of industrialized countries, with some of the highest nominal tax rates (e.g. Sweden) accompanying some of the most generous tax concessions.[11] All of these tax loopholes influence economic behavior and amount to government's influencing the economy and society just as if it taxed and spent for the same purposes.[12] Tax concessions are not, however, conventionally counted as part of the size of the public sector, as expenditures for the same purposes would be.

Government loans are another means through which government can influence the economy without ostensibly increasing the size of government. In the majority of industrialized countries governments make loans to nationalized industries that often are not repaid; these defaulted loans do not always show up as an item of public expenditure, however.[13] Even loans to individual citizens, for example to farmers, or to small businesses, often are not counted as expenditures, given the assumption that eventually they will be repaid. The involvement of government is even more subtle when, as in the United States, governments offer guarantees for private loans to companies in financial difficulty or to students who want to go to college. Such arrangements involve the actual expenditure of little or no public money but, again, produce a significant effect in the economy.

Not only do expenditures and other uses of financial resources fall on the boundary between the public and private sectors, but organizations do as well. There has been a significant increase in the number of quasi-public organizations in most countries during the post-war era.[14] In order to provide organizations with greater flexibility in making decisions, or to subject them to greater market discipline, or to protect them from potentially adverse political pressures, or simply to

Table 1.1 Public expenditure as a percentage of Gross Domestic Product[a]

Country	1960	1970	1980	1985	1990	1998
United States	27.5	30.3	33.4	33.2	34.1	34.0
United Kingdom	33.1	33.2	42.2	42.8	41.9	43.4
Sweden	28.7	37.1	57.2	51.9	48.8	49.9
Singapore	11.9	12.8	23.5	39.2	31.5	33.2
Colombia	8.4	16.2	14.9	17.1	16.4	18.9
Kenya	11.5	16.2	20.4	30.1	32.2	34.6
India	11.4	14.1	18.0	25.2	24.0	23.6

Sources: United Nations, *Statistical Yearbook* (New York: United Nations, annual); United Nations, *Yearbook of National Accounts* (New York: United Nations, annual); World Bank, *World Tables* (Washington, DC: World Bank, annual)

Note
a Gross Domestic Product at market prices

Table 1.2 Proportion of Gross Domestic Product derived from primary sector of economy (agriculture, forestry and fishing) (percentage)

Country	1960	1970	1980	1985	1990	1998
United States	4	3	3	2	2	2
United Kingdom	4	3	2	2	2	1
Sweden	7	4	3	3	3	3
Singapore	4	3	2	2	1	1
Colombia	32	26	26	18	16	16
Kenya	38	30	30	29	26	23
India	47	41	31	30	28	26

Sources: United Nations, *Statistical Yearbook* (New York: United Nations, annual); United Nations, *Yearbook of National Accounts* (New York: United Nations, annual); World Bank, *World Tables* (Washington, DC: World Bank, annual)

mask the true size of government, organizations have been created that straddle the public–private fence. In some instances these organizations are created anew as government enters a policy area for the first time – for example, the Corporation for Public Broadcasting in the United States. In other instances these are organizations that existed previously as a part of government but are then "hived-off" to a quasi-independent status, as many of the numerous non-departmental public bodies in the United Kingdom and Crown Corporations in Canada have been. As a part of the more radical reforms of the public sector undertaken in the 1980s and 1990s, large numbers of quasi-government organizations have been created that enable governments to pursue their policy goals while not appearing to be as "large" as in the past.

In addition to the obvious measurement problems these quasi-governmental organizations create, they give rise to even more important problems of accountability. As they have been divorced from direct control by government to some extent, the conventional political and legal means for enforcing accountability (see Chapter 8) may no longer be applicable. The result is that these organizations (and the politicians who are responsible for them) have opportunities for abuse of powers.[15] Further, given that they are at once public and private, the average citizen may find it difficult to ascertain who really is responsible for the services they provide. Somewhat paradoxically, as governments have sought to appear smaller and more efficient, the resultant confusion and perceived unaccountability may cause even greater harm to their reputations with the public.

Public spending

Although we now can see that it is difficult or impossible to measure the magnitude of government definitively, we can still gain insight into the changes that have taken place in the role of government by examining figures for public expenditure. This variable is the most widely used measure of the relative size of government and represents perhaps the most visible portions of governmental activity. A particular insight about the size of the public sector can be found in the

Table 1.3 Public expenditure as a percentage of readily extractable Gross Domestic Product (secondary and tertiary sectors)

Country	1960	1970	1980	1985	1990	1998
United States	28.6	31.3	34.4	33.4	34.2	34.2
United Kingdom	34.5	34.2	43.2	42.9	42.0	44.6
Sweden	30.9	38.7	59.0	52.2	49.5	51.1
Singapore	14.7	13.4	24.0	40.0	38.9	33.2
Colombia	12.4	21.6	20.0	20.8	19.6	20.1
Kenya	13.1	22.9	29.1	42.4	43.5	44.6
India	21.5	24.0	27.6	36.0	33.3	32.6

Sources: United Nations, *Statistical Yearbook* (New York: United Nations, annual); United Nations, *Yearbook of National Accounts* (New York: United Nations, annual); World Bank, *World Tables* (Washington, DC: World Bank, annual)

relationship between government expenditure and Gross Domestic Product (GDP), a standard measure of all the marketed goods and services produced in an economy.

As can be seen in Table 1.1, there are marked differences among nations in the proportion of GDP devoted to public expenditure. The most obvious differences are between the less-developed and the industrialized nations. Even the less-developed country with the highest level of public expenditure (Kenya) spends much less as a proportion of GDP than does the United States, which spends the least among the three industrialized countries in the table.[16] Of course, a sample of only seven countries is prone to great error, but similar findings probably would be present were there a much larger sample of nations. In addition, there are differences among the industrialized countries and among the less-developed countries. For instance, Sweden spends over 80 percent more in the public sector as a proportion of GDP than does the United States.

In addition to the differences among the countries, the rate of increase in public expenditure appears substantially higher in the less-developed countries than in the industrialized countries. India has almost quintupled the percentage of Gross Domestic Product devoted to public expenditure over the 35 years from 1950 to 1995, while Colombia has more than doubled the percentage in that time. Kenya almost tripled its percentage of GDP in the public sector from 1960 to 1990, although the increase has virtually stopped. The rate of increase in spending has been almost as rapid in Sweden as in the less-developed countries. The rate of growth of public expenditure has been much more modest in the other two industrialized countries, and has slowed or stopped in Sweden. A major exception to the increasing size of the public sector has been in Singapore, a "newly industrializing country," where the public sector has increased very little and there has been a great deal of emphasis on ensuring a good business climate for its rapidly growing private sector.[17]

Part of the reason for the relatively lower rate of public expenditure in the less-developed countries is that so much of their GDP comes from agriculture and especially subsistence agriculture, as is apparent in Table 1.2. This means that there are fewer "free-floating resources" in the economy that are readily taxed. The other way of saying that is that there are fewer tax handles for government to use in extracting resources. A cash transaction is easier to tax than if someone is simply growing his or her own crops in order to eat, or is trading by barter. If we calculate the level of public expenditure in relation to the secondary and tertiary sectors of the economy (manufacturing and services, respectively), we get a somewhat different picture of the rate of public expenditure in the less-developed countries. Using this calculation, Table 1.3 shows that Kenya, India, and Colombia spend about as much in relation to their readily extractable GDP as does the United States. Thus, the less-developed countries do tend to make rather substantial public expenditures when the difficulties of resource extraction are considered. In the terminology of Almond and Powell, since the extractive capabilities of these countries are weak, so too are their distributive capabilities.[18]

These data, while only illustrative, point out that government is a big "business," and continues to grow, albeit more slowly than in the recent past. Even in the less-developed countries, with their smaller public sectors, a minimum of one dollar (or whatever monetary unit) in seven goes into public expenditure. In the United States – among the least expenditure-prone of the developed countries – this figure is one dollar in three in the public sector. However, we must remember that when government spends money, it is not shovelled into a hole somewhere in Washington or Nairobi; the expenditures provide education, hospitals, highways, police protection and the whole range of government services that most citizens require.

In addition, especially in the less-developed countries, these funds can be used to promote economic growth. In those developing countries, government must function as a principal source of capital accumulation for future economic growth. In the more developed economies human capital appears to be the dominant issue in economic growth and government plays a crucial role in providing and/or promoting education and training.[19] Thus, simply reducing the size of the public sector is not necessarily the recipe for promoting economic growth as is sometimes assumed on the political right; at times the effect may be quite the opposite.

Table 1.4 Projected growth of population over 65 years of age (percentage)

Country	Year		
	2000	2025	2050
Australia	11.4	18.9	24.9
Germany	16.8	24.1	26.7
Japan	16.7	26.1	29.0
Sweden	18.1	23.0	23.1
United Kingdom	15.9	20.3	23.9
United States	12.6	20.3	23.2

Source: E. Bos, M. T. Vu, A. Levin and R. A. Bulutao, *World Population Projections, 1992–93 Edition* (Baltimore, MD: Johns Hopkins University Press, 1992)

The growth of government

Forgetting for the time being that the concept of "government" is difficult to measure in quantitative terms, we can proceed to inquire just why this institution – or set of institutions – increased in size and power after the end of World War II. There was a massive increase in the peacetime role of government after that War. In some European countries this reflected a pattern begun before the War, but there was at the time the resource base, and political will, to construct a larger and more influential role for government.

The experience of the public sector during the past several decades has been somewhat more ambiguous. During the period of conservative rule in the United States, Canada and the United Kingdom (among others) the public sector was able to resist many efforts to reduce its size. Even in countries such as the United States and the United Kingdom that had a decade or more of conservative government, there was little or no reduction in the scope of government, when measured by public revenues or expenditures as a percentage of GDP.[20] When the political pendulum again swung back toward the left, with the election of leaders such as Tony Blair, Bill Clinton, Gerhard Schroder and Lionel Jospin, there was surprisingly little will to expand government revenue and spending. The new version of the left accepts a much more limited role for government – at least financially – and often depends upon closer alliances between the public and private sectors to influence economy and society.[21]

There are almost as many answers to the question of why governments grow as there are scholars concerned with the subject, but several fundamental approaches can be used to relate that growth to the growth of public bureaucracy. Also, these same answers must be examined to determine whether government can also down-size in response to demands that the public sector become a less pervasive and intrusive aspect of life.

Entitlements

One dominant explanation for the growth of the public sector is that governments extended a variety of "entitlement programs" to their citizens during bountiful economic times and have been unable to rescind these entitlements as the economy has become less buoyant.[22] Examples of these programs are social security, public health insurance, and housing subsidies. These programs are especially difficult to curtail when they are supported by an earmarked tax that gives citizens the impression of actually purchasing something akin to an insurance policy.[23] Programs of this type constitute a major portion of the expenditures of government – approximately 42 percent in the United States, 45 percent in the United Kingdom, and almost 59 percent in Sweden. Further, when there are pressures to reduce public expenditures for either political or economic reasons, in the 1980s for example, the proportion of total public spending devoted to entitlement expenditures tends to increase rapidly as discretionary expenditures are eliminated.

Table 1.5 Growth of government: number of ministries

Period	States	Functions (average number)			
		Defining	Resource mobilization	Social	Total
Nineteenth-century origin	22	5.7	1.7	1.1	8.5
Twentieth-century origin	9	4.8	3.7	1.9	10.4
1913	25	5.9	4.0	1.6	11.5
1936	31	5.7	4.7	2.4	12.8
1972	32	5.6	9.1	4.4	19.1
1984	34	5.1	7.3	3.7	16.1
1992	34	5.4	6.0	4.1	15.5
1997	38	5.2	5.7	4.8	15.7

Sources: Richard Rose, "On the Priorities of Government: A Developmental Analysis of Public Policies," *European Journal of Political Research*, 4 (1976), 247–89, Table 1 and 2; *Statesman's Yearbook*, 1985, 1986, 1992, 1998

Entitlement programs in and of themselves would not necessarily produce increases in the relative size of the public sector were it not for the demographic shift occurring in almost all industrialized societies. These societies are aging, with a higher proportion of the population retiring each year. In addition to pensions, the elderly tend to consume more medical care per capita than do younger people, so expenditures for public medical care programs are also likely to increase as populations age; on average a person over 65 uses twice as much medical care as one 45–65 years old. This shift in the age structure of industrialized countries is quite rapid. For example, in the United States, which remains a relatively young country with just over 12 percent of the population over 65 as compared to over 18 percent in Sweden and 16 percent in Switzerland, the over-65 component of the population is increasing more than twice as fast as the population as a whole. The projected increases of the over-65 population shown in Table 1.4 will place a great deal of pressure on public expenditures in the years to come.

Fiscal pressures

The nature of public sector economics also tends to increase the size of the public sector relative to the rest of the economy. This proposition was advanced in its most extreme version by Adolph Wagner and has come to be known as "Wagner's Law."[24] The basic idea is that, as the economy of a nation grows, a larger proportion will be devoted to the public sector. The logic underlying this proposition is that, as the economy grows, the basic subsistence needs of the population will be met and consequently money for private consumption will have declining marginal utility. A number of empirical studies have found only slight support for this contention, and some scholars have argued that political pressures tend to keep public expenditures at the lowest acceptable level, rather than permit them to increase along with economic growth.[25] Further, the experience of rapid economic growth in the 1990s appears to be that individual desires for consumption are virtually insatiable.

A second financial explanation for the relative growth of the public sector was advanced by the British economists Alan Peacock and Jack Wiseman.[26] They argued for the existence of a "displacement effect," whereby public tolerance for taxation increased during times of stress, such as a war; and, after the end of the crisis, government would use newly created revenues to fund new programs. Thus, the public's acceptance of taxation was displaced upward during each successive crisis, allowing those within government to develop new policies and programs. Although originally discussed in terms of wars, other crises such as economic depressions or even natural disasters might have the same consequences.[27]

Although this "ratchet effect" has a certain plausibility, it appears equally plausible that politicians could reap an even larger benefit from reducing taxes rather than creating new programs. The public has expressed resistance to taxation in any number of polls. The problem with that logic is that the recipients of program benefits tend to be better organized than are taxpayers and representatives of the "public interest."[28] Therefore, it may not appear to politicians that they have as much to gain from opposing expenditures and benefits as they do from supporting the programs. The organization of taxpayers' interest groups and of political parties devoted to the reduction of public expenditure have helped to balance these pressures for more expenditure, but have not been totally successful. Even the radical anti-tax parties of Scandinavia, tax referenda and tax capping in the United States, and a decade of conservative rule in Germany and the United Kingdom, have done little more than slow expenditure growth.[29]

The third fiscal reason for the expansion of the public sector has been called "Baumol's disease" or, more technically, the Relative Price Effect.[30] Government is a labor-intensive "industry" and, therefore, tends to gain very little productivity from the application of capital expenditures. The majority of tasks performed by government, such as delivering the mail, providing education, or policing, have their costs reduced very little by the introduction of any but the most extensive technological advances. This dependence upon labor means that in an inflationary period the costs of governmental services will increase more rapidly than the costs of other types of goods and services, assuming that public sector pay remains on a roughly equal footing with private sector pay. Thus, in order to provide the *same* level of services, the costs of government will *increase*. At one time the British Treasury estimated this relative price effect to be 0.7 percent per year.[31] That is,

Table 1.6 Examples of privatization

United Kingdom	France	Japan
British Gas	St Gobain	Japan National Railways
British Telecom	Compaigne Générale	Japan Telephone and
British Airways	d'Electricité	Telegraph
Public Buses	Crédit Commercial de France	Japan Monopoly
British Petroleum	Mutuelle Générale Française	Corporation
National Freight		

just to provide the same level of public services, public expenditures would have to increase at an annual rate of seven-tenths of one percent. In ten years, with compounding, this rate would amount to an expenditure increase of almost 8 percent.

The labor intensity in government leaves public managers with two options: increase public expenditures (and with them taxes) or reduce public services. Neither of these is an attractive alternative for politicians or administrators working in contemporary governments. The relative labor intensity of government organizations was accentuated in the 1990s by the continuing tendency of private sector organizations to reduce their permanent workforces in favor of hiring temporary workers as and when they are needed. Although governments are also implementing similar programs to save money, many are constrained by civil service rules and union protections. They are also constrained by the need to maintain a public service ethic among workers, especially those dealing with sensitive materials (tax examiners) or in direct contact with the public (social workers).

Although the RPE may have had some impact on expenditures for much of the post-war period, toward the end of the century a reverse effect appeared to be in place. Now, the public sector appears to be *more* amenable to productivity changes from the use of computers than does the private sector.[32] Much of the work of the public sector involves the manipulation, storage and dissemination of information, the natural tasks of computers. Government work also involves a great deal of communications among its members, and electronic mail and other information services assist in that communication. There is some evidence that productivity in the public sector is now rising rapidly with the aid of computerization, as well as a deregulation of public employment practices.[33]

The political process

The third reason for the increasing size of government might be termed the "pogo phenomenon." That is, "We have met the enemy and it is us," or government grows because citizens demand more services from it. This expression of demand is rarely, if ever, made through mass political means such as political parties; on the contrary, politicians often appear to have been successful by promising to reduce the level of expenditure and taxation. Rather, the pressure for more generally comes through pressure groups that have ample access to government. Pressure groups have every incentive to press their demands on government. They can receive a special, concentrated benefit for their members – farmers can collect higher subsidies, businesses can acquire greater tax concessions, and the elderly can achieve higher pensions.[34] The costs of these benefits are dispersed widely across the population so that forming organizations to combat pressures from these more particularistic pressure groups is difficult. Relatively few individuals feel that they have enough to gain personally to invest sufficient time to organize against greater spending. As Lowi has pointed out, the public sector may be appropriated for private purposes, all funded by taxpayers' money.[35] These developments approach the "tragedy of the commons," in which behavior that is perfectly rational for the individual, or in this case the group, becomes extremely dysfunctional for the society as a whole.[36]

In many political systems there have been significant attempts to redress the imbalance between the forces of special interests and those of the "public interest." In the United States, organizations such as Common Cause have pressed for legislation and procedural changes to assist ordinary citizens when they must deal with government.[37] They have also sought to increase the power of those ordinary citizens in relation to the powers of "special-interest groups." Similar movements have occurred in many other industrialized countries. Some movements, such as the Greens in Germany, have gone so far as to institutionalize themselves as political parties, but the majority remain citizen action groups. These groups, sometimes referred to as *Burgerinitiativen,* tend to concentrate on a single issue and then perhaps to dissolve; but, while in existence, many have been quite successful in affecting the priorities of governments.[38] The difficulty of these developments for public administration, however, is that it is difficult to institutionalize interactions with interest groups that form and dissolve almost at will.

Finally, we should notice that the public does appear to have some sense of what the French would call *services publics,* or activities that are almost inherently the responsibility of the public sector.[39] When government attempts to rid itself of these services, it may encounter political difficulties in even the most market-oriented society. In less market-oriented systems, such as most of continental Europe, privatization or contracting out is likely to be opposed vigorously. For example, France has privatized some activities but retains substantial involvement in many industries.[40] In the Scandinavian countries there have been some reforms of state programs but government remains active in regulation and in attempting to equalize socio-economic conditions of citizens – there is still something of the "negotiated economy" left in many of the smaller countries of Europe.

Decline of late capitalism

One explanation for the growth of government in advanced, industrial countries has been the "decline of late capitalism." This approach, rather obviously, is based upon Marxist or neo-Marxist principles. It argues that the inherent contradictions of the capitalist system – most notably that the removal of profits by capitalists reduces the overall growth and productivity of the system – force governments to attempt to patch up the system by increasing public expenditures, especially for welfare programs. However, as more and more money is spent for social purposes, there is even less that can be used to maintain the economic viability of societies. The public sector will increase relative to the productivity of the entire economy, but ultimately the socio-economic system is doomed to come crashing down from the weight of its own contradictions.

This explanation for the increasing relative size of public expenditure is based on a particular ideology usually described as being on the political left. Further, with the end of the Cold War, Marxism might appear relevant only from a historical perspective. Interestingly, however, this analysis is similar in many ways to the analysis of public expenditure offered by conservatives on the political right. Both Marxists and conservatives would argue that social expenditure will slow the rate of economic growth, although one side argues that this is so because of profits while the other that there are too few profits. Further, in both ideological systems, social expenditures are a major cause of the decline of the economic systems in question. They differ, of course, in the proposed remedy, with Marxists assuming that the only solution is the end of capitalism, while the political right argue for the application of even more capitalist solutions.

The public bureaucracy

Finally, the public bureaucracy – our principal focus of inquiry – has itself been cited as a cause of growth of public expenditure, and of government generally. One of the many stereotypes of public bureaucracy is that of an acquisitive and expansive set of organizations. This view is perhaps most forcefully expressed in the work of William Niskanen.[41] He argues that bureau chiefs – these are assumed to be permanent civil servants – are budget maximizers, and that they will use their control of information and their ability to disguise the true costs of producing the public services they provide in order to increase their budgets to points far above the level necessary. In his model, Niskanen argues that the legislature has little or no ability to control the bureaus, because of the monopoly of information held by those bureaus. As a consequence, the legislature cannot make independent judgments on the budget and the costs of government increase rapidly. The solution Niskanen offered for controlling the public bureaucracy is to create something approximating a market, with multiple bureaus competing in the same service area to provide better services to more clients. This competition is assumed to keep costs down, with the threat of poorer performing organizations being driven out of business.[42]

This elegant economic analysis is based, however, on a number of very shaky assumptions, and bears limited resemblance to the real world of public administration.[43] The first and most basic is that individual bureaucrats in a formalized bureaucratic system have an incentive to maximize the size of their bureaus. The individual in such a bureau has little to gain personally from a larger budget, given relatively inflexible pay schedules based on formal position and longevity rather than on organizational size. It is true that those at the bottom or middle ranks of the organization may be able to advance more rapidly when new positions are opened, but the bureau chiefs – the budget maximizers in Niskanen's model – would themselves gain little or nothing. In fact, increasing the size of the bureau may only generate managerial difficulties for the bureaucrat, an outcome that would conflict with the other prevailing stereotype of the bureaucrat as being interested primarily in minimizing personal difficulty rather than maximizing budgets.[44]

This model of bureaucracy also seriously underestimates the capacity of the legislature to develop means for independent judgment. As we will be pointing out in greater detail later,[45] legislative bodies have made a concerted effort to reestablish their control over public expenditure and have developed independent sources of information about public expenditure and public programs. Even where the "counterbureaucracies" have not flourished, legislatures have attempted to organize and reorganize themselves for improved control over spending. In short, the passive, ignorant legislature assumed by the Niskanen model no longer exists, if it ever did.

Even if the Niskanen model were descriptive of the United States bureaucracy for which it was developed, it is doubtful whether it would be as descriptive of other countries, primarily because the independence accorded to bureaus in the United States is by no means typical of countries where the cabinet departments are more dominant.[46] Likewise, outside the United States the career for civil servants has been less restricted to within a single organization. As a consequence, individual civil servants may perceive their career future as being more within the public bureaucracy as a whole rather than within the one organization. Such a perception will then produce an emphasis on the creation of a record of trust and dependability rather than on the hiding of costs to produce growth for the one organization.

Finally, if the logical and conceptual arguments that can be mounted against this model are not sufficient, it has another basic flaw. It simply does not appear to work. Such empirical work as has been done to test the Niskanen model finds very little support.[47] This is true of the settings outside the United States to which the model has been applied, but it is even true within the model's country of origin. The role of the public bureaucracy in policy making and the dynamics of the budget process are both too complex and subtle to be represented adequately by any such simplistic model.

The "bureau-shaping" model is one interesting attempt to address the subtleties of the relationship between bureaucracies and public expenditure.[48] The argument of this model is that all public expenditures are not equal for the bureau chief, the main protagonist in this story.

Paradoxically, many reforms of the public sector designed to make government more efficient and effective may, in fact, make the realization of the negative outcomes envisaged by Niskanen more likely. For example, the increasing use of quasi-autonomous organizations, e.g. "agencies," to deliver public programs[49] provides the type of freedom for bureaucratic entrepreneurs to use their positions for advancing their own interests and the interests of their organizations. Likewise, the elimination of many internal civil service rules and the implementation of "pay for performance" has tended to make differential rewards more possible. Positions that once were restricted to civil service are now open to open competition and with that also some loss of commitment to public service and the values that may have restricted use of public offices for more personal purposes. Competition may have been instilled, but the loss of internal controls appears actually to have created the entrepreneurial world that Niskanen so deplored.[50]

Summary

Government has grown. By whatever measure we would want to apply, governments spend more money, employ more people, and constitute a more pervasive influence on the lives of their citizens now than for most of human history. More important in recent years has been a government's ability to withstand numerous attempts to reduce its size and scope. The reasons advanced for this growth and persistence are numerous, including those enumerated above. Some support as well as some contrary evidence can be found for each of the reasons advanced. What may be happening, in fact, is the confluence of all these reasons; there is no single cause for the growth of government, but rather a large number of factors. And growing along with government, the public bureaucracy has become a more important institution for making as well as implementing public policy.

The growth of administration

The public bureaucracy is rarely mentioned in constitutions, and generally does not figure in the design of political regimes, yet it has become central in government decision making, and is still increasing its influence within government. As Samuel Krislov put it:

> Bureaucracies are the late bloomers of modern political structure. They grew silently, inexorably in the underbrush – seldom noticed, little analyzed. Convenience and necessity, not ideology and legitimacy, are their life-blood: they are not loved and respected, but rather tolerated and depended on.[51]

Thus, although public bureaucracies are among the oldest political institutions, they have become powerful – or more likely have been seen to become powerful – only in recent decades. Certainly in ancient empires and other authoritarian states the public bureaucracy was a powerful actor, but it has only been in the post-World War II era that they have come to be widely perceived as powerful policy-making actors within democratic regimes.[52] The increasing power of the public bureaucracy has been indicated by growing levels of public employment, as well as by expenditures for general governmental purposes. It is also seen through the capacity of bureaucracies to regulate the economy and society.[53] On a less quantified level, the growth of bureaucratic power has been documented, discussed, and damned in a number of places.

In these discussions several conflicting stereotypes of the public bureaucracy have been developed. On the one hand, bureaucracy is seen as a Leviathan seeking to increase its powers and operating as an integrated, monolithic institution. The Niskanen view of bureaucracy mentioned above advances that power-seeking view of bureaucracy. Likewise, the growth of the European Union (EU) has promoted the view in much of Western Europe that the "Brussels bureaucracy" has taken control over policy in those countries, with a consequent democratic deficit threatening the legitimacy of the EU.[54]

On the other hand, bureaucracy is pictured as a court jester – a fumbling, bumbling collection of uncoordinated agencies that, at best, muddle through and, at worst, make absolute fools of themselves. The examples of the apparently foolish behavior of bureaucracies have been assembled in several places and include contradictory programs, meaningless memos, and other assorted blunders. So, as one federal agency (OSHA) requires backup sirens on construction equipment, another (EPA) bans them as violating noise-pollution regulations. One former U.S. senator, William Proxmire, made a name for his monthly "Golden Fleece Award" honoring the silliest government grant he could find, and the Citizen's Coalition in Canada publishes an annual list of what it considers wasteful grants. The *Washington Monthly* magazine has published a monthly "Memo of the Month" to honor the most ludicrous government memo of the month, and one television network runs a regular series on its nightly news asking whether we taxpayers really need one government program or another. In the United Kingdom the media have reported that failures to coordinate government activities have resulted in public organizations digging up the same street dozens of times in a two-year period. One can find published collections of seemingly nonsensical memoranda and decisions from bureaucracies in any number of countries. The examples of bumbling proliferate, and the negative stereotype of bureaucracy persists and even expands within the popular mind.

Both quantitative and qualitative trends in policy formation lead us to the conclusion that we must understand public bureaucracy in order to understand policy in contemporary political systems, and, further, that the power of bureaucracies is increasing steadily. The task here is to provide an explanation of these changes in the relative powers of institutions. To that end, we argue that the reasons for this change are primarily four: the quantitative growth of public problems and concerns, the qualitative growth of those concerns, the failures of two alternative institutions – the legislature and the political executive – to cope with the changes in the policy-making environment, and the nature of public bureaucracies themselves.

The quantitative growth of public concerns

To say that the scope of government has increased because there are more things being done in the public sector is tautological, but it is important to note the substantial array of goods and services now produced by collective action that either were unheard of, or were the subjects of private action, several decades earlier. The developmental scheme proposed by Richard Rose is one description of the changes in the range of activities in the public sector. Government began with its "defining functions" such as defense and tax collection and then added, first, resource mobilization activities (roads, canals, railways, etc.) and finally social activities to its portfolio of activities.[55] One bit of Rose's evidence, reproduced and updated, appears in Table 1.5, and demonstrates how these functions have changed in European countries.

There was a general pattern of increase in activity, as measured by organizations, until the mid-1980s. By the early 1990s the increasing privatization of public functions (examples of which are given in Table 1.6) produced a substantial reduction in the number of resource mobilization activities, albeit with little net change in the number of defining and social ministries.[56] Even then, however, if the various forms of government involvement were measured, e.g. devolved agencies performing services rather than ministries, government activities would

Table 1.7 Citizens' evaluation of government (percentage)

	1966	1967	1968	1969	1970	1971	1972	1973	1974	1975	1976	1977	1978	1979	1980	1981	1982	1984	1988	1990
United States																				
Agree, "Government wastes a lot of tax money"	61		61		70		67		76		76		80		80		68	66	64	68
Agree, "Income tax is too high"	52	58		66				64	69	72	73	69	70		74	72		64	57	61
Confidence in leaders of executive branch	41					23		18	28	13	11	23	14		22	26	35	19	17	24
United Kingdom																				
Prefer current level rather than more spending					51			47					47				26	17	12	10

Sources: Douglas A. Hibbs and Henrik Jens Madsen, "Public Reactions to the Growth of Taxation and Government Expenditure," *World Politics*, 33 (1981), 413–35; "Opinion Roundup," *Public Opinion*, 1 (July/August, 1978): 30–1; E. H. Hastings and P. K. Hastings, eds, *Index to International Public Opinion* (Westport, CT: Greenwood, annual); George F. Gallup, *International Gallup Polls* (Wilmington, DE: Scholarly Resources, annual)

probably be nearly as numerous.[57] Similar patterns would hold for other countries, although newly developing countries must often plunge into doing everything at once, given the expectations of their people. Thus, as well as increasing in the *level* of activity, reflected through the size of the public budget, government is also extending the *range* of its activities.

The increasing complexity of modern economic and social life is one obvious reason for the increased range of governmental activity. This complexity is, at least in part, a function of the technological content of modern life, in which telecommunications, the Internet, atomic energy, rapid commercial air service, space travel, and the mechanization of most production are but a few examples of dramatic increases in technology that impinge upon the citizen as consumer and voter. Further, increases in the rapidity of communication and transportation, and an increasing concentration of people in urbanized areas, have required collective decisions on matters that, in simpler societies, could be handled by individuals. Thus, in the phraseology of economics, the externalities of individual behavior have tended to increase as the size and concentration of the population have increased.[58]

Not only have the externalities of individual behavior increased, so too have the perceptions of those externalities. Unfortunately, little research exists to document changes in perceptions of this sort, but by using somewhat softer evidence we can get some idea of the attitude changes. Some such evidence is given by the increasing level of organization in a number of nations, of individuals attempting to secure regulation of matters such as environmental pollution, deceptive and unsafe business practices, land use, and even economic foreign policy. Likewise, society has been increasingly unwilling to allow individuals to live below minimum standards, although conservative governments during the 1980s and 1990s lessened those commitments. To the extent they do continue to exist, however, social programs represent some recognition of the possible externalities of poverty and despair, and at least some concern for the ability of collective action to improve the lot of fellow citizens. Thus, modern society produces situations in which mechanisms of collective action are perceived as virtually necessary for a high quality of life. These necessities are apparently accepted by much of the population, although variably both by classes of individuals and by nations, and the bureaucracy has become the institutional manifestation of those needs.

In addition to real or perceived externalities, changes in modern social structure have tended to place pressures on government to intervene in society. For example, the rapid increases in female participation in the labor force have produced demands for public day care, after-school programs, and other programs to assist working mothers. Also, the increase of leisure time enjoyed by most people has resulted in demands for more public recreational programs. Less positively, the "breakdown" in family life in many Western nations has resulted in programs designed to deal with disturbed, displaced, and delinquent youths. There is also a need for society to care for the increasing number of aged as their families become less willing or able to do so. Society has not been standing still, and government has become the means of addressing problems of social change.

The qualitative growth of public concerns

In addition to the increasing externalities of modern life and the popular desire to have some regulation of economic and social problems, the technological content of life, already alluded to, has definite implications for bureaucratic dominance in decision making. Increasingly, the things that government is called upon to regulate are matters which have significant technological content. This is true not only of things involving the natural sciences and engineering, but also of developing "social technologies" in areas such as education, chemical dependency and childhood development. Experts in government tend to be concentrated in the bureaucracy, with few legislative or executive structures employing many of their own experts. As the concerns of government are increasingly influenced by available technology, the public bureaucracy as the locus of the public sector's share of that technology comes increasingly to the forefront in decision making.

Just as it has influenced its relationship with other political institutions, the level of technological sophistication of the bureaucracy has also influenced relationships with the society. As programs such as atomic energy and space exploration have developed – requiring enormous capital investment, high levels of staffing, and some national security concerns – few if any private institutions would be capable of engaging actively in the problem areas, even if they were legally able. This leaves government as the sole supplier of certain socially important technological services. Private concerns that seek to engage in these technologically sophisticated activities – for example, a utility company building an atomic reactor – must seek the guidance and, more importantly, accept the regulation of the public bureaucracy. Further, research and development activities are diverted from what might be valued in the private marketplace into directions dictated more by political and bureaucratic demands. The spin-offs of these research efforts may have positive values for the citizens, but the impetus and direction of that research has changed from the private to the public sector.[59] Governments have found, however, that this situation does not always produce the most desirable research, especially when economic development must depend in part upon spin-offs from defense research. Hence, there is an increased emphasis on partnerships between the public and the private sectors; these create new problems of their own.

Finally, the role of government has, to some extent, been expanded by the internationalization of economies and of social life in general. Even analysts on the political right tend to recognize the importance of government for buffering a domestic economy from the international economy, in which other governments may not play by the same rules. Thus, somewhat paradoxically, as the international market is said to come to dominate domestic economic policies, government as the player in organizations such as the World Trade Organization become more rather than less important. If the economic success of a country, and its citizens, is dependent upon the international environment, as is the case for probably all countries, then government often must play the role of mediator and protector, given that no private sector organization has the right or the power to do so.

Institutional weaknesses

The remaining reasons for the increased power of bureaucracies in contemporary political systems are institutional, related both to the characteristics of bureaucracy as a political institution and the characteristics of other political institutions that are its competitors for power. The competition among institutions is rarely overt, but it does have the effect of delineating the power relationships among those institutions and the nature of the policies that are likely to be adopted. This segment of the chapter focuses on the weaknesses of the conventional, political decision-making institutions in government and then discusses the characteristics of bureaucracy that make it a powerful actor in the policy process in a later section.

The legislature.   The legislature has been the traditional locus of rule making in democratic political systems, and most nondemocratic systems also use a legislative body to legitimate their actions to their own people and to the outside world. Given this traditional and normative role of legislatures, it is necessary to understand why these institutions are apparently losing, if not the formal powers of decision, at least the actual role-making powers within many political systems. This will help in understanding why the gainer in this decline of legislative powers is generally the bureaucracy.

Rather obviously, the quantitative and qualitative growth of governmental concerns has contributed to this decline in power. Legislatures, by placing their organizational effort into discussion, debate, and elaborate procedures for the full and open consideration of viewpoints, consequently limit their ability to consider more than a handful of issues in any one session. For example, during the period 1979–95 the British parliament passed an average of approximately 55 acts per session; approximately half of these were bills consolidating and clarifying existing legislation or changing administration.[60] The issues that face a legislative body are usually the most important issues confronting a society, and they may set broad parameters of policy, but this still leaves a very large quantity of detail to be filled in by administrators. During the period 1979–95, while Parliament was making its 55 laws per session, an average of 2,000 statutory instruments elaborating legislation were adopted.[61] Further, the qualities valued in legislative recruitment, popular elections, or advancement within the legislature are rarely those needed to handle technically complex materials in large quantity.[62] The non-legislative careers of most legislators are hardly those that would prepare them for such law-making tasks, except perhaps in terms of the legalistic drafting of the legislation.

Associated with the questions of recruitment of legislators are questions concerning the structure of legislative institutions. Relative to the bureaucratic agencies that they must confront, legislative bodies are understaffed and under-specialized. Even when well-developed systems of legislative committees exist, as in the United States, Germany and Sweden, the members of those committees have any number of other duties that prevent their specialization in narrow policy areas.[63] Further, few legislative bodies are lucky enough to have any substantial functional specialization in committees to begin with, so that policy consideration in those bodies is often a haphazard thing. Finally, even when legislative committees exist as highly specialized bodies, rarely do they have independent sources of information to draw upon in considering policy; they commonly must rely upon information gathered and processed by a bureaucratic agency, which presumably has some interest in a particular outcome.

Finally, the relative instability of legislative bodies, as compared with the bureaucracy, places the legislature at a disadvantage in any power competition. Even in societies that have not had high levels of governmental instability or frequent elections, legislators and legislatures are certainly more transitory than are bureaucracies. Thus, a certain uncertainty surrounds the conduct of legislative business, and an opportunity arises for bureaucrats to engage in tutelage to new and inexperienced legislators. Further, the bureaucracy can always try to wait out the legislature, hoping that at the next election the people or parties in charge will change their minds or not be there at all.

Some analysts have argued that the desire for stability, or at least for stable personal careers, is accelerating the decline of legislatures as decision-making bodies. Fiorina and others have argued that, as legislators have sought to maximize their chances for re-election, they have found that the best way of doing so is to serve their constituents well. They can enhance their chances of re-election, for example, by helping with citizens' grievances and providing "pork barrel" benefits, rather than making statements about national policy issues.[64] Strong advocacy of a policy runs the risk of offending voters, while effective constituency service can only benefit voters. Thus, the safe path for the legislator is to vote when he or she must, but to concentrate on service. Such a stance, while rational for the individual, does not provide the sort of societal leadership that is needed from those in government.

The political executive.   Many of the problems identified for legislatures are also encountered in the political executives of contemporary governments. This is especially true in parliamentary systems, in which executives suffer from the instability of regimes and often inadequate policy staffs. This situation has been described as the "problems of party government" and reflects the difficulty of any political executive imposing its will upon the ongoing administrative offices.[65] There are four particular problems that political executives have in seeking to impose their wills over the policies of their own departments.

The first is a lack of skills relevant to understanding the policies that must be made, and a lack of time required to understand and manage those policies. Political executives must rely on their civil servants to shape policy and to advise them about the operations of the ministry. Headey, for example, calculates that of the 51 appointments to departmental ministerial posts in the Wilson government of 1964–70, only five had any substantial prior knowledge of the policy area, with another five or six having some background in the area.[66] In the 1970 Heath government, only four original appointees could claim specialist knowledge, with four more having some substantive background.[67] Many would argue that individuals appointed to the Thatcher and Major governments were appointed less on the basis of their substantive knowledge of issues, although there are some notable exceptions, than on the basis of their agreement on ideological issues.

Having been out of office for almost two decades, the Labour government elected in 1997 could not have been expected to have much experience in policy issues, although some ministers did have non-governmental experience and expertise in the policy areas for which they were made responsible, and others had been shadow ministers.

Britain may be less well served than other countries in regard to the expert knowledge of ministers, but hearings for cabinet posts in the United States, as well as cabinet reshuffles in any number of countries, indicate that a knowledge of the policy area is by no means a prerequisite for a cabinet appointment.[68] The Clinton cabinets, for example, have contained many knowledgeable people but also some individuals clearly appointed for political reasons. There is some evidence, however, that the development of "issue networks" around policy issues are becoming able to provide experts of almost any ideological stripe for a government that wants to employ them. These people may not get the top position in government, but can be brought into the next tiers in order to guide policy making.

Lacking any specialized knowledge, it would be helpful if those in the political executive had sufficient time to spend in running their departments. In fact, most spend a "dog's life" in their ministerial posts.[69] Again, this weakness may be especially evident in parliamentary systems, and even more particularly in Britain. In France and Norway ministers are prevented from also being parliamentarians, and that has greatly aided these ministers in running their departments, but in most countries ministers can, or must, remain active parliamentarians.[70] Likewise, the norms of parliamentary systems other than Britain (and other Westminster systems) concerning hours and the time spent in the legislatures may ease political burdens substantially. Even in political systems in which political executives are not members of the legislature, they are political figures and must spend time in public appearances, receive delegations of interest-group representatives, and engage in other political activities, with a consequent drain on the time available to contemplate policy questions. Thus the minister remains at a disadvantage in attempting to understand and control the work of full-time and relatively specialized civil servants.

If the disadvantages of time and prior training were not enough, the political executive is also seriously outnumbered in his or her attempts to impose external political goals upon a bureaucratic structure. Compared with the size of most administrative bodies, the number of political appointees who are imposed at the top of the organization is quite small, but the appointees are expected to control all activities within the organization. This number is, of course, variable by political system – the United States and France, for example, have considerably more political appointees than the United Kingdom or other Westminster systems – and across time with many governments adding more political appointees.[71] Further, the senior civil servants in some political systems – Germany and Austria for example – themselves have partisan affiliations so that they can be relied on to support the program of their minister more readily than might a neutral. Still, the number of committed people in a ministry pales in comparison to the size of the permanent, full-time bureaucracy.

Finally, the willingness of civil servants to accept the decisions of their political masters, and actually to put into effect a partisan program, is another obstacle to effective political control. Although few civil servants systematically sabotage or even obstruct the stated program of a minister, they still have their own departmental or ideological concerns, which may impede the smooth flow of work.[72] From all that is known about human nature and behavior in organizations, it is unlikely that civil servants who disagree with, or are genuinely neutral toward, a policy will administer it with the same alacrity and vigor as they will a policy they like. Further, given the handicaps under which many ministers labor, civil servants are frequently able to control the agenda of the minister sufficiently so that few programs actually hostile to the interests of the incumbent civil service will be considered. The power of civil servants to control agendas, and their general power in the policy process, has provoked the demand for a more committed civil service, even in countries such as the United Kingdom that have long prided themselves on a neutral service. Further, in transitional regimes, the need to change policies drastically places an even greater strain on the relationship between civil servants and their ministers.

The tendency of administrators to drag their feet, or at least to not administer programs vigorously, will be exacerbated in situations of high politicization both of particular policies and of the society in general.[73] For example, when a political system is divided communally and changes occur in the composition of the political leadership in cabinet, frequently this change may require the reshuffling of many senior civil servants so that the two sides – civil servants and politicians – can cooperate more effectively. Perhaps the most general point that can be made is that civil servants have little to gain by close and overt cooperation with particular politicians. Their careers are largely untouched by politicians in many countries (although not all), and it may, in fact, be detrimental for them to be too closely identified with a particular political party or politician – especially if they lose office.

The nature of bureaucratic institutions

Although bureaucratic institutions should not be blamed for (or credited with) the growth of the public sector, they do have some influence on the redistribution of powers away from elective institutions and in the direction of the bureaucracy itself. We will not adopt the totally cynical view that agencies are concerned only with the growth of the agency budget, but neither can we adopt the more naive view that agencies are concerned entirely with the performance of their constitutionally and legally designated tasks. The truth probably lies somewhere in between. Further, attempts at bureaucratic "empire building" may be closely related to the desire of the agency to survive and also to perform functions that it considers essential to a high quality of life for the society. Thus, despite the obvious attempts of the Pentagon at times to increase the military budget to feed its own needs, it is only fair to say that officials in the Department of Defense sincerely believe that they are supplying an essential service to the society. Or, as Cleaves once wrote of the Chilean bureaucracy:

Derogatory comments on bureaucracy's tendency to consolidate its power (e.g., empire building, prestige accrual) are value judgments to the extent that they are not examined in context of the agency's need to increase its capacity for goal-oriented behavior.[74]

In other words, one person's empire building is another person's need for survival, or even public service. In addition, the model of bureaucratic dominance in policy making assumes that agencies compete over scarce resources – the budget – and for control of policy choices. This competition appears to limit the extent to which any integrated bureaucratic governance might emerge, given that the bureaucracy would tend to behave as a set of competitive entrepreneurs rather than as a unified political force. However, it can also be argued that bureaucracies engage in competition primarily when their core interests are threatened; they rarely are competitive over issues that are peripheral to their survival or the performance of their basic tasks.[75] Likewise, in the budgetary process they can perhaps be best seen as satisfiers, rather than maximizers, again seeking to ensure survival of their organization rather than the domination of a policy field. Perhaps the best analogy would be with the balance of power in international affairs, in which all actors involved attempt to gain security through limited or tacit cooperation rather than overt competition.

Even if the bureaucracy as a whole does not constitute a unified political force, it may still constitute a formidable force within individual agencies. We have already noted the ability of the permanent staff in a ministry essentially to determine the agenda for their presumed political masters. This capacity becomes especially important in the presence of an agency ideology concerning the proper goals for the agency to pursue and proper means of attaining those goals. Through the ability to control information, proposals for policy, and the knowledge concerning feasibility, the bureaucracy is certainly capable of influencing agency policy, if not determining it. It requires an unusual politician to be able to overcome this type of control within an agency.

Thus, we can view the bureaucracy as being in a powerful position in competition with its ostensible political masters. Having control of information and of the instigation of policy alternatives, having an expert knowledge of the subject matter, and having a ministerial or departmental ideology concerning the manner in which the subject matter should be treated, the bureaucracy can control decisions actually adopted by the partisans at the top. Further, competition between agencies, which might serve to limit such powers, is usually confined to a small number of issues in which the basic interests of one or more agencies overlap. Within its purview, each agency remains supreme and consequently can dominate or influence its own political masters.

Countertrends in government growth

Lest we think that all goes well for the statist position in modern society, we should mention several important countertrends that have tended to restrain the growth of government and of the public bureaucracy. In fact, the experience of the last decade may make the reader wonder how one could defend the position that government remains a powerful actor. We must be careful, however, to separate the rhetoric of political leaders, including contemporary leaders such as Clinton, Blair and Schroeder among others, from the reality of what their governments have been doing and have become. Few if any government leaders in the industrialized democracies were successful in fundamentally altering the size and shape of their public sectors – New Zealand is perhaps the one clear example of a fundamental transformation of the public sector,[76] with the United Kingdom being another possible case of fundamental change. Real changes, of course, have occurred in the former communist countries and in some Third World countries that have truly rolled back the state, but now these countries face the problem of creating entire new state structures and governing procedures.

The rolling back of government in Eastern Europe and the former Soviet Union demonstrates the upper limits of the reaction against the power of government and bureaucracy.[77] In many Third World countries the same rolling back has been accomplished less by endogenous political processes than by the involvement of international organizations such as the World Bank and the International Monetary Fund.[78] Even here, however, the state has hardly been dismantled and, soon after the revolutions, powerful public institutions are seen to be necessary to help restructure the inadequate economic bases and deal with the problems of managing newly-freed societies.

The above having been said, there have been extensive amounts of privatization of public services in most democratic countries.[79] The difference has been largely that the same services that were public are now private, so that citizens must pay for those services as consumers rather than as taxpayers. Given that many of the privatized firms are monopolies, with their consequent ability to potentially charge exorbitant rates if not controlled in some way, there has been a need for public regulation. Government is now involved in those same economic sectors as a regulator rather than as a direct provider of goods and services.

Many of the changes that have occurred have been in the attitudes of citizens toward their government. One obvious fact has been the "taxpayers' backlash" and the associated strength of more conservative political parties, beginning in the late 1970s and lasting to the present. This was manifested in events such as the passage of Proposition 13 in California to limit the property tax and then numerous other similar anti-tax measures at state and local levels, and in the elections of Margaret Thatcher, Ronald Reagan, George Bush, Brian Mulroney, Helmut Kohl and bourgeois governments in Sweden (1976–82, 1991–94). Also, the strength of tax protest parties such as the Progress Parties in Denmark and Norway and "New Democracy" in Sweden illustrate the political power of groups seeking to dismantle some of the structure of the contemporary welfare state. It is debatable whether these reactions are against government in general, or only against certain aspects of taxation and expenditure. Wilensky and Hibbs and Madsen have argued that visible, direct taxes, rather than taxation in general, are what populations are protesting against by these votes.[80] However, for whatever reasons, words like "cutbacks," "privatization" and "deregulation" became common parlance in political circles that a decade or so ago might have been discussing new public programs, or the expansion of existing ones.

In addition to expressing their concerns by voting for political parties favoring reduced taxation, citizens have taken more direct action. The amount of increase in tax evasion is a matter of some debate, but there is general agreement that there has been such an increase. The rejection of the legal claims of government to their money may be taken as an indicator of a more general rejection by citizens of the government's claims on the society in general. In fact, the evidence is that tax evasion is more an indicator of political protest than it is an indicator of the real economic "bite" that taxes put on the (potential) taxpayer.[81] This is a revolution of sorts against government, albeit one that is bloodless and very quiet.

Associated with the changes in behavior have been changes in attitudes among the public. Tables 1.7 and 1.8 show that citizens are expressing substantially lower levels of support for government, and for the public bureaucracy in particular. By the 1970s and 1980s there were solid majorities against public expenditure in each country for which we can present data. These majorities have been especially strong in the United States, but it is interesting to note that citizens in one of the more advanced welfare states – Sweden – also respond with increasing reservations about increased expenditure and taxation. In other data (Table 1.8) the proportion of Swedes opposing cuts in the public sector declined by almost half from the early 1980s to the early and mid-1990s.

That reaction against big government, however, appears to have begun to moderate, once some of the consequences of a reduced public sector became more apparent to the respondents. Again, this has been manifested both in political behavior and in attitudes. In the middle to late 1990s, parties of the political left have returned to office in almost all European countries, and in the United States and Canada. These left parties may not be as ready to tax and spend as their counterparts in the past, but they do see a more positive role for government than the parties they replaced. Likewise, the attitudes expressed in opinion polls show that the public has assumed a somewhat more positive view of government

Table 1.8 Attitudes toward the public sector in Sweden, 1982–96

	Favor reducing size of the public sector	Oppose cuts in the public sector	Other/ no answer
1982	38	45	17
1985	42	42	16
1988	40	33	27
1990	56	18	26
1991	50	23	27
1992	41	34	25
1993	32	43	25
1994	35	38	27
1995	29	45	26
1996	23	49	28

Source: SOM Institute, *Trends in Swedish Public Opinion* (Goteborg: SOM Institute, University of Goteborg)

Table 1.9 Citizens' evaluation of public spending (percentage)

	1968	1973	1974	1975	1976	1977	1978	1979	1980	1981	1982	1983	1984	1985	1987	1989	1991
United States																	
Government spends too much for:																	
a) foreign aid	70	76	73	75	66	67		71		72		74		72	72	72	76
b) welfare	51	42	43	60	60	58		60	48		20			22	46	44	40
c) defense	38	31	31	27	23	22			15		20	32	37	46	42	41	28
d) helping blacks	22	21	24	25	25	19		19			20			16	22	23	22
e) urban problems	12	11	12	20	19	19		19			19			28	28	23	22
f) education	9	9	11	9	10	11		9	8		5	5		5	6	4	3
g) health	5	5	5	5	5	7		7			6			4	4	4	4
United Kingdom																	
Government spends too much for:																	
a) defense	37			21				24			27			22		56	45
b) health	21			12				4			4			2		1	1
c) education	18			15				3			6					7	2
d) roads	8			23				8			6			9		7	12
e) old-age pensions	2			3				1			1			1			1

Sources: "Opinion Roundup," *Public Opinion*, 1 (July/August, 1978): 32; "Opinion Roundup," *Public Opinion*, 6 (April/May, 1983): 27; E. H. Hastings and P. K. Hastings, eds, *Index to International Public Opinion, 1982–83* (Westport, CT: Greenwood, 1984); *Public Opinion*, 9 (April/May, 1986): 29; *Gallup Monthly Report* (Wilmington, DE: Scholarly Resources, monthly)

than in the 1980s, and see that the public sector can be important in providing the good life, just as is the market.

It is important to note, furthermore, that the majorities against "big government" often vanish when specific categories of public expenditure are discussed. In Table 1.9 we see that when citizens are asked about which public programs spend too much money and could be cut, there are very few majorities in favor of reducing expenditures. In many instances majorities, and even large majorities, could be found for *increasing* expenditures for particular public services, especially health, education, and services for the elderly.[82] Another survey taken in the late 1980s (Table 1.10) found majorities in favor of increased spending for half the programs asked about. The questions included a number of less popular programs (the arts, defense in most countries) and the sample contained none of the large public spending countries such as the Netherlands and those of Scandinavia. Still, there is reason to think that the public is more sophisticated in their assessment of the public sector than is often assumed.

It is important to remember, however, that some of the changes that have taken place in the modern public sector are more cosmetic than real. Some of these changes involve trading more intrusive and costly means of government intervention for less obvious and less directly costly instruments of governing.[83] Regulating the prices of a newly privatized electricity company may impose costs on the private sector, but it does not have the visible impact on budgets that running that same electric company would have if it had remained in the public sector. It is often the case that government can not realistically withdraw from a policy area completely, but instead it must find new and innovative means of achieving public purposes while, at the same time, limiting the visibility, and the costs, of its action to the public.

Table 1.10 Percentage of respondents wanting "much more" or "more" public spending for services, 1987

	Britain	USA	Australia	West Germany	Austria	Italy	Average
Health	88	60	62	52	62	81	67
Pensions	75	44	55	46	50	76	58
Education	75	66	64	40	38	63	58
Unemployment benefits	41	25	13	35	16	57	28
Law enforcement	40	51	67	30	23	48	45
Environment	37	43	32	83	74	61	55
Defense	17	20	46	6	13	12	19
Culture and the arts	10	16	10	14	12	33	16

Source: Peter Taylor-Gooby, "The Role of the State," in R. Jowell, S. Witherspoon and L. Brook, eds, *British Social Attitudes: Special International Report* (Aldershot: Gower, 1989)

Summary

This chapter should foreshadow what is to come in the remainder of the book. It establishes one crucial component of the environment within which contemporary public administration functions. This is that government in the late twentieth century is very big government, which makes the job of public administrators much more difficult. In the first place, the scale of contemporary government means that any organization being managed is likely to be a large organization with complex inter-relationships with other public and private organizations. Even small local governments now require skilled management to be effective and efficient. The issues about which governments now must legislate require skillful and expert decision makers. The second problem that arises is a constraint on resources available to the administrator: real resources, for example, money; and the "policy space" in which to function in making new policies.[84] Anything an administrator is likely to want to accomplish may involve him or her in a conflict with other organizations over money and "turf." With limited resources, the conflicts that arise among public organizations over the use of resources become more intense. Even if the administrator is cooperative, he or she will have major coordination problems that will require substantial skill and effort to overcome.[85]

Finally, citizens are now ever more wary and watchful of government in general, and of the public bureaucracy in particular. The majority of public administrators do not consciously "flee" from accountability for their actions, but the level of concern of citizens may make doing their job more difficult. Also, even in societies where public service has been a respected profession, the "bureaucracy" is increasingly a negative symbol of what is wrong with the country. This negative image cannot help but harm morale. That loss of morale, in turn, may so damage recruitment and retention that the low quality of the public bureaucracy, so often claimed by its critics, becomes a self-fulfilling prophecy.

Notes

1 P. Gould, *The Unfinished Revolution: How the Modernisers Saved the Labour Party* (London: Little, Brown, 1998).
2 This is true even for the Scandinavian countries. See J. G. Christensen, "The Scandinavian Welfare State: Institutions of Growth, Governance and Reform," *Scandinavian Political Studies*, 20, 367–86; 1998.
3 Brian W. Hogwood, "Developments in Regulatory Agencies in Britain," *International Review of Administrative Sciences*, 56 (1990), 595–612.
4 L. J. Sharpe, *Meso-Governments in Europe* (London: Sage, 1993).
5 For a review see Patrick D. Larkey, Chandler Stolp and M. Winer, "Theorizing About the Growth of Government," *Journal of Public Policy*, 1, 157–220; 1980.
6 B. Guy Peters and Martin O. Heisler, "Thinking About Public Sector Growth," in Charles L. Taylor, ed., *Why Government Grows: Measuring Public Sector Size* (Beverly Hills: Sage, 1983).
7 Prior to the change in systems, government was financed by small taxes but primarily from the trading revenues of the massive state sector. See M. A. Newcity, *Taxation in the Soviet Union* (New York: Praeger, 1986).
8 Joseph S. Nye, Philip D. Zelikow and David C. King, *Why People Don't Trust Government* (Cambridge, MA: Harvard University Press, 1997).
9 Christopher Howard, *The Hidden Welfare State* (Princeton, NJ: Princeton University Press, 1997).

10 Brian W. Hogwood, *Trends in British Public Policy* (Buckingham: Open University Press, 1992), pp. 64–9.

11 B. Guy Peters, *The Politics of Taxation: A Comparative Perspective* (Oxford: Basil Blackwell, 1992), pp. 198–208. In part this is because the higher the nominal rates of tax, the more any tax concession may be worth.

12 But see Aaron Wildavsky, "Keeping Kosher: The Epistemology of Tax Expenditures," *Journal of Public Policy*, 5 (1985), 413–31.

13 See T. Stanton, "Government Loans," in L. Salamon, ed., *Handbook of Policy Instruments* (New York: Oxford University Press).

14 Christopher Hood and Gunnar Folke Schuppert, *Delivering Public Services in Western Europe: Sharing Western European Experience of Para-Government Organizations* (London: Sage, 1988).

15 Christopher D. Foster and Francis J. Plowden, *The State Under Stress* (Buckingham: Open University Press).

16 The Kenyan government does spend more money in relation to GDP than Switzerland.

17 On the other hand, the state has been crucial for the economic development of the "little tigers" in Asia, including Singapore. The state has, however, acted more as a promoter than as a taxer and spender. See Peter B. Evans, *Emebedded Autonomy: States and Industrial Transformation* (Princeton: Princeton University Press, 1995).

18 Gabriel Almond and G. Bingham Powell, *Comparative Politics: A Developmental Approach* (Boston: Little, Brown, 1967), pp. 195–6.

19 S. Adjibolosoo, *Rethinking Development Theory and Policy: A Human Factor Critique* (Westport, CT: Praeger, 1999).

20 This was in part because economic growth was relatively lower during these years than in many other time periods, so the denominator did not expand very much,

21 The leaders of the new version of social democracy had a meeting in Florence to proclaim the virtues of their approach to governing and to lobby for "the Third Way." See Anthony Giddens, *The Third Way: The Renewal of Social Democracy* (Cambridge: Polity Press, 1998).

22 These benefits have been termed the "new property" created by the Welfare State. See Charles A. Reich, "The New Property," *Yale Law Review*, 73 (1964), 733.

23 Richard E. Wagner, *Charging for Government: User Charges and Earmarked Taxes* (New York: Routledge, 1991).

24 Adolph Wagner, *Finanzwissenschaft*, 3rd edn (Leipzig: C. F. Winter, 1890).

25 Bernard P. Herber, *Modern Public Finance*, 3rd edn (Homewood, IL: Dorsey, 1975), pp. 366–73; William D. Berry and David Lowery, *Understanding United States Government Growth* (New York: Praeger, 1987).

26 Alan T. Peacock and Jack Wiseman, *The Growth of Public Expenditure in the United Kingdom* (Princeton: Princeton University Press, 1961).

27 Even natural disasters may accentuate the need for an effective government and with that produce greater public acceptance of government revenue collection.

28 See A. G. Cuzan, "Political Profit: Taxing and Spending in the Hierarchical State," *American Journal of Economics and Sociology*, 40 (1981), 265–75.

29 Taxpayers' organizations have been successful at the state and local level in the United States and the Progress Parties in Denmark and Norway and the New Democracy Party in Sweden have made significant political gains into otherwise high-spending regimes.

30 William J. Baumol, "The Macroeconomics of Unbalanced Growth: Anatomy of Urban Crisis," *American Economic Review*, 57 (1967), 414–26.

31 H.M. Treasury, *Public Expenditure White Paper: Handbook on Methodology* (London: HMSO). The trimming of public employment may have reduced this figure, but on the other hand the privatization of many public sector enterprises that were more amenable to productivity improvements may have raised the figure.

32 See Christopher Hood, Desmond S. King and B. Guy Peters, *Understanding Changes in Public Employment*, Paper presented at Joint Workshops of European Consortium of Political Research, Bern, Switzerland, April, 1997.

33 John J. Dilulio, *Deregulating Government* (Washington, DC: The Brookings Institution, 1994).

34 James Q. Wilson, *The Politics of Regulation* (New York: Basic Books, 1980). Wilson argued that the nature of politics could be described in terms of the concentration or dispersion of costs and benefits.

35 Theodore J. Lowi, *The End of Liberalism*, 2nd edn (New York: W. W. Norton, 1979).

36 Garrett Hardin and John Baden, eds, *Managing the Commons* (San Francisco: W. H. Freeman, 1977); Elinor Ostrom, *Governing the Commons* (Cambridge: Cambridge University Press, 1990).

37 Lawrence S. Rothenberg, *Linking Citizens to Government: Interest Group Politics at Common Cause* (New York: Cambridge University Press, 1992).

38 Ruud Koopmans, *Democracy From Below* (Boulder, CO: Westview Press, 1996).

39 Christian Stoffaes, *Services Publics Comparees en Europe* (Paris: La documentation française, 1997).

40 *op. cit.*

41 William Niskanen, *Bureaucracy and Representative Government* (Chicago: Aldine/Atherton, 1971).

42 Not surprisingly, some governments of the political right have attempted to implement this suggestion, sometimes placing a public organization in competition with a private or quasi-private organization.

43 André Blais and Stéphane Dion, *The Budget-Maximizing Bureaucrat* (Pittsburgh: University of Pittsburgh Press, 1990).

44 See Alan T. Peacock, "X-Inefficiency: Informational and Institutional Constraints," in H. Hanusch, ed., *The Anatomy of Government Deficiencies* (Berlin: Springer, 1983).

45 See Chapter 8.

46 B. Guy Peters, "The European Bureaucract: The Applicability of *Bureaucracy and Representative Government* to Non-American Settings," in A. Blais and S. Dion, *The Budget-Maximizing Bureaucrat, op. cit.*

47 Christopher Hood, Meg Huby and Andrew Dunsire, "Bureaucrats and Budgeting Benefits: How Do British Central Departments Measure Up?," *Journal of Public Policy*, 4 (1984), 163–79; Patrick Dunleavy, *Democracy, Bureaucracy and Public Choice* (New York: Prentice-Hall, 1991).

48 Patrick Dunleavy, "Bureaucrats, Budgets and the Growth of the State: Reconsidering an Instrumental Model," *British Journal of Political Science*, 15 (1985), 299–328.

49 Brian W. Hogwood, D. Judge and M. McVicar (2000) "Agencies and Accountability," in R. A. W. Rhodes, ed., *Transforming British Government, Vol. 1: Changing Institutions* (Basingstoke: Macmillan).

50 Moshe Maor, "The Paradox of Managerialism," *Public Administration Review*, 59 (1999), 5–18.

51 Samuel Krislov, *Representative Bureaucracy* (Englewood Cliffs, NJ: Prentice-Hall, 1974), pp. 40–1.

52 B. Guy Peters, "Bureaucracy and Public Policy," in Douglas E. Ashford, *History and Context in Public Policy* (Pittsburgh: University of Pittsburgh Press, 1992).

53 See Cornelius Kerwin, *Rulemaking*, 2nd edn (Washington, DC: CQ Press, 1999); R. Baldwin, *Rules and Government* (Oxford: Oxford University Press, 1994).

54 This view is heard most commonly in "Euroskeptic" countries such as the United Kingdom and Denmark.

55 Richard Rose, "On the Priorities of Government," *European Journal of Political Research*, 4 (1976), 247–89.

56 The increase in the number of defining function agencies is in part a function of the increasing need to manage internal federal issues and other questions of regional political concern, as well as some increased needs to manage international affairs, including, in some cases, relationships with the European Community.

57 This is especially evident for the formerly communist countries that have begun to privatize state industries but continue a significant involvement in their industrial economies.

58 See R. H. Coase, *The Firm, the Market and the Law* (Chicago: University of Chicago Press, 1988).

59   Anthony Barker and B. Guy Peters, *The Politics of Expert Advice* (Edinburgh: University of Edinburgh Press, 1993).

60   See Brian W. Hogwood, *Trends in British Public Policy* (Buckingham: Open University Press, 1992), 156–9; updated by author. The figure of half of the acts being consolidated is an extrapolation from the work of Burton and Drewry. There has been a flurry of legislative activity – and extremely significant legislative activity – since Labour returned to office in 1997.

61   Hogwood, *ibid.*

62   A major exception to this generalization would be European countries such as Germany in which a large percentage of the legislature is made up of civil servants on leave from their posts in the bureaucracy. These civil servants are often trained as lawyers but many will have had substantial on-the-job experience with more technical matters.

63   Sanford F. Schram, *After Welfare: The Culture of Postindustrial Social Policy* (New York: New York University Press, 2000).

64   Morris P. Fiorina, *Congress: The Keystone of the Washington Establishment*, rev. edn (New Haven: Yale University Press, 1987).

65   Richard Rose, *The Problem of Party Government* (London: Macmillan, 1974); Francis G. Castles and Rudolf Wildenmann, eds, *Visions and Realities of Party Government* (Berlin: de Gruyter, 1986).

66   Bruce Headey, *British Cabinet Ministers* (London: George Allen and Unwin, 1974), pp. 83–109.

67   *ibid.*

68   For some idea of the variations in recruitment of ministers see Jean Blondel, "Ministerial Careers and the Nature of Parliamentary Government: The Cases of Austria and Belgium," *European Journal of Political Research*, 16 (1988), 51–71.

69   Edwin Marples, "A Dog's Life at the Ministry," in Richard Rose, ed., *Policy-making in Britain* (London: Macmillan, 1969), pp. 129–31.

70   B. Guy Peters, *European Politics Reconsidered* (New York: Holmes and Meier, 1991), pp. 66–9.

71   Paul C. Light, *Thickening Government* (Washington, DC: The Brookings Institution, 1996).

72   John Brehm and Scott Gates, *Working, Shirking and Sabotage* (Ann Arbor: University of Michigan Press, 1999).

73   *ibid.*

74   Peter S. Cleaves, *Bureaucratic Politics and Administration in Chile* (Berkeley, CA: University of California Press, 1974), pp. 310–11.

75   Anthony Downs, *Inside Bureaucracy* (Boston: Little, Brown, 1967).

76   Jonathan Boston *et al.*, *Reshaping the State: New Zealand's Bureaucratic Revolution* (Auckland: Oxford University Press, 1991).

77   Klaus König, "The Transformation of a 'Real-Socialist' Administrative System into a Conventional West European System," *International Review of Administrative Sciences*, 58 (1992), 147–62.

78   Joan M. Nelson, *Economic Crisis and Policy Choice: The Politics of Adjustment in the Third World* (Princeton: Princeton University Press, 1990).

79   For an interesting analysis of privatization see the introduction in L. Parotti and Vincent Wright, *Privatization* (Cheltenham: Edward Elgar, 1999).

80   Harold Wilensky, *The "New Corporatism," Centralization and the Welfare State* (Beverly Hills, CA: Sage, 1976); Douglas Hibbs and H. J. Madsen, "Public Reactions to Growth of Taxation and Government Expenditure," *World Politics*, 33 (1981), 413–35.

81   O. Listhaug and Arthur H. Miller, "Public Support for Tax Evasion: Self-Interest or Symbolic Politics," *European Journal of Political Research*, 13 (1985), 265–82.

82   See Peter Taylor-Gooby, "The Role of the State," in R. Jowell, S. Witherspoon and L. Brock, eds, *British Social Attitudes: Special International Report* (Aldershot: Gower, 1989).

83   See Lester M. Salamon, ed., *Handbook of Policy Instruments* (New York: Oxford University Press, 2001).

84   Brian W. Hogwood and B. Guy Peters, *Policy Dynamics* (Brighton: Wheatsheaf, 1983).

85   Eugene Bardach, *Getting Agencies to Work Together* (Washington, DC: The Brookings Institution, 1999).

Political culture and public administration

Citizens do not interpret the behavior of their governments and their public servants in a vacuum. Rather, they are equipped by their society with an image of
what constitutes good government and proper administration. This mental
"picture" of good government is composed of a set of complex cognitive and evaluative structures that tend to be (relatively) common among all members of the
society, although certainly many countries do have significant divisions with very
different ideas about politics and public administration. We refer to these generally shared psychological orientations as *political culture*.[1]

Although at times this common culture is directly imparted to children
through civics courses and patriotic exercises, the acquisition of a political
culture is usually part of the more general process of learning about living as
part of the society. Thus, just as the child learns the prevailing norms concerning economic behavior, social interaction, and table manners, he or she also
learns how to understand and evaluate politics and government. This process of
learning political values and political culture is referred to as *political socialization*.[2]

We have already seen that the social and economic systems of a country
place boundaries on the actions of government, and more specifically on public
administration. Political culture is equally important in setting boundaries,
although the boundaries are less tangible than those determined by economic
conditions. By defining what is good and bad in government, the culture may
mandate some actions and prohibit others. One component of this set of prescrip-
tions is the content of policy; governments must do certain things in order to be
considered a proper government, and they are also prohibited from engaging in
certain other activities.

Another component of the constraints on action is style; governments must
perform their requisite duties in certain ways. For example, although citizens now
expect governments to exert some control over the economy, there are some
means of doing this (regulation) that have become more acceptable than others
(public ownership). For public administration the manner in which members of
the public service meet the public and enforce their decisions is extremely important; one of the most common reforms of the public sector has been to attempt to
create a more client-centered approach to governing. Style issues may be especially important for public administration; both components are crucial for the
success of government.

Despite the seemingly abstract and vague nature of these cultural boundaries on behavior, governments can violate prevailing political norms only at their
risk. This is true no matter how antiquated and vestigial an element of the political
culture may be.[3] This is not to say that society's cultural values are immutable.
Culture is subject to change, and there is a constant interaction of culture and
actual politics that redefines the role of government.[4] For example, the latitude of
action allowed to governments at present would have been unthinkable before two
World Wars, one major economic depression, and a Cold War fundamentally
altered popular perceptions of the role of government, and that latitude has also
been enhanced by the relative success of the programs adopted to cope with the
crises. During the 1980s, however, the dominant culture in most industrialized
democracies was again modified to stress the limits, as well as the successes, of

government intervention, even in the Scandinavian countries that have a history of substantial state involvement in economy and society.[5]

Nevertheless, at the same time that the acceptable scope of government was tending to contract in the economic and social arenas, some of the other values supporting a democratic political system, such as freedom, equality and participation, have remained important or have actually increased in importance to citizens. Similarly, the activities now prescribed and proscribed for governments in Eastern Europe are vastly different than they were prior to the overthrow of the communist regimes. Some governments in Central and South America also have a diminished scope of action after the end of authoritarian rule, and the beginning of large-scale privatizations.[6]

Political culture has sometimes been considered a residual category for scholars of comparative politics seeking to explain similarities and differences among countries. That is, when all other explanations failed, the cause must have been political culture.[7] While this reductionist style of research has been perhaps too prevalent, there has also been a revival of interest in the explanatory capacity of cultural variables. For example, the concept of "policy style" has been used successfully to capture national differences in the process of policy making.[8] National "myths" have also been shown to have a pervasive influence on the conduct of government,[9] and policy sectors as well as countries have been shown to exhibit distinctive cultural features that influence policy choices.[10] Political culture is a difficult concept to isolate and measure precisely, but it is also a concept that is difficult to ignore, or to dismiss as meaningless for understanding politics and governing.

The remainder of this chapter examines the effects of political culture on the nature of the public administrative system. The comparisons made are of two varieties: (1) between political systems, commenting on the differences in administration in different countries, which may be a function of differences in their cultures; and (2) within systems across time. The second form of change is often undervalued, but given the vast transformations of governments in Eastern Europe and the former Soviet Union, Latin America and South Africa (to name the more obvious cases), cultural change across time within a system is a crucial element in understanding contemporary administrative behavior. Further, as well as participating in the total system transformations mentioned above, public administration itself may change in response to changing values, changing technologies, and changing expectations. Indeed, we will have one entire chapter on the reform of public administration as it attempts to adjust to marked changes in expectations about what a bureaucracy should do, and how those tasks should be done.

Administrative culture

For purposes of understanding public administration, we can think of culture as existing at three distinct levels: societal, political, and administrative. The conceptual relationship among these three levels can be seen in Figure 2.1. Notice that all three levels of culture influence the conduct of public administration. Very

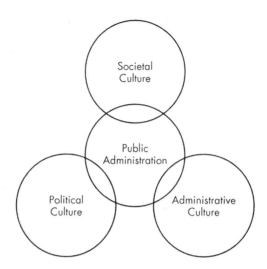

Figure 2.1 Culture and public administration

general value orientations in the society will influence the behavior of individuals working within formal organizations, as well as the manner in which those organizations are structured and managed. The political culture will also, in part, influence the relationships between political and bureaucratic elites, and between the population and the bureaucracy. Finally, the general orientation of the society toward management and impersonal authority in formal organizations will also affect the behavior of public officials. Public bureaucracies are sometimes portrayed as running roughshod over their societies, but they are bound by many thin but strong bonds to their societies, and the values of those societies.

We should also point out that individual organizations in government will develop their own cultures.[11] Some organizational cultures, such as that of the British Treasury, may be very elitist, while others (many social service agencies) may be extremely participatory and allow workers and clients substantial influence over decisions. In addition, organizations may provide their members with the means of interpreting general social and political values, so that very strong organizations can obtain somewhat greater freedom from control by prevailing social norms.[12] Organizational cultures, while important, are more suitably discussed when we consider management in the public sector and more micro-level considerations. In this chapter we will be concerned with cultural questions that affect virtually all public organizations within a country.

General societal culture

Let us first look at several aspects of societal culture that affect the performance of administration. The first of these cultural elements is the very basic question of the acceptability of "bureaucracy" as a means of large-scale organization in the society. A culture will have a basic set of evaluations of bureaucratic structures not only in government but also for all large-scale organization. Likewise, those societies that tend to adopt bureaucratic forms of management for one type of enterprise will tend to adopt bureaucratic means for all types of enterprise.[13] In discussing some aspects of these patterns, Reinhard Bendix made the distinction between entrepreneurial and bureaucratic societies.[14] Bendix used Great Britain as his example of an entrepreneurial society. This did not mean that business leadership was particularly aggressive or creative but rather that it was largely personal. The development and management of British enterprise has traditionally been through entrepreneurial action, despite the rather early acceptance of corporations and limited liability. The style of management has tended to remain personal, the development of a rather extensive administrative apparatus notwithstanding.[15]

The administration of public policy in Great Britain appears to follow many of the same entrepreneurial principles. Despite the development of the complex bureaucracy in Whitehall, the manner of functioning of public administration appears to be decision making through personal bargaining and negotiation as much as through the bureaucratic imposition of authority. Even the Treasury's pervasive authority over the public budget contains many elements of bargaining and negotiation. Much of the administrative process is conducted in an informal, personalistic manner based generally on personal acquaintances and personal trust.[16] The reforms of administration and the current reliance on chief executives to manage the "Next Steps" agencies make this personalistic bias in administration even more evident.[17] Finally, the nature of accountability in government has been highly personalized, with, in principle, the minister being responsible for everything that occurs in his or her department.[18]

The opposite of this entrepreneurial approach to administration is the institutionalized bureaucratic style of administration that has characterized Germany. This is, of course, a common stereotype of the culture of Germany but is also rather descriptive of styles of administration. Bureaucracy is a dominant form of social organization, in the public and private sectors, just as the relative informality of the committee is a common form of organization in Britain. Likewise, despite continuing change in the society, authority and status relationships may be more important in social relationships, including the family, than might be true in other industrialized societies.[19] In such a society, bureaucracy and its emphasis on authority relationships is a natural and acceptable form of public organization. This formality is considerably less acceptable in a society more oriented toward personal and informal decision making as in the United Kingdom, or the even more extreme case of the United States or some southern European countries.[20]

The differences between Britain and Germany are all the more interesting given that both societies are concerned with the equal and just application of the rule of law to individual citizens. There have been strains, however, as the increasing role of bureaucracy that has been characteristic of all modern societies collides with the more informal and increasingly egalitarian norms of Britain while bureaucracy has remained generally acceptable in Germany.[21] That having been said, there are also strains in the other direction, with increasing interest in postmaterial values (see below).

Bendix was primarily discussing differences among Western industrialized nations, but there are perhaps even more significant differences between that group of nations and the non-Western and non-industrialized nations. In general, the non-Western world is less accepting of the use of bureaucratic methods than is the Western world. Attempts to import this Western concept into the non-Western world have often resulted in the adoption of the formal aspects of bureaucracy while circumventing the procedural norms usually associated with those structures. Fred Riggs, in his discussion of the use of bureaucratic methods in underdeveloped countries, talks about the "sala" model of administration – structures having the form of a Western bureaucracy but actually filled with individuals operating according to more traditional norms of family and communal loyalty.[22] Even in an economically developed, albeit non-Western, society such as Japan, norms of personal and organizational loyalty may supplant bureaucratic reliance on authority, achievement and rules.[23]

The breakdown of the former Soviet Union, and the attempts of those countries to adapt to more democratic forms of management, has emphasized the existence of another style of administration. This might be termed a "control" system of administration. Rather than relying on individual initiative or the internal controls – hierarchy and law – of the bureaucracy, this form of administration is oriented toward using elaborate (and often extremely expensive) forms of external controls. For example, in most communist systems there were parallel structures of party and government that monitored each other. The ultimate goal of these systems was compliance of the individual administrator, and an assurance of close conformity to the preferences of the dominant regime.[24] This style of administration appears to have been characteristic of Russia under the Tsars as well as under communism, and to have been exported to other countries under Russian influence, e.g. Poland.[25] It may still be seen to some extent in the People's Republic of China.

As well as entrepreneurial, bureaucratic and control organizations, contemporary societies have been developing yet another type – the participatory organization. Rather than relying on the entrepreneurial actions of one or a few individuals, the authority of rules and structure, or on external controls, a participatory organization derives its energy from its members and their active involvement. This form of organization is common in voluntary organizations, but is less common in workplace organizations.[26] In business or government this form of organization is intended to take advantage of the desire of most people to participate in the decisions that affect their lives. Participatory organization also helps utilize the expertise that many lower echelon employees have about their jobs and about the performance of their organization. Participation is then a mechanism for harnessing the informal pattern of relationships that exists within any organization.[27]

Impersonal rules and organizations

Related to societal acceptance of bureaucracy as a means of organization is the acceptance of impersonality and universality of rules, a common theme in studying organizations and society. Talcott Parsons, in describing general patterns of cultural development, discussed this characteristic as one of his five pattern variables.[28] Likewise, Mary Douglas' conceptions of culture place an emphasis on the extent to which individuals are controlled by rules and other external restraints; what she calls "grid."[29] Likewise, in his empirical study of organizational values, Hofstede identified "individualism" as one of the four central values, with its antithesis appearing to be impersonality.[30] Wilson discusses political culture in terms of compliance ideologies, with "positional compliance" being very similar to an emphasis on bureaucracy and authority.[31] For their smooth functioning, bureaucracies depend on the acceptance of impersonality and universality of rules. If the rules of an organization must be renegotiated for each individual – whether employee or client – bureaucracies become not only inefficient, but superfluous as well. Bureaucracies have been developed to provide consistency and universality in the application of rules. These characteristics are demanded by law as well as by "modern" conceptions of fairness and justice. Other conceptions of justice, of course, depend more upon giving each individual an appropriate response, and in such a setting a bureaucracy may be of little real use. As governments tend to permit clients to have greater involvement in the administration of laws that affect them, and also more rights to complain about perceived administrative failures, formal bureaucracies become less valuable and less culturally acceptable.[32] Further, workers in public organizations may seek the same sorts of freedoms from rigid hierarchical controls.[33]

What sort of cultural systems tend to support the bureaucratic concept of universality and impersonality of rules? It can be associated with what has been called *rationalist* or *deductive* cultures.[34] These have been characteristic of developed countries in which political ideologies are relatively important, and are especially characteristic of the countries of continental Europe. These cultures tend to emphasize the deduction of specific statements and actions from general statements of principles. It is only a short step from this type of argument in the general social culture to the bureaucratic style of decision making, in which the decision about an individual case is made on the basis of deductive reasoning from a legal premise. This deductive variety of political culture is also to some degree manifested in the legal system of codified law, which attempts to detail every aspect of the law and thereby to minimize the need for personal discretion.[35] In these cases, if the deduction of the specific decision is performed correctly, there is little basis for argument. Both client and administrator can accept the adequacy and the justice of the ruling. The client will not always like the ruling made by the administrator, but the correctness of the impersonal nature of the application is difficult to question within such a cultural context. This is almost a stereotype of the Weberian bureaucracy, but also appears to function in some real-world settings.

The rationalist culture may be contrasted with the *pragmatic* or *empirical* culture that has been said to characterize the United Kingdom and much of northwestern Europe. In these cultures, generalities are derived from a series of individual decisions or inductively from observations. This type of culture is perhaps best typified by English (and American) common law, built up through centuries from individual decisions. This style of political culture is not so amenable to the development of bureaucracies or to impersonal decisions as are the rationalistic cultures described above. Each case is, to some degree, a new case and the particular individual circumstances may be sufficient to modify or overturn an apparent generality. In the inductive culture, administrative and legal decisions are almost inherently individualized and, although precedent certainly may rule, each case may be contested on its personal merits.[36]

The above statements should not be taken to indicate that the United Kingdom and the United States do not have bureaucratic organizations. By almost any definition of bureaucracy, that would be a foolish statement. Rather, they do mean that there tends to be less rigidity and impersonality accepted in these more inductive cultures than would be true in the more deductive, continental systems. In addition, the rulings made by administrators will be governed less by codified law than by precedent and perhaps by even less formalized conceptions of equity in law. The concept of individuality and individual rights, as one component of the more empirical culture, tends to make the job of the bureaucrat more difficult and forces more attention on specifics rather than on the generalities of the case.[37]

Katz and Eisenstadt point to an interesting case in which the norms of impersonality developed by a bureaucratic system are undermined by an influx of clients unaccustomed to those norms.[38] Israel was settled initially by Jews of European origin accustomed to the norms of impersonal and universal rule applications. These same norms were not held, however, by later waves of immigrants from the Eastern branches of Judaism. Socialized into the largely personalistic and barter cultures of the less-developed nations, the new settlers were unwilling to accept even the most basic universal rules, for example, that everyone who rides the bus should pay the same fare. Moreover, these immigrants were to constitute a major portion of the caseload for a number of social service agencies in Israel. Interestingly, both the clients and the administrative structures found it necessary to modify their behavior in order to accommodate the strains on their usual behavior patterns. The immigrants tended to adopt some of the basic ideas of impersonality, but the administrators also became more aware of personal differences among clients. Caiden found rather similar conflicts between the older immigrants to Israel, who had become accustomed to operating in a Middle-Eastern style, and the native-born *sabras*, who had become more oriented toward impersonality and bureaucracy.[39]

Much the same pattern of conflicts in values would be encountered in many less-developed societies where individuals raised in rural districts confront the more "modern" cultures that have evolved in urban areas. Such conflict may also be increasingly characteristic of government in developed democracies as the number of immigrants from the less-developed countries continues and public officials must interact increasingly with people with very different value systems. Even in wealthy and previously homogenous countries such as Switzerland, Denmark and Norway the influx of immigrants places some strain on the efficient administration of public policies.[40]

The above example points to three important aspects of the relationship between culture and public administration. The first is the "barter" nature of the political cultures encountered in a good portion of the underdeveloped world.[41] These nations present a variety and richness in cultural patterns, while universality and impersonal rules remain largely attributes of developed, Western societies.

In the non-Western world, and even in some portions of the Western world, all decisions are assumed to be subject to influence through personal bargaining and negotiation. Thus, formal rules promulgated by the bureaucracy merely constitute a place to begin the bargaining. Likewise, Riggs has noted that societies in transition from traditionalism to modernity, which he terms "prismatic," adopt a style of decision making that he refers to as "double-talk." Riggs notes:

> Even more typically prismatic is a law which provides for one policy although in practice a different policy prevails. A rule is formally announced but is not effectively enforced. The formalistic appearance of the rule contrasts with its actual administration – officials are free to make choices, enforcing or disregarding the rule at will. We have already seen that over-conformity and nonenforcement of laws is typically prismatic. It makes possible prismatic codes which, while appearing to promulgate a rule, in fact permit a wide variety of personalized choices by enforcement officials.... Apparent rules mask without guiding actual choices.[42]

Arguably, this form of administrative "double-talk" is prevalent in societies that have well-developed bureaucratic apparatuses but which lack the cultural infrastructure to support them. This would be true in some less-developed countries, such as in Africa and in parts of Latin America, as well as in many former socialist countries.[43] As control systems eroded in the countries of Eastern Europe and the former Soviet Union, the bureaucracy often persisted in the formal structures, but lost much of its impersonal and authoritative character.[44] Administration in those regimes has come to appear very much like Riggs' description of a prismatic administration,[45] and has also become plagued with the corruption often characteristic of administration in the Third World.[46]

Thus, we can imagine a rough continuum of cultural orientations toward impersonality and universalistic rules, ranging from the barter cultures described by Riggs and others to the highly rationalistic, impersonal attitudes apparently typical of continental European countries. On such a continuum, the pragmatic culture of the Anglo-American democracies might constitute something close to a halfway point. That is, compared with many non-Western political systems, the political culture of the Anglo-American countries would appear quite accepting of impersonal rules.[47] When compared with other advanced and industrial countries of Europe, however, the culture of the United Kingdom appears more personal and less bureaucratic than most other nations at similar levels of socio-economic development.

The second point emphasized by the Katz and Eisenstadt research is the importance of interaction in setting and changing the norms of administration. We have been stressing the importance of the lower echelons of administration and of their contact with clients. Not only is this type of contact crucial for the client, it may also be crucial for the organization in the formulation of its policies. In the case of Israel and the immigrants, we see the organization modifying its basic orientation toward clients and toward administration as a result of a problem in applying rules to specific clients. We can argue that, at least formally, the organization could have continued to apply rules impersonally. In this case, however, the organization chose to innovate, and did so successfully to meet client needs. Organizations willing to make this type of innovation generally will be more successful in the long run than organizations that maintain their rigid bureaucratic procedures even in the face of non-bureaucratic clients.

Evidence that more innovative organizations are more effective is limited, but behavior of that sort is potentially important for the effectiveness of administration. The limited work done in Israel and in less-developed societies can be supplemented by the more plentiful work done on "street level bureaucracy" in the United States, and on the "bottom up" view of implementation in a number of settings.[48] A general conclusion of this work is that organizations are more successful when they take into account the characteristics and needs of their clients rather than reacting in a stereotypically bureaucratic manner. The emphasis on "citizen involvement" as a part of contemporary administrative change is another indication of the belief in, and the reality of, a role for greater participation in bureaucracies.[49]

The third point raised by the research on Israeli immigrants is that the reaction of the immigrants to bureaucracy may be indicative of an emerging general pattern of interactions between citizens and government. All Western societies have undergone substantial cultural change since the 1960s, and those socialized politically in the 1960s and 1970s are now assuming major leadership roles in their nations. A major characteristic of that cultural change was a negative reaction to the impersonality and perceived inhumanity of large organizations in society and the desire to create less bureaucratized social and political systems.[50] While some of the ideas espoused at that time have been rightly criticized as utopian, there has been some real effect on politics and administration.

Politically, the desire for a more participatory and less bureaucratic society has been manifested in a number of political parties, and movements of the political left and right are attributable in part to this desire. These movements include the Greens in Germany (now a part of the governing coalition) and, in other parts of Western Europe, the Progress Party in Denmark and Norway and New Democracy in Sweden, and the more limited successes of the Social Democratic Party in Britain.[51] Thus there appear to be pressures that may be able, at least in part, to debureaucratize even highly bureaucratized Western societies. Further, increasing waves of international immigration are requiring civil servants in the more bureaucratized countries, like their Israeli counterparts mentioned above, to cope with clients who do not accept the norms of impersonal rules and laws.

In summary, we have examined two aspects of the general cultural values of society that are potentially important for understanding public administration. This is only a sample of these values, but any further enumeration runs the risk of being somewhat tedious. Further, it would distract attention from the more important relationships of the *political* culture of a country to the functioning of public administration. These political values tend to be more proximate to the decisions of civil servants, and to influence not only how they make their decisions but also the content of those decisions. We will now turn our attention to the examination of these political aspects of the culture, and their relationships to public administration.

Political culture and administration

When discussing political culture, we are concerned with the specific orientations of individuals in a society toward politics as one type of social action and collective decision making.[52] Public administration is a component of government and, therefore, may be analysed most effectively from the more politicized perspective, rather than being examined as simply another form of managerial activity. Some academics and practitioners have argued that public management is much the same as private management, but we will be arguing that there are, in fact, a number of significant differences.[53] Public administration is perceived as a managerial activity within public organizations themselves,[54] but is perceived more often by citizens as another component of government, albeit generally the least respected component of government. For citizens, public administration matters primarily because of the services it delivers rather than as an arena where managerial skills can be exercised.

Unfortunately for our purposes, the analysis and classification of political culture have been concentrated largely on the "input side" of the political system. Most attention has been given to attitudes and values concerning political participation, democratic procedures, political efficacy and political involvement. Much less scholarly attention has been devoted to classifying the orientations of citizens to the institutions of government, and to the outputs of the political system. Our knowledge of popular conceptions of public administration is even weaker than our knowledge of people's feelings concerning legislatures, the political executive and perhaps even the courts.[55]

It is difficult to avoid the general idea that most citizens do not like the bureaucracy, but have little direct evidence to support that idea. There is a great deal of anecdotal evidence about how people view the bureaucracy, but less systematic evidence.[56] There is now, however, an increasing body of information about the ways in which citizens evaluate their public bureaucracies, especially in industrialized societies, as is illustrated in Table 2.1. These data from a number of countries point to a varied conception of what governments should do and how they should do it. The public is rarely of one mind about the actions of their public servants.

How these data are evaluated may depend upon whether one believes that the glass is half empty or half full. On the one hand, given some of the exaggerated statements made about the incompetence and venality of public officials, the ratings of public officials are generally rather good. On the other hand, the ratings given generally are not as good for public sector employees as for private sector employees. Even for fairness, which should be the public sector's strongest point (see Chapter 8), the public sector did not generally rate as high as the private sector.[57] Further, some of the evidence suggests that actual contacts with the public service, even if favorable, have little impact upon attitudes; the evaluation of the public sector appears to be culturally determined as much or more than it is determined by the actual performance of government.[58] In the terms of role theory, the role which many societies have assigned to their public employees is one of incompetence, bungling and high-handedness, and empirical evidence may have little impact on citizens' evaluations.

Table 2.1 Popular evaluations of public bureaucracy

A. Fairness (percentage of those answering)			
	United States (Government)	Canada Government	Canada Business
Good and very good	43.8	68.9	84.4
So-so	29.2	21.1	10.6
Bad and very bad	27.0	10.1	4.9
Total	100.0	100.1	99.9

B. Government vs. Business (United States) (percentage)			
	Government Better	Government Same	Business Better	Business No answer
Considerate	11.5	47.8	37.5	3.2
Fair	18.8	33.6	44.5	3.1

C. Public employees are . . . (percentage responding yes)		
	United States	Australia
Too numerous	67	54
Working less hard than business	67	63

D. Descriptions of public administration (France) (percentage)				
	High integrity	Efficient	Competent	Accountable
Good description	79	54	67	41
Bad description	11	38	23	45
No answer	10	8	10	14
Total	100	100	100	100

Sources: David Zussman, "The Image of the Public Service in Canada," *Canadian Public Administration*, 25 (1982): 63–80; Daniel Katz *et al.*, *Bureaucratic Encounters* (Ann Arbor, MI: Survey Research Center, University of Michigan, 1975); *The Bulletin* (Sydney), 20 August 1977; J. L. Quermonne and L. Rouban, "French Public Administration and Policy Evaluation: The Quest for Accountability," *Public Administration Review*, 46 (1986): 401

As well as discussing relationships with civil servants, we can also see the public's evaluation of the public service by examining how well they think those services are performing. In the United Kingdom the public were asked how well a variety of organizations and institutions were run. In general, public institutions fared rather well in this evaluation. Banks were considered the best-run organizations in the society (Table 2.2), but the police, the BBC and universities (all public or quasi-public) came in second, third and fourth. The civil service was rated almost as highly as private industry in terms of its being well run. It is important to note, however, that most public organizations in Britain experienced a sizeable drop in positive evaluations even in the short period from 1983 to 1987, while private institutions improved slightly.

Table 2.2 Perceptions of management of institutions in the United Kingdom (percentage)

	"Well run"	
	1983	1987
Banks	90	91
Industry	43	48
Unions	29	27
BBC	72	67
National Health Service	52	35
Nationalized industries	21	33
Universities	–	65
Police	77	66
Civil service	42	46
Local government	35	29

Do the following (public) institutions work well?

Post Office	80	
Police	69	
Railways	65	
Hospitals	63	
Schools	57	
Social security	49	
Justice system	29	

Sources: Roger Jowell and Richard Topf, "Trust in the Establishment," in Roger Jowell, Sharon Witherspoon and Lindsay Brook, *British Social Attitudes, Fifth Report* (Aldershot: Gower, 1988); *L'Etat de l'Opinion*, 1996 (Paris: Editions de Seuil), p. 326

Also, if we examine the evaluations of public services and public servants in France and Italy, we can see that respondents in these two societies give rather positive evaluations of many of their public services. Indeed, their evaluations are, in many cases, more positive than for private sector organizations, including major market organizations. Both of these countries have had a large public sector, and France has been more reluctant to cut back the size of government than have most other European governments. The strength of the positive evaluation of government in France may be seen in the popular outbursts against several attempts to reduce public sector involvement in providing public service.[59]

Several other studies also point to generally positive evaluations of the performance of the public sector in delivering services. One study in Canada showed generally high levels of satisfaction with a variety of public services, with no service having more than a majority of the respondents saying they were dissatisfied with the services (Table 2.3). French respondents expressed somewhat less positive views of services, but only marginally so. Another Canadian study showed that a large, and increasing, proportion of the population considered public services to be "good value for money," although a similar British study revealed much less support for public services (Table 2.4). Another survey in France asked respondents whether they believed the quality of service provided would improve if the service were privatized.[60] For a majority of services the modal response was that privatization would make the quality of service worse, and only for hospitals did a majority think that privatization would produce an improvement (Table 2.5). In short, although the public service may have a

Table 2.3 Satisfaction with public services (percentage)

A. Canada (1990)					
	Very satisfied	Somewhat satisfied	Somewhat dissatisfied	Very dissatisfied	Don't know
Fire department	64	27	2	1	6
Garbage collection	61	29	4	3	3
Libraries	49	33	4	2	12
Medical services	48	38	9	4	1
Postal services	46	40	10	4	–
Police	46	41	8	3	2
Elementary schools	35	32	8	3	22
Recreation	33	42	11	4	10
High schools	29	33	12	4	22
Street repair	19	35	24	19	3

B. France (1987)			
	Satisfied	Not satisfied	Don't know
Fire services	96	1	3
Municipal services	90	7	3
Gas and electricity	85	14	1
Postal services	82	17	1
Hospitals	79	18	3
Social security	37	58	5
Tax collectors	35	62	3
Justice	32	53	15
Education	28	57	15

C. Italy					
	1976	1979	1985	1988	1995
Post office	47	44	64	53	53
Telephones	65	69	80	76	84
State railways	43	33	49	35	53
Medical services	–	–	–	31	22

Sources: Jean-Luc Bodiguel and Luc Rouban, *Le Fonctionnaire Détrôné?* (Paris: Presses de la Fondation Nationale des Sciences Politiques, 1991); DOXA, *Alcuni Aspetti dell'Opinione pubblica* (3 March 1995)

Table 2.4 Value for money in public services (percentage)

A. Canada		
	Good value	
	1983	1988
Fire protection	87	89
Medicare	86	87
Garbage collection	83	83
Police	79	82
Education	58	60
Postal service	47	58

B. Great Britain		
	Good value	
	1986	1988
Police	73	69
Garbage collection	71	69
National Health Service – GPs services	65	68
Sports and recreation	60	62
National Health Service – hospitals	57	56
Primary education	44	50
Family allowances	44	39
Universities	41	46
Housing	41	33
Elderly services	40	37
Roads	36	29
Secondary education	32	42
Pensions	31	25
Unemployment benefits	31	23
Maternity benefits	30	26

C. Italy		
	Honesty and commitment	Capacity and competence
1967	33	39
1974	6	7
1976	4	4
1984	19	29
1991	9	23
1993	8	21
1995	46	41

Sources: E. H. Hastings and P. K. Hastings, *Index to International Public Opinion, 1988–89* (Greenwood, CT: Greenwood Press, 1990); DOXA, *Alcuni Aspetti dell'Opinione pubblica* (3 March 1995)

Table 2.5 Perceived effects of privatization in France (percentage)

	Positive	Negative	No difference	Don't know
Health insurance	25	30	27	18
Postal service	27	27	32	14
Education	29	32	24	15
Prisons	20	23	20	37
Hospitals	30	29	24	17

Source: *Le Nouvel Observateur*, October 10–16 1986

negative public image in general, citizens do appear to appreciate the services it provides to them.

The above positive perception of public services may hold true for the industrialized world, but is much less true for the developing countries. The evidence is limited here, but there is a sense that much of the population has come to expect poor quality services and less than fair treatment from the service providers. For example, over half of the Zambian respondents to a survey said that they found four government services poor or very poor (Table 2.7). The same survey pointed out that the Zambian population found their civil servants incompetent, rude and unfair. Although the evidence is less quantified, several reform efforts in less-developed countries in Latin America are centered on improving the quality of public services.

Some of the negative evaluations of public servants encountered in surveys may be a result of very high popular expectations about the behavior of their public officials. For example, in one survey in Britain there were very different feelings about a manager taking a gift from a firm with whom he or she was doing business, depending upon whether the manager was employed in industry or in local government (Table 2.6). Three times as many people thought that such a gift was totally acceptable for someone in business than believed that it was acceptable for someone in government service. There are clearly different standards of behavior expected for public servants, and therefore, perhaps, greater disappointments when there are ethical failures.[61]

Evidence about citizens' attitudes toward the public bureaucracy is spotty in the developed countries, but it is extremely difficult to find for less-developed countries. Almond and Verba examined the administrative competence of citizens in five countries, including Mexico. They sought to determine the degree to which these citizens feel capable of influencing administrative decisions. There was considerable variation among the countries, with over half the respondents in Germany and Great Britain feeling capable of exerting such an influence, while only eight percent of Mexican respondents felt their protests would make any difference.[62] Eldersveld, Jagannadham and Barnabas, building on the work of Janowitz, Wright and Delany, have been able to make some comparisons between citizens' attitudes toward administration in the United States and in India.[63] Although the Indian respondents surveyed were more willing to work in public jobs than private jobs, their general evaluation of public administration was much less positive than that of a sample in Detroit. The Indian respondents felt that they

Table 2.6 Expectations about behavior in the public sector (percentage)

	Gifts from contractor for:	
	Company manager	Local Government official
Nothing wrong	39	13
A bit wrong	23	14
Wrong	29	43
Seriously wrong	7	28
Don't know	2	3

	Good descriptions of public administrators? (France) (yes)		
	1980	1989	1996
They love paperwork	71	75	76
They play favorites	40	33	–
They are honest	–	–	78
They work too little	–	40	39
They are competent	64	60	62
They are friendly	47	49	51

Sources: Michael Johnston and D. Ward, "Right and Wrong in Public and Private Life," in Roger Jowell and Sharon Witherspoon, eds, *British Social Attitudes, 1985* (Aldershot: Gower, 1985); *L'Etat de l'Opinion 1990* (Paris: Editions de Seuil, 1991), p. 188; *L'Etat de l'Opinion 1997* (Paris: Editions de Seuil, 1991), p. 155

were treated badly in their interactions with administrators and had a cynical view of corruption and favoritism in the public bureaucracy of India. This result may be accounted for, in part, by the "prismatic" nature of Indian government and its administration. It does point out, however, that, despite the findings of Levy and others, Americans are not entirely negative about their public administrators, especially when their attitudes are compared with those of citizens of underdeveloped countries. Other studies conducted in underdeveloped countries have pointed to the same negative evaluations of the civil service.[64]

Some recent studies from formerly communist Eastern Europe point to extraordinarily negative evaluations of the public bureaucracy.[65] This assessment is perhaps to be expected given the behavior of bureaucracies in the former communist regimes, and in many, the behavior of bureaucracies in previous regimes. It may, therefore, require years if not decades for bureaucracies to develop the legitimacy of bureaucracies within these governments, even if the political institutions are able to create greater legitimacy for their activities.

Leaving aside for the time being a lack of much direct evidence concerning popular orientations toward administration, we can undertake a more analytical discussion of the effects of political culture on administration. This should begin with some of the possible dimensions for analysis. As was mentioned previously, the majority of analyses of political culture have dealt almost exclusively with mass political participation. Thus, Almond and Verba speak of parochial, subject

and participant cultures on the basis of the willingness of the individual to participate on the input side of politics.[66] Almond and Powell use cultural secularization
as one of their three variables to describe political development.[67] Although this is
a broad concept, one of the primary components is an orientation toward politics
involving manipulation, and the attainment of individual goals through political
action. We do not want to paint with too broad a brush, however. Some discussions of political culture have been concerned with problems of authority and of
governmental institutions. Nettl used "constitutional" and "elitist" as the two basic
dimensions of his analysis of culture, with these two dimensions defined largely
by the authority relationships within the society and polity.[68] This is, therefore,
somewhat similar to Eckstein's discussion of authority as a crucial dimension of
the analysis of political culture.[69] Likewise, Elazar's discussion of the dimensions
of political culture in the United States rather explicitly involves a discussion of
the cultural acceptability of certain types of public policies, and authors following
his lead have found connections between culture and the policies adopted by state
governments. Thus, we do have some amount of guidance in attempting to relate
political culture to the activities of government and to major institutions.

Dimensions of political culture

There have been a number of attempts to classify political cultures. Perhaps the
two most useful general conceptualizations of political culture are those provided
by Lucian Pye in the introductory essay to *Political Culture and Political Development* and Mary Douglas' general conceptualization of culture in, among other
places, her essay "Cultural Bias."[70] Pye developed his four dimensions for the

Table 2.7 Perceptions of public services and public servants in Zambia

	Quality of public services			
	Very poor	Poor	Good	Very good
Education	23.8	39.1	32.1	5.1
Health	27.0	38.4	31.7	2.9
Local services	59.8	24.1	14.4	1.7
Post office	8.0	18.7	55.4	17.9
Police	29.6	28.0	35.3	7.2
	Evaluation of civil servants			
	Very poor	Poor	Good	Very good
Competence	41	47	11	1
Fairness	22	55	20	3
Politeness	12	53	30	5

Source: Mamadou Dia, *Africa's Management in the 1990s and Beyond* (Washington, DC:
The World Bank, 1994), pp. 65, 67

examination of political inputs, but these dimensions are also useful for our analysis of the administrative aspects of government. Although not explicitly linked, these dimensions can be related to Douglas' ideas about the underlying dimensions of culture.

Douglas discusses cultures as the intersection of two dimensions – "group" and "grid." The "group" dimension refers to the extent to which an individual is incorporated into a defined group, and hence the extent to which individual decisions are subject to group influences. "Grid" refers to the extent to which an individual's life is bound by externally imposed restrictions, and hence the extent to which individual factors and individual negotiations can determine life circumstances; in "high-grid" societies there is less room for individual autonomy. We will relate these concepts to those of Pye as we discuss the four dimensions of culture that Pye described. These two variables interact to form four cells with distinctive types of cultural relations.

Hierarchy and equality.   The first dimension of culture mentioned by Pye is hierarchy and equality. Most administrative structures have a hierarchical structuring of personnel and authority in formal organizations, and the cultural values concerning authority and impersonality of rules mentioned above are important for determining the acceptability of hierarchical management practices. Several other more basic political questions also surface when we consider hierarchy and equality in public administration.

First, what are the means of recruitment into administrative positions? Parsons has used the terms "achievement" and "ascription" to describe how societies recruit people to positions.[71] In an achievement-oriented society, an individual's place in society is determined by his or her ability. Advancement in society is determined by what the individual can do, not by conditions of birth. Ascriptive societies recruit individuals to positions in society (and the public bureaucracy) on the basis of ascriptive criteria – class, status, race, language, caste, gender – and the individual's position is determined by these largely immutable personal characteristics.

As one would imagine, achievement criteria have generally been linked with "modern" society while ascriptive criteria have been linked with "traditional" societies. As was discussed by Weber, as well as most other commentators on administration, bureaucracy and administration are inherently modern and achievement-oriented components of the political system.[72] Voters may choose a traditional elite to rule the country, but the bureaucracy would (in theory) still select the best people regardless of socio-economic position or other ascriptive characteristics. Even traditional, ascriptive rulers may want to have the best trained and most modernized bureaucracy possible. This is true in theory, but the actual application of the principle varies markedly from society to society.

In Douglas' terms, ascription and achievement criteria are a function of the group dimension of culture, or more specifically of a political culture. The question is to what extent are the opportunities of any individual for a leadership role in government a function of his or her group membership in the society? In a traditional society, that would be high on both the group and grid components of her scheme, the role of an individual would be determined largely by ascriptive criteria. Even if there were room for some bargaining on a personal basis ("low grid"), the ascriptive criteria would often play a strong role in determining the scope of the bargains. In such a society individuals would find it difficult to escape the circumstances of their birth, and would be locked in a "fatalist" position without much control over their destiny.

Equality in the recruitment of public administrators is discussed at length in Chapter 4, but a brief discussion is necessary here. The issue of equality of recruitment arose in the United Kingdom over the issue of social class. Kingsley's seminal discussion of representative bureaucracy in Britain found that the middle classes were heavily over-represented in the higher civil service.[73] The study was, however, ambivalent concerning the effects of that over-representation. It is probable that even bureaucracies recruited on the most achievement-oriented basis possible would still display this same dominance of the middle and upper classes because of the correlation between social class and the ability to take standardized tests, success in school and so forth. The fact that the bias detected may be produced by other social forces has not prevented recruitment from being a political issue. This is true of greater equality among the social classes and has also been true of greater equality among language groups, religions, regions and genders.

Equality in recruitment is especially important given the composition of the clientele of most public bureaucracies. While a number of public administrators are concerned with business and industry, agriculture, foreign policy, and defense, the majority of the clients served directly by public agencies are from the relatively disadvantaged segments of the population. With this we come to the common situation of middle-class administrators attempting to provide solutions for working-class, or "under-class," problems.[74] While both groups may share a common national culture, there are still often differences among social classes in their values. This problem is especially important when class lines coincide with ethnic, linguistic or other cleavages.

Because of the importance of ethnicity and class in the perception of government by clients, some reformers have advocated the recruitment of administrators on a quota basis to ensure that administration accurately reflects the society it is attempting to govern. This perception may be especially important for the lower echelons of the bureaucracy who interact frequently with the public. The proposed solution, of course, can easily be interpreted as running counter to the value of achievement-oriented recruitment, usually characteristic of modern administrative systems. Thus, somewhat paradoxically, attempts at generating one form of equality in service may be seen to require some inequalities in recruitment.

Equality raises a second question for public administration. As has been stated several times, bureaucratic organizations in Western societies have involved the use of hierarchical authority. Superiors in the organizations have always attempted to exercise their authority to tell subordinates what to do. Various cultural groups have been more willing than others to accept this authority. Crozier points to distinct differences in the acceptance of authority within French, British, American and Russian organizations.[75] He points out that French organizations are plagued by the inability of many of their members to accept authoritative commands from a superior, whereas patterns of deference ingrained in British culture made such an authoritative command quite acceptable. Massive changes in orientations toward authority have taken place in Western societies and in Russia, but many of the problems and differences cited by Crozier persist.[76] Likewise, several studies of public administration in developing societies point out that orders from a superior may be obeyed as a function of the personal characteristics of that individual, and personal loyalty, rather than from an acceptance of the authority of the position.[77]

Despite these differences, acceptance of authority has declined in all developed nations. This trend may be seen as a part of the new individualism of the "postindustrial society."[78] Alternatives to the traditional hierarchical structuring of organizations have been proposed with such titles as "dialectical organizations" and "collaboration–consensus" organizations.[79] Other analysts have advocated the need to "break through" or "break down" bureaucracy in public organizations.[80] These and myriad other proposed reforms have had in common the desire to replace authority with more spontaneous forms of organization based on greater equality among all the members of a work group. In these conceptions the "leaders and the led" characteristic of hierarchical organizations would be replaced by groups of collaborators.

Some of the most important efforts in the direction of equality in organizations have taken place in industrial management. Going under the general label of "industrial democracies," some organizations have replaced the leadership of the foreman with joint decision making by the work group. For example, workers at numerous Swedish industrial plants have been able to choose their own work leaders and own working pace and times. A number of companies, as well as an increasing number of public organizations, have also imported mechanisms, such as "quality circles" from Japan and "Total Quality Management" in a number of countries, in an attempt to create greater involvement of the workers in their jobs and improve the quality of the products.[81] Finally, in Germany and Scandinavia, companies are required to give virtual equality on their boards of directors to representatives of their workers, and less extreme versions of this practice of *Mitbestimmung* have been instituted in other industrialized countries.[82]

As I will point out in the chapter on administrative reform one contemporary strand of reform of the public sector is "participatory." The argument of these reformers is that government is too hierarchical, so that the lower echelons of the public service are not able to influence the decisions being made within the organization. This is argued both to deny the worker the right to feel involved in the organization and to deprive the organization of his or her expertise. Further, reducing hierarchical controls enables governments to eliminate large numbers of middle-management employees whose job was supervision.[83] In modern political cultures granting greater opportunities for participation is almost essential for good management, whether in the public or the private sector.

These new forms of organizational management pose a unique question for public organizations: what is the role of the client in relationship to the organization? Public organizations tend to be "people-processing" organizations in which the "product" has many of the same human needs as the "producer." As such, the position of the client as either subordinate or participant must be defined by the organization. Few public organizations could afford the luxury of making the client an equal partner in the decision-making process, no matter how normatively desirable such a form of organization might be to some observers (and clients). Still, the participatory reforms discussed above argue for more participation by clients, especially in the management of facilities such as schools and public housing.[84]

Public organizations also have legal and moral obligations to fulfill that prevent their being overly responsive to their clients. At the same time, public organizations do have the opportunity and ability to involve clients in some aspects of decision making concerning their cases, as well as in the general functioning of the organization. If nothing else, public organizations can ensure that their clients are treated fairly and are given the right to influence, if not control, decisions that affect them.[85] Indeed, clients may be more willing to accept adverse decisions if they have been allowed opportunities for participation and have had the reasons for the decision explained to them.

The evidence derived from the first decades of the post-industrial society indicates that clients are increasingly unwilling to accept a passive and subordinated position *vis-à-vis* the public organization – in Douglas' terms they seek lower grid positions. This is certainly true of more educated clients of programs touching large segments of the population – for example, public retirement programs such as Social Security – and is increasingly true of lower socio-economic classes for whom terms such as "empowerment" represent a desire to change their relationship with the bureaucracy.[86] Also, reforms such as "citizens' charters" make it more evident to the average citizens just what his or her rights may be *vis-à-vis* the bureaucracy.[87]

Liberty and coercion.   Closely allied with the ideas of hierarchy and equality is the dimension of liberty and its opposite, coercion. As a gross generality, most of the societies discussed here have been undergoing historical changes in their value systems, favoring decreased economic liberty and increased liberty of expression and social action. It is often the bureaucracy that must decide the limits of both types of liberty and also determine how much coercion is acceptable in enforcing these decisions. This is, of course, true for economic regulatory agencies, but we often fail to remember that the police are themselves one of the most ubiquitous forms of administration. The enforcement of social programs such as the "workfare" reforms being implemented in many industrialized democracies also involve imposing restraints on the liberty of some citizens.[88]

We can make the argument that the stability of a democratic society may depend upon the degree of value consensus among the enforcers of those rules and the majority of the citizenry. As numerous student activists during the late 1960s demonstrated, and continuing protests against racial inequality, nuclear weapons, nuclear power stations, and environmental degradation have continued to demonstrate, there is a great deal of value dissensus with respect to the amount of liberty felt to be desirable and, relatedly, the amount of coercion deemed necessary to enforce one side of the argument. Student rebellions in places such as South Korea and China also point to the fact that, in a society, freedom and coercion themselves can be central issues in the value dissensus. Finally, conflicts over issues such as abortion and divorce point to the re-emerging role of religion and culture, as well as generational differences, as a cause of value dissensus over the role of government in regulating activities.

Despite the above-mentioned conflicts and outbursts, the application of direct physical violence is less acceptable and probably less frequent in modern societies. On the other hand, the application of indirect coercion is becoming an increasingly frequent and controversial technique of political control. Here we are referring not only to the potential use of psychological devices to exercise thought control, in the manner of Orwell's novel *1984*, but we are also speaking of the ability of administrative agencies to impose their wills on citizens without the opposition of those citizens. This imposition of the wishes of the public sector can be done in a variety of manners, with the most common now being through claims on behalf of efficiency, and the appeal to technological criteria in decision making.[89]

It has become increasingly difficult for the average citizen, or even the exceptional citizen for that matter, to dispute the decisions made by a technologically competent and well-insulated bureaucracy. Government has therefore become an amalgamation of large organizations making decisions on their own terms and forcing them on individuals. Emmette Redford has said:

> The first characteristic of the great body of men subject to the administrative state is that they are dormant regarding most of the decisions made with respect to them. Their participation cannot in any manner equal their subjection. Subjection comes from too many directions for man's span of attention, much less his active participation, to extend to all that affects him. Any effort of the subject to participate in all that affects him would engulf him in confusion, dissipate his activity and destroy the unity of his personality. Democracy, in the sense of man's participation in all that affects him, is impossible in the administered society.[90]

We, and Professor Redford, may be guilty of overstating the case, but the possibility of administrative tyranny is apparent in even the best-administered modern societies. Some obvious examples would be the general absence of public involvement in a range of environmental and energy issues that have profound effects on citizens. The decisions surrounding these issues tend to be dominated by experts, albeit frequently by disagreement among experts, and citizens have little information and less opportunity to make choices.[91] We comment on this problem here only as a dimension of culture, and will leave the analysis of possible solutions until Chapter 9.

Furthermore, while the possibilities for manipulation are certainly great in the administered or postindustrial state, we must not lose sight of the fact that the degree of control exercised over the individual through non-coercive means may be as great or greater in traditional society. This is, in fact, very clear in Douglas' discussion of the restrictions on individual behavior within societies, and controls existing along both the group and grid dimensions.[92] Thus, the period of mass democracy and liberalism during the early and middle twentieth century may be merely a period of transition between two more "totalitarian" forms of government. In the traditional society, this use of non-physical coercion is justified on the basis of religious or ideological dogma. In the postindustrial society, it may be justified through appeals to efficiency and technology and the media, which constitute the dogma of the modern societies striving for cumulative social and economic rationality.

The increasing level of education of the population, and the consequent increase in the perception of their competence to participate in political decisions, may generate increasing tension within a postindustrial society. In one scenario, there will be sufficient citizens with sufficient competence to have real impacts on policy and administration. In a less optimistic scenario, the intellectual demands of the technology will increase more rapidly than will citizen competence, producing large-scale alienation from the political system itself.[93] These tensions are now being played out in conflicts over nuclear power, reproductive technologies, the environment, and defense policy. Whichever scenario is correct, and there is the possibility that both will be apparent in respect to different policy issues, public participation in a bureaucratic and technological society is likely to be a continuing problem of postindustrial society. Institutional change and public awareness of the opportunities for participation continue to promote involvement while the daunting technological demands make effective participation difficult.

The dangers of technological and elite domination of decision making in democratic societies is not recognized as a problem, but there are no easy solutions. One recommended solution is electronic democracy, with the public being given the opportunity to participate in decisions (at least as voters) through numerous electronic referenda. Other critics argue that this simple form of participation is inadequate, in part because the questions to be considered have been determined before the public becomes involved. These critics advocate more deliberative forms of democracy, with the public being involved throughout the process, and being given the opportunity for some reflection and discussion about the issues.[94] The critics of deliberation, in turn, raise questions about the practicality of this method.[95]

Loyalty and commitment.   The third dimension of political culture mentioned by Pye was loyalty and commitment, referring mainly to the terminal community to which the individual gives his or her ultimate loyalty. For many developing societies, and even for some industrialized societies, there is little identification with people outside the family. Even where the commitment to the family is *not* paramount, loyalties to language, religion, caste, or ethnic group diminish individual commitment to the national political system and produce the potential for political unrest and instability. Further, in Europe there is a growing transfer of allegiance to the European Union, so that identification with the nation-state is under attack from yet another direction.[96]

The implications of a lower level of commitment to the nation-state by the public for public administration are profound. This is especially true when those commitments are to subnational groupings outside the family. First, the existence of this type of social cleavage will tend to direct power upward toward the bureaucracy. Political decision making in situations of extreme social cleavage is a difficult if not impossible process, although some countries of Europe have been developing structural and behavioral mechanisms to circumvent the problem. For example, both the Netherlands and Switzerland have found consociational means of coping with divisions, with strong elite agreement used to manage the potential for conflict over language and religion.[97]

In most cases of cleavage, however, either immobilism or the necessity of imposed decisions will limit the effectiveness of legislative or executive decision making. In these cases, the public bureaucracy may be the only effective decision-making body in the nation. In addition, if the bureaucratic ethos expressed by Weber and others, that the bureaucracy is above politics is successfully inculcated into the population, the bureaucracy may be able to function quite effectively. It can present the image of acting independently and rationally, while at the same time make important policy decisions for the society when more conventional democratic institutions are inoperable. Certainly France in the Fourth Republic and, to some degree, contemporary Italy and perhaps Belgium, would fit this characterization, as would a number of Third World countries.[98] As that central decision-making role becomes apparent, however, the erosion of these conceptions of bureaucracy may limit the future effectiveness of the bureaucracy in immobilist or fragmented societies. The bureaucracy ceases to be an impartial arbiter of justice and becomes the object of manifest political appeals.[99]

A second implication of the segmented nature of many political cultures for public administration concerns the relationship of administrator and client. As pointed out when discussing the relationship of social class to recruitment, so we must, in this instance, give attention to differential hiring by ethnic groups. Domination by one group is common in countries of the Third World, especially where current national boundaries were drawn by former colonial powers with little regard for the social composition of the political unit being created. For example, ethnic conflicts in Rwanda, Burundi, Nigeria and other countries are in part over the domination of the public sector (including the army) by one group or another. These ethnic divisions are not, of course, confined to the Third World; they are found in such cases as the domination by Protestants in Northern Ireland and historically by the English-speaking community in Canada.

The implications of these divisions are not only for civil unrest, but also for day-to-day political tensions. One aspect of this tension between social groups is the usual position of the dominant-culture personnel in administrative agencies. These administrators are placed in positions administering programs involved in aiding mostly people from the subject culture. As noted with respect to social class, we generally find the majority of administrators coming from the dominant cultural groups in a society, while a disproportionate share of their clients come from the subject cultures. This situation not only contributes to the underlying tension between the groups, but may also place important limits on the effectiveness of the administrative structures.

Most public administration is people processing. It involves the communication of desires and demands from client to administrator, the administrator then making a decision, and the transmission of that decision to the client. This is obviously a communication process and, like all communication processes, it depends upon the existence of common values, symbols and cognitive structures. This consensus does not necessarily exist between members of different subcultural groups in a society. In these cases the probable result of interactions between administrators and clients is not the development of effective communication and empathy, but rather hostility, resentment, and the reinforcement of existing preju-dices. This will be especially true when the program involved is a social program affecting the values of the client and administrator. The majority of direct evid-ence in this regard comes from the study of interactions of different social classes, but if we generalize, we can agree with Sjoberg, Bremer and Faris concerning the "critical role of bureaucratic organizations in sustaining social stratification."[100]

Trust and distrust: a theory of bureaucratic power. The fourth and final aspect of political culture is the level of trust and distrust among the population. The politi-cal trust has become extremely popular as an explanation for the relative success of different political systems, and especially for different levels of success in build-ing political democracy.[101] In our discussion of this dimension of culture, we will attempt to develop a theoretical explanation for the differential development of the power of public administration in different political systems.

We argue that differences in the level and growth of administrative decision-making powers in contemporary countries are not due entirely to random or irra-tional forces, but instead, at least in part, reflect patterns of political cultures in these societies. The patterning of trust in the political cultures may play an espe-cially important part in this explanation. To begin with, we should distinguish two separate components of social or political trust. The first component is trust in individuals, as opposed to personal cynicism. This variable is conceptualized as the degree to which individuals in the society believe that others outside their immediate family can be trusted, or at least are not actively an enemy. In addition, trustful individuals tend to have a benign view of human nature.

Trust of humanity is not at all evenly distributed across cultures. Almond and Verba offer some of the best direct evidence of this variation. In their survey they found that 55 percent of the Americans, 49 percent of the British, but only seven percent of the Italians in their sample indicated that they believed that "most people can be trusted."[102] Rather similar distributions of trust and distrust were found on several other items. Social distrust has been well described in the French context by Wylie, who notes that many of the provincial French with whom he was familiar felt:

> since all individuals are on the whole malicious and since society never tames the deeper self, every individual is actually motivated by hidden forces which are probably hostile.[103]

While certainly French politics and social life have modernized substantially since Wylie wrote those lines, some of the underlying negative conceptions of human nature appear to remain.[104] More recent evidence confirms different levels of trust (see below).

The importance of trust and distrust in a political culture for the growth of administrative power is that the lack of social trust removes the possibility, or at least the probability, of informal and self-regulative activities in society. In more trusting societies, these types of activities can be used to supplement the activities of government in regulating relationships within the society. In political systems such as the United States, the United Kingdom, or Scandinavia, where social trust is high, non-governmental alternatives to public administration emerge quite readily. Individuals feel that they can safely form organizations and can allow those organizations some control over the lives of the members. Some rather obvious examples of this are the use of bar and medical associations to regulate important aspects of public policy.[105] A variety of mechanisms for the co-production of public services – block watches for crime and tenant management of housing projects – also fit into this category.[106] This dimension of trust can be further evidenced by the comparative powers of labor unions in these societies in the regulation of economic affairs, although the United States would represent something of an anomaly here. Thus, in cases where high levels of trust among individuals exist, we may expect a large number of otherwise public functions to be performed privately.

Robert Putnam has argued for the importance of different levels of "social capital" in explaining differences among societies.[107] In his conception, building successful democracy is dependent upon the capacity of individuals to form associations outside their family or immediate social groupings. These groups not only serve as what is in essence practice for democratic participation, but also indicate a willingness to work with people who are different from themselves. Further, these social organizations intervene between state and society, and thereby minimize the direct imposition of authority on individuals.[108] Putnam uses these differences to explain variance in regions of a single country (Italy), as well as differences in the one country across time.[109]

Here we can also see an instance in which political culture may be undergoing some systematic change. One of the common features of the programs of many right-of-center governments during the 1980s and into the 1990s has been the privatization of functions that previously were public. Even in societies that historically have assigned a very positive role to public sector action, e.g. France and Italy and many Third World Countries, many public functions have been privatized.[110] Whether this will be an aberration, with a return to more etatiste policies after the fashion of the "New Right" passes, has yet to be seen. It may be, however, that if the privatizations are reasonably successful, attitudinal changes will follow changes in behavior.

As well as the overt privatization of economic activities, the delivery of public services, now more than ever perhaps, depends upon the active involvement of not-for-profit organizations – the "Third Sector." A variety of public and private sector interactions now characterize the delivery of public services, with public–private partnerships being one of the more important. This pattern of service delivery is often efficient and effective, and permits some debureaucratization of the services. On the other hand, it raises questions of accountability and control and requires government to be able to monitor a variety of contractual and partnership arrangements, rather than simply using hierarchical controls.[111]

Indicators of interpersonal trust. Using the willingness to form associations as one indicator of trust among individuals, we again find high levels of variation by countries. For example, Almond and Verba found that 40 percent of Americans and 30 percent of the British preferred outgoing leisure-time activities, most of which involved some type of group membership.[112] In contrast, only seven percent of the Italian sample and 11 percent of the Mexican sample preferred activities of this type. A survey of French respondents, reported earlier, displayed equally low interest in outgoing activities (only 11 percent preferring activities involving any sort of group membership),[113] although some later evidence points to a rich, and growing, associational life in France.[114] A survey performed in a number of industrialized democracies showed that the French, Italians and Japanese were much less likely to join voluntary organizations than people from other countries (Table 2.8). When a common pattern of group membership and participation does not exist, the pattern of participation appears to be one of long periods of quiescence broken by periods of large-scale and even violent social movements.[115]

Another indicator of the willingness to form groups may be taken to be the proportion of the work force that belongs to labor unions. Unions have emerged as probably the principal organizational groups in Western society, especially in terms of their influence on the political system. Thus, if we look at the proportion of the economically active population involved in these organizations, we get some indication of the organizational skills and interest of the respective populations, as is illustrated in Table 2.8. Here we see that the smaller European democracies, the United Kingdom and Australia have disproportionately higher levels of union membership than the other nations. We have already mentioned the high levels of interpersonal trust in the United Kingdom, and the organizational propensities of the Scandinavian countries have been noted frequently.[116] Similarly, countries of the Third World lack a strong labor movement, reflecting in part the relatively low levels of interpersonal trust in these societies, as well as the relatively small portion of the labor force in the monetized sectors of the economy.

The most interesting aspects of Table 2.9 are the low percentages of union membership reported in Italy, the United States and Japan. As we have been seeing throughout this discussion of trust, Italy and France have low levels of social trust among their populations. This low interpersonal trust is manifested here in low levels of organizational activities. Not only is this a quantitative indication of the lack of organizational propensity, but qualitative studies also indicate weakness within the organizations that do exist. Rather than functioning as a cohesive whole, the labor movements in France and Italy are riven by ideological and political disputes that constrain their effectiveness in shaping and implementing public policies.

Given the findings concerning attitudes of social trust and the use of outgoing leisure-time activities, somewhat higher levels of union membership might be expected among Americans. This is apparently an isolated manifestation of a lack of interest in joining a particular type of organization, rather than a more general indication of the propensity to join organizations. Finally, although Japan is sometimes taken as the model of a group-oriented society, it has low rates of union membership. In this instance, low union membership appears to be a result of one organization (the company) replacing another (the union) as the focus of organization in the work force. If the current economic recession forces Japanese firms to begin to dismiss workers, this pattern may change.

Table 2.8 Membership in social organizations[a] (percentage)

	Japan	Great Britain	Ireland	France	Belgium	Germany	Netherlands	Spain	Denmark	Italy
One or more	29	52	53	27	42	50	62	31	62	26
None	71	48	47	73	58	50	38	69	38	74

Source: Leisure Development Center Study, cited in E. H. Hastings and P. K. Hastings, eds, *Index to International Public Opinion, 1982–83* (Westport, CT: Greenwood, 1984)

Note
a Charities, religious, political, professional, or environmental organizations, trade unions, etc.

Table 2.9 Trade union membership as a percentage of labor force

Iceland	94
Sweden	91
Finland	80
Denmark	76
Belgium	73
Norway	68
Austria	62
Luxembourg	61
Philippines	58
Poland	57
Ireland	53
Australia	51
Czech Republic	39
United Kingdom	39
Canada	37
Italy	36
New Zealand	36
Germany	35
Greece	34
Estonia	33
Switzerland	32
Netherlands	30
Argentina	27
Japan	26
Spain	20
Singapore	17
United States	15
Zimbabwe	13
South Africa	13
India	8

Source: M. Upham, ed., *Trade Unions of the World* (London: Cartermill, 1996)

Trust in government. A second aspect of trust is trust in government and political institutions. Here we are especially interested in the degree to which an individual believes that the "political" structures and politicians, as opposed to administrative structures, are worthy of trust. Also involved in this conception of political trust, or its reverse of political cynicism, is the idea that politicians will take the citizen's viewpoint into account when making decisions. The implications of this type of trust for the development of administrative power are perhaps more obvious than the implications of generalized social trust. If the majority of the population, or even a significant minority, does not trust government and politicians to be fair, honest and impartial, then government will have at best a very difficult time in ruling the country. Decisions of a highly distrusted political system will be difficult for the population to accept as legitimate; the assumption would always be that some sort of corruption, deception, or favoritism was involved in the decision.

We also find considerable variation across cultures on the level of political trust, just as we did for interpersonal trust. Almond and Verba present some directly comparable evidence, albeit now dated, about the distribution of this trait. When respondents in the five countries involved in their survey were asked if they believed themselves capable of influencing local and national regulations, 75 percent of the American and 62 percent of the British respondents felt that they could influence national regulations, while only 28 percent of the Italian respondents felt that they could exert such an influence.[117] Also, in a study of political socialization in France, the Netherlands and the United States, Abramson and Inglehart compared the trust expressed in a child's father and in the head of state. In the Netherlands and the United States, the children were very slightly more trusting of the political official; in France, the children were much more trusting of the father than the representative of the political system.[118] More recent research has found that French citizens trust politicians less than they do other occupational groups – including civil servants (see Table 2.10). Rather high levels of political trust have also been reported in Scandinavia and in the Low Countries, although even here the level of political trust appears to be in decline.[119]

If social researchers discovered significant variation in the level of trust in developed countries, the variations would be more extreme if substantial survey evidence were available from less-developed societies.[120] Some indication of the prevailing level of distrust can, however, be obtained through other methods. The general finding is a very low level of trust in government in those societies, and a feeling that anyone who goes into government employment must be doing so for personal gain.[121] This attitude, in turn, tends to be related to the prevalence of authoritarian regimes in those societies, given that other forms of government would have difficulty in gaining sufficient compliance from citizens to be effective.

Trust in government has been in decline in most industrialized countries since the time that Almond and Verba did their research. Nowhere has that decline been more precipitous than in the United States, where the traumas of the Vietnam War and Watergate followed so closely on one another. For example, in response to a question on whether they could expect the government in Washington to do the right thing all the time, most of the time, or only some of the time, 77 percent of Americans in 1964 said all or most of the time. By 1977 that percentage had dropped to 32 percent. Looking at the problem the other way, 22 percent of a sample in 1964 said that government could not be trusted to do what was right,

Table 2.10 Trust of politicians in France (percentage)

	"Do you believe that most politicians are more honest, less honest, or equally as honest as . . . ?":			
	More	Less	Equally	No opinion
Banks	6	15	68	11
Lawyers	7	24	53	16
Civil servants	4	42	37	17
Industrialists	6	24	52	18

Source: CSA/*Le Journal du Dimanche* Survey, April 5 and 6 1990

whereas in 1977, 64 percent said government could not be trusted unconditionally.[122] While trust in government to some degree rebounded in the United States during the Reagan administration, the "Irangate" scandal and the Congressional banking scandal produced additional declines in the confidence in government expressed by citizens, according to public opinion polls. For example, by 1993 only 24 percent of the public thought that government could be trusted to do what was right.[123]

Another way of looking at the trust of citizens in their government is to look at the confidence they express in the institutions of that government, especially those of the executive branch. Of nine major institutions in society asked about in 1979, the executive branch of government ranked next to last in people's confidence; only organized labor was lower. In 1966 the executive branch was tied for fourth. Some more recent surveys show an increase in the relative ranking of the executive branch and its surpassing the legislature in the confidence of citizens. In 1991 some 26 percent of respondents had confidence in the executive branch, but only 18 percent of respondents had confidence in Congress.[124]

The United States is by no means alone in having citizens who are skeptical about their government. This appears to be a common phenomenon in the industrialized democracies, perhaps in part because of the (relative) failure of governments to provide citizens with high economic growth and improved social conditions. For example, although 34 percent of a sample of Americans had little or no confidence in their civil service, 35 percent of a British sample said the same thing. Even more surprisingly, over one-fourth of a West German sample expressed the same negative sentiments toward their bureaucracy.[125] Thus, as we argued above, political cultures do change. It is unclear, however, whether the changes we see in the last part of the twentieth century are a short-term response to specific events or a more fundamental shift in the population's assessment of government.

Although there does appear to be some loss of confidence in government, the glass may be at least half full as well as half empty. For example, the European Community has been asking citizens of its member countries how satisfied they are with the performance of democracy in their country.[126] The average[127] level of satisfaction ("very satisfied" plus "somewhat satisfied") across the Community in 1989 was 60 percent, and dropped to 57 percent in 1998. These later figures are significantly higher than satisfaction in 1973 (47 percent) even with the addition of three countries (Greece, Portugal and Spain) with less than average levels of satisfaction.

There were also substantial differences in levels of satisfaction among the countries, with satisfaction with democracy in 1998 ranging from 28 percent (Italy – only one percentage point higher than in 1973) to 84 percent (Denmark). In general, the countries of southern Europe were less satisfied with their governments than those from other parts of the continent. In the best of all worlds we would want every citizen to be satisfied with the way in which his or her government functions, but there does appear to be a substantial reservoir of popular support for this set of governments.[128]

Likewise, when asked about their perceptions of their governing institutions, citizens of Western European countries demonstrated a good deal of confidence (Table 2.11). Regarding confidence in the civil service, there were marked differences among the countries, with very high confidence in countries such as Denmark and Ireland, but very low in others like Italy, Spain and Portugal. Further, in some countries (Denmark, France, Ireland) the public had more confidence in the civil service than in their parliament. Also, the public on average lost little confidence in the civil service during the 1980s.

Trust and administration. We have now developed two different dimensions of trust – trust in individuals and trust in government.[129] These two dimensions can be inter-related in a typology, as shown in Figure 2.2. In this typology, we attempt to explain different levels of political power and affect of the population toward administration from the positions on the two trust dimensions. In referring to political power of administration, we mean the decision-making power of the public bureaucracy relative to other decision-making bodies (for example the legislature) in the political system. Over time the policy-making power of administration has increased, but at different rates in different societies.

The second variable in this typology is the affect felt by the population toward the administrative structure. It may be difficult to love a bureaucrat, barring the chance that he or she is a member of your immediate family. Yet there are instances in which cultural orientations toward the administrative apparatus are at least benign, and perhaps even positive. Some populations hold the public bureaucracy in high regard as a traditional societal elite. In others this positive affect may be only a grudging respect for their administrative and technical competence, but it is still a positive view of administration.

Table 2.11 Trust in major institutions (latest year available) (positive responses, in percentage)

	Armed forces	Educn. system	Legal system	Press	Trade unions	Police	Parliament	Civil service	Major companies
Belgium	33	74	45	44	37	51	43	42	50
Denmark	46	81	79	31	46	89	42	51	38
France	56	66	58	38	32	67	48	49	67
Germany	40	54	65	34	36	70	51	39	38
Ireland	62	73	47	36	43	86	50	59	52
Italy	63	48	49	32	34	67	32	27	62
Netherlands	32	65	63	36	53	73	54	46	49
Norway	65	79	75	43	59	88	59	44	53
Portugal	47	51	41	36	29	44	34	32	45
Spain	42	62	45	51	40	58	43	37	49
Sweden	49	70	56	33	40	74	47	44	53
UK	81	47	54	14	26	77	46	44	48

Source: European Values Survey

Trust in Others

		High	Low
Political Trust	High	Low Administrative Power	Moderate Administrative Power (positive affect)
	Low	Moderate Administrative Power (negative affect)	High Administrative Power

Figure 2.2 Relationship of dimensions of social trust to administrative power

As is shown in Figure 2.2, we do not include all possible combinations of the two dependent characteristics of the typology in our predicted outcomes. Instead we have chosen to hedge our bets and have labeled two of the cells as having moderate administrative power. This is, however, something more than a simple hedge and is related to some characteristics of the political and social systems expected to fall into those cells of the typology. Following is a discussion of each of the four cells, with an attempt to explain and justify our predictions of administrative power.

The first cell of the typology contains societies that have high levels of interpersonal trust and high levels of trust in government. In these cases we would expect to find the weakest administrative structures. In these political systems the normal "political" branches of the government are reasonably successful in ruling the country and tend to maintain a strong hold on their decision-making prerogatives. They are able to make and enforce rules without excessive assistance from their public bureaucracy. At the same time there are successful decision-making bodies outside government that are capable of performing a number of regulatory functions that might otherwise have to be performed by the bureaucracy.

The most obvious example of a nation that would fit into this category of high interpersonal trust and high political trust is the United Kingdom. In this case, the Cabinet and, to a lesser extent, the Parliament, comprise an effective political decision-making body.[130] As Nordlinger pointed out, the level of political trust is sufficiently high in this system to permit the political decision makers extreme latitude after an election.[131] The population can thus exert direct political control over its elected politicians only at the time of an election, although a number of informal mechanisms for interim participation have been increasing in importance.[132] In addition, there has traditionally been a good deal of self-regulation by organizations within the society. Perhaps the best example of the reliance on self-regulation is the very low level of government involvement in regulating labor–management disputes. At various times Conservative governments have proposed and implemented some labor legislation, but even that put through by the Thatcher government has been quite meager when compared to that in the United States, or to members of the old Commonwealth countries.

This should not be taken as saying that the British bureaucracy is entirely dormant and uninvolved in making policy. There has, in fact, been substantial concern about the policy-making role of the civil service in Britain.[133] However, unlike the case in a number of other political systems, the Cabinet and, to a lesser extent, Parliament, retain more than rubber stamp powers over the actions of administrators. The tradition of parliamentary control of ministers has tended to prevent the accretion of bureaucratic authority experienced in other regimes, for example, France. Further, a succession of governments (including the Labour government elected in 1997) have been concerned with the powers of the public bureaucracy, and have been attempting to assert greater political control.[134] The United Kingdom, therefore, remains a political system with a relatively low level of administrative power and control.

In the opposite cell would be countries that have neither high levels of trust in the political system nor high levels of interpersonal trust. Among industrialized countries, France and Italy (despite their continuing social change) would come close to fitting into this category. Some indication of the level of interpersonal trust in developed democracies is given in Table 2.11, and certainly the respondents coming from those two countries do appear to be very distrustful of others. This characterization would also fit a large number of Third World countries, especially those nations with ethnic diversity that have been unable to build effective national institutions. In these nations, there is little or no basis for the construction of effective extra-governmental organizations that could be useful in the regulation of some economic or social affairs.[135] A number of authors have also noted the relative weaknesses of these organizations in France and Italy. These societies are certainly not devoid of interest groups, but the groups that exist tend to be fragmented and effective largely as defensive groups. They further lack the firm normative and political commitment on the part of their members that is so characteristic of groups in other societies; a major exception may be labor unions.[136]

The governing capacity of the *political* components of government in these societies is relatively weak, although years under the Gaullists and then the Socialists under Mitterrand in France certainly strengthened the system there. Some evidence of this tendency is given in Table 2.11. Politics has tended to be characterized by fragmentation, ideological argument, and "blockage."[137] These difficulties are in part a function of the institutions themselves and in part a function of the values of the societies that stress family and individual roles rather than the role of the government. Thus the population is less willing to accept the decrees of government than the needs of the family or the guidance of the local patron. In these cases, the bureaucracy may be required to step in to fill a power vacuum in the political system. The country must be run somehow, and the logical heir to powers ordinarily held by parliament or the executive is the bureaucracy. Unfortunately, perhaps, this pattern tends to be self-reinforcing. As more power and decision making pass to the bureaucracy, the popular image of government as authoritarian and impersonal is reinforced. This image further reduces the legitimacy of the political system in the eyes of the population and further prevents the legislative and executive bodies from becoming effective rule-making bodies. Thus, a cycle of bureaucratic domination tends to perpetuate itself, being broken mainly by "charismatic personalities" who are capable of producing effective political action either through or around normal political channels.

These problems in governance appear particularly pronounced in countries of the Third World, even those that have been making economic progress, and the countries of the former Communist Bloc. The new nations tend to lack interpersonal trust among the population, as well as trust of government.[138] This absence of trust is often traceable to the predominance of ethnic cleavages in the society, and the use of protective as opposed to promotional groups. Each segment of the society tends to protect its interests against all others, rather than offering an alternative means of social decision making; the conflicts in the former Yugoslavia and ethnic conflicts in Rwanda represent the extreme cases here. Likewise, the long history of colonial rule and the lack of a social and economic infrastructure usually associated with democratic government have made the bureaucracy and the army the two logical contenders for power in these societies.[139]

In some countries there is an alternative source of distrust of social organizations. In some countries in the Southern Cone of South America, for example, the state itself has been a powerful, and in some cases largely benevolent, actor so that third-sector organizations that seek to fulfill some of the purposes of the State are viewed with suspicion. As these governments attempt to conform to the managerial and neo-liberal styles of governing now becoming the norm around the world, their commitment to government as a means of solving problems may be a major barrier.

As well as being the choices by default, the bureaucracy and the army also have some of the characteristics of modernity that would qualify them for the management of developing economies and societies. Both institutions tend to have had relatively extensive contacts with more modern nations and to have values and attitudes that conform more closely to those of the modern state than to those of other political elites. Thus, just as with the developed countries of France and Italy, the bureaucracy in the underdeveloped world fills a power vacuum when it exists. One question that remains is whether this will be a continuing phenomenon or whether the underdeveloped countries will be able to develop the political and interpersonal trust that a large proportion of the developed world has been able to generate.

We move now to the two cases with mixed degrees of trust. These have been characterized as having moderate levels of administrative power, but they differ in the affect felt by the population toward the administrative system. The first is the case of low interpersonal trust and high trust for government. This would appear to be typical of the "consociational democracies" of the Low Countries, Austria, Switzerland and (once) Lebanon. In these societies, strong cleavage between religious and linguistic groups in turn produces relatively few feelings of interpersonal trust. Lorwin notes that in Belgium:

Flemings know little of Walloons' thinking: Walloons know little of Flemish thinking. People of each side therefore tend to see and resent the others as a solid bloc arrayed against them.[140]

Again, there has been substantial social modernization, but political conflict and even violence over language took place during 1987, resulting in the creation of a rather extreme form of federalism.[141] Similarly, traditionally Dutch political sociology emphasized the "pillarization" of their society, with the three major groups (Protestants, Catholics and the non-religious) vertically integrated and having relatively little contact with members of other "families."[142] Mass communications and secularization have reduced this isolation substantially, but some separation remains.[143]

These societies obviously have the inherent potential to develop the immobilism and the conflict that had been characteristic of French and Italian governments for some time. Fortunately, however, there is a well-developed sense of mutual trust among the elites of each of the "families," as well as a general feeling of political trust for the government. Thus, although vertically integrated, compromise and interaction at the elite level enable the political system to function effectively. It is also able to function with only a moderate level of administrative power. The legislative bodies are fragmented politically but, at the same time, have formed coalition governments with the continuing support of the population. This feeling of trust and respect for the government is carried over into the generally positive feelings of the population toward the administrative structures.

The final set of nations are those with relatively low trust in the political system but high levels of interpersonal trust. This pattern would appear to be displayed in the United States. The political culture of the United States has traditionally been one preferring individual and group action to governmental action.[144] A number of functions that might be performed by government, or at least with extensive governmental intervention, are still performed privately in the United States. The most notable example of this is health care, although a number of other professions and businesses have also retained the right to administer their own affairs and to make decisions that in other societies would be considered a matter of direct public concern. Despite this, survey evidence has shown that Americans at least expect fair treatment from the political system, although this expectation is not so high as in the United Kingdom. Moreover, when compared with levels of interpersonal trust, the government comes out a rather poor second. Thus, if we use the level of interpersonal trust as an "expected" level of trust, the level of trust found for government is low, and getting lower.

Whether or not the United States can be said to be indicative of this pattern, what are the consequences for administrative power? In the first place, we may expect a moderate level of administrative power. The use of non-governmental organizations for a variety of regulatory tasks lessens the work load of the administration; at the same time, the relatively bad image of the political arms of government forces a number of questions to be decided administratively rather than politically. The "political" branches of governments tend to be so weighted down with checks and balances that the bureaucracy must again be called on to fill something of a decision-making vacuum. This is apparent in part in the widespread utilization of regulations written by the bureaucracy in place of other legislation and in the difficulties that some presidents have experienced in trying to control the administrators whom they nominally command.[145] Even given the relative powers of the public bureaucracy, however, the general viewpoint of Americans *vis-à-vis* the bureaucracy is negative. Americans may have some respect for individual administrators, but the dominant theme of the culture is well indicated by the successful presidential campaigns of both Ronald Reagan and Bill Clinton, both campaigning very hard against Washington and the public bureaucracy.

In summary, a relatively simple typology of variations in the levels of trust among the population toward two different social objects – individuals and the government – can be useful in explaining differences in the degree of administrative power in modern governments. This typology and its conclusions are rather obviously an oversimplification of a complex reality. A number of other cultural and political factors must be taken into account in the final explanation or prediction of administrative power. However, the relatively strong correspondence between the predictions of the typology and this descriptive analysis of representative political systems offers some credence to the relationships hypothesized.

Culture and the internal management of organizations

Up to this point we have been examining the relationship between the societal and political cultures (types of which are given in Table 2.12) and the role prescribed for the public bureaucracy; that is, we have considered what role the bureaucracy performs within the political system rather than the manner in which it chooses to perform those tasks. We now turn our attention to the question of the impact of culture on the internal management of complex administrative organizations. This is a complex topic worthy of several volumes in itself. However, only two topics will be discussed here: the relationship between superiors and subordinates in an organization; and the cultural basis for the motivation of workers. As has been true for most other topics in this book, we are especially interested in the effects of these internal management practices on the policy outputs of the public organization.

Table 2.12 Types of social and political cultures

		Group	
		High	Low
Grid	High	Hierarchist	Fatalist
	Low	Egalitarian	Individualist

Culture and authority

The definition and acceptance of the authority of one individual by another is a function of culture and society. As with virtually all cultural values, there are individual interpretations of the norm, and hence individual variation, but certain modal patterns emerge. The use of impersonal and "rational–legal" authority as a means of controlling individuals, as suggested in formal models of bureaucratic management, is a culturally determined concept. First, it is intimately connected to the social–cultural patterns of the West, and even then to a rather small segment of Western thought. This managerial strategy, to be successful, would require the support of a generally hierarchical and bureaucratic society – the Germany of Weber, perhaps. A culture that stressed the virtues of individualism and personal equality would find it difficult to accept such an impersonal system of management.

Weber has presented the classical discussion of the sources of authority in society.[146] Much the same can be said of patterns of authority in organizations. Weber argued that authority had three sources: tradition, charismatic personality and rationality. The first was assumed to characterize most traditional societies. The authority exercised by an individual in government or in a private organization (such few as might exist in a traditional society) would be a function of the individual's position in the traditional hierarchy in the society. This hierarchy may be ordained by some alleged divine connection, or it may be a function of possessing property, but the source of authority is not subject to any rational challenge.

Charismatic authority is a transitional variety of authority. This source of authority stems from the force of personality of the individual. Weber spoke of charismatic authority largely in terms of social and political leadership, but the same type of authority could characterize organizational leaders. Some individual executives are capable of commanding respect and obedience through the force of their individual personality. Weber notes that, over time, charisma tends to be institutionalized and to be converted into rational–legal authority.

In the third variety of authority the individual employee willingly accepts the authority of the superior, simply because of the hierarchy of the organization or society. Thus, if an individual occupies a superior position within the organization, that is sufficient to provide the individual with authority. In Herbert Simon's terms, the subordinate willingly suspends judgment and accepts directions given by the superior with little consideration.[147] Individual leaders may squander this natural source of authority by what is in essence "negative charisma," but they begin with a reservoir of authority with which they can manage their organization.

A good deal of management thinking in the public sector is still bound to this Weberian conception of rational–legal authority, and of the right of the superior to command the subordinate. Fortunately or unfortunately, most real-life management does not actually depend upon such clear lines of authority and obedience. In his study of Weber's model of bureaucracy, Page points to the role of bargaining and informal power, even in what is assumed to be a prototype of the Weberian public bureaucracy (Germany).[148] Attempts at hierarchical management are increasingly impractical and, in fact, would appear to be one of the major causes for discontent in most large organizations in the Western world today. The cultural values of these societies have changed decidedly in favor of the right of people to decide their own futures. Workers, especially younger workers, are seeking greater involvement in decision making. This desire has been phrased largely in terms of the management of industrial enterprises, but much the same can be said of public organizations. The lower echelons of these organizations are also seeking new forms of management that facilitate participation by the people (themselves and their clients) affected by the decisions. Further, their organizational superiors (if that term continues to have much meaning) often support more participative management. In some governments major management reform programs, such as PS2000 in Canada and the National Performance Review in the United States, have been initiated to promote greater involvement by employees in the organizations,[149] with a further push for citizen engagement attempting to include clients as well as the lower levels of administration.

Another challenge to hierarchical authority is expertise. The appeal of technology and expertise in modern society is almost hypnotic in its effects. Expertise has become a new basis of charisma for leaders of an organization. The problem is that this source of authority often (usually?) conflicts with the rational–legal basis of authority. Victor Thompson long ago argued that this divergence between expertise and formal authority is the fundamental problem of modern organizations.[150] Authority is concentrated at the top of the organizational pyramid while expertise is concentrated at the bottom. The conflicts intrinsic in such a situation are obvious. In public organizations expertise is often not only technical, but also consists of direct knowledge of the clientele and their problems, which may be considered unimportant by those in the upper levels of the organization. Conflict, over both knowledge and values, in such a situation is virtually unavoidable.

The problems of authority and management in underdeveloped nations are rather different. The acceptance of hierarchy and rational–legal authority in many of these cases is formalistic at best. This pattern of authority conflicts with a persisting traditional basis of authority in most other relationships. Even under colonial rule, the traditional authority structure was often borrowed by the colonial power for its own uses,[151] and subsequent attempts to modernize have placed new strains on traditional power structures. In many cases, the ideology of modernization has required the destruction or bypassing of older systems of authority. The weakening of these authority systems has created a vacuum that has been difficult to fill on the basis of rational–legal authority. Thus, modern institutions may often serve as a thin disguise for traditional practices, much as expected in Riggs' dualistic model of administration. In addition, charismatic leaders supply another major source of authority both for government as a whole and for public bureaucracies.

In fairness, however, it is not only the administrative structures of Third World countries that contain vestiges of traditional and charismatic authority. Performance in many "central agencies" in developed countries is based upon the personal leadership of an individual leader.[152] Individuals remain a part of those organizations so long as they have confidence in, and the confidence of, the person in the executive position – be it president, prime minister, or whatever. Organizations with this personal authority constitute a small but crucial component of the administrative structures of most countries. In addition, the importance of these organizations may be increasing as political leaders find themselves frustrated by the existing career organizations and demand ways of breaking out of that mold. Likewise, there are increasing efforts to impose political criteria for appointment in a wide range of posts in public bureaucracies in order to ensure greater personal and political control.

Culture and motivation

How do you motivate workers to join an organization and to produce once they are members? To some degree, this is a part of the prior question of authority, in that Weber tended to assume that authority was itself a sufficient motivation for performance.[153] Beyond this seemingly naive expectation, how can the manager of a public organization activate his subordinates to perform their jobs effectively, and have at least a modicum of loyalty to the organization for which they work?[154] Answers range from using physical coercion, either real or threatened, to permitting enhanced participation by the organization's workers in decision making. In each instance, the choice of motivational strategy will be, to some degree, a function of the culture of the society.

In general, we can think of four basic motivational techniques that are available to managers. The first technique, if it may be given such a euphemistic title, is coercion. Fortunately, the contemporary world has largely left behind the period in which direct coercion might be used as a means of gaining organizational compliance. The use of indirect or implied coercion is still an actively used technique, however. The coercion is rarely physical but involves other types of deprivations to the employee. In particular, this can include the loss of prestige, status and acceptance through either loss of office or demotion. Newspapers carry stories of the deportation of out of favor administrators to the country's functional equivalent of Siberia (for example, Cut Bank, Montana, for the FBI in the United States). While this relocation is certainly better than a public flogging in most people's minds, it can still be a severe deprivation in both physical and psychological terms.

A somewhat more subtle form of coercion is the use of ideological or religious doctrines as a motivating force. Perhaps the two most famous examples of this are the Protestant ethic and the thoughts of Chairman Mao. The former religious and ideological doctrine has been cited as one of the principal reasons for the development of Western industrial society.[155] By equating success in business or profession with salvation, the Protestant ethic constituted an important motivating force for the growth of Western business and commerce. Even now, when direct belief in the correlation of success and divine election has waned, the culture of the West has been sufficiently influenced by this doctrine that success is valued as a good in itself. More recently, Moslem fundamentalism has played a similar role in motivating political and social behavior in several countries in the Middle East, most notably Iran.[156] The thoughts of Chairman Mao, although less widespread, constitute perhaps the best example of the use of a secular ideology as a motivating device. Exhortations to progress, development and efficient production through this ideology were an important if not crucial factor in China's economic development. This was true despite a number of economic inefficiencies dictated by the doctrine. On a more personal basis, the desire to fulfill the thoughts of Mao and to please him and the people of China as a whole served as important means of motivating the individual. As with the Protestant ethic, the threat of coercion has been internalized by the individual. The deprivations for the individual are more often than not internal, so that personal pressures of compliance constitute the major motivation for the individual. The thoughts of Chairman Mao, therefore, may have been an important transitional phase between the old China and a new China which at times appears to be operating closer to the ideals of the Protestant ethic than to Mao.[157]

It should be noted here that the use of ideology and religion can be at once a very expensive and a very inexpensive means of motivation. On the one hand, once the ideology is accepted by the population, it requires largely symbolic manipulation in order to be effective. This is certainly less expensive than having to pay people money to motivate them or to involve them in decision making. Thus, as with any cultural device, the ideology of a society (or organization) provides a set of symbols that can be manipulated by those in power. The ideology also provides a set of psychological deprivations for the individual for failure to comply with the ideology. At least psychologically, the manipulation of symbols can constitute something approaching coercion. Ideology used as a means of motivation becomes expensive when it restricts forms of action available to the organization. One of the defining characteristics of an ideology is that it prescribes and proscribes actions for individuals and groups that, in turn, limit the flexibility of action for the organization and society. Political leaders have been quite adept at justifying virtually any policy in terms of the dominant ideology, but this is costly both in the time required and in the probable weakening of commitment by some individuals. The same types of problems are encountered in attempting to change an ideology to meet changing social conditions. Thus an ideology can be an exceedingly inexpensive motivational method in the short term, but it may impose a number of long-term costs. The rational assessment of the net benefits of this particular motivational strategy will therefore depend upon the discount attached to long-term costs as well as the level of short-term demands.

The third motivational technique available to managers is monetary reward. Probably the prevailing concept of management in Western societies has been that monetary rewards are a sufficient inducement to gain the compliance of workers with the demands of the organization. The importance of money as a means of management and motivation is that, in many ways, it is the cheapest means of motivation, particularly in administrative organizations. Here, the main "product" is not goods or services, but rather decisions. If the majority of the work force can be motivated through their paychecks, then the need to allow their participation in decision making is eliminated. This will allow greater latitude of action for decision makers than can be found in ideological or involvement systems of management. This type of motivation was, in fact, a major assumption of Weber's ideal type of bureaucracy. It makes bureaucracy virtually a neutral instrument that can be used for almost any purpose by its managers, with the monetary reward being a major reason for joining. While this assumption is rather obviously overstated, the latitude granted to managers through monetary motivation is an important consideration for any manager. The choice, however, is probably not individual but cultural.

The spread of market-based ideas for public sector management is increasing the use of monetary incentives for motivating public servants. "Pay for performance" has been one of the most commonly adopted ideas in this spate of reforms. This may be implemented by individual contracts for senior managers, through to individual performance measurements of lower echelon workers who are eligible for bonuses. This technique may have improved motivation for some members of the public service but it also appears to have demotivated others. Many public employees consider themselves in the business of serving the public rather than working in the usual manner, and find pay for performance almost insulting.[158]

The questions of the decision making and service bring us to the fourth source of motivation. This is the involvement of the workers in decision making in the organization. There are some countries in which workers' involvement is especially well developed, such as it was in the former Yugoslavia and to some degree still is in China.[159] It appears, however, that this method of management has varied across time more than across cultures and is generally considered to be a product of the "postindustrial" or "postwelfare" society. In general, this method of management employs the ability of the worker to perceive that he has greater control over his life and work as a means of motivation. Studies of motivation have shown that the major source of motivation for professional and white-collar employees is the ability to perceive that they are doing something significant and the ability to feel that they could control what happened to them in their jobs. Given the level of education and training required for most administrative jobs, the same type of motivational structure can be expected among administrators. Moreover, the ideology of participation is apparently increasing in importance as an increasing number of workers at all levels of administration demand an influence on the decisions that affect them. This development is rather obviously in contradiction to the ideal-type bureaucratic model and to a significant body of literature in public management stressing the importance of executive control and the duty of leadership at the top.

One interesting aspect of this increasing demand for involvement in decision making is that it has spread not only among administrators, but also among the clients of administration. Thus a new force has to be taken into account by management, and managers must think of motivating the clients of the organization to gain their compliance in somewhat the same way that managers must think about motivating workers. The inducements for compliance are not only of the monetary (service delivery) variety, but now also include involvement in decision making. In some instances, this involvement will extend to the co-production of the service, for example tenant management of public housing.[160] Some of the methods now deemed necessary to make government services more efficient and effective, e.g. recycling refuse and neighborhood policing, all involve a great deal of involvement by the public.[161]

With both workers and clients, involvement is an expensive means of gaining organizational compliance. It reduces the latitude available to a manager and provides possibly very little in return for the management of the organization. Unlike an ideology that can be readily used in "normal" times to satisfy employees, involvement requires a constant redefinition of goals and priorities. And, like ideological change, these types of changes are generally quite costly to the organization in terms of both time lost and personal cost to the losers in the struggle. In public organizations, goal change also involves a redefinition of some aspects of public policy that may require negotiations of other political institutions. Thus the losses in continuity of programs, in the reanalysis of priorities, and in the personal reshaping of work priorities make the granting of involvement an exceedingly expensive means of motivation. Nevertheless, in some cases it may be the only means of motivation that will be successful. Increasingly, organized labor has sought to negotiate means for becoming more involved in decision making in plants; some countries, such as Germany, have developed successful mechanisms for co-management of firms.[162] Teachers and other professionals in government demand to have their professional judgment considered in the making of policy. We should expect that even in times of economic difficulty labor negotiations will be directed at the problem of participation as well as wages, and greater participation may become an alternative to enhanced financial rewards.

We should not be totally negative concerning the use of involvement in decisions as a motivational device for organizational employees. In terms of human values it is probably the best means of management devised. Furthermore, it may be one means of solving Thompson's dilemma concerning the comparative misplacement of expertise and authority within organizations.[163] Increased worker (and client) involvement can diminish any monopolies of information within the organization, and let top managers know what is really happening. In the short term, this method of management has been successful, although its long-term effects have yet to be gauged. Involvement with little real change in the circumstances of the participating individuals may actually be an alienating experience, given that the worker must also invest more heavily in the organization. Given the character of contemporary culture, however, demands for involvement can no longer be denied.

We have, to this point, avoided the traditional notion that the motivation of the public servant is solely or primarily serving the public interest. This was not done to denigrate the long service of the large number of dedicated individuals working in the public bureaucracy.[164] Instead, we view the majority of individuals in public organizations to be little different in their motivational structure (although perhaps they are in their value structures) from individuals working in other types of organizations. The concept of public service would therefore be classified analytically as just another of the many cultural or ideological convictions that have motivated individuals to participate in organizations. A strong commitment to the public service will, however, compensate for some of the financial deprivations sometimes associated with working in the public sector. The problem many public servants now face, however, is that the public service idea is denied by the society and their political masters but the financial rewards are still lower than in the private sector.

Summary

This chapter has attempted to show the influence of patterns of political culture and general cultural values on the operation of the administrative system. We have examined this influence as it affects not only the outputs of the administrative system, but also the internal management of the organizations. In both cases, we find that culture has a significant impact on the behavior of public administration. Unfortunately, the assessment of this impact had to remain at a somewhat impressionistic level because of the lack of much hard evidence on these relationships. One of the main problems with the concept of culture, and especially of political culture, is that it generally tends to be a vague and amorphous concept that can be twisted to include virtually anything a researcher wishes. We hope we have avoided this pitfall as much as possible and have presented the evidence in as unbiased a manner as possible. But we are the products of our own culture and see the world from our own perspective. It is difficult if not impossible to escape the imperatives of a culture taught to us from birth. Any significant progress in the field of relating cultural values and their effects on administration (or other aspects of politics) must come from a more complete empirical delimitation of culture and an examination of its dimensions. It is hoped that this discussion has been a step in the direction of analysing the potential and probable effects of culture so that more informed empirical analysis can test for these effects.

Notes

1   See Lucian W. Pye and Sidney Verba, *Political Culture and Political Development* (Princeton, NJ: Princeton University Press, 1965); John R. Gibbins, ed., *Contemporary Political Culture* (London: Sage, 1989).

2   See Harry Eckstein, "A Culturist Theory of Political Change," *American Political Science Review*, 82 (1988), 791–3.

3   For example, the seemingly antiquated elements of British political culture have been argued to be extremely functional for the preservation of that political system. See Richard Rose, "England: A Traditionally Modern Political Culture," in Lucian Pye and Sidney Verba, eds, *Political Culture and Political Development* (Princeton, NJ: Princeton University Press, 1967). In contrast see the arguments of Stephen Haseler, *The End of the House of Windsor – The Birth of a British Republic* (London: I. B. Tauris, 1993), for views that have seemingly become more popular year after year.

4   Aaron Wildavsky, "Choosing Preferences by Constructing Institutions: A Cultural Theory of Preference Formation," *American Political Science Review*, 81 (1987), 3–22.

5   See Jan Erik Lane, "The Decline of the Swedish Model," *Governance*, 8 (1995), 579–90.

6   See Phillipe C. Schmitter and Terry Karl, "Types of Democracy Emerging in Southern and Eastern Europe and South and Central America," in Peter M. E. Volten, ed., *Bound to Change: Consolidating Democracy in East Central Europe* (Boulder, CO: Westview Press, 1992).

7   David J. Elkins and Richard E. B. Simeon, "A Cause in Search of An Effect; Or What Does Elite Political Culture Explain?," *Comparative Politics*, 11 (1979), 117–46.

8   Jeremy J. Richardson, *Policy Styles in Western Europe* (London: George Allen and Unwin, 1982); Franz Van Waarden, "Persistence of National Policy Styles," in B. Unger and Van Waarden, eds., *Convergence or Diversity?: Internationalization and Economic Policy Response* (Aldershot: Avebury, 1995).

9   John Girling, *Myths and Politics in Western Societies* (New Brunswick, NJ: Transaction Books, 1993).

10   Gary Freeman, "National Styles and Policy Sectors: Explaining Structured Variation," *Journal of Public Policy*, 5, 467–96.

11   J. Steven Ott, *The Organizational Culture Perspective* (Pacific Grove, CA: Brooks/Cole, 1989); B. Guy Peters, "Administrative Culture and Analysis of Public Organizations," *Indian Journal of Public Administration*, 36 (1990), 420–8.

12   On the importance of *strength* of culture in shaping the capacities of an organization, see John P. Kotter and James L. Heskett, *Corporate Culture and Performance* (New York: Free Press, 1992).

13   Paul J. Dimaggio and Walter W. Powell, "The Iron Cage Revisited: Institutional Isomorphism and Collective Rationality in Organizational Fields," *American Sociological Review*, 48 (1991), 147–60.

14   Reinhard Bendix, *Work and Authority in Industry* (New York: John Wiley, 1956).

15   Just as in the United States, enterprises are often associated with one individual, e.g. Richard Branson of Virgin, or Muhammed Al-Fayed of Harrods.

16   Hugh Heclo and Aaron Wildavsky, *The Private Government of Public Money* (Berkeley, CA: University of California Press); Colin Thain and Maurice Wright, *The Treasury and Whitehall* (Oxford: Clarendon Press, 1995).

17   A. Davies and J. Willman, *What Next?: Agencies, Departments and the Civil Service* (London: Institute for Public Policy Research, 1992).

18   In practice this has become something of a useful fiction, but the principle remains a central part of the constitution. See Geoffrey Marshall, *Ministerial Responsibility* (Oxford: Oxford University Press, 1995).

19   See Petra Bauer, "Politische Orientierungen im Ubergang," *Kolner Zeitschrift fur Soziologie*, 43 (1991), 433–53.

20   All industrialized countries have some bureaucratic tendencies, but see Joseph LaPalombara, *Democracy, Italian Style* (New Haven, CT: Yale University Press, 1987).

21   Roger Jowell, Sharon Witherspoon and L. Brock, eds, *British Social Attitudes, 1986* (Aldershot: Gower, 1986).

22   Fred W. Riggs, *Administration in Developing Countries: The Theory of Prismatic Society* (Boston: Houghton-Mifflin, 1964).

23   Yung H. Park, *Bureaucrats and Ministers in Contemporary Japanese Government* (Berkeley, CA: Institute of East Asian Studies, 1986).

24   See John Brehm and Scott Gates, *Working, Shirking and Sabotage* (Ann Arbor: University of Michigan Press, 1999) for a discussion of compliance in bureaucracies.

25   A. V. Obolonsky, "The Modern Russian Administration in the Time of Transition," *International Review of Administrative Sciences*, 65 (1999), 569–77.

26   Blau and Scott discuss organizations in terms of *cui bono*, or "who benefits," and argue that commonweal organizations such as clubs tend to be organized in this participatory manner. See Peter M. Blau and W. Richard Scott, *Formal Organizations* (San Francisco: Chandler, 1962).

27   See Camilla Stivers, "The Public Agency as *Polis*: Active Citizenship in the Administrative State," *Administration and Society*, 22 (1990), 86–105.

28   Talcott Parsons and Edward A. Shils, *Toward a General Theory of Action* (Cambridge, MA: Harvard University Press, 1951), p. 77 ff.

29   Mary Douglas, *In the Active Voice* (London: Routledge and Kegan Paul, 1982).

30   Geert Hofstede, *Culture's Consequences* (Beverly Hills, CA: Sage, 1980).

31   Richard W. Wilson, *Compliance Ideologies: Rethinking Political Culture* (Cambridge: Cambridge University Press, 1992).

32   Organization for Economic Management and Development, *Administration as Service, The Public as Client* (Paris: OECD, 1987); *Implementing the UK Citizen's Charter* (Ottawa: Canadian Center for Management Development, 1992).

33   See O. P. Divedi and James Gow, *From Bureaucracy to Public Management: The Administrative Culture of Canada* (Peterborough, ONT: Broadview Press, 1999).

34   Giovanni Sartori, "Politics, Ideology and Belief Systems," *American Political Science Review*, 43 (1969), 398–411.

35   Mirjan R. Damaska, *The Faces of Justice and State Authority: A Comparative Approach to the Legal Process* (New Haven: Yale University Press, 1986).

36   This is especially the case given the large number of (often conflicting) precedents available.

37   As we will see in Chapter 9, one strand of reform in the 1980s and 1990s has stressed the need to enhance participation and the power of clients to influence decisions.

38   Elihu Katz and S. N. Eisenstadt, "Some Sociological Observations on the Response of Israeli Organizations to New Immigrants," *Administrative Science Quarterly*, 5 (1960), 113–33.

39   Gerald Caiden, *Israel's Administrative Culture* (Berkeley, CA: University of California, Institute of Government Studies, 1970); see also Gregory Mahler, *Israel: Government and Politics in a Maturing State* (San Diego, CA: Harcourt, Brace Jovanovich, 1990).

40   Rey Koslowski, *Migrants and Citizens: Demographic Change in the European State System* (Ithaca, NY: Cornell University Press).

41   Fred W. Riggs, *Administration in Developing Countries, op. cit.*, pp. 200–2.

42   Riggs, *ibid.*, p. 201.

43   David J. Gould, "Administrative Corruption: Incidence, Causes and Remedial Strategies," in Ali Farazmand, ed., *Handbook of Comparative and Development Public Administration* (New York: Marcel Dekker, 1991).

44   Obolonsky, *op. cit.*

45   Joachim Jens Hesse, *Administrative Transformation in Central and Eastern Europe* (Oxford: Blackwell, 1993).

46   Atilla Agh, "Eastern and Central Europe," in Joachim Jens Hesse, Christopher Hood and B. Guy Peters, eds, *Paradoxes of Administrative Reform* (Berlin: Duncker and Humblot, 2001).

47   Richard Topf, "Political Change and Political Culture in Britain, 1959–87," in John R. Gibbins, ed., *Contemporary Political Culture* (London: Sage, 1989).

48   Michael Lipsky, *Street Level Bureaucracy* (New York: Russell Sage, 1980); M. Adler and S. Asquith, *Discretion and Power* (London: Heinemann, 1981); Stephen H. Linder and B. Guy Peters, "A Design Perspective on Policy Implementation: The Fallacies of Misplaced Precision," *Policy Studies Review*, 6 (1987), 459–75.

49   This style of reform has been particularly popular in Canadian government. See, for example, Jane Jenson and Martin Papillon, "The Changing Boundaries of Citizenship: A Review and a Research Agenda," Paper presented at Research Planning Conference, Canadian Centre for Management Development, Ottawa, May, 2000.

50   Ronald Inglehart, *The Silent Revolution: Changing Values and Political Styles Among Western Publics* (Princeton, NJ: Princeton University Press, 1977); *Culture Shift in Advanced Industrial Society* (Princeton, NJ: Princeton University Press, 1990).

51   Paul Taggart, "The New Populism: The Case of *New Democracy* on Swedish Politics," Paper presented at Annual Meeting of the Midwest Political Science Association, April 1993; Ferdinand Muller-Rommel, *New Politics in Western Europe* (Boulder, CO: Westview, 1996).

52   John R. Gibbins, "Introduction to Contemporary Political Culture," in Gibbins, *Contemporary Political Culture, op. cit.*

53   Hal G. Rainey, Robert W. Backoff and Charles H. Levine, "Comparing Public and Private Organizations," *Public Administration Review*, 36, 234–42; B. Guy Peters and Vincent Wright, *The New Handbook of Political Science* (Oxford: Oxford University Press, 1997).

54   For alternative views see Graham Allison, "Public and Private Management: Are They Fundamentally Alike in All Unimportant Respects," in Frederick S. Lane, ed., *Current Issues in Public Administration* (New York: St Martin's Press, 1986).

55   See Anke Grosskopf, *Citizen Support for Supreme Courts*, Ph.D. Dissertation, Department of Political Science, University of Pittsburgh.

56   One example among many is E. Brunet, *La Betise Administrative* (Paris: Albin Michel, 1998).

57 David Zussman, "The Image of the Public Service in Canada," *Canadian Public Administration*, 25 (1982), 63–80.

58 Daniel Katz *et al.*, *Bureaucratic Encounters* (Ann Arbor: Survey Research Center, University of Michigan, 1975); Charles T. Goodsell, *The Public Encounter: Where Citizen and State Meet* (Bloomington, IN: Indiana University Press, 1981).

59 See B. Guy Peters and Christian Hunold, *European Politics Reconsidered*, 2nd. edn (New York: Holmes and Meier, 1998).

60 But see F. Lemaitre, "La gestion des enterprises de service public en Europe se rapproche de celle du secteur privé," *Le Monde*, 6 October 1996.

61 Richard A. Chapman, ed., *Ethics in the Public Service* (Edinburgh: University of Edinburgh Press, 1993).

62 Gabriel A. Almond and Sidney Verba, *The Civic Culture* (Boston: Little, Brown, 1963), pp. 70–3.

63 Samuel J. Eldersveld, V. Jagannadham and A. P. Barnabas, *The Citizen and the Administrator in a Developing Democracy* (Glenview, IL: Scott, Foresman, 1968).

64 Randall Baker, "The Role of the State and Bureaucracy in Developing Countries Since World War II," in Ali Farazmand, ed., *Handbook of Comparative and Development Public Administration* (New York: Marcel Dekker, 1991).

65 Adam Sarapata, *A Portrait of Bureaucracy* (Delft: Akademos, 1992).

66 Gabriel Almond and Sidney Verba, *The Civic Culture*, Chapter 1.

67 Gabriel A. Almond and G. Bingham Powell, *Comparative Politics: A Developmental Approach* (Boston: Little, Brown, 1966), 57–63.

68 Peter Nettl, *Political Mobilization* (New York: Basic Books, 1967).

69 Harry Eckstein, "Authority Patterns: A Structural Basis for Political Inquiry," *American Political Science Review*, 67 (1973), 1142–61.

70 Lucian W. Pye, "Introduction: Political Culture and Political Development," in Pye and Verba, *Political Culture and Political Development, op. cit.*; Mary Douglas, *Cultural Bias* (London: Royal Anthropological Society, 1975).

71 Parsons and Shils, *Toward a General Theory of Action, op. cit.*

72 H. H. Gerth and C. Wright Mills, *From Max Weber: Essays in Sociology* (New York: Oxford University Press, 1946, pp. 198–200).

73 J. Donald Kingsley, *Representative Bureaucracy* (Yellow Springs, Ohio: Antioch University Press, 1944).

74 For one view of the problem see Steven Wineman, *The Politics of Human Services* (Boston: South End Press, 1984).

75 Michel Crozier, *The Bureaucratic Phenomenon* (Chicago: University of Chicago Press, 1964).

76 Geert Hofstede, *Culture and Organizations: Software of the Mind* (New York: McGraw-Hill, 1991); Philippe d'Iribarne, *La logique de l'honneur: Gestion des enterprises et traditions nationales* (Paris: Editions de Seuil, 1989).

77 This familiar pattern of patronialism and clientelism is also found in some areas of Southern Europe.

78 Ronald Inglehart, *The Silent Revolution, op. cit.*

79 See Orion F. White, "The Dialectical Organization – An Alternative to Bureaucracy," *Public Administration Review*, 39 (1969), 32–42; Robert Denhardt, *In the Shadow of Organization* (Lawrence, KS: University of Kansas Press, 1981).

80 Michael Barzelay, *Breaking Through Bureaucracy* (Berkeley, CA: University of California Press, 1992).

81 David Osborne and Ted Gaebler, *Reinventing Government* (Reading, MA: Addison-Wesley, 1992).

82 Hans Diefenbacher and Ulrich Schasse, *Mitbestimmung, Norm und Wirklichkeit* (Frankfurt: Campus Verlag, 1984).

83 This reduces the costs of government by eliminating individuals who contributed little to the direct delivery of services. This has been one of the major strands of reform in the

National Performance Review in the United States. See B. Guy Peters, "Institutional Theory and Administrative Reform," in Per Laegreid and Morten Egeberg, eds, *Organizing Political Institutions* (Oslo: Scandinavian University Press, 1999).

84   E. Sorenson, *Public Administration*; Hess, G. A., "School Based Management as a Vehicle for School Reform," *Education and Urban Society*, 26 (1994), 248–63.

85   Numerous reforms in the late 1980s and early 1990s – the Citizen's Charter in the United Kingdom and CS2000 in Canada as examples – have sought to provide a much greater role for clients in decisions taken by government organizations. These will be discussed in greater detail in Chapter 7, dealing with accountability.

86   Some argue that this view of postindustrial politics is too idealistic and that what modern citizens – whether clients or not – want is more self-indulgent. See Bo Reimer, "Postmodern Structures of Freedom: Values and Lifestyles in the Postmodern Age," in John R. Gibbins, ed., *Contemporary Political Culture, op. cit.*

87   See M. Connolly, P. McKeown and G. Milligan-Byrne, "Making the Public Sector User Friendly?: A Critical Analysis of the Citizen's Charter," *Parliamentary Affairs*, 47 (1994), 23–37.

88   See Paul Pierson, "The New Politics of the Welfare State," *World Politics*, 48 (1996), 143–79.

89   Anthony Barker and B. Guy Peters, *The Politics of Expert Advice* (Edinburgh: University of Edinburgh Press, 1993); but see Werner Bussmann, "Von der Doppelbodigkeit des Verhaltnisses zwischen Wissenschaft und Politik," *Schweizerisches Jahrbuch fur Politische Wissenschaft* (Bern: Paul Haupt, 1989).

90   Emmette Redford, *Democracy in the Administrative State* (New York: Oxford University Press, 1969), p. 66.

91   Paul Sabatier, "An Advocacy Coalition Framework for Policy Change and the Role of Policy-Oriented Learning Therein," *Policy Sciences*, 21 (1988), 129–68.

92   Douglas, *op. cit.*

93   Samuel P. Huntington, "Post-Industrial Politics: How Benign Will It Be?," *Comparative Politics*, 6 (1974), 163–91.

94   See Jon Elster, *Deliberative Democracy* (Cambridge: Cambridge University Press, 1998).

95   J. Knight and J. Johnson, "What Sort of Equality does Deliberative Democracy Require?," in J. Bohman and W. Rehig, eds, *Deliberative Democracy* (Cambridge, MA: MIT Press, 1997).

96   See Bernhard Wessels, "Development of Support: Diffusion or Demographic Replacement?," in O. Niedermayer and R. Sinnott, eds, *Public Opinion and Internationalized Governance* (Oxford: Oxford University Press, 1995).

97   With the increasing secularization of society the religious cleavage may be less volatile, but the same accommodative strategies are available to manage other divisions, including those arising because of immigration.

98   The bureaucracies in many Third World countries may appear inefficient to outsiders but may be more efficient than the political institutions, or even the private sector.

99   That having been said, the Supreme Court in the United States, and to some extent the Constitutional Court in Germany, have maintained their legitimacy despite overt policy-making roles. See Anke Grosskopf, *op. cit.*

100 Gideon Sjoberg, Richard A. Bremer and Buford Faris, "Bureaucracy and the Lower Class," *Sociology and Social Research,* 51 (1966), 325.

101 This to some extent began with Robert Putnam's provocative discussion of Italian politics. It has been followed by others such as Frances Fukuyama, *Trust: Social Virtues and the Creation of Prosperity* (New York: Free Press, 1995).

102 Gabriel Almond and Sidney Verba, *The Civic Culture*, p. 213.

103 Laurence Wylie, "Social Change at the Grassroots," in Stanley Hoffmann *et al., In Search of France* (New York: Harper and Row, 1963).

104 James F. Hollifield, "Still Searching for the New France," in Hollifield and Ross, eds, *Searching for the New France* (New York: Routledge, 1991).

105 In the United Kingdom the Thatcher government moved to reduce the self-regulative

powers of professional organizations. This was done in part because they were seen as monopolies that inhibited the free working of the market.

106 Steven G. Koven, "Coproduction of Law Enforcement Services; Benefits and Implications," *Urban Affairs Quarterly*, 27 (1992), 457–69; Max Neiman, "Government Directed Change of Everyday Life and Coproduction: The Case of Home Energy Use," *Western Political Quarterly*, 42 (1989), 365–89; Charles H. Levine, "Citizenship and Service Delivery: The Promise of Coproduction," *Public Administration Review*, 44 (1984), 178–87.

107 Robert D. Putnam, with Robert Leonardi and Raffaella Y. Nanetti, *Making Democracy Work* (Princeton, NJ: Princeton University Press, 1993).

108 This is similar to the argument that Kornhauser made about mass society. See William Kornhauser, *The Politics of Mass Society* (Glencoe, IL: Free Press, 1959).

109 Robert D. Putnam, *Bowling Alone: The Collapse and Revival of American Community* (New York: Simon and Schuster, 2000).

110 See Jeffrey R. Henig, Chris Hamnett and Harvey B. Feigenbaum, "The Politics of Privatization: A Comparative Perspective," *Governance*, 1, 4 (1988), 442–68; "Italy: Stopping the Rot," *The Economist*, 324 (September 12, 1992), 51; Attiat F. Ott and Keith Hartley, *Privatization and Economic Efficiency: A Comparative Analysis of Developed and Developing Countries* (Aldershot: Edward Elgar, 1991); Salamat Ali, "Barons vs. Bureaucrats," *Far Eastern Economic Review*, 15 (April 18, 1991), 60 ff.

111 Kevin Kearns, *Managing For Accountability: Preserving Trust in Public and Non-Profit Organizations* (San Francisco: Jossey-Bass, 1996).

112 Almond and Verba, *The Civic Culture*, p. 270.

113 SOFRES, *Sondages*, 25, 2, 1963.

114 Francois Bloch-Laine, "Le renouveau du mouvement associatif," in Jean-Daniel Reynaud and Yves Grafmeyer, *Francais, qui etes-vous?* (Paris: La Documentation Francaise, 1981), pp. 363–8.

115 Charles Tilly, *The Contentious French* (Cambridge, MA: Belknap Press, 1986).

116 Johan P. Olsen, *Organized Democracy* (Oslo: Universitetsforlaget, 1986); Henry Milner, *Sweden: Social Democracy in Practice* (Oxford: Oxford University Press, 1990), pp. 73–100; Olof Petersson, *Medborgnas makt* (Stockholm: Carlssons, 1989).

117 Almond and Verba, *The Civic Culture*.

118 Paul R. Abramson and Ronald Inglehart, "The Development of Systemic Support in Four Western Democracies," *Comparative Political Studies*, 2 (1983), 419–42.

119 See K. A. Rovik, *Den "Syke" Stat* (Oslo; Universitetsforlaget, 1992).

120 For some evidence, see Geert Hofstede, *Culture's Consequences* (Beverly Hills, CA: Sage, 1980), pp. 115–18; Ali Kazan, "Bureaucracy and Egalitarianism," *Public Administration Review* (Lahore), 22 (1984), 19–40; see also the evidence concerning Zambian administrators cited above (pp. 50–1).

121 Keith Hart, "Kinship, Contract and Trust," in Diego Gambetta, ed., *Trust: Making and Breaking Cooperative Relations* (Oxford: Basil Blackwell, 1988).

122 "Opinion Roundup," *Public Opinion*, 1 (July/August, 1978), p. 31.

123 *The Public Perspective*, 4 (March/April, 1993), 89; see also Seymour Martin Lipset and William Schneider, *The Confidence Gap: Business, Labor and Government in the Public Mind*, rev. ed. (Baltimore, MD: The Johns Hopkins University Press, 1987), 47–60.

124 *The Public Perspective*, 3 (November/December, 1992), 85.

125 *The Public Perspective*, 3 (November/December, 1992), 96. An East German sample had almost half of the respondents express little confidence in the civil service.

126 Commission of the European Community, *Euro-Barometer* (Brussels: European Community) quarterly,

127 This average is not weighted by population; rather, each country counts as one observation.

128 As well there might be. Most have been fully democratic for a number of years and also provide a host of Welfare State benefits to their citizens.

129 There is also some literature on trust in public organizations by their workers. See David

G. Carnevale and Barton Wechsler, "Trust in the Public Sector," *Administration and Society*, 23 (1992), 471–94.

130 Geoffrey Marshall, ed., *Ministerial Responsibility* (Oxford: Oxford University Press, 1989).

131 Eric Nordlinger, *The Working Class Tories* (Berkeley, CA: University of California Press, 1967).

132 A. F. Heath and Richard G. Topf, "Political Culture," in Jowell, Witherspoon and Brook, *British Social Attitudes, The Fifth Report, op. cit.*

133 Kevin Theakston, *The Labour Party and Whitehall* (London: Routledge, 1992).

134 Donald J. Savoie, *Thatcher, Reagan, Mulroney: In Search of a New Bureaucracy* (Pittsburgh: University of Pittsburgh Press, 1993); Andrew Grice and Colin Brown, "Blair Turns Up Heat on State Sector," *The Independent*, 9 July 1999.

135 On the development of civil society in Africa, see E. Gyimah-Boadi, "Civil Society in Africa," *Journal of Democracy*, 7 (1996), 118–32.

136 Dominique Labbe and Maurice Croisat, *La Fin des Syndicats?* (Paris: L'Harmattan, 1992).

137 Michel Crozier, *La société bloquée* (Paris: Seuil, 1970).

138 S. Fortescue, "Soviet Bureaucracy and Civil Society," in D. Lovell, C. Kukathas and W. Maley, eds, *The Transition from Socialism: State and Civil Society in Gorbachev's USSR* (Melbourne: Longman Cheshire, 1991); see also Norbert Lechner, ed., *Cultura politica y democratizacion* (Santiago de Chile: Salesianos, 1987).

139 M. A. H. Wallis, *Bureaucracy: Its Role in Third World Development* (London: Macmillan, 1989).

140 Val R. Lorwin, "Belgium," in Robert A. Dahl, *Political Oppositions in Western Democracies* (New Haven: Yale University Press, 1966), p. 174; The consociational nature of Belgium has been declining as the system has become increasingly federalized.

141 John Fitzmaurice, *The Politics of Belgium: A Unique Federalism* (Boulder: Westview Press, 1996).

142 Kenneth Gladdish, *Governing From the Center: Politics and Policymaking in the Netherlands* (DeKalb, IL: Northern Illinois University Press, 1991), 33–48.

143 H. J. G. A. van Mierlo, "Depillarisation and the Decline of Consociationalism in the Netherlands, 1970–85," *West European Politics*, 9 (1986), 97–119.

144 Robert N. Bellah, *Habits of the Heart: Individualism and Commitment in American Life* (Berkeley: University of California Press, 1985).

145 Cornelius Kerwin, "Rulemaking," 2nd edn (Washington, DC: CQ Press, 1998).

146 Gerth and Mills, *From Max Weber*, pp. 295 ff.

147 Herbert Simon, *Administrative Behavior* (New York: Free Press, 1947).

148 Edward C. Page, *Bureaucratic Authority and Political Power: A Comparative Analysis*, 2nd edn (New York: Harvester, 1992).

149 *Public Service 2000: The Renewal of the Public Service in Canada* (Ottawa: Privy Council Office, 1990).

150 Victor Thompson, *Modern Organizations* (New York: Alfred A. Knopf, 1961).

151 This was particularly true for British colonial management in Africa. See L. Rubin and B. Weinstein, *Introduction to African Politics* (New York: Praeger, 1974), pp. 34–41.

152 Colin Campbell and George Szablowski, *The Superbureaucrats: Structure and Behaviour in Central Agencies* (Toronto: Macmillan of Canada, 1979).

153 Gerth and Mills, *From Max Weber, op. cit.*, pp. 199–202

154 John Brehm and Scott Gates, *Working, Shirking and Sabotage, op. cit.*

155 Max Weber, *The Protestant Ethic and the Spirit of Capitalism* (London: George Allen and Unwin, 1930); R. H. Tawney, *Religion and the Rise of Capitalism* (New York: Harcourt, Brace, 1926).

156 Jamil E. Jreisat, "Bureaucratization in the Arab World," in A. Farazmand, ed., *Handbook of Comparative and Development Public Administration* (New York: Marcel Dekker, 1991).

157 Kenneth Lieberthal and Michel Oksenberg, *Policymaking in China: Leaders, Structures and Processes* (Princeton: Princeton University Press, 1988); P. Christopher Earley, "Social Loafing and Collectivism: A Comparison of the United States and the People's Republic of China," *Administrative Science Quarterly*, 34 (1989), 565–81.

158   Patricia W. Ingraham, "Of Pigs and Pokes and Policy Diffusion: Another Look at Pay for Performance," *Public Administration Review*, 53 (1993), 348–56.

159   Wen-fang Tang, "Workplace Democracy in Chinese Local Industries," *American Journal of Political Science*, 1993, 37, 920–40.

160   See Richard Hula, "Alternative Management Strategies in Public Housing," in William T. Gormley, Jr, ed., *Privatization and Its Alternatives* (Madison, WI: University of Wisconsin Press, 1991).

161   Of course, the clients of these types of services are often middle class and generally more efficacious and organizationally skillful than the clients of most social service programs.

162   S. Pejovich, *The Codetermination Movement in the West: Labor Participation in the Management of Business Firms* (Lexington, MA: Lexington Books, 1978).

163   Victor Thompson, *Modern Organizations, op cit.*

164   We will discuss the role of public service as an incentive for recruitment and retention of public servants in Chapter 4.

The recruitment of public administrators

Before anyone can make much progress toward administering a public program, the political system must enlist and train a group of public administrators. This fact is common sense, but it simply points to the importance of recruitment in the study of public administration. In order to be capable of saying what a public organization will do (and how it will do those things), we must first have some conception of *who* will perform its tasks and for what purposes – public or personal – the personnel will act. Unlike earlier assumptions concerning organizational management, such as Weber's ideal-type conceptualization of the bureaucrat or the Taylor scientific-management school, individuals who occupy positions in public organizations are not interchangeable parts.[1] This is widely understood for partisan political leaders – presidents, prime ministers, etc. – but the same ideological and personality characteristics generally assumed to affect political leadership often are not assumed to influence bureaucrats and their behavior in office.

Public servants, as well as any other political elite, bring to their jobs a host of values, predispositions, and operating routines that will greatly affect the quality of their performance in the bureaucratic setting, as well as the type of decisions they will make.[2] Some of those predispositions are a function of their social, ethnic and economic backgrounds. Other decisional premises arise out of the academic and professional preparation of the civil servants. Still other influences will come from the work experiences, both within and outside the public sector, of these employees. It is therefore very important to understand how governments select their employees, and who within the societies seek to work for government and why they do.

Again we must emphasize that public administrators, even those at relatively low levels in the organizational hierarchy, are indeed public decision makers. The proverbial story of the judge having burned toast for breakfast and then sentencing the defendant to death may be as true, albeit in less extreme situations, of thousands of administrators deciding on thousands of demands for government services from clients each day.

This chapter examines the way in which governments select administrators, and thereby one of the ways in which they narrow the range of possible outcomes of the policy-making process. As well as being a question about predicting behavior and improving management, recruitment is also a question about democracy. One standard of good government is that it, and its decisions, should be representative of the public that is being served. Therefore, we will also be interested in the extent to which the public service in a range of countries reflects the public and the consequences that this representativeness or lack of it may have on services rendered.

Merit versus patronage

Several somewhat conflicting themes have dominated the discussion of administrative recruitment. The first of these has been the search for efficiency through merit recruitment. One of the defining characteristics of Weber's model of bureaucracy was that civil servants should be selected on the basis of achievement criteria and merit, rather than ascriptive criteria such as caste, race, class, or language. This has been referred to as selection by "neutral competence."[3] The criteria used to select personnel, therefore, may be either their training and expertise for certain identified positions in the bureaucracy, or their general competence and intellectual abilities. In either case, the assumption underlying merit selection of personnel is that bureaucracy must be able to recruit the best possible personnel, and merit recruitment is the logical means of filling the available positions with the best qualified personnel.

It should be remembered, however, that in some instances ascriptive criteria may be important for achieving the purposes of a public organization. An organization that must provide services to members of minority communities can, everything else being equal, do a better job by using a large number of minority employees in contact with the community than by using members of the dominant community. The concept of "merit" in public office is more complex than it is sometimes assumed to be, and race, creed, color and gender of public employees may be important in determining how well government really will deliver its services.[4] As ethnicity, gender and other ascriptive criteria continue to increase in importance as political cleavages within both industrialized and developing countries, issues of representativeness along those dimensions are likely to be even more crucial in the future.

In developmental terms, a second impetus for adoption of merit recruitment was the desire to remove the appointment of administrative positions from political patronage and to require merit qualifications.[5] Thus, in addition to removing the inequalities and possible inefficiencies of ascriptive recruitment, the merit reforms of civil service were intended to remove the inefficiencies and favoritism of political appointment. As desirable as the idea of employing the best person possible for each job in the public service may be from the perspective of enforcing the achievement norms of a modern society, and perhaps of achieving contemporary goals of social equality in a developing society, some important inefficiencies may result from merit recruitment.

The potential inefficiencies of merit recruitment may be especially noticeable when contrasted with the alternative: political appointment. Merit recruitment appears to imply the more mechanistic conception of the administrator or bureaucrat as the value-free administrator of programs who will administer public policies regardless of their intentions or impacts on society. It is assumed that sufficient legal and technical criteria will guide their choices and that personal commitment to the program being administered, or rejection of it, will have little influence on behavior. This conception of the administrator simply does not conform to the realities. Individuals selected by a spoils system were at least more disposed toward the programs of the political party in power than the supposedly neutral appointees of a merit system who may, in fact, be hostile to that program. A committed bureaucracy requires that political appointees be selected for some combination of political disposition and administrative talent, however, and not for their political predisposition alone. Thus, "responsive competence" may be more important than "neutral competence" in assuring that the tasks of government are accomplished well.

This difference between political and merit appointment is, of course, one of degree. Virtually all political systems have some level at which appointments are quite clearly political – frequently referred to as "policy-making" positions – and they also have jobs for which appointment is made on a relatively routine basis on some sort of merit system. The question, then, is how far up the ladder of the administrative hierarchy merit appointment, or at least not overtly political appointment, is intended to go; and conversely, what are the limits of political appointment?

The differences between two major administrative systems – the United States and the United Kingdom – illustrate the range that may exist in appointment. A president in the United States can appoint approximately three thousand people to office, and four or even five echelons of political appointees may stand between a career civil servant and the cabinet secretary.[6] In the United Kingdom each ministry will have only a few political appointments other than the minister or secretary of state in charge – the largest number now is the Treasury with six appointments – but even then, the major interface between political and administrative leaders occurs between the minister and a single career civil servant, the permanent secretary.[7] The reforms of the British civil service have, however, opened up a number of positions to appointments, including the chief executives of agencies and also positions in a growing number of "quangos."[8] These systems are obviously different, but each seems to function effectively within its own context and own political culture.

What accounts for the differences among countries in the extent to which political appointments are employed as a means of attempting to ensure compliance within an organization? One argument is that bureaucratic structures simply have evolved through history and no one has seen any real reason to alter them.[9] A more rationalist hypothesis would be that the more fragmented the decision-making structures of a government, the more likely it is to provide its ministers with a number of political appointees to provide some integration of political intentions and actual administration. The relative integration of the political elite and policy system in the United Kingdom, contrasted with that of the United States, could be taken to argue that the United Kingdom simply does not need so many political appointees on top to create compliance within the machinery of government.

We have been using the United States as the example of a country with a large number of political appointees, but several continental European countries could be used equally well. In many of those European cases, however, the political appointees, rather than being inserted directly into the structure of the departments or ministries, are linked directly to the minister and his or her private office.[10] This system removes some of the direct authority that the appointees might have over the department, but it provides the minister with both policy advice and a group of people whom he can use anywhere within the ministry. In other systems, the minister may be able to exercise some choice over the civil servants who will serve him or her, dismissing some and calling others to office. To some extent this system combines the expertise of the career civil servant with the commitment of the political appointee.

In addition to using political appointment through cabinets and other policy advisors, there is an increase in more overt forms of politicization.[11] For example, there is an increasing number of appointments available in quasi-governmental organizations and the newly-created boards and agencies that permit political leaders to attempt to control these organizations through appointments.[12] In addition, the deinstitutionalization of many civil service systems provides additional opportunities for making political appointments to positions that previously had been reserved for career civil servants.

Representative bureaucracy

A second dominant theme in a discussion of recruitment into public administrative positions is that of equality of opportunity and representativeness of the public bureaucracy.[13] Since Kingsley coined the term "representative bureaucracy," there has been concern over the extent to which the bureaucracy does, or should, represent the characteristics of the population in whose name it administers policy. Thus, just as some scholars have emphasized the necessity of merit in the recruitment of public administrators, others have stressed the importance of producing a set of administrators whose social and economic characteristics are similar to those of the people with whom they will be working. The arguments are twofold. The first is that narrow recruitment from any social stratum will tend to bias programs and policies. This is an especially important factor in social programs, because there is a higher probability that these personnel will be working members of minority communities and may tend to impose dominant group values. Studies of teachers, social workers, the police and other types of public employees indicate a tendency to reward those clients who correspond to accepted values in the dominant culture and to punish those who do not.[14] This difference in value structures may not only impair the personal interaction of client and administrator, but will also tend to prevent a number of qualified individuals from receiving services.

The second argument in favor of greater representativeness is that the ability of the public bureaucracy to hire personnel should be used as a positive means to alter the social and economic structure of the society. Thus, hiring minority community members can serve not only to attack any prejudices within the society but also to provide a means of economic advancement for members of the minority community. In the United States this has taken the form of "affirmative action" programs in which employers (especially government) are pledged to make positive efforts to hire women and members of racial minorities.[15] In India the government is similarly required to attempt to hire members of castes and tribes that traditionally have been discriminated against in Indian society.[16] In ethnically plural societies in which the differences among the ethnic communities are not necessarily those of dominance and submission, or in which the ethnic cleavages are intensely politicized, the argument for representative recruitment can be altered to say that it can be used to *preserve* the social structure and the rights of each of the ethnic communities in administering policy.[17]

In both versions of this argument, however, exists the underlying premise that bureaucracies should be representative not simply because it is democratic for them to be so, but because the pattern of recruitment will have a fundamental effect on social structure and social stratification across time. Thus, government may have a special responsibility for fostering greater equality of employment and, over time, creating greater social equality.[18] This recruitment pattern may be adopted to enhance social equality per se but may even be important for improving the efficiency and effectiveness of service delivery by the public sector. This representativeness is especially important as a means of creating a bureaucracy that will be similar to the clients with whom they come into contact on the job.

The political debate over representative bureaucracy has not ended, and continues at the present. In the spring of 2000 the Labour government in Britain expressed a variety of concerns about the alleged elitism of leading British universities and recruitment to the civil service, demanding that the universities and the civil service look more like the country as a whole. As a consequence the government advocated additional means of enhancing the representativeness of the public service.[19] The issues being raised were not at all dissimilar to those raised by Kingsley in 1944, emphasizing both the efficiency and democratic elements of the representative's argument.

Caveats = long formal notice

Before anyone goes too far with the idea of representative bureaucracy, however, several important caveats must be advanced. The first is that research on representative bureaucracy has consistently found an over-representation of middle-class (broadly interpreted) backgrounds among civil servants. This is to be expected. The civil service is in itself a middle-class occupation, and the sons and daughters of the middle class tend to have a much higher probability of attaining middle-class occupations than do the sons and daughters of the working class. This tendency toward middle-class recruitment is due in part to the nature of educational recruitment which, even in modern "welfare states," tends to substantially over-represent the middle class, and due in part to the nature of the motivations and incentives inculcated in middle-class households.[20] In either case, the number of middle-class offspring in the civil service is not a particularly damning finding for the nature of the bureaucracy but, rather, reflects general patterns of social stratification and mobility in society. Interestingly, this pattern of recruitment persists in societies that have sought to eliminate class barriers in public life, such as China and the former Soviet Union.[21] Such evidence as we have indicates that individuals occupying positions in the upper echelons of these civil service systems tend to come from families of fathers who also held "middle-class" occupations. The civil service in particular tends greatly to over-represent individuals coming from civil service and political families.

A second caveat is that the advocacy of representative bureaucracy assumes that the social class of parents will tend to determine the behavior of their offspring. This is an underlying assumption in a large amount of elite research, but the empirical research attempting to link background with behavior provides quite disappointing results.[22] Putnam described the assumption that social background influenced behavior in public office as "plausible, but ambiguous and unsubstantiated."[23] Socialization is a lifelong process, and as administrators from working-class backgrounds attain middle-class status, they tend to adopt the values of that class rather than their class of origin.[24] Further, although members of minority ethnic groups may not be able to change their status quite so readily, those who are in posts (especially senior posts) in the public bureaucracy will tend to support the values of the dominant community at a higher rate than other members of the minority group.[25] This phenomenon produces something of a paradox. Regardless of the degree of representativeness in the recruitment of civil servants, there will tend to be relatively great homogeneity of social and political values. We must remember, however, that the composition of the civil service may be as important for symbolic and political purposes as it is for "real," decision-making purposes.

Finally, we must understand that there may not necessarily be as broad a gap between merit recruitment and programs of "affirmative action" as there might appear to be at first glance.[26] To some degree, the possession of relevant ascriptive criteria may be an important qualification for the efficient administration of public programs, especially at the client-contact level of the bureaucracy. Language, race, or class differences may prevent the adequate administration of public programs because clients may perceive these differences as a measure of the program's commitment to their needs. To prevent those differences from becoming too significant in administration, some attention to ethnic or gender balancing of personnel must be given. Thus, to some degree, defining the person best able to carry out a job can depend upon their demographic characteristics just as it can depend upon formal education and the possession of certain skills.

Public versus private employment

A final general question about the recruitment and retention of civil servants is the relationship between the advantages of public and private employment in terms of salaries, benefits and working conditions. Most citizens want an efficient and well-qualified civil service, but many do not want that civil service to compete excessively with the private sector for the best personnel. The attractiveness of public jobs is especially great in times of recession because of the relative security of a government job. The argument against making civil service employment too attractive is that, through taxation, employers are actually coerced into supporting their competition in the labor market; further, the public sector lacks any effective means of pricing most of its products. Therefore, governments can, to a point, drive up the price of labor to an unreasonable level from the viewpoint of actual productivity of personnel if they were employed in the market economy. This diseconomy may become especially evident when public personnel are allowed to unionize. Thus, we come down to a rather simple question of the relative demand for public and private goods and the consequent willingness to pay for each type of goods. The evidence would appear to argue that there is considerably less demand for publicly produced goods – especially as they take on the characteristics of public goods – compared with the demand for private goods.[27] Citizens appear to value a new car or a new TV more than they value a new park. This lower demand for public goods may accentuate the diseconomies of public employment. There may be no ready solution for this problem, but it is one that must be considered when we discuss the extent and type of recruitment into the public bureaucracy.

If we leave aside the economic arguments for hiring "the best and brightest" versus an adequate civil service (sometimes at best), there are political and administrative questions that must be addressed.[28] One is that even if the public does not express an overwhelming demand for publicly provided services, those services are still important; we have already argued that, in fact, they are increasingly crucial for contemporary societies. Therefore, there may be a need to hire higher-quality personnel than a simple economic model of the public sector might dictate. Further, again there is a symbolic factor to be considered, and few citizens would want much of their fate determined – whether that fate included a pension, air traffic control or nuclear destruction – by someone who is just "good enough" for the job. The public sector does provide sensitive and important services, and having skilled and capable personnel is important.

Methods of recruitment

In addition to the rather broad questions concerning recruitment outlined above, several issues deal with the more specific methods of recruitment and assessments of qualifications for positions. These questions are, of course, greatly simplified if political patronage or other sorts of non-achievement criteria are used, for then only simple appointment by the appropriate political official is required.

Education and training

The first question is the type of training required for a position and, associated with it, the type of testing employed. Here we are interested primarily in the recruitment of the upper echelons of the bureaucracy rather than the clerical positions for which relatively uniform skill requirements can be established. In general, recruitment to policy-making positions requires some sort of post-secondary education, with the major question becoming the degree of specialization of that education. This brings us to the now standard argument between the advocates of generalists versus specialists in public bureaucracy.[29] The generalist school, as typified by practice in the United Kingdom, selects individuals for the top roles in the civil service largely on the basis of general intellectual abilities and performance in post-secondary education. The Northcote–Trevelyan Report of 1854 not only called for the establishment of a merit-based civil service in the United Kingdom but also noted that training in the classics was perhaps the best preparation for a future administrator.[30] The assumption was, and largely still is, that general intelligence (rather than specialized education or training) is all that is required to master the task of sifting information and preparing advice for ministers.

The tradition of the "talented amateur" has persisted in Britain despite the increasing technological content of government work, and despite attacks on the policy by the Fulton Report (1968) and other public and private investigations of the civil service.[31] As is shown in Table 3.1, arts and humanities graduates decreased somewhat as a percentage of all entrants to the senior civil service, but that percentage remained well over half of the total in 1987. Certainly those entering the higher civil service in Britain are extremely talented intellectually and will be able to master much of the required material while on the job, but they begin their careers at a severe disadvantage when dealing with technical (including economic) questions.

Recruitment to the civil service in the majority of continental European countries represents a different form of generalist education. In the majority of those countries the role of the administrator is quite similar to that of the jurist, and a law degree is a requirement for almost all senior positions. For example, in one study 66 percent of the senior civil service *(Beamte)* in the Federal Republic of Germany have legal degrees.[32] Other studies have shown somewhat similar levels of recruitment of lawyers in other continental European civil services.[33] Even then, however, the degree of reliance on lawyers may differ by ministry. In one study of the Austrian civil service several ministries (Interior Justice) had more than 80 percent lawyers among upper echelon employees, while others (Health, Agriculture) had less than ten percent.[34] As with British civil servants, some training in technical matters will take place on the job, although it is much more common for German and other continental civil servants to take advanced degrees in more technical subjects, especially economics. In addition, in Germany there is a national civil service academy to provide training and education for those working within the career structure so that they can more readily acquire the needed technical education.

The United States and France represent two different forms of specialist training for civil service careers. In the United States people are recruited to many positions in the civil service on the basis of having some particular educational qualifications prior to entry. For example, if an individual is seeking a job with the Department of Agriculture, he or she is usually expected to have training in

Table 3.1 University concentrations of recruits to the higher civil service in the United Kingdom (percentage)

	Arts and humanities	Social science	Natural sciences/ applied science	Other
1961–67[a]	62	24	11	3
1975[b]	54	28	17	–
1985	56	27	17	–
1989	56	32	12	–

Sources: A. H. Halsey and I. M. Crewe, "Social Survey of the Civil Service," *The Civil Service* (London: HMSO, 1968), vol. 3, pt. 1, p. 93; House of Commons, Expenditure Committee, 11th Report, 1976–7, *The Civil Service* (London: HMSO, July 25, 1977); Civil Service Commission, *Annual Report* (London: HMSO, 1985); Civil Service Commission, *Annual Report* (London: HMSO, 1989)

Notes
a Direct entrants to the administrative class; percentage of total concentrations mentioned
b Recruits for administrative trainee positions

agronomy, agricultural engineering, or some other relevant specialty. As a consequence of that pattern of recruitment, well over one-third of higher civil servants in the US federal government have formal scientific or professional qualifications of some type.[35] In fairness, legal degrees are often a generalist qualification for working in government rather than being used just for law-related positions.

In France, the specialized training needed for one to become a top civil servant is provided by government itself. The principal source of entry into the higher civil service is the Ecole Nationale d'Administration (ENA), which provides instruction in finance, management and law. The engineers and technical staff needed by government in its economic roles are trained in the several *grandes ecoles*, such as the Ecole Polytechnique. Lower-level administrators are trained in the Instituts Regionaux d'Administration (IRA). In total, the French government runs approximately eighty different types of school for the training of civil servants.[36] In this system the government can prepare its future employees in exactly the manner it wants, either as administrators (ENA and IRA) or as technical and scientific staff.

Less developed countries are in a more difficult position when deciding between generalist and specialist recruitment strategies. In the first place, when countries have recently gained independence, they are frequently left with a civil service trained by the former colonial power and thereby trained according to the traditions of that European country.[37] Further, most underdeveloped countries generally lack technical talent and must opt for a more generalist stance in recruitment into new positions. Some countries have attempted to replace an indigenous technical force with one drawn from Western countries – usually the former colonial power – but the demands of national pride and the need for jobs for their own people frequently require that jobs be given to individuals from within the nation, even if they are not always as skilled as potential hires from abroad. At the same time that the administrative system may be somewhat deficient in specialized talent from an absolute point of view, it may have a relative monopoly on such talent within the country. A principal characteristic of many developing countries is that the political system is forced into the position of becoming the major directive force in social and economic reform. As one commentator put it:

> While there is no uniform pattern the experience of many newly independent countries shows a growing emphasis on centralized planning, direction, and implementation of development programs. Thus, the government relies more on the bureaucracy than the private sector to carry out the task of nation and state building, economic growth, and social reforms – activities which are preeminent in the consciousness of the rulers and the ruled.[38]

Reliance on the private sector has been increasing in most developing countries, in part because of external pressures, but compared to most developed countries there is less implementation capacity on which to rely.

There is, however, no single pattern of recruitment for governments in developing countries. For example, the countries of South and Central America that have been independent for a number of years have had time to develop their own distinctive patterns of recruitment. In some instances these recruitment patterns are generalist and highly politicized, while in others they may be more technical and merit based.[39] Most of the African countries and many Asian countries, e.g. India and Pakistan, follow patterns inherited from their former colonial masters, often without the modernization of managerial and organizational techniques implemented over the past decades. Pressures from donors, e.g. the World Bank and the United Nations, are pushing all these countries toward recruitment and management practices more like those found in the developed "First World."

The Western model of development – speaking broadly, as the Western economic and social systems evolved by several significantly different paths – was blessed with a long time span and the absence of developmental pressures from mass publics and organized segments of the society.[40] The developing countries today are faced with producing change within the context of widely disseminated information about the glories of development and consumerism. Their leaders face demands for increased production of consumer goods at the same time that they know the need for investment in capital projects. Those investments should bear greater productive benefits in the long run but require a short-term retreat from a consumer-oriented economy toward a more state-directed economy. They face additional pressures from abroad to abandon substantial elements of state intervention in the economy in order to "let the market work." Given these problems and countervailing pressures, it is apparent that these societies have a pressing need for specialized administrators capable of proposing some solutions to these problems, and a large number of skilled personnel to actually manage economic enterprises that may be run directly by the state.

The centrality of administration and administrative functions as described above for the undeveloped countries, if taken to the logical extreme, might be a relatively accurate description of nature of bureaucracy in the former Soviet Union and, to a lesser extent, other formerly communist countries.[41] These characterizations remain largely true of countries such as China and Cuba.[42] As the state became not only an economic planner, regulator and adviser, but also the chief entrepreneur, the need for specialized talent tends to increase in government. Thus the average Soviet administrator, even if not administering a highly technical project, tended to have scientific or social science training. For example, by the 1960s, over 80 percent of all politburo members and regional elites had technical training and this pattern persisted through the end of the Soviet Union.[43] Interestingly, the more generalist talents of ideological argument and broad knowledge of the intended purposes of the Soviet state appeared to be devalued by this set of upper-level administrators, who differed little in this respect from public administrators in other societies.[44] They had the same, if not greater, demands for production that faced other managers, and they are often confronted with highly technical problems that only someone with a technical background may fully understand. Even more important is the fact that political leaders as well as the administrative elites tend to have that technical education in their backgrounds, so the civil service did not have the degree of monopoly over skills and information it might in other countries.[45]

The above discussion has dealt with the recruitment of the higher civil service. At some point in the civil service hierarchy almost all recruitment is done on the basis of narrow, job-specific criteria. Typists, for example, are hired because of their ability to type. In terms of sheer numbers, therefore, most civil service recruitment is on the basis of specialized criteria and the ability to perform a specific job. The changing nature of work in modern societies, however, is altering the need for many of the specialized skills previously needed in large numbers – many managers now do their own typing on word processors. Increasingly the emphasis in public employment will be on conceptual rather than mechanical skills.

Job placement

Related to the type of training a prospective civil servant is expected to have is the question of the means through which the applicant and the position are expected to find each other. Again, there are two principal answers: centralized personnel organizations, or recruitment by each individual agency seeking employees. Centralized placement is practiced by the United States, the United Kingdom, France, Belgium, Italy and the majority of Third World countries. The last set of countries has used centralized placement in large part as a function of inherited systems of administration. In the centralized pattern of recruitment there is a central civil service organization of some sort that is responsible for advertising new positions, testing applicants and selecting some smaller set of applicants for final selection by the agency seeking the employee.

The usual procedure for centralized placement is that a line agency notifies the personnel organization of the existence of a vacant position, a competitive examination is held, and then the agency seeking the person is sent a list of three or more names from which to select the new employee. The selection may be made on the basis of personal interviews or simply by taking the individual with the highest score on the examination or by any other rational or irrational criteria. This means of recruitment obviously meets the requirements of merit recruitment. Competitive tests are used to fill the position; these tests are centrally administered to prevent bias, and the hiring organization accepts only those deemed qualified on the basis of the examination. In practice, there may be ways around the merit system, especially for those who have professional qualifications, such as physicians, lawyers, librarians and the like. They may be judged qualified simply on the basis of their degrees and certificates and require no further examination. In addition, recruitment to the senior civil service may be done not so much on the basis of particular needs in particular departments, but on the basis of creating a cadre of administrative elites that will have lifetime careers somewhere within government.

The second means of hiring and recruitment is used primarily by the northern European countries, Spain, and many Latin American countries. In these systems there is no central personnel organization; rather, each agency is responsible for hiring its own personnel. The most common procedure is for the hiring agency to publish a notice of a vacancy and accept applications from prospective employees. These applications are generally judged on the basis of appropriate minimum qualifications for the job – especially legal training in the Scandinavian countries (Sweden, Denmark, Norway), Germany, and Austria. After the individual is deemed minimally qualified, selection may be made on the basis of less achievement-based criteria.

This system of decentralized recruitment obviously allows considerable latitude for the use of partisan and ascriptive criteria in hiring public officials, who can become tenured in office and virtually impossible for subsequent regimes to remove. Charges of partisanship in the civil service are indeed made in these systems, even in Sweden and Denmark with their long histories of civil service independence and prestige. For example, there were some concerns expressed as to whether a bureaucracy recruited during the 35 years of Social Democratic government could serve the bourgeois coalition elected in Sweden in 1976. A similar question emerged after the 1991 elections which produced another right-of-center government with an apparently more radical program of market-based reforms.[46] It is a simple matter to hire partisans when there are no formal restrictions to prevent it, and the parties in power would be extremely foolish if they did not try to provide employment for their own supporters. They can also employ administrators likely to be favorably disposed toward the programs they will be administering. As with many administrative practices, this is not a simple case of recruitment by merit or by patronage, but rather something of an intermediate means of recruitment that combines some features of both ideal-type methods. There is the potential for substantial patronage, but these opportunities are restrained in practice by the norms, procedures and pride of the administrators. In each country in Europe in which the recruitment of administrators by agency is practiced – with the possible exception of Spain – the civil service is a sufficiently institutionalized and respected profession that few practitioners would seek to demean it by an excessive or blatant use of the personnel powers they find themselves possessing.

The nature of recruitment by agency is made more complex when federalism is introduced as another variable. In Germany and Switzerland recruitment to public administrative positions is done not only by the individual agencies, but also by separate and in some cases highly independent subnational political units, which are, in turn, responsible for the administration of national programs.[47] This system is further complicated by the Swiss bureaucracy's need to preserve some balance among regional, linguistic and religious subpopulations within the civil service.[48] In general, the use of subnational bodies to perform the recruitment function may provide even greater possibilities for the use of non-merit criteria in recruitment. Nevertheless, in Germany and Switzerland we find again that the norms of the bureaucratic system are sufficiently ingrained so that merit criteria are strenuously enforced. Those who are hired have the necessary qualifications for the position – legal training and prior legal experience – must pass an examination and then they are made to undergo some sort of post-entry training in the work of administration before they are granted permanent positions as administrators.[49] There is an attempt – in practice a rather thorough one – to employ people who are formally qualified according to the requirements of the law. Thus, in this case as in others, although the rigidity of bureaucracies is often an impediment to innovation, it can also serve as an important protective device for the society in preventing illegal or immoral actions on the part of government.

Career distinctiveness

A third question concerning recruitment is the extent to which the public service is a distinct career, one for which the individual may prepare specially and that is regarded as a separate career hierarchy from the rest of the economy. It is interesting to note that movement back and forth between public and private employment – especially in policy-making positions – has been used as an indicator of two rather different relationships between society and the political systems. On the one hand, such movement is frequently taken to indicate a healthy congruence between the value structures of polity and society, a means of ensuring the representativeness of the bureaucratic structures, and even a means through which "typical" citizens can exert some influence on public policy. If the public bureaucracy is a more open career, then it is more likely that they will act in ways that the public would find legitimate and acceptable.

On the other hand, such movement among sectors can also be taken to indicate the colonization of the society by bureaucrats or, conversely, the colonization of the public service by representatives of certain vested interests in the society. The former of these negative perceptions is best illustrated by the concern of the French over the *pantouflage*, or "parachuting," of upper echelon civil servants into important and lucrative positions in the private economy.[50] This is taken as an indication of the attempt on the part of *fonctionnaires* and technocrats to manage the whole of economy and society and not just the governmental apparatus. It also means that a great deal of executive talent developed at public expense is exported to the private sector free of charge. A somewhat similar pattern is found in Japan, where civil servants who have finished one career in government (especially in MITI – the Ministry of Trade and Industry – and other economics ministries) are then hired into powerful and prestigious positions in the private sector.[51] This type of movement may help ensure that government in Japan continues to be supportive of the private sector.

The second, and negative, conception of the lateral movement between the public and private sectors is observed in the United States. The sentiment is often voiced that too much of American government is being run by administrators currently on leave from major corporations, major unions and other significant interests in the society.[52] Consequently, there is a belief that much of government is managed for the benefit of those interests rather than for the benefit of the public at large. Of course, in the United States there is also a good deal of movement from government careers into management positions in the private industry, especially from the military and civilian defense positions into defense contracting firms. The Ethics in Government Act passed during the Carter administration has, however, limited the rapidity with which such movements can be made legally.[53] Other countries have also sought to regulate the movement of civil servants into positions in the private sector that are potential sources of a conflict of interest.[54]

The degree of concern over, or distrust of, lateral movements between public and private sectors would appear to be a function of several normative concerns of the society, especially as they relate to the administrative roles of government. One concern is the perception of the values, job and norms of the public bureaucracy as being distinct from those of the private sector. In the French case, the *fonctionnaires* are perceived as a special group within society, by themselves and by the general population. This perception contains some positive and some negative elements, but the most common is that *pantouflage* is a means through which they may seek to impose their conception of society onto the society. This is especially true of placing former employees of the public sector into key economic positions to ensure close coordination of the economy with the policies of government.[55]

In other societies that seek as much as possible to distinguish bureaucratic careers from private careers, it is rather clear that employment as a public administrator is *supposed* to carry with it a rather distinct set of values and decisional premises. For example, in Germany and Sweden the public administrator has been traditionally conceived of in a modified legal role.[56] It is assumed that he or she will act much as would a judge in impartially administering programs *pro bono publico* and in accordance with the letter of the law. This may be too much to expect from a mere human, but this separation and idealization of administrator and career patterns has been useful in justifying decisions made by administrators in societies that rely heavily on administration in the conduct of public business. The tradition of the United Kingdom, Canada and other "Anglo-American Democracies" has also been of a separation of public and private careers but without a judicial interpretation of the role. Rather, the role of the public servant is conceived to be just that – someone who will devote a working lifetime to the service of the public.[57]

A second and related normative concern is the extent to which the society fears bureaucracy and therefore seeks to prevent the development of a large and inflexible bureaucratic structure atop society. There are a number of means of controlling the development of such a bureaucracy, and lateral entry at the upper echelons is certainly one of them.[58] This is perhaps the logical extension of the idea of the amateur in administration, but it is one way in which general social values can be injected into the conduct of government and administration, recognizing all the while that this will likely reduce the efficiency of organizations already attacked as being inefficient.

Civil service systems differ markedly in the extent to which their members have experience outside government. At one end of the dimension is the United Kingdom, where civil servants rarely have experience outside government and tend to remain in government for their entire working lifetime. For example, in one study of careers in the British civil service, it was found that only 29 percent of senior civil servants had any working experience outside central government. Of that 29 percent, eight percent had experience in some other type of government and 12 percent had experience in teaching. Only seven percent had worked in private sector firms.[59] That particular study is over a decade old, and there have been some changes in the recruitments of senior managers in the British public sector. The continuing separation of policy and implementation, with implementation functions being vested in agencies often headed by managers hired from outside the civil service, has opened the system somewhat.[60] To the extent that there have been changes, however, they have been to allow individuals from the private sector to come into public positions, rather than allowing those in the civil service to work elsewhere for short periods of time. The

Swedish civil service also had been relatively distinct from the private economy, but managerialist pressures have helped to open the system, at least in principle. In practice, very few senior managers have chosen to leave the private sector to take similar positions (Directors General) in the public sector.[61] A study in Switzerland showed that in most cantonal civil services there has been reduced movement between the public and private sectors, but that for the federal civil service younger civil servants are somewhat more likely to have had some experience outside government.[62]

There are three patterns that assume less separation of the civil service from the rest of the economy and society. One is the American revolving door, or the "government of strangers" described by Heclo.[63] In this system there is a great deal of movement back and forth between the public and private sector, with most people staying in government only a few years. They may, however, return to government at a later date. The majority of these "in and outers" would be in political appointments made by the President and his cabinet, but they would be in positions normally occupied by civil servants in other countries. Although these appointees occupy the major positions in government, there is still a large permanent civil service that can keep government functioning during the transition from one regime to the next.[64] The French government has used a variant of this approach by making political appointments to top posts in the administration in order to maximize both political control of the bureaucracy and career opportunities for politicians.[65]

A second pattern is that in which individuals leave government at a certain stage in their careers and go to work for the private sector. In the United States this has been a move primarily of retired military officers who go to work for defense manufacturers, but it is more common in France and Japan for civilian administrators. It has been considered a normal part of the career, for example, for top civil servants from MITI to take lucrative posts in the private sector after retiring early from government.[66] Civil servants of other ministries, to a lesser extent, may find similarly lucrative places to land after leaving government. The search for a position after retirement is facilitated when there are a number of public or quasi-public corporations into which the retiree can be placed.[67]

Finally, there are interesting cases in which being a civil servant is not considered incompatible with a political career. This pattern is most evident in Germany, where the individual, once granted the status of *Beamte*, retains that status almost without exception. The civil servant can leave government service temporarily while pursuing a political career and then return to service or be retired early with a full pension. In a typical lower house of the parliament *(Bundestag)* one-half or more of the members will be civil servants on leave for a political career.[68] Likewise in France the members of the *Grands Corps* remain so whether they are actually serving in that capacity or not, and the National Assembly and the ministries are well-stocked with members of the *Corps*. Of course, in China, the former Soviet Union, and other communist and single-party countries, the connection between administrative and political careers was very close, and that closeness is necessary as the hegemonic party provides an all-purpose elite for the management of the country.

Incentives and motivation

We have already mentioned the question of incentives when discussing one of the more general aspects of recruitment in public bureaucracies. We now discuss more of the methods available to public administration to recruit and maintain their personnel. In a general overview of organizations and membership in organizations, Clark and Wilson developed a classification of the types of incentives that an organization can offer its members; the three types of incentives mentioned were material, purposive and solidary.[69] Material incentives are factors such as pay, benefits and direct financial rewards. Purposive incentives are related to the ability of the individual within the organization to have some influence over the shape of public policy adopted and implemented by government, or simply to get something done on the job. Finally, solidary incentives derive from the social aspects of employment and group membership, which in the case of public employment may, in some countries, involve belonging to one of the more prestigious organizations in the society.

Each of these incentives has, almost as a mirror image, a possible disincentive for working in the public sector. Some people may be attracted by the salaries of government jobs, but in most countries the top jobs in government are paid substantially less than jobs with similar responsibilities in the private sector.[70] Likewise, many people are attracted by the opportunity to achieve policy goals through working in government, but others are frustrated by the slowness with which government often appears to move and the barriers to action. Finally, public employees have become the targets of increasingly adverse publicity and attacks on their skills and integrity – often from their own political masters – that have deterred more people from joining the government service.[71] Thus, we can find out why people say they choose not to join the public service, and why they leave, as well as looking at why they say they join.

Any organization will potentially provide some of each of these three types of incentives to employees. However, there are cross-national differences in the extent to which each of the three is perceived as an effective means of motivation by current and potential administrators. Some evidence about these differences can be gained through survey data, although such data are available for only a limited number of systems, largely from Western nations. As is shown in Table 3.2, there are some differences in response patterns even in this relatively homogeneous set of countries. In the first place, it is interesting to note that purposive incentives, which might have been thought to be the most significant means of influencing people to join the bureaucracy, are not that important. In the cases for which we have data, one of the other incentives, most often solidary, is mentioned by a larger percentage of the respondents. The only exception to that generalization is Japan, where responses from new entrants into the civil service demonstrate a very high level of purposive incentives. This reflects in part the elite nature of Japanese public bureaucracy and its central position in governing Japan.[72]

It might be thought that the relative undervaluing of purposive incentives was a function of the subgroup within the civil service about which we have most information. This group is composed largely of administrators near the top of the

Table 3.2 Incentives in recruitment and retention of civil servants (percentage)

Incentives	United Kingdom[a] (1967)	United States[b] (1985)	France[c] (1969)	New Zealand[d] (1966)	Spain[e] (1967)	Italy[f] (1978)	Turkey[g] (1965)	India[h] (1968)	Switzerland[i] (1987)	Australia[j] (1975)		Japan[k] (1990)
										Join	Stay in	
Material	20	37	24	36	21	48	25	38	20	34	30	7
Purposive	19	23	32	27	39	11	12	6	52	13	27	49
Solidary	56	40	34	21	30	36	56	29	22	26	15	6
Other	6	–	10	16	10	6	6	26	6	–	–	38
Total	101	100	100	100	100	101	99	100	100	73	72	100

Sources:

a Brian Chapman, "Profile of a Profession: The Administrative Class of the Civil Service," in The Civil Service (Fulton Report) (London: HMSO), v. 3, pt. 2, p. 12

b US General Accounting Office, Reasons Why Career Members Left in Fiscal Year 1985 (Washington, DC: US Government Accounting Office, 1987) GAO/GGD-87-106FS

c Ezra Suleiman, Politics, Power and Bureaucracy in France (Princeton: Princeton University Press, 1974), p. 120

d R. L. Green, M. R. Palmer and T. J. Sanger, "Why They Leave," New Zealand Journal of Public Administration, 30 (1967), p. 27

e Manuel Gomez-Reino and Francisco Andres Orizo, "Burocracia Publica y Privada," in Anales de Moral Social y Economica, Sociologica de la Administracion Publica Espanola (Madrid: Raycar, 1968), p. 267

f Franco Ferraresi, Burocrazia e politica in Italia (Milan: Il Mulino, 1980), pp. 120–1

g Leslie L. Roos and Noralou P. Roos, Managers of Modernization: Organizations and Elites in Turkey (Cambridge, MA: Harvard University Press, 1971), p. 123

h Richard P. Taube, Bureaucrats Under Stress (Berkeley, CA: University of California Press, 1969)

i Paolo Urio, Sociologie politique de la haute administration publique de la Suisse (Paris: Economica, 1989)

j Royal Commission on Australian Government Administration, Report, Appendix 3 (Canberra: Australian Government Publishing Service, 1976). Percentage listing each type as "important" or "very important"

k Ministry of Civil Service, Japan, Annual Report (Tokyo: Ministry of Civil Service, 1990), p. 6

administrative hierarchy; they have been in office for some time and may therefore be expected to have developed greater identification with the organization rather than with the ostensible purposes of the organization. In Anthony Downs' terminology, they may have become conservers rather than advocates or zealots.[73] The limited evidence reported from an Australian survey seems to dispute this, however, and the reasons reported for joining the civil service are less purposive than those reported for remaining in the service.

The differences between the several sets of administrators for which we have data are not particularly striking, but do lead to three rather interesting points. The first is the extremely high percentage of administrators in the United Kingdom who gave answers in terms of solidary incentives when questioned about their jobs. This result would appear to conform nicely with the stereotype of British administration as a set of "old boys" who conduct administration in a collegial, gentlemanly fashion and whose role as talented amateurs may prevent any effective policy initiative from arising from within the bureaucracy. Of course, numerous recent studies of the administrative apparatus of the United Kingdom indicate that although they may not be educated as experts in any particular technical specialty, many administrators discharge quite significant roles in the formation of policy – in fact, that has been known by the practitioners themselves for quite a long time.[74] Still, it is interesting to note the extent to which the practitioners give more social reasons for either joining or staying in their positions.

Of the countries on which we have data, the French upper-echelon administrators reported the highest levels of purposive incentives.[75] This finding also conforms to the prevailing conception of the French bureaucracy as the *groupe dirigeante* for the entire society.[76] Traditionally, the way of getting things done in French government has been through administration, and we may expect that administrators would perceive a relatively great ability to accomplish things through their jobs. Finally, the Italian administrators gave a very high proportion of material answers, indicating the often cited tendency to use the bureaucracy as a means of personal advancement rather than as a force for policy change.[77]

Another study of motivations and incentives for working in the United Kingdom contrasted the motivations of public and private sector employees directly.[78] This study also contrasted the incentives deemed most important by men and women. All groups examined tended to rate the challenge of the work and certain solidary benefits as most important in their choices of jobs (Table 3.3). Public sector employees, however, also tended to rank the security of their positions· very highly. In fairness, they also rated their potential contributions to society (a purposive incentive) very highly while this value was very low in the ratings reported by private sector employees. For public sector employees, material incentives such as high earnings and fringe benefits were among the least important incentives available. While the differences between the sectors were not great, they do support most other findings and our general understanding of the differences between the public and private sector work forces. They also substantiate the earlier finding of strong solidary incentives in the United Kingdom. A similar study in Canada, for example, found less importance attached to solidary incentives, although employees in the public sector there were also less concerned with material rewards than were private sector employees.[79]

If the evidence on incentive structures for Western administrative systems is rather spotty, then the information on non-Western administrative systems appears virtually non-existent. The data for a by now rather dated sample of Turkish administrators, however, show a close similarity to Western nations.[80] Another study of administrative cadres in the People's Republic of China found that material incentives were the most commonly cited, but that purposive incentives were a rather close second.[81] Further, from a number of more descriptive studies, we can rather quickly develop the hypothesis that the major incentives for joining bureaucratic systems in non-Western societies are solidary and material rather than purposive. In the first place, given the colonial backgrounds of most of these societies, the pattern of goal achievement through administration was not well ingrained into these systems at the time of independence. Moreover, in the Latin American systems, which have been independent longer, the administrators are not always protected by merit systems and tenure, so any attempt to use administration to alter the existing social and economic arrangements in other than certain ways often meets with a prompt dismissal from office.[82] There are also more positive aspects to the attraction of the bureaucracy for many prospective employees. The public bureaucracy is a stable and relatively remunerative institution of the society, and compared with opportunities that may exist in the private economy, the opportunity to work in the public bureaucracy is frequently an extremely attractive economic option.[83]

The operation of the solidary incentives in administrative systems in developing countries is perhaps less obvious. One of the social and cultural bases of many underdeveloped countries has been an emphasis on status and rank in defining social behavior. Also, in most of these societies the public bureaucracy has been able to establish itself as a high-status occupation. This status may be in part related to the relatively brief separation in time from the period in which recruitment to these governmental positions was determined almost entirely by ascriptive criteria, and, in fact, the best families frequently chose to send their sons into the public service. As Kearney and Harris said in speaking of then Ceylon (now Sri Lanka):

> The great prestige enjoyed by the public servant has, however, probably contributed at least as much as material advantage or employment security to the attractiveness of a bureaucratic career. The social prestige of the modern bureaucrat is in large measure a heritage of Ceylon's feudal and colonial past.[84]

These authors go on to point out that the "social exclusiveness and supreme confidence" of colonial administrators tended to reinforce the impression that administrative positions were to be equated with superior social position.[85] Even after the passage of decades from the time of colonial domination, some of these values persist. Further, in societies that value social position above the more achievement-based criteria usually associated with Western societies, one may expect a high level of solidary incentives among those joining the bureaucracy.

The incentives of administrators joining the bureaucracy in the underdeveloped world are obviously different from the types of incentives that we would expect to characterize bureaucrats charged with bringing about important social and economic changes. We have already noted the load being placed upon administration in these transformations, and we find here a great disparity between the requirements of social change and the motivations of the people being recruited.[86] This situation cannot, of course, provide an optimistic outlook for the future of administered change.

The study from the United Kingdom shown in Table 3.3 is particularly interesting, since it represented the reaction of a group of senior civil servants then under fire by an administration that sought to limit bureaucratic control over policy and to limit the pay and prestige that the service had enjoyed. Here, too, the reasons given for leaving senior government positions were a balance of incentives (or disincentives). It is especially interesting that solidary concerns, such as the denigration of the civil service and political interference in personnel management, were more important than some of the more tangible attacks (e.g. on pay) then being made.[87] Other subsequent surveys of senior government positions, and some similar albeit less quantitative work on the British civil service weathering similar attacks, confirmed the impression that pride in service is an important factor in recruitment and retention of top civil servants. The same pride in service has been found even more strongly in studies of the Canadian public service.

To conclude this discussion of incentives, it is possible to make some highly conjectural statements about the nature of the bureaucracy in China, the former Soviet Union and other communist countries. On the basis of descriptive accounts and descriptions of prior administrative systems, one can hypothesize that the incentive structures of these bureaucrats will be rather similar to those found for administrators in Western societies. That is, there is a balance of material, purposive and solidary incentives. The purposive incentives are rather obvious, given that even more than most Western societies, communist regimes are heavily oriented toward administration as the means of achieving goals. It might be expected that individuals would perceive some real ability to accomplish certain goals through working in the administrative structures. The material incentives may appear rather odd in supposedly classless societies, but we know well that there are, if not classes, at least groups for which there are differential economic

Table 3.3 Most important characteristics of jobs for employees in the United Kingdom

Public sector		Private sector	
Females	*Males*	*Females*	*Males*
Challenge	Challenge	Challenge	Challenge
Friendly people	Security	Location	Autonomy
Security	Societal contribution	Friendly people	Friendly people
Societal contribution	Friendly people	Well-regarded organization	Well-regarded organization
Location	Autonomy	Being appreciated	Influence

Source: Beverly Alban Metcalfe, "What Motivates Managers: An Investigation of Gender and Sectors of Employment," *Public Administration*, 67 (1989) pp. 95–108.

rewards.[88] The public bureaucracy is one such group; being a member of the "apparatus" of the state will generally pay off not only directly, but also indirectly through access to scarce consumer goods. Finally, one traditional description of Russian administration was as a set of small and closely knit primary groups operating within the context of a larger governmental structure.[89] We may hypothesize that this same sort of small group were still operating within the Soviet bureaucracy, so there was a high level of solidary motivation for the workers within such groups. Also we might expect that there would be differences by age among public servants in these regimes. Those with their roots in the early days of the revolutions and World War II might think of their work in more patriotic, solidary terms, while younger workers might see the civil service as simply a well-paid occupation in a more stable society. Of course, these are only conjectures about the motivations of these administrators, but there is evidence that each of the incentives is likely to be effective. What is not known is the relative strength of these motivations and incentives.

Pay in the public sector

It has been established that money may not be the only, or even the best, means of motivating potential employees to accept governmental careers, or to continue in those careers once they have been employed. However, pay is an important issue in the public sector, not least because many citizens believe that government employees receive large salaries for little work.[90] In addition, it is not only the pay received during the working lifetime of the employees that produces popular resentment, but also the variety of benefits received by civil servants, not least of which is an inflation-proofed pension. The comparability of compensation in the public sector with that of the private sector is an important consideration in determining the satisfaction of government workers with their jobs, and for determining the satisfaction of citizens with their public servants.

Determining appropriate levels of compensation for government employees is not as simple a task as it may appear. It is true that many public sector jobs are directly comparable to jobs in the private sector; the tasks of a secretary in government are almost identical to those of a secretary in the private sector.[91] However, some jobs in government have no private sector counterparts, and many jobs that appear comparable may not be. Being a police officer is different from any private sector job, even that of a private security guard. And although the job of a government executive may resemble that of a private sector manager of a similar-size firm, the private sector manager is spared the political responsibility, media exposure, the managerial difficulties (for example, the convoluted personnel management practices of a civil service system) of a manager in government. In addition, determining the value of an index-linked pension, or of the relative security of public employment, involves a number of assumptions about the future rates of inflation, future rates of unemployment and the preferences of workers for future versus current income. President Ronald Reagan once suggested that civil servants be paid 94 percent of what would be earned for comparable jobs in the private sector; the missing six percent was for the pension and for job security.[92]

This figure was, however, only a guess at best of what the true value is of those components of the civil service compensation package.

Most studies of pay comparability between the public and private sectors find that government employees at the lower echelons are better paid than their private sector counterparts.[93] This is especially true of workers in unskilled or semi-skilled positions, such as sanitation workers or bus drivers. This relative advantage of public sector workers derives, at least in part, from the ability of these workers to exert pressure on political leaders by real or threatened strikes, as well as the absence of the "bottom line" that would constrain a private employer. However, as responsibilities increase, government employees are paid less well than workers in the private sector. Those working at the very top of public organizations frequently earn only a fraction of what they would be earning for jobs with similar responsibilities in the private sector.[94]

There are some significant exceptions to the above generalization about the rewards of public office. In societies with traditions of strong and prestigious government, senior civil servants are often well paid. For example, in the United Kingdom the very top officials of the civil service (the "open structure") are well paid in comparison to the majority of similar executives in the private economy, although their pay has been gradually falling behind since the late 1970s.[95] Even though the pay of the top British civil servants has been falling (relative to the private sector) they have done well relative to the rest of the civil service, whose pay has slipped even more.[96] These civil servants lack some of the perquisites, such as an automobile, of highly-placed private sector employees, but they do have an index-linked pension to look forward to after retirement. Also, in societies dominated by government, such as the former Soviet Union or many contemporary Third World countries, government is by far the most rewarding place to be employed. Indeed one of the best paid civil service cadres is in the "Little Asian Tiger," Singapore, whose President reputedly has said that ". . . if you pay people peanuts you get monkeys."

The relative position of public and private sector pay is demonstrated in Tables 3.4 and 3.5 which relate average pay in the public sector to that in the private sector in a number of countries, and more detailed information about rewards of high office in a more limited number of countries. While there are inherent difficulties in making these comparisons – for example, differences in the occupational structure within the civil service and the private sector – these data are, to some degree, indicative of the relative position of the two sets of workers. In most industrialized democracies, civil servants earn on average about what is earned in the private sector, while in most underdeveloped countries they earn substantially more.[97] This is indicative of the important position of government, and its employees, in the management and development of these societies. The position of top managers in industrialized democracies is not, however, so good and they tend to be substantially less well paid.

Pay determination in the public sector is more than a question of personnel management. It is also a crucial element in economic management. Since government now employs a very large proportion of the total labor force (18 percent in the United States, 31 percent in the United Kingdom and 42 percent in Sweden), pay determination in the public sector influences economic conditions for the

Table 3.4 Pay of top civil servants as a percentage of average pay in the economy

Country	Civil servants' pay
United Kingdom	541
Germany	487
France	461
Belgium	444
Switzerland	385
Denmark	302
Sweden	223
Norway	189

Source: Unpublished data from Christopher Hood and B. Guy Peters, *Rewards of High Public Office* (London: Sage, 1994)

Table 3.5 Ratio of central government wages to per capita income

Nation	
Burundi	15.11
Senegal	9.90
Cameroon	7.39
Egypt	5.70
India	4.80
Austria	1.06
Australia	1.16
Singapore	1.16
Norway	1.48
Sweden	1.49

Source: Peter Heller and Alan A. Tait, *Government Employment and Pay: Some International Comparisons* (Washington, DC: International Monetary Fund, 1983)

economy as a whole. This is one aspect of the economy that government can influence most directly, and when there is an attempt to implement an incomes policy, public sector wages serve as guidelines for the remainder of the economy.[98] Further, when governments come into conflict with labor unions over wages, the settlement reached can be used as an indicator of the power and resolve of the government; for example, Conservative governments in the United Kingdom in 1974, 1982 and in 1985. In contrast, the French government caved in to union demands several times during the 1990s with the consequence that the French public sector continues to absorb more resources than those in most other European countries.

Pay for public sector employees is determined in a number of ways. One is to link pay directly to changes in the private sector, or to consumer prices. For example, in the Netherlands, civil service pay has been adjusted biennially to take into account changes in private sector wages, while in Australia pay is adjusted annually on the basis of changes in prices.[99] Pay for civil servants in the United States is nominally based upon comparability with the private sector, although the

President and Congress make independent judgments about appropriate levels of compensation. In the 1980s the President and Congress consistently passed pay increases below the comparability figures recommended by the more independent Advisory Committee on Federal Pay. The Pay Act of 1990 delinked civil service pay from Congressional pay so that another political barrier to appropriate compensation for civil servants was eliminated.[100] In several countries pay movements in the public sector are directly linked to changes in compensation in the economy as a whole. This helps remove the incentive for politicians to hold down the pay of civil servants. As noted above (pp. 65–7), attacking the civil service in their pocketbooks is good politics in most countries, and politicians can earn substantial credit by being tough on pay awards.

Negotiation with unions is the other major means of setting public sector pay. In Denmark this bargaining occurs as a part of negotiations for wages throughout the economy, whereas in Italy, Canada and a number of other countries, the negotiation is independent of other labor negotiations. In all negotiations, however, comparability is at least an implicit part of the bargaining process. Germany has a modified version of unionized pay setting in which the salaries of ordinary civil servants *(Angestelle)* are set by negotiations with unions; then Parliament determines pay for top civil servants *(Beamte)*. The *Beamte* have a legal right to a living suitable for their status as representatives of the state (the "alimentation principle").[101]

The traditional means of rewarding civil servants is to pay all individuals at the same grade of the service the same amount, adjusted perhaps for seniority, or social factors such as the number of children supported by the employee. The spread of managerialist ideas during the 1980s and 1990s has produced a greater use of merit pay in the civil service, with differential rewards to employees based upon their perceived performance.[102] In some instances the better performers are given bonuses, while in other systems their salaries are adjusted upward on a more permanent basis. Further, in some of the bonus systems there are well-regulated means of determining those rewards, but in others a huge amount of discretion is available to political and civil service leaders to reward their subordinates, and the bonuses are virtually secret.[103] In some instances merit is determined in advance, with many top government managers hired on performance contracts that differ markedly across individuals.[104] A few merit pay systems also provide for reductions in salaries for poor performers, although it is generally difficult to prove that performance is sufficiently poor to warrant reductions.

All merit pay systems, however, assume that civil servants are motivated more by these material rewards than by the solidary incentives characteristic of standard pay systems. These plans also assume that it is possible to measure merit adequately and fairly.[105] That may be relatively easy for many of the lower level positions, e.g. typists or technicians, but becomes difficult for top managerial and professional positions. It becomes especially difficult for the civil servants whose primary responsibility is policy advice for ministers. To the extent that this is true, merit pay programs tend to emphasize the managerial and technical nature of civil service jobs and may devalue the policy advice functions of those positions.

Despite differences in the manner in which public sector pay is determined, several generalities can be made. First, a balance must be struck between fiscal constraints and the need to attract and retain qualified personnel. This is obviously more of a problem at the upper levels of government than at the bottom but may become a problem in regard to people with specialized skills, such as computer operators, as well as to executives. Second, in times of economic constraint or insecurity, public sector pay is a convenient target for those who want to control the costs of government. This is true despite the fact that personnel costs constitute a relatively small proportion of total costs of government. For example, central government wages and salaries in Sweden are only six percent of total expenditure at that level; in the United States they are 11 percent.[106] In both countries wages and salaries for all levels of government are higher than for just central government, but still are less than one quarter of all expenditures. Public sector wages and salaries are a larger proportion of total expenditures in less-developed countries; for example, salaries are over half of total expenditures in Kenya and many other African countries.[107] For much of the developed world, however, holding down public sector pay, despite its symbolic value, may be a small portion of the total fiscal restraint needed to control public expenditure.

A third important factor about public sector wages is that public sector employees, by virtue of their central positions in the economy and society (public transportation workers, firemen, defense, etc.) and their increasing levels of unionization, are in powerful positions to influence their own levels of pay. Finally, pay itself is only a part of the total compensation package; to understand fully the benefits of public employment, one must also take into account factors such as index-linked pensions.[108] Further, as noted above, employment in the public sector may be a stepping stone to more lucrative private sector occupations, so that lower wages in the short term may be an acceptable trade-off for very high long-term rewards.

Methods of recruitment

We have been discussing the methods by which administrators are chosen and some of the issues involved in the choice of methods. This section examines the effects of these choices by scrutinizing the actual patterns of recruitment of administrators. Again, we are somewhat constrained by the lack of availability of data for administrative systems, especially those of the less-developed countries. Despite these constraints, it is possible to identify substantial recruitment information on the administrative systems of over 25 countries, although the timeliness of those data is varied. The data are on several dimensions of social background, academic preparation, and representativeness that can give important information about how administrators are chosen. However, some important caveats should be noted. This information was gathered by different individuals, at different times, and on somewhat different segments of the bureaucratic population. The majority of data is concerned with upper-echelon administrators, but in some cases the coverage is broader. Therefore, care must be exercised in the interpretation of differences among these countries. Nevertheless, the data serve an important function of illustrating the general directions of recruitment in each country. In each case, the source, year and definition of the administrative population (if different from "top" administrators) are noted.

The first dimension upon which there are data is the socio-economic background of the administrators. Given that public administration is essentially a middle-class occupation, the major variance here is in the occupation of the fathers – or the class of origin – of these administrators. We see from Tables 3.6 and 3.7 that not only is public administration a middle-class occupation, but the origins of the administrators are also primarily middle class. The definition of class of origin is somewhat fuzzy, especially the difference between upper class and middle class, but the largest single class of origin in each case is the middle class. This is even more striking when the categories are collapsed into working class and bourgeois (by adding together middle and upper classes). In each case, few if any children of workers ever make it into the ranks of upper administration, with the most open system apparently being that of the United States, where almost one quarter of the federal executives came from working-class backgrounds. Despite the elitist image, the French civil service also had a relatively large percentage of inductees from the working class. Despite this apparent openness, the Mitterrand government developed a third means of entering ENA, directed at union officials and others of working-class backgrounds.[109] This program had very little real success, was subsequently terminated, but then reinstituted in the early 1990s. Germany would appear to be the most unrepresentative of the civil service systems, for in at least one sample of upper administrators, none came from working-class backgrounds.[110] Other studies show a more representative recruitment pattern in Germany, but not a great deal more representative than other European countries. Somewhat different samples used by Aberbach, Putnam and Rockman show France to have fewer civil servants from working-class backgrounds than does Germany, and the number of working-class inductees into the civil service in France appears to be decreasing.[111] As noted, these differences are a function of different samples, different definitions of the higher civil service, and different definitions of class origins.

Lest we become too critical of the bureaucratic systems, we should note that this pattern of elitist recruitment is far from entirely the fault of elitism within these institutions. The bureaucracies are at the mercy of the educational system, and despite efforts by governments in most industrialized countries to make postsecondary education more widely available, it still remains a sanctuary of the upper and middle classes. Given the job requirements for the vast majority of higher administrative positions, be they for specialists or generalists, a postsecondary education is a virtual necessity, and in most countries – even ones with social democratic histories – relatively few working-class children are provided that opportunity. This educational nexus is, in fact, the probable reason for the rather positive showing of the United States. Post-secondary education is more available in the United States than elsewhere, and consequently the pool of potential applicants for the senior civil service is that much larger.[112]

We should not, on the other hand, be too quick to absolve the bureaucracies of all guilt for their rather unrepresentative nature. All organizations tend to replicate themselves, and there is a definite tendency to recruit people like those already in the positions. This type of organizational bias is especially strong

Table 3.6 Social class backgrounds of senior civil servants (percentage)

Social class origin	United Kingdom[a] (1995)	United States[b] (1959)	France[c] (1971–5)	Germany[d] (1987)	Denmark[e] (1974)	Sweden[f] (1972)	Switzerland[g] (1980)	Italy[h] (1965)
Upper	28	19	40	1	47	42	61	17
Middle	58	44	30	69	43	44	16	65
Working	14	21	14	11	10	14	23	5
Other/unknown	—	16	16	19	9	—	—	13
Total	100	100	100	100	99	100	100	100

Social class origin	Canada[i] (1977–88)	India[j] (1947–63)	Turkey[k] (1962)	Republic of Korea[l] (1962)	Spain[m] (1967)	Pakistan[n] (n.d.)	Zambia[o] (1969)	Netherlands[p] (1988)
Upper	44	17	29	13	—	22	5	55
Middle	19	66	62	70	96	76	43	23
Working	36	—	1	7	4	2	23	18
Other/unknown	—	17	8	10	—	—	27	4
Total	99	100	100	100	100	100	98	100

Social class origin	Australia[q] (1970)	Belgium[r] (1973)	Norway[s] (1976)	Brazil[t] (1972)	Finland[u] (1970–80)	Israel[v] (1986)	Greece[w] (1988)
Upper	} 78	13	} 71	36	31	18	—
Middle		59		53	59	59	86
Working	22	11	14	11	4	23	—
Other/unknown	—	17	15	—	6	—	14
Total	100	100	100	100	100	100	100

Sources:

a Peter Barberis, *The Elite of the Elite* (Aldershot: Dartmouth, 1996); I. M. Crewe, *Social Survey of the Civil Service*, vol. 3, pt. 1 of *The Civil Service* (The Fulton Report) (London: HMSO, 1968) p. 19

b W. L. Warner et al., *The American Federal Executive* (New Haven: Yale University Press, 1963), p. 29

c Pierre Racine, "L'origine sociale des enarques," *La Fonction Publique. Cahiers Français* (La Documentation Française, 1980)

d Hans-Ulrich Delien and Renate Mayntz, *Einstellungen der politisch-administrativen Elite des Bundes 1987* (Bamberg: University of Bamberg Lehrstuhl für Verwaltungswissenschaft, 1988)

e T. Rau, *Den dansk cenraladministration og dens embsmand* (Copenhagen: University of Copenhagen, Institut forsamfundsfag, 1974)

f U. Christofferson, U. Molin, B. Mansson and L. Strömberg, *Byråkrati och politik* (Stockholm: Bonniers, 1972)

g Paolo Urio, *Sociologie politique de la haute administration publique en Suisse* (Paris: Economica, 1989), p. 146

h Paolo Ammassari, "L'estrazione sociale dei funzionari dello Stato e degli enti local," in Ammassari et al., *Il Burocrate di fronte alle burocrazia* (Milan: Giuffe, 1969), p. 21

i Jacques Bourgault and Stéphane Dion, *The Changing Profile of Federal Deputy Ministers 1867-1988* (Ottawa: Canadian Center for Management Development, 1991)

j V. Subramanian, *Social Backgrounds of India's Administrators* (New Delhi: Ministry of Information, 1971), p. 145

k C. H. Dodd, "The Social and Educational Backgrounds of Turkish Officials," *Middle Eastern Studies*, 1 (1964), p. 271

l Dong Suh bark, "Korean Higher Civil Servants: Their Social Backgrounds and Morale," in Byung Chui Koh, *Aspects of Administrative Development in South Korea* (Kalamazoo, MI: Korea Research Publication, 1967), p. 27

m Juan J. Linz and Amando de Miguel, "La elite funcionarial Española ante la reforma administrativa," in *Añales de Moral Social y Economica, Sociological de la Administracion Publica Española* (Madrid: Raycar, 1968), pp. 208-9

n Ralph Braibanti, "The Higher Bureaucracy of Pakistan," in Ralph Braibanti, ed., *Asian Bureaucratic Systems Emergent from the British Imperial Tradition* (Durham, NC: Duke University Press, 1966), p. 271

o Dennis L. Dresang, "Ethnic Politics, Representative Bureaucracy and Development Administration; The Zambian Case," *American Political Science Review*, 68 (1974), p. 1609

p F. M. van der Meer and L. J. Roborgh (1993), *Ambetenaren in Nederland* (Alphen aan den Rijn: Willink), p. 334

q Royal Commission on Australian Government Administration, *Report* (Canberra: Australian Government Publishing Service, 1976); Appendix 3

r Andre Molitor, *L'Administration en Belgique* (Brussels: Centre de Recherche et d'information socio-politique, 1974)

s Per Laegreid and Paul Roness, "De statliga anställlda i Norge," in Lennart Lundquist and Krister Ståhlberg, *Byråkrater i Norden* (Åbo: Åbo Akademi, 1983)

t Paolo Roberto Motta, "The Brazilian Bureaucratic Elite," unpublished Ph.D. dissertation, University of North Carolina, 1972

u Krister Ståhlberg, "De statliga Anställlda i Finland," in Lundquist and Ståhlberg, *op. cit.*

v David R. Nachmias, "Israel's Bureaucratic Elite: Social Structure and Patronage," *Public Administration Review*, 51 (1991), p. 414

w George Vendendrakis and Catherine D. Papastathopoulous, "The Higher Civil Service in Greece," *International Review of Administrative Science*, 56 (1990), p. 474

Table 3.7 Educational level of senior civil servants (percentage)

	United Kingdom[a] (1967)	United States[b] (1984)	France[c] (1984)	Germany[d] (1983)	Switzerland[e] (1987)	Canada[f] (1977–88)	USSR[g] (1950–66)	Japan[h] (1975–86)	Republic of Korea[i] (1988)
High school	2	3	0	}5	12	}2	10	1	2
Some college	27	10	7		–		50	–	1
College graduate	52	55	93	29	42	34	}40	99	}97
College+	19	32	–	66	45	65		–	
Total	100	100	100	100	99	101	100	100	100

	Turkey[j] (1962)	Pakistan[k] (1948–64)	Burma[l] (1962)	Israel[m] (1969)	Netherlands[n] (1988)	Finland[o] (1977)	China[p] (1989)	Belgium[q] (1973)	Italy[r] (1961)
High school	2	0	–	–	33	}72	30	}19	}18
Some college	–	–	24	49			8		
College graduate	98	35	76	28	}67	21	47	}81	}82
College+	–	65	–	23		7	15		
Total	100	100	100	100	100	100	100	100	100

	Spain[s] (1996)	Sweden[t] (1978)	Denmark[u] (1996)	Norway[v] (1970–74)	Brazil[w] (1972)	Greece[x] (1988)	Nigeria[y] (1979–83)
High school	40	}20	}6	}11	}14	}10	2
Some college	–						75
College graduate	}60	}80	}94	}89	}86	50	19
College+						40	
Total	100	100	100	100	100	100	96

Sources:

a A. H. Halsey and I. M. Crewe, Social Survey of the Civil Service, Vol. 3, pt. 1 of The Civil Service (The Fulton Report) (London: HMSO, 1968), p. 64

b US Office of Personnel Management, Statistics of Federal Civilian Workforce, 1986 (Washington, DC: USOPM, 1986)

c Jean-Louis Quermonne, L'appareil administratif de l'État (Paris: Editions de Seuil, 1991) d Hans-Ulrich Derlien and Renate Mayntz, *Einstellungen der politisch-administrative Elite des Bundes 1987* (Bamberg: University of Bamberg, Lehrstuhl für Verwaltungswissenschaft, 1998)

e Paolo Urio, *Sociologie politique de la haute administration publique en Suisse* (Paris: Economica, 1989)

f Jacques Bourgault and Stéphane Dion, *The Changing Profile of Federal Deputy Ministers 1867–1988* (Ottawa: Canadian Center for Management Development, 1991)

g Philip D. Stewart, *Political Power in the Soviet Union* (Indianapolis: Bobbs-Merrill, 1968), p. 142

h B. C. Koh, *Japan's Administrative Elite* (Berkeley: University of California Press, 1989), p. 221

i Pan S. Kim, "Who Serves the State: Educational Backgrounds of South Korean and Japanese Bureaucrats," unpublished paper, Department of Urban Studies and Public Administration, Old Dominion University, 1991

j C. H. Dodd, "The Social and Educational Background of Turkish Officials," *Middle Eastern Studies*, 1 (1964), p. 273

k Ralph Braibanti, "The Higher Bureaucracy of Pakistan," in Ralph Braibanti, ed., *Asian Bureaucratic Systems Emergent from the British Imperial Tradition* (Durham, NC: Duke University Press, 1966), pp. 279–81

l James F. Guyout, "Bureaucratic Transformation in Burma," in *ibid.*, p. 424

m Nimrod Raphaeli, "The Senior Civil Service in Israel; Notes on Some Characteristics," *Public Administration*, 48 (1970), p. 174

n F. Van der Meer and J. Raadschelders, "Senior Civil Service in the Netherlands," in E. C. Page and V. Wright, eds, *Bureaucratic Elites in West European States* (Oxford: Oxford University Press, 1999)

o Charles Debbasch, *La fonction publique en Europe* (Paris: CNRS, 1980); total civil service

p Xiaowei Zang, "Elite Formation and the Bureaucratic-Technocracy in Post-Mao China," *Studies in Comparative Communism*, 24 (1991), pp. 114–23

q Andre Molitor, *L'Administration en Belgique* (Brussels: Centre de recherche et d'information socio-politique, 1974)

r Franco Ferraresi, *Burocrazia e politica in Italia* (Milan: Il Mulino, 1980)

s I. Molina, "Spain: Still the Primacy of Corporatism," in E. C. Page and V. Wright, eds, *op. cit.*

t Ulf Christofferson, "De statligt anställdia i Sverige," in Lennart Lundquist and Krister Ståhlberg, eds., *Byråkrater i Norden* (Åbo: Åbo Akademi, 1983)

u H. N. Jensen and T. Knudson, "The Danish Central Administration," in E. C. Page and V. Wright, eds, *op. cit.*

v Per Laegreid and Paul Roness, "De statligt anstälida i Norge," in *ibid.*

w Paolo Roberto Motta, *The Brazilian Bureaucratic Elite*, unpublished Ph.D. dissertation, University of North Carolina, 1972.

x George Vendendrakis and Catherine D. Papastathopoulos, "The Higher Civil Service in Greece," *International Review of Administrative Sciences*, 55 (1989), pp. 603–29

y Bola Dauda, "Fallacies and Dilemmas: The Theory of Representative Bureaucracy with a Particular Reference to the Nigerian Public Service 1950–1986," *International Review of Administrative Sciences*, 56 (1990), p. 477

during the personal interviews generally required for appointment to upper-echelon positions; the foreign service of most countries is the most obvious locus for class bias in personnel selection. Bureaucracies also utilize formal rules, such as the requirement for degrees or the difficulties in moving from one class of civil servant to another (for example, the administrative and executive classes in the British civil service prior to the Fulton Report), as a means of maintaining their recruitment patterns even in the face of democratization of the society and cultures of most Western societies. This tendency to preserve a more elitist recruitment pattern may not even be conscious, and those doing the recruiting may simply be functioning with a mental picture of a good candidate that eliminates potentially very good working-class talent.

Education

We now have some inkling that education may be an important characteristic in describing public administrators, and especially those at the upper levels of the hierarchy. Again, there is less than comprehensive data, but we can get some impression about the educational levels that differ across cultures and educational systems. As much as possible, we have attempted to group the data into categories that are comparable across countries and are meaningful to most readers. Doing this may have some costs in lost precision, but that disadvantage should be offset by increased comparability of the data.

The previous discussion of the relationship of education and class in the selection of administrative personnel should have led us to expect a well-educated group of people serving as upper-echelon administrators. This expectation is well justified by the data. Almost universally, higher-level administrative personnel tend to have some form of post-secondary education, with the majority having completed the equivalent of a bachelor's degree. In some cases, this education may be within the confines of a specialized administrative college, but there is nonetheless a definite post-secondary phase of education for most administrators. This is true even for less-developed countries that have a scarcity of educated personnel. The data taken from Aberbach, Putnam and Rockman indicate that civil servants tend to be more educated than employees in similar types of positions in the rest of the economy.[113] This should be expected in most cases simply because such education is a formal requirement for appointment. Interesting here is that the United States and Canada, which are frequently cited as having more "democratic" political cultures, tend to have larger percentages of their upper civil services lacking any post-secondary education than do most other industrialized democracies. Israel, however, has by far the most open administrative structures, in part because of the newness of the country and in part because of the relatively poor pay levels.

As well as having completed college or its equivalent, upper-level public administrators frequently have attended the more prestigious colleges and universities. Studies of the British civil service, for example, have shown over two-thirds of the senior civil service as having gone to Oxford or Cambridge. The civil service appears to have declining appeal for "Oxbridge" graduates, however.[114]

In his study of the backgrounds of Indian administrators, Subramanian reported that "the majority of recruits come from the six older and better known [universities] ... The significance of education in the right college is unmistakable."[115] Suleiman also reports that the majority – and, in fact, over three-fourths – of the entrants to the ENA had their university education in Paris. Forty-two percent of these ENA entrants had their entire education in Paris. A later study shows over half of all ENA students having had all their education there, with another quarter having had their higher education there.[116] The dominance of top universities is especially pronounced in Japan, where the University of Tokyo and the University of Kyoto are the principal sources of talent for the senior civil service.[117] A similar pattern is found for Seoul National University in South Korea and for the Universities of Athens and Salonika in Greece.[118] Thus, in these cases, the importance of not only attending college but also attending the right college is indeed unmistakable.

The American pattern of recruitment from universities is somewhat different from that of other political systems. The (somewhat dated) analysis by Warner *et al.* of the college attendance of American career executives shows a rather strong influence of large state-supported universities in the education of administrators.[119] If foreign-service executives are excluded, none of the Ivy League schools is among the top ten in terms of number of degrees held, and only three are in the top 30. Among foreign-service executives, however, three of the Ivy League are in the top ten, and all eight schools are in the top 30. Later evidence tends to confirm the position of large state universities, especially those of the Midwest, as the breeding ground of future civil servants. These data would appear to offer some support for the conception of American society and its administrative system as being somewhat more open than most. It further supports the contention that public service in the United States has been an important means of social mobility, a factor we will elaborate on when discussing the ethnic representativeness of the civil service.

The last question to be asked concerning the educational backgrounds of these administrators is the type of degree obtained. Here we are interested in the degree of technical or functional expertise that the administrators are likely to be carrying into their work as a function of their college education. We have already reported some data of this type for the United Kingdom, and they are reproduced in Tables 3.7 and 3.8 along with data for such other countries as were available. There is considerably more variance in the *types* of education received than in the *level* of education, with apparently three rather distinct groups of educational degree types in this non-random sampling of administrative systems.

The first pattern is represented by the United Kingdom, with a great emphasis on general education, the arts and humanities, and consequently less emphasis on technical ability. As was noted, this is indicative of the generalist conception of administration in the United Kingdom. A second type is typified by Germany, Austria and Sweden. These systems place heavy emphasis on legal training, and consequently about two-thirds of their administrators have legal backgrounds. Many of the remainder also possess some form of professional qualification, such as engineering, medical, or educational degrees. France is somewhat similar but goes a step further by providing most of the future

Table 3.8 College majors of senior civil servants (for those with college backgrounds)

Major	United Kingdom[a] (1970–4)	United States[b] (1986–8)	Germany[c] (1987)	Japan[d] (1986)	Republic of Korea[e] (1982)	Turkey[f] (1963)	India[g] (1947–63)	Canada[h] (1977–88)	Switzerland[i] (1987)	Israel[i] (1986)
Natural science	26	32	8	23	5	34	33	28	20	17
Social science	—	—	—	—	16	6	9	—	7	21
Humanities	52	23	—	18	13	13	21	42	11	27
Economics and business	—	28	18	—	32	16	36	53	12	25
Law	3	19	63	59	32	18	—	19	49	10
Other	18	—	12	—	15	13	1	—	2	—
Total	99	102	101	100	100	100	100	142	101	100

Major	Netherlands[k] (1988)	Belgium[l] (1976–84)	Italy[m] (1972–4)	Denmark[n] (1993)	Finland[o] (1980)	Norway[p] (1980)	Brazil[q] (1972)	Greece[r] (1988)	Spain[s] (1996)	France[t] (5th Republic)
Natural science	20	20	10	—	14	8	22	14	20	2
Social science	39	28	—	11	19	26	22	}67	5	42
Humanities	—	12	37	—	—	12	—		7	7
Economics and business	—	—	—	20	—	—	—	19	20	6
Law	32	35	54	10	43	38	22	—	45	73
Other	19	6	—	19	24	17	34	—	3	—
Total	100	101	101	100	100	101	100	100	100	140

Sources:

a Joel D. Aberbach, Robert D. Putnam and Bert A. Rockman, Bureaucrats and Politicians in Western Democracies (Cambridge, MA: Harvard University Press, 1981), p. 52

b Joel D. Aberbach, Hans-Ulrich Derlien, Ranate Mayntz and Bert A. Rockman, "Hauts fonctionnaires féderaux americains et allemands: attitudes technocratiques et politiques," Revue internationale des sciences sociales, 12 (1990), p. 7

c Hans Ulrich Derlien and Renate Mayntz, *Einstellungen der politisch-administrativen Elite des Bundes 1987* (Bamberg: University of Bamberg, Lehrtuhl für Verwaltungswissenschaft, 1988)

d B. C. Koh, *Japan's Administrative Elite* (Berkeley: University of California Press, 1989) p. 137

e Pan S. Kim, "Who Serves the State: Educational Backgrounds of South Korean and Japanese Bureaucrats," unpublished paper, Department of Urban Studies and Public Administration, Old Dominion University, 1991

f Republic of Turkey, Office of the Prime Minister, State Institute of Statistics, Government Personnel Service Statistics I (Ankara: State Institute of Statistics, 1965), pp. 32–9

g V. Subremanian, *Social Background of India's Administrators* (New Delhi, Ministry of Education, 1971), p. 155

h Jacques Bourgault and Stéphane Dion, *The Changing Profile of Federal Deputy Ministers 1867 to 1988* (Ottawa: Canadian Center for Management Development, 1991)

i Paolo Urio, *Sociologie politique de la haute administration publique en Suisse* (Paris: Economica, 1989), p. 40

j David Nachmias, "Israel's Bureaucratic Elite: Social Structure and Patronage," *Public Administration Review*, 51 (1991), pp. 418–19

k F. van der Meer and J. Raadschelders, "Senior Civil Service in the Netherlands," in E. C. Page and V. Wright, eds, *op. cit.*

l R. Depre and Annie Hondeghem, "Recruitment, Carriere et formation des fonctionnaires superieurs en Belgique," in Desire De Saedeleer *et al.*, *La haute fonction publique en Belgique et dans les pays industrialisés* (Brussels: International Institute of Administrative Science, 1988)

m Aberach, Putnam and Rockman, *Bureaucrats and Politicians*

n H. N. Jensen and T. Knudsen, "Danish Central Administration," in E. C. Page and V. Wright, eds, *op. cit.*

o Krister Stahlberg, "De statliga anstälida i Finland," in *ibid*.

p Per Laegreid and Paul Roness, "De statligt anstälida i Norge," in *ibid*.

q Paolo Roberto Motta, "The Brazilian Bureaucratic Elite," unpublished Ph.D. dissertation, University of North Carolina, 1972

r George Vendendrakis and Catherine D. Papastathopoulos, "The Higher Civil Service in Greece," *International Review of Administrative Sciences*, 55 (1989), pp. 603–29

s I. Molina, "Spain: Still the Primacy of Corporatism," in E. C. Page and V. Wright, eds, *Bureaucratic Elite in West European States* (Oxford: Oxford University Press, 1999)

t L. Rouban, *Les Prefets de la Republique* (Paris: Cevipof, 2000)

upper-echelon of the administration legal, management and economics training through ENA. All of these systems have a strong emphasis on the legal role of the civil service so that this pattern of education is crucial for success within the system.

The final pattern of educational backgrounds is typified by the United States and several underdeveloped countries. The principal characteristic of these countries is the relatively large percentage of natural science (including engineering) backgrounds in the civil service. As was noted above, the United States tends to hire people with specialized backgrounds to do specialized jobs rather than hiring generally qualified personnel. In the Third World countries there is a need to concentrate the available technical talent in the country and to make the most efficient use of this scarce resource. One way of doing this is to hire as much talent as possible in government and then use the government as the means of allocating total societal resources. Moreover, given the relatively underdeveloped state of the economies of many of these countries, the only real employment options for educated individuals may be to work for the government.[120] Many political considerations may prevent the public bureaucracy in underdeveloped countries from fulfilling their potential for administering programs of social and economic change. It would appear, however, from these data that many of the countries do have the raw material, in terms of personnel within their bureaucracies (especially relative to the pool of educated and trained talent available) that might make those socio-economic reforms successful.

Ethnic representativeness

Another question to be looked at in the presentation of background data on civil services is the ethnic representativeness of the bureaucracies. Just as there is some cause for concern about the representativeness of public bureaucracies according to social class, so is there concern over their equality in recruitment of various minorities within the society. We may expect the same sort of pattern as was found with respect to class, with the dominant community having a disproportionate share of the members of the civil service, especially in elite positions. As the data in Table 3.9 show, these suspicions are confirmed. In most cases, there is a distinct over-representation of the dominant racial, language, or religious group. As with the findings for social class, this may be the result of applying the usual educational criteria, not the result of overt discrimination.

Three special points should be made with respect to ethnic representation in the public bureaucracy. The first is that the data that are presented are primarily for upper-echelon personnel; as we go farther down the bureaucracy, the importance of the representativeness of the organization should increase rather than decrease. We have noted the importance of the client-contact personnel of agencies for the success of the agency in serving its clients. Such limited information as does exist on the lower echelons of public agencies indicates that they are more representative than are upper, managerial positions.[121] These more representative lower echelons may therefore be expected to be more successful in dealing with their clientele than would top management. Also, the public sector

Table 3.9 Ethnic representativeness of public bureaucracies (percentage)

Ethnic group	United States[a] Total (1990)	United States[a] Higher (1990)	Canada[b] Total (1978)	Canada[b] Higher (1977–88)	Israel[c] (1985)	Malaysia[d] (1960)	India[e] (1974)	Zambia[f] Total (1975)	Zambia[f] Higher (1975)	Papua New Guinea[g] Total (1975)	Papua New Guinea[g] Higher
Dominant	63	8	73	70	81	67	96	72	27	92	50
Minority	37	92	27	30	19	33	4	28	73	8	50
Total	100	100	100	100	100	100	100	100	100	100	100

South Africa[h]

	Total (1989)	Excluding laborers (1989)
White	41	82
Colored	17	3
Asian	4	1
Black	38	14
Total	100	100

Lebanon[i]

	(1955)
Maronite	40
Sunni	27
Shi'ite	4
Greek Orthodox	12
Greek Catholic	9
Druze	7
Total	99

Switzerland[i]

Language (1992)		Religion (1987)	
French	24	Catholic	38
German	72	Protestant	58
Italian	4	Other/none	4
Romansh	—	Total	100
Total	100		

Nigeria[k]

	(1988)
Igbo	18
Hausa/Fulani	6
Yoruba	54
Other/Don't know	22
Total	100

Sources:
a United States Office of Personnel Management, Affirmative Employment Statistics (Washington, DC: USOPM, biennial); minority = non-white
b P. K. Kuruvilla, "Public Sector Recruitment in Canada," Indian Journal of Public Administration, 26 (1980), p. 86 Jacques Bourgault and Stéphane Dion, The Changing Profile of Federal Deputy Ministers 1897–1988 (Ottawa: Canadian Center for Management Development, 1991); minority = francophone
c David Nachmias, "Israel's Bureaucratic Elite: Social Structure and Patronage," Public Administration Review, 51 (1991), p. 415; minority = Sephardim
d Robert O. Tilman, "Public Service Comissions in the Federation of Malaya," Journal of Asian Studies, 10 (1961), p. 194; minority = non-Malays
e B. A. V. Sharma and K. M. Reddy, Reservation Policy in India (New Delhi; Light and Life, 1982); minority = scheduled castes and tribes
f Dennis O. Dresang, The Zambia Civil Service (Nairobi; 1975); minority = non-Zambian
g P. Pitil, "Public Personnel Administration," in O. P. Dwevidi and Nelson E. Paulia, eds, The Public Service of Papua New Guinea (Boroko; Administrative College of Papua New Guinea, 1986), p. 168; minority = expatriates
h Sunette van der Walt, "Employment in the Public Sector of South Africa," SAIPA, 27 (1992), p. 23
i Ralph E. Crow, "Confessionalism, Public Administration and Efficiency in Lebanon," in Leonard Binder, ed., Politics in Lebanon (New York: John Wiley, 1966), p. 172
j R. E. Germann, Administration Publique en Suisse (Berne: Haupt, 1996), p. 155
k Bola Dauda, "Fallacies and Dilemmas: The Theory of Representative Bureaucracy with a Particular Reference to the Nigerian Public Service 1950–1986, International Review of Administrative Sciences, 56 (1990), 467–95; approximate figures based on state of origin

may not be perceived as being as unrepresentative as it actually is, simply because the clients may deal only with the relatively more representative lower echelons.

The second point about ethnicity and representativeness is that this is frequently a point of bargaining in societies attempting to manage severe internal ethnic divisions. In some societies, most noticeably Belgium, this has gone to the extent of dividing several ministries by ethnicity (in this case, language) and actually providing two ethnically homogeneous units instead of one integrated unit that might tend to advantage one group or another. Another variant of the same pattern is the Austrian method of carefully dividing the posts in each ministry according to ethnicity or, more specifically in this case, religious or non-religious preferences.[122] Similarly, the division of posts in the Lebanese administrative system among the numerous religious groups in that society was an important part of the bargain holding that otherwise tenuous union together prior to 1975.[123] Thus there is no necessity for having unrepresentative bureaucracies in ethnically plural societies, but the equalization of the service often requires explicit bargaining and a recognition of the role of the bureaucracy in institutionalizing ethnic cleavage.

The third point is that even when there are active programs to recruit members of minority populations, they may not alter the representativeness of the civil service. Affirmative action programs do not appear to make that much difference in the recruitment of non-whites in the American civil service. Similarly, legal provisions to benefit certain "scheduled" castes and tribes in India that have been discriminated against historically have produced very few members in the civil service, and especially few at the upper echelons.[124] As with the representativeness of the civil service by class, educational and other social barriers may have to be overcome before legal efforts at greater ethnic representativeness have the intended effects.

A final point to be made about the ethnic representativeness of the civil service is that the civil service has served as a means of social advancement for minority groups, in part because of its reliance upon relatively objective criteria for recruitment. For example, while blacks and Hispanics constitute a rather small percentage of the civil service in the United States, they actually comprise a higher percentage there than in total employment in the economy. This would be especially true of non-white employment in white-collar and managerial positions, although the relative decline of public sector salaries combined with the increasing openness of business to minority employees has made the public sector a less attractive employer in the United States. Similarly, the civil service has served as a means of social and economic advancement for Italians from the poorer southern region; in 1978, 56 percent of the Italian civil service came from the southern part of the peninsula and Sicily, although only 33 percent of the population lived in these regions.[125] This pattern of regional recruitment does not appear to be changing rapidly, even with pressures from northern political groups who increasingly appear to resent being governed by southerners.[126]

The European Community represents a special case of a political system attempting to ensure equality of recruitment in the public service. Community laws and regulations call for recruitment of civil service personnel in proportion to the populations of the member countries, but there are wide disparities in the extent to which member nationals have been offered and accepted positions in the European bureaucracy (Table 3.10). It is not surprising that there are relatively more Belgian and Luxembourger employees, given that most EC offices are located in Brussels and Luxembourg, but there still is a differential attraction of senior positions in the EC bureaucracy. Spain is markedly under-represented at all levels of the EC bureaucracy, as are the United Kingdom and Germany to a lesser extent. This pattern appears related to the differential attractiveness – in career and financial terms – for senior civil servants in different countries, as well as some attempt to ensure that all countries have some representation in the upper levels of the Brussels bureaucracy. The differential recruitment may, however, represent a political problem for countries who believe that they do not receive enough good jobs for their people and that EC decision makers may be stacked against them.

Sexual equality

A final dimension of representativeness is gender. The issue of equal treatment of women has become increasingly important in all phases of social and political life, and the public bureaucracy is no different. The issue in the civil service is, in general, not about the total number of women employed; most governments already employ large numbers of women, and in many countries more than half of total public employment is female.[127] Even in countries that historically have assigned an unequal role to women, there have been some increases in employment of women.[128] The issue of gender equality centers primarily on the types of positions in which women are employed. Women often comprise a large

Table 3.10 Employment in the European Community bureaucracy and population by country (percentage)

	Upper echelon positions	Total positions	Population
Belgium	7.9	12.0	3.1
Denmark	3.6	6.5	1.6
France	17.8	15.2	17.2
Germany	15.5	10.2	18.9
Greece	5.6	6.2	3.1
Ireland	3.6.	2.0	1.1
Italy	12.5	17.3	11.5
Luxembourg	2.3	8.7	0.1
Netherlands	5.6	6.3	4.5
Portugal	4.3	3.7	3.2
Spain	6.3	3.9	12.0
United Kingdom	14.9	8.1	17.6

Source: House of Lords Select Committee on the European Communities, 11th Report, *Staffing of Community Institutions*, HL 66 (London: HMSO, 1986)

proportion of public sector employment, and over half in some, but they are concentrated in lower level positions. The majority of women in the civil service of almost every country are employed in lower-level jobs, such as clerks and typists, rather than in the higher civil service.

Table 3.11 clearly shows the disparity between the total number of women employed in the public sector and the number employed in upper-echelon government positions. Although, in some cases, over half of total civil service employment is comprised of women, in no case does the higher civil service have more than 15 percent women. Further, that 15 percent figure is reached only in Norway; the average is only 4.6 percent women in the higher civil service.[129] Women have fared somewhat better in subnational governments, with over a quarter of top employees in some German Lander being women.[130] There is, however, some evidence that the proportion of women in senior positions has been increasing rapidly.

As with the cases of class and ethnic representativeness, we must consider whether these observed employment patterns are the result of overt discrimination or reflect other social, economic or historical factors. It would be difficult to dispute that there has been overt discrimination against women in recruitment to senior posts in government, although the civil service has probably been more open than many other occupations. In addition, historically there have been relatively few women putting themselves forward for the top government positions, or even having the necessary educational qualifications. As the more overt discrimination lessens, it will still require time for larger numbers of women to be recruited into entry-level positions for the higher civil service and then to work their way up the career ladder. Countries that have more open career structures, such as the United States, will be able to accommodate to these changes more rapidly than will those with closed structures requiring years to work up a ladder.

Summary

Noted here are several more general points about the composition and the representativeness of public bureaucracies. The first is that although these may be highly unrepresentative institutions, they are generally less unrepresentative than other public elites in the same countries. Parris notes, for example, that in Britain the membership of the House of Commons is at least as unrepresentative, if not more so, than the administrative class of the civil service:

> If there is an excessive proportion of Oxbridge graduates in the Administrative Class, so is there in the House of Commons. The electorate ought to be blamed for making the wrong choice just as much as the Civil Service Commissioners. If too few civil servants have scientific and technological backgrounds, the same criticism can be made of industrial managers. Thus, management in both the public and private sectors reflects the values of the society about what is needed to make organizations function well.[131]

Table 3.11 Employment of women in the civil service (percentage)

Country	Total in civil service	In higher civil service
Australia	39	2
Belgium	40	7
Canada	47	23
Czechoslovakia	67	?
Finland	51	4
France	48	13
Greece	31	7
Guadeloupe	51	?
Guyana	39	?
Hong Kong	?	7
Israel	52	3
Italy	35	4
Netherlands	19	2
New Zealand	?	2
Norway	47	15
Spain	14	?
Sweden	42	5
Switzerland	26	2
United Kingdom	55	7
United States	51	16
Germany	47	9

Sources: Charles Debbasch, ed., *La fonction publique en Europe* (Paris: CNRS, 1981); Andre Molitor, *L'Administration de la Belgique* (Brussels: Centre de recherche et d'information socio-politique, 1974); Per Laegreid and Johan Olsen, *Byråkrati og Beslutningar* (Bergen: Universitetsforlaget, 1978); John P. Burns, "The Changing Pattern of Bureaucratic Representation: The Case of the Hong Kong Civil Service," *Indian Journal of Political Science*, 27 (1981), pp. 398–429; Royal Commission on Australian Government Administration, *Report*, appendix 3 (Canberra: Australian Government Publishing Service, 1976); P. K. Kuruvilla, "Public Sector Recruitment in Canada: Some Perspectives and Problems," *Indian Journal of Public Administration*, 26 (1980), pp. 62–90; Jacques Bourgault and Stéphane Dion, *The Changing Profile of Federal Deputy Ministers 1867–1988* (Ottawa: Canadian Center for Management Development, 1991); Phillipe Clerdieu and Christian Theresine, "La fonction publique en Guadeloupe – Comparisons avec les autres DOM," *Revue Française d'Administration Publique*, 31 (1984), pp. 89–120; *La fonction publique de l'État* (Paris: La Documentation Française, 1998); Richard Rose *et al.*, *Public Employment in Western Nations* (Cambridge: Cambidge University Press, 1985); David Nachmias, "Israel's Bureaucratic Elite: Social Structure and Patronage," *Public Administration Review*, 51 (1991), p. 415; Robin Williams, "The Staffing and Structure of the Public Sector," in R. M. Alley, ed., *State Servants and the Public in the 1980s* (Wellington: New Zealand Institute of Public Administration, 1986); US Office of Personal Management, *Affirmative Employment Statistics* (Washington, DC: USOPM, biennial); Data from Comparative Public Service Project, Department of Politics, University of Strathclyde

The simple point is that elites are unrepresentative by the very function of their being elites. Success in society is related to social background, educational opportunities and interests, and the elite that a society may *select* to govern it will differ only at the margins in most cases from an elite *appointed* to govern – at least in terms of their social and educational backgrounds. The dangers of elitism and unrepresentativeness in public life are general, therefore, and not confined simply to the public bureaucracy. They are only more apparent in the bureaucracy where the emphasis on merit criteria and open recruitment makes it a more ostensibly democratic institution in its selection. But, as Max Weber pointed out:

> Democracy takes an ambivalent attitude toward the system of examinations for expertise. On the one hand the system of examination means, or at least appears to mean, selection of the qualified from all social strata in place of rule by the notables. But on the other, democracy fears that examinations and patents of education will create a privileged "caste" and for that reason opposes such a system.[132]

These words should not be taken as an exoneration of bureaucracies for their often elitist practices, but rather as a means of placing the problem of representative and unrepresentative bureaucracy in clearer perspective. Further, we should remember that most of the studies pointing to the unrepresentativeness of the civil service are studies of the *higher* civil service, and that the service as a whole does tend to be more representative. As the lower echelons of the service interact directly with clients, government may in fact appear more representative and therefore more democratic than it is.

The second point is that all the furor over social class and ethnic background of administrators, especially top administrators, may be a somewhat misplaced attack on the institutions. Much analysis has shown that social background tends to have a rather slight effect on behavior in public office. This is true of legislators, judges and administrators. A more important determinant of behavior would appear to be the nature of the organization and the goals of the agency. Again, this may be especially true at upper echelons; there may need to be greater representativeness at lower levels simply to be able to cope adequately with the clientele that an agency may serve. This is not to say that this need be simply a cosmetic gesture on the part of the agency; rather, it is a real need to be effective in interacting with and serving the clientele. But the more general point remains that in order to change the policy outcomes from the public bureaucracy, one may have to do more than simply gradually replace administrators drawn from one social class with administrators recruited more broadly from society. The operating routines of agencies, the tendency toward conservatism in organizations in general, and the process of organizational socialization all tend to reduce the variability of individuals in the organization, regardless of their social background. Thus, changing policy may be a considerably more complex topic, and it is one that will be probed extensively during the remainder of this volume.

Public policy does involve a human element. This chapter opened with a discussion of the failure of traditional models of bureaucracy to take into account human differences and variability. The differences, however, may be as much (or more) in values, motives and goals than in social background. We touched on this briefly when discussing the incentive structures of public bureaucracies, and also when discussing the administrative cultures of society. Thus, studies of recruitment need to delve somewhat into the nature of the personnel recruited to administrative careers, to determine not only where they came from but, more important, where they think they (and the society) are going. The values that are relevant are not just those about the specific programs that the individuals will be administering, but should also extend to questions of accountability and political control of bureaucracy. These values are not necessarily related to education or background but may say more about the suitability of the recruit for working in government, especially a democratic government.

Notes

1 Max Weber, "Bureaucracy," in H. H. Gerth and C. Wright Mills, *From Max Weber: Essays in Sociology* (New York: Oxford University Press, 1964), pp. 196–244; Frederick W. Taylor, *Principles and Methods of Scientific Management* (New York: Harper, 1911).

2 Robert D. Putnam, "The Political Attitudes of Senior Civil Servants in Western Europe," *British Journal of Political Science*, 3 (1973), 275–90; Joel D. Aberbach, Robert D. Putnam and Bert A. Rockman, *Bureaucrats and Politicians in Western Democracies* (Cambridge, MA: Harvard University Press, 1981).

3 Herbert Kaufman, "Emerging Conflicts in the Doctrine of Public Administration," *American Political Science Review*, 50 (1956), 1059–73.

4 Even in South Africa, issues of equal employment opportunities and affirmative action in the public sector have been placed on the agenda. See the special issue of *SAIPA* (South African Institute of Public Administration), 27 (1992).

5 Ari Hoogenboom, *Outlawing the Spoils* (Urbana, IL; University of Illinois Press,1968); Jane Caplan, "Profession as Vocation: The German Civil Service," in G. Cocks and K. Jarusch, *German Professions, 1800–1950* (Oxford: Oxford University Press, 1990).

6 See Paul C. Light, *Thickening Government* (Washington, DC: The Brookings Institution, 1997).

7 Some other smaller systems, e.g. Finland, have even fewer political appointees than the British, to the point that ministers find that they do not have adequate support for decision-making.

8 Chris Skelcher, *The Appointed State: Quasi-Governmental Organizations and Democracy* (Buckingham: Open University Press, 1997).

9 See Bernard S. Silberman, *Cages of Reason: The Rise of the Rational State in France, Japan, the United States and Great Britain* (Chicago: University of Chicago Press, 1993).

10 These political appointees are usually in personal offices or ministerial cabinets. For France, see Monique Dagnaud and Dominique Mehl, "L'Elite de la Cohabitation," *Pouvoirs*, 42 (1987), 137–53; see also Axel Murswieck, "Policy Advice and Decision-making in the German Federal Bureaucracy," in B. Guy Peters and Anthony Barker, eds, *Advising West European Governments* (Pittsburgh: University of Pittsburgh Press, 1993).

11 See B. Guy Peters and Jon Pierre, *The Politicization of the Civil Service?* (forthcoming).

12 Skelcher, *op. cit.*

13 J. Donald Kingsley, *Representative Bureaucracy* (Yellow Springs, Ohio: Antioch University Press, 1944); Kenneth J. Meier, "Representative Bureaucracy: An Empirical Assessment," *American Political Science Review*, 69 (1975), 526–42.

14 For example see Ellen E. Pinderhughes, "The Delivery of Child Welfare Services to

African American Clients," *American Journal of Orthopsychiatry*, 61 (1991), 599–605; Laura A. Schmidt, "Problem Drinkers and the Welfare Bureaucracy," *Social Service Review*, 64 (1990), 390–406; David Burn, "Ethical Implications of Cross-Cultural Counseling and Training," *Journal of Counseling and Development*, 70 (1992), 578–83.

15 T. Edward Kellough, "Affirmative Action in Government Employment," *The Annals*, 583 (September, 1992), 117–30.

16 B. A. V. Sharma and K. M. Reddy, *Reservation Policy in India* (New Delhi: Light and Life, 1982).

17 The intense political activity that often surrounds personnel issues in the European Community is one example of this point. See Morten Egeberg, "Organization and Nationality in European Commission Services," Paper presented at ECPR Joint Sessions Bourdeaux, France, April, 1995. These appointments are perceived to be crucial to the influence of each country in the Community.

18 For the argument for government as a "model employer," see P. B. Beaumont, *Government as Employer – Setting an Example?* (London: Royal Institute of Public Administration, 1981).

19 John O'Leary, "Four-year Study Looks for Bias in Entry to Oxford," *The Times* 14 August, 2000.

20 See, for example, Pierre Bourdieu, *La Noblesse d'État* (Paris: Minuit, 1989), pp. 101–39.

21 See Xiaowei Zang, "Elite Formation and the Bureaucratic–Technocracy in Post-Mao China," *Studies in Comparative Communism*, 24 (1991), 114–23.

22 Samuel J. Eldersveld, *Political Elites in Modern Societies: Empirical Research and Democratic Theory* (Ann Arbor, MI: University of Michigan Press, 1989).

23 Robert D. Putnam, *The Comparative Study of Political Elites* (Englewood Cliffs, NJ: Prentice Hall, 1967), p. 44.

24 See Albert Somit and Stephen A. Peterson, "Political Socialization of US and Japanese Adults," *Comparative Political Studies*, 13 (1980), 3–32.

25 This may be in part self-serving. The working class or minority members who are successful can say that they "made it," and therefore others can as well, if they have the talent and determination.

26 See Jack Rabin, ed., "The Future of Affirmative Action and Equal Employment Opportunity: A Symposium," *Review of Public Personnel Administration*, 4 (1984), 1–82.

27 For a classic statement see Anthony Downs, "Why the Public Budget is Too Small in a Democracy," *World Politics*, 12 (1960), 541–63.

28 One official of the Reagan administration in the United States argued that he only wanted a competent civil service, so that the "best and brightest" would be in the private sector. Terry W. Culler, "Most Federal Workers Need Only be Competent," *Wall Street Journal*, 21 May 1986.

29 F. F. Ridley, *Specialists and Generalists: A Comparative Study of the Civil Service at Home and Abroad* (London: Routledge and Kegan Paul, 1968).

30 Sir Stafford Northcote and Sir Charles Trevelyan, *Report on the Organization of the Permanent Civil Service*, reprinted in *Committee on the Civil Service Report* (the Fulton Committee), Vol. I, Appendix B (London: HMSO, 1968).

31 See John Garrett, *Managing the Civil Service* (London: Heinemann, 1980).

32 Hans-Ulrich Derlien, "Repercussions of Government Change on the Career Civil Service of West Germany: The Case of 1969 and 1982," *Governance*, 1 (1988), 50–78.

33 Aberbach, Putnam and Rockman, *Bureaucrats and Politicians*, p. 52; James W. Fesler, "The Higher Public Service in Western Europe," in Ralph Clark Chandler, ed., *A Centennial History of the American Administrative State* (New York: Free Press, 1987).

34 Heinrich Neisser, "Die Rolle des Burokratie," in Heinz Fischer, ed., *Das Politische System Osterreichs* (Vienna: Europaverlag, 1978).

35 For the Senior Executive Service almost one-third of the members are scientists or engineers, with another quarter having other professional qualifications. US Office of Personnel Management, *The Fact Book: Federal Civilian Workforce* (Washington, DC: OPM, June, 1992).

36   Serge Salon, "Recrutement et formation," in *La Fonction Publique*, Vol. 2 (Paris: Les cahiers Français, 197, 1980), 2–7

37   At the extreme, the bureaucracies of Latin America are still argued to have been influenced by their colonial experiences over a century and a half ago. See M. Hanson, "Organizational Bureaucracy in Latin America and the Legacy of Spanish Colonialism," *Journal of Inter-American Studies*, 16 (1974), 199–219. At the other extreme, countries of Eastern Europe are only recently left with bureaucracies trained according to the style of the former Soviet Union. See Jaroslaw Piekalkiewicz and Christopher Hamilton, *Public Bureaucracies Between Reform and Resistance* (Providence, RI: Berg, 1991).

38   Fred A. Clemente, "Philippine Bureaucratic Behavior," *Philippine Journal of Public Administration*, 15 (1971), 119–47.

39   Harry Taylor, "Public Sector Personnel Management in Three African Countries: Current Problems and Possibilities," *Public Administration and Development*, 12 (1992), 193–208.

40   See John A. Armstrong, *The European Administrative Elite* (Princeton, NJ: Princeton University Press, 1974); Rolf Torstendahl, *Bureaucratization in Northwestern Europe, 1880–1985: Domination and Governance* (London: Routledge, 1991).

41   Jerry Hough and Merle Fainsod, *How the Soviet Union is Governed* (Cambridge, MA: Harvard University Press, 1979); E. Huskey, *Executive Power and Soviet Politics: The Rise and Decline of the Soviet State* (Armonk, NY: M. E. Sharpe, 1992).

42   Kenneth Liberthal and Michel Oksenberg, *Policymaking in China: Leaders, Structures and Processes* (Princeton, NJ: Princeton University Press, 1988).

43   T. H. Rigby, *Political Elites in the USSR: Central Leaders and Local Cadres from Lenin to Gorbachev* (Aldershot: Edward Elgar, 1990).

44   Jerry F. Hough, *The Soviet Prefects* (Cambridge, MA: Harvard University Press, 1969), pp. 292–305.

45   Rolf H. W. Theen, "Party and Bureaucracy," in *The Soviet Polity in the Modern Era*, Erik P. Hoffman and Robbin F. Laird, eds (New York: Aldine, 1984), pp. 254–65.

46   There are strong legal requirements that prevent blatant use of patronage for positions. Also, the "Swedish" model was beginning to change prior to the election of the right-of-center government. T. Petterson and K. Geyer, *Varderingsforandringar i Sverige: Den svenska modellen, individualism och rattvisa* (Stockholm: Brevskolan, 1992).

47   Klaus von Beyme and Manfred Schmidt, *Policy and Politics in the Federal Republic of Germany* (London: Gower, 1985).

48   Paolo Urio *et al.*, *Sociologie politique de la haute administration publique de la Suisse* (Paris: Economica, 1989).

49   Wolfgang Pippke, *Karrieredeterminaten in der offentlichen Verwaltung* (Baden-Baden: Nomos, 1975).

50   Jean-Louis Quermonne, *L'Appareil Administratif de l'Etat* (Paris: Editions de Seuil, 1991), pp. 185–6.

51   This has been referred to as the "descent from heaven." See Chalmers Johnson, *MITI and the Japanese Miracle* (Stanford, CA: Stanford University Press, 1982), pp. 65ff.

52   See G. Calvin Mackenzie, *The Politics of Presidential Appointments* (New York: The Free Press, 1981); *The In and Outers* (Baltimore, MD: Johns Hopkins University Press, 1987).

53   The Act, however, lacks the teeth that critics of the military-industrial complex would like for it to have. Also, other sectors of the government are not even this closely regulated. See US General Accounting Office, *DOD Revolving Door: Processes Have Improved but Post-DOD Employment Reporting Still Low* (Washington, DC: USGAO, 1989), Report GAO/NSIAD 89–211.

54   Kenneth Kernaghan, "Promoting Public Service Ethics: The Codification Option," in Richard A. Chapman, ed., *Ethics in Public Service* (Edinburgh: University of Edinburgh Press, 1993).

55   This is often less than fully successful. See Harvey Feigenbaum, *The Politics of French Oil* (Princeton: Princeton University Press, 1986).

56   This career distinctiveness of Swedish civil servants is beginning to change. Attempts to

impose a managerialist conception of its role on the civil service have opened the system to outsiders, although not to the extent hoped by its advocates.

57 Kieran Walsh and John Stewart, "Change in the Management of Public Services," *Public Administration*, 70 (1992), 499–518.

58 Some of the managerialism associated with administrative reform in the 1980s attempted to open the public service to outsiders, especially from business. See Andrew Massey, *Managing the Public Sector* (Aldershot: Edward Elgar, 1993).

59 Peta E. Sherif, "Outsiders in a Closed Career: The Example of the British Civil Service," *Public Administration*, 50 (1972), 397–418.

60 See Anne Davies and John Willman, *What Next?: Agencies, Departments and the Civil Service* (London: Institute for Public Policy Research, 1992).

61 D. Soderlind and O. Petersson, *Svensk forvaltningspolitik* (Uppsala: Diskurs, 1988), p. 169.

62 Paolo Urio *et al.*, *op. cit.*, p. 46.

63 Hugh Heclo, *A Government of Strangers* (Washington, DC: The Brookings Institution, 1978).

64 As the number of appointees has increased and experience in the civil service has declined, with many people leaving because of low pay and morale, the continuity of the system is becoming increasingly threatened.

65 Jean-Luc Bodiguel, "A French Style Spoils System," *Public Administration*, 61 (1983), pp. 295–300; Monique Dagnaud and Dominique Mehl, "L'elite rose confirmee," *Pouvoirs*, 50 (1989), 149ff.

66 For a detailed description, see B. C. Koh, *Japan's Administrative Elite* (Berkeley, CA: University of California Press, 1989), Chapter 8.

67 Hans-Ulrich Derlien, "Wer macht in Bonn Karriere? Spitzenverbande und ihr beruflicher Werdegang," *Die offentliche Verwaltung*, 43 (1990), 311–19.

68 This figure includes school teachers and lower level public servants as well as *Beamte*; one authority cites just over one third of the *Bundestag* as being from the *Beamte* group. Russell J. Dalton, *Politics in Germany*, 2nd edn (New York: HarperCollins, 1993), pp. 216–20.

69 Peter B. Clark and James Q. Wilson, "Incentive Systems: A Theory of Organizations," *Administrative Science Quarterly*, 6 (1962), 129–66.

70 Hood and Peters, *op. cit.*

71 Charles H. Levine, "The Quiet Crisis of the Civil Service," *Governance*, 1 (1988), 115–43.

72 National Personnel Authority, *Handbook on Japan's Civil Service Statistical Overview* (Tokyo: National Personnel Authority, 1990).

73 Anthony Downs, *Inside Bureaucracy* (Boston: Little, Brown, 1967), pp. 96–101.

74 Christopher Hood, "De-Sir Humphreying the Westminster Model of Bureaucracy," *Governance*, 3 (1990), 205–14.

75 For a less quantitative view of the incentives, see Direction Generale de l'Administration et de la Fonction Publique, *Les Administrateurs civils dans les services centraux de l'Etat face a leur carriere et a leur travail* (Paris: La Documentation Francaise, 1991).

76 This characterization of the French civil service may be less true in the 1990s than it had been in the past. See Jean-Luc Bodiguel and Luc Rouban, *Le fonctionnaire detrone?* (Paris: Presses de la Fondation Nationale des Sciences Politiques, 1991).

77 The factor of self-advancement is especially important for Italy where the civil service is often utilized as a route of economic advancement for people from the southern part of the country. See Sabino Cassese, "The Higher Civil Service in Italy," in Ezra N. Suleiman, ed., *Bureaucrats and Public Policy* (New York: Holmes and Meier, 1984).

78 Beverly Alban Metcalfe, "What Motivates Managers: An Investigation by Gender and Sector of Employment," *Public Administration*, 67 (1989), 95–108.

79 Jak Jabes and David Zussman, "Motivation, Rewards and Satisfaction in the Canadian Federal Public Service," *Canadian Public Administration*, 31 (1988), 204–25.

80 Leslie L. Roos and Noralou P. Roos, *Managers of Modernization: Organizations and Elites in Turkey* (Cambridge, MA: Harvard University Press, 1971).

81   Wen-Fang Tang, William Parish and Guansan Yang, "Bureaucracy in China," unpublished paper, Department of Political Science, University of Pittsburgh, 1993.

82   Ben Ross Schneider, *Politics Within the State: Elite Bureaucrats and Industrial Policy in Authoritarian Brazil* (Pittsburgh: University of Pittsburgh Press, 1991); Fernando Uricoechea, *Estado y burocracia en Colombia* (Bogota: Universidad Nacional de Colombia, 1986).

83   M. A. H. Wallis, *Bureaucracy: Its Role in Third World Development* (London: Macmillan, 1989).

84   Robert N. Kearney and Richard L. Harris, "Bureaucracy and Environment in Ceylon," *Journal of Commonwealth Political Studies*, 2 (1964), 254–5.

85   *Ibid.*, p. 255.

86   John W. Thomas and Merilee S. Grindle, "After the Decision: Implementing Policy Reforms in Developing Countries," *World Development*, 18 (1990), 1163–81.

87   See Patricia W. Ingraham, "Building Bridges or Burning Them?: The President, the Appointees and the Bureaucracy," *Public Administration Review*, 47 (1987), 425–35.

88   M. S. Voslenski, *Nomenklatura: The Soviet Ruling Class* (Garden City, NY: Doubleday, 1984); Bruno Rizzi, *The Bureaucratization of the World* (New York: Free Press, 1985).

89   Michel Crozier, *The Bureaucratic Phenomenon* (Chicago: University of Chicago Press, 1964), pp. 228–9.

90   Fortunately or unfortunately the recent politicization of issues of public sector pay has made the rewards of political and administrative officials in government more apparent to the public. See Christopher Hood and B. Guy Peters, eds, *The Rewards of High Public Office* (London: Sage, 1993).

91   Even here, however, a public sector employee may have special obligations and duties. A secretary in a government office may type numerous letters of the utmost political sensitivity and is assumed to be able to exercise the appropriate discretion in not recounting to others what she or he has seen.

92   Peter M. Benda and Charles H. Levine, "Reagan and the Bureaucracy: The Bequest, the Promise, the Legacy," in Charles O. Jones, ed., *The Reagan Legacy* (Chatham, NJ: Chatham House, 1988).

93   Siv Gustaffson, *Lonebildning och lonestruktyr inom den statliga sektorn* (Stockholm: Almqvist and Wicksell, 1972); INSEE, "Remunerations des Agents de l'Etat en 1987 et 1988," *INSEE Premiere*, 50 (1989), 1–4.

94   One Swedish civil servant is reported as having said in a meeting with private sector counterparts that he expected their comments to be twice as good as his, given that they were paid twice as much. See Barbara Czarniawska, "The Ugly Sister: On the Relationship of the Private and the Public in Sweden," *Scandinavian Journal of Management Studies*, (1985), p. 93.

95   *Review Body on Top Salaries, Report No. 33*, Cmnd. 2015 (London: HMSO, 1992) reported a three percent drop in the real earnings of senior civil servants, in contrast to a 41 percent increase of income for top managers in the private sector in the period of 1985 to 1992.

96   Christopher Hood, "Rewards at the Top," in Hood and Peters, *Rewards of High Public Office*.

97   Peter S. Heller and Alan A. Tait, *Government Employment and Pay: Some International Comparisons* (Washington, DC: International Monetary Fund, 1983).

98   J. L. Fallick and R. F. Elliott, *Incomes Policies, Inflation and Relative Pay* (London: George Allen and Unwin, 1981).

99   Renk Robough and Wendy Kooistra, "Rewards in the Public Sector: The Case of the Netherlands," Paper presented at Conference on the Rewards of Higher Public Office, Erasmus University/Riksuniversiteit Leiden, Februrary, 1993.

100   Desmond S. King and B. Guy Peters, "Rewards of Higher Public Office: The United States," in Hood and Peters, *The Rewards of Higher Public Office*.

101   Hans Ulrich Derlien, "The Structure and Dynamics of the Reward System for German Bureaucratic and Political Elites," in Christopher Hood and B. Guy Peters, *The Rewards of Higher Office* (London: Sage, 1993).

102 This is true even in countries such as Sweden, Norway and the Netherlands with histories of low differentiation of wages in the public sector and a "solidaristic" wage policy in the economy as a whole. Per Laegreid, "Lonspolitsike reformforsok i staten," *LOS Senteret Notar* No. 52 (Bergen: LOS Center, 1989); Lennart Lundquist, *Ambetsman eller direktor* (Stockholm: Norstedts, 1993); Robough and Kooistra, "Rewards in the Public Sector: The Case of the Netherlands," in Christopher Hood and B. Guy Peters, *Rewards of High Public Office* (London: Sage, 1994).

103 Luc Rouban, "Rewards of High Public Offices in France: Political Arguments and Institutional Changes," in Christopher Hood and B. Guy Peters, *The Rewards of High Public Office* (London: Sage, 1994); Marlene Brans, "Public Office and Private Rewards: Rewards for High Public Office in Belgium," in Hood and Peters.

104 On Sweden, see Maivor Sjolund, *Statens Lonepolitik 1966–1988* (Stockholm: Publica, 1988).

105 See James L. Perry, "Merit Pay in the Public Sector: The Case for a Failure of Theory," *Review of Public Personnel Administration*, 7 (1986), 57–69.

106 International Monetary Fund, *Government Finance Statistics Yearbook*, Vol. 14 (Washington, DC: International Monetary Fund, 1990). Much of the total expenditure of the government of any developed country is transfer expenditures such as pensions and other social benefits. These tend to far exceed civil service costs.

107 *Ibid.* In part, government may become an employer of last resort in order to prevent high levels of unemployed people in urban areas. Also, overt corruption and putting friends and supporters on the public payroll accounts for some of these inflated figures.

108 Christopher Hood and B. Guy Peters, *The Rewards of High Public Office* (London: Sage, 1994).

109 Jean-Luc Bodiguel, "Nouveaux concours, nouveaux enarques," *La Revue Administrative*, 186 (1978), 610–18. Also, there has been some increase in the number of direct entrants, even into the *grands corps* such as the Cours de Comptes.

110 Wolfgang Zapf, *Wandlungen der Deutschen Elite* (Munich: Piper, 1966), pp. 180–2. The later study by Derlien and Mayntz found only five percent of senior civil servants with a working-class background. Hans-Ulrich Derlien and Renate Mayntz, *Einstellungen der politisch-administrativen Elite des Bundes 1987* (Bamberg: Universitat Bamberg, Lehrstuhle für Verwaltungswissenschaft, 1988).

111 Joel D. Aberbach, Robert D. Putnam and Bert A. Rockman, *Bureaucrats and Politicians in Western Democracies* (Cambridge, MA: Harvard University Press, 1981). See also Bodiguel and Rouban, *Le fonctionnaire detrone*, pp. 104–10.

112 This appears to be true even though American higher education is fee-paying while it is free in many European countries.

113 Aberbach, Putnam and Rockman, *Bureaucrats and Politicians*, pp. 48–9.

114 Gavin Drewry and Tony Butcher, *The Civil Service Today*, 2nd edn (Oxford: Blackwells, 1991); Nicholas Holgate, "Is Fifty-Nine Percent Enough?," *FDA News* (June, 1990), 2

115 V. Subramanian, *The Social Background of India's Administrators* (New Delhi: Ministry of Information and Broadcasting, 1971), p. 39.

116 Pierre Bourdieu, *La Noblesse de L'Etat* (Paris: de Minuit, 1989).

117 Koh, *Japan's Administrative Elite*, pp. 86–94.

118 Pan S. Kim, "Who Serves the People: Educational Backgrounds of South Korean and Japanese Bureaucrats," unpublished paper, Old Dominion University, Department of Public Administration, 1990; George Vernardakia and Catherine D. Papastathopoulos, "The Higher Civil Service in Greece," International Review of Administrative Sciences, 55 (1989), 603–29.

119 W. Lloyd Warner, *The American Federal Executive* (New Haven: Yale University Press, 1963), p. 372.

120 Critics would argue that this state domination is one of the major barriers to socio-economic development in these countries.

121 As noted above, representativeness may be particularly important at this level of the public sector. See M. Adler and S. Asquith, *Discretion and Power* (London: Heinemann, 1981).

122 This practice is becoming less established. See Barbara Liegl and Wolfgang C. Mueller, "Senior Officials in Austria," in Edward C. Page and Vincent Wright, eds, *Bureaucratic Elites in Western European States* (Oxford: Oxford University Press, 1999).

123 Ralph E. Crow, "Confessionalism, Public Administration and Efficiency in Lebanon," in Leonard Binder, ed., *Politics in Lebanon* (New York: John Wiley, 1966), pp. 71ff.

124 Sharma and Reddy, *Reservation Policy in India*.

125 Franco Ferraresi, *Burocrazia e Politica in Italia* (Milan: Il Mulino, 1980), 114–17.

126 Sabino Cassese, "Italy's Senior Civil Service," in Page and Wright, *op. cit.*

127 See the evidence presented in Richard Rose *et al.*, *Public Employment in Western Nations* (Cambridge: Cambridge University Press, 1985).

128 Monirah Rawaf, "The Changing Status of Women in Management in the Public Administration of Saudi Arabia," *Public Administration and Development*, 10 (1990), 209–20.

129 Several of the individual Lander in Germany have achieved over 15 percent employment of women in the senior civil service. See *This Week in Germany*, September 10 (1993), 7.

130 "Higher-Echelon Positions Remain Largely a Male Domain in the German Bureaucracy, Though Some Improvement May Be Seen," *This Week in Germany*, September 10 (1993), 7.

131 Henry Parris, *Constitutional Bureaucracy* (London: Allen and Unwin, 1969), p. 315.

132 Gerth and Mills, *From Max Weber*, p. 240.

Chapter 4

Problems of
administrative structure

Concern over the structure and design of organizations has traditionally dominated the study of public administration. The focus may result from the absence of any readily quantifiable measures of organizational performance – such as profit – in public organizations, so that greater attention must be devoted to practical and theoretical questions of organizational design.[1] Moreover, the responsibility of public organizations to external political actors and institutions, and the general opprobrium associated with the word "bureaucracy" also have placed pressure on public administrators to design the perfect organization. For whatever reason, public administration has been almost obsessed with constructing the best organizational structures for implementing public programs.[2]

The tendency to focus on structure reached one zenith during the 1920s and 1930s with the presumably scientific theories of administration, dismissed by Simon as the "proverbs of administration," advocating concepts such as unity of command, span of control and POSDCORB management.[3] The 1980s and 1990s have been another high point in the search for the best possible forms of administrative structure. The reforms implemented in this period have had a number of procedural and behavioral elements, but they also had a strong structural component (see Chapter 9).

In addition, the structure of the public sector depends very significantly upon history and economic and social conditions, as well as upon ideas about the purposes of government. The reform of government is a common activity, but no reform, however well informed by organization theory, is likely to be able to overcome all the inherited traditions embodied within the machinery of government.[4] Unless that macro-level of organizational constraint is understood, any attempt to alter the character of the internal functioning of the organization is doomed to failure.

This chapter has two objectives. The first is to describe in a brief fashion five major administrative systems, representing a range of variation along a number of dimensions of public administration. These descriptions should provide the reader with some basic information about how administrative systems are structured, and how various components fit together to form a more or less coherent whole. Second, the chapter will examine several points concerning governmental structures that are raised by organizational theory and assess the responses made by governments as they structure and restructure their administrative systems. The range of these answers can be used to gain a better idea about the relationship of organizational structure to the functioning of the public sector.

Germany

Germany is the heir to a long tradition of administrative development, beginning with the Prussian reforms of 1807–11. This development has produced a highly professionalized civil service, based upon a merit system of recruitment and possessing a high degree of commitment to the service of the state. The nature of the civil service has been altered very little by the numerous political changes that have taken place in Germany since the days of the Hohenzollern empire. Much of the old civil service law remained in place in East Germany as well as in West Germany, so that, after the reunification, the legal requirements for participating in the civil service, if not their implementation, had been similar in the two parts of the country.[5]

The contemporary structure of administration is highly decentralized in some ways, although some aspects of administration remain centralized. A relatively small percentage of the total number of civil servants in Germany were employed directly by the central (*Bund*) government. The central ministries of the *Bund* government are small planning organizations that develop policies to be implemented by the state (*Land*) governments.[6] The major exceptions to this generalization are the military, the post office and the relatively few remaining nationalized industries. Of the approximately 5.1 million public employees in Germany, only approximately 11 percent are employees of the central government (Table 4.1). However, despite the decentralization of the implementation structures, the procedures and standards of public administration remain centralized. All public employees must meet the same general standards for employment, as well as those of the particular positions for which they are employed, and all are subject to the legal strictures. Likewise, their training after entry into the public service is centralized and supervised by the central government. And, unlike the situation in the majority of other nations, the similar legal requirements and procedures apply to many of the employees of the nationalized industries such as those remaining in the state railways.

Public employment in Germany is divided into several broad classifications, with admission to each dependent upon specific educational qualifications. The highest level are civil servants, or *Beamten*, and their conditions of employment are determined by civil service law. This level of employment requires university education and passing an examination administered by a board composed of practicing civil servants and professors (actually, in Germany, professors *are* civil servants). The *Beamten* might be seen as roughly equivalent to the Senior Executive Service in the United States, or the old Administrative Class in the British civil service. They occupy the principal decision-making posts in the bureaucracy and consequently can substantially influence the outcomes of policy making. A second category of employment, the *Angestellen Dienst*, is not strictly made up of civil servants but it constitutes the major body of clerical and other lower-level white-collar employees.[7] Finally, there are the *Arbeiters* (workers), who constitute the blue-collar work force in the nationalized industries and in conventional governmental functions, such as sanitation and streets.

Most civil servants who become *Beamte* will have a university degree in law (the *Justiemonopol*), although those who will pursue more specialized and technical careers may have degrees in economics or science and engineering. The continuing importance of law, however, does point to the continuing legalistic conception of administration in Germany (the concept of the *Rechtstaat* – government and governing being defined by law – is dominant in German administration). Public administration is commonly seen as the application of the law to particular circumstances, rather than policy making. This is, of course, a mechanistic conception of the inherently political process of administration, but it is one that has

Table 4.1 Reduction in the number of local government units

Country (basic unit)	Number of units		Population per unit
	1951	1982	1982
France (commune)	37,983	36,391	1,500
United States (all general purpose)	41,029	38,732	6,700
Germany (municipality)	24,500	8,510	7,200
Norway (municipalities)	746	454	9,000
Belgium (commune)	2,670	596	16,700
Netherlands (municipalities)	1,014	820	17,000
Sweden (commune)	2,500	279	29,800
United Kingdom (districts)	c.1,500	484	115,100

Sources: Richard Rose, *Understanding Big Government* (London: Sage, 1984); US Bureau of the Census, *Statistical Abstract of the United States* (Washington, DC: Government Printing Office, annual)

persisted long after Weber wrote about administration in such terms. This reliance on law also constituted a problem for reunification, given that legal training in communist East Germany was totally different from that in West Germany and the civil service inherited from the East was not of much use in implementing laws drawn primarily from the West German system.[8]

Contrary to practice in most Anglo-Saxon countries, once the individual obtains the status of civil servant, it remains with him or her. Thus, the status is vested in the individual, not in the position that the individual occupies at any particular time. This system allows the civil servant to engage in political activities, although if the individual is successful in obtaining elective office then he or she will have to resign the civil service position. As important as the status of civil servant is, however, the position may be more subject to influence by political leaders than would be true in many other countries. The political leaders have the power to pension off any members of the higher civil service (those positions being defined as "political" despite their legalistic trappings) and to appoint any qualified person to fill the resulting vacancy. A number of civil positions may be filled by external candidates, especially when there is a change in political parties organizing government. Thus, although this is a career civil service, it is a career service with substantial room for political influence and outside appointment to top posts.[9]

A special case of the connection between politics and administration in Germany is the attempt to prevent students who have been involved in radical political activity from becoming civil servants (the *Berufsverbot*). This was especially important during the period of student activism in the late 1960s and early 1970s, but continues as a means of ensuring that those employed by government are favorably disposed toward the continuance of the democratic political institutions established in post-war Germany, a policy perhaps supported by a fear of the fragility of those institutions.[10] While there have been legal challenges to this principle, it remains largely intact, and most recently has been applied to members of the Church of Scientology.[11] It has also proved extremely useful in sorting out the civil servants coming from the former East Germany and deciding who could continue to serve the state and who could not.

Thus, the administrative structures of West Germany present an internal contradiction. On the one hand, the role of the public servant is considered to be highly legalistic, and the definition of the activities attached is strictly defined by statutes. On the other hand, there is considerable involvement in politics by administrators, and some political involvement in administration. The legalistic, Weberian definition of administration simply does not apply to a complex political system administering a wide variety of politically sensitive programs, but there is a desire to maintain some of the high status and quasi-judicial trappings of the civil servant. This mixture need not be dysfunctional, for the legalism and high status of the *Beamte* can be utilized as a means of making what are patently political decisions more acceptable to the public.

The United Kingdom

Attempting to capture the complexity of British administration in a few pages is a difficult task, and becoming increasingly so as the system is reformed. Unlike that of many of the other countries under discussion, British administration has evolved over centuries with few attempts (and even fewer successful ones) to rationalize and reorganize the machinery of government. Further, unlike the case with the continental countries, bureaucracy and administration have not played a prominent role in British thinking about government. As a consequence of both of those factors, British administration has developed by accretion with relatively little planning and, arguably, without a central organizational format that would make the system more comprehensible. The major exception to this exception was the experience of the Thatcher and Major governments, and their planned reforms decentralizing many of the functions of government to a series of quasi-autonomous executive agencies.[12]

To gain some understanding of this complexity of administration, it is first necessary to identify the major organizations in British government. There are six major types, each of which stands in a different relationship to the political authority of Parliament and Cabinet. The *executive departments*, such as the Department of Health and Social Security, are most closely connected to that authority. These are typically staffed by civil servants (in the restrictive sense of the term), are headed by a politician sitting in Cabinet, and have somewhat similar forms of organization. There is generally a Permanent Secretary at the top of the civil service pyramid who serves as the link between a small number of political leaders and the permanent officials. However, despite their importance and their familiarity to most citizens, these organizations employ a relatively small and declining proportion of total public employees in the United Kingdom (now less than six percent). Their actions, however, establish the legal framework within which most other organizations and public employees function. Also, the Treasury and the Cabinet Office at the heart of this collection of organizations help to determine overall government policy

The Thatcher government moved a number of the administrative and implementation functions of the executive departments into a series of *executive agencies*, in an exercise referred to as "Next Steps."[13] These agencies are each linked to a department, but also have a great deal of autonomy in how they organize themselves. The plan was that these organizations would act almost as private corporations seeking to maximize their revenue from service if they can sell their services, e.g. the Passport Office, or trying to minimize costs if they had a firmly established budget. Further, the heads of the agencies are not technically civil servants but are hired on performance contracts so that they are rewarded by how well the agency performs, and can be dismissed more easily than could civil servants.

The third form of organization is *local government*. The United Kingdom is a unitary government, so the number and functions of local authorities are controlled by the central government, and much of the cost of local government is borne by the central government. Despite this centralization, local authorities enjoy some freedom in the way in which they structure their own organizations, and to some degree in the qualifications they impose on their employees. They have almost as much latitude in those regards as subnational governments in federal Germany, although much less latitude in making policy.

The breakup of the six metropolitan governments and the Greater London Council by the Conservative government has introduced greater complexity, with a number of special-purpose authorities, such as transportation, covering metropolitan areas.[14] Also, it should be noted that one component of the United Kingdom – Northern Ireland – has its own civil service. Devolution to Scotland, and to a lesser extent Wales, means that these governments also exercise executive powers and have their own employees. The picture one gets at the subnational level in Britain is one of great complexity, even in the face of increased central government dominance over policy. These governments are also rather large in employment terms (approximately 70 percent of total public employment) and are responsible for implementing many central government programs as well as their own functions.[15]

The fourth major group of public employees comprises the *health services*. These employees stand in a variety of relationships to government, depending upon how they are employed and what functions they perform. In general, the employees of the National Health Service are definitely public employees, but they are not civil servants. Consequently, many of the benefits – and restrictions – of civil service employment do not apply to them. Hospital physicians (consultants) and all other employees of hospitals are salaried public employees, although they are employees of the National Health Service and not of government per se. General practitioners, on the other hand, are paid on the basis of the number of patients on their register, as well as for performing certain services for their patients, and function under a contract with the National Health Service.

Finally, there are a number of *non-departmental public bodies* in the structure of British government. These bodies are, in turn, divisible into two groups. One consists of the nationalized industries, such as British Railways, British Steel, the National Coal Board, and others. These industries have a sponsoring department, and, although their employees are definitely public employees, they lack the status of civil servants. Some attempt is made to keep management of these industries at least partially removed from government, to provide as much market discipline for their activities as possible. The nationalized industries are a declining share of British government as the government has been selling off industries – British Telecom, British Airways and British Gas, for example – for which buyers could be found. Within the classification of nationalized industries there are also some 150,000 industrial civil servants, with full civil service status, employed primarily in government-owned enterprises supplying the Ministry of Defense. With the end of the Cold War and the advance of a market conception of government, employment in this category is being cut drastically.

In addition to the nationalized industries there are a number of non-departmental bodies, commonly referred to as *quangos* (quasi-non-governmental organizations) which, in fact, represent a large number of different types of organizations standing in various relationships to the government.[16] Some are simply sections of cabinet departments that have been "hived off" for some reason or another – the Manpower Services Commission and its successor the Employment Service, for example – and may still be staffed by civil servants.[17] These bodies would be quite similar to independent executive agencies in the United States in that they perform executive functions but are not components of cabinet departments. The universities represent another set of non-departmental bodies that, while clearly in the public sector, are kept at arm's length from government for reasons of academic freedom. During the 1980s and 1990s, however, the universities have been brought closer to government for purposes of cost control and mandating increased levels of service.

Finally, there are the true quangos, organizations that are private, or partially private, but that spend public money and exercise the authority of government.[18] Also, there are a number of advisory bodies for ministries included among the quangos. These bodies at the fringe of government represent great difficulties in administrative accountability and control and were subject to a round of "quango-bashing" during the Thatcher government.[19] It should be pointed out, however, that some actions of the Thatcher government, such as reorganization of local government in the large metropolitan areas, actually have added to the number of quasi-independent bodies in British government, a trend that continued under John Major and under the Labour government.[20]

The types of public employees staffing these institutions are almost as varied as the institutions themselves, and in our discussion we will concentrate on the civil service, and particularly the top civil service. The British civil service made its first major movement toward modernization as a result of the Northcote-Trevelyan Report of 1854, which stressed the value of a highly qualified civil service recruited on the basis of merit.[21] Also, the qualifications stressed by this report were of an abstract, intellectual variety, rather than the more specific and practical qualifications traditionally employed in the United States. This report and its sequels resulted in a civil service dominated by class composed almost entirely of honors graduates in the humanities (especially Classics) who, though intelligent, did not have the training in the economic and technological issues that they were increasingly called upon to administer. The careers of this administrative class were varied, with frequent changes among positions and even among departments; these civil servants did not specialize in the work of any particular department until rather late in their career. The administrative class was a closed career; if someone was not selected initially for this bracket in administration, the opportunity to work one's way up was extremely limited. Also, lateral entry from the private sector was virtually unknown. All in all, this system produced a civil service composed of "talented amateurs."

The British civil service came under frequent attacks on the basis of these characteristics. The most comprehensive of these attacks was the Fulton Report, published in 1968, which recommended abolishing the existing internal divisions by class within the civil service.[22] In their place would be put a series of grades, similar to the general schedule in the United States, from the top to the bottom of the non-industrial civil service, with promotion up this schedule being based upon performance in previous positions. In addition, the Fulton Report advocated abolishing the separation of a number of technical and professional services from the remainder of the civil service – a system that kept the technical personnel "on tap, never on top," even in departments whose subject matter was highly technical. The Fulton Report also recommended that the civil service become less of a closed profession, that it be opened for lateral entry from the private sector at almost any point in the career structure. Some of these points have been reiterated in subsequent reports concerning the civil service, for example, the Megaw Report.[23]

As might have been predicted, the response to Fulton by those already in positions in the civil service was less than joyous. A number of weaknesses were pointed out in the document. After a process of negotiation and bargaining, some of the report's proposals for reform were adopted. The divisions between the Administrative Class, the Executive and the Clerical Classes were formally abolished, with an Administrative Group being substituted, and then the "open structure" at the top of the civil service being substituted. Further, socially and in terms of training, the composition of this group have remained quite similar to that of the prior administrative class. Also the separation between the technical and professional groups and the rest of the civil service has largely been maintained, as has the isolation of the civil service from lateral entry from the private sector or even local government. In short, with cosmetic changes, the system of the "talented amateur" – the rallying cry of the defenders of the system against the Fulton reforms – has been to a great degree maintained. Even as the technological demands of contemporary government have increased and become even more evident, recruitment continues to be disproportionately from the humanities and the "softer" social sciences. To some extent the civil service has been opened to outsiders, especially in managerial positions, but the dominant pattern is still to have an entire career within government.[24]

Another of the important characteristics of the British civil service has been its political neutrality. It has been assumed that a civil servant could serve any political master, be it Conservative, Labour, or whatever. This principle has also come under attack. One group of critics has argued that Britain needs a civil service committed to the program that it is administering and as a consequence more posts – especially senior posts – should be obtained by political screening and appointment.[25] Some commentators believe that the Conservative governments have in fact done just that over the past 15 years, to the extent possible under existing arrangements, and that the system has become more politicized, especially in the appointment of very top officials.[26] In addition, the civil service in general may be far from uncommitted. Its members are often committed to policy goals, especially the preservation of the status quo within their own departments. The civil service may be neutral in partisan terms, but it is far from neutral in policy terms.

The Thatcher and Major governments have also produced some greater openness in the personnel system of the British government. First, Mrs Thatcher did not trust the advice offered to her by career civil servants so she brought more personal advisors into government. More importantly, the "Next Steps" reforms mentioned above made the executive positions of the newly created agencies open to private sector as well as public sector applicants so that many principal managerial positions were occupied by individuals with limited public sector experience. The major policy advice positions remained in the hands of career civil servants, although the Blair government has been adding even more political advisors (especially in the Prime Minister's office). Also, it is argued that recent governments have asked much more than previous governments "Is s/he one of us?" This question may be related to style as much as to partisan affiliation, but is still an important question about political influence over appointments.

In summary, the British system of administration has adapted slowly to external pressures for change. It retains much of its character as a group of (very) talented amateurs, with a good deal of internal differentiation. Despite the pressures from almost a decade and a half of Conservative governments skeptical about their abilities, top public administrators remain the "mandarins" of the political system. Private sector techniques, and private managers, have made some inroads, but public administration remains a major cog in the machinery of government.

France

France has had a long tradition of centralized and strong government, going back at least to the reign of Louis XIV. Many of the administrative institutions developed by Napoleon as emperor to govern France are still being used, and the principal direction for government activity in France continues to emanate from Paris. This dominant role for the center is true despite several decentralizing reforms introduced by the Mitterrand and Chirac governments, and the activism of the newly created regions in dealing with the European Community. French government has been, if not dominated by bureaucracy, at least highly bureaucratic. It has been argued that because of the numerous changes in regimes in France, and the instability of governments during the Third and Fourth Republics, if France was to be governed at all it had to be governed by the central bureaucracy. This view may be overstated, but the bureaucracy continues to play a very significant role in French government and politics.[27]

Although it is centralized, the French bureaucracy also has a number of internal divisions. First, there are the vertical divisions between classes of administration (now A through G), which roughly represent educational qualifications needed for positions, with the F and G categories being the top administrative positions requiring at least a university-level education. The lower categories may require secondary education with the lowest requiring no particular education. As with the older conception of the administrative, executive and clerical classes in the British civil service, movement between these classes is rare. Again, this remains true despite attempts by the Mitterrand government to make advancement to the upper civil service more open to the lower echelons.[28] Further, within each of these classes there are divisions based upon the nature of the position, specialty of the individual occupying the position, and so on. Attempts at forming a unified civil service in 1946 were to prove hopeless, given the long tradition of these divisions in French public administration.

Perhaps the most important of all the divisions is the separation of class A into the *grands corps*, as well as some civil servants who do not belong to any of the corps. The *grands corps* constitute a vestige of Napoleonic administration and have been copied in other administrative systems influenced by the Napoleonic system – Spain, Italy and some Latin American countries. The corps represent organizations within the civil service and have some of the attributes of fraternal organizations.[29] When an individual becomes a member of a corps, he or she remains a member for the duration of his or her career. There are two principal technical corps – *Mines* and *Ponts et Chausses* – and five major administrative corps – *Inspection des Finances, Conseil d'Etat, Cour des Comptes,* the diplomatic corps, and the prefectoral corps as well as several minor corps. The names attached to these corps reflect their functional tasks for government, e.g. financial management, but an individual remains a member of his or her corps regardless of whether or not that function is being performed. Further, the individual remains a member of the corps even if working in the private sector, and indeed the contacts between public and private sectors are increased (perhaps to detrimental levels) by the number of civil servants who have "parachuted" into the private sector.[30] The several *grands corps* represent something approaching governments within the government, as the informal contacts among members constitute a means of doing business even when formal channels are blocked.

An individual becomes a member of one of the corps on the basis of performance at one of the two major schools channeling people into the civil service. One of the schools, which provides personnel for the technical corps, is the *École Polytechnique*, established by Napoleon to provide the engineers he required to modernize France and to modernize its army. The other school, the *École Nationale d'Administration* (ENA), supplies recruits for the administrative corps. ENA was established in 1946 as the training ground for future public servants.[31] Its curriculum stresses law, administration and, to a lesser extent, finance, emphasizing the legalistic conception of administration in France – not dissimilar to the conception held in Germany. Entry to the ENA is gained by one of two national examinations: one given to students completing their education at the university, and another for those already employed by government in lower-echelon positions. A third examination – for those working in the private sector and especially for workers, union leaders and the like – was introduced by the Socialist government but later abandoned. It produced very few successful candidates and, as the size of the public sector was being reduced in the late 1980s, the demand for new "ENAcrats" diminished markedly, along with the opportunities to make the senior civil service more representative.

Yet another division in French administration, one common to most administrations but perhaps rather more intense in France, is among the departments and agencies. French administration has a traditional bureaucratic structure, with departments divided into a number of sections and subsections. This structure and the competitive nature of policy formation in the system makes the units in the administrative system extremely protective of their budgets and their access to cabinet and to the presidency.

The members of the *grands corps*, and indeed any French civil servant, may become involved in politics. The members of the *grands corps* are particularly valued as political contacts because of their ties with the powerful and well-connected membership of their organizations. They are particularly visible as members of the *cabinets* of individual ministers.[32] These *cabinets* are bodies of advisors for the minister of a government department, and it has been considered essential to have members of the corps, such as the *Inspection des Finances*, in a *cabinet*. The Socialist government tended to involve higher civil administrators in *cabinets* and to purge the older, elitist corps. This purge was specially evident in the personal entourages of Prime Minister Mauroy and President Mitterrand.[33] When the coalition of Gaullists and Giscardians won the National Assembly elections in 1986, the corps made something of a comeback and continue to dominate French administration, even in the Jospin government.

Thus, the civil service in France does not work under the same assumptions of impartiality as in Britain. Many senior civil servants are openly political and even participate in politics and hold public office. In fact, a large proportion of government ministers are civil servants or former civil servants. Of course, when a civil servant becomes involved politically, he or she may become *persona non grata* for subsequent governments. In that case, there are always opportunities outside government for members of the *grand corps*.

A large percentage of French public employees are not civil servants but, rather, work for nationalized industries or parastatal organizations (see Table 4.1). Despite some change, France has not progressed as far with privatization as many other European countries, so that there are still a large number of industrial public employees.[34] The employees of public enterprises are clearly public employees but do not necessarily have the same civil service perquisites of other government employees. There is an attempt to impose as much market discipline on these organizations as possible, and for this reason their employees are not tenured (except by arrangement with unions) and their salaries are not so tightly controlled by the *grille* as those of civil servants. Other public enterprises, notably *Postes, Telegraphes et Telephones* (PTT), are components of the government, and their employees are civil servants. All of these public corporations are subject to pressures for privatization, so that the French state may not remain the powerful economic actor that it has been.

Local governments in France have only limited independence from the central government. The criteria for employment in local and regional governments are prescribed nationally. In addition, the major function of local government in most counties – education – is a national function, and the employees of local schools are actually direct employees of the Ministry of Education in Paris. Likewise, many local public works are controlled centrally through the technical *grands corps*, so the latitude available to local governments to invest in capital projects as they wish is also limited.

The latitude of local governments has been limited even further by the prefectoral system.[35] France is divided into 95 *départements*, each named after a particular geographical feature. These divisions are also a Napoleonic device designed to eliminate the traditional provinces in France, such as Burgundy and Normandy, which were perceived to limit loyalty to the nation. The *préfet*, also a Napoleonic invention, was designed to ensure that each of the *départements* was governed in the manner desired by the central government in Paris. Each *département* had a *préfet* who was responsible to the Ministry of the Interior for the administration of government policy in his or her area. Prior to reforms beginning in the 1960s and 1970s almost any little thing a local government wished to do – repair a local street, for example – required the approval of the *préfet* and perhaps even officials in Paris. The powers of the *préfet* have been weakened further by the Socialists.[36] Some changes have been symbolic, for example, changing the title to "Commissioner of the Republic." Others changes are more genuine, with most executive power in the department now residing in the President of an elective departmental council. The "Commissioners" do continue to exercise some supervisory powers, although their powers of *tutelle* (instruction) have been abolished. Now, instead of being able to block local actions they consider illegal by Fiat, they must sue in an administrative tribunal. The Commissioners do continue to have some importance in making sure that the *saupoudrage* ("pork barrel") spending continues to flow into their department and to its local governments.[37]

In summary, French administration is a vast and somewhat contradictory institution. It has been a major weapon of a centralizing national government but is itself deeply divided and internally fractious. An administrative system that was formerly highly centralizing is now becoming more decentralized than many administrations that have appeared more open to local influence. French administration is highly legalistic in its own definitions of its work and in its relationships with citizens, but at the same time it is deeply involved with politics. Individuals derive great status from their connections with the *grands corps* but may spend some or most of their career in the private sector. This system has been capable of governing France when there was little alternative governance available from politicians, but it is not entirely clear that it can always govern itself as effectively.

Sweden

Although it did not industrialize until much later, Sweden developed a skilled central bureaucracy quite early in its history. This development began during the reign of Gustavus Adolphus, whose entry into the Thirty Years War required the development of a competent bureaucracy if tiny Sweden was to be governed at home and fight a major foreign war.[38] Sweden had more civil servants per capita than did most countries during the eighteenth and nineteenth centuries, and the civil service that developed had an image of competence and honesty.

Although its total numbers have been greatly expanded by the programs of the contemporary welfare state, much the same could be said of the modern Swedish civil service. The public bureaucracy remains large relative to that of other industrial democracies and is also generally quite competent. In addition to being competent, the bureaucracy is also held more stringently accountable than almost any other in the world, so the opportunities for bureaucratic excesses are more limited than in other countries. This degree of control has not made the Swedish civil service immune to complaints about abuses of power but it has ensured them a more positive public image than that enjoyed by most bureaucracies.

The organization of Swedish government is a combination of centralized and decentralized features. This characterization applies both to the overall structure of government and to the practices within government. First, although Sweden is technically a unitary government, there is a long tradition of local government liberty. Both the lowest tier of government (the communes) and the intermediate tier (the *lan)* have a number of policy-making powers, including control of some types of taxation, which they can exercise independently. The *lan* governments, for example, are very heavily involved in providing hospital care and appear to compete among themselves over quality of facilities and services. The *lan* governments are composed of an elective legislative body and a governor general appointed by central government for life – another mixture of centralized and decentralized features.

In addition to the division between levels of government, there are also a number of nationalized industries, as well as public participation in a number of joint-stock companies.[39] In these commercial ventures the dividing line between public and private sectors becomes extremely vague. In general, however, the employees of the joint-stock companies are not in any way considered to have civil service jobs, whereas those in the fully nationalized industries – especially the traditional ones such as forestry – do tend to have that status. As is true for other industrialized democracies, many Swedish nationalized industries have been privatized and many others are under the threat of privatization. The pressures for privatization have increased under the bourgeois government elected in 1991.

The formal structures for carrying out public business also have something of a decentralized character, even within the central government itself. The central ministries in Sweden are relatively small organizations, charged primarily with planning and policy formulation. The major task of implementing policy falls to the boards (*styrelsen* or *ambetsverk*), which in many ways are independent of the ministries supervising their work.[40] The separation of these organizations appears related to the tendency in Swedish government to specify as clearly and unambiguously as possible the roles that organizations are to play. The boards are, however, coordinated with the ministries by law and through the all-important budgetary process.[41] These boards that implement policy are governed in one of three ways. A few continue with the traditional pattern of a collegial management by top officials on the board, almost in the manner of a multi-member court, with day-to-day management by a director general. Another group is controlled directly by a director general, an appointee of the crown (in practice, the government). The largest – and still growing – number of boards are managed by a lay board convened by the director general, but containing a variety of representatives of important interests in the particular policy area. In all these instances, however, the boards are the major employers of public servants, and it is they who do the day-to-day work of administering Swedish government.[42]

Personnel policy in Swedish public administration is more decentralized than in most other political systems. Agencies are given the latitude to advertise for and hire their own personnel. There is, however, a legal framework for public employment, so although there is latitude to select individuals, the individual selected must meet the necessary requirements and the field from which the choice can be made may be limited. The history of Sweden, with government by the Social Democrats from 1935 to 1976, again from 1982 until 1991 and from 1994 onwards, has produced an indirect politicization of the civil service. Government has been so closely associated with that one party and its programs that the civil service has tended to attract primarily adherents of that party. The bourgeois government elected in 1991 has complained about the civil service they inherited and has sought to redirect government with its own appointees.

There are also internal divisions within the civil service, much as has been noted in French, German and British administrations. Further, although Sweden is frequently cited as a prototype of a socialist society (a description in many ways patently untrue), these distinctions are as institutionalized in Sweden as in any of the other countries. Members of the civil service at different levels are not only on different pay plans, they are in different unions. Those with a university education belong to SACO-SR, the union that represents only graduates, while those who are in white-collar positions but who lack a university education tend to belong to TCO.[43] Finally, those in blue-collar jobs belong to LO, the principal labor federation. Further, those in the top positions, the *tjansteman*, have a status similar to that of the *Beamte* in West Germany, although the position lacks most of the quasi-judicial trappings found in Germany.

Another of the apparent internal contradictions in Swedish administration is the emphasis on efficiency in a government that is (relative to population size) one of the largest in the world, and has been controlled for most of modern history by a moderate socialist party. Government has had an active policy of managerial improvement and has been able very effectively to control the size of managerial and clerical employment (albeit not health and education workers).[44] Further, in contrast to the emphasis on equality in much of Swedish political life, a system of merit pay has been introduced in an effort to further improve the efficiency of Swedish government.[45]

The United States

The administrative system of the United States may be thought to be derived in some ways from that of the United Kingdom, and indeed there are some important common features. That having been said, public administration in the United States also represents the particular historical experiences of that country, as well as attempts to meet continuing administrative challenges. Many Europeans stereotype the United States as having a small public sector dominated by issues of national defense and the other "defining functions" of government. The reality, however, is that the public sector in the United States employs almost 20 million people, with the vast majority of those working in education and social policy organizations (Table 4.1). The tendency of non-Americans to assume that the public sector in the United States is small is a function of the location of approximately five in six of those public employees in state and local governments, rather than in Washington.

As well as the high level of decentralization in American administration, another important feature of the system is a relatively high level of political involvement. At the national level there are approximately 3,000 political appointments in the executive branch, many more than would be found in other industrialized democracies. Further, the number of these appointments has been increasing, as presidents and cabinet secretaries attempt to ensure control over the operations of the departments and agencies.[46] Although this high level of politicization may be a threat to good management, the good news is that the majority of the people now appointed to these posts have a good deal of expertise in the policy area. They are a part of the "policy communities" around these issues and are working on the same issues whether they are in or out of government.

In addition to the political appointments at the top of public organizations, there is a large career civil service hired on merit principles. This civil service is divided first into large groups based on the type of work performed, and then classified into a series of grades.[47] The tendency is to hire these individuals (especially at managerial levels) based on their expertise in a particular policy area rather than as generalists. The creation of the Senior Executive Service in 1978 was an attempt to create more of a general management cadre in the federal government, but the system is still one in which experts remain within a single department for most of their careers.[48] The meaning of "merit" in the merit system has become more ambiguous as a result of reforms during the past decade, but there is still a strong sense that a demonstration of objective qualifications is required.[49]

There is a variety of types of organizations in the US federal bureaucracy.[50] First, there are 14 cabinet departments, the secretaries of which (along with several other officials) comprise the president's cabinet. There are also over 50 independent executive agencies which also report to the president but which are not included in the cabinet – examples are the National Aeronautics and Space Administration (NASA) and the Small Business Administration.[51] There are also a number of independent regulatory commissions that are, in principle, removed from control by president and Congress but which are subject to some control through the budgetary process. There are also some government corporations existing either independently or within one of the other types of structures. Finally, there are some important organizations responsible to the legislative branch rather than the executive branch of government, including the General Accounting Office and the Congressional Budget Office.

The accountability system of American bureaucracy is extremely complex, given that the typical public servant reports both to the secretaries of the cabinet departments, or some other official in the executive branch, and also to the Congress and its committees that oversee the operations of executive-branch organizations.[52] The United States also has a more developed system of administrative law than many other Anglo-American systems, with the Administrative Procedures Act of 1946 providing a set of guidelines for administrative rule-making and adjudication.[53] In addition, there are internal, managerial checks on behavior through the Inspectors General located within each large organization. Finally, the performance management system being developed in conjunction with the Government Performance and Results Act is providing yet another avenue for enforcing accountability.

The structure of administration

Perhaps the most fundamental question of administrative structure is the basis of organization for the administrative apparatus. How will the public service be structured to execute its assigned tasks? Rather early in the study of public administration, Luther Gulick proposed that the organization of public administration could be founded on four alternative principles: geographical area covered, processes employed, types of persons or things dealt with, or purpose served.[54] Examples of these forms of organization are readily available. The area served is frequently used as an organizational principle at the subdepartmental level, as in the use of regional offices. The principle may also be institutionalized at the departmental level, as in the office for the South in Italy,[55] the Scottish and Welsh Offices in the United Kingdom,[56] or what were in essence regional ministries in Canada.[57]

Organization by process is also commonly encountered at subministerial levels, with divisions or bureaus of accounting, legal services, engineering and the like. This principle may, however, also be found at the ministerial level, and has tended to do so increasingly as financial strains have placed demands for tighter supervision and management on "central agencies."[58] Types of persons or things dealt with would include organizations such as the Veterans Administration in the United States, similar organizations in other countries, the Ministry for Maori Development in New Zealand, and various boards and commissions for (or against) foreign workers and immigrants in most European countries. Finally, the purposes served are the most frequent basis of organization, as the ubiquitous departments or ministries of defense, education and health and so forth would indicate.

Each of these modes of organization has some assets and some liabilities, which have been rather thoroughly discussed by Gulick and others working on the problem since then.[59] There is no need to engage in an extensive discussion of that theoretical literature here. Rather, let us begin to examine how these four categories of organization can be used to analyze differences in administrative systems cross-nationally, and what the implications of these differences are for administration. No government will use any one of these as the sole basis of organization, so the question becomes under what conditions each should be selected, and how they should be integrated for greatest effectiveness. The bulk of our analysis is on modes of organization other than by purpose, since that mode is the most common and the one with the fewest comparative differences.

150

Organization by area served

Organization by area provides the most interesting comparative differences across cultures. These differences in administration are largely related to broader organizational questions for the entire political system, especially the degree of centralization to be imposed upon the country by the central government. In fact, the two most important variants of areal administration emanate from quite different solutions to this problem. One solution is for the central government to attempt to control and supervise closely the execution of its policies throughout the nation. One of the most powerful means to ensure such uniformity is the use of prefectoral officers in localities. In a general sense, prefects are officers of the central government responsible for the execution of national programs at the subnational level. Each ministry may have its own field service, but these are coordinated and, to some degree, supervised by the prefect, who is responsible to the Ministry of the Interior or some other ministry charged with supervising administration. In France, and other countries following the Napoleonic tradition, the prefect also has been responsible for local governments, especially their finances. While the decentralization programs described above have reduced that authority in France, the prefects do continue to monitor local government. There are differences in the exact ways in which prefectoral systems operate, but the common thread of such systems – as in France, Italy and Japan – is that one officer should coordinate and be responsible for public policies delivered in one subnational area.[60]

Prefectoral systems in practice often operate quite differently from the formal model of central control. In addition to serving as representatives of the national government to the locality, prefects also represent their locality – and themselves – to the center. That is, prefects frequently are co-opted by their localities and will support claims for local variances in national programs. Worms and Thoenig, among others, have noted a number of points of convergence between the interests of prefects and similar central government officials and the interests of local politicians.[61] Other analyses of the policy roles of the prefect in France tend to point to local rather than central dominance.[62] The prefect, in practice, is often the man in the middle, linking the demands of the local constituency for special treatment and rapid action to the demands of the central government for uniformity. Prefects must also think of their own careers, so that it may benefit them to cooperate with their localities in order to obtain smooth and successful execution of the tasks for those local authorities.[63]

The other common answer to the question of central control is not to try too hard, and is implemented through a variety of schemes for administrative devolution and administrative federalism. These either transfer control of administration downward to a subnational unit or provide deconcentrated control of the administration. Probably the most extreme versions of this form of organization are found in Germany and Switzerland, where the functions of the national bureaucracy are confined primarily to program development in the ministries and running the state railroads, the post office and several nationalized industries. The vast majority of the work of administering public policies (federal and subnational) is done at the level of the equivalent of states (*Lander* in Germany, Cantons in Switzerland).[64]

Although the federal ministers have the responsibility for ensuring that programs are administered properly, they have few resources to enforce uniformity, other than the law and the legalism of both administrative systems.[65] Indeed full uniformity is not a goal in many administrative settings, because of historical, cultural and practical differences among the component parts. This has been especially true for Switzerland, but is now increasingly the case for Germany after the addition of former East Germany. Such a decentralized administrative system raises a number of important problems concerning public accountability for policy and, associated with that, possibilities for public control of policy and administration. The centralized system may be inflexible and possibly autocratic, but at least responsibility for policy is clear. Thus, as with the internal management of public organizations, the conflict between centralization and its associated responsibility for decision, and decentralization and its associated flexibility, rages at the broader level of the organization as a whole.

The decentralization of administration in Germany is somewhat extreme, but virtually all central governments use their subnational governments to administer national policy. For example, in the United States, the majority of federal social programs – Medicaid, the reformed program of social welfare, and many others – are administered by state and local governments. The central governments of Canada and Australia, two other geographically large federal governments, also depend upon their provincial or state governments to administer large shares of social and economic policy. Even in more centralized governments local authorities administer central government programs. In the nominally unitary Scandinavian countries, for example, major functions such as health, education and even tax collection may be devolved to counties or communes.[66]

The United Kingdom has become an especially interesting study in decentralization within a largely unitary system. With devolution in 1999, the former Scottish and Welsh offices have been terminated in favor of greater self-government in these regions. Likewise, a new Northern Ireland government took over a large number of activities from London in spring, 2000, albeit for only a short time in the first instance. That having been said, the central government still administers some programs in these regions, and differences in the administration of the law (and in some cases the law itself) remain in these parts of the country.[67] In addition, local (regional and district) governments administer policies such as housing, criminal justice and education for the central government.[68] Also, there can be conflicts between local governments and the central government over the manner in which the policies are implemented – for example, the (Labour controlled) Lambeth council refusing to implement controls on public expenditure for health, and Liverpool refusing to implement a number of central government policies during the Thatcher government. These particular conflicts have been politically motivated, but conflicts could easily arise over the interpretation of the law. Further, even in centralized governments, local governments are usually capable of obtaining some autonomy in the management of a number of policies.[69]

Administrative decentralization is now a widely used tactic for coping with problems of ethnic and regional differences in what might otherwise be centralized countries. For example, in Spain there has been a movement to decentralize administration to ethnic and linguistic areas that have demands for special considerations, and in Belgium the separation of the regions is almost complete.[70] The decentralization of economic planning in France into the rather new regions, and the regionalization of Italian government, are in response to demands for greater autonomy, as well as real needs of government to respond more flexibly to local conditions.[71]

Another version of administrative decentralization is emerging within the European Community. Despite numerous complaints by politicians in the 12 countries about the "bureaucracy in Brussels," the public service in the European Community itself is rather small – approximately 2,000, leaving aside the interpreters and clerical staff. Like the central government in Germany, the European Community depends upon a lower level of government – in this case the nation-states – to implement its policies.[72] In this case the administrative and legal traditions are much more diverse than among the *Lander* in Germany (even after the inclusion of the former East German *Lander*) so that much greater variation may be expected.[73] In addition, many EC laws depend upon the member states adopting them as a part of national law, so that there are also variations in the extent to which national legislatures have acted to comply with European policies.[74]

Related to the decentralization of decision making is a second areal question relating to the size of administrative units, or the size of local governments themselves. There has been a consistent tendency among governments to reorganize administration and local government (the two may be synonymous) into larger and larger units. As Table 4.1 indicates, Sweden, for example, reorganized over 2,500 local governments into 279, with similar changes occurring in other Scandinavian countries, the United Kingdom and Germany. These reforms have generally been justified by economies of scale in the production of public goods and services and by the ability of the larger units to provide a broader array of public services.[75] Further, urban areas in particular require the integration of a range of services (transportation in particular) that, in turn, require large local government areas.

There is, however, little systematic evidence that these presumed benefits actually materialize. First, as the size of governmental units increases, there is a tendency for overhead expenditures to increase as a proportion of total expenditures; after some point, gains from the economies of scale are absorbed by increases in overhead.[76] Further, each service has a different-size unit at which it is most efficiently produced. Refuse collection appears to be very efficient on a very large scale, while policing can be argued to be more efficient for smaller units. Unless very complex systems with multiple single-purpose governments are to be created, no single-size government will be most efficient for all services.[77] That complex array of single-purpose governments has actually been evolving in some countries, in response to demands for greater efficiency, to privatization, and to fiscal strains on local governments. For example, during the past several decades the United States added over 400 special-purpose governments per year.[78] Similarly, the breakup of large metropolitan governments in Britain has produced a number of authorities providing a single service, especially in transportation. In Belgium, France and numerous other countries intercommunal associations continue to be formed as a means of addressing the need for certain services that cannot be fulfilled by the communes themselves.

Leaving aside economics, as the size of the unit increases, there may be a decrease in satisfaction with the services. This is perhaps a function of the perceived cost of government in relation to the services actually provided. On the other hand, as Fesler points out, as the size of government increases, so does the perception of its remoteness, and consequently so does the alienation of the population.[79] This alienation is one of the causes of a somewhat contradictory trend: the increase in neighborhood government and organization in large cities. These neighborhood organizations may be general-purpose units functioning within the context of city government, or they may be special-purpose organizations created for the "co-production" of a service, for example, "neighborhood watch" programs for crime prevention. In either case, they help to create an enhanced feeling of participation and citizen efficacy. Thus the argument can be made for the retention of small and "inefficient" administrative divisions, even in the face of demands for greater efficiencies and increased services.

Organization by process

Government can be organized by process, or by the communality of the processes employed by the members of the organization and the communality of their professional skills, rather than by purpose of the organization. Taken to an extreme this principle might mean, for example, that all accounting or purchasing activities for government would be concentrated in single agencies, or that all engineers or lawyers would be concentrated in bureaus of engineering or law, and their services provided to other agencies as required.

Line and staff. The above examples may appear inefficient – and they probably are – but such options do exist for the organization of government. They can be justified as a means of concentrating skilled individuals, as a means of imposing relatively uniform professional practices across the public sector and as a means of streamlining the operations of other organizations. The most common process distinction in the literature on public administration is between "line" and "staff" agencies. Line agencies are those that directly deliver services to the public, while staff agencies are responsible for coordinating the line agencies and providing central services needed by all of government.

Initially, the concept of staff was reserved for personal advisors to an executive – the Richelieus, Mazarins and Oxenstiernas – that directly advise the executive. As the tasks of the political executive have broadened, however, so has the definition of staff. Executives have found that their own staffs expanded to the point where they could no longer be personally supervised, and differentiated organizations performing staff functions have been developed. For example, the Executive Office of the President in the United States, currently employing 1,700 people, is perhaps the largest staff organization in the world. However, the expansion of the Executive Office has been mirrored in the expansion of similar offices in a number of countries. For example, the Office of the Prime Minister in Britain has expanded from a few dozen employees to over 300 people, and the *Bundeskanzlersamt* (the office of the Chancellor) in Germany now employs over 500 people.[80]

We have been employing the term "staff functions" rather facilely. Just what are the functions that a staff person or agency is expected to undertake? Personnel from line or operating agencies might be tempted to say that their principal function is to prevent those actually providing a public service from having access to the executive. This is hardly their real function, but it points to a potential conflict between staff and line agencies. The ostensible purpose of staff agencies is to do those things that line agencies have neither the time, the power, nor the competence to do. Perhaps the most important of these tasks is coordinating the programs of line agencies. Line agencies, having a limited scope of operations and consequently narrow perspectives on the tasks of government, are not really in a position to attempt to coordinate their own programs. In fact, their incentives – if we assume that agency growth is a prime bureaucratic goal – are to attempt to spread their services into policy areas already occupied by other agencies and thereby to provide, if not duplicate services, at least competing services. Thus, the chief executive and his/her staff (here interpreted broadly as either personal staff or staff agencies) must intervene in order to prevent unnecessary duplication. Such duplication as develops among government agencies need not be the result only of bureaucratic aggrandizement, but may represent a genuine willingness to do a job well, and a frustration over inability to coordinate effectively with other organizations.

The "central agencies" of government are primarily responsible for controlling duplication and enforcing coordination in government.[81] These agencies include the central financial and budgetary organizations, such as the Office of Management and Budget in the United States or the Treasury in the United Kingdom. They also include central personnel organizations, such as the Office of Personnel Management in the United States or the Civil Service Commission in Canada. Planning is also an important aspect of coordination and budgeting. Line agencies tend to be so heavily involved in their ongoing work that they frequently lack the time for non-essential things such as planning what to do in the future, and any sort of comprehensive planning may involve a wider viewpoint than that of a single agency. Planning agencies tend to be directly attached to the executive and to provide a broader overview of the future. The planning that is done in these agencies may be for government programs themselves, or may be planning for the economy and society that will require the intervention of the public sector.

Several differences appear in the use of staff agencies. Peter Self provides an interesting discussion of staff functions in the United States and Great Britain. He notes that staff functions typically have not been institutionalized in Britain as they have in the United States, in part as a function of the differences in the forms of government. Specifically, in British Cabinet government, problems of coordination are in the main horizontal rather than vertical, with a number of (allegedly) equal departments competing for funds and programs.[82] Since the heads of these departments are all members of the Cabinet, the problem of coordination becomes one of imposing collective decision, rather than analysis and coordination by executive decree. Further, rather than being performed by an isolated presidential agency such as the Office of Management and Budget, most coordination in Britain is done by one of the departments – the Treasury – whose leader is among the members of the Cabinet.[83] There was an experiment with coordination of personnel through a civil service department, but that function was returned to the Treasury after 13 years. As Self and others have pointed out, such a system of coordination could not work in an administrative system less homogeneous and less well integrated than that of Britain.[84] Self further notes that, with the exception of Treasury control, there is virtually no formal means of coordination within government. The past several decades have produced important changes, with the growth of the Prime Minister's Office and a larger staff at No. 10, but still in comparison to most other governments the central coordination apparatus in British government is subtle and, at times, almost invisible.[85]

Attempts to achieve coordination have included the creation of very large departments; any potentially duplicating or competitive services can be included within the confines of a single department and be subject to hierarchical coordination by a single minister.[86] Likewise, there have been attempts to impose "overlords," or superministries, on the existing Cabinet structure to ensure effective policy control. In practice, it would appear that as the size of the ministries is increased, the old administrative proverb of "span of control" would be increasingly violated, so that in practice one might actually get less coordination, or at least the need for more extensive staff work within the department.[87]

Despite the managerial problems that they may create, larger ministries are in vogue at the beginning of the twenty-first century.[88] This pattern is especially obvious for social service departments that have become integrated with health and/or labor ministries to provide more comprehensive services to their clients. The management of these large departments is being facilitated by the availability of information technologies that enable a senior official to monitor operations and communicate with subordinates with much greater ease than in the past.

Further, fewer ministries also tends to mean fewer ministers so that decision making in cabinet, as well as prime ministerial leadership, can be facilitated. The reduction in the number of ministries is, to some extent, being supplemented by the creation of more junior ministers, or deputy prime ministers, with portfolios that are explicitly to produce greater coordination across a range of programs. The junior ministers are often given responsibility for groups that require services and consideration from a variety of ministries, e.g. women, families and immigrants. These developments reflect that it has now become clearer to governments that one of their most difficult tasks is to manage horizontally across the range of their activiities.[89]

We have at several points intimated the existence of conflict between line and staff agencies. Conflicts are almost inherent in this system of organization. The line agencies tend to regard the other side as ivory-tower planners far removed from the day-to-day problems of program administration but still able to sell themselves as experts with more access to decision making than the operating agencies. The staff agencies are also identified as formidable obstacles to organizational growth.[90] On the other side of the conflict, staff agencies often become highly suspicious of the motives of line agencies in resisting attempts to coordinate and "rationalize" public services, and may resent the ability of the line agencies to mobilize political support for their programs outside the bureaucracy. Staff may come to regard the line agencies as spendthrifts, raiders on the public purse and captives of the special interests that they serve. Thus, one of the inherent limitations that organization by process, especially in terms of line and staff, may have is the tendency for intraorganizational conflict and resistance to coordination and streamlining of services. These tensions among line and staff are as old as government, but have been accentuated by the increased emphasis on management and efficiency.

The potential conflict between line and staff may occur not only at the level of the whole government, but also within individual departments. Just as national executives require staff services to perform functions that their operating agencies cannot do, executives of the operating agencies have the same need. At the departmental level, these staff services are also concerned with coordination of programs and activities. If, as noted above, ministerial departments are tending to become larger, then the needs for coordination and control within the department may become as great as those among departments.

One of the more notable examples of staff services within a department is the ministerial *cabinet* in France and Belgium. Each minister in the French government has the opportunity to appoint a *cabinet* consisting of a dozen or more members to provide a variety of staff services such as policy advice, press relations, control of potentially recalcitrant civil servants, communications and planning. Although appointments to these *cabinets* are ostensibly at the will of the minister, in practice they involve extensive political considerations in addition to concerns over the quality and political reliability of the staff work produced.[91] Especially important in terms of the actual direction of policy is the job of the *conseilleur technique*, who serves as a political appointee linking the formal bureaucratic organization of the ministry to the politically appointed *cabinet*. Interestingly, the socialist government which came to power in 1981 did not change as many members of *cabinets*, or their directors, as might have been expected.[92] They too needed expertise in managing and coordinating policy. Given their extensive reform agenda and the legacy of Gaullism, they perhaps needed new advisors more than most governments. Much the same occurred when the political right returned to power, although the Socialist Jospin government appears to have cleaned house more intensively.[93]

The use of ministerial *cabinets* is even more extensive in Belgium, to the point that they have been termed "counter-administrations."[94] The divisions of Belgian society along several dimensions make it desirable to employ *cabinets* staffed by people known to be reliable, as opposed to civil servants who may be highly politicized and consequently may not be politically loyal to the minister. Again, some contrast with British and American practice may be in order. One might argue for the need for the ministerial *cabinets* in large part because of the relative inability or unwillingness of French and Belgian ministers to rely on their civil servants. This, in turn, necessitates the use of political appointees to drive the control of the minister farther down into the organization than would otherwise be possible and provides more of a check on the execution of ministerial directives within the organization. In the United States, the existence of several layers of political appointees between the cabinet officer and the upper echelons of the career civil service is one type of "staff" organization, although the appointees may actually hold positions in "line" agencies to ensure political control over presumably independent-minded civil servants. The opportunities for political control have been extended, as the Senior Executive Service has been opened to political appointments. The Reagan Administration took full advantage of its opportunities to employ loyalists in what formerly had been career civil service positions,[95] and subsequent presidents have also utilized their personnel powers in an attempt to control government.[96]

Britain and some Commonwealth systems such as Canada are unusual in the apparent willingness of political ministers to accept advice from career civil servants, and the willingness of the ministers to allow those civil servants to control most day-to-day business within the ministry.[97] Even here, however, analogues of the *cabinet* system may be tried. For example, the Mulroney government in Canada created the post of Chief of Staff within each department, allowing the minister to make political appointments that mirrored the career civil service structure at the top of the ministry. The Blair government in Britain has also been adding some political advisors to the public payroll at the ministerial level. Neither of these is as well-institutionalized as the *cabinet* system but do represent some movement in that direction.

One interesting variant of organization by staff and line, or more generally organization by process, occurs in Sweden and Finland.[98] Here the two usual functions of the public bureaucracy – development and the execution of public policy – are organizationally divided into two separate organizations. First, the ministries are charged with the development of public policy. The ministries are small, and their work is confined to staff type work – planning, coordination and program development. The actual execution of public programs is left to a set of administrative boards, which are independent of the ministries, although linked through the budgetary process and a number of other ways, and perform "line" functions of actually implementing programs.

Although the distinction between functions is clearest in Sweden, to some extent all contemporary governments are developing such distinctions. First, countries such as the United Kingdom, New Zealand and the Netherlands are developing administrative structures more similar to those of Sweden.[99] The use of agencies was one of the most pervasive features of administrative reform in the 1980s and 1990s. More generally, the separation of politics and administration is being achieved through privatizing implementation of many public activities, and using "third-party" mechanisms of service delivery.[100] In essence, government organizations continue to perform the staff work while private or quasi-public organizations perform the line functions.

The use of cabinets and the politicization of the upper echelons of government point to the extent to which organization by line and staff corresponds to the old adage about the separation of politics and administration.[101] Staff functions can be equated with the political functions of advocating programs and formulating policy, and assuring that the independent civil servants do what their political masters intended. Line functions are more normally associated with the execution of policy in a rather routine fashion. As we have pointed out – and will deal with more extensively later – the dichotomy between politics and administration is largely a false one, but it is important to note the extent to which it has been incorporated into public administration.

The corps. Another possibility for organization by process is organization by corps or by some other internally homogeneous administrative bodies. The corps system is best developed in France but has been copied by a number of other countries, especially those derived from a French or Napoleonic administrative tradition.[102] The concept of the corps is a body of administrators with similar educational backgrounds and similar professional skills. Each of the *grands corps* is, in theory, specialized by function; in practice they have a pervasive influence on French administration and have adopted somewhat broader roles. Suleiman noted that it was virtually obligatory to have a member of the *Inspection des Finances* as a member of a ministerial *cabinet* or for *directeur*, if for no other reason than to have a ready avenue for appeal and consultation on the budget.[103] The Socialists have been less dependent upon that one *Inspection* than previous governments, but it remains a powerful component of French administration. Members of the other corps are also included in a number of *cabinets*. In Spain the *cuerpos* also tend to dominate a particular ministry, although again some of the more influential have a pervasive impact in government.[104]

These corps are specialized by function but together provide a high level of leadership within the public service, which might be lacking without the corps structure and the *esprit de corps* that such a system engenders. Moreover, the isolation of the *grands corps* from a number of the usual administrative pressures, their prestige and their individual intellectual and managerial capabilities allow them to enforce standards of uniformity throughout the administration, so that this form of organization by function contributes to the maintenance of centralized government in France.

Several functions have been found to be amenable to organization by corps or process. Engineering has been one, and any number of countries have specialized engineering corps within their national civil services or militaries, for example, the Army Corps of Engineers in the United States. If we look at administration broadly, the military officer corps and the diplomatic services could be considered as specialized corps, and as rather obvious cases of organization by function or process. Also, as with the Inspectorate of Finances in France, financial inspectors are frequently organized as a separate branch of administration, to ensure their impartiality in auditing public accounts. This precaution goes so far, in the United States, as to isolate them almost entirely from the rest of the public service (in the General Accounting Office). Other inspectorates in government, such as H.M. Inspectors of Schools in Britain or Inspectors General in the United States, also benefit from separation from the remainder of the public bureaucracy.[105] Thus, we can say that those functions that can benefit from being organized by process tend to be those that require: (1) technical training or highly professional skills; (2) a high degree of internal commitment and *esprit de corps*; or (3) impartiality and isolation from other portions of the bureaucracy and from political pressures. With the erosion of many *ex ante* controls over bureaucracy, as a result of the reform processes, governments are turning more often to inspectorates as means of providing effective and independent *ex post* controls.[106]

Multiple advocacy. Another possible implication of organization by process is that an organization may build in competing visions of policy and with that multiple advocacy. For example, the Federal Trade Commission in the United States is organized with economists and lawyers in different divisions of the Commission.[107] Before the FTC can act, these two divisions must discuss the case and reconcile their competing professional and theoretical visions of anti-monopoly legislation. Further, of the two anti-trust organizations in the federal government, the FTC is more dominated by economists while the anti-trust division of the Department of Justice is more controlled by lawyers. The organization by process may appear redundant but it does prevent organizations from developing excessively narrow standard operating procedures. It has the potential of correcting policy and implementation errors before they occur.

Summary. In summary, organization by process can make some useful distinctions between the tasks of various civil servants and agencies, but as a general organizing principle it appears to be unwieldy. Even in its limited form, it tends to engender political conflicts between those who (at least from their own perspective) do the work of the civil service, and those who "merely" plan, coordinate and control. Likewise, organization by corps as a special example of organization by process can engender similar political conflicts and rivalries directed against an elite group with broadly defined competencies who appear all too ubiquitous in the exercise of their tasks, and all too close to those who are responsible for making decisions. Thus, as will be said again, the organization of the public service is a problem not only for the administrative scientist, but for the politician as well. Both must attempt to provide smooth and efficient government, and both must try to protect their own interests through organizational devices.

Organization by clientele

The third possible basis for organization is the clientele served by the organization. Clientele groups who are presumed to have special needs or whose lifestyles, industries, or other characteristics are considered sufficiently distinctive may justify a separate organization for them and their interests. There have been two apparent reasons for developing clientele-based organizations: (1) to be able to provide better services for a special set of clients (especially those with political clout), such as veterans, urban dwellers and farmers; or (2) conversely, at once to assist and to *control* segments of the population lacking such political clout, such as Native Americans and foreign workers.

The important fact about both of the justifications for clientele groups is that they result in an organization that can become an obvious avenue of political influence by the clientele. That is, organization by clientele, even when undertaken for the purpose of regulation, generally results in more direct group influence on administration than might be found in other forms of organization. The reasons for this are perhaps obvious; they will be developed more in Chapter 6, discussing of the politics of administration.[108] But we should point out here that in client-based organizations, a process of exchange and mutuality almost inherently results. The clientele group needs the access to government decision making provided by the public organization, and the agency in turn requires popular support from its clientele in political conflicts. Further, those public organizations may owe their existence to the activities of particular clientele groups and must therefore cater to the demands of those groups more than by others in the "public interest."

Perhaps the most important manifestation of this tendency toward co-optation and symbiosis between clientele and administration occurs in so-called independent regulatory boards. The underlying conception of these boards, as they are constituted in the United States and used increasingly in other political systems, is that they should serve as administrative *qua* judicial bodies controlling the activities of some portion of the economy or society. The boards are made independent to prevent excessive partisan influence from being exerted over their decisions. They are intended to regulate in the public interest and without regard for political considerations.

No matter how commendable the idea of independence may be in theory, they are almost certainly doomed to failure in practice. Many of the activities that these boards were intended to regulate are among the most sensitive and societally important, including transportation, energy and communication.[109] But, by being isolated from political demands in their tasks of regulating these industries, the boards are isolated from political support as well. They essentially lack any strong and direct connection with the executive and cannot, therefore, easily appeal for assistance in financing, staffing and general support for their regulatory functions. Any such executive interference might be regarded as antithetical to the depoliticized and non-partisan conception of these boards. Thus the independent regulatory boards must seek other sources of political support, with the most likely source being the very interests they were designed to regulate. The point of this argument, then, is that organization *by* clientele may rapidly change into organization *for* clientele.

The "capture" idea concerning regulatory commissions has come under substantial intellectual attack. It is argued, for example, that the fundamental point that they often do develop special relationships with the regulated industry remains intact.[110]

Organization on the basis of clientele may also be implemented at the sub-departmental level and may have many of the same consequences at that level. At this level, however, the consequences will be primarily intra-organizational conflict, rather than through isolation and subversion of the public purpose. As a department or agency develops bureaus devoted to assisting or even regulating a particular client group, those bureaus frequently become captives of that group and become spokesmen for them in policy-related matters. Like the organization of departments by client, the sub-departmental agencies may also need political support for political conflicts. Their clientele can provide such support, but the price of that support is favorable treatment or regulation.

It is often difficult to distinguish client-based organizations from area-based organizations. Many of the same problems of organizations being captured arise with either basis of organization. Two interesting and countervailing examples of the interaction of organizations with client groups are those of the forest rangers and the engineering corps. In these examples, local communities, or, more specifically, local business interests, operate as clients. In the case of the United States

Forest Service, the organization attempts to counteract possible local influences on regulation. One task of a forest ranger is to regulate the use of national forests for commercial purposes such as lumbering and grazing. The Forest Service uses as a general guideline that no ranger should remain in the same community for more than two years. This policy is to prevent him from becoming too closely integrated into the local community and therefore too sympathetic to pleas from local businessmen for excessive use of the forests.[111]

An alternative example is provided by civil engineering corps in both France and the United States – and probably elsewhere. These organizations generate a significant portion of their political support by integrating themselves into local communities and, at times, providing special treatment for the localities. Providing these services to local communities produces a huge reservoir of political support should the executive or legislature seek to curtail the autonomy of the corps.[112] The first of these examples shows an attempt to prevent clientele organization from subverting the formal goals of the organization; the second shows a use of client organization to enable the agency to succeed in its political conflicts (albeit perhaps at the expense of a broader public interest).

Everything else being equal, organization by client is likely to become more common in the future. Part of the reform agenda of many governments during the 1980s and 1990s has been greater concern for the role and rights of clients as the "consumers" of government services.[113] This shift in the focus of management will mean that even organizations that are not organized primarily around clientele may have to organize at a sub-departmental level to ensure that they are responsive to their clients. This change in structure may, in turn, build-in some of the same problems of capture by the clientele and conflicts with overall public sector goals that are encountered with organizations built around their clients. Further, and somewhat paradoxically, it will generate more general problems of democratic accountability.[114]

Organization by clientele is at times difficult to avoid. There are powerful political pressures to organize government to benefit certain groups in society, and there is a certain logic to such organization when the needs of a clientele are distinctive. On the other hand, this form of organization has a number of possible dangers. It is difficult for the agency organized in this manner to remain detached from its clientele and to be able to administer programs objectively and in the "public interest." They may trade their politically powerful connections to one group for separation from, and often conflict with, the remainder of government.

Organization by purpose

The final possibility for organizing administration is the principal purpose, or goal, of the organization. This mode of organization is not always clearly distinguishable from the others already discussed. For example, is a Ministry of Agriculture organized on the basis of its major purpose – the promotion of agriculture – or is it organized around a ready-made clientele group – farmers? Organization by purpose, perhaps more than the other criteria mentioned, highlights the lack of exclusiveness of this set of categories of studying government structure. In some ways most government organizations have some aspects of all four principles.

Organization by purpose does, however, raise some important issues in public administration. The first is, where do organizational goals and purposes come from? Presumably, the legislation establishing an organization will specify the tasks to be performed by that organization. In most cases, however, these tasks are put forth in only the barest outline, allowing substantial latitude for future elaboration and interpretation. In theory, the elaboration of these organizational goals will be primarily a political process involving the imposition of externally developed goals by politically selected leaders. However, given the barriers facing those political masters, the impact of external leaders on organizational goals is less than would be thought by listening to the formal discussions of the roles of civil servants and politicians.[115]

If the goals of public organizations are not determined by their political leaders as usually thought, where do they come from? The most obvious answer is that they are generated internally. If that is true, we come to one of the most commonly noted pathologies of formal organizations: the displacement of goals.[116] There is a tendency in organizations gradually and almost imperceptibly to shift from what might be called public goals to what may be termed private goals. Even though the organization was established to fulfill some need in society, over time organizational survival and possibly organizational development may supersede that societal goal. Anthony Downs discusses this process in terms of the tendencies of individuals within organizations to shift from zealot to conserver roles.[117] When young, organization members seek to achieve societal goals through their actions in the public service, but over time, because of a natural aging process, the growth of personal responsibilities, and perhaps cynicism about the possibility of social change, they become less interested in producing change but more interested in personal gain and security. Their major goals in office become: (1) to continue the existence of the agency; (2) possibly to expand its role and budget; and (3) finally to do something for the society. Similarly, L. B. Mohr identifies a difference between transitive goals of organizations and reflexive goals. Transitive goals are those directed at some outside target group, such as a clientele, while the reflexive goals are those directed at internal maintenance.[118] Even when there are attempts to create measureable goals for an organization, the organization may attempt to shift these in its own favor.[119]

Even if we do not accept the cynical view that after some (unspecified) point in their existence agencies become self-serving, we must understand that over time the goals pursued by an agency generally come to mean what the incumbents of the roles want them to mean. In other words, government organizations develop cultures and ideologies concerning the tasks that lie before them and the means of completing those tasks. Further, by controlling selection, socialization and, to some degree, retention of their members, organizations tend to preserve this ideology even when confronted with new members.[120] The organizational conception of goals and the means of achieving those goals are often functions of the period of political and organizational socialization of the incumbents to the leadership positions within the organization. For example, most social service agencies in the United States were developed or expanded dramatically during the New

Deal era. The basic philosophy of social improvement at the time was to throw money at the problem, and to some extent to impose middle-class values on clients of the agency.[121] These organizations were not particularly receptive to innovative or client-centered approaches to social problems, and so new organizations had to be created outside the existing framework to take new initiatives in social policy.

The existing organizational cultures led to the creation of new organizations such as the Office of Economic Opportunity in President Johnson's War on Poverty with a (then) very different means of addressing the problems of poverty; there is a contemporary analog in the "social exclusion" units in the Blair government in the United Kingdom. Similarly, social service organizations all over the world now have to face the (attempted) imposition, by the political system, of new goals about lower-cost service, privatization and self-reliance. Fulfilling these new goals may also require some restructuring and the creation of new organizations. In France, the need to produce rapid action outside the structure of existing organizations produced the *administrations de mission*, which are given a very specific mission, and often a specific lifetime as well.[122] The problems of organizations being locked in time and committed to a particular manner of doing things is not confined to domestic agencies. For example, the foreign offices of many Western nations are still very heavily influenced by a "Munich mentality," which dictates that any attempt at compromise with an enemy is a sign of weakness and a prelude to further threats and demands.

A final example of differences in goals held by an organization and those which others expect it to hold is found in many Third World countries that inherited essentially elitist and conservative civil services from their former colonial masters. These civil services frequently have not been organized or staffed to undertake the massive programs of social and economic development expected of them, and some were even hostile to these programs ideologically. Thus there have been frequent expressions of hostility from the political leaders of these countries toward these seemingly recalcitrant civil servants who were impeding programs of rapid social change.[123] The major point to be made in this discussion of goal setting is that the purpose of a public agency is not necessarily the one outlined in the enabling legislation or in official policy statements. Setting goals is a political process, and often it is an intra-organizational political process hidden from public scrutiny and public control.

Following the question of origin of goals is the question of what the agency does when it runs out of things to do. There are a number of rather amusing examples of agencies that have long outlived their stated purposes and have become essentially sinecures for the remaining employees. Our concern is not with blatant inefficiency and redundancy, but rather with the problem of the succession of goals in an organization. That is, how can an agency shift its principal concerns and orientations from one objective to another? Given the discussion above, we must first assume that this would be a difficult task, but we do know that organizations undergo such shifts in order to survive. There are a number of examples of this type of goal succession in private organizations; two commonly cited examples are the March of Dimes and the YMCA.[124] The examples from public organizations are perhaps less clear, but they exist. One of the most common in European nations of late has been the transformation of agencies formerly concerned with the management of colonial territories into offices of overseas development and aid to underdeveloped countries. While these agencies are still dealing with essentially the same clienteles geographically, their goals, operations and politics have been greatly changed. Similarly, the end of the Cold War has forced the military in many countries to reconceptualize its mission and take on tasks such as "peace-keeping," involving retraining and restructuring. We can see that agencies can and do shift goals, but it requires some strong impetus to do so, with the loss or decline of agency support – both from the budgetary process and the public – being the most important impetus in public organizations.

The discussion of organization by purpose has focussed on agencies that have, or at least hope to have, a stable mission and a long and healthy life. We should remember, however, that governments sometimes attempt to deal with a mission with short-term, temporary organizations. This is true whether the purpose is to provide a particular type of service or to coordinate the programs already being provided by other, more permanent organizations. While the conventional wisdom is that temporary public organizations *are* permanent, we should still investigate the use of short-term approaches to solving problems.

One form of organization of this type is a function of the need to coordinate activity in a policy area in which a number of existing organizations have some role without assigning any one of those organizations a pre-eminent role. The creation of the posts of "Drug Czar" and "AIDS Czar" in the United States is an example of this strategy. It is, to some extent, like creating a central agency (see above, pp. 155–6) but differs in two respects. First, these are hoped to be temporary institutions that will cease to exist once the problem is "solved." Second, these offices deal with a single issue and a narrow range of organizations rather than attempting to coordinate policies and spending across government. Indeed, these organizations often become advocates for the policy area as well as referees among contending organizations, rather than allocators of scarce resources (money, personnel, authority) among organizations.

Another organizational device for solving the coordination problem in a particular policy area is to create interministerial or interdepartmental committees. One of the most elaborate structures of this type exists in France, which has committees existing at three levels (civil servants, ministerial and presidential) to cope with conflicts and overlaps.[125] Rather than employing a single "czar" that can utilize authority to impose that coordination, the coordination in this model results from bargaining and the exchange of information. A similar pattern can be found in the Scandinavian countries that utilize large advisory committees for ministries. These committees generally include representatives of other ministries that have some interests and activities in the policy area.[126]

Summary

We have discussed four broad methods of organizing government and public administration. As was noted, the lines between these categories are not always clear. What is clear is that none of them offers the perfect solution to the problem of organizing public services, and each has its advantages and disadvantages. The decisions to use one or another should be dependent upon two factors. One is the nature of the service to be delivered. Some services, such as police and fire protection, require dispersion by area, while others work very well with a highly centralized structure. Some services, such as accounting, appear to function better when all the experts are concentrated, while others function better when expertise is dispersed. The architect of the public service must be clear that he or she understands the nature of the service to be provided by any organization being created.

The second factor that must be understood is the nature of the political system in which our architect is functioning. For example, a political system that is deeply divided by language or race or other primordial sentiment will – everything else being equal – function better with as many functions as possible organized by area or client. On the other hand, a society that values expertise and control will – again, everything else being equal – function better with as many organizations as possible organized by purpose. The nature of public organizations must conform not only to the wishes of organizational theorists, but also to the political realities of the nation.

Internal organization

To this point we have been largely examining the problems of organizing the public service at the national level, with some attention to problems within agencies that are analogous to those at a more macroscopic level of analysis. We turn now to a brief discussion of internal organization and management, particularly problems of hierarchical control and communication within public sector agencies.

Hierarchical control, or the chain of command, and the associated need to communicate information and decisions form a central core of the study of formal organizations.[127] Those who draw neat, pyramidal organization charts assume that the individuals on the top of the hierarchy are responsible for making decisions and that their decisions are binding for all members of the organization. Likewise, it is assumed that it is the task of subordinates to communicate all relevant information upward, so that the right decisions can be made by those at the top. Unfortunately for those who would like to see organizations function this way, such orderly management of organizations is rarely encountered in practice. In fact, many argue that the best way to understand organizations is not as a system of hierarchy but as a system of cooperation and bargaining.[128] In such an approach to organizations, all levels of the organization are seen as having resources and power.[129] Consequently, management increasingly involves building coalitions, within and across organizations, rather than issuing commands.

The non-hierarchical approach to organizations may be especially applicable to the public sector. In the first place, public sector organizations lack clear definitions of success or failure; they have no analogue of profit in the business world.[130] Managers therefore can be less certain about the orders that should be given and the relative effectiveness of employees. Also, the employees of most public-sector organizations are still permanent – or almost permanent – civil servants. This makes it difficult to employ many of the threats and incentives that would be available in private sector organizations.[131] Third, because of their public nature, government organizations must consider not only their workers but also their clients when coalitions are being built. Thus they must be especially sensitive to the needs of those clients as well as of the lower-echelon workers who have regular contact with the clients. Finally, because of the mixture of political and civil service personnel in most public organizations, there are often differences in the long-term commitments of individuals to the organization, different motivations and different perceptions of the time in which change should be brought about.[132] All these factors make the effective management of public organizations a particularly trying task.

The major purpose of hierarchical control is to create uniformity of an action by subordinates within the organization. One of the hallmarks and presumed benefits of bureaucratic organization is the elimination of personal discretion and caprice from the decisions taken by the organization. Such uniformity and predictability may be especially important for public organizations because they must be sure that clients are treated fairly and that their rights are respected. Unfortunately for those attempting to manage organizations, individuals like discretion and power, not so much to be able to deal capriciously with their clients as to have the opportunity to exercise some personal initiative. Further, they enjoy being able to establish personal relationships – for example, those not strictly governed by the rules of the organization – with both superiors and subordinates. Many formal organizations tend to deny these opportunities to their members, with any number of adverse consequences both for individuals and for goal attainment within the organization. Leaving aside the consequences for individuals, let us look at the consequences for the organization.

One of the most important consequences of hierarchy is the isolation of strata within the organization.[132] Superior–subordinate relationships tend to become rigidified, with diminished opportunity for other than formal communication across strata. Each stratum becomes socially isolated from others, and each tends to develop its own norms of compliance with the directives of superiors. These norms are rarely in violation of the formal norms of the organization; in fact, there is a tendency to comply ritualistically with rules and directives while possibly subverting the real purposes of the organization. Thus, complaints about bureaucratic red tape and inefficiency may largely result from the need of lower echelons to protect themselves from their superiors by complying with the letter of regulations and refusing to take any personal initiative outside those regulations that might subject them later to punishment. Their compliance is real, but, paradoxically, by complying with the rules they may reduce the effectiveness and efficiency of the organization. This is another aspect of goal displacement, in that the rules become an end in themselves rather than a means to accomplish the goals of the agency. While, to some extent a universal phenomenon, strata isolation and formalistic compliance does appear to be especially characteristic of some cultures, especially those that do not like face-to-face authority relationships.[133]

Associated with the isolation of strata is a tendency for organizations to foster the development of redundant channels of communication that can be beneficial to an organization.[134] Redundancy was a tactic adopted by Franklin Roosevelt as president to prevent the existing bureaus from sabotaging or delaying his New Deal programs. The existence of dual hierarchies in Soviet administrative practice was perhaps an extreme version of redundancy intended to ensure that there is a check on information and performance at all stages of the administrative process. With the end of Communist Party rule a hierarchy loyal to the president replaced that of the party and the redundant party and government hierarchies. To some degree the existence of ministerial *cabinets* in France and Belgium, and the Executive Office of the President in the United States, are further uses of redundant structures to check on the performance of administration. Downs further mentions the possibility of building in overlapping and redundant structures as a means of ensuring the flow of relatively unbiased information within organizations.[135] Likewise, Niskanen and others – adopting an economic approach to the study of public bureaucracy – have argued that redundancy and competition could improve the efficiency of government and reduce its total cost.[136] Interestingly, all these schemes involve the construction of organizations quite at odds with those that might be advocated by traditional students of management and public administration, for whom unity of command and the lack of overlapping functions were seen as two of the prime elements of proper organization.

Variations in internal organization

The problems of internal organization are general, and we should expect variation by both nation-state and the characteristics of the particular policy area being administered. Differences occur between those two broad categories of Western and non-Western systems, or developed and underdeveloped countries.[137] Despite their own variations, Western cultures are more accepting of impersonality, hierarchy and bureaucracy than are non-Western cultures. Thus we might expect the dysfunctions of bureaucracy outlined above to be more evident in non-Western cultures if attempts were made to enforce such a system. Attempts to depersonalize administration and policy through rules and procedures have been shown in a number of instances to be rather ineffective as a means of achieving ends in those systems. The formal structures of most bureaucracies in the non-Western world do conform quite closely with those of Western administration, in part as a function of colonial inheritance and in part because of the need to comply with certain formalities in order to receive aid from developed nations and international organizations. However, the actual operations of these structures tend to be quite different from the form, with non-bureaucratic criteria still tending to supersede the rules, procedures and hierarchy of the formal structure. Some of the bureaucratic dysfunctions related to communication may be overcome by a reliance on communalism and non-bureaucratic criteria in recruitment, as may in fact some problems of rigidity with clients. What is given up is the entire justification for having bureaucratic structure in the first place; namely, a high level of uniform behavior and client treatment. Such behavior is not, however, highly valued in many Third

World countries and actually may be regarded as being as immoral as Westerners might regard graft or nepotism. Western nations appear to show substantial variation in their prospects for effective bureaucracy. These were discussed to some extent in the discussion of the "administrative cultures" of these countries.[138] What is important is the extent to which cultural differences tend to ease or exacerbate dysfunction in bureaucracy. One of the tendencies noted by Crozier in discussing these problems is the influence of general conceptions of authority and equality on the bureaucratic structure of organizations.[139] For example, he noted that, perhaps as a function of generalized patterns of deference and acceptance of authority, the organizational structure of British ships tended to be substantially less complex and less dependent upon impersonal rules than those of American ships. American crewmen, apparently socialized in more individualistic mores, were less willing to accept the personal authority of a superior, and formalized rules had to be devised to take the personal element out of rule enforcement. At the other end of the spectrum, societies in which authority is both accepted and revered, and where those in authoritative positions tend to view their roles somewhat paternalistically, can function with simple organizational structures and a relative absence of bureaucratic rules and still obtain high levels of uniformity in behavior. In their study of managerial attitudes cross-nationally, Haire, Ghiselli and Porter found that there were several distinct blocs of Western nations in terms of their conceptions of the management role: Nordic, Anglo-American and Latin-European.[140] The differences among these groups were rather subtle but pointed to important differences in attitudes toward managerial practice and authority even among Western nations. Also, Roos and Roos found that cultural variables were important in explaining how Turkish managers approached their tasks of promoting development.[141] More recently, Hofstede identified distinct groups of countries on the basis of their managerial cultures.[142] Differences between types of organizations also depend on the tasks they are intended to perform. This is a major argument of *contingency theory* as an approach to understanding organizations in both the public and the private sectors. Unfortunately, however, such work as has been done in the public sector has found relatively little relationship between the variables usually used in this approach and the structuring or performance of public organizations.[143]

On the other hand, Amitai Etzioni has provided one useful set of broad categories.[144] He classifies organizations according to the type of power that the organization seeks to use over its members and the type of compliance of the members. Etzioni classifies power as either coercive, remunerative, or normative. The compliance of organizational members may be alienative, calculative, or moral. Although there may be mixed organizations, the three model types of organizations in this typology are coercive–alienative, remunerative–calculative and normative–moral. Rather obviously, a normative–moral organization such as a church or even a highly-committed public bureau is able to do its job effectively with a simpler organizational structure, fewer impersonal rules and less dysfunctional activity than would other types of organization. On the other hand, such an organization would have more difficulty in modifying its goals and retaining its personnel than would an organization relying on remunerative power. Some public organizations of all three types exist, and managers, although they may not conceptualize it in exactly these terms, have to know how to employ the appropriate incentives with each type of organization.

Other schemes for classifying organizations depend more on the nature of the services they provide. Blau and Scott use a classification of organizations based upon the criterion of *cui bono*, or who benefits.[145] Most public organizations fall into their category of commonweal organizations, in that the public at large is the prime beneficiary. Other public organizations would be service organizations in that the prime beneficiaries are the clients; for example, social service agencies. Again we can see that the dynamics of organizations whose intention it is to provide a service to the public at large, generally free and with no exclusions, will have different organizational problems than an organization whose intention is to serve only a limited number of individuals, on the basis of the particular needs of those individuals. Moreover, the clients (consumers of services) for the commonweal organization tend to be considerably less dependent upon those organizations than clients of service agents, so that, for service organizations, most conflicts emerge with the political representatives of the public at large over expense and responsibility.

One successful attempt to analyze organizations using some aspects of the contingency approach can be found in the work of Perrow (along with that of Thompson and Tuden).[146] This scheme attempts to relate the characteristics of the problem of policy area to the type of decision making that is likely to occur.[147] Although both schemes (see Figure 4.1) were intended to have universal applicability, they also have relevance to problems of public administrative agencies. In Thompson and Tuden's scheme, the same types of variation in the agreement on ends and the agreement on means occur among public agencies as they do more generally. The examples in Figure 4.1 may not be universally agreed upon, but they should point out that, first, there is such variation, and second, that it will have consequences for public organizations. Likewise, the Perrow scheme, based

| | **Preferences** | |
	Agreement	Disagreement
Perception of Causation — Agreement	Programmed Decisions (public health)	Bargaining (incomes policy)
Perception of Causation — Disagreement	Pragmatic (comprehensive education reform)	Inspiration (research and development)

Figure 4.1 Typology of policy problems for administration

Sources: Derived from James D. Thompson and Arthur Tuden, "Strategy, Structure, and Process of Organizational Decision," in *Comparative Studies in Administration* (Pittsburgh: University of Pittsburgh Administrative Science Center, 1959); Charles Perrow, *Organizational Analysis* (Belmont, Calif.: Wadsworth, 1970, pp. 80–91)

largely on the characteristics of technology and raw materials, has also been given examples from among public organizations. The assumption is that organizations dealing with a stable (or stabilized) raw material, such as prisons, will have a vastly different type of organizational structure than will those dealing with essentially unknown materials, such as research and development agencies.[148] Of course, the characteristics of the individuals likely to be employed in such agencies and the tasks set out for them will also have an impact, but it does appear useful to look at the correspondence between organizations and the raw materials – most commonly human – with which they must deal.

Reorganization

To this point we have been discussing administrative structure in a largely static manner; we have been looking at a still photograph. Unfortunately – both for analysts and for many people in government – such stability is rarely achieved, and in fact there is a great deal of change and reorganization in government structure. It may be more accurate to look at a moving picture. In fact, it appears that when governments have little else to do, or when they feel themselves impotent to make any real changes, they settle for reorganization.[149] By doing so, at least they can appear to have done *something* and they can tell their critics that some changes are being implemented to solve the problems. This is not to deny that reorganization can make a difference, just as the structure of government itself makes some difference in performance. Organizational change is not, however, the panacea that some politicians and some students of public administration believe that it is.

The 1980s was a decade of very intense organizational activity in government. One of the most common forms of activity was the division of large cabinet departments into a number of smaller, quasi-independent organizations. These go under the title of agencies (United Kingdom), special operating agencies (Canada) and a variety of other names. At its most extreme in New Zealand, this form of organization leaves a very small center for government and places most operations in quasi-independent agencies or "corporations."[150] These new organizational forms move the implementation structures of these governments in the direction of that of Sweden mentioned above. The impact of these reforms has been to grant greater autonomy to organizations involved in implementation and often to expose them to pressures for accountability through the market rather than through conventional political means.

Many of the efforts at reform during the 1980s and early 1990s were more procedural than structural. There has been a greater emphasis on public management, as opposed to traditional civil service values, as the means of directing action within organizations.[151] Even in countries such as France and the Scandinavian countries with well-respected public services there were large-scale movements to "modernize" and "renew" the public service.[152] In addition to the decentralization to agencies and similar sub-departmental bodies, there have been a number of structural reforms of civil service systems. In particular, the idea of the Senior Executive Service contained in President Carter's Civil Service Reform Act[153] was transplanted to a number of other countries.[154] In general, these reforms have created a cadre of senior executives that can be deployed within the public sector to address important managerial problems.

As important as the changes in the industrialized democracies have been, those occurring in the formerly communist countries of Eastern Europe are even more dramatic.[155] These changes have involved not only eliminating the ideological character of the communist regime but attempting to catch up with decades of managerial and organizational changes that have occurred in Western countries. This is all being done in the context of broader social, economic and political change, and in the context of relative economic scarcity. This is a formidable task, and it is still too early to comment on the success or failure of the efforts. They do, however, constitute interesting laboratories for understanding processes of administrative change.

We cannot hope to review the vast literature on government reorganization in all countries in the world in this one section, nor perhaps in several large books.[156] We will, however, make several principal points about administrative reorganization and change in its comparative context. The first of these points is that change in government is more common than many people believe. One school of thought argues that government organizations border on the immortal: once they are created they never go away and rarely change. This school of thought is very popular among the general public – especially those generally critical of government – and has been championed by some academics as well.[157]

This characterization of immortality and immutability, however, does not appear to be accurate; change is very common among government organizations. In one study of government organizations in the United States, we found almost 2,000 organizational changes in the federal government between 1933 and 1986.[158] Some of these changes were terminations, some were formations of entirely new organizations, but most were changes of existing organizations and groups of organizations. Similar patterns were found for organizations in the United Kingdom and more tentative analysis of the structure of government in Sweden and France reveals rather similar patterns of organizational change.[159] Thus, if we look at government at a sufficient distance, it appears to be a constant – for example, the United States has added only nine cabinet departments since the first cabinet was formed – but if we look more carefully, the picture of stability is rapidly replaced by one of reorganization and change. Therefore we need to understand organizational change better than we do.

A second point to be made about reorganization is that it matters, but not too much. Reorganization is sometimes denigrated as simply being an exercise in shuffling boxes on organization charts. This may be the case, but simply changing the location of an organization may determine how it operates and how it makes public policy.[160] For example, the Coast Guard in the United States has been located in a number of cabinet departments in its 200-year history; most recently it was moved from the Department of the Treasury to the Department of Transportation. This movement means that, everything else being equal, it will now receive more memos about boat safety and fewer about smuggling. Thus reorganization may have a subtle but nonetheless real impact on the pattern of policy that emerges from a government organization.

On the other hand, reorganization for efficiency may be, as one scholar and practitioner argued, a "will o' the wisp."[161] From the point of view of efficiency, all forms of organization may be equally good or bad. That is, broad factors, such as whether or not it is public and what the particular organizational culture of the society is, will typically have a greater impact on efficiency than will the particular form of organization selected. In fact, the major efficiency benefit from reorganization appears to derive simply from doing it; the shake-up of an organization in the reorganization process may be as beneficial as any particular organizational format that could be chosen. Even drastic organizational changes, such as privatization, may have only ephemeral efficiency benefits. These findings about reorganization have not, of course, prevented politicians, practitioners and academics from expending a great deal of time and energy in discussing and advocating specific reorganizations. It is simply too appealing and apparently too obvious a thing to do to stop simply because it may have few demonstrable effects.

The final point to be made about government reorganization is that it is manifestly a political exercise. It is easy, if one believes that efficiency gains really are possible, or if one believes in the proverbs of good administration discussed above, to think that reorganization is primarily a managerial or administrative activity. Structural changes in government, however, are better considered as an exercise in which political benefits are created. Some, or perhaps even most, of these benefits may be symbolic. Reorganization activity is an indication that government is addressing a problem and that it has some real concern about the citizens impacted by the problem. On the other hand, some of the political benefits may be real. Reorganization of government in a multi-ethnic society for example, may give a group that considered itself oppressed by a dominant culture greater representation in decision making and perhaps the ability to manage a portion of its own affairs.[162] Even when there are no ethnic sensibilities involved, reorganization may give greater power to some groups. For example, the almost continuous reorganization of the Department of Trade and Industry in the United Kingdom has variously advantaged different groups concerned with different economic development and regional issues in that country.[163]

In summary, governments continue to attempt to get their organizational structure right, but may be doomed to failure. There may be no right structure, only structures that are more or less satisfactory. Reorganization is still, however, a valuable activity in government. It is valuable in part because it may be able to shape policy outcomes in ways desired, if the flow of communications and influence is altered. It is also valuable as a political recognition of the importance of some issues and of some elements of the society. So long as the real benefits are understood, along with the symbolic values, government reorganization need not be the waste of time it is sometimes considered to be.

Summary

This chapter has provided a brief overview of the complex topic of the structure of public organizations. As such, it has been largely an introduction to the problems and questions that arise, rather than a set of definitive answers to those questions. Nevertheless, it should be clear that the design and redesign of public administra-

tion is more than a technical exercise. There are a number of rather broad questions concerning the nature of the establishment as a whole that must be answered
by political leaders or constitution writers rather than by the civil service. These
answers may, in turn, greatly influence the overall effectiveness of the public establishment as well as the satisfaction of the public with that establishment.

Beyond these questions, there are any number of problems with the internal
organization of agencies and with the managing of an ongoing public enterprise.
These must be considered in the light of the particular nation in question and the
characteristics of the task involved. The basic task of organizational analysis,
however, is to design organizations that enable their officials to have at least the
possibility of providing effective services to the population. No organization chart
or diagram of responsibilities can ensure this, so the task of the manager is
largely to make it possible and perhaps even probable. The ultimate success or
failure of the agency will remain with the individuals who inhabit it.

Notes

1 That having been said, there is relatively little recent work on the design of public organizations. For several notable exceptions see Karen Marie Hult and Charles E. Wolcott, *Governing Public Organizations: Politics, Structures and Institutional Design* (Pacific Grove,
   CA: Brooks/Cole, 1990); David Weimer, *Approaches to Institutional Design* (Dordrecht:
   Kluwer, 1995).
2 See, for example, Jack H. Nott and Gary J. Miller, *Reforming Bureaucracy: The Politics of
   Institutional Choice* (Englewood Cliffs, NJ: Prentice-Hall, 1987).
3 Gulick and Urwick, *Papers on the Science of Administration* (New York: Institute of Public
   Administration, 1937); Herbert Simon, *Administrative Behavior* (New York: Free Press, 1947).
4 On the role of traditions see B. Guy Peters, "The Anglo-American Administrative Tradition," in John Halligan, ed., *Public Administration in the Anglo-American Countries* (Cheltenham: Edward Elgar, 2001).
5 Heidrun Pohl, "Verwaltungsrechtsschütz," in Klaus König, ed., *Verwaltungsstrukturen der
   DDR* (Baden-Baden: Nomos, 1991).
6 See Klaus Konig, H. J. van Oertzen and F. Wagener, *Öffentliche Verwaltung in der Bundesrepublik Deutschland* (Baden-Baden: Nomos, 1981).
7 These are employed under general labor law rather than under the statutes governing the
   Beamten.
8 Some members of the inherited civil service were also compromised by their too faithful
   implementation of some of the more repugnant acts of the East German government and
   could not be accepted into the service of the unified State.
9 Hans Ulrich Derlien, "German Unification and Bureaucratic Transformation," *International Political Science Review,* 14 (1994), 319–34.
10 Gerhard Braunthal, *Political Loyalty and the Public Service in West Germany: The 1972
   Decree Against Radicals and its Consequences* (Amherst, MA: University of Massachusetts
   Press, 1990).
11 For a view from the perspective of the Scientologists, see Herbert Druks, *Discrimination
   Against Scientology in Today's Germany* (New York: H. M. Druks, 1997).
12 See Patrick Dunleavy, "The Architecture of the British Central State," parts 1 and 2, *Public Administration,* 67 (1989), 249–75, 391–417; Anne Davies and John Willman, *What's Next?: Agencies, Departments and the Civil Service* (London: Institute for Public Policy Research, 1991).
13 "Symposium on Improving Management in Government," *Public Administration,* 66
   (1988), 429–55.

14   See, for example, Ken Young, "Metropolis R.I.P.?," *Political Quarterly* (1986), 36–46.

15   Derived from Brian W. Hogwood, "Towards a New Structure of Public Employment in Britain," *Policy and Politics*, 26 (1999), 321–41.

16   D. C. Hague, Bruce L. R. Smith and Anthony Barker, *Public Policy and Private Interests: The Institutions of Compromise* (London: Macmillan, 1975); Brian W. Hogwood, "Quasi-Government in Scotland: Scottish Forms within a British Setting," in Anthony Barker, ed., *Quangos in Britain* (London: Macmillan, 1982)

17   Mike Fogden, "Managing Change in the Employment Service," *Public Money and Management*, 13 (1994), 9–16.

18   Christopher Hood, "The Hidden Public Sector: The Quangoization of the World?," in Franz-Xaver Kaufmann, Giadomenico Majone and Vincent Ostrom, *Guidance, Control and Evaluation in the Public Sector* (Berlin: deGruyter, 1986).

19   P. Holland and M. Fallon, *The Quango Explosion* (London: Conservative Political Centre, 1978).

20   Quangos are convenient in part because they provide a number of patronage positions with which government can reward its supporters.

21   Sir Stafford Northcote and Sir Charles Trevelyan, *Report on the Organization of the Permanent Civil Service* (London: House of Commons, 1853).

22   Committee on the Civil Service, *Report* (June, 1968), Cmnd. 3638 (The Fulton Report).

23   *Inquiry into Civil Service Pay* (The Megaw Report), Cmnd. 8590 (London: HMSO, July, 1982).

24   There is now also somewhat more mobility between local and central government, but still not so much as in Germany.

25   Sir John Hoskyns, "Whitehall and Westminster: An Outsider's View," *Fiscal Studies*, 3 (1982), 162–72.

26   See Gavin Drewry and Tony Butcher, *The Civil Service Today*, 2nd edn (Oxford: Basil Blackwell, 1988), pp. 166–70.

27   Thierry Pfister, *La Republique des fonctionnaires* (Paris: Albin Michel, 1988).

28   Jean-Luc Bodiguel and Luc Rouban, *Le fonctionnaire detrone* (Paris: Presses de la Fondation nationale des sciences politiques, 1991), pp. 99–103.

29   Marie-Christine Kessler, *Les grands corps de l'Etat* (Paris: Presses de la Fondation nationale des sciences politiques, 1986).

30   Luc Rouban, *Les cadres superieurs de la fonction publique et la politique de modernisation administrative* (Paris: Fondation nationale des sciences politiques, 1992).

31   Jean Francois Kesler, *L'ENA, la societe, l'Etat* (Paris: Berger-Levrault, 1986).

32   Rene Remond, Aline Coutrot and Isabel Boussard, *Quarante Ans de Cabinets Ministeriels* (Paris: Presses de la Fondation des sciences politiques, 1982).

33   Anne Stevens, *"L'Alternance* and the Higher Civil Service," in Philip G. Cerney and Martin A. Schain, eds, *Socialism, the State and Public Policy in France* (London: Frances Pinter, 1985); Monique Dagnaud and Dominique Mehl, "L'Elite Rose Confirmee," *Pouvoirs*, 50 (1989), 142.

34   Alice Rawsthorn, "So Far the Omens Are Not Ideal," *Financial Times*, June 24, 1993.

35   Howard Machin, *The Prefect in French Public Administration* (London: Croom Helm, 1978).

36   Jean-Paul Costa and Yves Jegouzo, eds, *L'administration françaises face aux défis de la decentralisation* (Paris: Editions STH, 1988).

37   Jack Hayward, *Governing France: The One and Indivisible Republic*, 2nd edn (New York: Norton, 1983), pp. 24–5.

38   Kurt Samuelsson, *From Great Power to Welfare State* (London: George Allen and Unwin, 1968).

39   See B. Guy Peters, "Sweden: The Explosion of Public Employment," in Richard Rose *et al.*, *Public Employment in Western Nations* (Cambridge: Cambridge University Press, 1985).

40   D. Soderlind and O. Petersson, *Svensk forvaltningspolitik* (Uppsala: Diskurs, 1988).

41   See Daniel Tarschys and Maud Eduards, *Petita* (Stockholm: Petita, 1975); Bengt Jacobssen, *Hur styrs forvaltningen* (Lund: Studentlitteratur, 1984).

42   Hugh Heclo and Henrick Madsen, *Policy and Politics in Sweden: Principled Pragmatism* (Philadelphia, PA: Temple University Press, 1987), pp. 10–12.

43 Peters, "Sweden: The Explosion of Public Employment," in Richard Rose *et al.*, *Public Employment in Western Democracies* (Cambridge: Cambridge University Press, 1985).

44 See A. Beckerus and A. Edstrom, *Doktrinskiftet: Nya ideal i svenskt lederskap* (Stockholm: Svenska Dagbladet, 1988).

45 Maivor Sjolund, "Rewards at the Top: The Swedish Case," in Christopher Hood and B. Guy Peters, *Rewards of Higher Public Office* (London: Sage, 1993).

46 Paul C. Light, *Thickening Government* (Washington, DC: The Brookings Institution, 1996).

47 The large divisions are the General Schedule composed largely of white-collar workers and the Wage Schedule largely for blue-collar workers. The Post Office has its own pay and grading system as do some other organizations such as the Tennessee Valley Authority and the CIA.

48 Patricia W. Ingraham and Carolyn Ban, *Legislating Bureaucratic Change: The Civil Service Reform Act Of 1978* (Albany: SUNY Press, 1984).

49 Patricia W. Ingraham, *The Foundation of Merit: Public Service in American Democracy* (Baltimore, MD: Johns Hopkins University Press, 1995).

50 See Harold Seidman, *Politics, Power and Position*, 5th edn (New York: Oxford University Press, 1998).

51 The SBA is kept outside the Department of Commerce in large part because it is felt that commerce is more interested in big business than in smaller businesses.

52 Typically each organization will report to a functional committee in each house and also to an expenditure subcommittee in each house.

53 Christopher F. Edley, *Administrative Law: Rethinking Judicial Control of the Bureaucracy* (New Haven, CT: Yale University Press, 1990).

54 Luther Gulick, "Notes on the Theory of Organizations," in L. Gulick and L. F. Urwick, eds, *Papers on the Science of Administration* (New York: Institute of Public Administration, 1937), pp. 3–50; Schuyler Wallace, *Federal Departmentalism* (New York: Columbia University Press, 1941).

55 The Office for the Mezzogiorno is actually located in the office of the Prime Minister.

56 Richard Rose, *Ministers and Ministries* (Oxford: Clarendon Press, 1987).

57 These have now been turned into agencies within a single ministry but the area structure remains.

58 Colin Campbell and George Szablowski, *The Superbureaucrats: Structure and Behaviour in Central Agencies* (Toronto: Macmillan of Canada, 1979).

59 Gulick, "Notes on the Theory of Organization. . .," *op. cit.*

60 Robert Fried, *The Italian Prefects* (New Haven: Yale University Press, 1967).

61 Jean-Pierre Worms, "Le prefet et ses notables," *Sociologie du Travail*, 12 (1966), 249–75; Jean-Claude Thoenig, *L'Ere des Technocrates* (Paris: L'Harmattan, 1987).

62 Douglas E. Ashford, *Policy and Politics in France, Living With Uncertainty* (Philadelphia: Temple University Press, 1982).

63 *op. cit.*

64 Ulrich Kloti, "Switzerland," in Donald C. Rowat, ed., *Public Administration in Developed Democracies* (New York: Marcel Dekker, 1988); Heinrich Siedentopf, "West Germany," in *ibid.*

65 Mirjan R. Damaska, *The Faces of Justice and State Authority* (New Haven, CT: Yale University Press, 1986).

66 See Jorgen Gronnegaard Christensen, "The Scandinavian Welfare State: Institutions of Growth, Governance and Reform," *Scandinavian Political Studies*, 20 (1997), 367–86.

67 See chapters by Richard Parry, Ian Thomas and P. N. Bell in Richard Rose, *Ministers and Ministries* (Oxford: Clarendon Press, 1987).

68 R. A. W. Rhodes, *Beyond Westminister and Whitehall* (London: Unwin Hyman, 1988).

69 This was decreasingly true in Britain during the Thatcher government as the conflict over the community charge (poll tax) revealed. See Arthur Midwinter and Claire Monaghan, *From Rates to the Poll Tax* (Edinburgh: University of Edinburgh Press, 1993).

70 Michael Keating, "Does Regional Government Work?: The Experience of France, Italy and Spain," *Governance*, 1 (1988), 162–83.

71 Robert D. Putnam, Robert Leonardi and Raffaella Nanetti, *Making Democracy: Civic Traditions in Modern Italy* (Princeton, NJ: Princeton University Press, 1993).

72 Joseph Jamar and Wolfgang Wessels, *Community Bureaucracy at the Crossroads* (Bruges: De Tempel, 1985); Heinrich Siedentopf and Jacques Ziller, *Making European Policies Work: The Implementation of Community Legislation by Member States* (London: Sage, 1988).

73 Yves Meny, Pierre Mueller and Jean-Louis Quermonne, *Adjusting to Europe* (London: Routledge, 1998).

74 Rory Watson, "Who Tops the Table in Europe," *The European*, July 11, 1993.

75 One of the most complete evaluations of these changes is Jorgen Westerstahl, *Ett forskningsprogram: Den kommunale sjalvstyrelsen* (Stockholm: Almqvist and Wiksell, 1971).

76 See Jeffrey S. Sax, "Is There a Leviathan in Your Neighborhood?," *American Economic Review*, 79 (1989), 560–7.

77 See Kirkpatrick Sale, "The Polis Perplexity: An Inquiry into the Size of Cities," *Working Papers for a New Society* (January/February, 1978), 64–77.

78 US Department of Commerce, Bureau of the Census, *Census of Governments*, 1992 (Washington, DC: Government Printing Office, 1995). See also Kathyrn A. Foster, *The Political Economy of Special Purpose Government* (Washington, DC: Georgetown University Press, 1997).

79 James S. Fesler, *Area and Administration* (University, AL: University of Alabama Press, 1949).

80 F. Muller-Rommel, "The German Chancellor's Office," in B. Guy Peters, R. A. W. Rhodes and Vincent Wright, eds, *Administering the Summit* (London: Macmillan, 2000).

81 Campbell and Szablowski, *The Superbureaucrats* (Toronto: Macmillan of Canada, 1979).

82 Peter Self, *Administrative Theories and Politics* (London: Allen and Unwin, 1972), p. 128.

83 The head of the Treasury – the Chancellor of the Exchequer – is more than just another minister, and has substantial authority within Cabinet, especially when in agreement with the Prime Minister. See Peter Hennessy, *Cabinet* (Oxford: Basil Blackwell, 1986).

84 Self, *Administrative Theories and Politics*, pp. 133–4. Mrs Thatcher as Prime Minister attempted to perform some of the coordination function herself, along with a much expanded Prime Minister's Office.

85 The Blair concept of "joined up government" is, however, placing a greater emphasis on this coordination capacity at the center.

86 See B. Guy Peters, "The Structure of Government: Issues of Concepts and Theory," in Colin Campbell and B. Guy Peters, eds, *Organizing Governance: Government Organizations* (Pittsburgh, PA: University of Pittsburgh Press, 1988).

87 For an analysis, see William H. Starbuck, "Organizational Growth and Development," in James G. March, ed., *Handbook of Organizations* (Chicago: Rand-Mcnally, 1965), pp. 496–8.

88 Geert Bouckaert, Derry Ormond and B. Guy Peters, *A Governance Agenda for Finland* (Helsinki: Ministry of Finance, 2000).

89 B. Guy Peters, "Managing Horizontal Government: The Politics of Coordination," *Public Administration*, 76 (1998), 295–312.

90 This is especially true of financial departments responsible for examining and controlling public budgets. See Chapter 7.

91 Remond, Coutrot and Boussard, *op. cit.*

92 Anne Stevens, *op. cit.*

93 Luc Rouban, "La politisation des Fonctionnaires en France: Obstacle ou Necessite?," *Revue francaise d'administration publique*, 86 (1998), 167–82.

94 Leo Moulin, "The Politicization of Administration in Belgium," in Dogan, *The Mandarins* (New York: John Wiley, 1975), pp. 163–84.

95 Peter M. Benda and Charles H. Levine, "Reagan and the Bureaucracy," in Charles O. Jones, ed., *The Reagan Legacy* (Chatham, NJ: Chatham House, 1988).

96 Paul C. Light, *Thickening Government* (Washington, DC: The Brookings Institution).

97 But see F. F. Ridley, "The British Civil Service and Politics: Principles and Traditions in Flux," *Parliamentary Affairs*, 36 (1983), pp. 28–49.

98 Jon Pierre and Peter Ehn, "The Welfare State Managers: Higher Civil Servants in Sweden," in E. C. Page and V. Wright, eds, *The Higher Civil Service in Western Europe* (Oxford: Oxford University Press, 2000).

99 Jonathan Boston, "Reorganizing the Machinery of Government," in John Martin Boston, June Pallot and Pat Walsh, *Reshaping the State* (Auckland: Oxford University Press, 1991); J. L. Boxum, J. de Ridder and M. Scheltema, *Independent Administrative Bodies* (Kluwer: Deventer, 1989).

100 Donald F. Kettl, *Sharing Power: Public Governance and Private Markets* (Washington, DC: The Brookings Institution, 1993); Christopher Hood and Folke Gunnar Schuppert, *Delivering Public Services in Western Europe* (London: Sage, 1988).

101 Colin Campbell and B. Guy Peters, "The Politics/Administration Dichotomy: Death or Merely Change?," *Governance*, 1 (1988), 79–109.

102 See B. Wunder, ed., "The Influence of the Napoleonic 'Model' of Administration on the Administrative Organization of Other Countries," Special issue of *Cahiers d'Histoire de l'Administration*, 4 (1995).

103 Ezra Suleiman, *Politics, Power and Bureaucracy in France: The Administrative Elite* (Princeton: Princeton University Press, 1974), pp. 188–91.

104 Carlos Alba, "Spain," in Jon Pierrre and B. Guy Peters, eds, *Politicians and Bureaucrats in Administrative Reform* (London: Routledge, 2001).

105 Paul C. Light, *Monitoring Government: Inspectors General and the Search for Accountability* (Washington, DC: The Brookings Institution, 1993); Gerald Rhodes, *Inspectorates in British Government* (London: Allen and Unwin, 1981).

106 Christopher Hood, Colin Scott, Oliver James, George Jones and Tony Travers, *Regulation Inside Government* (Oxford: Oxford University Press, 1999).

107 Marc Allen Eisner, *Antitrust and the Triumph of Economics* (Chapel Hill: University of North Carolina Press, 1991).

108 See Chapter 5.

109 Richard A. Harris and Sidney Milkis, *The Politics of Regulatory Change* (New York: Oxford University Press, 1989).

110 For a general discussion of these questions see Mathew D. McCubbins, "The Legislative Design of Regulatory Structure," *American Journal of Political Science*, 29 (1985), 721–48.

111 Herbert Kaufman, *The Forest Ranger: A Study in Administrative Behavior* (Baltimore: Johns Hopkins University Press, 1967), pp. 176–83. This rapid movement from place to place has the additional organizational advantage of building the image of the service as a distinct organization and career.

112 Arthur Maas, *Muddy Waters: The Army Corps of Engineers and the Nation's Rivers* (Cambridge, MA: Harvard University Press, 1951); Daniel Mazmanian and J. Nienaber, *Can Organizations Change?: Environmental Protection, Citizen Participation and The Army Corps of Engineers* (Washington, DC: Brookings Institution, 1979); Thoenig, *L'Ere des technocrates, op. cit.*

113 Organization for Economic Cooperation and Development, *Administration as Service, The Public as Client* (Paris: OECD, 1987); Kenneth Kernaghan, "Career Public Service 2000: Road to Renewal or Impractical Vision?," *Canadian Public Administration*, 34 (1991), 551–72.

114 B. Guy Peters, "Is Democracy a Substitute for Ethics?," in Richard A. Chapman, ed., *Public Sector Ethics in the New Millennium* (Aldershot: Ashgate, 2000).

115 See Richard Rose, *The Problem of Party Government* (London: Macmillan, 1976); B. Guy Peters, "Public Bureaucracy and Public Policy," in Douglas E. Ashford, ed., *History and Context in Comparative Public Policy* (Pittsburgh: University of Pittsburgh Press, 1992).

116 Robert Merton, "The Unanticipated Consequences of Purposive Social Action," *American Sociological Review*, 1 (1936), 894–904; "Bureaucratic Structure and Personality," *Social Forces*, 18 (1940), 560–8.

117 Anthony Downs, *Inside Bureaucracy* (Boston: Little, Brown, 1967), pp. 98–9.

118 Lawrence B. Mohr, "The Concept of Organizational Goal," *American Political Science Review*, 67 (1973), 470–81.

119   J. Bohte and K. J. Meier, "Goal Displacement: Assessing the Motivation for Organizational Cheating," *Public Administration Review*, 60 (2000), 173–82.

120   Joanne Martin, *Cultures in Organizations* (New York: Oxford University Press, 1992).

121   Edward D. Berkowitz, *America's Welfare State: From Roosevelt to Reagan* (Baltimore: Johns Hopkins University Press, 1991).

122   Gerard Timsit, *Administrations et Etats: etude comparee* (Paris: Presses universitaires de France, 1987), pp. 98–110.

123   See, for example, Merilee S. Grindle, ed., *Politics and Policy Implementation in the Third World* (Princeton: Princeton University Press, 1980); Jean-Claude Garcia-Zamor, "Problems of Policy Implementation in Developing Countries," in Ali Farazmand, ed., *Handbook of Comparative and Development Public Administration* (New York: Marcel Dekker, 1991).

124   One of the classic works is David L. Sills, *The Volunteers* (Glencoe, ILL: The Free Press, 1957).

125   Jacques Fournier, *Le travail governmentale* (Paris: Dalloz, 1987).

126   Robert B. Kvavik, *Interest Groups in Norwegian Politics* (Oslo: Universitetsforlaget, 1976); Olof Petersson, *Maktens Natverk: En undersokning av regeringskansliets kontakter* (Stockholm: Carlssons, 1989).

127   Arthur L. Stinchcombe, *Information and Organizations* (Berkeley, CA: University of California Press, 1990).

128   An early statement of this is Mary Parker Follett, "The Process of Control," in L. Gulick and L. F. Urwick, *Papers on the Science of Administration, op. cit.*

129   See Chester Barnard, *The Functions of the Executive* (Cambridge: Harvard University Press, 1960).

130   Neil Carter, Rudolf Klein and Patricia Day, *How Organizations Measure Success: The Use of Performance Indicators in Government* (London: Routledge, 1992).

131   Of course, the marketizing reforms of the last two decades have placed more public employees on short-term contracts.

132   Michel Crozier's analysis of organizations depends heavily upon the concept of isolation of strata. See his *The Bureaucratic Phenomenon* (Chicago: University of Chicago Press, 1964), pp. 190–208.

133   The prototype as developed by Crozier was France. Much the same may be true of Third World countries in which face-to-face authority relationships may be a threat to existing social orders.

134   Martin Landau, "The Rationality of Redundancy," *Public Administration Review*, 29 (1969), 346–58.

135   See Gordon Tullock, *The Politics of Bureaucracy* (Washington, DC: Public Affairs Press, 1965), pp. 137–42; Jonathan Bendor, *Parallel Systems* (Berkeley: University of California Press, 1985).

136   William Niskanen, *Bureaucracy and Representative Government* (Chicago: Aldine/Atherton, 1971); for an assessment of this argument, see Andre Blais and Stephane Dion, eds, *The Budget-Maximizing Bureaucrat* (Pittsburgh: University of Pittsburgh Press, 1992).

137   Donald J. Horowitz, "Is There a Third-World Policy Process?," *Policy Sciences*, 22 (1989), 197–212.

138   See pp. 43–50.

139   Crozier, *The Bureaucratic Phenomenon*, pp. 231–6.

140   Mason Haire, Edwin E. Ghiselli and Lyman W. Porter, *Managerial Thinking: An International Study* (New York: John Wiley, 1966).

141   L. L. Roos and N. P. Roos, *Managers of Modernization* (Cambridge, MA: Harvard University Press, 1971).

142   Geert H. Hofstede, *Culture's Consequences: International Differences in Work-Related Values* (Beverly Hills, Sage, 1984).

143   D. C. Pitt and B. C. Smith, *Government Departments: An Organizational Perspective* (London: Routledge and Kegan Paul, 1981).

144   Amitai Etzioni, *A Comparative Analysis of Complex Organizations* (New York: Free Press, 1961), pp. 3–21.

145 Peter Blau and Richard Scott, *Formal Organizations* (San Francisco: Chandler, 1962).

146 Charles Perrow, *Organizational Analysis: A Sociological Vie*w (Belmont, CA: Wadsworth, 1970); James D. Thompson and Arthur Tuden, "Strategy, Structure and Process of Organizational Design," in *Comparative Studies in Administration* (Pittsburgh: University of Pittsburgh Administrative Science Center, 1959).

147 For a general argument on the importance of the differences among policy areas, see Gary Freeman, "National Styles and Policy Sectors Explaining Structured Variation," *Journal of Public Policy*, 5 (1985), 467–96. Unlike the contingency schemes discussed below, Freeman discusses nominal policy areas such as health, education and defense.

148 W. Henry Lambright and Albert H. Teich, "The Organizational Context of Scientific Research," in Paul C. Nystrom and William H. Starbuck, *Handbook of Organizational Design* (Oxford: Oxford University Press, 1981).

149 See Robert Miewald and Michael Steinman, eds, *Problems in Administrative Reform* (Chicago: Nelson-Hall, 1984).

150 Jonathan Boston, "Reorganizing the Machinery of Government," in John Martin Boston, June Pallot and Pat Walsh, *Reshaping the State* (Auckland: Oxford University Press, 1991); Graham Scott, Peter Bushnell and Nikitin Salle, "Reform of the Core Public Sector: The New Zealand Experience," *Governance*, 4 (1990), 138–67.

151 Christopher Pollitt, *Managerialism and the Public Services* (Oxford: Basil Blackwell, 1990); Andrew Massey, *Managing the Public Sector* (Aldershot: Edward Elgar, 1992).

152 Luc Rouban, "La modernisation de l'Etat et la fain de la specificite francaise," *Revue francaise de science politique*, 40 (1990), 521–45; Johan P. Olsen, "Modernization Programs in Perspective," *Governance*, 4 (1991), 133–57.

153 Patricia W. Ingraham and Carolyn Ban, *Legislating Bureaucratic Change: The Civil Service Reform Act of 1978* (Albany: State University of New York Press, 1984).

154 Patricia W. Ingraham and David Rosenbloom, *The Promise and Paradox of Civil Service Reform* (Pittsburgh: University of Pittsburgh Press, 1992); Colin Campbell and John Halligan, *Political Leadership in an Age of Constraint* (Pittsburgh: University of Pittsburgh Press, 1992).

155 See Theo A. J. Toonen, "Analyzing Institutional Change and Administrative Transformation: A Comparative View," *Public Administration*, 71 (1993), 151–68; Joachim Jens Hesse, "Administrative Modernisation in Central and East European Countries," *Staatswissenschaft und Staatspraxis*, 2 (1991), 197–217.

156 See Gerald Caiden, *Government Reorganization Comes of Age* (Berlin: DeGruyter, 1991); Johan P. Olsen and B. Guy Peters, *Learning From Administrative Reform* (Pittsburgh: University of Pittsburgh Press, Scandinavian University Press, 1996).

157 Herbert Kaufman, *Are Government Organizations Immortal?* (Washington, DC: The Brookings Institution, 1976); Paul C. Nystrom and William H. Starbuck, *Handbook of Organizational Design* (Oxford: Oxford University Press, 1981), pp. xv–xvi.

158 B. Guy Peters and Brian W. Hogwood, "The Death of Immortality: Births, Deaths and Metamorphoses in the US Federal Bureaucracy," *American Review of Public Administration*, 18 (1988), 119–33.

159 Brian W. Hogwood, "Much Exaggerated: Death and Survival in British Quangos," Paper presented at meeting of Political Studies Association, Leicester, April, 1993.

160 Lester Salamon, "The Question of Goals," in Peter Szanton, ed., *Federal Reorganization: What Have We Learned?* (Chatham, NJ: Chatham House, 1981).

161 Rufus Miles, "Notes for a President Bent on Reorganization," *Public Administration Review*, 37 (1977), 155–62.

162 The most extreme example of this would be splitting the culturally relevant ministries in Belgium, e.g. education and communications, into French and Flemish sections each with cabinet status.

163 Brian W. Hogwood, "The Rise and Fall and Rise of the Department of Trade and Industry," in Colin Campbell and B. Guy Peters, eds, *Organizing Governance, Government Organizations* (Pittsburgh: University of Pittsburgh Press, 1988).

Politics and public administration

The preceding chapters were, in essence, the foundation for this and the following three chapters. We have discussed the relationship of public administration to its environment through an elaboration of the social and economic surroundings of administration, the cultural milieu in which administration functions, attempts of public administration to recruit personnel from that environment and the patterns of organizational structure within the bureaucracy. In this chapter we begin to examine the relationship of politics to the conduct of public administration and to the policy decisions made by administrators. It is sometimes appealing to think about public administration as management, but this would be misleading. The interaction of administration with both formal and informal political actors in the society has a profound impact on the behavior of administrators and on their decisions. The extent of this influence, and the manner in which it is exerted, are the subjects of investigation in this chapter and those that follow.

Perhaps the best place to begin this discussion is by again noting the survival of the ancient proverb of public life that politics and administration are separate enterprises and that such a separation is valid both in the analysis of the institutions and behaviors of government as well as in the actual conduct of public business.[1] Although any number of authors have attempted to lay this proverb to rest, it has displayed amazing powers of survival and reappears in any number of settings in any number of political systems.[2] We must therefore assume that this proverb, if not entirely or even partially valid from an analytic perspective, serves some purpose for administrators and politicians. What does the artificial separation of these two activities assume to do that makes the survival of this "useful fiction" so desirable for both sets of actors?

For administrators, this presumed separation of administration and politics allows them to engage in politics (organizational rather than partisan) without the bother of being held accountable politically for the outcomes of their actions. Further, they can engage in policy making – presumably using technical or legal criteria for their decisions – without the interference of political actors who might otherwise recognize political or ideological influences on policies and make demands upon them for the modification of those policies.[3] Thus, the actions of administrators may be regarded by politicians, the public and even by themselves as the result of the simple application of rational, legal, or technical criteria to questions of policy. This apparent professional detachment may make otherwise unacceptable decisions more palatable to the public.[4] This appearance of rational and technical decision making is heightened when, as in the Anglo-American democracies, great efforts are made to make the civil service politically neutral between parties in office.

The separation of politics and administration also allows a certain latitude to politicians which they might otherwise lack. In essence, the separation of these two types of institutional choices facilitates many of the difficult decisions of modern government being made by individuals who will not have to face the public at a subsequent election.[5] Thus it may allow politics to shape, or at least influence, an important decision that will be announced by a "non-political" institution that will not be held publicly accountable. Further, this conception that political and technical decision making can be separated in public life has allowed political reformers to remove many important public decisions as far as possible from the realm of "politics" – meaning largely corrupt machine politics and other pejorative aspects of political life. Doing this results in many important governmental functions being transferred from partisan political control to independent agencies, bureaucracies and technocratic elites.[6]

It is obviously assumed that the administrators who make decisions in these settings are, in fact, insulated from political pressures and are able to make decisions *pro bono publico* because of that insulation. As we will show, however, these artificial separations of the political and administrative functions, instead of removing decisions from political influence, may actually subject them to different and more invidious types of political influences. These influences are believed to be more invidious because, having already been defined out of existence, they are difficult for the citizenry to identify and even more difficult to control. Further, the capacity of the bureaucracy to make binding rules for society may be hidden to all but the most astute members of society, given the relatively arcane procedures used.[7]

Having still not completely exorcised the demon of the separation of political and administrative choice, we are now at least in a position to understand why the actors in the policy process may be willing to accept such a doctrine and why scholars may come to believe them. Thus, although scholars may discount the dichotomy between politics and administration in the abstract, when they confront the realities of how the actors perceive their roles, they must accept at least the psychological reality of the separation. We will therefore go on to discuss the political environment of administrative decision making as well as the political influences on those decisions. In so doing, it is useful to distinguish several basic dimensions of the political activity of administrators.

The first of these dimensions is labeled "internal–external," or perhaps more appropriately "policy–survival." On one end of this dimension is political activity within the agency which seeks to take a variety of inputs from pressure groups, partisans, the political executive, and any number of other sources and develop a policy. On the other end of the continuum are political activities directed toward the maintenance and growth of the organization – purposive and reflexive goals in Mohr's terminology.[8] These two forms of politics are rarely so neatly separated in real life, and each contributes to the successful accomplishment of other goals. However, we can usefully distinguish the two forms for analytic purposes and discuss the types of influences likely to be brought and the major loci of political conflict for each.

The second dimension of administrative politics is one of officialdom, or formality. Administrators interact both with other governmental officials (legislators, the political executive, other administrators, representatives of sub-national governments) and with unofficial political actors (largely the representatives of pressure groups). Again, these interactions are not always clearly separable, for officials often carry with them a continuing commitment to the cause of particular interests, and pressure groups may function in quasi-official capacities. However, it is useful to make such a distinction for analytic reasons because the style of the interaction, its legitimacy and its probable influences on policy will vary considerably as a function of the type of actor involved as well as a function of the type of agency activity involved.

The two dimensions of political activity by public administration, along with examples of each category of activity, are presented in Figure 5.1. We show four categories based upon a cross-classification of the two dimensions. Thus we will be looking at administrative politicized actions that have a characteristic of being both formal and informal, and directed more toward policy formation or survival. Our example of internal (policy)–formal administrative politics is the relationship between an upper echelon civil servant and the cabinet minister he or she is designated to serve.[9] Ministers, who are charged with extensive political chores in addition to managing a large and complex bureaucratic organization, cannot be reasonably expected to have a sufficient grasp of the issues involved or of the information available for many policy decisions; such decisions will, therefore, be produced through either consultation with, or delegation to, their senior administrative officials.[10] Consequently, interactions between ministers and civil servants have become one of the dominant features of the policy-making process and must be better understood in order for the analyst to predict the outcomes of the policy process in contemporary political systems. Some progress has been made in formulating models to assist in that understanding, but substantial refinement and conceptualization are still required.[11]

External–formal administrative politics are perhaps best identified in two ways. The first is the process of public budgeting, in which administrative agencies have to seek their continued and expanded funding from other institutions of government. A number of authors note that this is perhaps the most crucial locus of administrative politics because of its pivotal role in the future programs of the agency.[12] It is certainly a political activity that is the focus of an enormous amount of effort on the part of the agencies and one that has received considerable attention in the popular and scholarly literature. Budgeting involves the mobilization of considerable political support for the agency, if it expects to be successful in obtaining its desired funding, and consequently is an activity that will involve considerable informal politics – lobbying by both interest groups and the agency itself – as well.

The second important type of external–formal politics is the politics of public accountability through which other formal bodies may seek to curb the autonomy of the public bureaucracy. Any number of institutions in the public

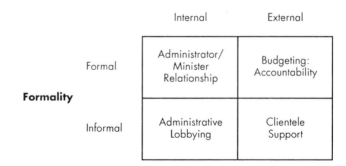

Figure 5.1 Types of bureaucratic politics

sector have some responsibility for seeing that the public bureaucracy does not abuse its discretion and acts in accordance with the laws that established its organizations and the laws that it administers. Given the importance of both of these types of "external–formal" politics in contemporary politics, they will be discussed in chapters of their own.[13]

Internal–informal administrative politics is probably best characterized by the relationship of pressure groups and administration in the formation of policy. In virtually all political systems, attempts are made by interest (or pressure) groups to influence public decisions.[14] The openness of public administration to these influences and the relative success of groups in obtaining the policies they seek are again a function of a number of institutional, political and cultural factors that will require further discussion and elaboration. However, except in the most totalitarian society, there is generally considerable opportunity for group action and for group influence on the process of policy formulation in bureaucracy.

Finally, external–informal administrative politics is best characterized by relationships between interest groups, the public at large, and public bureaucrats attempting to develop support for their programs and for the continued success of the agency in the budgetary process. Those bureaucrats have several means of trying to influence even the inattentive public, including advertising and the promotion of a positive image among the public, for example, "the Marine Corps needs a few good men."[15] As was noted above, this type of political activity is inextricably bound to the ability of pressure groups to influence policy and the ability of agencies to survive in a competitive environment.

Now that we have some general picture of the scope and variety of administrative politics, we begin our more intensive discussion of the politics of administration by examining the informal side of these interactions – that is, the relationship between administration and pressure groups, political parties and other unofficial political groups who are seeking to influence the course of public policy or whom the administrators rely upon in justifying their future programs and funding. Our discussion of the relationships of political parties to administration is substantially briefer than that of pressure groups. This is so in large part because the major influence of party appears to be manifested through official mechanisms, when members of the party occupy formal positions of government and attempt to impose their views on the bureaucracy. Since, almost by definition, political parties are motivated principally by the opportunity to hold public office rather than the opportunity to influence policy through lobbying activities, it makes more sense to look at the official rather than the unofficial side of partisan activities. The major exception to that generalization would be small parties that know they have little or no chance of holding office and hence function in many ways as interest groups.

Bureaucracy and pressure groups

We must suppose that the conflict between the demands of pressure groups and the role of bureaucracy in decision making is, in most societies, one of the most basic in government. On the one hand there is an institution of government, representing the authority of the state, impartiality, and in the *Rechtstaat* tradition of Germany even a judicial temperament. On the other side of the conflict are groups that by their very nature represent only specialized narrow interests seeking some preferential treatment from government. This type of division of the role of the state and the role of interests is perceived differently in different political cultures. The conflict may not be as intense in Norway as in, say, France, and may not be so intense in either of those as in many less-developed societies. Interestingly, however, the conflict between bureaucracy and interest groups has been sufficiently ameliorated in most societies so that the two sets of organizations are able not only to coexist but even to cooperate effectively.[16] Further, it is especially interesting that societies that have had among the most positive conceptions of the public bureaucracy – Germany, the Netherlands and the Scandinavian countries – have been much more successful in accommodating the role of pressure groups into policy making than have political systems that have a less exalted conception of their civil servants.[17] In fact, a relatively positive evaluation of the civil service may be *required* to allow the civil servants sufficient latitude in dealing with the pressure groups and in making accommodations to their demands for this relationship to be successful.

Given the apparent conflict in the roles of these two sets of political actors and institutions, how are they able to cooperate so well, and so often in making policy? In the first place, the stereotypical descriptions of the policy roles of these two sets of actors obscure some of the reality of their interaction. The civil service rarely speaks or acts as a unified entity. Rather, it is divided into numerous organizations, each with its own narrow policy interests that happen to correspond to the interests of certain pressure groups. Thus, agencies within the bureaucracy, especially a public bureaucracy as decentralized as that of the United States or the Scandinavian countries, may have a great deal in common with the interest groups concerned with the same policy issues. Furthermore, pressure groups in most Western democracies have found that acting in a less blatantly self-interested manner in politics may produce greater policy benefits for them and their members in the long run.

Second, conflict between interest groups and the bureaucracy is minimized, as both sets of actors need each other to be successful. Administrators need the political support and influence of pressure groups in their external relationships with other political institutions, and they also need the information supplied by pressure groups for making and defending policies. Likewise, the pressure groups need access to the political process and influence over the decisions that are taken. This mutual need, given the fragmentation of decision making in modern governments, is the basic dynamic explaining the frequent cooperation between public bureaucracies and pressure groups.[18] We are now left with the more formidable task of describing how the two partners in this exchange interact, and what the effects are of differing patterns of interaction.

We can classify the interactions between pressure groups and bureaucracies into four basic types. This classification, along with the presumed characteristics and effects of each type, are illustrated in Table 5.1. This classificatory scheme places the interaction between bureaucrats and pressure groups into four broad categories, constituting an informal continuum from situations in which pressure-

Table 5.1 Types of interaction between pressure groups and bureaucracy

Types	Scope	Influence	Style	Impact
		Characteristics		
Legitimate	Broad	Great	Bargaining	Redistribution/self-regulation
Clientela	Narrow	Moderate	Symbiosis	Self-regulation/distribution
Parantela	Narrow	Moderate	Kinship	Regulation/distribution
Illegitimate	Variable	None/great	Confrontation	None/redistribution

group influence on policy is regarded as illegitimate to cases where it is regarded as legitimate and necessary. These four categories are themselves rather broad and may contain substantial variation, but it is still useful to use such a scheme to begin to understand the broad differences in relationships between these actors. Associated with each of these patterns of interaction are categories describing the manner in which the relationship is carried on and its impact on policy.

Legitimate interactions

The first category of interactions between bureaucrats and pressure group actions is labeled "legitimate." This denotes that in some political systems, not only are pressure groups an accepted fact of political life, but they are also legally and officially involved in the process of making and administering public policy. Indeed, in this conception of government the involvement of interest groups with the public sector is not only legitimate, it is almost necessary. The major examples of this type are found in Germany, the Low Countries and Scandinavia, but a number of other countries have adopted legitimate roles for pressure groups in more limited forms.

Corporatism and public administration.   One variant of the legitimate relationship between interest groups and government has been described as "corporatism" or "neocorporatism."[19] This is actually a rather extreme version of the legitimate relationship in that it tends to restrict the number of interest groups involved in the policy process and, to some extent, to incorporate that limited number into the state apparatus rather directly. Phillipe Schmitter defines corporatism as an arrangement characterized by a "limited number of singular, compulsory, non-competitive, hierarchically ordered and functionally differentiated" groups that are given a virtual license to represent their particular area of competence.[20] He further differentiates *societal corporatism*, in which the private associations dominate the state in policy making, from *state corporatism*, in which the state is the dominant actor.[21] This definition of corporatist arrangements implies a monopolistic relationship of interest groups in a particular policy area and sanctioning of this relationship by some state organization. This pattern stands in contrast to the more open bargaining arrangements thought to characterize pluralistic interest group systems.

Gerhard Lehmbruch develops a somewhat less restrictive version of corporatism, in which the relationship between interest groups and government is less formalized and there is greater bargaining among the groups themselves during the process of policy making.[22] This variant, which is more reminiscent of pluralism, is termed "liberal corporatism," or "corporate pluralism."[23] Subsequent research and writing on corporatism has differentiated the concept even further, using terms such as "meso-corporatism" and "the negotiated economy" to describe somewhat less restrictive variations of the general pattern of relationships between the public sector and private interests.[24]

As initially formulated, none of these approaches to the relationship between interest groups and government had very much to say concerning the relationship of groups and the public bureaucracy. The major policy area discussed by the theorists of corporatism was the setting of national economic policy, as in "Harpsund Democracy" in Sweden or *Konzertierte Aktion* in the Federal Republic of Germany. These meetings of the major peak organizations of labor and management with the government involved negotiations about the future course of wages, prices and profits. This was "high politics," directly involving top government officials, rather than the more mundane politics of policy making by bureaucracy.[25]

But corporatism does have some relevance for this more ordinary type of policy making. One of the major effects, similar to those that will be pointed out for the *clientela* relationships between interest groups and the bureaucracy, is to restrict the advice and ideas coming into the bureaucracy.[26] In the (arguably) corporatist arrangements between government and interest groups in Japan, for example, labor has been excluded, while business groups dominate.[27] If the strict corporatist definitions put forth by Schmitter do indeed apply, then there will be a one-on-one relationship between interest group and agency. In such an arrangement, only the position of the official interest groups will be heard through this channel. Similarly, this form of relationship will likely produce even greater incoherence in government than might exist otherwise. If agriculture groups are talking to agriculture officials (be they political or administrative), labor groups to labor officials, and so on, then governmental priorities and decision making will tend to be highly fragmented. This is especially so if there is also a fragmentation in the political executive, for example, through cabinet committees able to transmit this individualized priority setting into the highest reaches of government.[28] A corporatist arrangement would not be without benefits, however; the presence of a captive interest group assisted in legitimating actions and in implementing them certainly aids a governmental agency. Further, as the relationships between peak interest groups and their members are deemed to be hierarchical, there could be reasonably high levels of control exercised over pressure groups that may present potential challenges to the legitimacy of policies.

Corporatist arrangements for making and then delivering public policy have taken on additional importance as governments have come under increased pressure to adopt alternative mechanisms for service delivery. With "government by proxy" or the "hollow state" being more important, services may be delivered by interest groups, by other not-for-profit organizations, or through private sector methods such as contracting.[29] Governments have been quite active in seeking the involvement of interest groups and in promoting partnerships between the public and the private sector that can both deliver a service and provide legitimacy for the policy.[30] The legitimating function becomes especially important as public trust and confidence in government declines.

In general, corporatism may be of limited importance for understanding how government manages its relationships with interest groups. The entire pattern of relationships appears to be under threat now, as the fiscal pressures that almost all developed economies confront have made interest groups less cooperative with government and less willing to be co-opted.[31] In addition, even at its high point, corporatism describes only a relatively small portion of the activities of interest groups – even those accorded some legitimate rights of participation in government – as they deal with government. Finally, for some of the more well-developed corporatist systems in Western Europe, the movement into the European Union means breaking up some of the cozy relationships that have existed at home.

Networks and communities

Most forms of corporatism imply some limitation on the number of groups involved in interactions with government. Corporate pluralism is something of an exception to that generalization, and several more recently developed conceptualizations about the relationship of interest groups with government, as well as among public organizations themselves, provide greater latitude for a range of interest groups to influence government. There has been a growing body of literature focussing on "policy communities" and "issue networks" as rather loose aggregations of groups involved in a policy area and having (in general) legitimate interactions with the public sector.[32]

The basic concept behind network theory is that every policy area is populated by a large number of interest groups. Each of these groups is attempting to have its own views of policy adopted as law, and works with other groups to press their views. They do this through making contacts with legislatures and the bureaucratic agencies responsible for the policy. They also interact with other interest groups that have similar orientations to the policy in question in order to create coalitions to further those interests. These "networks" are also populated by other government organizations that have conflicting and complementary interests in the policy. As well as having an influence at the formulation stage, these networks also become involved in implementing policies, much as in the corporatist arrangements.

The scholars who work in this field have engaged in a number of debates over the different meanings of "networks" versus "communities," and even over different types of communities (policy versus epistemic).[33] We will not attempt to go very far into that debate here, but will point out that "network" tends to be a more neutral term, implying only that groups interact. The term "community," on the other hand, tends to imply that there is some sharing of common orientations to the policy area. For example, an epistemic or interpretative community relies on a shared vision of the policy problem and a relatively common scientific and professional basis for working with that problem. The increasing importance of the European Community for public policy provides an especially interesting example of networks, given that there are at times markedly different perspectives on policy among the 12 member countries.[34] The European case may be, however, merely a special case of the growing importance of international actors in domestic policy, with the international "regimes" surrounding policies having domestic impacts.[35]

This network literature has performed a number of important services for students of politics. Most importantly it has pointed out that even though governments may at times attempt to limit the number of groups involved in a policy area, that is difficult to do in a democratic political system. This difficulty is apparent even when the more important groups also attempt to limit participation to preserve their own oligopolistic position. There will always be groups with the resources to participate in some way, even if only illegitimately. This does not mean that the outcome of these interactions can be predicted,[36] but only that there is an enhanced capacity to predict who will be involved, and to describe the patterns of their interactions.

Another virtue of the network approach is that it focusses attention on interactions between government agencies and other actors – other government organizations, politicians and private interest groups. These interactions are important whether or not they occur within the context of formalized committees or other advisory structures. There is an increasing body of evidence about who talks with whom in the process of deciding about public policy. For example, in Sweden research from the "power project" has mapped patterns of interaction between departments and agencies and other important actors in their environments.[37] A good deal of empirical research in Norway has also pointed to the extensive level of interaction between the public and private sectors there.[38] Knoke and Laumann in the United States mapped patterns of interaction in two policy areas very thoroughly.[39] In all these cases there was a very large number of interactions, involving a wide variety of public and private organizations surrounding the policy maker.

The empirical nature of this research approach enables us to compare interest group influence over policy in a way that other approaches might not. For example, in general we would expect interactions in less-developed countries to contain a higher percentage of contacts from institutional groups and other government departments than would be true in more developed systems. Likewise, there could be differences among policy areas in the number, variety and type of interactions. For example, a complex policy area such as health care may have a wider range of interactions than would a somewhat simpler policy area such as agriculture or defense.[40] For example, in the Swedish data mentioned above, the defense department had on average many fewer contacts than did other departments, with environment and energy having a very high level of interaction.[41]

A final positive aspect of the network literature is that it does not necessarily assume cooperation and agreement on policy as appears implied in the corporatist literature. If groups are to be official in the corporatist world they appear to have to accept much of the existing policy framework. In a network or community world, on the other hand, conflict is permitted and even expected. Sabatier, for example, argues that policy change should be understood through the conflicts of several "advocacy coalitions" constructed around different interpretations of the policy issues and problem solutions.[42] In this view there are several networks that are involved in a political struggle to control any issue. This appears a more realistic view of most issues than does the more consensual one almost inherent in corporatist models.[43]

Despite its analytic virtues, the network literature also has some problems as a means of understanding the way in which interest groups influence policy.[44] The most important of these problems is the indeterminacy of a network. The approach argues, quite rightly, that groups may be interested in making policy, but does relatively little to explain how one view wins and another loses.[45] Are there not factors that explain the relative success and failure of groups in pressing their demands? The simpler corporatist and clientelistic approaches are much better at predicting, albeit not always accurately. Further, given that networks must be created and managed, the real prediction of success may be that government organizations will dominate, rather than the interests coming from the society.

Other patterns of legitimate interaction

The two means of interaction described below, although they are involved to some extent in corporatist and network arrangements, are more generic and affect a much wider range of behavior in the public sector. They may be found in corporatism but may also be found in other systems that do not have such highly formalized patterns of interaction.

Required consultation. The required-consultation mechanism for legitimating pressure group involvement in policy making is, as the name implies, the result of a variety of rules that require administrative bodies preparing new regulations to consult with the relevant pressure groups for their opinions and to solicit advice and information from them. In some cases this is done in the preparation of legislation to be sent to a legislative body for enactment; in other cases required consultations are used for regulations that the administrative body can issue as a result of delegated legislative authority. In either case, required consultation permits an interest group direct access to the making of administrative policies.

One method of ensuring such input is through the use of *remiss* petitions as in Sweden and Norway. In both these countries, when policy modifications are being considered, the administrative agencies are required to ask for *remiss* from interest groups. These documents state the views of the group as well as some of the information that the group considers relevant to the case. Originally the device was used only for pressure groups directly affected by the new set of regulations (for example, agricultural groups affected by new regulations from an agricultural marketing board). More recently, the system has been extended to include virtually any organized group that wishes to submit an opinion although there are still power differentials among the groups.[46] While such a system provides no guarantee that the advice of the group will be heeded, it does ensure access to the relevant decision makers. Further, since it is customary for the *remisser* to be passed on with any proposed legislation, the system also provides some assurance that those who must finally pass legislation are also informed of interest group opinion. In Germany, public agencies seeking to write new legislation or regulations are required by law to seek advice from interested pressure groups. In Germany the array of pressure groups consulted on any one issue is not generally so wide as in the Scandinavian countries, but the mechanism does allow direct and legitimate input of information and opinions.[47]

While the *remiss* system relies on formal written communications for pressure groups to make their views known, other methods of required consultation employ more personal approaches. Most notable in this regard is the use of advisory committees, especially in Scandinavian administrations.[48] The majority of public committees in these countries will include representatives of some organized interests. For example, in a study of Danish committees, Johansen and Kristensen found that functional interest groups were represented on the majority of committees and that local interests and institutional interests within government itself were also frequently represented.[49] A subsequent study showed an increase in interest group representation and a slight decline in the proportion of official representation.[50] In Norway each committee will contain a variety of administrative and interest group personnel charged with advising the respective administrative body on the proper course of public policy. These committees provide a forum for the interest group to present their evidence and to make a case for their particular views in an open forum. Interestingly, however, most representatives on these committees do not consider their role as that of an advocate of a particular position, but rather as more that of a technical expert and manager.[51] This role conception is obviously useful in facilitating compromise in those committees on even difficult questions of policy. Further, the presence of all affected interests in the committee requires openness and permits the analysis of evidence from all parties in a manner that can facilitate compromise.

The use of advisory bodies is not confined to the Scandinavian countries, and in fact is a relatively common feature of administrative life around the world. In Germany, interest groups are represented on advisory boards for the ministries as a matter of legal right. These advisory boards and commissions exist in virtually all countries. France had some 3,700 in the 1960s, with more being added continually, and one more recent estimate put the number at 15,000.[52] The biennial report on advisory committees in the United States lists several thousand and, although less formalized, many also exist in the United Kingdom.[53] Richardson also argues that the use of advisory committees is a characteristic feature of British public administration.[54]

What may distinguish the use of advisory committees in Germany and Scandinavia is the official sanction given to the role of the groups in the process of making policy.[55] As Kvavik notes, these systems move the role of pressure group influence from that of input to that of "withinput"; that is, in non-Eastonian language, the political system recognizes pressure groups as an integral part of the decision-making process and therefore accords them some of the same status accorded to other official participants in the policy process.[56] In Germany this situation may be viewed as a continuation of some of the traditional corporate conceptions of the state, but in all systems this type of influence provides an important alternative to the usual liberal means of representation through elections and legislatures.[57] Moreover, with the rapid growth of administrative policy making, it may soon surpass the liberal means in its impact on public policy.

Implementation. The second major form of legitimate interest group involvement in administration is the use of the groups as agents of implementation for public policies. Interest groups serve as quasi-official arms of the political system in implementing some programs about which they are assumed to have expert knowledge and skills. Again, this means of group involvement is particularly apparent in Scandinavia and also frequently occurs in the Low Countries.[58] One of the most common areas in which administration of this type occurs is agriculture, where either commodity groups or local farmers' organizations administer regulations, acreage allotments or contractual relationships with the government. In Sweden the implementation of many portions of the labor law is left to the individual groups most affected by the law.[59] Similarly, in the Netherlands a large, but declining, portion of that country's complex system of economic regulation has been administered by boards composed largely of interest group representatives charged with the "self-policing" of a particular industry in order to maintain the delicate economic balance within the country.[60]

In all of these cases of implementation with the aid of interest groups, the government essentially allows the groups to engage in activities in the name of the public, with only indirect "political" control over their actions. They tend to be somewhat restrained by having competing interests represented on the same administrative boards, but this is obviously a manner in which interest groups can have a quite direct impact on the shape of public policy and its execution. In most European societies this role is well institutionalized although the theoretical separation of state and society in most Anglo-American systems makes these implementation structures more suspect.

Again, we should point out the degree to which the need of governments to implement their policies in a cheaper or less obtrusive manner has given increased importance to the legitimate role of interest groups as implementing agents.[61] In such interactions the state, of course, must be willing to trade some of its authority in return for ease of implementation, and possibly even greater legitimacy among those who will consume the service. In some instances, such a trade-off might have been resisted, but fiscal and popular pressures in the beginning of the twenty-first century are sufficient to make it extremely palatable. In the language of state theory, states must become weaker and less autonomous as they become increasingly enmeshed with, and dependent upon, private interests.[62]

Although we usually think about the impact on government organizations, interest groups also lose some autonomy when they become a part of the apparatus of state policy making and implementation. They run the risk of becoming co-opted by government, with maintaining their relationship to government becoming as important a goal as changing policy.[63] The maintenance of the loyalty and commitment of interest group leaders to the wishes of the rank and file members is an enduring problem in voluntary organizations.[64] It is especially pronounced when leadership roles involve regular participation in important negotiations over policy, and frequent contacts with government officials. There is a danger that interest groups become too much a part of the system of government to represent adequately the wishes of their members to government.

Institutional groups. Institutional pressure groups appear to constitute a special class of legitimate pressure groups. By definition, these groups are important social or political institutions that are seeking to influence public policy.[65] Some rather obvious examples are the church, the army, and the public bureaucracy itself. Local governments, even in unitary regimes, may also act as institutional groups. Institutional groups, like all interest groups, seek to obtain benefits for themselves or their members, and their actions are legitimated through the prestige of the institution, or perhaps the threat of extreme actions in the case of the army in some societies. Johansen and Kristensen point out that these groups are increasing more rapidly than functional interest groups in their representation on public committees in Denmark.[66] Likewise, in France, Tournon argues that these are the most effective groups in the system.[67]

Even in countries that tend toward legitimate patterns of interaction between interest groups and the bureaucracy, institutional interest groups may actually be better conceptualized as a special class of *clientela* groups in that they have legitimate access when a number of competing groups may not, and they tend to seek more particularized special-interest outputs than tends to be true in legitimate pressure group systems. This is often particularly true of local government organizations that lobby for support from the central government, whether as a group or for their own particular community.[68] In many developing countries the military (and to some extent also the bureaucracy) is a special case of the powerful institutional interest group, lobbying, or threatening, in order to get what it wants from a relatively weak government.

As is noted in Figure 5.1, which characterizes the interactions of administrators and pressure groups, the scope of interaction between the two in "legitimate" situations tends to be quite broad. A single pressure group may be consulted on a variety of policies, and virtually all policy areas may be the subject of inputs from interested parties. Also, the influence of the legitimate groups on policy may be expected to be great relative to other types of interaction patterns. The legitimacy of the groups, their frequency of interaction with administrators and their official or quasi-official status all make it possible for groups to have an impact that they would not have elsewhere. In part this is a function of not having to expend organizational resources simply to gain access, and in part a function of the roles adopted by the interest group participants in the process. These perceived roles contribute to the bargaining style of their interactions. As is noted by Kvavik, the dominant-role type in these negotiations is the expert who supplies information and opinion but who does not serve merely as an advocate of his particularistic viewpoint.[69] This bargaining activity was described by Stein Rokkan, and the basic pattern has changed little since he wrote that:

> The crucial decisions on economic policy are rarely taken in the parties or Parliament: the central area is the bargaining table where the government authorities meet directly with the trade union leaders, the representatives of

the farmers, the smallholders, and the fishermen, and the delegates of the Employers' Association. These yearly rounds of negotiations have in fact come to mean more in the lives of rank-and-file citizens than have formal elections. In these processes of intensive interaction the parliamentary notions of one member, one vote and majority rule make little sense. Decisions are not made through the counting of heads, but through complex considerations of short-term advantages in alternative lines of compromise.[70]

When the influence of pressure groups must be more covert, this important bargaining mode of interaction is, of necessity, eliminated through the politics of gaining access, necessitating that few groups rather than many will be involved in any one decision. This characterization does not hold true, of course, in the corporatist arrangements described above, in which there is a one-on-one relationship between pressure group and government. The relationship may not be as particularized as in *clientela* relationships described below, but it lacks the broad bargaining style associated with most legitimate patterns of interaction.

Finally, the policy consequences of this pattern of interaction between pressure groups and administrators are generally confined to two types (phrased in terms of the Lowi and the Salisbury and Heinz typologies, which continue to have substantial relevance for the political examination of public policy): redistribution and self-regulation.[71] That is, in situations in which administrators are capable of imposing the choices made by groups through a bargaining and negotiation process, the decisions taken are likely to take from one group and give to another. This means of bargaining over policy is, however, a relatively safe manner (politically) in which to adopt redistributive policy, since it ensures the participation of both winners and losers as well as ensuring the application of technical knowledge to the choice. These two characteristics – the technical knowledge of the participants and the presence of all competing sides – were in fact the criteria selected by respondents in Kvavik's sample as most important in legitimating their decisions.[72] Rather similar patterns of participation and involvement are found in Olsen's later work.[73] Elvander and others likewise note that, in Sweden, the inclusion of all competing groups is important for the smooth implementation of policies adopted by pressure group representatives cooperating with the government.[74] In addition, Heisler and Kvavik point out that continued access to policy making may be sufficient motivation in itself to produce compliance with the decisions taken, even in the face of adverse decisions in the short term.[75]

In political situations in which the elite may lack the cohesion and consensus necessary to implement a redistributive decision, these legitimate interactions between interest groups and administrators may result in policies of self-regulation.[76] In these cases organizations are generally allowed to manage their own affairs and thereby essentially manage a sector of public policy for the government. One example of this type of policy outcome is in the area of agriculture, where the conflict within the sector is relatively slight so that there may be little need for directly redistributive decisions, and where some policies – such as the allocation of acreage allotments – may have little effect on other groups.[77] Even in these cases there is potential conflict, for example, between agricultural groups wanting high subsidies, and therefore high food prices, and labor groups wanting low prices and therefore lower subsidies; or agricultural groups may want to use pesticides while environmentalists do not.[78] The choice between redistributive and self-regulative policies may depend on the breadth of groups involved in any one decision as well as the integration of the elites making and enforcing the decisions. In other policy areas, one group may have such a monopoly of information and expertise that it is given the responsibility of self-regulation on the basis of that expertise. This has been especially true of medical and legal groups in the United States and is a prevalent finding for similar groups in a variety of other political systems.[79]

The economic difficulties which most Western democracies encountered during the 1970s and even into the 1990s have had contradictory effects on legitimate patterns of interaction between interest groups and the public bureaucracy. On the one hand, we have already pointed to the increasing use of interest groups or other aspects of "third-party government" to relieve some of the administrative burden of government and to enhance the legitimacy of programs.[80] On the other hand, corporatism and other forms of legitimate involvement of pressure groups appear much better suited to dividing a growing economic pie in the public sector than to deciding where the cuts must be made.[81] Access is important when there is more to be given out, but it becomes almost a burden for the interest groups when there is little good news to distribute. For government, however, there is a temptation, when faced with stress and a large number of conflicting demands, to reduce its involvement with outside groups and make its own decisions. The exact manner in which these contradictory pressures are manifested in actual decisions will depend upon a number of cultural and situational factors, but formalized relationships between government and interest groups are undergoing examination and some change. Also, although the patterns are perhaps clearest in Western countries, some of the same changes have been occurring in the less-developed countries, especially the increased reliance on the third sector for policy delivery.[82]

Clientela *relationships*

The second type of interaction between interest groups and administration is one of the two major types discussed by LaPalombara. A *clientela* relationship is said to exist when an interest group, for whatever reasons, succeeds in becoming, in the eyes of a given administrative agency, the natural expression and representative of a given social sector which, in turn, constitutes the natural target or reference point for the activity of the administrative agency. What that rather long definition implies is that a single interest group becomes the exclusive representative of a sector, and there is a close connection between the one organization and a single agency.

This type of interaction is characterized by a perceived legitimacy on the part of administrators of a *single* interest group rather than a formal statement of the legitimacy of all or virtually all groups. The consequences of this seemingly slight difference are, however, quite important. In the first place, the scope of interaction of pressure groups and administration tends to be rather severely constrained. Each agency tends to select a single pressure group as *the* legitimate representative of its particular social sector and to avoid most other groups seeking to present information and advice. Thus, whereas in the "legitimate" arrangement mentioned previously the agency might be able or required to consult a broad range of groups, in a *clientela* relationship it will entertain a quite narrow range of information and advice. This narrowing is especially evident when two or more groups seek to organize a single sector of the society but only one is accorded regular access to decision making. This situation tends to skew the sources of information, generally in the direction toward which the administrators tended in the first place. Suleiman and others have noted that in France – and certainly elsewhere – legitimate groups tend to be those whose economic strength is undeniable and whose demands are in general accord with government policy.[83] The pattern appears to persist after substantial modernization of many aspects of French government and administration.

The second consequence of this form of interaction is that, while the influence of one group may be increased, the overall influence of pressure groups on public policy will be lessened. Not having legitimacy in any formal sense obviously reduces the acceptability of special-interest influence on policy for the general public, and the ability of the bureaucracy to accept advice is also limited. Further, each pressure group must expand relatively more of its organizational resources on the pursuit of access, so that less is available for the information and influence functions. Moreover, in this process of seeking access, any conception of the "public interest" – even as an aggregate of pressure group interests – tends to be lost and replaced with a set of private interests, each represented in government by a single agency.[84] Associated with the above is a need to keep the negotiations and interactions of interest groups and administrators private and informal, thereby removing them even further from public scrutiny and accountability. All these characteristics of the scope and manner of interaction indicate that the pressure group universe will tend to be less broadly influential over policies, with virtually any influence that does occur having something of a taint of illegality among the general public.

If we remove this taint of illegality from the idea of interactions between interest groups and government, it is difficult to distinguish *clientela* relationships and corporatist arrangements that have developed along sectoral lines, especially in policy sectors such as agriculture, with very close collaboration between government and groups in almost every country.[85] That "taint" is, of course, important in defining the dynamics of the interactions and in influencing the legitimacy of the outcomes, but it is a very subtle distinction.

The description of the interactions of interest groups and public administration in *clientela* politics leads to the characterization of these relationships as symbiotic. As in biological symbiosis, this relationship implies a mutual dependence of the two participants. The administrative agency depends upon the pressure group for information, advice, prior clearance of policy decisions and, most important, for political support in its competition with other agencies for the scarce resources within government. The pressure groups, on the other hand, depend upon the agency for access to decision making and ultimately for favorable decisions on certain policy choices. For both sides the existence of a *clientela* relationship serves to regularize the political environment and to develop friendships in what might otherwise be a hostile political world.

This form of pressure group relationship with administration, noted by LaPalombara in Italy, has been used by several authors as a means of describing much of the politics of policy in the United States, and it would seem to be prevalent in a number of other political systems that have strong interest groups but where the interactions of these groups and the government is at the margin of acceptability.[86] Heclo and others have argued, however, that this clientelist pattern is now less descriptive of the United States than it once was, and a much broader array of interests has come to be represented in Washington.[87] While this may appear virtuous on grounds of democracy, it does make the policy-making process substantially less predictable than it had been. On the other hand, the by now standard lament on the impact of "single-issue politics" on American government may lead one to continue to accept the clientelist description.[88]

Further, although the United States has been a principal example of *clientela* politics, it is by no means the only example. Even countries that have more legitimate interactions in some areas may find certain sectors, or sometimes a broader array of sectors, behaving in a clientelistic manner.[89] As noted, agriculture often operates in a clientelistic manner, and financial interests have been able to preserve this position even in countries being governed by left-leaning governments.[90] Likewise, given the plethora of possible groups from which to choose, the European Union also appears to relate to interest groups by selecting a particular client through which to channel influence.

Finally, the policy consequences of the *clientela* arrangement produce essentially self-regulative and distributive outcomes. LaPalombara notes that regulation is one of the defining characteristics of a *clientela* relationship but goes on to note that the regulative activities undertaken are not necessarily those that would promote the "public interest."[91] Rather, they are activities that quite directly promote the interests of the regulated. This pattern of regulation, as has been noted, has been referred to as "self-regulation." Again, this tendency toward self-regulation appears endemic to administrative agencies and especially independent regulatory commissions in the United States. Lowi has argued that "interest group liberalism," or the appropriation of the power of the state for private ends, is in fact the dominant characteristic of contemporary public policy in the United States.[92] McConnell observes that the "outstanding political fact about independent regulatory commissions is that they have, in general, become the protectors and promoters of the industries they have been established to regulate."[93] Evidence from other political systems, however, is that this phenomenon is not confined to the United States but is a more general feature of industrial societies. In a variety of settings the need for political support is sufficient to necessitate the replacement of regulation with clientelism and self-regulation. Administrators may lack the resources and the central political support to enforce programs of regulation in the face of opposition of powerful and well-organized groups, so in essence they must gain support from those groups. However, as with Heclo's analysis of *clientela* politics in the United States, there is an interpretation that regulatory capture is less prevalent in the United States than it once was, especially for the

"New social regulation," in which the regulatory bodies have jurisdictions that cut across a variety of industries.[94] Further, there is increasing attention to the design of regulatory structures that can minimize the chances of capture.[95]

Besides self-regulation, *clientela* relationships also tend to be associated with distributional outcomes, which may be merely more tangible manifestations of self-regulative programs. In distributional politics, however, instead of being allowed to make its own regulations, a group is granted continuing benefits. In Lowi's terminology, distributional politics "create privilege, and it is a type of privilege which is particularly hard to bear or combat because it is touched with the symbolism of the state."[96] A further feature of distributional politics is its tendency to accord benefits to all groups accepted as legitimate rather than select some as worthy and others as less worthy. The close relationship between the interest group and the government agency can ensure that the clients continue to receive something of value from government, and that questions of redistribution and the need for adjustment of the relative benefits are rarely subjects of discussion.

Again, if we examine the impact both of a decline in the confidence of populations in government's ability to solve society's problems and of the declining budgetary resources enjoyed by most governments, there are contradictory implications for *clientela* relationships. On the one hand, the crisis mentality that pervades government when faced with declining legitimacy and less money tends to produce more attempts at central control. Central agencies concerned with budgets and with the management of the public sector as a whole attempt to impose their priorities on the policy process, rather than allowing the departments and agencies to work so closely with private interests in shaping policy.[97] No longer are distribution and self-regulation so acceptable as policy outcomes, but government is seen to need to set priorities and make hard decisions among programs. As we will see in Chapter 7, a number of methods have been developed to cope with these problems, but all depend upon the priorities set and the choices made.

On the other hand, the fiscal pressures on government, and the crisis of confidence in the system of governing in many countries, may have forced public administration closer to organized interests and, therefore, may have accentuated tendencies to form clientele relationships. If government needs an interest group to implement a policy, or to provide advice and information which government organizations themselves are increasingly hard-pressed to produce, then it is difficult for them to impose tighter controls on the self-regulatory policies that have benefited those interests. As was noted above, this may be the means by which clientele relationships lose their taint and become legitimate. Again, how these pressures are played out will depend on cultural and situational factors.

The development of clientele politics is heavily influenced by the peculiar politics and economics of public bureaucracies. Despite the arguments that consider bureaucracy and bureaucrats as integrated and homogeneous actors, seeking collectively to assume control of the political system (at a minimum), many bureaucratic systems are highly fragmented institutions. By being so fragmented, they may be forced into competition simply because there is rarely an effective central means of allocating resources according to the merits of programs or the needs of society. This is true even if there are pressures for more priority setting arising from scarcity of resources. Bureaucratic competition for resources can be overstated very easily, as it is in much of the "public choice" literature on bureaucracy, and much of what competition does exist is a function of sincere commitments to programs rather than of a desire to maximize budgets.[98] But fragmentation within the public sector does contribute to the development of *clientela* politics.

The budgetary process then tends to force public bureaucracies to seek public support and make distributive accommodations in order to gain that support. This outcome is further magnified by the division among the other actors in the budgetary process and their needs for other types of benefits and accommodations. The clientelism that extends between the pressure group and the administration may extend to a type of clientelism between legislative committees and the administrative agencies they are ostensibly overseeing.[99] This situation is, in part, a function of the stability of the actors involved in the process, as in the United States Congress, but more generally is related to the joint need of administrators and legislators to serve a constituency. For example, legislators interested in agricultural matters tend to come from predominantly agricultural districts; any attempt to curtail the activities of an agricultural program would not be well received in their constituencies and would thereby threaten their chances for re-election.[100]

Institutional interest groups comprise a special class of group in their relationships with the bureaucracy. In the case of clientele relationships, there are a variety of important patterns of relationship, although these too are under some pressure. In industrialized societies these are local government groups, as well as interest groups within the government itself.[101] In less-developed countries, these groups might include the church, the military, or the bureaucracy itself. These groups all have claims upon government that are difficult or impossible to deny, and, as with other *clientela* groups, these special claims are pressed for special privileges.

Again, we would characterize the effects of *clientela* politics between the public bureaucracy and interest groups as a tight intermeshing of interest groups, administration and legislators, all of whom have something to gain by increasing certain types of public expenditures. These interconnections produce patterns of policy similar to those predicted by Salisbury and Heinz in such situations: the parceling out of goods and services available through the public budget in a manner that will provide each organized sector with some portion of the benefits.[102] This, in turn, produces a lack of coordination and coherence in the public sector as a whole.[103]

Parantela *relationships*

This is the second type of administrative pressure group relationship mentioned by LaPalombara in his discussion of Italian interest groups. A *parantela* relationship describes a situation of "kinship" or close fraternal ties between a pressure group and the government or the dominant political party.[104] These relationships are generally characteristic of preindustrial societies or of ideological regimes, but our discussion will show them occurring in a number of political systems in which there is a single dominant party or faction. In these cases pressure groups must gain access and legitimacy through their attachment to that particular party rather than through their ability effectively to represent a sector of the society.

Parantela relationships between pressure groups and bureaucracies involve an indirect linkage between those actors rather than the direct linkage discussed in the *clientela* relationship. The important added linkage is the political party – most commonly a hegemonic party – with which the pressure group must develop some feeling of consanguinity. In these cases, the pressure groups obtain their access to administrative decision making through the willingness of the party to intercede on its behalf with the bureaucracy and therefore in essence to control bureaucratic policy making. In considering *parantela* relationships, we must be sure to think of organizations such as think tanks and consulting firms as being relevant interest groups. With ideological parties at the helm of government, there may be a need to ensure that the advice given to them is sufficiently "pure." Of course, the party itself may wish to provide such advice, but they may also wish to endorse other organizations as providing acceptable ideas and policy advice.[105]

There must, therefore, be a domination of policy making by a political party, something that is not usually associated with Western democratic systems but that is still present in those systems. LaPalombara, for example, found relationships of this type existing in Italy with the Christian Democratic Party.[106] In France, the Gaullists during the first part of the Fifth Republic involved themselves directly with the bureaucracy to favor one interest group over another, especially in the area of agriculture.[107] Likewise, when the Socialists came to power they tended to press policy and the bureaucracy toward closer alliance with a smaller but more leftist agricultural group.[108] While this issue was complicated by many issues internal to agricultural politics in France, the fundamental point of the imposition of party control over administration in order to favor one group is clear. During periods of cohabitation the presidency and the prime minister may be supporting different *parantela* groups.[109]

This type of interaction does occur in Western political systems, but it is more typical of a number of political systems – the former Soviet system, a majority of African single-party states and many Latin American countries – in which one party or coalition is dominant.[110] As in the case of France, it is also found where partisan competition may exist but where there has been a tendency for one party to dominate government – for example, Italy, Japan, India and Mexico.[111] It is also common in more competitive political systems in the relationship that exists between organized labor unions and political parties, such as the relationship between the Trades Union Congress and the Labour Party in the United Kingdom, or LO and the Social Democratic Party in Sweden. Further, interest groups may be able to exert an influence over the parties by having their members adopted into political party roles such as candidates for office.[112]

Another type of *parantela* interest group that has frequently existed in democratic societies represents an attempt on the part of government to organize some aspect of society traditionally difficult to organize. For example, in the United States, urban renewal and model cities programs required the development of organizations in the affected neighborhoods that would represent the interests of the residents. Such organizations have rarely been successful in that role and more often have been co-opted by government as a means of social control in the neighborhoods.[113] Also, in several Western European countries, government has taken an active part in organizing consumers' groups – also traditionally difficult to organize – and these groups have frequently been criticized for becoming co-opted by government. One very clear example of government's forming organizations to organize difficult segments of the society and using those organizations for its own benefit is the growth of para-political organizations in Singapore.[114] The People's Action Party has formed a large number of organizations that cut across traditional lines in the society and form yet another political base for that party.

The effects of *parantela* relationships tend to be quite pervasive. It is, in fact, one tendency of these political systems that the hegemonic party will seek to impose its control over as much of the society and economy as is possible. One principal means of effecting this is the fostering of *parantela* relationships in a number of social sectors through the co-optation of existing interest groups or through the creation of new groups directly allied with the party. The above example from France is a case of the party taking the side of an existing interest group in its struggle with other groups seeking to represent the same social interests; and the previous Spanish regime's organization of the workers into official or semi-official syndicates is an example of a party creating its own interest group structure.[115] In either case, this is an effective means through which the party can extend its scope downward into the society to control the nature of the inputs being generated and regularize the behavior of that social sector in accordance with the dictates of the party. This means of control through organization has been especially common in the former communist countries, challenged only when free organizations such as Solidarity (in Poland) can gain something approaching legitimate status. It also serves as a means of checking bureaucratic autonomy within that particular policy area.

The above would seem to imply that pressure groups involved in a *parantela* relationship are little more than the pawns of a dominant political party, and such an interpretation would be justifiable in many instances. Weiner, for example, describing the relationship of the Congress Party in India and its affiliated labor union, writes:

> The Indian National Trade Union Congress – in reality the labor wing of the Congress Party – is organized along these principles of political responsibility and supports the basic program of the present government. Its leaders proudly declare that their demands are in the national interest, not in behalf of sectional interests. Their first loyalties are to the Congress Party, then to the present government, to the nation, and last of all to the workers who belong to the union.[116]

While the Indian case is illustrative of many *parantela* relationships, it is by no means an entirely general finding. Even in the case of pre-democratic Spain, Anderson can write:

the conventional picture of unrepresentativeness and ineffectiveness of the syndicates can be greatly overdrawn. The government and the syndicates did not speak with one voice on public policy. The syndical leaders were expected by the system itself to play the role of militant spokesmen for labor.... In their language and style of militancy many of the syndical leaders were not unlike their counterparts in other Western nations. They were brokers, and they bargained for their clients, though in the last analysis they accepted the judgment of the constituted authorities.[117]

The behavior of militant members of the Trades Union Congress in the United Kingdom with respect to the policies of Labour governments represents the logical extremes of independence of *parantela* partners.[118] The pressure groups in these arrangements are frequently capable of exerting substantial influence over the course of public policy, and for many of the same reasons that motivate *clientela* pressure groups. The symbiosis between a hegemonic party and a pressure group is certainly not as important as that between the *clientela* partners, but it is present. The pressure groups can be expected to have some impact on bureaucratic choice because of their special relationship with the dominant party. Typically in such a case the hegemonic party will have colonized the bureaucracy as well as created its own interest group partners. Further, both the party and the bureaucracy gain the benefit of the specialized knowledge of the group, thereby reducing their own direct costs for policy development and planning. Moreover, the party's direct costs of social control may be reduced by their developing subsidiary organizations to perform functions that might otherwise have to be performed centrally. The above-mentioned example of the relationship between the syndicates and the government in Spain is one example of this type of control, as is the relationship between communist parties and their unions in both hegemonic and competitive situations. The numerous party-sponsored organizations in China are perhaps the epitome of this relationship between party and organizations.

Interestingly, the development of *parantela* organizations may also alter the behavior of the hegemonic party and may pluralize (at least slightly) politics within a one-party state. The politics may begin to resemble those of *clientela* relationships, with greater specificity by policy area. Dittmer writes that modernization in communist political systems has been associated with the rise of "quasi-interest groups" who practice "cryptopolitics." Although they are not autonomous, and cannot command the range of resources available to interest groups in pluralist systems, they have been able to exert increasing influence upon policy within the functionally specified fields in which they are assumed to have some professional competence. Such groups do not perceive themselves to be representative of broadly popular constituencies, so this development is hardly "democratic," but it is consultative, better informed and meritocratic.[119]

To some degree the policies adopted by the participants in *parantela* relationships are a function of the ideology and program of the hegemonic party and as such may vary from programs of the far left to the far right. In general, however, there is a tendency toward distributive programs. This means there is a tendency toward distributing various goods and services among the faithful and directing groups to develop claims on certain public goods and services as the appropriate representatives of certain social sectors. In this sense, the party is acting as something of a "canteen" for its adherents and for official groups by essentially subsidizing their existence in the marketplace of pressure groups – and thereby essentially depriving any competing, or potentially competing, groups.[120] This may be especially important when the dominant political party also has virtually complete control over the economic resources of the society and can distribute both political and material rewards.

Thus, in some ways, the *parantela* arrangements closely resemble the corporatist pattern of interest group relationships described above, especially the state corporatist model.[121] Individuals would receive benefits under such an arrangement as a function of their membership in the appropriate corporate entity, rather than as a matter of individual right. Moreover, *parantela* relationships tend to be antithetical to the conception of modern politics about the universalism of the distribution of economic, social and political benefits. Such benefits – even the most basic political benefits of the rights of organization and participation – are, in *parantela* systems, most definitely the function of having the proper political affiliations, and the influence that any group may expect to have over the outcomes of the decision-making process will be a function of this consanguinity.

A second effect of *parantela* relationships is also obviously regulative. This is true not only of the attempts of the party to regulate the outputs of the bureaucracy through regulating the advice that it receives, but more broadly to regulate the society as a whole through the use of intermediary groups. These intermediary groups not only structure inputs but may also serve as means of implementing the programs of the regime. The *parantela* relationships then serve as two-way streets; information – and to a lesser extent power – can flow in both directions. The extent to which power can flow upward is, however, ultimately determined by the willingness of the dominant political party to entertain modifications and challenges.

Illegitimate group processes

The final category of interactions between administrators and pressure groups is labeled "illegitimate." This term is used to describe a variety of political situations in which the interaction of pressure groups with bureaucracy may be defined as outside the pale of normal political actions, but these interactions occur anyway. This style of interaction may be a function of the nature of the political system as a whole, which may attempt to suppress autonomous groups in society, or it may be a function of the nature of particular groups, which are defined as being illegitimate as representatives of the social sector that they purport to represent. In the first three types of interactions discussed, some or all pressure groups were accepted as legitimate spokesmen for some social sector or another. In the case of the illegitimate pressure groups, neither the system as a whole nor individual administrators may be willing to accept the legitimacy of the inputs of some or all interest groups. It is rarely the case, however, that a political system will attempt to exclude all interest groups. Even the most "totalitarian" can find groups useful and will attempt to form *parantela* style organizations.[122]

As might be expected, influence from pressure groups of this type is not the normal pattern of policy making. Such influences tend to be indicative of some rather fundamental failures of the policy-making system in satisfying demands of one or more sectors of the society. Thus these individuals feel constrained to go outside the bounds of "normal" politics to seek what they want from the political system. We may, therefore, be discussing in large part the behavior of "anomic" pressure groups in their attempts to exert influence through protest, demonstrations and violence. It is not necessary, however, to confine this discussion entirely to groups using violence as a means of expression, for there are a number of situations in which pressure groups declared as illegitimate in *parantela* or *clientela* arrangements may still seek influence and may occasionally exert some influence on policies. The latter instances are rare. As one of LaPalombara's respondents in Italy noted on this topic:

> I know of no policy within the Ministry of Industry and Commerce that says that there *are* certain groups in Italian society whose representatives will not at least be received. It is true that once this is done we will assign different importance or give varying weight to the proposals made to us by such groups, but they are free to approach us.[123]

Suleiman notes that in France groups defined as *groupes de pression* (in contrast to the acceptable "professional" groups) may be received by the administrators but are unlikely to be able to produce the results they desire.[124]

The illegitimate groups continue to play the political game by the administrator's rules and politely present their petitions and remonstrances, often knowing that their probability of success is nearly zero. We may ask why these groups continue in these seemingly irrational behaviors. There is the odd chance that they may actually have an influence. More commonly, however, they persist simply because this is what their members expect them to do. This is the reason the members pay their dues or give their allegiance to the group, and the leaders must carry out a seemingly pointless exercise.[125] Finally, having attempted to play by the rules of the game, they may make future extraordinary political activity appear more acceptable.

If normal politics cannot work for a group, then they appear more justified in using violent or inflammatory means, even in societies that are usually very willing to accommodate the demands of interest groups. This has been true, at least in part, of "social movements" in a number of industrialized countries.[126] These groups have not had the permanent organizational structures that would be desirable for continuing cooperation with government, and have tended to eschew such relationships for ideological reasons. Although usually associated with the political left – anti-nuclear groups, the peace movement, tenants' organizations, etc. – there also have been social movements on the right. In all cases, they have been willing to use confrontational tactics, if not violence, to attempt to press home their political points.

The interaction between illegitimate pressure groups and administration tends to produce high levels of frustration and alienation for those groups. The rather arbitrary categorization of pressure takes place even in political systems generally receptive – if not partial – to group influences. For example, in the United States, with a long history of pressure group influence on agriculture policy, one group – the National Farmers' Organization – was for all practical purposes classified as illegitimate; members reacted by descending on Washington, DC, with their tractors.[127] The level of frustration may be even greater in political systems that attempt to suppress – rather than simply ignore – the activities of interest groups declared to be illegitimate. The suppression of Solidarity by the Polish government is an example of this type of behavior which comes most readily to mind.

We can better understand the characterization of the influences of these illegitimate groups as coming essentially from extralegal activities – through some sort of conflict with the system – and their influence as being at best episodic. Likewise, the impacts of their activities on public policy are extremely difficult to predict, if they occur at all. Despite these limitations, it is important to understand that these influences may occasionally be productive of important changes. The French student movement of May 1968, and its associated activities, have been used as an example of virtually every political phenomenon known to humankind, but that should not restrain us from pointing out that this is one example of an essentially illegitimate pressure group having a substantial impact on a regime and on the shape of subsequent public policy.[128] The American students and their protests against the Vietnam War constitute another example, while in some Latin American countries the argument can be made that accomplishing almost any type of policy change requires the kind of fundamental challenge to the system that can be offered by illegitimate groups.[129] Also, the early successes of Solidarity in Poland produced some liberalization in the regime, although the ultimate result was the imposition of martial law.

When illegitimate groups are successful, the impacts of their activities tend to be redistributive, if for no other reason than they may force the system to recognize a set of demands that it could previously declare as being outside its concern. Most illegitimate pressure groups seek to transform the existing political system and its output distribution in the direction of a redistribution of privilege, be it political, social or economic. Some of the most obvious examples would be attempts of minority racial and ethnic groups to have their claims for civil rights and equal treatment accepted when previously they had been excluded from the political process.

In addition, there are other significant differences among these four classes of interactions we have discussed. First, the activities of illegitimate pressure groups are clearly the most distinctive. The other three patterns accord some legitimacy to the activities and influence of one or more groups, so that there are accepted patterns of interaction between the groups and the bureaucracy. In the case of illegitimate groups, such interactions – at least if they are to have any significant effect on policy outcomes – occurs almost by definition only in times of political crisis. Thus, the three more or less legitimate patterns imply a certain stability and institutionalization of influence, whereas the illegitimate pattern implies episodic influence, or no influence at all.

Second, the legitimate pattern of interaction is the only one of the four in which there is little or no politics of access. In this arrangement, access exists for virtually any group that seeks it – even for those that almost certainly would be declared illegitimate in other settings. In one well-known example, organized street gangs in Amsterdam have been given a representational role; *organization* appears to be the most crucial variable here. By removing access from politics, such an interaction pattern may in fact make the pluralist's dream of a self-regulating universe of pressure groups formulating public policy a possibility, if not a reality.[130] As long as access remains a scarce and closely regulated commodity, the possibility of finding the "public interest" among a set of conflicting pressure groups is remote, if not non-existent. Having legitimate interactions of pressure with administration – and, perhaps more importantly, open interactions of pressure groups with each other in advising the administrators – by no means ensures that such a mystical entity as the "public interest" will emerge, but it is more likely to appear when interests are forced to bargain than when each interest is able to capture its own portion of the administrative structure. This capture tends to convert public policy into private policy. Likewise, unless one considers the hegemonic political party as an accurate representation of the interests of the population, the control of pressure groups and bureaucracy by such a party is also likely to produce distortions of outputs from what would emerge from a bargaining table, especially when many interests may be defined out of existence by the dominant party. To put this in the terms of our original typology of interactions, serious distortions of policy from what would emerge from a simple bargaining process among competing groups are likely to occur when the politics of policy making cannot be removed from the politics of organizational survival.

We should also note that we have not been able to argue clearly that any particular pattern of interaction characterizes any one nation or another, although the examples tend to point to some important patterns. In the first place, political systems with hegemonic political parties, be they ostensibly democratic or not, tend toward *parantela* relationships between interest groups and administrators, if for no other reason than that the hegemonic party is able to use these relationships as one means of social control and regulation. Second, legitimate interactions tend to be characteristic of the Northern European countries, which have had long histories of the involvement of organized groups in social and political life, and whose leaders have perceived a need to manage potentially divisive conflicts within the society, either ethnic or socioeconomic in origin. Third, *clientela* arrangements tend to be quite common in any number of societies, especially when there is a fragmentation of interests and a lack of overall coordinating mechanisms in the political system (for example, a dominant political party or institution), that can regulate the competition among interest groups or among the competing agencies within the bureaucracy; the United States is a major, but by no means the sole, example. Finally, illegitimate interest groups may arise in virtually any setting but tend to be most important in settings where they are least likely, for example, in societies that seek to suppress interest groups or at least a wide variety of interest groups. That is to say, these groups are most important in settings where they serve as a fundamental challenge to the regime. This means that their day-to-day interactions with administrators will be unfruitful if they occur at all, but that they may produce substantial transformations of a political system.

Just as there is little pattern of interest group–bureaucratic interaction by political system, there is also little pattern by type of interest or policy area. There is some tendency for interest groups that can be clearly defined geographically to be able to establish clientele relationships with administration, perhaps because of the ability to mobilize political support more easily. The most obvious example of this pattern is agriculture, which has been notoriously successful in utilizing clientele relationships in almost all political systems. Likewise, interest groups that may be vertically integrated with political parties – frequently labor unions with labor parties – may develop *parantela* relationships, even within the context of competitive political systems.[131] Finally, groups that may be regarded as outcasts in normal social affairs, or that are not regarded as having differentiated political viewpoints by the dominant community – racial minorities, students, women – may tend to act through illegitimate relationships with bureaucracies, if they are able to form any relationship at all.

Social movements and the bureaucracy

Interest groups represent the majority of social and economic groups in society, but by no means all. Changes in the structure of society and in the issues being confronted by government have spawned a variety of social movements.[132] These groups differ from conventional interest groups in several ways. First, they are often short-lived, created to address a single issue and then disbanded when that issue is resolved or loses saliency. Second, they are more commonly associated with non-economic issues such as the environment, peace, human rights, etc., than with "bread and butter" economic issues. Finally, their organization tends to be less stable and institutionalized than is true for most interest groups or political parties.

As noted above, social movements tend to function most often as illegitimate interest groups, often refusing on principle to cooperate more directly with government. Movements are often created because the existing close collaboration between certain interest groups and the bureaucracy is perceived to exclude other equally important segments of society from being heard. Thus, the members of social movements may perceive most existing interest groups as being in *parantela* or *clientela* relationships with government, even when those other groups themselves believe that the relationships are more open and broadly legitimate. Thus, a good deal of the politics of social movements revolves around defining issues and defining participation (whether with the bureaucracy or more generally) in ways that have not been conventional in the political system.

As noted, any individual social movement tends not to persist long in the political life of a country. They generally simply disband, but some also become more institutionalized and become interest groups much like others, or even political parties. The environmental movement is the clearest example of these changes over time. Although some more fundamentalist environmental groups still behave like social movements, the majority have become part of the normal interest group environment of government, especially when there is broad legitimacy of interest group activity. In many European countries these former social movements have become institutionalized as "green" political parties and have become part of the governing coalition, most notably in Germany.

Bureaucracy and political parties

In most contemporary political systems, the direct impact of partisan concerns on bureaucracy has been consciously limited by a number of structural and procedural devices. The most important of these, of course, is the institutionalization of the merit system for appointment and retention of administrators so parties can no longer force large-scale changes of administrative personnel when there is a change in governing parties. While some patronage arrangements certainly do exist in all political systems, any widespread use of patronage is generally regarded in Western countries as evidence of corruption and mismanagement. This self-serving view is somewhat less easy to justify since the 1980s, as a number of Western countries have begun to politicize their civil services, and to recruit more specialist political advisors for ministers.[133]

A number of non-Western countries, despite the tutelage of their former colonial countries, have continued or reinstituted non-merit systems of appointment to administrative posts – even the most routine and trivial of posts. This is justified largely on the need for national unity and mobilization in the face of the difficulties of development. In such situations, loyalty to the nation – or more exactly to the current regime – is considered more important than the possession of certain scores on objective tests or the possession of requisite diplomas. This practice is by no means universal in the non-Western world, but a number of one-party regimes tend to recruit their bureaucracies in this fashion. As Kwame Nkrumah once said in relation to administration in Ghana:

> It is our intention to tighten up the regulations and to wipe out the disloyal elements of the civil service, even if by so doing we suffer some temporary dislocation of the service. For disloyal civil servants are no better than saboteurs.[134]

Also, in French-speaking Africa, a number of one-party regimes have attempted to use partisan control to replace "selfish individualism" with "patriotic socialism."[135] While the language is less colorful there, political leaders in a number of Western democracies have stated their wishes to develop a "committed" civil service that would follow the wishes of the dominant political party.[136] A smaller number of such countries have in fact developed the mechanisms for creating such a politically loyal civil service. As yet, these mechanisms have remained within the bounds of civil service law, if not always within previously prevailing customs and understandings. The potential for waste and abuse, and the reinstitutionalization of the spoils system is, however, quite apparent. In this context, we must remember that the politically neutral civil service that we in Anglo-American democracies in particular consider to be normal is really only a century old, while the desire for political loyalty is much older and perhaps much stronger.

While the increasing politicization of the civil service is one option in the context of an age of "conviction politics," another option is the diminution of the political and policy-making roles of the civil service.[137] If, no matter how loyal and committed they appear, the civil service still has the "taint" of objectivity and neutrality, then they may not be perceived as being really trustworthy. Again, these doubts would be present even in countries that have become fully accustomed to a civil service with substantial power in policy making. Thus, one reaction to the perceived need for greater political loyalty by the civil service may be an even greater acceptance of the traditional politics–administration dichotomy, at least among those who actually work in government.

The most obvious example of the utilization of partisan control over the state bureaucracy occurred in the former Soviet Union and other European communist countries, and continues in China and in some authoritarian governments on the right. This control is achieved to a great extent through dual hierarchies – one party and one administrative – used simultaneously to execute policies and to check for the political orthodoxy of personnel.[138] Such a system of duplication appears redundant and inefficient to many Western analysts of organizations, but it is deemed crucial in systems in which political orthodoxy is so important. As with the non-Western systems of the underdeveloped world, partisan control and the use of the bureaucracy as a mechanism for fundamental social and economic change appear to go hand-in-hand. Where political neutrality is not really acceptable, much less valued, then many of the Western dogmas concerning nonpartisan merit appointment are simply not feasible as criteria for evaluating the recruitment and executive actions of administrators.

Summary

We have developed a means of classifying and analyzing the politics of bureaucracy. Beginning with the notion that it is not useful to separate the political from the administrative in either real life or analysis, we have attempted to provide some means of better understanding how administration becomes involved with politics and political actors. This chapter has dealt primarily with administrative involvement with pressure groups, showing the extent to which these two political actors depend upon each other in their attempts to shape public policy and to survive in what might otherwise be an extremely hostile political environment. In three of the four patterns of interaction discussed, some type of legitimating relationship was developed so that a stable pattern of interaction between group and bureaucracy could be used in policy formation – the internal aspect of bureaucratic politics. These relationships could, in turn, directly (through clientelism) or indirectly (through *parantela* and legitimate interactions) produce some support for the programs and the continued existence of the specific bureaucratic agency involved. These are then two political actors who need each other in order to carry out their respective purposes in as efficient a manner as possible. Both operate on the fringes of political respectability and need friends in their battles. The symbiosis that tends to develop between bureaucracy and pressure group is readily explicable in terms of these needs for legitimation and support. The major question that remains is whether this symbiotic relationship is to be accepted – as with the legitimate groups – or forced further into the gray areas of politics.

We turn now to bureaucratic politics, more directly concerned with power and policy than access. These are the politics arising from the public bureaucracy dealing with other formal institutions of government. Each of these institutional actors has access to the arenas of political conflict, and their positions in those arenas are more secure than that of the bureaucracy. Here, then, the bureaucracy must engage in substantially different types of political behaviors, both to preserve its autonomy as an organization and to have an impact on public policy. In some way the role of the bureaucracy becomes that of gaining access to legitimate political power, just as the interest groups had to do when dealing with it.

Notes

1   This separation is usually attributed to American theorists of public administration such as Woodrow Wilson, "The Study of Administration," *Political Science Quarterly*, 2 (1887), 209–13. The doctrine was elaborated by scholars such as Willoughby, Pfiffner and Goodnow. The attack on it was led by Paul Appleby in *Policy and Administration* (University, AL: University of Alabama Press, 1949).

2   See, for example, Colin Campbell and B. Guy Peters, "The Politics/Administration Dichotomy: Death or Merely Change?," *Governance*, 1 (1988), 79–100.

3   Richard Rose, "Giving Direction to Permanent Officials," in Jan-Erik Lane, ed., *Bureaucracy and Public Choice* (London: Sage, 1987).

4   Despite the general public's dislike for bureaucracy, the institution often does have respect for being apolitical or for being the repository of technical expertise. See Morris P. Fiorina, "Flagellating the Federal Bureaucracy," *Society*, 20 (1983), 66–74. More recent attempts to make bureaucracies more closely aligned with political authority may therefore threaten their capacity to legitimate. See Joel F. Handler, *Down From Bureaucracy* (Princeton: Princeton University Press, 1996).

5   B. Guy Peters, "Public Bureaucracy and Public Policy," in Douglas E. Ashford, ed., *History and Context in the Study of Comparative Public Policy* (Pittsburgh: University of Pittsburgh Press, 1992).

6   For a classic discussion of this phenomenon, see Karl Mannheim, *Ideology and Utopia* (New York: Harcourt, Brace and World, 1946), pp. 105ff.

7   See Cornelius Kerwin, *Rulemaking*, 2nd edn (Washington, DC: CQ Press, 1999); Robert Baldwin, *Rules and Government* (Oxford: Oxford University Press, 1996).

8   Lawrence B. Mohr, *Explaining Organizational Behavior* (San Francisco: Jossey-Bass, 1982).

9   See, for example, Colin Campbell, "Review Article: The Political Roles of Senior Government Officials in Advanced Democracies," *British Journal of Political Science*, 18 (1988), 243–72.

10   Policy advice then becomes a crucial aspect of governance in modern societies. See William Plowden, *Advising the Rulers* (Oxford: Blackwells, 1987); B. Guy Peters and Anthony Barker, eds, *Advising West European Governments* (Pittsburgh: University of Pittsburgh Press, 1993).

11   See Robert D. Putnam, "Political Attitudes of Senior Civil Servants in Britain, Germany and Italy," in Mattei Dogan, ed., *The Mandarins of Western Europe* (New York: Halsted, 1975); B. Guy Peters, "Politicians and Bureaucrats in the Politics of Policymaking," in Jan-Erik Lane, ed., *Bureaucracy and Public Choice* (London: Sage, 1987); Donald J. Savoie, *Governing From the Centre* (Toronto: University of Toronto Press, 1999).

12   See Eduardo Zapico Goni, "Many Reforms, Little Learning: Budgeting, Auditing and Evaluation in Spain," in Andrew Gray, Bill Jenkins and Bob Segsworth, eds, *Budgeting, Auditing and Evaluation: Functions and Integration in Seven Governments* (New Brunswick, NJ: Transaction, 1993); Dirk-Jan Kraan, *Budgetary Decisions: A Public Choice Approach* (Cambridge: Cambridge University press, 1996).

13   See Chapters 7 and 8.

14   See Graham Wilson, *Interest Groups* (Oxford: Basil Blackwell, 1991); Jeremy Richardson, ed., *Pressure Groups* (Oxford: Oxford University Press, 1993); David S. Goodman, *Groups and Politics in the People's Republic of China* (Armonk, NY: M. E. Sharpe, 1984); Clive S. Thomas, *First World Interest Groups* (Westport, CT: Greenwood Press, 1994).

15   In this case the advertising is directed as much to the members of the organization as to the general public. Public service advertising, e.g. about drug abuse, is targeted more generally.

16   See Johan P. Olsen, *Organized Democracy* (Oslo: Universitetsforlaget, 1983); Frank L. Wilson, *Interest Group Politics in France* (Cambridge: Cambridge University Press, 1987); Marcia Drezon-Tepler, *Interest Groups and Political Change in Israel* (Albany: State University of New York Press, 1990).

17   See, for example, Olof Ruin, "Sweden in the 1970s: Police-making [sic] Becomes Difficult," in Jeremy Richardson, ed., *Policy Styles in Western Europe* (London: George Allen and Unwin, 1982).

18   Edward C. Page, *Bureaucratic Authority and Political Power*, 2nd. edn (Brighton: Wheatsheaf, 1992).

19   Grant Jordan, "Iron Triangles, Woolly Corporatism and Elastic Nets: Images of the Policy Process," *Journal of Public Policy*, 1 (1981), 95–123; Phillipe C. Schmitter and Gerhard Lehmbruch, *Trends Toward Corporatist Intermediation* (London: Sage, 1982).

20   Phillipe C. Schmitter, "Still A Century of Corporatism?," *Review of Politics*, 36 (1974), 93.

21   *Ibid.*

22   Schmitter's more restrictive view of corporatism may be a function of his initial work in Latin American and Iberian corporatism.

23   Gerhard Lehmbruch, "Liberalism and Party Government," *Comparative Political Studies*, 10 (1977), 91–126; Martin O. Heisler, "Corporate Pluralism Revisited: Where is the Theory?," *Scandinavian Political Studies*, 2 (1979), 277–97.

24   Alan Cawson, *Organized Interests and the State: Studies in Meso-Corporatism* (London: Sage, 1985).

25   Hugh Heclo and Henrick Madsen, *Politics and Policy in Sweden* (Philadelphia: Temple University Press, 1987); H. Adam, *Die konzierte Aktion in der Bundesrepublik* (Cologne: Bund Verlag, 1972).

26   See below, pp. 196–200.

27   Harmon Zeigler, *Pluralism, Corporatism and Confucianism: Political Associations and Conflict Regulation in the United States, Europe and Taiwan* (Philadelphia: Temple University Press, 1988), p. 164.

28   Thomas T. Mackie and Brian W. Hogwood, *Unlocking the Cabinet: Cabinet Structures in Comparative Perspective* (London: Sage, 1985).

29   Donald F. Kettl, *Government by Proxy: (Mis?) Managing the Federal Government* (Washington, DC: CQ Press, 1988); Brinton Milward, " 'Symposium on the Hollow State', Capacity, Control and Performance in Interorganization Settings," *Journal of Public Administration Research and Theory*, 6 (1996), 193–5.

30   Donald F. Kettl, *Sharing Power: Public Governance and Private Markets* (Washington, DC: The Brookings Institution, 1993); Jon Pierre, *Partnerships in Urban Governance* (London: Macmillan, 1999).

31   Brigitta Nedelman and Kurt G. Meier, "Theories of Contemporary Corporatism: Static or Dynamic?," in Phillipe C. Schmitter and Gerhard Lehmbruch, *Trends Toward Corporatist Intermediation* (London: Sage, 1982); Peter Gerlich, "A Farewell to Corporatism," *West European Politics*, 15 (1992), 132–46.

32   Walter Kickert, Erik-Hans Klijn and Joop Kooppenjan, *Managing Complex Networks*

(London: Sage, 1997); Edward Laumann and David Knoke, *The Organizational State* (Madison, WI: University of Wisconsin Press, 1987); Olof Petersson, *Maktens Natverk* (Stockholm: Carlssons, 1989).

33 Ernst B. Haas, *When Knowledge is Power* (Berkeley, CA: University of California Press, 1990); Michael M. Atkinson and William D. Coleman, "Policy Networks, Policy Communities and the Problems of Governance," *Governance*, 5 (1992), 154–80.

34 Sonia Mazey and Jeremy J. Richardson, *Lobbying in the European Community* (Oxford: Oxford University Press, 1993).

35 Yves Meny, "The National and International Context of French Policy Communities," *Political Studies*, 37 (1989), 387–99.

36 Some of the structuralist literature in sociology is attempting to produce just such predictions but the results are as yet not promising. See David Knoke, *Political Networks: The Structural Perspective* (Cambridge: Cambridge University Press, 1990).

37 Olof Petersson, *Maktens Natverk* (Stockholm: Carlssons, 1989).

38 Tom Christensen and Morten Egeberg, "Noen trekk ved forholdet mellom organisasjionene go den offentlige forvaltningen," in Christensen and Egeberg, eds, *Forvaltningskunnskap* (Oslo: Tano, 1993).

39 Knoke and Laumann, *The Organizational State*.

40 These sectoral differences have been argued to be a more appropriate basis of comparison than country. See Gary P. Freeman, "National Styles and Policy Sectors: Explaining Structured Variation," *Journal of Public Policy*, 5 (1985), 467–96.

41 Petersson, *Maktens Natverk*, p. 172.

42 Paul A. Sabatier, "An Advocacy Coalition Model for Policy Change and the Role of Policy-oriented Learning Therein," *Policy Sciences*, 21 (1988), 129–68.

43 The one case in which the corporatist model is more appropriate is the tripartite bargaining over economic policy during the 1960s and 1970s. There was broad agreement on the economic model that best described the relevant issues (Keynesianism) and it was also clear that there were just the three relevant actors.

44 See Keith Dowding, "Model or Metaphor: A Critical Review of the Policy Network Approach, *Political Studies*, 42 (1995), 136–58.

45 Walter J. M. Kickert, Erik-Hans Klijn and Joop F. M. Koopenjaan, *Managing Complex Networks* (London: Sage, 1997).

46 Michele Micheletti, "Interesseorganisationerna – i gar, i dag, i morgon," *Statsvetenskaplig tidskrift*, 91 (1988), 41–54.

47 Nevil Johnson, *State and Government in the Federal Republic of Germany*, 2nd edn (Oxford: Pergamon, 1983), pp. 105–43.

48 Neil Elder, Alastair H. Thomas and David Arter, *The Consensual Democracies* (Oxford: Martin Robertson, 1982), pp. 105–43; Tom Christensen and Morten Egeberg, "Noen trekk ved forholdet mellom organisasjoene og direktorat," in Christensen and Egeberg, eds, *Forvaltningskunnskap* (Oslo, Tano: 1997).

49 Lars Norby Johansen and Ole P. Kristensen, "Corporatist Traits in Denmark, 1946–76," in Gerhard Lehmbruch and Phillipe C. Schmitter, eds, *Patterns of Corporatist Policy-Making* (Beverly Hills, CA: Sage, 1982), pp. 199–203.

50 Jorgen Gronnegard Christensen and Peter Munk Christiansen, *Forvaltning og omgivelser* (Herning: Systime, 1992), p. 74.

51 Kvavik, *Interest Groups in Norwegian Politics*; Micheletti argues that, in Sweden, the groups have become more partisan and less expert. See Michele Micheletti, "Interest Groups in Transition and Crisis," in Clive S. Thomas, *First World Interest Groups* (Westport, CT: Greenwood Press, 1993).

52 Yves Weber, *L'administration consultative* (Paris: Librarie Generale du Droit et Jurisprudence, 1968); Frank L. Wilson, *Interest Group Politics in France* (Cambridge: Cambridge University Press, 1987).

53 Office of the Federal Register, *Federal Advisory Committees* (Washington, DC: Government Printing Office, 1998).

54   Jeremy J. Richardson, "Interest Group Behaviour in Britain: Continuity and Change," in Richardson, *Pressure Groups*.

55   Jakob Buksti, "Interest Groups in Denmark," in Richardson, *Pressure Groups*.

56   Robert B. Kvavik, *Interest Groups in Norwegian Politics* (Oslo: Universitetsforlaget, 1976), pp. 68–73.

57   Klaus von Beyme, "West Germany and the New Germany: Centralization, Expanding Pluralism, and New Challenges," in Clive S. Thomas, *First World Interest Groups* (Westport, CT: Greenwood, 1993), pp. 166–7.

58   See Jan Van den Bulck, "Pillars and Politics: Neo-corporatism and Policy Networks in Belgium," *West European Politics*, 15 (1992), 35–55.

59   Jonas Pontusson, "Labor, Corporatism, and Industrial Policy: The Swedish Case," *Comparative Politics*, 23 (1991), 163–79.

60   See M. P. C. M. van Schendelen and R.J. Jackson, eds, *The Politicisation of Business in Western Europe* (London: Croom Helm, 1987): A 1999 report by the Audit Commission in the Netherlands still identifies dozens of regulatory bodies involving interest groups as major players.

61   Lester M. Salamon, "Rethinking Public Management: Third Party Government and the Changing Forms of Public Action," *Public Policy*, 29 (1981), 255–75.

62   Much of the recent literature has been challenging the idea of autonomy and the comparative strength of states, but these notions that states have more or less power *vis-à-vis* organized interests is still an important means of understanding their actions. See Michael M. Atkinson and William D. Coleman, "Strong States and Weak States: Sectoral Policy Networks in Advanced Capitalist Nations," *British Journal of Political Science*, 19 (1989), 47–67; see also Jon Pierre and B. Guy Peters, *Governance, the State and Public Policy* (Basingstoke: Macmillan, 2000).

63   See Martin O. Heisler with Robert B. Kvavik, "Patterns of European Politics: The 'European Politics Model'," in M. Heisler, ed., *Politics in Europe* (New York: David McKay, 1974); Michael Saward, "Cooptation and Power: Who Gets What from Formal Incorporation," *Political Studies*, 38 (1990), pp. 588–602.

64   The classic case is that of political parties. See Robert Michels, *Political Parties: A Sociological Study of the Oligarchical Tendencies in Modern Democracies* (London: Collier-Macmillan, 1962).

65   Gabriel A. Almond and G. Bingham Powell, *Comparative Politics: A Developmental Analysis* (Boston: Little, Brown, 1966), pp. 77–8.

66   Johansen and Kristensen, *op. cit.*, pp. 200–3.

67   Jean Tournon, "Les pressions publiques: les pouvoirs publics sont le premier lobby de France," in Maurice Duverger, ed., *Jean Meynaud ou l'utopie revisitee* (Lausanne: Universite de Lausanne, 1988).

68   R. A. W. Rhodes, *Beyond Westminster and Whitehall* (London: Unwin Hyman, 1988).

69   Robert B. Kvavik, "Interest Groups in a Cooptive Political System," *op. cit.*, pp. 111–12.

70   Stein Rokkan, "Norway: Numerical Democracy and Corporate Pluralism," in Robert A. Dahl, ed., *Political Oppositions in Western Democracies* (New Haven, CT: Yale University Press, 1968), p. 107.

71   Theodore J. Lowi, "The Public Philosophy: Interest Group Liberalism," *American Political Science Review*, 61 (1967), 19; Robert H. Salisbury and John Heinz, "The Analysis of Public Policies: A Search for Theories and Roles," in Austin Ranney, ed., *Political Science and Public Policy* (Chicago: Markham, 1968).

72   Kvavik, "Interest Groups in a Cooptive Political System," *op. cit.*, 113.

73   Johan P. Olsen, *Organized Democracy* (Bergen: Universitetsforlaget, 1986).

74   Nils Elvander, *Interessorganisationerna i dagens Sverige* (Lund: CWK Gleerup, 1969); Lennart Lundquist, *Forvaltning och demokrati* (Stockholm: Norstedts, 1991), pp. 154ff.

75   Heisler with Kvavik, *op. cit.*

76   See Leonardo Parri, "Neo-corporatist Arrangements, 'Konkordanz', and Direct Democracy: The Swiss Experience," in Ilja Scholten, *Political Stability and Neo-Corporatism* (London: Sage, 1987).

77   For a brief discussion see Salisbury and Heinz, "Analysis of Public Policy," *op. cit.*, 55–9.

78   Peter J. May and Soren Winter, "Regulatory Enforcement and Compliance: Examining Danish Agro-Environmental Policy, *Journal of Public Policy Analysis and Management*, 18 (1999), 625–51.

79   Robert Alford, *Health Care Politics* (Chicago: University of Chicago Press, 1975); Ellen M. Immergut, "Institutions, Veto Points and Policy Results: A Comparative Analysis of Health Care," *Journal of Public Policy*, 10 (1990), 391–416.

80   Donald Kettl, *Government by Proxy, op. cit.*; Christopher Hood and Gunnar Folke Schuppert, *Delivering Services in Western Europe* (London: Sage, 1988).

81   See Jorgen Hermansson, Torsten Svensson and Per-Ola Oberg, "Vad blev det av svenska korporativismen," *Politica*, 29 (1997), 365–84.

82   E. A. Brett, "Adjustment and the State: The Problem of Administrative Reform," *IDS Bulletin*, 19 (1988).

83   Suleiman, *Politics, Power and Public Policy in France, op. cit.*, pp. 338–9.

84   Wolfgang Wirth, "Control in Public Administration: Plurality, Selectivity and Redundancy," in Franz-Xavier Kaufmann, Gidomenico Majone and Vincent Ostrom, eds, *Guidance, Control and Evaluation in the Public Sector* (Berlin; deGruyter, 1986).

85   For Japan, see John Creighton Campbell, "Bureaucratic Primacy: Japanese Policy Communities in an American Perspective," *Governance*, 2 (1989), 5–22; Wayne Moyer, *Agricultural Policy Reform: Politics and Process in the EC and the USA* (Ames, Iowa: Iowa State University Press, 1990); Jeffrey Ira Herbst, *State Politics in Zimbabwe* (Berkeley: University of California Press, 1990).

86   Theodore J. Lowi, *The End of Liberalism*, 2nd edn (New York: W. W. Norton, 1979); John T. S. Keeler, *The Politics of Neocorporatism in France* (New York: Oxford University Press, 1987); Cinzia Dato Giurickovic, *Senso dello Stato e anarchia delle lobbies* (Naples: Edizioni Scientifiche Italiane, 1990).

87   Hugh Heclo, "Issue Networks and the Executive Establishment," in Anthony King, ed., *The New American Political System* (Washington, DC: American Enterprise Institute, 1978); Jack L. Walker, *Mobilizing Interest Groups in America: Patrons, Professions and Social Movements* (Ann Arbor: University of Michigan Press, 1991).

88   Robert H. Salisbury, "The Paradox of Interest Groups in Washington – More Groups, Less Clout," in Anthony King, ed., *The New American Political System*, 2nd edn (Washington, DC: AEI Press, 1990).

89   Olsen, *Organized Democracy*, pp. 157ff; Ruin, "Sweden in the 1970s," *op. cit.*

90   Jack Vowles, "New Zealand: Capture the State," in Clive S. Thomas, *First World Interest Groups* (Westport, CT: Greenwood Press, 1993).

91   LaPalombara, *Interest Group Politics*, pp. 272–4.

92   Theodore J. Lowi, *The End of Liberalism*, 2nd edn (New York: W. W. Norton, 1979).

93   Grant McConnell, *Private Power and American Democracy* (New York: Knopf, 1966), p. 287.

94   William Lilley III and James C. Miller III, "The New Social Regulation," *The Public Interest*, 4 (1977), 49–61.

95   Jonathan R. Macey, "Organizational Design and Political Control of Administrative Agencies," *Journal of Law, Economics and Organization*, 8 (1992), 93–110; Mathew D. McCubbins, Roger G. Noll and Barry R. Weingast, "Structure and Process, Politics and Policy: Administrative Arrangements and the Political Control of Agencies," *Virginia Law Review*, 75 (1989), 431–82.

96   Lowi, "The Public Philosophy. . . ," p. 19.

97   Peter Aucoin, "Organizational Change in the Machinery of Canadian Government: From Rational Management to Brokerage Politics," *Canadian Journal of Political Science*, 14 (1986), 3–27; Donald Savoie, *Governing from the Centre* (Toronto: University of Toronto Press, 1999).

98   See Andre Blais and Stephane Dion, eds, *The Budget-maximizing Bureaucrat* (Pittsburgh: University of Pittsburgh Press, 1992).

99   Von Beyme, for example, found that there was a concentration of legislators with interest group connections on committees in the *Bundestag* that were concerned with the same policy area. See Klaus von Beyme, "West Germany and the New Germany," 170.

100   See B. Guy Peters, *American Public Policy*, 3rd edn (Chatham, NJ: Chatham House, 1993), p. 71.

101   For an example of a particularly strong government lobby see Ulrich Kloti, "Political Ideals, Financial Interests and Intergovernmental Relations: New Aspects of Swiss Federalism," *Government and Opposition*, 23 (1988), 91–102. The Intergovernmental lobby can be important even in centralized regimes, e.g. Pierre Gremion, *La Pouvoir Peripherique* (Paris: Seuil, 1976).

102   Salisbury and Heinz, "Analysis of Public Policy," p. 48.

103   See B. Guy Peters, "Managing Horizontal Government: The Politics of Coordination," *Public Administration*, 76 (1998), 295–312.

104   LaPalombara, *Interest Group Politics*, pp. 306–7.

105   This occurs even in competitive political systems. For example, the major political parties in Germany each has a party foundation that functions as a think-tank for the party as well as funding some academics that may be beneficial to the party. The Adam Smith Institute in Britain was a source of advice and advisors for the Thatcher government, and the Heritage foundation served something of the same function for the Reagan administration. The close links between labor movements and social democratic parties across much of the world is another example.

106   LaPalombara, *Interest Group Politics*, pp. 308–15; see Paul Furlong, *Modern Italy* (London: Routledge, 1994), pp. 149–51.

107   Philip M. Williams and Martin Harrison, *Politics and Society in De Gaulle's France* (Garden City, NY: Doubleday, 1972), pp. 339–42.

108   Sarah Sokoloff, "Socialism and the Farmers," in Philip G. Cerny and Martin A, Schain, eds, *Socialism, The State and Public Policy* (London: Frances Pinter, 1985).

109   On cohabitation see Maurice Duverger, *La Cohabitation des Francais* (Paris: Presses Universitaires de France, 1987).

110   See, for example, Friedrich-Ebert Stiftung, *Organisationen und Verbande in der DDR* (Bonn: Neue Gesellschaft Verlag, 1987).

111   See the relevant chapters in Kay Lawson, ed., *How Political Parties Work: Perspectives from Within* (Westport, CT: Praeger, 1994)

112   Muller-Rommel, for example, found that the major parties in (then) West Germany all had numerous members of the *Bundestag* with direct ties to interest groups. See F. Muller-Rommel, "Interessengruppenvertretung im Deutschen Bundestag," in Uwe Thaysen *et al.*, *US-Kongress und Deutscher Bundestag* (Oplanden: Westdeutscher Verlag, 1989).

113   Marilyn Gittel, *Limits of Citizen Participation: The Decline of Community Organizations* (Beverly Hills, CA: Sage, 1980).

114   Seah Chee Meow, "Parapolitical Organizations," in Jon T. S. Quah, ed., *Government and Politics of Singapore* (Singapore: Oxford University Press, 1985), pp. 173–94.

115   Charles W. Anderson, *The Political Economy of Modern Spain* (Madison: University of Wisconsin Press, 1970), pp. 30–4.

116   Myron Weiner, *The Politics of Scarcity* (Chicago: University of Chicago Press, 1962), p. 78. This quote is perhaps more illustrative of the theoretical case than the relationship between the Congress Party and unions in contemporary India.

117   Anderson, *The Political Economy of Modern Spain*, p. 69. On the changes in the relationship between unions and government since the Francoist regimes, see Victor Perez-Diaz, *El Retorno de la sociedad civil* (Madrid: Instituto de Estudios Economicos, 1987).

118   Colin Crouch, "The Peculiar Relationship: The Party and the Unions," in Dennis Kavanagh, ed., *The Politics of the Labour Party* (London: Allen and Unwin, 1982).

119   Lowell Dittmer, "Comparative Communist Political Culture," *Studies in Comparative Communism*, 16 (1983), 17.

120   The term "canteen" to describe this particularistic relationship between party and interest groups was developed by Fred W. Riggs, *Administration in Developing Countries: The Theory of Prismatic Society* (Boston: Houghton Mifflin, 1964), pp. 105–9.

121   Schmitter, "Still the Century of Corporatism?," p. 93.

122   Victor C. Falkenheim, *Citizens and Groups in Contemporary China* (Ann Arbor: University of Michigan Press, 1987).

123   LaPalombara, *Interest Group Politics*, p. 265.

124   Ezra N. Suleiman, *Politics, Power*, pp. 340–6; see also his *Private Power and Centralization in France: The Notaires and the State* (Princeton: Princeton University Press, 1987).

125   This conflicts rather obviously with Mancur Olson's view that individuals will tend not to join groups if they receive no tangible benefits from that membership. See his *The Logic of Collective Action* (Cambridge, MA: Harvard University Press, 1968).

126   J. Paluski, *Social Movements: The Politics of Moral Protest* (Melbourne: Longman Cheshire, 1991); Thomas R. Rochon, *Mobilizing for Peace: The Antinuclear Movements in Western Europe* (Princeton: Princeton University Press, 1993); Chris A. Rootes, "The New Politics and the New Social Movements: Accounting for British Exceptionalism," *European Journal of Political Research*, 22 (1992), 171–91; Sidney Tarrow, *Power in Movement: Social Movements and Contentious Politics*, 2nd edn (Cambridge: Cambridge University Press, 1998).

127   William P. Browne, *Private Interests, Public Policy and American Agriculture* (Lawrence, KS: University Press of Kansas, 1988).

128   Michelle Salvati, "May 1968 and the Hot Autumn of 1969: The Responses of Two Ruling Classes," in Suzanne Berger, ed., *Organizing Interests in Western Europe* (Cambridge: Cambridge University Press, 1981).

129   See Peter Snow and Luigi Manzetti, *Political Forces in Argentina* (Westport, CT: Praeger, 1993).

130   Martin J. Smith, "Pluralism, Reformed Pluralism and Neopluralism: The Role of Pressure Groups in Policy-Making," *Political Studies*, 38 (1990), 302–22.

131   Lewis Minkin, *The Contentious Alliance: Trade Unions and the Labour Party* (Edinburgh: University of Edinburgh Press, 1991).

132   Tarrow, *loc. cit.*

133   Sir John Hoskyns, "Whitehall and Westminster: An Outsider's View," *Fiscal Studies*, 3 (1982), 162–72; *Revue française d'administration publique*, Special issue on politicization, April–May, 1998.

134   Kwame Nkrumah, *I Speak for Freedom: A Statement of African Ideology* (New York: Praeger, 1961), p. 173.

135   William Tordoff, *Government and Politics in Africa* (Bloomington: Indiana University Press, 1993), Chapter 10.

136   Hoskyns, "Whitehall and Westminster...".

137   Richard Rose, "Loyalty, Voice or Exit?: Mrs. Thatcher's Challenge in the Civil Service," in Thomas Ellwein *et al.*, *Yearbook on Government and Public Administration*, 1987/88 (Baden-Baden: Nomos, 1989).

138   Rolf H. W. Theen, "Party and Bureaucracy," in Gordon B. Smith, ed., *Public Policy and Administration in the Soviet Union* (New York: Praeger, 1980).

The politics of bureaucracy

The previous chapter discussed the political relationship of bureaucracy to "informal" political actors such as pressure groups and political parties. We now turn our attention to the political relationships of the bureaucracy to formal institutional actors in government. In these relationships – labeled "formal-internal" and "formal-external" in our typology – the relative legitimacy of the bureaucracy is changed. When dealing with pressure groups, the bureaucracy represents the majesty of the state; when dealing with legislatures, prime ministers, presidents and the courts, the bureaucracy often appears as an extra-constitutional interloper in the affairs of government. Thus, like the pressure groups in our previous analysis, the bureaucracy must either seek to have its actions legitimated formally or be capable of bargaining successfully to gain influence over decisions. It must also bargain for funds to continue its existence and operations. Without carrying the analogy too far, these options for bureaucracies dealing with political institutions might correspond to the legitimate and *clientela* options available to pressure groups in their dealings with bureaucracy.[1]

The task of the bureaucracy in gaining access to decisions is rarely as taxing as that of the pressure groups; if anything, the tendency has been for the more representative and legitimate political institutions to throw power at the bureaucracy rather than resist its pleas for influence. These representative institutions are incapable of formally abdicating powers (even if they might want to), but they must bargain to get the assistance in policy making and implementation that only the bureaucracy can provide. Bureaucracies have the information and expertise that contemporary governments require for effective policy making. Hence, the representative institutions must find a means of acquiring that information, even if that means informally abdicating their responsibilities.

The shifting power relationships between bureaucracies and more representative institutions involves a delicate political process and some attention to public opinion. Most members of the public continue to regard their elected officials as responsible for the conduct of public business, and these officials must therefore continue the form (if not the substance) of policy making in their interactions with the public bureaucracy.[2] Both sets of actors in this exchange of power, influence, information and money have a great deal to lose by a clumsy handling of the process, and a political "game" of conflict and compromise results. Most of this game is hidden from the public eye, but it is an essential component of government and, despite its apparent illegitimacy, actually improves the quality of policy decisions in most instances.

Two elements must be examined for us to understand better the role played by bureaucracy in modern government. The first is an analytical understanding of the requirements for governing, whether that governing be by the legitimate political institutions or by the bureaucracy. The second is a thorough review of the existing knowledge about the role of bureaucracy in policy making with that analytical picture firmly in mind.[3] We would not expect political institutions to abdicate their rights to bureaucrats, nor do we expect a declaration of bureaucratic government to emanate from the depths of some office building in Foggy Bottom, Whitehall, or Karlavagen. Rather, we are interested in the degree to which – given the lack of leadership alleged to be besetting traditional institutions of government and the difficulties that even skilled leaders have in managing government departments – the bureaucracy is capable of providing needed direction and leadership. This has been largely assumed by theorists of postindustrial society; we now intend to provide some direction in conceptualization, measurement and analysis.

Bureaucratic government

What must any group of actors in politics do to effectively govern a country? The root word for "government" implies control and steering; can any group really be said to be controlling the large and complex societies and economies of industrialized countries? Further, the increasing globalization of economic and social life places an additional constraint on the ability of those in government to govern. This has been true for Third World countries for some years, but it is also increasingly true for industrialized economies.[4] Governments often do not have control over powerful forces within their own countries, much less over other countries or over international organizations such as the International Monetary Fund or the World Bank.

Richard Rose has provided a set of criteria that a political party must fulfill if it is to provide government after it has been elected.[5] If these criteria are modified to remove the components that apply strictly to political parties, they can be restated as follows and applied to any group attempting to govern a society:

1   The group must formulate policy intentions for enactment in office.
2   These intentions must be supported by statements of "not unworkable" means to the ends.
3   There should be some competition over the allocation of resources.
4   The group should be in sufficient numerical strength in the most important positions in the regime.
5   Those given office must have the skills necessary for running a large bureaucratic organization.
6   High priority must be given to the implementation of goals.

As was noted, these criteria are somewhat modified and condensed versions of those developed for political parties, but the damage done to the original intentions of the analysis does not appear mortal. The basic idea that in order to govern, it is necessary for individuals with ideas about policy to be able to implement those ideas through the existing structures of government comes through clearly, even in this modified version of the model. Let us now begin to examine these criteria separately in order to assess the importance of each for the role of bureaucracy in governance.

Policy intentions: the agency ideology

The first criterion for government is one that ordinarily might be regarded as the crucial shortcoming of public bureaucracy as a workable alternative to other forms of government. The bureaucracy has traditionally been regarded in most societies as lacking ideas about what to do with the machinery of government that it appears to control. However, bureaucratic organizations frequently have their own well-developed ideas about what government should do.[6] These ideas are not general statements, such as might be found in a political party platform, but rather are confined to the narrow area of expertise of the agency. Another way to think about these ideologies is as analogous to the "organizational cultures" increasingly used to explain the behavior of private sector organizations. To understand these "agency ideologies" better, it is necessary to differentiate two types of ideologies, here labeled as "soft" and "hard."

The "soft" version of the agency ideology is that the existing program itself is a set of ideas that are favored by the bureaucracy, out of familiarity if for no other reason. Stated more positively, we may regard the ongoing program of an agency to constitute something of an agency ideology. Political executives coming into nominal positions of power over bureaucratic structures have almost invariably reported overt or covert resistance by their civil servants and the existence of a "departmental view" about policy that limits the effectiveness of any political leader. For example, it has long been argued that the British Foreign Office is pro-Arab in Middle-Eastern politics, and that the Department of Education is in favor of the expansion of the public sector of education even in the face of Conservative ministers' seeking to expand the private sector. Thus, ministers coming into office with views contrary to those would have difficulty overcoming the biases of his or her "servants."[8] There are few commentators on bureaucracy or executive leadership in industrialized societies who have not commented on the existence of this "soft" version of a bureaucratic ideology, so if we can accept this as a minimalist version of the existence of ideas about policy in a bureaucracy, then clearly such ideas do exist.

The "hard" version of the policy intention criterion is that not only must the bureaucracy be interested in the preservation of the existing policies of the agency, but it must also be interested in imposing a new set of policy priorities. In part, this is because civil servants are, or become, experts in their policy areas and develop ideas about how policy might be done better. Given that, on average, civil servants remain in their positions longer than do politicians, theoretically they could, over time, alter policies in the way they saw fit, but the civil servants' conceptions of good policy are also subject to change over time.

Civil servants' policy ideas could change in several ways. First, bureaucrats and bureaucracies are increasingly interconnected via organizational and professional memberships, so what they want in policy may change over time to correspond to "best practice" in their profession. Some organizations to which civil servants belong may be strictly "bureaucratic," or concerned entirely with public sector management, while others may be organizations of subject-matter specialists in health, education, sanitary engineering and so on. In either case the bureaucracy may, through its professional contacts, generate challenges to existing policies on the basis of new ideas or the diffusion of policy innovations.

In Western Europe, transnational organizations such as the European Community facilitate such diffusion and the development of bureaucratic policy agendas. These agendas commonly involve mandated or suggested standards of service that usually are generated from within the public bureaucracy rather than from the more political level of government.[9] International organizations such as the United Nations, the International Labor Organization and the World Bank are also responsible for diffusing ideas about what governments should do, and these serve as sources of ideas for public bureaucracies.[10] The day-to-day contacts between national governments and international organizations are a major way in which ideas spread, especially to members of the bureaucracy.

Even without diffusion, however, bureaucrats do have policy ideas. These typically derive from increasing professional qualifications and training of members of the public bureaucracy. Mosher dates the rise of the "professional state" from the mid-1950s.[11] This form of state organization is characterized by the dominance of specialized professional knowledge concentrated in bureaucratic agencies. Mosher was speaking primarily of the United States; in other countries – for instance, France – such a form of state organization may have arisen earlier.[12] The professionals in the agencies become the source of new policies within their sphere of competence, having both expert knowledge and some interest in the expansion of their agencies. Those bureaucrats interested in changing policies may have to wait a number of years before implementing their ideas, so that sufficient popular and political support can be generated. The movement for Medicare and the development of community mental health programs in the United States are examples of policy changes generated within the bureaucracy that required a very long time between formulation and implementation.[13]

Taking either conception of the bureaucratic role in the generation of policy ideas, we would expect significant cross-national differences in the role of bureaucracy. One source of these differences would be the relative independence of agencies from centralized political control. Thus, in the United States or Sweden, where agencies (or *styrelsen*) have substantial independence and where they must compete directly for funding, we would expect greater policy advocacy than in political systems with more centralized administrative systems, such as those with something analogous to Treasury control in the United Kingdom.[14] Likewise – although Diamant's arguments would appear to refute the contention – the absence of effective political leadership appears to allow greater bureaucratic discretion and policy advocacy than would a more stable and effective political executive.[15] For example, in France during the Third and Fourth Republics, "long-range policies had been the work of officials rather than politicians. . . . The situation was a by-product of ministerial instability; however undesirable in theory, it was preferable to no long-range policies at all."[16] In countries that must endure long periods between governments as coalitions are being formed, and then have coalition governments composed of many parties – the Netherlands, Denmark and Belgium are obvious examples – a strong and effective public bureaucracy may be a necessity.[17] Much the same would be true for Third World countries, although here the problems would be general political instability and an absence of effective political leadership.

By way of contrast, the doctrinal emphasis on ministerial responsibility in the United Kingdom makes even ineffective political leaders powerful in theory, if not always in practice. When that doctrine is combined with an effective political leader, such as a Churchill or a Thatcher, the capacity for leadership is very great indeed. Changes in the style of governance in Britain and other Whitehall regimes has tended to accentuate the power of the prime minister and to "presidentialize" the office.[18] At the same time, however, pressures to decentralize departments have tended to give managerial, if not necessarily policy-making, powers to civil servants.[19]

A third factor affecting policy advocacy is the length of time civil servants remain in an agency. We would expect that bureaucratic personnel systems that permit individuals to remain within a single agency or a limited number of agencies during an entire career would experience greater bureaucratic policy advocacy than would administrative systems with more diverse career patterns. Thus the Scandinavian countries, in which civil servants are hired directly by agencies or ministries rather than through centralized personnel agencies, or the United States, where careers tend to be within a single department, would be more likely to have strong policy advocacy by bureaucratic agencies than would the United Kingdom or France, where the senior civil service will have held a number of different positions, albeit within the context of a *grand corps* in France.[20] Germany frequently provides even greater diversity in careers, by recruiting at least some senior federal officials from state and even local government bureaucracies.[21] In the United States the formation of the Senior Executive Service, with greater movement of these top civil servants among agencies, was intended to make at least a part of the American administrative system more like its European counterparts.[22]

Finally, there are definite attitudinal configurations that appear related to policy advocacy by bureaucracy. Aberbach, Putnam and Rockman have discussed such attitudinal configurations among their samples of higher civil servants from six industrialized countries, and related studies have added to that body of information.[23] A number of less quantitative studies have also discussed cultural and dispositional elements of an active public bureaucracy.[24] In some instances there is as much variation within a country as there is between countries, but the attitudes that individuals have toward an active role for the civil service will play an important role in determining that role.

The availability of "not unworkable" means

If politicians are generally considered the masters of policy ideas, then certainly the bureaucracy is considered the master of routine and techniques. Thus, there should be little question about the bureaucracy being able to present feasible means to carry out a program. In fact, the danger runs the opposite way – what is feasible is often translated into policy. Thus, as with Lindblom's idea of reconstructed preferences, bureaucrats are frequently capable of molding not only techniques but also policies by their definition of what is feasible.[25] This definition of feasibility is often manifested in what programs are considered to be "implementable," so the administrative criterion of the ease of implementation may come to dominate ideas of desirable policy based on other criteria.[26]

The ability to mold preferences by appeal to feasibility may make the agency as much a victim of its own procedures as the master. The bureaucracy may wish to be innovative but frequently is limited by a reliance on accepted procedures for a definition of what can – and should – be done. Feasibility may be defined in terms of the ability of the program to be administered through the standard operating procedures of the agency, as was implied with Allison's concept of the organizational process model of policy making.[27] Thus, while agencies may indeed develop feasible mechanisms for implementing a program, these means may in turn blind both bureaucrats and politicians to the range of available policy alternatives. As Majone has pointed out, feasibility is not nearly as constraining as it is sometimes thought to be, and the creative administrator or policy maker can make programs appear feasible that might not at first appear to be so.[28]

The impact of feasibility and standard operating procedures can be seen in the area of industrial policy. The governments of the United States, Western Europe and other industrialized countries are all involved in some form of industrial policy. To a great extent the differences appear to be differences of what are considered feasible programs. In the United States, programs of regulation, tax subsidy and limited direct subsidies are the common approaches.[29] In the majority of European countries – even those with conservative governments – the common approach has been to nationalize industries or for the government to otherwise become directly involved in the economy. There has been substantial privatization in most European countries but there is still much greater public ownership remaining than in the United States.[30] In Japan the involvement of government directly in the financing of industrial ventures and its active involvement with industry is considered possible and desirable.[31]

Bureaucracies may clearly have procedures to implement any program they may wish to, but, rather than being an undivided asset, this may at times be a liability. Agencies may be able to implement a weak conception of program advocacy as mentioned above but may be impeded in making any substantial changes in programs because of accepted procedures and methodologies. Their agenda may be defined by how they are accustomed to doing business rather than by what they would like to do. There is a tension, therefore, between the role of the bureaucracy as advocates of innovation in policies and their role as conservers of procedures.[32]

The role of bureaucracies as conservers of procedures is a variable, as is their role as policy advocate. It varies in part as a function of tradition and culture, but it is also related to more specific political and structural features. One of these is the legalistic emphasis given to public administration in some countries. If the self-definition of governing and administration is inclined toward judicial activity, then formal procedures will almost inevitably come to dominate.[33] A second important aspect is the extent to which there are external pressures for control that would make administrators wary of actions unjustifiable as part of the usual procedures. In all democratic – and some non-democratic – countries, there have been growing pressures for increased accountability of the public bureaucracy.[34] With such pressures, there is a natural tendency for civil servants to retreat behind a wall of procedures for protection, with a consequent loss of innovation and flexibility. As with so many situations dealing with public administration, there is an obvious trade-off between two important attributes here, and no firm basis upon which to make a decision.

225

Competition among agencies

One criterion for governance usually associated with democratic and partisan government is competition among contenders for office. Bureaucrats already have office and are unlikely to lose it. What they do not have is money. Thus, while the currency of partisan competition is votes, the currency of bureaucratic competition is currency. The competition for budgets among agencies may provide many of the same benefits at an organizational level that partisan competition is assumed to provide in democratic politics. Just as partisan competition is presumed to allow voters to choose among alternative governments, which in turn are supposed to be related to alternative policies, bureaucratic competition allows political and administrative personnel to choose more directly among alternative policies.[35] This competition is frequently conducted without the direct involvement of elected officials, as with many spending decisions made within the British Treasury or the ministries of finance of most countries.

An entire chapter will be devoted to the budgetary process, but here we emphasize the strictly competitive and policy-choice aspects of the budgetary process. There is substantial disagreement among analysts of bureaucracy as to both the nature and efficacy of this competition among agencies. Some argue that the conflict is intense and pervasive, with the principal intention being to maximize the agency's budget.[36] Others have argued that the competition is less frequent and more restrained, seeking to preserve a "fair share" for the agency and even seeking cooperation in dividing the available budget pie.[37] Some would argue, in fact, that agencies will frequently avoid conflict and agency growth if that growth may threaten their basic purpose and perhaps expose weaknesses in their existing programs.[38] In addition, Downs among others has argued that competition among bureaucracies, just as with industries in the model of the free market economy, is a positive force encouraging policy innovation and also serving as a check on bureaucratic autonomy.[39] In any of the above conceptions, however, competition among agencies does have a place as a means of allocating resources among competing policies and thus allowing some organizations to flourish and some to languish or, less frequently, to die.[40]

No matter what the stakes of bureaucratic competition may be, such competition will occur to a different degree in different bureaucratic systems. The structure of some governments – for example, the decentralized systems of the United States or Sweden – allow more latitude for bureaucratic competition and bargaining over budgets than is true in more centrally-managed systems.[41] The existence of a large number of agencies with relatively little coordination except through the budgetary process – and the ability of those agencies to argue directly for their own appropriations and to mobilize political support – makes competition a relatively important part of the lives of the agencies and very important for their survival. This means that these agencies will be more capable of providing an alternative source of governing – at least within a single policy area – than will agencies more constrained by central political and administrative control. Thus, bureaucratic competition appears to go hand-in-hand with the "hard" conception of policy advocacy, if for no other reason than that policy ideas provide one means by which the competition is conducted.

226

The nature of bureaucratic competition has two principal effects on politics and government. First, it may in part account for some of the massive growth of the size of government – as reflected in public spending – over the past several decades.[42] Old programs become institutionalized as commitments of governments – and entitlements for citizens – and the need to compete for increased funding produces new programs and new policies from the agencies.[43] Some authors have argued exactly the opposite – that, in fact, competition among agencies would decrease the size of government, but that analysis seems severely to underestimate both the persistence of agencies and their ability to limit the scope of competition to areas outside their "heartlands."[44] It does appear that competition for funding and for new policy initiatives are related to an expansion of public expenditure. The cause may not be entirely the desires of the bureaucracy, however, as politicians may also favor the expansion of government because it provides them with more benefits to distribute among constituents and thus a better chance for re-election. One study of the growth of American government, for example, argued that the major source of expansion had been Congressmen seeking to use new programs to make names for themselves.[45] That study, however, was undertaken prior to the time that conservative ideas became more fashionable and Congressmen have come to compete over who can do the most to reduce public expenditures. Even in this more conservative era, however, Congressmen still continue to press for spending that directly benefits their constituents.[46]

The second major effect of bureaucratic competition is that it limits the internal consistency or coherence of governments. The bureaucracy does not act as an integrated tool of the public instrument, but rather as a set of subgovernments, each serving a clientele group crucial in the political game of survival. Depending upon whether one adopts a more rigid "iron triangle" conception or the more flexible "issue network" perspective, such subgovernments are either immutable and totally self-centered or merely an important aspect of the professionalization and specialization of government.[47] But with highly competitive agencies, there may be bureaucratic governments but no bureaucratic government. As Natchez and Bupp put it, "Priority setting in the Federal bureaucracy resembles nineteenth-century capitalism; priorities are established by aggressive entrepreneurs at the operating levels of government."[48] Again, the reassertion of conservative political ideas, combined with economic problems, has changed the dynamic of expenditure growth. Central agencies such as the Office of Management and Budget in the United States, or the Ministry of Finance in many countries, now have greater (but by no means total) control over agenda setting and attempt to restrict levels of expenditure.[49]

The incumbency of positions

Another necessary condition for the ability of a bureaucracy to provide an alternative source of governance is that officials must occupy the most important positions in policy making, and further, they must be in sufficient numbers to be able to make their decisions effective. The bureaucracy clearly satisfies the quantitative aspect of this criterion, even though it is never certain that those in the lower echelons of the bureaucracy will always comply with the directives of their superiors. However, the bureaucracy may not be able to fulfill the qualitative aspect. Politicians have been thought to be in the most important positions for policy making, and bureaucrats only in a position to implement decisions.

There are two points, however, that qualify the traditional assumption. First, the contact of the bureaucracy with the environment of the organization, as well as the concentration of technical expertise in the lower echelons of organizations, tends to give bureaucracies a substantial control over information and expertise crucial for policy making. Thompson's analysis of the separation of expertise and authority in modern organizations is most important here, and the ability to control information is a major influence over policy in the hands of the bureaucrat.[50] Further, to the extent to which information is passed through the bureaucratic hierarchy, it is selectively distorted. Thus, although there may be enough people in the bureaucracy – and perhaps a few extra – there may still be an important gap between those making decisions located at the top and those with the information needed for making those decisions at the bottom.

Political institutions have been attempting to break the monopoly on information that the bureaucracy appears to hold by creating their own independent sources. These "counterbureaucracies" are most numerous in the United States – for example, the agencies of the Executive Office of the President, the Congressional Budget Office, and the ever growing committee staffs of Congress – but they also exist in a number of other political systems.[51] Some have sought to provide this information through ministerial cabinets,[52] while others have established research offices in government or have strengthened the Prime Minister's office – for example, the expansion of the *Bundeskanzlersamt* in Germany.[53] Still other governments have tried unsuccessfully to use their political parties as instruments for policy research. Despite these efforts, the bureaucracy retains a central role in the development and dissemination of policy-relevant information and thereby retains a powerful position in policy making.

A second factor vital to assessing the relative importance of bureaucratic and political positions in policy making is the weight assigned to implementation in defining policy. As has already pointed out, it can be easily argued that "policy" is what happens, rather than what is stated in legislation. Some have argued, in fact, that policy *should* be defined by the lower echelons of the bureaucracy, given that they have greater knowledge about the objective conditions which government policy is meant to address.[54] Many public programs allow a substantial degree of latitude for the implementers of a policy, such as in police work or in defining the eligibility of applicants for social programs, and the lower echelons of the bureaucracy may be as important as those in the nominal policy-making positions in defining the realities of a policy.[55]

Finally, it should be emphasized again that the bureaucracy retains one principal advantage in a struggle over power and policy – it is simply so numerous. The sheer immensity of the task of controlling a large, complex and knowledgeable public bureaucracy possessing substantial political support may defeat all but the hardiest politician. Even in the United States, where Presidents have a very large number of political appointees compared with most other countries, the size of the bureaucracy and its relationship to important political forces make it difficult to control. As one presidential aide said, "Everybody believes in democracy until they come to the White House," meaning that Presidents would like to have more control over government than they sometimes have.[56]

In summary, bureaucrats may occupy the most important positions in government simply because they occupy the most positions. In addition, they occupy positions that involve both the direct delivery of services and the definition of what the programs really signify for clients. This may mean that they will disagree with the political leadership of their organization, except perhaps on the crucial question of whether the organization should survive. Their ability to loosen up some of the fetters of political control, given their numbers and their expertise, may have some of the same results mentioned for competition among agencies. There is an increased ability for agencies and their personnel to go their own ways, with ever-increasing incoherence among government programs.

6 *The possession of managerial skills*

Political leaders frequently lack the managerial skills necessary to manage a large, complex organization such as a government department.[57] It is assumed that the bureaucrats who occupy these organizations permanently do have the skills, if for no other reason than they appear to keep the organizations running on a day-to-day basis. So, just as they frequently find themselves boarding a policy train that has a great deal of momentum, politicians coming on board their departments find that the organizations of which they are nominally in charge tend to run on their own with little direction from above.

When compared to some absolute scale, rather than to the abilities of politicians, the skills of bureaucrats are not so overwhelming. In fact, many of the standard complaints about bureaucracy, and more specifically about public bureaucracy, concern their internal managerial dysfunctions. Discussions of "red tape," displacement of goals and general chronic inefficiency have filled the literature on bureaucracy.[58] Therefore we must be concerned whether these internal problems are sufficiently great to limit the ability of bureaucracy to provide effective governance when conventional political institutions have proven themselves ineffective.

The "publicness" of the public bureaucracy and the lack of measurable outputs both contribute to the difficulties of managing public organizations. Being public, these organizations must be more concerned about the adherence to laws, norms, procedures and so on than private organizations. They are responsible for public money and act in the name of the people, and they must therefore be held accountable to the people. Accountability, in turn, may force the bureaucrat to protect himself or herself against possible complaints, with the only protection being in the strict or even rigid adherence to rules and procedures.[59] This protection is as important when dealing with superiors as it is when dealing with clients, and policy dealership from the top of the organization may be thwarted by bureaucratic rigidities and procedures within the organization. The best conceived policy innovation will fail if the administrators implementing it are more concerned with their own protection than the success of the program.

These general problems of control are exaggerated by the absence of measurable outputs for most public organizations. The major means of evaluating success in a public bureaucracy generally is consumption rather than production.[60] That is, the standard measure of success is a larger budget rather than more services rendered to the public. Therefore, lacking a single measure such as profit, which would allow an assessment of effectiveness, public sector managers are forced to use rules, regulations and hierarchical control more than would be true for other types of managers. What is attained more often than not is dysfunction rather than smooth operation.

The internal managerial dysfunctions that beset public bureaucracy are the accumulation of many factors. Some are purely organizational dysfunctions that appear endemic to large structures, while others appear related to cross-cultural differences in conceptions of authority and hierarchical control.[61] Many of the dysfunctions are universal but are particularly apparent in some settings. For example, societies with a resistance to the imposition of impersonal authority are more likely to experience bureaucratic dysfunctions than others more accepting of authority.[62] Likewise, and somewhat paradoxically, the greater the extent to which individual public servants are likely to suffer punishment as a result of an improper action, the more likely bureaucratic dysfunctions will be; the individual public servant will retreat behind a wall of rules, regulations and delays for protection.

These managerial problems, and their importance in the eyes of many politicians as well as citizens, have produced a number of responses from government.[63] These are directed at producing better internal management and enhanced capacity for control from the center. One example would be the Financial Management Initiative in the United Kingdom, which has sought to impose on government the same logic that applies in business, such as "cost centers."[64] In Sweden an organization – *Statskontor* – has been established within government to promote improved management, especially through management information systems and other technological changes. In virtually all governments, productivity – and finding incentives to boost worker productivity – is a major concern of government managers.[65]

Finally, it has become a truism to say that, in the management of modern governments, there is an increasing interdependence of the public and private sectors.[66] Not only does policy have to descend from above, but it must be cleared from below. This places bureaucrats in a strategic position to link the public and private sectors, but it also makes their jobs more difficult. Not only must there be compliance within the public organization, but there must also be compliance in the society, with many more built-in "clearance points."[67] These naturally make management more difficult and increase the probability of bureaucratic delay and failure. These managerial problems are accentuated as government utilizes more mechanisms, such as "third-party government" and privatization, that involve the private sector more directly in the delivery of public services. While these techniques are sometimes sold as panaceas for the problems of government, they may actually create rather than solve problems.[68]

A high priority given to implementation of policy

Some of the problems of internal management within public organizations have already been discussed. There are also numerous problems with communication that inhibit the flow of information upward and internal rigidities that block the smooth flow of authority downward.[69] The sixth criterion for government is directly concerned with the translation of decisions made at the top of the organization into effective actions in the field. As has been noted, the "real" policy of a government is the policy as implemented, rather than the statements of legislatures, political executives and others. A number of studies have documented the variety of pressures on field workers that may limit their ability to take the program passed by the legislature and put it into effect as planned.[70] This concern with lower echelon administrators complying with the law as written may appear to conflict with our earlier concern about flexibility and the exercise of discretion. However, that concern with "red tape" focussed on compliance with the procedures of the organization rather than with the substance of the policy.

A significant portion of this failure of implementation can be explained by political rather than organizational factors. As an administrator finds himself or herself farther and farther from the center of organizational power, there is a loss of political support and policy reinforcement. The administrator becomes more subject to political pressures from outside the organization, if for no other reason than that these pressures are more relevant and immediate than those from the home office. Kaufman's now-classic study of the US Forest Service is a case in point of local pressures on a field officer.[71] Pressman and Wildavsky's study of implementation illustrates this problem in an intergovernmental context, as do the problems of ensuring compliance in the decentralized administrative structure of Germany.[72] Even the French *prefet* (now officially entitled the "Commissioner of the Republic") must negotiate and attempt to co-opt local forces in order to govern his or her territory successfully.[73] Even in a (seemingly) centralized country such as France, the need to implement policy in a local setting places a great deal of power in the hands of local politicians and even the local populace.

The necessity of mobilizing political support for policy, and its attendant need to bargain away some policy intentions of central government, may be fundamental to the political process when one is attempting to put legislation into effect. However, it is the one area of the policy process, as Pressman and Wildavsky pointed out some years ago, about which we have the least reliable information.[74] One school of thought about implementation, especially prevalent in Europe, argues that the only way to understand what happens in government is to understand how the very lowest echelons of government work, how they interact with each other and how they interact with citizens.[75] If this is the case, then governance by bureaucracy is at once more important and more difficult. It is important because it will define what happens. It is difficult because it is extremely difficult to obtain coordination and control in such a decentralized environment.

Given the relative lack of information about the implementation process – a weakness that is being remedied rapidly – it is difficult to make reasonable hypotheses about the sources of variation in effective implementation. One obvious hypothesis is that, in highly decentralized administrative systems, such as in Germany, there will be greater problems in ensuring implementation than in more centralized systems. Likewise, the degree of sectionalism and local autonomy would be related to failures of implementation, as would the abilities of political leaders with strong sectional bases to place pressures on the bureaucracy for special considerations for their areas.[76] Several studies in implementation in Third World countries have emphasized the importance of local power relationships and patron–client relationships in limiting effective policy implementation.[77] Also, the degree of vertical separation of the client-contact levels from the center of the organization may make it more likely – and more necessary – that lower-echelon workers bargain with local and client interests. Finally, the lack of political support for an organization, as with the independent regulatory commissions in the United States, may make it crucial for organizations to develop operative policies somewhat different from those intended in their enabling legislation.[78]

In addition to the political pull of clients and geographical interests, there are other factors within public bureaucracies that limit effective implementation. These organizational factors have been documented in a number of studies.[79] More important, as is outlined above in the discussion of agency ideologies, organizations may have goals of their own and consequently may not accept the goals of their nominal political superiors. Opposition to the policies of politicians is rarely overt, as this might violate the formal relationships between elective and permanent officials in government. More commonly, bureaucrats defeat politicians by obfuscation, delay and the use of rules, regulations and procedures.[80] Politicians, being short-term occupants of their positions, rarely understand either the procedural mechanisms or the substance of policy as well as their nominal servants and, consequently, are frequently at the mercy of civil servants. This is particularly so when the policy in question falls among several departments so it is the result of the "groups of officials in the thousands of interdepartmental meetings, luncheons, and telephone calls that take place every day."[81] An interorganizational network exists in government, both among departments and among levels of government, and an individual needs substantial length of service in order to learn the network and how to get what he or she wants out of it.[82] Civil servants have that longevity, whereas politicians rarely do.

We should not count politicians out too readily, however. They have developed a number of mechanisms to attempt to restore their control over the structures and policies of government, increasingly considered to be dominated by bureaucracy. We have already mentioned the use of ministerial *cabinets* in France and Belgium, as well as the role of the Central Policy Review Staff in the United Kingdom. There is also an increasing use of political appointees in positions in which they were previously infrequent. Even in the United Kingdom, which has had a long history of a politically neutral civil service, the Thatcher government has made appointments in senior civil service posts that *appear* political, in addition to the appointment of some manifestly political advisors in the Treasury.[83] There has been an increase in the appointments of political officials in some of the Scandinavian countries as well.[84] In countries such as Germany, where a civil service career and political commitment have not been seen as so incompatible, the use of political appointments has become more obvious and more important than in the past.[85] Further, development of "matrix organizations" in the *Bund* ministries has been, in part, an attempt to improve control within these organizations since it is so difficult to exercise control over the *Land* administrations charged with implementation.[86] Those difficulties are especially pronounced when there are partisan differences between the central government and *Land* governments.

Implementation is a central problem in contemporary political systems. Breakdowns of implementation represent a fundamental failure of those systems to translate political ideas into effective action. Bureaucracies are a central component of this failure, although usually not from malice but more from the rigidities built into their structures, or from their members' sincere beliefs in the policies already being pursued or regarded as preferable. While implementation is important for governance, it is not the only problem. At times there may be a tendency to design a program for ease of implementation without asking whether that is really how government should undertake to "solve" a particular policy problem.[87] As in the earlier discussion about the domination of procedures over substance in public bureaucracies, implementation considerations can come to dominate real policy considerations, and governments may do what they think they *can* do rather than what they *should* do or even *want* to do. Certainly the true meaning of a policy is the actual policy that is implemented rather than what is written on an official piece of paper. However, there is little point in having a policy implemented if it is the wrong policy in the first place. Thus we cannot blame policy failure only on the implementation of a program but should attribute it also to more fundamental problems with the conceptualization and design of the program itself.

Summary

We have been exploring the question of the ability of bureaucracy to provide government with a set of coherent policy intentions and the implementation of those intentions in contemporary political systems. The conclusion is that, although bureaucracy may be able to go some distance in providing such leadership, it is also thwarted by many of the same problems that limit politicians seeking to exercise governance. Those whose primary concern is democratic politics and popular control of government may welcome this analysis initially but upon reflection may be chastened. This analysis indicates that there are difficulties in public management and government that are more basic than the short-term political and economic forces cited as the causes of most contemporary problems.

One term for the very fundamental problems which contemporary governments face in governing is "overload." This term, though coined in the 1970s, continues to have substantial relevance for governments today.[88] These problems arise from a loss of confidence by citizens, the decline of obedience and quiescence by citizens, the inability to provide meaningful new benefits and – last but certainly not least – the very machinery of government itself. The sheer bulk and inertia of bureaucracy, combined with its needs for external political support from clientele groups, tend to fragment control and divert attention from problems of governance to problems of organizational survival. The political life and, to some extent, the values of bureaucratic agencies are tied up in questions of organizational survival.

Thus government by bureaucracy is a problem. Bureaucracy may be capable of supplying government, but unlike political parties that supply by "directionless consensus," government supplied by bureaucracy may be government by "non-consensual directions." The government supplied will go in many directions, dependent upon the agency and its relationship to its clientele. For the same reason it will be non-consensual and incoherent government. There would be no integrating ideology or philosophy, only a set of specific ideologies about specific policy problems. These ideologies, rather than integrating the activities of government, tend to fragment government and render it a set of competing, or at least not cooperating, fiefdoms. Even popular leaders, such as Ronald Reagan, Margaret Thatcher and Pierre Trudeau, with long periods in office, find it difficult to overcome these deep-seated centrifugal forces in government. This centrifugal tendency is all the more pronounced in poorly integrated governments, e.g. that of the European Community or those of less-developed countries.[89]

Strategies in bureaucratic politics

Even if we can agree that government by bureaucracy, meaning by an integrated and purposive civil service elite, is not a likely occurrence, this does not mean that the struggle over power and influence on public policy between elective officials and permanent officials will not go on still.[90] In this struggle, each side has important weapons and important stratagems at their disposal. This section will discuss some of these weapons and how they may be employed.

The resources of bureaucracy

The first and perhaps most important resources of the bureaucracy are *information* and *expertise*. To the extent that government has information at its disposal, this information is concentrated in bureaucratic agencies. Accompanying that information is the technical expertise to understand and interpret it. This relative monopoly of information can be translated into power in several ways. The most blatant is the argument that since they (the agency) know more about the subject, they should be given control over it. In other words, they are likely to do a better job (technically) of making policy in a certain issue area than would the relatively ignorant political executive and legislature. If that argument fails, as it often does, and the politicians are sufficiently audacious to attempt to make policy themselves, then the major source of information for formulating those policies will still be the bureaucracy.[91] This means that the bureaucracy is in a situation in which it can at least implicitly trade information for influence over policy, and indeed information may be produced selectively to make one type of decision a virtual inevitability. In the same vein, Bartlett has referred to legislatures "subsidizing" bureaus in order to get information about their operations, that is, trading information for money.[92]

A second power at the disposal of the bureaucracy is the *power of decision*. Despite the "metaphysical pathos" about the red tape and inefficiency of bureaucracy (especially public bureaucracy), compared with many political institutions – especially legislative institutions – they seem a model of efficiency.[93] Having few procedural rules concerning free discussion, voting and the like, bureaucracies are in a position to act more rapidly than legislatures on many issues. There are, of course, some procedural safeguards and delays for would-be bureaucratic rule-makers – for example, the Administrative Procedures Act in the United States – relatively speaking, the bureaucracy can act quickly.[94] In part because of the capacity of bureaucratic organizations to make decisions quickly, and to utilize technical information more readily than do legislatures, there has been a continuing trend to delegate authority to them.[95] Also, bureaucratic agencies do not have to be as sensitive to the political pressures that may be coming from constituents in making their decisions. Political executives may share the advantage of rapid decision making in situations where they are independent of the legislature, as, for example, authoritarian leaders, or the French or American presidencies within a range of action, but they are more commonly bound in democratic systems by a reliance on legislative action and approval.

Third, just as political institutions have their *political supporters*, so do bureaucratic institutions. In the previous chapter we discussed the relationship between bureaucracy and interest groups. In two of the four types of interactions there is a definite political linkage between an interest group and an agency. The bureaucracy has the ability to mobilize these political supporters in making claims for funding or for policy autonomy. The political support of other political institutions tends to be less policy-specific than that of agencies, and the agency can consequently mobilize a more interested and vocal group of supporters on an issue than would be likely for any legislative group that sought to oppose it.[96] This is especially true given the internal difficulties of decision making within the legislature. This issue-specific political support can be of special importance because of the fragmented nature of decision making in many legislative bodies, with committees or other specialized bodies having a substantial influence over policy and funding. The agency is able to mobilize support before the appropriate committee, which may not have the interest or latitude to consider alternative uses for funds, and can develop the case that indeed there is a large demand for the agency's services. The bargain struck with the client group, allowing access and influence, is generally consummated in front of a legislative committee.[97]

Having discussed the political powers of the bureaucracy, we now proceed to discuss the advantages they have by being *apolitical*. This may appear to be a contradiction, but it is an important means of understanding how bureaucracies are able to compete successfully for influence and power in decision making. Bureaucracies have the advantage of being formally divorced from partisan politics. Civil servants do not have to stand for election, are not faced with constituency pressures or pressures for conformity from their own party, and have been effectively neutered politically in most societies. This isolation from partisan politics allows them to argue that not only are they expert in what they do, but also that their decisions will not be affected by the need to placate voters. This partisan impartiality goes hand-in-hand with the expertise of the bureaucracy to make a strong argument that their decisions will be superior on technical grounds to those that would be taken by political institutions. If for no other reason, the longer time horizon of the bureaucracy and their willingness to make long-term plans may produce superior decisions.

As was already mentioned, bureaucracies develop *agency ideologies* as a means of justifying their actions. These ideologies are important weapons in the struggle over influence, as they tend to be impervious to the argument and evidence of outside "non-experts" and to be self-serving for the agency. One of the classic examples of such an agency ideology is the doctrine of strategic bombing held by the United States Air Force. This doctrine, stated simply, is that the best means (if not the *only* means) of bringing an enemy to its knees is through strategically bombing its means of war production. This is alleged to have brought about the demise of Germany and Japan in the Second World War, and these cases are cited as proof of the doctrine. Such evidence as does exist on the effects of the bombing, however, indicates that if anything, production of war material increased during the bombing rather than decreased.[98] The Air Force – for obvious reasons – persists in its claim that bombing is the answer to the problems of war. Even with so-called "smart" munitions the record of bombing during the Gulf War was filled with failures to hit key targets (e.g. the SCUD missiles) but this has not deterred the continued articulation of the ideology of strategic bombing.

There are a number of other examples of the rigid adherence of military bureaucracies to ideologies of this sort, but some of the same behavior can be found in social and economic bureaucracies as well. Even though most social agencies at least pay lip service to the idea that most social problems are multidimensional, they tend to see them and act on them largely in terms of their own expertise, to try to capture clients rather than sending them on to seek other types of help, and to argue for increased funding in terms of the ability to solve social problems through their particular program. The numerous problems of agency coordination in social services are one indication of the reliance on agency ideologies about policy and solutions to those problems.[99]

To return to the central point of this discussion of bureaucratic ideologies, we can see that the existence of such an ideology is important for the success of the agency in dealing with political institutions. Political actors rarely have a ready reply to such policy-specific ideologies. They labor under a number of disadvantages in competing with the bureaucrats, not the least of which is a frequent lack of any specific policy ideas. Many political leaders, when put into a ministerial or cabinet role, simply do not have the background in the policy area to contribute much in the way of policy direction, and the demands of the job often prevent them from developing such a direction. The civil servants who work within the department – even the generalists at relatively high levels – rarely have such difficulties and are quite capable of providing a direction for the department's program.

Finally, the bureaucracy has the advantages of *permanence* and *stability*. It is difficult to fire a civil servant and may even be difficult to have one transferred. Civil servants can always adopt a strategy of waiting and delay. Ministers come and go, but the basic work of civil servants does not change, simply because the ministers rarely have time to learn what has to be changed or to put such a program into effect. In addition, the longer time perspective of the permanent civil service allows them to pick solutions to problems that may take a long time to come to fruition but that may ultimately solve a problem rather than offering only a "quick fix" before the next election.

The resources of political institutions

Perhaps the ultimate weapon at the disposal of political institutions is their *legitimacy*. Associated with legitimacy is the formal and constitutional authority to do the things that government is intended to do. Few constitutions even mention bureaucracies, much less vest any formal powers of decision making in them. Therefore, whether by delegation, funding, or acquiescence, bureaucratic actions must be legitimated by constitutionally prescribed actors. More often than not this legitimation comes through inaction and acquiescence rather than through formal action, but it still involves a transfer of authority.

Almost as important as the formal power and authority to perform tasks is the wherewithal to do them: money. The second major power held by political institutions, then, is the *power of the purse*. In order to survive, prosper and grow, agencies require money and must be able to influence political institutions to provide them with it. The budgetary process – or the politics of survival, as we referred to it earlier – is one of the crucial points of interaction in bureaucratic politics. The bureaucracy seeks money and the autonomy to spend it, while the political institutions seek control of their funds and also seek to ensure accountability as to how it will be spent. The importance of the budget for both sets of actors has led to the development of a number of techniques on both sides to attempt to counteract the powers of the other.

Third, and certainly related to the first two items, is something that we might call *latitude,* or *autonomy for the agency*. In general, agencies seek to acquire as much latitude as they can. This refers primarily to latitude to make policy; they might seek a blanket grant of authority in an area of policy. It may also refer to budgeting; they might seek some latitude in the way in which funds may be spent. Given the volume of business and the complexity of modern government, bureaucracies are likely to be given greater latitude. On the other hand, the power to grant such latitude is a powerful weapon for political institutions and can be used to gain concessions of information, or compliance on other issues. It is the constitutional role of political institutions to control policy and its implementation. Moreover, they must be responsible politically for what happens to the country, and they want to control policy if they are to be held responsible for it. Thus, in addition to bargaining over money, agencies and political institutions must also bargain over the degree of autonomy to be granted, the responsibility for funds and accounting, and the procedures for delegating authority.

The powers of political institutions mentioned to this point are largely formal and legal. These institutions have substantial resources as well, if for no other reason than they are, to some degree, *representative of the public*. It may be argued exactly how representative the institutions are along several dimensions, but they are generally the most representative institutions available.[100] As such they are able to mobilize political strength through their relationship to the public, political parties and interest groups. The public will rarely rise up as a mass in righteous anger, but the politicians are quite capable of making it seem that way. By any number of means – investigation, publicity, electoral campaigns, speeches, debates – the political institutions may be capable of pitting the "people" against the bureaucrats. Given the careers and insulation of public bureaucracy, there is little the people are capable of doing even in their aroused state, but the bureaucracy can ignore public opinion for only so long. Moreover, the arousal of public opinion may make it considerably easier for the political institutions to employ the formal powers at their disposal.

Bureaucratic ploys

Having discussed the weapons available to both sides in the struggle over policy and money, we proceed to the dynamic means through which those powers can be exercised. This of necessity will be only a partial listing of all the ploys available but it still should provide an idea of the ways in which both bureaucrats and political leaders play the game of politics within formal organizations.

We begin with a set of devices, stratagems and structures that greatly assist the bureaucracy in achieving its ends of control over policy and stable if not expanding budgetary commitments. In most cases these ploys are related to the ability of the bureaucracy to mobilize information and expertise, and secondarily to the ability to mobilize bias in the form of pressure group support for programs. These ploys largely involve removing policy from consideration by political officials and placing it in the hands of presumably neutral, expert and objective administrators. As admirable as this may sound in theory – at least to those who advocate "rational" policy making in government – it represents a movement away from the ability of elected or even selected leaders to control government and supply the quality and quantity of goods and services demanded by the public.

Planning. The first and perhaps most important of the strategies of expanding bureaucratic influence is public planning. This device began as a means of controlling the economy but has been extended to a variety of social and economic spheres such as land use, transportation, urban areas and even social services.[101] Even in the 1990s, where government planning received a bad name among most of the public, it was still a powerful weapon for the bureaucracy.

The need and justification for planning is obvious from a number of perspectives. In the first place, planning involves the systematic application of knowledge to important areas of human concern and allows some long-range manipulation of the state of the economy and society. Likewise, it can make the nature of the economy more amenable to the desires of the public and, by removing many decisions from the marketplace, allow for investment in areas that, while socially desirable, may not be particularly profitable in a private market. By removing to some extent macro-economic policy from the political agenda, the device may successfully defuse many important political conflicts, especially where politics is heavily influenced by segmental disputes within the society. As Abert said of economic planning in the Netherlands, "... the technical process of economic planning is accorded a position of major influence [because of] the lack of a political consensus that might resolve economic issues through the electoral process."[102] Thus the tendency toward adopting planning as a means of making long-range policy tends to remove some aspect of public policy from the partisanship and divisiveness of politics, and transport it to the rarefied atmosphere of "rational" decision making.

It should be clear that planning is an important weapon for the bureaucratic politician. It places the regulation of the national economy or some other aspect of national policy in his or her hands. If planning is accepted as the "proper" means of making policy for the nation, then the proper policy becomes the one that the planners advocate, and the burden of proof falls on those who advocate anything else. This may be especially true of policy areas other than the economy where the effects of the policy decisions are not as apparent to the public through such factors as inflation and unemployment, and where the requirement of capital investment means that the effects will be years in the future.[103]

A second item in favor of bureaucracy planning, especially economic planning, is that it is difficult for the average layperson – or politician – to understand. Much current economic planning is done through such devices as mathematically sophisticated econometric models processed by computer and dependent upon large quantities of economic theory. Few members of the political community have the skills, or are willing to invest the time required to acquire the skills, to understand fully the reasoning behind these planning methods or the assumptions on which they are built. The politicians are at the mercy of the planners in having the programs and their implications explained to them.[104] Some political systems have gone even farther in having the plan go into effect unless actively blocked by the political institutions.[105] Given that this would be a difficult and time-consuming activity with very little probable payoff to a politician, since his or her constituents probably wouldn't understand it anyway, this active blocking will rarely be undertaken.

A third item favoring the bureaucracy and the planners is the integration of the plan. Almost by definition, planning offers something of an integrated and comprehensive view of some aspect of social or economic life and an integrated set of policies for achieving certain ends in that policy area. Therefore, any attempt by political institutions to modify the plan can be opposed as upsetting the whole plan. As Shonfield put it:

> if parliament is to play an effective part in the business of national planning – and if it does not the outlook for the future of democracy is bleak – then members of parliament will also have to recognize some theoretical as well as practical limitations on the exercise of their collective sovereignty. These theoretical limitations apply to the whole procedure of introducing a parliamentary amendment to a set of planning proposals, whose merit is their intellectual coherence and self-consistency. If any significant element in them is changed, the whole structure must be adapted to accommodate the alteration.[106]

239

He goes on to argue that such adaptability is crucial on the part of the planners, but the presence of an integrated plan makes it difficult for any political organization to make the types of alterations and modifications at which they are perhaps most adept. The burden of proof would again appear to fall on those who want to change the plan rather than those who want to accept it. This was written during the heyday of planning but may be even more true as governments must make comprehensive plans about the environment, health care and a variety of other complex policy areas.

Following from the above, it is difficult for political institutions to attack the efficacy of the planning process as a means of allocating resources. Certainly some plans are more successful than others, but with the exception of a few societies that approach being totally planned, there are always sufficient areas of independence so that plan failures can be blamed on those non-planned sectors of the economy, or on oil prices, or on drought. This not only can be used as a means to argue for more public control of the marketplace, but also prevents the public and its representatives from measuring bureaucratic or planning output in the same way they might measure the output of other governmental programs such as garbage collection or water supply. Planning is, thus, one of the public goods mentioned previously that often defy accurate pricing.

In this discussion we should be careful not to assume that planners and the rest of the bureaucratic establishment are necessarily homogeneous. In many cases, in fact, there is significant friction between the traditional bureaucracy and planning agencies that exist outside that conventional framework. As with the conflict between line and staff, the presence of planning agencies threatens line agencies, and planning tends to direct resources away from the pet projects of line agencies. However, the planning process must be seen as directing political control and authority away from "political" institutions and toward bureaucratic (especially when each agency or department does its own planning) or technocratic agencies.

Planning constitutes a major weapon in the hands of the bureaucracy, both at agency and societal levels. It provides a technical means of reinforcing and quantifying the positions of the bureaucracy and at the same time removes many important and sensitive matters from the hands of partisan decision makers. Planners can argue that their decisions will be objectively superior to those reached by partisan institutions, that they can impose a longer time perspective on the problem than the politicians, and that they can prevent special interest considerations from determining policy. Despite these to-some-degree commendable attributes of planning, the major effect that we must be concerned about in this context is removing those decisions from the hands of politically responsible officials and placing them into the hands of the bureaucratic elites. This shift may be seen by a large portion of public opinion as undemocratic. It may be seen by those on the political right, who had greater political influence in the 1980s, as removing public decisions even further from influence by their favorite solution for social problems, the market.

Budgeting. An entire chapter is devoted to the role of budgeting in the life of public agencies, but some points should be made here briefly, since budgeting is such an important weapon for both bureaucrats and politicians. On the bureaucratic side, a number of highly sophisticated and technical approaches to the problem of allocating resources have been useful in mystifying the process of making budgets. These techniques, in turn, placed the more amateur political leaders at something of a disadvantage. These approaches to budgeting, such as PPBS (Planning-Programming-Budgeting System, or simply program budgeting), ZBB (Zero-Base Budgeting), RCB (the French version of program budgeting) and volume budgeting in Britain (the PESC system), were undertaken with the admirable intention of improving the objective quality of public decisions and of relating budgeting more directly to the final products of public programs. Interestingly, if anything, these reformed systems of budgeting were designed to break the strangle hold of the bureaucracy on the budget through incrementalism. Their effect, however, would appear to have been actually to strengthen the position of the agency in relationship to parliaments or political executives. Many of these programs were discredited shortly after their introduction but keep reappearing in other manifestations in other countries.

In the first place, program budgeting requires considerably more information about the activities of the agencies than is required for traditional line-item budgeting. Where is that information to come from? Clearly it must come from the agencies themselves. Assuming that the agencies do not directly lie about the operations of their agencies, this informational role still gives them a substantial impact over the outcomes of budgeting. Program budgeting requires a considerable investment of time and money to be effective, so programs as well as agencies are selected for more intensive analysis in any one year. Frequently, centralized budget agencies – if they exist – lack sufficient staff to scrutinize the activities of agencies fully or to collect independent information. The bureaucracy may therefore not be effectively restrained by this device in its search for secure funding.

A second point is that program budgeting, although it requires priority setting at the very highest levels of government, forces some decentralization of control within the bureaucracy. One effect of the programming process is to allow each bureau chief considerably more latitude than would be allowed under a line-item budget. Instead of funds being allocated for items such as personnel, equipment and the like, they would be allocated for doing a job. The bureau chief would be allowed latitude in how he used the funds. For example, if he found that he could build roads more cheaply by using less sophisticated machinery and more hand labor, a bureau chief would be able to do so. While this may, and should, have the effect of producing better policy outputs at a lower or equal cost, the *political* effect is to make it more difficult to impose central control on the operations of the bureaus and agencies, although priorities will be determined centrally.

Third, few political bodies are likely to be willing or able to invest the time and money required to undertake their own program review of agencies. They rarely have the staff to compete with those of the agencies, so the competition for control becomes a conflict between a "computer and slide rule."[107] Even if legislatures or political executives were to respond favorably to the imposition of such management techniques – and the evidence is largely that they have not – they might still be at a severe disadvantage in attempting to understand and alter the outputs of program budgeting by the agencies and centralized budgeting agencies.

Related to both planning and program budgeting is what we might call "technical budgeting." By this we refer to a tendency to assign the budgetary function to a special body having highly developed technical skills and little if any political responsibility. Another variant of budgeting with some of the same implications is a tendency to develop middle-range budgetary forecasting, with projected budgets made for five-to-seven-year periods.[108] The formulation of the national budget in Norway has been perhaps the best example of technical budgeting. The budget is still largely formulated by a group of civil servants and technicians using a quite complex model of the Norwegian economy.[109] These "technocrats" develop a draft budget that is then scrutinized by a select committee of civil servants and the government, is reformulated, and is finally passed by the parliament.

Storting. This procedure gives significant powers over the formulation of the Norwegian budget to one set of civil servants. As Higley *et al.* argue:

> It is in the nature of the process that the choices of the civil servants who collect and analyze the mass of data from which the national budget is constructed are of fundamental importance to the outcome. It is so because the civil servants have a virtual monopoly of the technical knowledge necessary to the process and because the process gives the initiative to them throughout.... Moreover, many of the communications from the civil servants to the government take the adversary form: civil servants tell the government how the national budget should be composed. Thus, not only are they in control of the general framework in which decisions are made, but they also define the important questions, influence the directions of the politicians' attention, and argue for their proposed solutions with the help of esoteric knowledge that is difficult to refute.[110]

The authors point out that elected ministers can and do have an impact on the final shape of the budget, but the choices they make are likely to be small relative to the overall content of the budget, and these choices tend to be within the general parameters already established. Planning the reformulation of one aspect of the budget will tend to require a reformulation of the entire document, and the substitution of the judgment of ministers and politicians for that of experts. This is quite a burden for politicians to bear in attempting to retain control over policy. Some control has been regained as the economic problems of the 1980s and 1990s reached even prosperous Norway, but planning is still an important mode of decision making.[111] Here again, as with the conflict between planners and line bureaucrats, we find that the "bureaucracy" as a whole rarely marches to the same drummer. There is an almost inherent conflict between the spending ministries and the financial ministry. They are all bureaucrats in the generic sense but show here a lack of any common interest that might make them a unified body controlling public policy. We might be better able to understand the outcome of what happens in budgeting in terms of the *conflicts* of these agencies.

This would in fact be the conflict of differing types of expertise: one of policy areas and one of economic effects. In any case, despite who may win that conflict, the political institutions of legislatures and presidents may be excluded from it. The anticipated reactions of the actors may be influenced by the threat of the imposition of political authority, but in day-to-day operations, it is a bureaucratic war.

Advisory bodies. Another useful device for the bureaucracy in gaining control over policy areas is the use of advisory bodies or committees in the formulation of policy. We have previously discussed bodies of this type that are attached to ministries, but they also provide a useful means for our understanding something of the influence of administration on policy. It is, in fact, in part because of the pressure group connection that these bodies can become so successful in assisting bureaucratic power. In the societies where the use of advisory bodies is so important in making policy – principally Scandinavia and the Low Countries – the imprimatur of pressure groups is important in legitimating policy. Since these advisory boards are attached to the ministries and thereby interact largely with civil servants, there is the possibility of substantial reciprocal influence over policy. Further, many of the members of the advisory bodies are themselves members of the civil service. For example, one study in Norway showed that in 1966, 272 civil servants held 623 positions in 351 (of 954) advisory committees.[112] Later studies indicate that two-thirds of all civil servants, and almost 90 percent of top civil servants, participate on committees of this type.[113] In France, although the numerical membership of civil servants in ministerial advisory boards is generally not large, they tend to hold the more important positions of chairman and *rapporteur*, so what the committee advises is at least interpreted by the civil service before dissemination.[114] In Japan the civil service serves as the staff for the numerous advisory committees (*shingikai*) and is often accused of manipulating the content of their recommendations.[115]

Thus the civil service can be expected to have a significant influence over the findings of ministerial advisory boards, and these boards often have a crucial role in determining the final outcome of policy. Board or committee findings tend to have the approval of both pressure groups and the civil service, have substantial informational backing and, therefore, become quite difficult for anyone to oppose politically. Thus the vertical integration of many pressure groups into the ministries, and the general ability of the ministries to dominate one policy area, make the formulation of much public policy in practice – if not officially – the product of negotiation between representatives of pressure groups and the civil service. One Swedish official report, for example, argued that:

> Many agencies have been built and have developed their identity on different sectors of the welfare state. Contacts between these agencies and their sector's interest groups are often intimate. Therefore agencies and specialized departments have often functioned as embassies of these special interest groups.[116]

A second type of advisory committee tends to be independent of any particular ministry, although it may be working on a problem clearly identified with the concerns of the ministry. We have already discussed bodies such as royal commissions, presidential task forces and the like when discussing pressure group impact on policy.[117] These advisory bodies tend to have substantial bureaucratic input as well, and, if anything, the influence of the bureaucracy has been increasing in recent years.[118] This growing influence has been partly a function of the growing technical expertise of the bureaucracy in a variety of policy areas and partly a recognition of the need to obtain cooperation from the civil service if a program is to be effective once adopted.

It should be obvious that, no matter who benefits directly by the use of such advisory bodies, it is not the political actors who will be ultimately held responsible for their actions and policies. These political actors gain in the short term by having a sensitive issue defused, but in the long term, the likely effects are to increase bureaucratic influence over the policy. Further, the issues likely to be sent to commissions of this type are the truly sensitive ones that cannot be resolved easily by political actors. Thus, if we are willing to admit that most routine decisions are determined largely administratively and now we see that many extremely broad and sensitive decisions are increasingly influenced by bureaucracy, the roles of the political institutions are being diminished rather dramatically. They do not have the time or staff to handle most routine decisions, and they lack the consensus to handle most major decisions, so they are left with the task of setting broad policy guidelines on issues where there is already a certain amount of consensus. This may be an extreme statement, but the evidence to this point in the analysis would seem to support it.

The listing of the various ploys and strategies available to the bureaucracy and, in fact, often unwittingly placed in their hands, gives some idea of the way in which their expertise, internal organization and position in the structures of government can be translated into effective political power. The devices listed above have relied largely on the expertise and information available to the bureaucracy and, consequently, have assumed the lack of same on the part of the political institutions. In the next section we look at the ways in which the political institutions have sought to counterattack against growing bureaucratic influence on policy.

Politicians' ploys

Given the imposing list of formal powers that the political institutions have been said to have, it may seem strange that they would need to search out new means of asserting their power and their control over policy and the budget. However, the skills and expertise of the bureaucracy (at least in relative terms) and the largely antiquated structure of many political institutions have made such a search necessary. Legislatures may be good at deliberation but are often poor at making decisions, and political executives often lack the skills necessary to manage large public organizations.

Special budgetary institutions.   One of the first things that the political institutions must seek to recover from the potentially dominant civil service is some effective control over the public budget. In order for them to do so, several forms of specialized budgetary institutions have been devised. The most common is something following the style of the Office of Management and Budget (OMB) in the United States.[119] The idea of these bodies is to develop an expert institution responsible directly to the political executive rather than to the bureaucracy. Most budgeting systems require a review of agency requests by other civil servants in a ministry of finance, treasury or some other similar body, but few provide for an office so directly responsible to a political actor or institution. It is expected that the existence of such a body will allow the executive to be able to have an independent watchdog on expenditures and to have a policy staff directly concerned with expenditures and policy. A vigorous bureaucratic agency such as the British Treasury or the Swedish Ministry of Finance may be able to provide something of the same type of control, but the linkage to the chief political executive may not always be so clear. This lack of linkage will often result in deliberations between civil servants over policy rather than the imposition of executive guidelines.

Unfortunately, little is actually known about the ability of OMB to control expenditures effectively either in the aggregate or in an allocative sense. Such accounts of the ability of the agency to impose presidential goals suggest that the success is partial, and, as is often true, the weakness tends to be rather far down the bureaucratic hierarchy. In this case it is with the individual budget examiners attached to the agency. Their job is to keep a close eye on the spending of the agency and to work with the agency in the preparation of expenditure requests for the coming fiscal year. It is often easy for a budget examiner to become a captive of the agency he is supposed to control.[120] The typical examiner sees considerably more of the people whose budget is being monitored than he or she does of those for whom he is ostensibly controlling it and he may tend to adopt their view of policy priorities rather than that of the budget bureau. On the other hand, the informal norms concerning careers in OMB have been that it pays to cut budgets, and only those with records of cutting budgets successfully are likely to advance within the organization. Those norms were especially evident during the time that David Stockman ran the organization.[121] It is further evident in the dominance of the B(udget) component of the organization over the (M)anagement component.

Although OMB may be far from totally successful in imposing its (and the President's) will on the budgetary process, it is at a distinct advantage compared with the task allotted to many chief executives in seeking to control their budgets. As has been noted, most countries use essentially a bureaucratic agency as a means of performing the budget-examining functions – the Treasury in Britain and the Ministry of Finance in most countries. Despite the norms of these organizations, they remain essentially civil service organizations and, as such, may not willingly accept the goals of an executive attempting to improve his political future. In addition, many parliamentary political systems tend to be apprehensive about a prime minister attempting to control the budget from his office rather than through the collectivity of the cabinet, so that the internal negotiations over the budget may become so difficult that bureaucratic domination is inevitable.

Even in Germany where the Chancellor is in a stronger position than most parliamentary executives, the use of his position to impose priorities in budgeting is not well received, and much of the power devolves to the Ministry of Finance. In fact, the Minister of Finance is given a special position in the cabinet that makes it difficult for his decisions, and those of his department, to be overturned. Thus, although independent executive budgeting agencies may be far from a perfect solution to controlling public expenditure and the powers of the bureaucracy, they are probably a better solution than has been found in many political systems.

Legislatures have also begun to evolve a number of specialized institutions for dealing with the problem of budgeting. The development of the Congressional Budget Office in the US Congress, and its provision of a rather large and well-qualified staff, is one obvious example of a legislature attempting to regain some control over levels of public expenditure and economic policy.[122] In this case, the conflict is obviously with both the bureaucracy and the presidency. In Britain there have been rather successful attempts to revive the Public Accounts Committee as an effective policy, as well as a financial instrument of Parliament. In addition, the Treasury and Civil Service Select Committee has provided another legislative institution that monitors the financial activities of the executive.[123] While these efforts are certainly steps in the proper direction from the point of view of the legislatures, they are as yet unproved, and the general direction is actually toward giving the legislature less of a role in the budgetary process.

Organizational differentiation. The formation of committees such as those noted above is a part of a general tendency toward organizational differentiation that is manifesting itself in many political institutions seeking to control public expenditure and policy. In order to be able to counteract the specialization and differentiation of the bureaucracy, executives and legislatures have adopted some similar organizational tactics. In general, there has been a growth of the organization within the office of the chief executive, even in countries such as Britain, where the individual power of the chief executive tends to be restricted by a number of conventions. For example, the personal staff of the Prime Minister in No. 10 Downing Street has now increased to over 70 people – small in comparison to the Executive Office of the President of the United States but large in historical terms.[124] The tendency to develop and differentiate organizations has been especially apparent in single-party states faced with either opposition or a lack of enthusiasm in the bureaucracy. This situation has forced political leaders in those countries to develop their own means of monitoring the implementation of programs or actually implementing them through their own executive organizations.

The ability of many public organizations to differentiate is often limited by law, so the institutions will be at a severe disadvantage in attempting to compete with the bureaucracy. For example, in France, the National Assembly is constitutionally limited to six committees, which in turn greatly limits their ability to compete with a highly developed bureaucracy and political executive. Further, Congressional actions have limited the ability of the American President to reorganize his office and expand its staff. Again, some limitation of the differentiation, undertaken for political reasons, will have the effect of limited ability to manage effectively.

Counterstaffs. One extremely important means which political leaders can employ in attempting to control the powers of the bureaucracy is the development of their own staffs and independent sources of information. These enable them to remove the bureaucratic bias in the information received. These independent sources of information may be institutionalized, as in the Executive Office of the President of the United States and the Office of the Chancellor (*Bundeskanzler-samt*) in Germany or they may be the more casual use of outside consultants.[125] In either case, the stratagem involved is to break the monopoly that the bureaucracy has had on expertise. It also enables the political leader to break the strangle hold that the bureaucracy often has on the initiation of policy.

The use of counterstaffs varies rather markedly across political systems and policy areas. In the first place, there must be a source of counterinformation, and until recently this has not existed in policy areas such as atomic energy, space technology, or defense. Also, in most underdeveloped countries, the available scientific and technical ability of the country tends to be concentrated in the public bureaucracy so there may simply be no other source of internal information. It is also more likely that counterstaffs and information – often by the ton – will be available on highly politicized issues, those that involve well-developed professional organizations and those in which pressure groups have a direct interest. However, most of these issues are ones on which the average politician is also likely to have information or a strong ideological commitment; consequently, much of this information may be redundant.

A principal reason for the use of counterstaffs is the problem of segmentalization and politicization in the society. In the first place, there may be conflict or, at a minimum, distrust between a minister who belongs to one social or ethnic group in the society – for example, Catholic, francophone, or Ibo – and a civil servant of a competing group. Politics itself may serve to generate segmental conflicts, and frequently political leaders of newer countries cannot trust their civil servants, many of whom may be expatriates or were trained under the colonial regime. If those civil servants who are indigenous to the country in question are from a different group of the society the level of trust may be no higher.

Even in more developed political systems, many incoming political leaders feel that they cannot trust the advice of civil servants left over from the previous cabinet. This is especially true for ministers from leftist political parties, who tend to regard the civil service – perhaps properly – as a conservative institution.[126] This is not to say that civil servants would purposely obstruct or sabotage a program – there is little evidence of that – but rather that perhaps unwittingly their implementation of programs and their granting of proper advice would not be as energetic as it might be.

The second form of politicization that affects the use of existing staffs by political leaders is the level of institutional politicization or the perceived conflict between different political institutions for control of policy in government. For example, in the United States one of the major reasons for the development of large executive staffs by the President, and for the development of increasingly large staffs by Congress, is the perception that these two branches of government are in conflict over the control of the policy-making machinery.[127] The less well institutionalized presidential systems of Latin America are prone to more severe institutional conflicts of this type, with each attempting to increase its policy-making capacities.[128] In the bicephalous executive of France, there can be conflicts between the President and the Prime Minister, with the need for creating a set of institutions to coordinate their activities.[129]

In countries with long histories of strong bureaucratic control of policy, or at least perceived bureaucratic control of policy, there will be a similar perception of conflict with the bureaucracy. So, in France, the ministerial *cabinets* constitute a counterstaff designed in part to combat the influence of the departmental bureaucracy.[130] On the other hand, a society that is more integrated politically in both segmental and institutional terms, such as Britain, will develop relatively few staff personnel directly accountable to politicians.[131] The norms that the civil service is sufficiently trustworthy and sufficiently devoid of any ideological dispositions allow politicians to accept their advice even after long periods in opposition. While there is little objective evidence of the impartiality of those civil servants, Britain is perhaps less well served in policy terms because of this belief. Although in comparison with most politicians, civil servants are experts, compared with the types of policy staffs developed in other countries, the British may remain "talented amateurs." As a result, much policy is determined by "muddling through" or by "directionless consensus." The Thatcher government, however, attempted to counter both a perceived amateurishness and an even more strongly perceived ideological bias in the civil service by hiring more personal staffs and floating ideas for reform that could include *cabinets* similar to those found in France and Belgium.[132]

Managerialism. Another ploy that was used in the 1980s to strengthen the role of political officials and institutions was managerialism. That is, politicians have increasingly sought to make their civil servants managers rather than policy advisors and certainly not policy makers. This conception of the role of the civil service is associated particularly with governments of the political right, with the most pronounced changes occurring in Britain and other Westminster systems.[133] Even some governments of the Left, e.g. France with a program of "modernization" and "gestion," have stressed a management role for their civil servants. The World Bank and other international donor agencies have also forced managerialism on the governments of Third World countries.[134]

It is difficult to deny that management in the public sector is a difficult task and one which can occupy the time and energy of senior civil servants. Further, the demands for greater economy and efficiency in government have placed even more pressure on civil servants to manage their organizations as effectively as possible. Despite those factors, the pressures for managerialism often have been motivated more by the desire to reduce the influence of civil servants over policy than to enhance their capacity to manage effectively. The strategy has been to separate policy and administration as much as possible and to ensure that politically reliable people are in control of public policy.

Managerialism provides another check on the power of the public bureaucracy by using performance contracts and other merit-related instruments to motivate and punish senior managers in government. Whereas civil service systems typically have protected public employees from dismissal in other than extreme circumstances, performance contracts often make dismissal rather easier. These mechanisms generally go no further down the hierarchies than middle management, and depend upon the capacity of supervisors (presumably often politicians) to measure performance, but they do constitute yet another check on the power and permanence of the bureaucracy.[135]

Customer-driven government. Another of the trends affecting government in the 1990s was the premise that government exists to serve the "customer" and that the functioning of agencies should reflect that fundamental value. The goal of civil servants in such as system is to satisfy that segment of the public identified as their "customers." This is clearly a premise drawn from the private sector, along with a good deal of the emphasis on managerialism. Serving the customer tends to drive power in bureaucracies downward to the echelons that have direct contact with the customers and who must make the service decisions about them. The usual role of top management in defining rules for the delivery of service and the behavior of personnel is devalued in this version of government.[136]

It is hard to argue that government should not serve its citizens well. However, as well as reducing the policy-making powers of top civil servants in setting policy, this ploy on the part of politicians may have some perverse consequences. The most important is that, to some degree, it alters the role of the citizen to that of a consumer with a more limited set of rights and obligations *vis-à-vis* the state. Further, it is not always clear who is the customer of a particular agency. Is the customer of a customs bureau the traveler (and potential smuggler) or is it the public at large who seek protection and fair tax collection? Are not citizens as taxpayers the owners of their public services as well as the customers, and thus have a variety of (often conflicting) roles to play? The implications of this changing focus for governance have yet to be explored fully, but some of these implications appear to set back the relationship of the citizen with his or her government.

Control of staff. One principal weapon available to the civil service in any attempt to gain control over policy is its permanence. Politicians come and go; the bureaucracy remains. This not only presents several long-term strategies to administrators who are not pleased with the current political "master," but it also presents those political masters with some quite difficult problems of controlling their civil servants. Counterstaffs are one solution to this problem, but there may also be solutions within the context of the civil service and personnel policy.

The most obvious means of allowing political control over the civil servants is enabling politicians to select their own, at least those who will be their immediate subordinates and, more importantly, their policy advisors. This can provide some of the advantages of the counterstaff without involving its redundancy and dual lines of authority. Given the limitations of most civil service systems, this means that the choice must come within the confines of the available civil servants; but some systems, such as France, allow the minister to select among the available personnel for his *directeurs*.[137] In Germany, the minister may be given quite a wide scope for choice and may be able to retire (at least temporarily) senior civil servants who occupy posts that he or she wants to fill.[138] The system in the United States is similar in its effect, but the immediate subordinates of political executives are political appointees rather than civil servants. They are therefore not protected by any statutory guarantees of tenure and can be shuffled at will. Thus, in the United States, political appointees fill policy-advisory and managerial posts that are filled by senior civil servants in other democratic political systems, allowing considerably more direct political supervision of implementation and more directly partisan policy advice.[139] Even in the United Kingdom, where the civil service has been independent of political control, the Thatcher government became more deeply involved in the selection and placement of senior personnel, most importantly top Treasury officials.[140]

Many Latin American countries have yet to fully institutionalize norms of civil service impartiality and tenure, so any changes in the government may also occasion changes in the civil service.[141] These may occur primarily at the upper echelons of the civil service, so the routine tasks of government continue to be performed much as they always have been, but this system does allow some flexibility for political leaders in seeking advice from civil servants. It is, of course, roundly condemned by advocates of "proper" public personnel procedures and may affect the behavior of bureaucrats who want to remain in office regardless of the regime. However, for a political situation in which the policy differences among parties are likely to be great, this sort of flexibility in personnel is a crucial means of managing the senior civil service. Further, we must remember that the effects of party change are not so different from those that might be found in a number of European or North American countries that presumably have fully-developed civil service systems.

The party. Another powerful weapon at the disposal of some political leaders is the existence of a strong political party or movement that can be used to ensure the compliance and control of the civil service. This mechanism was available most notably in the former communist countries and remains so in single-party states in the Third World. In these situations the existence of the party and its associated ideology perform a dual service in controlling policy initiatives by the public bureaucracy. First, the party provides definite ideological and policy guidance which an astute civil servant can either internalize or at least follow in making and advising on policy. Since the inception of an ideological regime is usually associated with a significant reshuffling of the civil service, most of those placed in positions of authority are likely to have internalized the ideology and program, but even in cases in which the existing civil service continues – often from the lack of any available alternative personnel – the existence of an ideology can provide them with some ready guidance in what to propose and implement. Again, we must remember that dominant political parties may play something of the same role in democratic political systems, as does the Social Democratic Party in Sweden or the Christian Democratic Party in Italy.

The second means through which the existence of a strong ideological party assists the ability of politicians to reduce bureaucratic initiative and dominance of policy making is that it can provide a check on performance and usually a means of correcting unsuitable performance. In such political systems, the party tends to be more involved in everyday life than in most democratic political systems, to check more thoroughly on bureaucratic actions and to be more resentful of bureaucratic domination of policy than even in democratic systems. Thus, for example, in the People's Republic of China the communist party and ideology serve as a means of guiding and correcting bureaucratic policy, either through direct action or through self-criticism.[142] In the former Soviet Union and Eastern European countries, although it was difficult at times to distinguish political from administrative personnel, the dual hierarchy of party and bureaucracy served as a mutual check on policy formulation at each level of government. This does not necessarily mean that policy making in the Soviet Union was any less bureaucratic than elsewhere, to the extent that we mean bureaucratic policies are those divorced from control by market forces or public opinion. It does imply, however, that the bureaucracy that did make public policy was likely to be more sensitive to political cues than are other bureaucracies. With the political structures shadowing public organizations they will be generally more willing to comply with the demands of a political elite and, given the presence of an expressed ideology, they may also be more capable of finding what the leaders want to do. Thus, although the policies that ensue may be divorced from direct control by popular opinion, they may paradoxically be more responsive to some political forces than are policies made in democratic systems. The conflict between "Red" and "Expert" may not always be resolved in favor of "Red," but the divergence is rarely as great as occurs in less ideological regimes.[143]

The military.   The military may constitute a special case of party or ideological governments. It is a special case largely because of the military's greater willingness to employ physical coercion to obtain its ends, among them the submission of the bureaucracy to the demands of politicians – in this case military politicians. In addition to an ideology and a set of coordinating principles – or, at times, instead of them – the military may just have guns. It does not follow, however, that military governments must always employ force to gain their ends when dealing with the bureaucracy. In the many cases in which the military and the bureaucracy are primarily conservative forces, they often willingly coalesce against forces of the political left or even against more moderate reformers.[144] This pattern has been more common in Latin America, whereas the pattern of the military representing modernizing ideals in opposition to a conservative bureaucracy – frequently with a number of members and practices inherited from colonial days – has been, and remains, somewhat more common in Africa.[145]

Summary

This chapter has been primarily concerned with the extent to which bureaucracies have come to play significant, if not dominant, roles in governing. Have modern societies come to the point where a new elite structure based on information, technical expertise, position and policy ideas has come to determine who gets what, when, where and why?

Our answer to this question is ambiguous and would depend in part on whether one thought in terms of an integrated bureaucratic elite producing policies, having common values, and essentially conspiring to remove authority from more responsible political decision makers, or whether one thought in terms of a number of independent policy elites whose powers are confined to one specific policy area and who were frequently in conflict with other similarly placed elites. If we wish to speak about an integrated bureaucratic power elite – as some rather apprehensively have – running a nation from a computer-equipped ivory tower, then we believe that no such creature actually exists, and Rose's characterization of government emerging by "directionless consensus" may be appropriate. On the other hand, if we wish to talk about a cartel of bureaucratic elites, each responsible for a particular area and functioning with a virtual monopoly over information in that area, then there does seem to be some verisimilitude in the idea of "bureaucratic government." However, as was pointed out, this would be government by "non-consensual directions." One of the characteristics of contemporary government may be its increasing incoherence and the associated lack of true governance.

The conclusion that emerges from this analysis is that the public bureaucracy is in quite a strong position *vis-à-vis* other potential policy-making institutions. It has the expertise, the time, the stability and the techniques required to be an effective policy maker in a modern age. What is required, however, is legitimacy and popular control. The legitimacy can perhaps be gained in part through effectiveness, and if largely bureaucratic processes of decision making are capable of producing results valued by the population, then the institutions are likely to be accepted as appropriate decision makers. They may lack formal legitimacy, but in terms of having operational legitimacy, they may become the appropriate collective allocators of values.

The question of popular control is perhaps more difficult. This has two possible interpretations. The first is the ability of the public to make its preferences known to the bureaucracy, through some as yet unspecified means, and to have the bureaucracy make decisions consistent with those expressed preferences. If we extend the arguments presented in this chapter, then the general public must be seen as being in an even more difficult position in dealing with the bureaucracy than the political elite. The second possible meaning of popular control is the ability of the citizens to obtain redress of grievances for certain administrative actions that violate the rights – economic or civil – of individuals. This is more of an *ex post facto* control, for which a number of procedural devices have been developed and which have met with a variety of successes and failures. These problems of popular and democratic control will be addressed in Chapter 8, where we will concentrate more on the application of broad policies, determined in the manner we have discussed here, to individual cases, and the remedies available when they are applied unfairly. However, before turning to that topic, we will discuss the budgetary process as another example of policy making within bureaucratic structures and perhaps the principal arena in which conflicts between political and bureaucratic elites are resolved.

Notes

1   See Chapter 5.
2   That form, however, often involves attempting to provide services to constituents and "pork barrel" benefits for the folks back home rather than deal effectively with broad national issues. This tendency is particularly pronounced in American legislatures but is found almost everywhere.
3   B. Guy Peters, "Public Bureaucracy and Public Policy," in Douglas E. Ashford, ed., *History and Context in the Study of Public Policy* (Pittsburgh: University of Pittsburgh Press, 1992).
4   Donald J. Savoie, "Globalization and Governance," unpublished paper, Canadian Centre for Management Development, Ottawa, 1993; Roger Wettenhall, "The Globalization of Public Enterprises," *International Review of Administrative Sciences*, 59 (1993), 387–408.
5   Richard Rose, *The Problem of Party Government* (London: Macmillan, 1974); see also Francis G. Castles and Rudolf Wildenmann, *Visions and Realities of Party Government* (Berlin: De Gruyter, 1986).
6   For a more global view, see Michael E. Urban, The *Ideology of Administration* (Albany: State University of New York Press, 1982).
7   J. Steven Ott, *The Organizational Culture Perspective* (Pacific Grove, CA: Brooks/Cole, 1989).
8   See, for example, Kenneth Theakston, *The Labour Party and Whitehall* (London: Routledge, 1992); see also, David Marsh and R. A. W. Rhodes, *Implementing Thatcherite Policies* (Buckingham: Open University Press, 1992).
9   Joseph Jamar and Wolfgang Wessels, *European Community Bureaucracy at the Crossroads* (Bruges: College d'Europe, 1985); B. Guy Peters, "Bureaucratic Politics and the Institutions of the European Community," in Alberta Sbragia, ed., *Euro-Politics* (Washington, DC: The Brookings Institution, 1992).
10 These ideas are often more than suggestions. The International Monetary Fund, for example, tends to impose its will on governments in exchange for gaining support for their currencies. The World Bank increasingly imposes financial and other restrictions as a condition of receiving loans.
11 Frederick C. Mosher, *Democracy and the Public Service* (New York: Oxford University Press, 1968), pp. 105ff; "Professionals and Public Service," *Public Administration Review*, 38 (1978), 144–50.
12 The Napoleonic system of *grands écoles* and the *grands corps* laid the ground work for a professional bureaucratic state in the early nineteenth century. See John A. Armstrong, *The European Administrative Elite* (Princeton: Princeton University Press, 1973).
13 Henry A. Foley, *Community Mental Health Programs: The Formative Process* (Lexington, MA: D. C. Heath, 1975); Martha Derthick, *Policymaking for Social Security* (Washington, DC: The Brookings Institution, 1979), pp. 17–37.
14 Bengt Jacobssen, *Hur Styrs Forvaltning* (Lund: Studentlitteratur, 1984).
15 Alfred Diamant, "Tradition and Innovation in French Administration," *Comparative Political Studies*, 1 (1968), 251–74.
16 Philip Williams, *Crisis and Compromise: The Politics of the Fourth Republic* (New York: Doubleday Anchor, 1965), pp. 365–6.
17 Michael Laver and N. Schofield, *Multiparty Government: The Politics of Coalitions in Europe* (Oxford: Oxford University Press, 1991).
18 See chapters by George Jones and Peter Aucoin in Colin Campbell and Margaret Jane Wyszormirski, eds, *Executive Leadership in Anglo-American Systems* (Pittsburgh: University of Pittsburgh Press, 1991).
19 Anne Davies and John Willman, *What Next: Agencies, Departments and the Civil Service* (London: Institute for Public Policy Research, 1991); Christopher Pollitt, *Managerialism and the Public Services* (Oxford: Basil Blackwell, 1990).
20 Marceau Long, "Les corps," *Cahiers français*, 194 (January, 1980).

21 Hans-Ulrich Derlien, "Repercussions of Government Change on the Career Civil Service in Germany," *Governance*, 1 (1988), 59–78.

22 The evidence on its success is rather spotty, at best. See Patricia W. Ingraham and David H. Rosenbloom, *The Promise and Paradox of Civil Service Reform* (Pittsburgh: University of Pittsburgh Press, 1992).

23 Joel D. Aberbach, Robert D. Putnam and Bert A. Rockman, *Bureaucrats and Politicians in Western Democracies* (Cambridge, MA: Harvard University Press, 1981).

24 See, for example, the cases reported in Ezra N. Suleiman, ed., *Bureaucrats and Policymaking* (New York: Holmes and Meier, 1986); see also Hans-Ulrich Derlien, "Observations on the State of Comparative Administration Research in Europe – Rather Comparable than Comparative," *Governance*, 5 (1992), 279–311.

25 Charles E. Lindblom and Edward J. Woodhouse, *The Policymaking Process*, 3rd edn (Englewood Cliffs, NJ: Prentice-Hall, 1993), pp. 24–7.

26 Stephen H. Linder and B. Guy Peters, "Research Perspectives on the Design of Public Policy: Implementation, Formulation and Design," in Dennis J. Palumbo and Donald J. Calista, eds, *Implementation in the Policy Process* (New York: Greenwood Press, 1990).

27 Graham T. Allison, *The Essence of Decision* (Boston: Little, Brown, 1972).

28 Giadomenico Majone, "On the Feasibility of Social Programs," *European Journal of Political Research*, 3 (1975), 259–75.

29 Lester M. Salamon and Michael S. Lund, eds, *Beyond Privatization: The Tools of Government Action* (Washington, DC: Urban Institute Press, 1989).

30 J. R. Hening, C. Hammnett and Harvey B. Feigenbaum, "The Politics of Privatization: A Comparative Perspective," *Governance*, 1 (1988), 442–68; Ralph H. Kramer *et al.*, *Privatization in Four European Countries* (Armonk, NY: M. E. Sharpe, 1993).

31 See Samuel Kernell, ed., *Parallel Politics: Economic Policymaking in Japan and the United States* (Washington, DC: The Brookings Institution, 1991).

32 This tension is reflected in the "garbage can" model of organizational decision making in which means seek ends rather than vice versa. See Michael D. Cohen, James G. March and Johan P. Olsen, "The Garbage Can Model of Organizational Choice," *Administrative Science Quarterly*, 17 (1972), 1–25; see also Nils Brunsson, *The Organization of Hypocrisy* (New York: John Wiley, 1989).

33 See, for example, the marked legalism of German administration described above (Chapter 5) as contrasted to the more managerial and political styles of Britain and the United States.

34 Paul C. Light, *Monitoring Government: Inspectors General and the Search for Accountability* (Washington, DC: The Brookings Institution, 1993); Dawn Oliver, *Government in the United Kingdom: The Search for Accountability* (Milton Keynes: Open University Press, 1991); see also Chapter 8.

35 Breton speaks of this as moving the competition from a public to a private arena. See Albert Breton, *The Economic Theory of Representative Government* (Chicago: Aldine, 1974), pp. 162–3.

36 The classic statement of this view is William Niskanen, *Bureaucracy and Representative Government* (Chicago: Aldine/Atherton, 1971).

37 Robert E. Goodin, "The Logic of Bureaucratic Backscratching," *Public Choice*, 24 (1975), 53–68.

38 Matthew Holden, "Imperialism and Bureaucracy," *American Political Science Review*, 60 (1966), 943–51.

39 Anthony Downs, *Inside Bureaucracy* (Boston: Little, Brown, 1967), pp. 198–99.

40 Public organizations do die more frequently than is sometimes assumed. See B. Guy Peters and Brian W. Hogwood, "Births, Deaths and Metamorphoses in the U.S. Federal Bureaucracy 1933–83," *The American Review of Public Administration*, 18 (1988), 119–34.

41 B. Guy Peters, "The European Bureaucrat," in Andre Blais and Stephane Dion, eds, *The Budget-Maximizing Bureaucrat* (Pittsburgh: University of Pittsburgh Press, 1991).

42 See Gary Miller and Terry Moe, "Bureaucrats, Legislators and the Size of Government,"

American Political Science Review, 77 (1983), 297–322; Patrick Dunleavy, "Bureaucrats, Budgets and the Growth of the State: Reconstructing an Incremental Model," *British Journal of Political Science*, 15 (1985), 299–320.

43 Ole P. Kristensen, "The Logic of Bureaucratic Decision-Making as Cause of Government Growth: or Why the Expansion of Public Programmes is a Private Good and their Restriction is a Public Good," *European Journal of Political Research*, 8 (1980), 249–64.

44 Downs, *Inside Bureaucracy, op. cit.*

45 Advisory Commission on Intergovernmental Relations, *The Federal Role in the Federal System* (Washington, DC: ACIR, 1980).

46 R. Douglas Arnold, *The Logic of Congressional Action* (New Haven: Yale University Press, 1990).

47 A. Grant Jordan, "Iron Triangles, Woolly Corporatism or Elastic Nets: Models of the Policy Process," *Journal of Public Policy*, 1 (1981), 95–124.

48 Peter B. Natchez and Irving C. Bupp, "Policy and Priorities in the Budgetary Process," *American Political Science Review*, 67 (1973), 963.

49 See Allen Schick, "Governments Versus Budget Deficits," in R. Kent Weaver and Bert A. Rockman, eds, *Do Institutions Matter?* (Washington, DC: The Brookings Institution, 1993).

50 Victor Thompson, *Modern Organizations* (New York: Knopf, 1961).

51 See William T. Gormley, Jr., "Counter-bureaucracies in Theory and Practice," paper presented at 1993 meeting of the American Political Science Association, Washington, DC, September, 1993.

52 Guy Thuillier, *Les cabinets ministeriels* (Paris: Presses universitaires de France, 1982).

53 Gordon Smith, "The Resources of a German Chancellor," in George W. Jones, ed., *West European Prime Ministers* (London: Frank Cass, 1991).

54 Richard F. Elmore, "Backward Mapping: Implementation Research and Policy Decisions," *Political Science Quarterly*, 94 (1980), 601–16.

55 M. Adler and S. Asquith, *Discretion and Welfare* (London: Heinemann, 1981). For a different view, see Chris Ham and Michael Hill, *The Policy Process in Modern Capitalist States* (London: Hemel Hempsted: Harvester Wheatsheaf, 1993), Chapter 8.

56 Thomas Cronin, "Everybody Believes in Democracy Until He Gets to the White House," *Law and Contemporary Problems*, 35 (1970), 573–625.

57 Edward C. Page, *Bureaucratic Authority and Political Power*, 2nd edn (Brighton: Harvester, 1992).

58 See Herbert Kaufman, *Red Tape* (Washington, DC: The Brookings Institution). For a contrary view, see Charles T. Goodsell, *The Case for Bureaucracy*, 3rd edn (Chatham, NJ: Chatham House, 1994).

59 Michel Crozier, *The Bureaucratic Phenomenon* (Chicago: University of Chicago Press, 1964), pp. 213–20.

60 Martin Cave, Maurice Kogan and Robert Smith, eds, *Output and Performance Measurement in Government: The State of the Art* (London: Jessica Kingsley, 1990).

61 See Chapter 3

62 One of the best statements of this point remains Michel Crozier, *The Bureaucratic Phenomenon* (Chicago: University of Chicago Press, 1964), pp. 213–20.

63 Christopher Hood, "A Public Administration for All Seasons?," *Public Administration*, 69 (1991), 3–19.

64 Andrew Gray and William Jenkins, "The Management of Change in Whitehall: The Experience of FMI," *Public Administration*, 69 (1991), 125–41.

65 For a variety of examples, see Gerald Caiden, *Administrative Reform Comes of Age* (Berlin: de Gruyter, 1991).

66 See, for example, John Waterbury, *Exposed to Innumerable Decisions: Public Enterprise and State Power in Egypt, India, Mexico and Turkey* (Cambridge: Cambridge University Press, 1993).

67 Jeffrey L. Pressman and Aaron Wildavsky developed a model of implementation based upon the notion of clearance points. See their *Implementation* (Berkeley: University of

California Press, 1974). For a critique, see Judith Bowen, "The Pressman-Wildavsky Paradox," *Journal of Public Policy*, 2 (1982), 1–21.

68 Donald F. Kettl, *Sharing Power: Public Governance and Private Markets* (Washington, DC: The Brookings Institution, 1993). These changing techniques of managing the public sector have been adopted even in societies with a history of a large and powerful public sector such as France and Sweden. See Jean-Luc Bodiguel and Luc Rouban, *Le fonctionnaire detrone?* (Paris: Presses de la Fondation nationale des sciences politiques, 1991).

69 See Arthur L. Stinchcombe, *Information and Organizations* (Berkeley: University of California Press, 1990).

70 See Alan Peacock, *The Regulation Game: How British and German Companies Bargain With Government* (Oxford: Basil Blackwell, 1984); B. Hudson, "Michael Lipsky and Street-Level Bureaucracy: A Neglected Perspective," in L. Barton, ed., *Disability and Dependence* (London: Falmer, 1989).

71 Herbert Kaufman, *The Forest Ranger* (Baltimore: Johns Hopkins University Press, 1960), pp. 75–80.

72 Jeffrey Pressman and Aaron Wildavsky, *Implementation* (Berkeley, CA: University of California Press, 1973); Renate Mayntz and Fritz W. Scharpf, *Policymaking in the German Federal Bureaucracy* (Amsterdam: Elsevier, 1975).

73 Yves Meny, "Decentralization in Socialist France: The Politics of Pragmatism," *West European Politics*, 7 (1984), 70ff.

74 Pressman and Wildavsky, *Implementation, op. cit.*

75 Benny Hjern and David O. Porter, "Implementation Structures: A New Unit of Administrative Analysis," *Organisational Studies*, 2 (1981), 211–27; Kenneth Hanf, "Enforcing Environmental Laws: The Social Regulation of Co-production," in Michael Hill, ed., *New Agendas in the Study of the Policy Process* (Hemel Hempsted: Harvester Wheatsheaf, 1993).

76 This has been true in a number of countries, even those that are nominally centralized. See Basil Chubb, "Going Around Persecuting Bureaucrats: The Role of the Irish Parliamentary Representative," *Political Studies*, 11 (1963), 272–86. See also Thomas D. Lancaster and W. David Patterson, "Comparative Pork Barrel Politics: Perceptions from the West German Bundestag," *Comparative Political Studies*, 22 (1990), 458–77.

77 Merrilee S. Grindle and John W. Thomas, "Policy Makers, Policy Choices and Policy Outcomes: The Political Economy of Reform in Developing Countries," *Policy Sciences*, 22 (1989), 213–48.

78 This is the standard argument about the "capture" of regulatory organizations. An increasing body of literature has pointed out that such capture is not inevitable but can be at least diminished by appropriate organizational and legal designs. See Randall Calvert, Mathew McCubbins and Barry Weingast, "A Theory of Political Control and Agency Discretion," *American Journal of Political Science*, 33 (1989), 588–611.

79 One of the best enumerations remains Christopher Hood, *The Limits of Administration* (New York: John Wiley, 1976).

80 For one discussion of these interactions, albeit in a more positive vein, see Colin Campbell, "Review Article: The Political Role of Senior Government Officials in Advanced Democracies," *British Journal of Political Science*, 18 (1988), 243–72.

81 Dudley Sears, "The Structure of Power," in Hugh Thomas, ed., *The Crisis in the Civil Service* (London: Anthony Blond, 1968).

82 Michael M. Atkinson and William D. Coleman, "Policy Networks, Policy Communities and the Problems of Governance," *Governance*, 5 (1992), 154–80.

83 Treasury and Civil Service Committee, *Seventh Report*, 1985–6, 728ff.

84 Krister Ståhlberg, "Politicization of the Public Service: Notes on Concepts, Causes and Consequences of Politicization," *International Review of Administrative Sciences*, 53 (1987), 363–82.

85 Derlien, "Repercussions of Government Change," *op. cit.*

86 Fritz W. Scharpf, "The Joint-Decision Trap: Lessons from German Federalism and European Integration," *Public Administration*, 66 (1988), 239–78.

87   Stephen H. Linder and B. Guy Peters, "A Design Perspective on Policy Implementation: The Fallacies of Misplaced Precision," *Policy Studies Review*, 6 (1987), 459–76.

88   See B. Guy Peters, "Overload in American Government," in Richard Maidment, ed., *Democracy in America* (Milton Keynes: Open University Press, 1993).

89   M. Donnelly, "The Structure of the European Commission and the Policy Formation Process," in Sonia Mazey and Jeremy J. Richardson, eds, *Lobbying in the European Community* (Oxford: Oxford University Press, 1993).

90   Barbara Wake Carroll, "Politics and Administration: A Trichotomy?," *Governance*, 3 (1990), 345–66.

91   William Plowden, *Advising the Rulers* (Oxford: Basil Blackwell, 1990).

92   Randall Bartlett, *The Economic Foundations of Political Power* (New York: The Free Press, 1973), pp. 63–4, 70–5.

93   Alvin W. Gouldner, "Metaphysical Pathos and the Theory of Bureaucracy," *American Political Science Review*, 49 (1955), 496–507.

94   Gary C. Bryner, *Bureaucratic Discretion: Law and Policy in Federal Regulatory Agencies* (New York: Pergamon, 1987).

95   For a critical study of delegation, see David Schoenbrod, *Power Without Responsibility* (New Haven: Yale University Press, 1993).

96   This is the familiar politics of diffuse costs and concentrated benefits described by James Q. Wilson, *Bureaucracy: What Government Agencies Do and Why They Do It* (New York: Basic Books, 1989).

97   Philip Norton, "Legislatures in Perspective," *West European Politics*, 13 (1990), 143–52.

98   Harold Wilensky, *Organizational Intelligence* (New York: Basic Books, 1977), pp. 24–34.

99   Hugh Heclo, "Towards a New Welfare State," in Peter Flora and Arnold J. Heidenheimer, eds, *The Development of Welfare States in Europe and America* (New Brunswick, NJ: Transaction Books, 1981).

100   See David M. Olson and C. E. S. Franks, *Representation and Policy Formation in Federal Systems: Canada and the United States* (Berkeley: Institute of Governmental Studies, University of California, 1993).

101   See Rob Flynn, "Restructuring Health Systems: A Comparative Analysis of England and the Netherlands," in Michael Hill, *New Agendas in the Study of the Policy Process* (New York: Harvester-Wheatsheaf, 1993).

102   J. G. Abert, *Economic Policy and Planning in the Netherlands, 1950–1965* (New Haven: Yale University Press, 1969), p. 39.

103   Areas such as this are becoming less common, given that there are now interest groups organized around almost every policy issue and the media expose most issues to greater public scrutiny, at least by the more interested public.

104   Richard Topf, "Advice to Government – Some Theoretical and Practical Issues," in B. Guy Peters and Anthony Barker, eds, *Advising West European Governments* (Edinburgh: University of Edinburgh Press, 1993).

105   This need not be undemocratic if there are adequate means of public participation in the planning process. See Frank Fischer and John Forester, eds, *The Argumentative Turn in Policy Analysis and Planning* (Durham, NC: Duke University Press, 1993).

106   Andrew Shonfeld, *Modern Capitalism* (London: Oxford University Press, 1965), p. 235.

107   Rudolf Klein, "The Politics of PPBS," *Political Quarterly*, 43 (1972), 280–1.

108   Frieder Naschold, "Probleme der mehrjahringen Finanzplanungen des Bundes," in V. Ronge and G. Schmieg, eds, *Praxis* (Munich: Piper, 1971), 125–54.

109   Higley, Brofoss and Groholt, "Top Civil Servants," *op. cit.*

110   John Higley, Karl Erik Brofoss and Knut Groholt, "Top Civil Servants and the National Budget in Norway," in Mattei Dogan, *The Mandarins of Western Europe* (New York: Halstad, 1975), pp. 266–7.

111   For the contrast, see Tom Christensen and Morten Egeberg, "Ministerial Budget Making: Behavioral Characteristics and Organizational Constraints," paper presented at Joint Sessions of European Consortium for Political Research, Paris, April, 1989.

112 Higley, Brofoss and Groholt, "Top Civil Servants," 262–3.

113 Per Laegreid and Johan P. Olsen, *Bureaukrati og Beslutningar* (Bergen: Universitetsforlaget, 1978).

114 Yves Weber, *L'Administration consultative* (Paris: Librarie general du droit et jurisprudence, 1968), p. 3.

115 Frank Schwartz, "Of Fairy Cloaks and Familiar Talks: The Politics of Consultation," in Gary D. Allison and Yasunori Sone, eds, *Political Dynamics in Contemporary Japan* (Ithaca, NY: Cornell University Press, 1993), 89–104.

116 *Nya Villkor for Ekonomi och Politik*, SOU 1993: 16, p. 166.

117 See Chapter 5.

118 Schwartz, "Of Fairy Cloaks and Familiar Talks"; see also Chapter 5.

119 David G. Mathiasen, "The Evolution of OMB," *Public Budgeting and Finance*, 8 (1988), 3–14.

120 The greater emphasis on political reliability has tended to lessen the freedom of examiners, but see James W. Davis and Randall B. Ripley, "The Bureau of the Budget and Executive Branch Agencies: A Note on their Interaction," *Journal of Politics*, 29 (1967), 749–69.

121 David A. Stockman, *The Triumph of Politics: How the Reagan Revolution Failed* (New York: Harper and Row, 1986).

122 Allen Schick, *Congress and Money* (Washington, DC: Urban Institute Press, 1980), pp. 131–65.

123 The Treasury and Civil Service Committee tends to operate before expenditures are made, while the Public Accounts Committee operates after the fact. See Gavin Drewry, *The New Select Committees* (Oxford: Clarendon Press, 1985).

124 Colin Campbell, *Governing Under Stress: Political Executives and Key Bureaucrats in Washington, London and Ottawa* (Toronto: University of Toronto Press, 1983), pp. 16–22.

125 Phyllis Berry, "The Organization and Influence of the Chancellory During the Schmidt and Kohl Chancellorships," *Governance*, 2 (1989), 339–55.

126 Anne Stevens, "L'Alternance and the Higher Civil Service," in Philip G. Cerny and Martin A. Schain, eds, *Socialism, the State and Public Policy in France* (London: Frances Pinter, 1985).

127 That conflict often has resulted in "gridlock" and difficulties in making any decisions. See James L. Sundquist, "Needed: A Political Theory for the New Era of Coalition Government in the United States," *Political Science Quarterly*, 103 (1988–9), 613–35. For an opposite view, see David Mayhew, *Divided We Govern* (New Haven: Yale University Press, 1991).

128 Matthew Soberg Shugart and John M. Carey, *Presidents and Assemblies: Constitutional Design and Electoral Dynamics* (Cambridge: Cambridge University Press, 1992); Scott Mainwaring, "Presidentialism in Latin America: A Review Essay," *Latin American Research Review*, 25 (1989), 157–79.

129 Jacques Fournier, *Le Travail Gouvernemental* (Paris: Dalloz, 1987).

130 E. Searls, "Ministerial Cabinets and Elite Theory," in J. Howarth and Philip G. Cerny, eds, *Elites In France* (London: Frances Pinter, 1981).

131 See Donald Savoie, *Thatcher, Reagan and Mulroney: In Search of a New Bureaucracy* (Pittsburgh: University of Pittsburgh Press, 1994).

132 John Gaffney, "The Political Think Tanks in the UK and Ministerial Cabinets in France," *West European Politics*, 14 (1991), 1–17.

133 Christopher Pollitt, *Managerialism and the Public Service: The Anglo-American Experience* (Oxford: Basil Blackwell, 1990); Peter Aucoin, "Contraction, Managerialism and Decentralization in Canadian Government," *Governance*, 1 (1988), 144–61.

134 World Bank, *The Reform of Public Sector Management: Lessons from Experience* (Washington, DC: The World Bank, Country Economics Department, 1991).

135 Jonathan Boston, "Assessing the Performance of Departmental Chief Executives: Perspectives from New Zealand," *Public Administration*, 70 (1992), 405–28.

136 Donald F. Kettl, "Reinventing Government," *LaFollette Report* (Madison: LaFollette Center, University of Wisconsin, 1993).

137 Jean-Luc Bodiguel, "A French Style Spoils System?," *Public Administration*, 61 (1983), 295–9.

138 Hans-Ulrich Derlien, "Regierungswechsel, Regeimewechsel und Zusammensetzung der Politisch-Administrative Elite," *Leviathan*, 12 (1991), 253–70.

139 Hugh Heclo, *A Government of Strangers* (Washington, DC: The Brookings Institution, 1978); Patricia W. Ingraham, "Building Bridges or Burning Them: The President, the Appointees and the Bureaucracy," *Public Administration Review*, 47 (1987), 425–35.

140 There is some debate concerning just how politicized appointments have become. See F. F. Ridley, "Politics and the Selection of Higher Civil Servants in the United Kingdom," in F. Meyers, ed., *La politisation de l'administration* (Brussels: Institut internationale des sciences administratives, 1986).

141 K. Ruffing-Hilliard, "Merit Reform in Latin America: A Comparative Perspective," in Ali Farazmand, ed., *Handbook of Comparative and Development Administration* (New York: Marcel Dekker, 1991).

142 See Gu Jiaqi, "Restructuring Government Organization in China and Transforming Government Functions for an Efficient and More Productive Bureaucratic Performance," *Governance*, 5 (1992), 391–401.

143 Baohui Zhang, "The State Central Economic Bureaucracies and the Outcome of Systemic Economic Reform: An Institutional Explanation for the Soviet and Chinese Experiences," *Governance*, 5 (1992), 312–41.

144 This is the by now familiar argument of Guillermo O'Donnell, *Modernization and Bureaucratic Authoritarianism: Studies in South American Politics* (Berkeley: Institute of International Studies, University of California, 1979).

145 See Henry Bienen, "Public Order and the Military in Africa," *The Military Intervenes* (New York: Russell Sage, 1968).

Paying for government: the budgetary process

The budgetary process is part of the political process that affects the public bureaucracy the most. Clearly, if an administrative agency is to accomplish any or all of its mandated tasks it requires an adequate supply of money. In addition to the instrumental need for money, there is a more affective reason for desiring budgetary success. Success in getting money is one means for agencies to demonstrate their political clout and their importance to the remainder of the political system.

On the other side of the green baize table, the budgetary process may be the arena in which political officials demonstrate their power and their concern for the average taxpayer by limiting the amount of money allocated to the public sector, and especially to the less popular programs of government. With increasing pressures on government both to provide services and to contain or reduce its costs, the budgetary process has become a crucial political battleground. It influences not only the prospects of each single governmental agency, but also the prospects of elected officials, the prospects of many citizens for a high quality of life and perhaps the success of the entire economy.

Basic questions

When the process of budgeting is considered cross-nationally, there are several basic questions that should be addressed. These questions arise in any political system, but the manner in which they are answered, or indeed can be answered, will vary according to a number of political, social and economic characteristics of individual nations. Also, since each country in the world is facing many of the same budgetary constraints, the world can serve as a useful laboratory for understanding the possibilities of controlling public expenditure through innovative mechanisms and procedures. We must, however, be careful in assuming that lessons learned in one country can easily be transported to another political or social system.[1] We must be equally careful not to assume that controlling expenditures is the only purpose of budgeting; promoting efficiency and effectiveness is also important.

Macro-allocation

Inherent in the process of budgeting is the problem of the allocation of resources, and the first form of allocation that must be considered is the allocation between the public and private sectors of the economy. Government must decide just how much it is willing – and able – to tax its citizens in order to provide benefits through public expenditure. In industrialized countries these decisions produce public sectors (measured in terms of tax revenues) that range from over 52 percent of Gross Domestic Product (Netherlands) to 14 percent (Japan).[2] Despite the importance of this decision for economic management and the nature of public programs, several factors limit the ability of governments to make definitive decisions about the "size" of government, and that limitation must be recognized when attempting to understand how governments decide to spend money.

probl gov has

The first problem a government encounters when attempting to control the size of its public sector is that public expenditure is not as easy to control as is assumed by many critics of government. For example, as of 1988, over 77 percent of US federal expenditures were considered uncontrollable in any one budget year.[3] The programs that comprise the $800 billion in expenditure are primarily entitlement programs such as social security, Medicare and unemployment compensation, for which expenditure levels are determined as much by demographics and economic conditions as by policy decisions. Interest on the public debt is also an uncontrollable expenditure; it must be paid lest investors lose confidence in the economic system of the United States. The majority of other industrialized countries would have even higher proportions of uncontrollable expenditures than does the United States, given the larger scale of social programs and smaller defense budgets. Our estimates of uncontrollable expenditures for the United Kingdom would be 81 percent of the budget, while for Sweden it would be 84 percent. An official of the Swedish government once argued that only two percent of the budget was not affected to some degree by automatic changes.[4]

Just as the numerator of the fraction determining the relative size of the public sector may not be controllable, so too the denominator is not readily controllable. Governments have taken upon themselves the control of the economy since at least the end of World War II, but despite the successes in the 1950s and 1960s, governments now appear less capable of producing sustained economic growth. The best thought-out budgetary allocations and calculations can be overturned by fluctuations in the economy. Governments invest a good deal of time and effort in forecasting the future state of their economies but often fail miserably. This failure results in part from the time span over which the estimates must be made – the budgetary process is often initiated 18 months prior to the implementation of the budget – and results also from the still-inadequate knowledge of economic dynamics in industrialized economies.[5]

Governments also have an interest in presenting optimistic forecasts to their citizens. Doing this not only allows them to appear to be managing the economy successfully (at least until the real figures appear), but also allows them to spend more without increasing the apparent budget deficit. Some idea of the magnitude of error that can creep into forecasts is presented in Table 7.1. Even in socialist economies, where control is assumed to exist over the major elements of the economy, there are still difficulties in forecasting the state of the economy for more than a few months in advance.[6] The problems with budget forecasting will be pronounced for governments of the Third World, especially for those heavily dependent upon primary commodities for their economic fortunes.[7]

Another factor limiting the efficiency of macro-allocations is the simple fact that there is almost invariably more than one level of government involved in deciding how much the public sector will spend. This is especially true of federal political systems in which sub-national governments have substantial fiscal autonomy. State governments in the United States, for example, make their revenue and expenditure decisions almost entirely independently from the federal government, with the major impact of federal expenditure priorities caused by the stimulative effects of matching grants.[8] Several central governments in federal systems

Table 7.1 Accuracy in predicting economic growth

| Year | Sweden | | United States | |
	Predicted	Actual	Predicted	Actual
1992	−0.7	1.1	2.7	2.0
1991	−0.6	−1.4	3.4	−1.2
1990	1.1	0.3	3.5	2.6
1989	2.2	2.1	3.4	2.8
1988	3.2	2.3	2.2	2.5
1987	2.2	1.8	4.0	3.8
1986	1.6	1.7	4.0	3.2
1985	2.1	2.2	4.0	2.1
1984	2.6	3.4	5.6	2.7
1983	1.5	1.9	6.1	6.4
1982	1.0	0.08	−1.2	−1.7
1981	0.7	−0.8	2.8	1.9
1980	3.6	1.8	−0.6	−0.2
1975	3.0	0.9	−3.3	−1.1
1973	2.5	1.5	6.75	5.2

Sources: Ministry of Finance, *The Swedish Budget* (Stockholm: Almanna Forlaget, annual);
Office of Management and Budget, *Budget of the United States Government* (Washington, DC:
US Government Printing Office, annual); Bureau of the Census, *Statistical Abstract of the United
States* (Washington, DC: US Government Printing Office, annual)

have found this degree of fiscal autonomy unacceptable and have developed mechanisms to better coordinate spending at all levels of government (see pp. 286–7).

Finally, for the majority of actors involved in the budgetary process, the ratio of public expenditure to available economic resources is not the primary consideration in making the budget. For spending agencies, whether they are managing "uncontrollable" programs or not, the primary consideration is their own success, or what they can extract from the central pool of resources.[9] In behavioral terms, this means that spending agencies will tend to coalesce to oppose attempts at controlling expenditures by finance ministers and/or the chief political executive. If their collective success in extracting resources means that the ratio of expenditures to GNP would increase, that would be someone else's problem, and it is always the other agency's program that should be reduced or terminated. This problem is not confined to participants in government. Not only do those participants in the budgetary process think in terms of what they can extract from the process, but most citizens do as well. Citizens tend to have schizophrenic views of the public budget: they oppose taxes but want more public expenditures, especially expenditures that benefit them directly.[10] In such a political environment it is difficult for any politician, even if he or she really wanted to, to limit expenditures, especially for programs supported by powerful clientele groups. In fact, those politicians generally have more to gain by spending than they do by limiting expenditures.

Micro-allocation

The last point concerning macro-allocation brings us to the stage of budgetary process, called here micro-allocation. In this stage, choices must be made among the huge number of competing programs in government, each one considering itself especially worthy and each one competing with all other programs for limited total funding. The separation of these decisions from the macro-allocation decisions may be artificial, since the constraints imposed upon funding any particular agency are, at least in part, a function of the desire of those controlling the economic management functions of government to restrain total expenditures. When that level of expenditure is low, compared with previous levels of expenditure and levels of inflation, then programs with the fewest uncontrollable elements will be the targets for disproportionate cuts. This has been occurring in many countries that have been attempting to put a brake on public expenditure. The discretionary elements of public expenditure, especially in non-defense programs, have already been squeezed heavily. For example, in the United States, the uncontrollable element of the budget increased from 72 to 77 percent of all federal expenditures from 1980 to 1992.[11] In Sweden, the comparable figure is estimated to be an increase from 82 to over 91 percent.[12]

Micro-allocation makes up most of the politics of budgeting. It is at this level that the priorities of individual political leaders interact to produce the allocation of resources within government. Despite the enormity of the task of assembling the public budget in any modern public sector, there is a tendency to consider budgeting as a rational process that produces an allocation of resources that matches the policy preferences of the public, or at least the preferences of their elected officials.[13] But there are a number of barriers preventing the process from reaching its goal of such an optimal allocation.

One of the principal factors threatening the rationality of the allocation is the disaggregation of the budgetary process into isolated segments. Frequently, separate committees or sections of budgetary review organizations perform the major analyses and make the major decisions about budget. For example, in the United States the most important decisions about the budget in Congress are made in sub-committees of the appropriations committee, and each of these sub-committees tends to have its own perception of national priorities. In Canada, the "envelope" system of budgeting (see pp. 280–1) placed considerable power in the dozen or so priorities committees which allocate funds among competing programs within their area and whose decisions tend to dominate the final determination of expenditures.[14] Similarly, in Sweden, the allocation of funds among the boards (*styrelsen*) under a ministry is a process that allocates predetermined blocks of expenditures rather than comparing marginal values of expenditure across the range of functions. At even more of an extreme, the Danish coalition government assembles a budget from a series of negotiations and deals in the individual ministries, with each deal possibly supported in parliament by different political parties.

It is only in a financial ministry preparing an overall budget statement or in the government's cabinet meeting, where the entire budget is (at least in theory) open to determination, that any detailed considerations of competing priorities can be made. Even in those settings, however, the outcome may be determined by the deliberations of staffs, or by the personality of a few dominant members of the cabinet, so that the systematic confrontation of all the alternative utilizations of public funds will not occur. Contemplating the entirety of a budget running into billions of dollars may be too much for any set of political leaders, especially given the many other claims on their time.

A second crucial factor affecting the range of consideration of budgetary alternatives, and pushing toward incremental outcomes, is the status quo. The sheer magnitude of the budget in a modern government makes it difficult for legislatures – or even an expert budgetary analysis organization such as the Office of Management and Budget or a ministry of finance – to make an extensive analysis of the many possible patterns of expenditures. As a consequence, there is a tendency to accept the previous year's allocation as a given and to examine primarily changes from that allocation. This incremental result is, in fact, explicitly written into the French budgetary process, where items in the *services votes* are accepted unless there is an explicit challenge and only new items (*mesures nouvelles*) are given detailed scrutiny.[15]

There is also a tendency to regard not only the existing distribution of expenditures, but also the rate of increase in spending as acceptable. Evidence exists that agencies tend to have the same rates of increase in their allocations from year to year. This rate of increase is not the same across agencies – in some instances there might be significant differences – but for each agency there is an accepted rate of increase on top of the accepted base, which allows the budget to increase predictably from year to year. Many innovations in the budgetary process have been advanced for the explicit purpose of rectifying the incrementalism in budgeting.

Competing bureaucracies

The above discussion of the process of allocating spending authority has already indicated another important feature of the budgetary process: budgeting, more than any other area of the policy process, forces a conflict between central staff agencies and line agencies.[16] Schick discusses these conflicts in terms of the opposing demands of "claimants" and "conservers." Central agencies, such as the Office of Management and Budget in the United States, H.M. Treasury in the United Kingdom, or the ministry of finance in most countries, are the conservers. They have the task of preparing the budget and in the process develop a proprietary interest in protecting the public purse. But these agencies, despite their centrality and close relationship with the chief executive may be "ganged up" against by the claimants – the spending agencies.[17] This is especially true in cabinet government, where the spending ministers and the financial ministers must sit together in the same political body making budgetary decisions, and the financial minister may be supported only by the prime minister, if that.

Again, although we might like these decisions to be made on a rational basis, the decisions between competing bureaucracies over the budget are inherently political, and each side has at its disposal several important weapons. The central agencies and their ministers have the advantage of being closely connected with the chief executive and frequently ministers of finance are in essence deputy prime ministers. This association with political authority makes it more difficult for the spending agencies to oppose the decisions that are made; in fact, the central agencies may be able to make some decisions by fiat, or, as in the case of Germany, special circumstances may be required in cabinet to over-rule decisions of the Finance Minister.[18] Similarly, the Minister of Finance in Sweden can decide that a remiss petition[19] will not be sent to certain interest groups when it is clear that all they want to do is spend more money. The Minister of Finance in Finland may decide unilaterally not to spend money or fill positions if financial circumstances require greater frugality.[20] In addition, financial agencies are specialized and can devote their full energies to budget issues, whereas spending agencies and their ministers have numerous other responsibilities and, although the budget is significant to them, it is but one consideration.

On the other hand, spending agencies have a political advantage in that they provide services directly to citizens and consequently have constituencies that support them in their quest for more money. Also, the constituencies of the agencies are constituents of elective officials and, consequently, the agencies can appeal over the head of the central financial agencies, and perhaps even the chief executive. Finally, the administrative agencies control information and are capable of deceiving the central budgeters about the true cost of producing their services.[21] Central agencies may be put in the position of trading money for information so that they can manage the national economy better. Thus here the macro-management role of central financial agencies may interfere with their micro-management role.

The relative success of the two sets of bureaucracies will depend upon situational factors as well as their own relative powers in the political process. One obvious factor is economics. Times of economic insecurity advantage the central financial managers in their quest for budgetary restraint. This power is enhanced when external financial agents such as the International Monetary Fund, or foreign banks threatening to call in loans, are involved. Budgetary decisions of many less-developed countries often are dependent upon decisions by those international organizations.[22] The IMF and other international agents, including private actors, are increasingly important even in highly-developed economies. On the other hand, the perception of specific needs for expenditures, such as a perceived need to increase spending on economic infrastructure or health, tend to favor the spending agency in question. Few spending ministers are willing to sacrifice their own expenditures in order to finance another minister's expansion, and consequently if one ministry is able to gain extra funding for a special need, it is likely that the total spending may increase.

Finally, the introduction of any of a number of innovations in budgeting may provide financial agencies with a variety of weapons – one of them is the complexity and obscurity of the method itself – that can be used to exercise control of spending ministries. For example, innovations such as performance budgeting and an increased emphasis on evaluation allow central agencies to impose a new set of criteria to control spending agencies.[23] The power of these instruments may frequently be overstated, however; technique is a complement to politics, not a substitute for it.[24]

The importance of resources

One important factor affecting the style of budgeting exercised by a country is the economic climate within which the budget is constructed. Aaron Wildavsky argued that two economic factors are crucial in determining the style of budgeting: wealth and predictability.[25] Wealth is self-explanatory, but the concept of predictability may require some explanation. We have already discussed the difficulties that even wealthy, industrialized countries have in predicting their revenues and expenditures. These difficulties are even greater for Third World countries whose economies are subject to huge fluctuations resulting from weather, changes in the international economy and internal political and economic changes. The chief executive of an industrialized country may have his or her calculations altered by changes in the international environment but those changes can completely destroy the calculations of leaders in less affluent countries.

In Wildavsky's analysis of the impact of the environment on budgetary behavior, affluent nations with certain revenues and expenditures should have incremental budgeting. This is indicative of a stable political process where government can fund its commitments with little need to make difficult choices among competing expenditure priorities. On the other hand, poor countries with uncertain revenues will engage in repetitive budgeting and will, of necessity, construct a succession of budgets during a fiscal year in order to adjust to changing conditions. Political systems that are relatively poor but that can predict their revenues accurately for a year will engage in "revenue budgeting." They will spend what they can collect – no more and no less – but lack the type of predictable, incremental patterns of change that would characterize more affluent political systems. Finally, wealthy but uncertain budgetary systems will alternate between incremental and repetitive budgeting as a reflection of political instability, or their administrative incapacities will lead them to supplemental budgeting. In this latter form of budgeting, the basic budget document will remain in force, but supplements will be added throughout the fiscal year as the revenue and expenditure figures become clarified.

When Wildavsky originally presented this argument, it was assumed that industrialized countries, such as the United States and the United Kingdom, would have incremental budgetary processes. However, within one year of the publication of this book, economic conditions had forced the United Kingdom to issue three budgets in a single year, thus following the pattern of a poor and uncertain country. The United States also began to engage in repetitive and supplemental budgeting to an extent unheard of prior to the economic difficulties that began in the mid-1970s. This pattern has become especially pronounced in the late 1980s and early 1990s, with the entire annual spending plan being passed several months after the official beginning of the fiscal year in the form of a resolution rather than appropriations acts, and supplemental appropriations becoming an increasingly important element of total federal spending.[26]

Incrementalism in the budgetary process

The Wildavsky typology hypothesizes that incrementalism is peculiar to the budgetary environment of relatively few affluent countries. However, despite the special conditions under which incrementalism is argued to arise, it has become a prevailing description of the budgetary process for all countries. Even in countries clearly beyond the range of incrementalist nations in the Wildavsky typology, there are pressures for incrementalism in the preparation of budgets that may over-ride the relative poverty or unpredictability of a budgetary environment. The budgetary process itself appears to push toward incrementalist outcomes, even in economic environments that appear to call for "rational decrementalism."[27] This section will discuss some of the pressures toward incrementalism in budgeting, to be followed by two sections discussing the variety of mechanisms by which political systems attempt to manage those pressures, with the goal of outcomes more objectively suited to changing social and economic conditions.

The nature of incrementalism

Incrementalism is both a descriptive and a prescriptive concept. Descriptively, it refers to observed patterns of change in budgets and other outcomes of the policy process in which those outputs increase in a stable and predictable fashion. For example, in a major empirical work on incrementalism, Davis, Dempster and Wildavsky analysed changes in the appropriations of a number of federal agencies in the United States.[28] They found that the majority of the changes in appropriations could be described as a simple linear function of the preceding year's expenditures. There was a pronounced tendency in the data examined by these three scholars for Congress to appropriate the same percentage increases in an agency's budget year after year. Although there were significant differences in the percentage increases provided to different agencies, for each agency the increase tended to be stable. In short, this legislative body (as well as many others that have been studied) tends to allocate money on the basis of simple, stable decision rules.

Prescriptively, this stability and predictability in decisions is regarded positively by incrementalists. It makes planning simpler for agencies and reduces decision-making costs in the legislature. Legislatures are able to minimize decision-making costs and concentrate on exceptional cases rather than ordinary decisions. More importantly, it is argued that attempts at more comprehensive (synoptic) decision making would not necessarily produce better decisions, because of the absence of information about the future and because of inadequate understanding of social and economic problems addressed through the budget.[29] In addition, major departures from the budgetary status quo may be irreversible without extreme expense. Therefore, incrementalists argue that the most rational approach to budgeting is to make relatively minor departures from the status quo, monitor the effects of those new policies and then adjust the policies in future decision making. If decision makers do anything else they run the risk of major mistakes, although incrementalism itself may perpetuate small mistakes.[30]

Critiques of incrementalism

Critiques of incrementalism have also been directed at both its descriptive and prescriptive features. The degree of incrementalism found in budgets appears to be a function of the level of aggregation at which the researcher looks: the larger the program or organization, the more incremental the outcomes appear. There is a great deal of variation in the levels of program appropriations, as some are initiated and others are terminated.[31] Critics also point out that the incrementalist approach may be adequate to explain or describe changes in the majority of programs for the majority of years but provides no mechanism for explaining changes in those percentage increases across time, nor for explaining differences in the percentage increases allotted each year to different agencies. Indeed, in their later work, Davis, Dempster and Wildavsky pointed to the importance of events that upset the stability of incremental decision-making systems.[32]

Prescriptively, it has been argued that the incrementalist approach to decision making tends to institutionalize the status quo and to curtail more creative thinking about possible uses of scarce resources. This is especially true during a period in which "decrementalism" is more appropriate than incrementalism. That is, the approach to cutting budgets that has most often been used is to apply the same percentage cut across the board to all programs. The result may be insignificant to a large program but be effective termination for a small program.[33] This is not incrementalism per se but has the same logic – minimizing decision costs – that characterizes incrementalism. In addition, critics point out that incremental decisions are not necessarily reversible, as a program expansion may well add clients who will expect continued benefits.[34] In fact, the more often incremental adjustments are made in a program, the more probable it is that the program will continue, as each small change constitutes a vote of confidence in the fundamental validity of the program.

Pressures toward incrementalism

Two fundamental factors in the budgetary process tend to work in favor of incremental outcomes. The first is the sheer magnitude of the process itself. The typical public budget in industrialized countries involves making decisions that allocate between one-third and one-half of the total goods and services in the economy. In the United States, where the federal budget is "only" 23 percent of Gross National Product, it still involves allocating approximately *$1.1 trillion* among hundreds of programs. In addition, the decisions to spend all of this money must be made in a relatively short time period under substantial political pressure. Consequently, there is a tendency to accept the existing distribution of expenditures as a given, and therefore to concentrate time and attention on the relatively few deviations from existing patterns. The French budgetary process institutionalizes this distinction with *mesures nouvelles* receiving extensive scrutiny while *services votes* receive almost none. The budgetary process at the federal level in the United States, through its use of the Current Service Budget, also informally uses this distinction. Congress can see just how much it will need to spend to maintain a constant level of services and then build on that "base." Thus, since there is not the time and the analytic staff to completely rework the budget each year, legislators tend to accept the existing budget and to employ very simple rules of thumb when making deviations from that pattern, such as the stability of the constant percentage changes.

The massive size of the public budget results in what has been called the "law of triviality."[35] The size of the budget is now so great that the average member of a legislature charged with using the power of the purse to control the executive really cannot comprehend the amount of money being spent. Therefore, the average legislator will concentrate time and effort on items of a magnitude he or she can comprehend – for example, a few thousand dollars or pounds or francs to hire an additional staff person – and will allow expenditures of millions or billions to be approved with little or no consideration. So long as the percentage changes appear reasonable, the legislature is likely to approve the spending proposals.

The second feature of the budgetary process that helps to produce incremental solutions is the sequential and repetitive nature of budgeting. A new budget must be created each year, or sometimes even more often. Consequently, both administrators and legislators tend to assume that errors made in one year can be corrected in subsequent years. Further, the actors involved in making the budget – bureaucrats, legislators and analysts – tend to retain their positions for long periods. This is especially true where, unlike in the United States, a change in government involves very few changes in those responsible for constructing the budget, or where a central agency with a permanent and expert staff tends to dominate the budgetary process as does, for example, the Treasury in the United Kingdom.[36] The long tenure in office of the principal actors in budgeting results in their having the opportunity to develop an accommodation among themselves and to shape the budget in the manner they find acceptable. Therefore all they must do on an annual basis is to make marginal adjustments from the accepted pattern.

Any actor wishing to make any significant departure from existing patterns have strong incentives to adopt cautious strategies. They should be aware that they are involved in a long-term "game" and that slow adjustments are far more probable than sudden shifts in budgetary priorities. Further, all actors must play the "confidence game" and gain the trust and respect of others involved in the budgetary process to be effective in getting what they want.[37] This cautious and conservative behavior in budgeting produces considerable frustration for those who come into political office with new ideas and priorities and expect to generate change in the budget overnight.

In addition to the very fundamental factors tending to push toward incremental results in the budgetary process, some more technical factors tend to have the same impact. One is that many public expenditures are now indexed, or automatically adjusted for inflation.[38] This procedure is especially common for social programs such as social security, but in some countries public sector wages and salaries have also been indexed.[39] When there are legal commitments to keep expenditures in line with increases in prices, or wages with those in the private sector, government loses a great deal of its control over expenditures. Given that the thresholds at which taxes are levied are also indexed, governments do not receive any automatic increases in revenue that would help fund those expenditures.[40]

Politics and incrementalism

Although there may be strong pressures toward incrementalism in the budgetary process, there are some political pressures that may produce real change. The most important of these is a change in the partisan control of government. This is most likely when there is a major change in government, such as a revolution from the right or left, that installs a new ideological regime. It can, and does, occur with less extreme changes in partisan control. For example, Bunce finds that a change in leadership in government does have a significant impact on the priorities expressed in the public budget.[41] This is true even for communist countries, where leadership changes while the party in control remains the same.

A second but less obvious political influence on budgetary change is a consequence of politicians' need in democratic governments to be perceived to be doing *something* to benefit their constituents. Simply keeping the existing constellation of programs operating well may be insufficient to present that image. Although clients of existing programs want their old programs maintained, many politicians find it advantageous to associate themselves with new and innovative approaches to public problems. While new programs may merely nibble at the edges of the expenditures governed by the incremental dynamic, the felt need for adopting them is a force for change and some reallocation of budgetary priorities.

Alternatives to incrementalism

The wealthy, predictable world so conducive to the development of incremental budgeting no longer exists in the majority of industrialized countries – and never existed for most other countries.[42] In response to fiscal pressures in virtually all political systems in the 1970s and 1980s, politicians and administrators devised a number of mechanisms intended to break the grip of incremental solutions on resource allocation in the public sector. These solutions demonstrate the creativity of politicians and civil servants when faced with genuine problems, but they have had varying degrees of success. Apparently none of the approaches has, however, altered the fundamental pattern of slow, evolutionary growth in expenditures characteristic of budgetary incrementalism.

It is not just the "fiscal crisis" that produces an interest in alternative budgeting mechanisms. Even during periods of affluence, several more "rational" approaches to budgeting have been advocated, primarily because of their appeal to human rationality and their potential for breaking the incremental cycle. The simple, and apparently irrational, decision rules involved in incrementalism have been an affront to those who believe that there must be better ways of making decisions in government, and even when resources are plentiful, there is no need to waste them. Government should, it is argued, get the most "bang for the buck" (or *frappe* for the franc) and should allocate resources so that a Pigovian optimum is obtained.[43] That is, the budget should be adjusted so that the marginal utility of the last dollar spent for each of the numerous functions of government is equal. Of course, in the real world such an optimal allocation of resources would almost certainly be unknowable and unattainable, but it is argued that the public sector should still aspire to reach that "perfect" allocation.

The following discussion considers budgetary mechanisms developed to produce more efficient allocation, as well as those developed as specific responses to contemporary fiscal problems. In some instances this distinction is artificial, but it may be useful in understanding how governments have attempted to respond to a basic problem in governance: deciding how to decide what is important.[44] First we discuss several of the more general methods advanced for enhancing rationality in budgeting. These methods have been popular principally in the United States but then have been exported to other countries. Several methods have been developed outside the United States as responses to particular problems arising from the governance of that country. These have not been exported as frequently, but have found some uses outside the one country.

Program budgeting

The most familiar alternative approach to budgeting is program budgeting or PPBS (Planning, Programming, Budgeting System), as it was practiced in the United States. Although commonly associated with the Defense Department under Robert McNamara, PPBS actually came to Washington during World War II and was introduced into several domestic agencies, notably the Department of Agriculture.[45] This approach to budgeting has been exported to several countries. For example, program budgeting has been one of several stages of budgetary reform in Canada, and France developed a system of program budgeting entitled *Rationalisation des Choix Budgetaires* (RCB).[46] Also the United Nations adopted the concept of program budgeting as the most appropriate means for Third World countries to manage their scarce economic resources and to link the public budget with developmental goals.[47] Therefore, for a period of time, some of the countries of the world least capable of meeting the data and analytic requirements of PPBS were expected to meet those standards in order to receive aid from the United Nations.

Program budgeting is based upon a systems concept of policy and government. In contrast to the usual organizational or programmatic basis of budgeting, program budgeting assumes that organizations are not sacrosanct or independent, but rather that all programs are interconnected and that there may be many means for attaining the same goals. PPBS attempts to identify the goals of government and how those goals can be best achieved. Program budgeting also depends heavily upon policy analysis and data in order to attempt to derive optimal solutions to budgetary problems. It requires that all the actors involved in budgeting identify alternative courses of action, along with the financial implications of those alternative courses, and justify the selection of one program over the others.

This approach to budgeting is obviously just as much a system of budgeting for wealthy countries as is incrementalism. It requires an abundance of information and analytic ability, as well as some predictability of the revenues and expenditures of government. Program budgeting is also a budgeting system for relatively centralized and elite-dominated political systems. It is almost inherently centralizing, as it requires the identification of goals at a very high level and the central authority to implement program-based decisions.[48] Thus, a political system such as that of the United States, which is highly decentralized and depends upon the goal setting of relatively autonomous administrative agencies, is not likely to find program budgeting very compatible. On the other hand, a more centralized political system such as France or even Sweden might find the PPB system compatible.[49] Similarly the importance of the legislature in the political system affects the acceptability of program budgeting.

Program budgeting, because it allocates resources to programs rather than to the line items so conducive to legislative control, tends not to be favored by legislatures. Also, strong legislatures like to be able to allocate resources to their favorite organizations and to protect those organizations during budgetary battles. Program budgeting does not lend itself to that degree of legislative involvement, but interestingly, in political systems dominated by a strong executive, such as Fifth Republic France, program budgeting may make the criteria for allocation more subject to legislative scrutiny than they might otherwise have been.[50] This is, in large part, because it makes the choices being made more apparent than they might otherwise be using more conventional forms of budgeting.

Different policy areas also appear more amenable to program budgeting than others. Defense has been the policy area to which program budgeting has most commonly been applied. This may be so simply because of the absence of any means of verifying the validity of the data and scenarios used to defend the budget requests – short of actually going to war.[51] The sophistication of the methods used in these forecasts and the absence of alternative information make it difficult for outsiders to question the results. On the other hand, areas such as social policy, which are more commonly understood and in which value assumptions are more clearly involved, are likely to produce obvious budget conflicts and greater involvement of legislative and non-governmental actors. Consequently, the technocratic and centralized decision making associated with program budgeting is less appealing in these areas.

Program budgeting has made something of a minor comeback in the early 1990s. In some of the more managerialist oriented industrialized countries, e.g. Australia, the systems concept and the analysis of alternative uses of funds has been appealing to managerialists.[52] Also, although it has rarely persisted as the central mechanism for resource allocation in governments, program budgeting has survived as a planning device in many countries.[53] It appears that the process of identifying goals, and the interactions among different categories of public expenditure, is a very useful way of understanding government. It is, however, too divorced from the political realities of most governments to be used as the central budgeting mechanism in any but the most technocratic political system, or a technocratic policy area within a political system. Program budgeting has all the virtues of rationality but, even when market values have come to permeate the public sector, the method still does not conform to the political realities that dominate government.

Zero-Base Budgeting

A second form of "rational" budgeting, which has been confined almost exclusively to the United States, is Zero-Base Budgeting. Incremental budgeting, either explicitly or implicitly, assumes that there is a budgetary base – the previous year's level of appropriation – that is guaranteed, and that there is only a question of how much of an increment will be given.[54] As was pointed out above, however, this appears to be true at the level of the department or agency but not true of individual programs. Even if it is not entirely true, it is a common perception about budgeting, and Zero-Base Budgeting (ZBB) was designed to solve this perceived problem.[55]

The most fundamental idea behind ZBB is that the agencies should have to justify its entire budget from the ground up each year. This is somewhat impractical, given the magnitude of the task for any national government budget, and therefore, ZBB forces each budget unit to develop contingencies for several possible levels of funding. The most basic level of appropriations is the "survival package," which is the minimal level of funding needed for the organization to survive and to provide for its minimum services. Agencies might also be asked what they would do in the face of five or ten percent cuts in their budgets, and what they would require to maintain their current levels of service provision. Finally, decision packages reflecting various alternative packages of new programs are presented as the priorities of the organizations for expanding their programs. The Canadian government at one time used a system called "A, B and X" to get at the same range of alternatives.[56] The decision packages are reviewed at successive levels in each organization to develop a set of "consolidated decision packages," reflecting the priorities of the executive department along with those of its various components.

This form of budgeting does not contain the complicated and threatening assumptions of programs dominating organizations. It therefore may be more suitable for less-developed countries than the more complex program budgeting system.[57] Zero-Base Budgeting does, however, have a number of problems that limit its political acceptability. Obviously, organizations do not like outsiders to know what the minimum amount of funding they need to survive really is. Also if there is an assumption that the survival level of funding for an organization is open to very fundamental challenges each year, political conflicts are perpetuated and old disputes opened annually.[58] This may be especially threatening to programs, such as some social programs, that lack broad popular support or a well-organized constituency group to defend them. Finally, legislatures and many citizens tend to think in terms of percentage increases, rather than in terms of "packages," so that the zero-based approach to budgeting may be difficult to "sell" politically.

Management by Objectives

Although it is not strictly a budgeting system, Management by Objectives (MBO) does have implications for public expenditure and should be discussed briefly in this context.[59] Like Zero-Base Budgeting, MBO is a transplant from the private sector. Also like ZBB, the concept behind MBO is deceptively simple and almost common sense. The basic concept behind MBO is that managers should establish clear objectives and develop plans for attaining those objectives, and individuals in the organization should be rewarded on the basis of their attainment of objectives. In the public sector, these seemingly simple ideas have some very serious complications for both managers and the recipients of the programs.

One of the political complications is that MBO can be very centralizing. A common feature of government is that there may be as many objectives as there are organizations, and if any agreed-upon list of objectives is to be envisaged, it must be conceived by central political (or possibly administrative) officials.[60] As with program budgeting, this centralization of the process of goal determination did not conform to the usual patterns of American government, with its tradition of highly decentralized goal formulation. The Nixon Administration was the primary advocate of MBO at the federal level in the United States; these centralizing tendencies may have been exacerbated by some of the individuals involved in that administration, but it is likely that similar problems would arise under any president. If government is to determine the priorities it will seek to attain, the central officials must be very heavily involved and ultimately determine these objectives.

A second problem that besets MBO, PPBS, or any system attempting to install "rational" policy analysis in government is that operational indicators of the attainment of objectives must be developed in order for the connected system of performance evaluation to be effective. Unfortunately, the search for such indicators rivals the search for the philosopher's stone in its apparent futility.[61] Many of the actions that government takes are taken through the public sector (as opposed to be private sector) simply because they involve vague, ill-defined, possibly contradictory and unmeasurable consequences. At best we can develop measures of the activities of government organizations, but in reality those activities may be inversely related to the attainment of the real objectives of government. For example, we can measure the number of people receiving welfare payments, but the ultimate purpose of the social service system is to make its recipients self-sufficient.

The implementation of MBO is also limited by personnel systems in many governments that still do not permit the flexibility in pay and other rewards assumed necessary by the majority of advocates of MBO. Pay levels for the majority of public employees are determined by their length of service and their job classifications. Relatively few personnel systems – for example, the Senior Executive Service in the United States and the managerial grades in Norway – allow more individualized determination of compensation.[62] The central premise of public pay schedules appears to be equality within the classification, with the classification being determined as much by the job as by the individual, so that there is little opportunity either to reward adequately the more effective employees or to punish the less effective.

Thus, while MBO is an admirable idea that few would oppose at the theoretical level, it runs counter to many of the established practices of government. Perhaps most important, MBO forces decisions upward toward the chief executive and the top administrators. It forces those individuals to determine the goals of government, while government is composed of many organizations and individuals with conflicting objectives. Thus the goals espoused may tend to be either so bland as to be meaningless or simply not accepted by many who may be charged with their implementation. This is especially true of countries with highly decentralized political systems, such as the United States or Canada, but may also be true of systems that are nominally more centralized.

The Public Expenditure Survey

In the United Kingdom, although there were certainly some elements of crisis management involved, the Public Expenditure Survey Committee (PESC) system was designed during the 1960s and 1970s to make better expenditure decisions about the allocation of public expenditures, regardless of the degree of fiscal restraint required.[63] PESC had five processes that it was intended to perform in the management of public expenditure. The first was planning. One of the common shortcomings of the budgetary process is its failure to take into account the long-term implications of an expenditure decision made in one year. A program may be small at its inception, but if it has the ability to accept clients at its discretion, or if there is an open-ended entitlement, the program may grow very quickly to have a substantial level of expenditure. PESC involved forecasts of expenditure requirements for all programs, as well as medium-term forecasts of the balance of public expenditure with the rest of the economy.

PESC also involved allocation among the competing purposes of government. Suggestions for this allocation were by the committee, but those suggestions obviously had to be validated by the Treasury and the Cabinet. As with any "rational" approach to policy making, however, the results of the PESC exercise carry a substantial degree of weight.

The PESC system was also charged with the execution of the budget. Another common problem in budgeting is ensuring that actual expenditures match the projected expenditures. This is a legal problem of ensuring that all expenditures are made legally, but it is also an important economic problem for a modern government that attempts to use the budget as a central mechanism for controlling its economy. If expenditures are above or below the levels projected, there may be serious economic repercussions.

The PESC system also involved evaluation of public expenditures. As with program budgeting, this system included an attempt to assess the cost effectiveness of public expenditure and to propose alternative means of reaching policy goals. Until the demise of the Programme Analysis and Review (PAR) system, PESC was supplemented in these efforts by the more extensive policy-analytic capabilities of PAR.[64] Later the remnants of PESC were supplemented by the selective review exercises of the Efficiency Unit (the Rayner Scrutinies).[65] More recently the vestiges of the system can be seen in accrual budgeting.

Finally, PESC was involved with accounting for the expenditures made by government. This function is an after-the-fact control on expenditure, whereas the control functions of PESC mentioned above constituted more continuous monitoring of expenditure levels throughout the year. The post-audit is a long-standing function in government, but continuous control has become more important as the size of the public budget has increased and the importance of that budget for the national economy has increased proportionately.[66]

When PESC was first introduced, in the 1972–3 fiscal year, the primary emphasis was on planning and the forward look. Relatively speaking, this was a period of affluence for Britain, and the major problem was perceived to be making appropriate decisions about future public expenditure. However, as there were numerous shocks to the British economy after that time, the emphasis quickly switched from planning to controlling expenditure.[67] The PESC system was founded on the concept of volume budgeting (consideration of the actual output of services rather than their cost in current prices), which is an excellent, rational means of viewing the development of the budget when resources are not in short supply. Then, when scarcity was reintroduced to the system, there was a need for more stringent controls.[68] There is still a fundamental emphasis on rational allocation in the program, even when the major concern has become monitoring current spending rather than forecasting the future. However, the changes that have been made in PESC have altered it almost entirely, so the assumptions of the PESC system continued in name only and there is a substantially different system of expenditure control in effect.

Bulk budgeting

New Zealand was perhaps the first country to experiment extensively with what it then called "bulk budgeting."[69] The concept is quite simple. Instead of an organization receiving funds in the conventional input categories such as personnel or equipment, they are allocated a lump sum of money and told to get on with their job. It is assumed that managers will utilize the input categories for the preparation of their budget requests, but after the funds are allocated, the manager will be free to do anything legal with them in order to achieve the stated goals of the organization. This budgeting system is assumed to permit the program managers greater flexibility in achieving their goals, and especially in responding to changing circumstances. Once a spending figure is decided upon, managers are charged with delivering the service and are then evaluated on the basis of the results. In many ways, this form of budgeting resembles PPBS, but without all the intellectual apparatus and without the implicit threats to the survival of organizations.

Implementing bulk budgeting successfully requires several conditions not always available in government. One necessary factor is a good information system that will allow managers to judge performance and effects of their choice of instruments to achieve goals.[70] It also requires an effective and professional auditing organization to ensure that the money really is spent properly and perhaps to provide – as does the General Accounting Office in the United States or *Riksrevisionsverket* – some independent advice on the efficiency and effectiveness of public programs.[71] Bulk budgeting also requires some flexibility both with staff ceilings, a means by which the growth of government has been controlled in difficult economic times, and in pay to provide incentives for managers to use their flexibility to the utmost. As we have already seen, just as legislatures want to control budgets through line items, they want to control the civil service through both personnel ceilings and standard pay schedules. However, despite these difficulties and caveats, bulk budgeting offers an interesting opportunity to allow public sector managers to manage and then to be judged by the success of their efforts.

The concept of bulk budgeting is now being spread more widely, although now more commonly under the rubric of "frame" or "framework" budgeting.[72] Frame budgeting is one component of a general shift toward focussing managerial attention on the outputs rather than the inputs of government. The most recent thrust of management reform in the public sector has been an emphasis on performance, the measurement of goal attainment and linking performance with budgets and with individual pay.[73] If public managers are provided the latitude to make more of their own decisions about the use of funds, then it becomes more feasible to judge their performance in reaching goals agreed upon with their political or administrative superiors.[74]

Reactions to stress

We have already mentioned in passing some of the changes implemented across the years in the Public Expenditure Survey in Britain as the result of changing economic fortunes. The cycle of changes in PESC constitutes but one of many reactions to the fiscal stress in Western political economies that have been manifested through the budgetary process. We will first discuss the several changes in PESC and then go on to other alternative methods for allocating resources – through both the macro- and the micro-budgetary processes – that have been developed in response to real and perceived fiscal stress.[75] Of course, for many of the poorer countries of the world the fiscal stress was never absent, and somewhat greater stress in the richer countries appeared rather manageable to those less-affluent regimes.

Cash limits

In the PESC program as it was formulated originally, expenditure forecasts were made in terms of constant pounds (although the base for calculation was modified frequently). That is, PESC allocated resources according to the volume of services to be provided rather than according to the costs of those services in the current monetary units. In an inflationary period, this meant that the cost of services in terms of the pounds or pence that the average citizens were paying as taxes might increase very rapidly, whereas the value in constant terms might not increase at all. The system made control by Parliament difficult since the calculations were in the form of "funny money," and additionally there was little constraint on the administrators, who never quite knew how much they could – or should – spend until long after the time had passed.

Because of both the political and the administrative difficulties arising from this form of volume budgeting, cash limits were imposed in April 1976. These imposed an absolute expenditure limit in current pounds on approximately 75 percent of public expenditure. The limits applied only to year one of the five-year PESC exercise, but since that is the most important year – the year's budget actually being executed – it represents the domination of control over planning in response to the increasing financial crisis of British government. Associated with the introduction of cash limits was the use of the contingency reserve in public expenditure as a means of short-term control rather than as a general "honey pot" that anyone who overspent could dip into.[76] Interestingly, after the introduction of cash limits, there was a tendency for government organizations to underspend and, indeed, to underspend significantly. While fiscal conservatives may regard that as a positive outcome, those attempting to manage the public budget in order to manage the economy – not to mention the possible beneficiaries of the expenditures – did not regard the outcome so positively. The difficulties associated with underspending and cash limits have produced some interest in greater flexibility for public managers in dealing with money left in their accounts at the end of the year.[77] In almost all public fiscal systems this money must revert to the general treasury rather than being retained by the agency that was sufficiently frugal to save it.[78]

The British government has now abandoned cash limits as originally implemented in favor of a system involving cash limits in the present budgetary year with future budgets being expressed in terms of cash but with forecast price levels. One analyst has called this system "hiccup money," as it is a new kind of volume budgeting expressed in cash terms. The same analyst has argued that the major effect of this change will be increased confusion over the published budget figures.[79]

Cash limits served as a useful stop-gap measure for the British government to gain control over public expenditure. The same instrument has been adopted in some version in most other developed countries, and in several less-developed countries, for the same reason.[80] They are, however, a very blunt instrument, especially for governments with a large volume of entitlement programs. Cash limits have the further effect of pointing out to a public that may not have understood the complexity of contemporary budgeting that when using the more sophisticated techniques for making allocations, such as PESC or PPBS, the usual mechanisms of budgetary control are actually more difficult to implement. This makes the familiar (and largely false) analogy between household budgets and central government budgeting more appealing to the public.

Envelope budgeting

Another approach to the problems posed by economic deceleration during the 1970s and early 1980s was the system of envelope budgeting developed in Canada.[81] This approach to budgeting depends upon two levels of allocation. At the first level budget resources were allocated among eleven "envelopes," or policy areas, such as defense and social affairs. These envelopes were allocated their total resources in part on the basis of tradition and in part on the basis of priorities developed by the Cabinet and by the Treasury Board Secretariat and the Ministry of Finance. Within each of these envelopes the ministers concerned would meet to allocate the scarce resources. Because there is a fixed amount of money allocated to each "envelope," increases in one program would have to be offset by reductions in others. The affected ministers and their deputies (civil servants rather than politicians) are handed the difficult task of making the allocations within the envelope. Their decisions are still subject to review and confirmation by the plenary Cabinet and by the Parliament but, in general, survive as the final allocation of resources.

Envelope budgeting is an interesting approach to the problem of allocating scarce resources, first proposed by the short-lived Clark government in 1979. The political leaders of this Progressive Conservative government sought a means to impose greater fiscal discipline on the component ministries. This "scrap and build" approach to controlling public expenditures is not confined to Canada. For example, as a part of its COPE system (Committee of Officials on Public Expenditure), since 1980, departments in New Zealand requesting new programs have been required to specify how they can achieve commensurate savings from others of their programs. There may still be room for new programs, but some attempt must be made to create room by cutting back on old programs. This approach differs from that in Canada by keeping the consideration strictly on a departmental basis, with the trade-offs between different agencies being achieved by COPE and by the Treasury, but it again places politicians in the position of balancing the importance of new and old programs. Although less formalized, a similar system has been adopted in Australia, and budgeting with a "scrap and build" philosophy has been common in Japanese government. Finally, the Budget Enforcement Act in the United States, adopted in 1990, requires a "pay-as-you go" (usually referred to simply as PAYGO) approach to new programs, finding savings or new revenues before a new spending program is adopted.[82]

This system of budgeting is very good at forcing ministries and civil servants within the various policy areas to make decisions about their collective priorities. What it does not do so well, however, is to make the initial allocative decisions about how much is to be devoted to each of the major portfolios. This must still be done by a means not dissimilar to the manner in which budgets have always been made. The method does, however, provide some means of addressing real scarcity in ways that "spread the pain" that are perhaps most acceptable to the parties involved.

Structural budget margin

Although macro-budgeting is a logical first step in the preparation of the budget, the final budget figures frequently reflect as much the aggregation of decisions about individual programs as they do the result of decisions about the allocation of goods and services between the public and private sectors. The use of the structural budget margin is a mechanism for institutionalizing macro-control over the amount of public expenditure, and for attempting to institutionalize some balance between the two sectors. Further, this budgeting system is based upon medium- or long-term trends in the growth of the economy and therefore should minimize the short-term political considerations that have tended to motivate a great deal of budgetary decision making.

Structural budgeting begins with a calculation of the effects of economic growth and inflation on government receipts. Because of the progressive tax structure of industrialized countries, either inflation or real growth will produce a greater proportion of government revenue relative to the private sector. This "fiscal dividend" is then available for either tax reductions or expenditure increases. As this system functioned in the Netherlands in the 1970s and 1980s, the plan was to keep the public sector at approximately the same size (relative to the private sector) as it had been when the program was initiated.[83]

As it was practiced, structural budgeting in the Netherlands bore a strong resemblance to the concept advanced by the Brookings Institution in the United States called the "full employment budget."[84] The Brookings concept was to calculate what the budget – in terms of both receipts and expenditures – would be if the economy were operating at full employment. Naturally, if it were operating at less than full employment, tax receipts would fall and expenditures for a variety of social programs would increase. This would create a "full employment deficit," which under this approach to budgeting would be justifiable as a means of bringing the economy back to full employment. However, any deficit beyond that level would not be economically justifiable but would be the product of politicians attempting to purchase votes through programs paid for not from taxes but rather through borrowing.[85] Germany has employed similar thinking in its annual calculation of a "cyclically neutral" budget to be used for planning purposes.[86]

Structural budgeting is, to some extent, a decision about making decisions. It establishes the limits on bargaining within the budgetary process by defining maximum appropriate total increase. As such, the mechanism is particularly suited to the nature of Dutch politics.[87] The degree of partisan fragmentation and the linkage of interest groups to their respective ministries make an attempt to develop budget control from the bottom up, as in the PESC system, rather difficult. By imposing at least a tacit ceiling on expenditures (based on the amount of money available without any increases in taxes, and perhaps after some tax reductions), this method cannot eliminate difficult political decisions about the competing uses of resources, but it can limit the macro-level outcomes in a manner perceived to foster greater economic growth. It also makes the consideration of these issues less short-term decisions made primarily on political grounds and more decisions based upon long-term economic growth and development. Further, a somewhat depoliticized budget commission was organized to advise the Dutch government on procedural and substantive adjustments to the budget process. These mechanisms all arguably make budgetary decisions more technocratic and reduce partisan political control over a crucial element of public policy.

The structural budget margin also illustrates the interdependence of budgeting and other aspects of economic policy. Given that a major component of the total costs of government is the wage bill of its employees (approximately 30 percent of the budget in the Netherlands in 1979 when the program was implemented), a policy of limiting the expansion of the budget could not work effectively without some coordination with wage and price policy.[88] If this coordination is achieved, government can maintain the relative purchasing power of its employees at the same time as it attempts to control total public expenditure.

Efficiency

Everyone talks about efficiency in government but, as the resources that were once readily available became increasingly scarce, some people in government have begun to do something about it. Efficiency in any strict sense of the term is probably not possible in the public sector, given that it is difficult if not impossible to measure and assign a meaningful value to the output of many government programs.[89] On the other hand, procedures can be introduced that force government managers to consider better, and perhaps cheaper, approaches to doing what they do.

One very simple means of making managers think about promoting efficiency is to give them less money and tell them to do what they had planned to do previously. In an unsophisticated version, this is the across-the-board cut so familiar to students of government cutbacks,[90] and called the "cheese slicer" by Swedish budgeters.[91] The Swedish concept that is now practiced, called more formally the "main alternative," is a more sophisticated answer to the problem. Swedish budgeting is designed to take into account effects of inflation in making allocations among programs; it begins as a version of volume budgeting. Once inflation is included in the expenditure forecast, however, the "main alternative" is to reduce the resultant figure by two percent. The idea is simple. Even the public sector, where productivity gains may be difficult to bring about, should be able to increase efficiency by this modest figure. In fairness, the Swedish government simply does not require the managers to come up with ideas on their own for productivity gains; several government organizations have been established to assist in that task, such as the internal consulting organization – *Statskontor* – and the state audit agency – *Riksrevisionsverket* – that advises on efficiency as well as on the legality of expenditures. The Danish government has a very similar program, but has permitted the negotiation of spending and efficiency targets between the ministries and the Ministry of Finance. In the trial efforts, the targets sometimes surpassed the simple two percent used in most Swedish cases.[92] A similar system is in place in Irish government.[93]

A more sophisticated approach to improving efficiency in government, one first popularized in Britain, is called the Financial Management Initiative (FMI).[94] The concept behind this innovation in the public sector is drawn directly from business; managers in the civil service must think about their organizations as "cost centers" (the idea of "profit center" might be rather farfetched in government). When managers accept this concept, they can begin to look at what they are producing and the costs of producing each unit, as well as at an overall corporate strategy. The task then becomes to reduce the cost of production of each unit. In so doing, they could systematically consider options involving using the private sector.[95] In short, the FMI involves systematic application of management information to the consideration of the costs of government, with an aim of generating strategies that improve the efficiency of service production.

When stated simply, the goals of FMI appear quite benign. In practice, however, many critics believe that they are anything but a simple examination of the functioning of government services. First, this initiative was developed in the context of substantial "civil service bashing" by the Thatcher government, and was interpreted by critics as just another mechanism for denigrating government and extolling the private sector.[96] A second associated factor is that one impact of the FMI is to make senior civil servants managers rather than policy advisors and indeed policy makers. This is another denigration of the role of the civil service and may make the career less attractive to the high-quality applicants that it needs to maintain its high standards.[97] The final and more technical point is, as noted above, that measuring output and efficiency in the public service is difficult or impossible. Thus the FMI may simply involve quantifying the unquantifiable and in that process potentially making spurious judgments about policy and public management. All these points having been raised, however, the Thatcher government was committed to the FMI and the managerial and efficiency values that characterized it. The Major and the Blair governments continued much of the same emphasis on managerialism in the public sector, although FMI per se had been largely abandoned.[98]

Australia had its own version of FMI called the Financial Management Improvement Programme (FMIP).[99] It also sought to disaggregate government into a series of cost centers and to permit the managers to make decisions about how best to achieve desired results with the funds allocated. This approach and the quite similar program called Increased Ministerial Authority and Accountability (IMAA) in Canada fall into the general category of "deregulating government" by moving an increasing number of budgetary, purchasing and personnel decisions downward to ministries and removing controls imposed by central agencies.[100] To the extent that controls remain in place, they will be negotiated between the Treasury Board Secretariat (Canada) or the Department of Finance (Australia) and the individual ministry.[101]

Outside evaluations

The Financial Management Initiative involves importing management ideas from the private sector to attempt to make government work better. Another group of efficiency exercises has involved actually importing individuals from the private sector or using management experts within the public sector. As with the Financial Management Initiative, the idea has been to make government function more like a business and to use business executives as advisors.

The largest exercise of this sort was the President's Private Sector Survey of Cost Control – called the Grace Commission after its chairman, Peter Grace.[102] Several thousand private sector executives were brought to Washington for a period of months to examine all the operations of government. They then produced some 2,478 recommendations about how government could save money. While many of the recommendations have been deemed unfeasible by experts in government management, and many ignored the political realities of government, this endeavor may still have resulted in significant cost savings for the federal government.[103] Most state governments in the United States have undertaken similar exercises and have produced relatively more significant savings.[104]

Government in the United States is more open to outsiders than is government in most countries, and hence it is easier to use groups such as the Grace Commission to develop efficiency recommendations. When government is more closed, as in the United Kingdom, other means must be found to achieve the same end. In Britain, Sir Derek Rayner (now Lord Rayner) was brought into government from the Marks and Spencer department store chain and asked to conduct reviews of specific management issues in government.[105] He was given a small staff of young, "high-flyer" civil servants to assist him in this task, and each "Rayner Scrutiny" was given a short time to complete an evaluation and to make its recommendations. The implementation of those recommendations was then carefully monitored from the Efficiency Unit attached to the Cabinet Office. While the results of this program have not been everything that might have been expected, especially by those who regard the private sector as the best exemplar for the public sector, some clear managerial improvements have resulted.[106]

The United States and the United Kingdom are by no means the only countries that have sought to interject some private sector management techniques into their government, or that have sought to review government policy. The Canadian government utilized a process rather similar to the Grace Commission – the Nielsen Commission – to recommend spending reductions. This differed from Grace, however, in that it was composed half of career public servants and half of outsiders.[107] In Sweden a systematic review of government programs was undertaken as even Social Democrats argued that the public sector had become too large. The reconsideration of the size of government continued under a conservative government, and continued after the Social Democrats returned.[108] That rethinking of government was accelerated under a conservative government in the early 1990s. In the Netherlands a "reconsideration" process forces a number of items of government policy, and a significant share of the budget, to be considered and justified each year.[109] As with all the instruments of budgeting and financial control we have been discussing, these scrutinies are incomplete and imperfect. These investigations, however, do represent yet another weapon at the disposal of those in government – civil servants and politicians alike – who want to exercise greater control over the level of public expenditure.

The return to rationality?

We have discussed a number of innovations in the latter part of 1980s and 1990s as being reactions to stress, but we can also see some elements of an attempt to impose rational solutions on the budgetary process. The Financial Management Initiative and its analogs in the Commonwealth countries has a number of elements of rationalism rather central to its operation. It assumes, for example, that the output of the public sector can be measured rather unambiguously and that clear corporate management strategies would be exert the control required to attain that efficiency. These methods further assume that budgetary decisions should be based on those levels of output. These methods depend more upon local, organizational solutions to the efficiency problem rather than the global solutions contained within methodologies such as program budgeting.

As noted, even methods such as program budgeting have been making something of a comeback. In Australia the budget reforms of the 1980s included a version of program budgeting as a means of conferring greater flexibility on managers. This version of program budgeting was adopted in the context of constraint on the budget rather than in the context of governmental expansion as had been the case in the 1960s. The intention, however, was to permit bureau managers to make better decisions than could be made centrally, rather than simply to reduce the total level of public expenditure.

There has also been a strong return to performance criteria and attempts to link organizational performance with budget decisions. For example, the Government Performance and Results Act of 1993 (GPRA in the language of Washington), requires the development of performance plans and indicators by all agencies, followed by assessment of their attainment of those goals; the General Accounting Office is used as the principal scorekeeper in this process.[110] Although removing politics from budgeting is almost impossible, the strategy of GPRA is to make the process driven as much by performance criteria as possible, and to make the process "rational" and automatic.

General problems of budgeting

The above are examples of a wide range of innovations that have been undertaken in response to the "fiscal crisis" of Western governments and economies.[111] Many of the same problems are endemic in less-developed countries but differ in not being a change from a more affluent past. These examples illustrate, however, the types of problem that must be addressed, as there is a perception that government spending has grown out of control. These methods are all to some degree perceived as short-term responses to short-term problems, although they may be reflective of more long-term considerations. There are, however, several other problems that have not been addressed in these programs, and these are problems that any government will have to face when deciding how much to spend and how to spend it.

Intergovernmental budget control

A problem that is especially important in federal countries is the coordination of expenditure policies across levels of government. Even in unitary governments, the sub-national levels may have sufficient control over their own expenditures to prevent the development of a coordinated fiscal policy. The importance of coordination arises from the utilization of budget as a means of regulating the economy, requiring that the central government obtain the overall balance of revenues and expenditures, not just on its own accounts. If the central government should choose to adopt an expansionary policy and reduce taxes, the effects of that decision may be nullified by the actions of sub-national governments increasing taxes. For example, some of the impact of the Kennedy administration's tax cut in 1963 were mitigated by increases in state and local taxes in the same and subsequent years.[112] In the United Kingdom, a unitary regime, local authorities have at times opposed both the general nature of the government budget and its particulars. They have sometimes spent more or less than was desired by the central government, in part through their ability to raise revenues via local property taxes – the rates.[113]

The Thatcher government addressed this problem in several ways. The first approach was to utilize "rate capping," which limited the amount of money that the local authorities could raise on their own, and to undertake a detailed review of spending by each local authority. The second approach was to replace the rates with a "community charge," or poll tax, that would be the same for all citizens in a local community.[114] This tactic would have the effect of limiting the amount of money that local authorities could raise, given that the tax is so regressive few local authorities would be willing to increase it. This, and the central control of business property taxes, were intended to return greater fiscal policy control to central government. The community charge proved so unpopular that one of the early actions of the Major government that replaced that of Mrs Thatcher was to repeal in favor of a return to a version of the formerly used local property tax.[115]

Germany has developed a more sophisticated mechanism for dealing with the problem of intergovernmental fiscal control. During "normal" years, state (*Land*) and local governments can decide how much they want to tax and spend (although *Land* and federal revenues are closely linked).[116] However, there are provisions whereby the federal government can impose its wishes on *Land* use of economic instruments such as tax rate changes, government credit provisions and the use of contingency funds, if there is a declared economic crisis.[117] The invocation of these provisions would not direct the state governments on how to spend their money and could only indirectly affect total expenditures. But this mechanism does provide greater opportunity for fiscal policy coordination, especially when combined with the consultative bodies of the economic council and the Financial Planning Council.

This coordinated approach to financial management should improve the ability of the central government in a federal system to produce the types of economic outcomes it desires – a conclusion reinforced by the success of Germany's economy relative to that of other industrialized countries for much of the post-war period. Other federal governments, such as Austria, Canada and Australia, have provisions for consultations on economic stabilization, but none has developed the degree of fiscal coordination present in Germany.[118]

Problem 2.

Annual budgets

Another classic problem with budgeting is that it has a very short time horizon, especially in a modern world of large-scale capital investments, long development times for technical and scientific programs and a need to control possible fiscal expansion over a period of time. The traditional pattern of budgeting was to produce an annual statement of revenue and expenditure and to have some accounting of deficit or surplus at the end of the year. This was a very comprehensible form of budgeting and it allowed legislatures to maintain a close check on spending by the executive.

Reforms are now pushing for longer-term budgets. At a minimum budgets now have rolling two- or three-year projections with the opportunity for decision makers to revise their predictions year after year. In particular this pattern is good at detecting programs that may have small expenditures in an initial year but which may then have rapid growth in subsequent years as entitlements are created and information about the program is disseminated. Of course, there is no reason to expect the advocates of these programs to be totally honest about their implications, or even perhaps to be aware of their implications, but a longer-term analysis may at least cause some of the participants in the process to think about the implications.

Some countries are now taking multi-year budgeting more seriously. The Finnish government, for example, has been doing multi-year rolling budgets for approximately a decade but, in the year 2000, used a harder ceiling on spending in the multi-year frame.[119] In addition, these ceilings will now have to be approved by the legislature. The idea behind involving the legislature is to commit the legislature to these figures so that there will be no question after the fact that this spending plan was not adequately reviewed. Further, by making these figures a matter of confidence, the government is able to have its program adopted with a great deal of political strength behind it, something especially important in a multi-party coalition government such as Finland.

Problem 3

Capital budgeting

Most government budgeting is discussed in terms of the operating budget, but governmental decisions concerning the allocation of capital resources in the society are equally important.[120] The problem of allocating capital is especially pronounced when there are a large number of nationalized industries that depend upon the government for their capital requirements. Making capital decisions presents a number of significant questions to government. The most important question is whether the available capital stock of the country could best be utilized in the public or the private sector. This is, to some degree, the same choice imposed when the operating budget is constructed, but capital budgeting may have even greater long-term implications for the society. First, decisions to build in the public sector will create a "stock" of certain types of goods that will influence future policy making and limit future choices. For example, decisions by previous British governments to build a very large stock of public housing posed a policy problem for the Thatcher government, which was committed to more privatized provision of housing. Also, using resources to build and buy capital goods in the public sector means that fewer will be purchased in the private sector, with the possibility of a subsequent slowdown in economic growth.[121]

Finally, there has been a tendency to use public capital funds, especially when speaking of nationalized industries, to bail out losers rather than to subsidize winners.[122] That is, given the political importance of nationalized industries as providers of employment, any government will be under pressure to allocate capital to existing organizations already providing identifiable jobs to identifiable workers, rather than attempting to allocate the same funds to subsidize the development of new growth industries. In a similar fashion, even where parliamentary bodies exercise strong control over expenditures, they are, on average, less reluctant to spend on capital – especially for their own district – than they are on operating items. Capital expenditures create identifiable monuments for the legislators, who can thereby demonstrate to their constituents that they have been effective legislators. But finally, if legislators do wish to build monuments to themselves, they may be better advised to build statues rather than hospitals, schools, or defense establishments. Statues require only an occasional cleaning, while all the other forms of public capital investment involve ongoing maintenance and operating expenditures that soon surpass the initial capital costs.

It is difficult to discuss and evaluate the various forms of allocation developed for capital funds. Many different approaches have been adopted, few of which fit into neat theoretical niches, but several general points should be raised. One is that capital budgeting is frequently conducted in a highly deceptive fashion, although it is unclear who is fooling whom. That is, it is a common practice to allocate to nationalized industries, or other ailing industries, capital loans, although almost everyone with any understanding of the situation knows that these loans will never be repaid. It is simply more palatable to give a loan through the visible budget (and loans may, in fact, not be shown in the budget) and then later to write that debt off at a future, less visible moment. Likewise, some capital allocations can be made without the government directly spending a penny, as when governments guarantee private loans to industry.[123] Unless the firm fails to make its loan payments, this practice does not involve any direct expenditure from government but merely requires a signature that will back the loan with the taxing power of government. But the resources are diverted into the firm – for example, Lockheed or Chrysler in the United States – although those loans would not be economically justifiable in the private sector without the guarantees from the public sector.

The final point to be made about capital budgeting is that it is the least incremental form of budgeting. Capital expenditures constitute the easiest type of expenditure to avoid, since they involve few, if any, ongoing commitments to individuals. There may be situations in which a previous capital expenditure requires some additional expenditures in order to lend it productivity but even if those expenditures are not made, there will merely be a loss of potential benefits rather than the removal of benefits from an individual. Therefore when governments are in a period of forced retrenchment, capital expenditures are among the first items to be cut. Doing this may be "penny-wise and pound-foolish," for capital expenditures are often related in the short term to operating savings in the long term, as in the installation of newer and less labor-intensive machinery or the construction of newer, energy-efficient buildings. Further, if capital budgeting is done on an annual basis, there is the danger of beginning projects that will not be completed if a budget cut is needed, wasting money as well as real resources.

Problem h

Coordination of taxation and expenditures

Another problem that besets politicians and administrators making budgets is the coordination of taxation and expenditures. These two elements of the public budget are closely interconnected; depending upon the perspective, available revenues stimulate expenditures, or the pressures from increased expenditure demands require increased revenues. In either case, it is difficult to know how much to spend without knowing how much revenue will accrue, and it is difficult to tax without knowing the amount of spending intended. Despite the close connection of these two elements of the public budget, decisions are frequently made by quite independent processes, with the obvious possibilities of discrepancies. This occurrence is less likely in a country with a parliamentary government, which is able to exercise relatively close control over policies through the cabinet, than would be true in a presidential regime with greater legislative power. However, even in a parliamentary regime, the revenue bills and expenditure bills are often voted upon at different times and may be developed by different institutions. For historical reasons, or as the result of organizational politics and a desire to concentrate expertise, institutions charged with developing expenditure plans may be separated from those charged with developing revenue proposals.[124] This system may make good organizational sense but appears to make little sense if a balanced budget is a desired end of the process.

The effects of the institutional separation of taxation and expenditure decisions, as well as their psychological separation in the minds of many citizens and political decision makers, produces a tendency toward unbalanced budgets.[125] In the 44 years from 1950 to 1993 the US government passed 40 unbalanced budgets, although this was mostly in a time of substantial economic growth. The United States was not alone: during that same time period the government of the United Kingdom passed 42 unbalanced budgets and Italy and Ireland had a deficit in every year. Even the fiscally prudent government of Germany passed unbalanced budgets for 30 years.[126] Thus it need not be economic crises that create fiscal deficits in government; the very nature of the decision-making process that separates revenue and expenditure decisions may contribute to that outcome. This is compounded by the political fact that it is much more acceptable to spend money on constituents than it is to tax them.

If the process of coordinating taxation and expenditure is difficult in affluent, industrialized countries, it is even more difficult in the Third World. The ability to predict either component of the budget balance is very limited, and the combination of errors in both predictions makes budgeting a process of vague estimations and frequent adjustments. It also means that these countries must first attempt to shift their revenue sources toward those that may be less buoyant in times of economic growth but have the offsetting advantage of being more predictable in the event of adverse economic shifts. It may also mean that these countries will become increasingly dependent upon the loans and grants of multinational financial institutions: the International Monetary Fund, the World Bank, the Inter-American Development Bank, and the like. When there is a budget surplus, there will be great political pressures to spend it, given the generally poor state of the economic and social conditions of less-developed countries. And when there is a deficit, there are few places to turn for support other than the international bodies.

Problems

Off-budget operations

A final general problem with the budgetary process is that not all that government does is actually included in the principal budget document and calculations of most countries.[127] Further, "off-budget" activity appears to be an increasing proportion of government activity in many countries.[128] There are a number of forms of off-budget activity. One application is keeping certain types of funds – both revenue and expenditure – separate and running them independently of the rest of government. Social security in a number of countries is managed in this manner, with payroll taxes being earmarked for pensions, health care and similar purposes, and the entire system operating almost as if it were a private insurance company, as legally they are in many countries.[129]

At the next level of insulation from the budgetary process are financial instruments such as loans which, if we assume they will be repaid, over time are not a real expenditure and escape inclusion in the budget in many countries.[130] If they are included, it is sometimes only as a ceiling on the lending authority rather than as a part of the general appropriations process. There are also policy instruments, such as insurance and loan guarantees, which involve little or no expenditure of funds in the short run but may entail very large contingent liabilities, future costs against which government may not be adequately protected. Finally, there are benefits given through the tax system – so-called tax expenditures or, less politely "loopholes" – whereby government shifts real economic resources in the society without making expenditure decisions.[131]

There are very good reasons, both political and administrative, for the large increases in the use of off-budget operations by government. First, politically, off-budget operations have become the means through which government can provide goods and services to their citizens while minimizing the *apparent* financial costs to the public. Thus, when government is being pressed by citizens to be both a service provider and to keep its costs down, these off-budget operations allow political leaders to do the seemingly impossible. Likewise, through the utilization of policy instruments such as tax expenditures, government provides incentives for action but most of the actual expenditure remains private.

Second, it may be important to isolate certain types of funds either to protect their sources of revenue from potential raids or to preserve the convenient fiction that they are not really a part of government. Social security is the obvious example of this type of activity; it is convenient for citizens to believe that they are making contributions to an insurance fund rather than paying a tax directly to government. Finally, some operations of government, such as its insurance activities, may well be conceived of as separate, quasi-business activities. These activities may be better managed if they are removed from the center of political conflicts, as expressed through the public budget, and are managed as if they were truly in the private sector.

Maintaining adequate financial and policy control over off-budget spending

291

programs is difficult and, at times, impossible. Some off-budget activities, such as tax expenditures, cannot be limited in the usual way that spending can but rather depend upon the behaviors of individual citizens responding to the available incentives, and may be influenced by factors such as changes in prices or interest rates.[132] Other policy instruments, such as insurance, depend upon the weather (crop insurance or flood insurance) or on the international marketplace to determine how much government will have to spend. The net expenditure for loans may depend upon the honesty, or even good memory, of those who received them. In short, if government is attempting to control total public expenditure as a means of controlling the economy, there are a number of commonly used instruments of government that can undermine that goal.

Summary

The public budget has always been a principal concern for government. It is at once a plan of what government hopes to do in its economy and society and an expression of political power. If anything, the importance of the public budget has been enhanced in the 1980s and 1990s, as a result of a more conservative political atmosphere in many countries and a desire to limit the size of government taxation and expenditure. Its importance has also been a function of the failure of many countries to align taxation and expenditure, with large government deficits as a major result. Finally, general economic problems in most countries have made the flow of funds into the public treasury less certain than in the past. Any contemporary political leader must be very concerned with what is happening with the public budget.

Although seemingly powerful, that political leader will have a difficult time controlling his or her budget. First, there is not even a clear and universally accepted definition of what is included in a budget or what a deficit is.[133] Second, the forces of incrementalism and uncontrollable expenditures make the exercise of discretion and control difficult. Third, many decisions about how much will be spent are not in the hands of government officials but in the hands of private citizens and private organizations.

Finally, political pressures to spend more are always present, while very few pressures are present to tell a political leader to tax more. Major forces for spending more are the organizations within government. As we have looked at the dynamics of public administration, we have seen that the budget process must be a central focus of attention for government organizations. It determines whether they will survive or not and, if they do survive, at what level and with what flexibility. There are also psychological and prestige elements associated with the budgetary process that may surpass the importance of minor differences in appropriations from year to year, or from agency to agency. Success in the budgetary process is a means of tabulating the winners and losers in political struggles, and budgetary outcomes may indicate tides in the interests and priorities of government.

Budgets have become even more crucial as citizens in a number of countries have begun to question the desirability of many components of public expenditure, and to question particularly the desirability of paying taxes to finance those expenditures. A number of procedural and institutional changes have been made to respond to these concerns. All have been well intentioned, but the common evaluation appears to be that if there is not a real commitment to control expenditure, then the procedures are useless. If there is such a commitment, then the procedures may be redundant. Institutions and procedures are certainly important but cannot substitute for the determination and abilities of the inhabitants of the structures of government.

Notes

1   Richard Rose, *Lesson Drawing in Public Policy* (Chatham, NJ: Chatham House, 1993).
2   International Monetary Fund, *Government Financial Statistics Yearbook* (Washington, DC: IMF, annual).
3   Office of Management and Budget, *Budget of the United States, FY-1989* (Washington, DC: Government Printing Office, 1988).
4   Bjorn Ericksson, "Sweden's Budget System in a Changing World," *Public Budgeting and Finance,* 3 (1983), 64–80.
5   See Howard A. Franck, "Expenditure Forecasting" and William Earle Klay, "Revenue Forecasting: A Learning Perspective," in Jack Rabin, ed., *Handbook of Public Budgeting* (New York: Marcel Dekker, 1992).
6   Rudolph G. Penner, "Forecasting Budget Totals: Why Can't We Get It Right?," in Michael J. Boskin and Aaron Wildavsky, eds, *The Federal Budget: Economics and Politics* (San Francisco: Institute of Contemporary Studies, 1982).
7   Eddy Omolehinwa and Emery M. Roe, "Boom and Bust Budgeting: Repetitive Processes in Nigeria, Kenya and Ghana," *Public Budgeting and Finance,* 9 (1989), 43–65; Naomi Caiden, "Unanswered Questions: Planning and Budgeting in Poor Countries Revisited," in Ali Farazmand, ed., *Handbook of Comparative and Development Administration* (New York: Marcel Dekker, 1991).
8   Edward Gramlich, "Intergovernmental Grants: A Review of the Literature," in Wallace E. Oates, ed., *The Political Economy of Fiscal Federalism* (Lexington, MA: D. C. Heath, 1977), 217–37.
9   Jorgen Gronnegard Christensen, "Hierarchical and Contractual Approaches to Budgetary Reform," *Journal of Theoretical Politics,* 4 (1992), 67–91.
10 David O. Sears and Jack Citrin, *Tax Revolt: Something for Nothing in California,* enlarged edn (Cambridge, MA: Harvard University Press, 1985).
11 The US federal government has changed its classification from "uncontrollable" to "mandatory." These figures are estimates attempting to apply the older classification. See *Budget of the United States, FY1993* (Washington, DC: Government Printing Office, 1992).
12 Author's estimate, based on *The Swedish Budget* (Stockholm: Ministry of Finance, annual).
13 For a good critique, see Peter Self, *Government by the Market?: The Politics of Public Choice* (Boulder, CO: Westview, 1993).
14 Rick Van Loon, "The Policy and Expenditure Management System in the Federal Government: The First Three Years," *Canadian Public Administration,* 26 (1983), 255–84.
15 Guy Lord, *The French Budgetary Process* (Berkeley: University of California Press, 1973); R. de la Geniere, *Le budget* (Paris: Presses de la Fondation nationale des sciences politiques, 1976).
16 For the definition and importance of central agencies, see Colin Campbell and George Szablowski, *The Superbureaucrats: Structure and Behaviour of Central Agencies* (Toronto: Macmillan of Canada, 1979).

17 Hugh Heclo and Aaron Wildavsky, *The Private Government of Public Money* (Berkeley: University of California Press, 1974), p. 160.

18 Nevil Johnson, *State and Government in the Federal Republic of Germany; The Executive at Work,* 2nd edn (Oxford: Pergamon, 1983), p. 113.

19 See Chapter 4.

20 Pertti Ahonen and Esa Tammelin, "Muddling Through, Too: Evaluative Auditing of Budgeting in Finland," in Andrew Gray, Bill Jenkins and Bob Segsworth, eds, *Budgeting, Auditing and Evaluation* (New Brunswick, NJ: Transaction Books, 1993).

21 This is a central argument in William Niskanen, *Bureaucracy and Representative Government* (Chicago: Aldine/Atherton, 1971).

22 Caiden, "Unanswered Questions," *op. cit.*

23 Christopher Pollitt and Geert Bouckaert (Oxford: Oxford University Press, 2000).

24 See Peter S. Cleaves, *Bureaucratic Politics and Administration in Chile* (Berkeley: University of California Press, 1974), pp. 316–18.

25 Aaron Wildavsky, *Budgeting: A Comparative Theory of the Budgetary Process,* 2nd edn (New Brunswick, NJ: Transaction, 1986), pp. 14–20.

26 James D. Savage, *Balanced Budgets and American Politics* (Ithaca, NY: Cornell University Press, 1988).

27 Daniel Tarschys, "Rational Decremental Budgeting," *Policy Sciences,* 14 (1981), 49–58; "Curbing Public Expenditures: Current Trends," *Journal of Public Policy,* 5 (1985), 23–67.

28 Otto A. Davis, M. A. H. Dempster and Aaron Wildavsky, "A Theory of the Budgetary Process," *American Political Science Review,* 60 (1969), 529–47.

29 William Ascher, *Forecasting: An Appraisal for Policy Makers and Planners* (Baltimore: Johns Hopkins University Press, 1978); Stephen H. Linder and B. Guy Peters, "From Social Theory to Policy Design," *Journal of Public Policy,* 4 (1984), 237–59.

30 Robert E. Goodin, *Political Theory and Public Policy* (Chicago: University of Chicago Press, 1982).

31 P. B. Natchez and I. C. Bupp, "Policy and Priority in the Budgetary Process," *American Political Science Review,* 67 (1973), 951–63

32 Otto A. Davis, M. A. H. Dempster and Aaron Wildavsky, "Toward a Predictive Theory of Government Budgeting," *British Journal of Political Science,* 4 (1974), 419–52.

33 Robert E. Goodin, *Political Theory and Public Policy* (Chicago: University of Chicago Press, 1982).

34 See Brian W. Hogwood and B. Guy Peters, *Policy Dynamics* (Brighton: Wheatsheaf, 1983).

35 See Gisli Blondal, "Balancing the Budget: Budgetary Practices and Fiscal Policy Issues in Iceland," *Public Budgeting and Finance,* 3 (1983), 55.

36 Brian W. Hogwood, *From Crisis to Complacency?: Shaping Public Policy in Britain* (Oxford: Oxford University Press, 1987), 129–51.

37 H. Heclo and A. Wildavsky, *The Private Government of Public Money* (Berkeley: University of California Press, 1974).

38 R. Kent Weaver, *Automatic Government: The Politics of Indexation* (Washington, DC: The Brookings Institution, 1988).

39 This practice has been eliminated in most countries in response to the need to control government spending. This is true even in Italy where the *scala mobile* (escalator) of wages had been a major factor institutionalizing inflation.

40 Prior to indexing these thresholds, governments received a "fiscal dividend" from inflation as more income earners moved into higher tax brackets.

41 Valerie Bunce, *Do New Leaders Make a Difference?* (Princeton, NJ: Princeton University Press, 1981).

42 Naomi Caiden and Aaron Wildavsky, *Planning and Budgeting in Poor Countries* (New York: Wiley, 1974); Peter N. Dean, *Government Budgeting in Developing Countries* (London: Routledge, 1989).

43 A. C. Pigou, *A Study in Public Finance* (London: Macmillan, 1928).

44   This is the problem of "meta-policymaking" described by Yehezkel Dror in *Public Policy-making Reexamined* (San Francisco: Chandler, 1968).

45   David Novick, "Origin and History of Program Budgeting," *Rand Corporation Paper* No. P-3427 (Santa Monica, CA: Rand Corporation, October, 1966).

46   Jacques Bravo, "Le R.C.B et le Management de l'Etat," *Revue de Science Financiere*, 64 (1972), 289–356; Douglas Hartle, *The Expenditure Budget Process in the Government of Canada* (Toronto: Canadian Tax Foundation, 1978).

47   A. Premchand, *Government Budgeting and Expenditure Control: Theory and Practice* (Washington, DC: International Monetary Fund, 1983); G. Timmaiah, "Budget Innovation in India: An Evaluation," *Public Budgeting and Finance*, 4 (1984), 49.

48   Aaron Wildavsky, "A Budget for All Seasons: Why the Traditional Budget Lasts," *Public Administration Review*, 38 (1978), 501–9.

49   Rolf Sandahl, "Connected or Separated?: Budgeting, Auditing and Evaluation in Sweden," in Andrew Gray, Bill Jenkins and Bob Segsworth, *Budgeting, Auditing and Evaluation* (New Brunswick, NJ: Transaction Publishers, 1993).

50   Jean-Claude Ducros, "The Influence of RCB on Parliament's Role in Budgetary Affairs," in David Coombes, ed., *The Power of the Purse* (London: George Allen and Unwin, 1976).

51   The troubles that the United States military have encountered in exercising a peace-keeping function in several places at once has pointed to some deficiencies in the planning and budgeting of the Pentagon.

52   See John Halligan, "Australia and New Zealand," in J. J. Hesse, C. Hood and B. G. Peters, eds, *Paradoxes of Public Reform* (Berlin: Decker and Humblot, 2001).

53   Naomi Caiden, "Comparing Budgetary Systems: The ASEAN Countries," *Public Budgeting and Finance*, 5 (1985), 38; Maurice F. Doyle, "Management of Public Finances in Ireland," *Public Budgeting and Finance*, 3 (1983), 75–76.

54   John R. Gist, "'Increment' and 'Base' in the Congressional Appropriations Process," *American Journal of Political Science,* 21 (1977), 341–52; Michael T. Hayes, *Incrementalism and Public Policy* (New York: Longman, 1992).

55   Peter Phyrr, "The Zero-Base Approach to Government Budgeting," *Public Administration Review*, 37 (1977), 1–8.

56   A. M. Premchand, *Government Budgeting and Expenditure Control: Theory and Practice* (Washington, DC: International Monetary Fund, 1983), 335.

57   A. Q. Yoingco and M. M. Guevera, "Budgetary Politics and Developments in the Philippines," *Public Budgeting and Finance*, 4 (1984), 107.

58   Aaron Wildavsky, "A Budget for All Seasons: Why the Traditional Budget Lasts," *Public Administration Review*, 38 (1978), 501–9.

59   Rodney H. Brady, "MBO Goes to Work in the Public Sector," *Harvard Business Review* (1973), 65–74.

60   Richard Rose, *Managing Presidential Objectives* (New York: Free Press, 1976).

61   See *Public Money and Management,* Vol. 13, 4 (October, 1993), entire issue.

62   In the case of the Senior Executive Service, the differentiation in pay is only for bonuses rather than for base salaries. See pp. 109–10 for a more complete discussion of performance pay.

63   Sir Richard Clarke, *Public Expenditure Management and Control: The Development of PESC* (London: Macmillan, 1978).

64   Andrew Gray and Bill Jenkins, "Policy Analysis in British Central Government: The Experience of PAR," *Public Administration*, 60 (1982), 429–50.

65   See p. 285.

66   See Gray, Jenkins and Segsworth, *Budgeting, Auditing and Evaluation.*

67   Maurice Wright, "From Planning to Control: PESC in the 1970s," in M. Wright, ed., *Public Spending Decisions: Growth and Restraint in the 1970s* (London: George Allen and Unwin, 1980).

68   Hogwood, *From Crisis to Complacency?*, pp. 131–9.

69   June Pallot, "Financial Management Reform," in Jonathan Boston, John Martin, June Pallot and Pat Walsh, eds, *Reshaping the State* (Auckland: Oxford University Press, 1991).

70   On policy instruments, see Stephen H. Linder and B. Guy Peters, "Instruments of Government: Perceptions and Contexts," *Journal of Public Policy,* 9 (1989), 35–58.

71   See Frederick C. Mosher, *The GAO: The Quest for Accountability in American Government* (Boulder, CO: Westview, 1989). See also Gray, Jenkins and Segsworth, *Budgeting, Auditing and Evaluation.*

72   Christopher Pollitt and Geert Bouckaert, *Public Management Reform: A Comparative Analysis* (Oxford: Oxford University Press, 2000), p. 65.

73   Hal Rainey and P. Steinbauer, "Galloping Elephants: Developing Elements of a Theory for Effective Public Organizations," *Journal of Public Administration Research and Theory,* 9 (1999), 1–32.

74   Of course, this begs the question of the validity and reliability of the measures being used. See Christopher Pollitt and Geert Bouckaert, *Public Management Reform: A Comparative Perspective* (Oxford: Oxford University Press, 2000).

75   Allen Schick, "Macro-Budgetary Adaptation to Fiscal Stress in Industrialized Democracies," *Public Administration Review,* 46 (1986), 124–34; "Micro-Budgetary Adaptation to Fiscal Stress in Industrialized Democracies," *Public Administration Review,* 48 (1988), 523–33.

76   Sir Leo Pliatzky, *Getting and Spending: Public Expenditure, Employment and Inflation* (Oxford: Blackwell, 1982).

77   Peter Mountfield, "Recent Developments in the Control of Public Expenditures in the United Kingdom," *Public Budgeting and Finance,* 3 (1983), 97–8.

78   The recommendations of the Gore Commission in the United States, for example, are to permit agencies to retain a significant portion of any budgetary savings they are able to generate. See *Creating a Government That Works Better and Costs Less: Report of the National Performance Review* (Washington, DC: US Government Printing Office, 1993).

79   Harold Copeman, "Analyzing Public Expenditure: (1) Planning, Control and Price," *Journal of Public Policy,* 1 (1981), 289–306.

80   Allen Schick, "Macro-Budgetary Adaptations to Fiscal Stress in Industrialized Countries," *Public Administration Review,* 46 (1986), 124–34.

81   Jerry McCaffrey, "Canada's Envelope Budget: A Strategic Management System," *Public Administration Review,* 44 (1984), 316–23.

82   Congressional Budget Office, *The Economic and Budget Outlook, 1992–96* (Washington, DC: Government Printing Office, 1991).

83   J. Diamond, "The New Orthodoxy in Budgetary Planning: A Critical Review of the Dutch Experience," *Public Finance,* 32 (1977), 56–76.

84   Alan S. Blinder and Robert M. Solow, "Analytical Foundations of Fiscal Policy," in A. S. Blinder *et al., The Economics of Public Finance* (Washington, DC: The Brookings Institution, 1974), 3–14.

85   This disjuncture between the political desirability of expenditures and the political costs of taxation is one of the underlying conflicts in any political system. See B. Guy Peters, *The Politics of Taxation* (Oxford: Basil Blackwell, 1991).

86   Roland Sturm, "Budgetary Politics in the Federal Republic of Germany," *West European Politics,* 8 (1985), 56–63.

87   Kenneth Gladdish, *Governing from the Center: Politics and Policy-Making in the Netherlands* (DeKalb, IL: Northern Illinois University Press, 1991).

88   J. L. Fallick and R. F. Elliot, "Incomes Policy and the Public Sector," in Fallick and Elliot eds, *Incomes Policies, Inflation and Relative Pay* (London: George Allen and Unwin).

89   Neil Carter, Rudolf Klein and Patricia Day, *How Organisations Measure Success* (London: Routledge, 1992).

90   Charles H. Levine, "Organizational Decline and Cutback Management," *Public Administration Review,* 38 (1978), 315–57; Andrew Dunsire and Christopher Hood, *Cutback Management in Public Bureaucracies* (Cambridge: Cambridge University Press, 1989).

91   Ericksson, *op. cit.*

92   Ministry of Finance, Department of Budget, *Improving Productivity in Central Government*

(Copenhagen: Ministry of Finance, 1987); more recent information is in Ministry of Finance, *Budgetanalyse af politiet* (Copenhagen: Ministry of Finance, 1999).

93   T. P. Hardiman and Michael Mulreany, *Efficiency and Effectiveness in the Public Domain* (Dublin: Institute of Public Administration, 1991).

94   Geoffrey K. Fry, "The Thatcher Government, the Financial Management Initiative, and the 'New Civil Service'," *Public Administration,* 66 (1988), 1–20.

95   Local governments have been required to put many services out for competitive bidding. See Andrew Massey, *Managing the Public Sector,* 182–6.

96   See Donald J. Savoie, *Reforming the Bureaucracy: Reagan, Thatcher and Mulroney* (Pittsburgh: University of Pittsburgh Press, 1994).

97   The attacks on the civil service may become a self-fulfilling prophecy in which the failure to attract qualified candidates may make employees in the public sector as bad as their critics argued all along. See B. Guy Peters, "Burning the Village," *Parliamentary Affairs,* 39 (1986), 79–97.

98   Christopher Pollitt, *Managerialism and the Public Service* (Oxford: Basil Blackwell, 1990); Andrew Massey, *Managing the Public Sector* (Aldershot: Edward Elgar, 1993).

99   Department of Finance, *FMIP and Program Budgeting: A Study of Implementation* (Canberra: AGPS, 1988).

100   James Q. Wilson, *Bureaucracy: What Government Agencies Do and Why They Do It* (New York: The Free Press, 1991).

101   Treasury Board Secretariat, *The IMAA Handbook: A Guide to Development and Implementation* (Ottawa: Supply and Services, 1988).

102   President's Private Sector Survey on Cost Control, *War on Waste* (New York: Macmillan, 1984).

103   Congressional Budget Office and General Accounting Office, *Analysis of the Grace Commission's Major Proposals for Cost Control* (Washington, DC: Government Printing Office, February, 1984); Donald J. Savoie, *Reagan, Thatcher, Mulroney: In Search of the New Bureaucracy* (Pittsburgh: University of Pittsburgh Press, 1994).

104   B. Guy Peters, "State Cost Control Commissions," unpublished paper, Department of Political Science, University of Pittsburgh.

105   Norman Warner, "Raynerism in Practice; Anatomy of a Rayner Scrutiny," *Public Administration,* 62 (1984), 7–22.

106   Gavin Drewry and Tony Butcher, *The Civil Service Today* (Oxford: Basil Blackwell, 1988), pp. 202–3.

107   Vincent S. Wilson, "What Legacy?: The Nielsen Task Force Program Review," in K. A. Graham, ed., *How Ottawa Spends, 1988/89* (Ottawa: Carleton University Press, 1988).

108   Asser Lindbeck, Torsten Persson and Agnar Sandmo, "Options for Economic and Political Reform in Sweden" (with commentary), *Economic Policy,* 17 (October, 1993), 219–64.

109   D. J. Kraan, "Towards More Flexibility of Government Expenditure: Some Recent Developments in the Netherlands," *Policy Sciences* 16 (1984), 413–27.

110   Beryl A. Radin, "The Government Performance and Results Act (GPRA): Hydra-Headed Monster or Flexible Management Tool?," *Public Administration Review,* 58 (1998), 307–16.

111   See Maurice Wright and Christopher Hood, *Big Government in Hard Times* (Oxford: Martin Robertson, 1981).

112   Federal income tax revenues increased a very slight 2.5 percent from 1963 to 1965 – roughly the rate of inflation. State income tax revenues increased 12.9 percent during the same period. In that period one state initiated an income tax and ten others increased their income tax rates.

113   George W. Jones and John D. Stewart, "The Treasury and Local Government," *Political Quarterly,* 54 (1983), 209–22; Arthur Midwinter and C. Mair, *Rates Reform: Issues, Arguments and Evidence* (Edinburgh: Mainstream, 1987).

114   G. Bramley, "Explaining the Puzzles in Policy Change: Local Finance Reform in Britain," *Journal of Public Policy,* 10 (1990), 45–65.

115   Chris Game, "The Underwhelming Demand for the Poll Tax," *Public Money and*

Management, 8 (1988), 55–8; Arthur Midwinter and Claire Monaghan, *From Rates to Poll Taxes: Local Government Finance in the Thatcher Era* (Edinburgh: University of Edinburgh Press, 1993).

116   Hans Klausen Korft, "Planning and Budgeting in the Federal Republic of Germany," *Public Budgeting and Finance,* 3 (1984), 57–70.

117   Jack H. Knott, "Stabilization Policy, Grants-in-Aid, and the Federal System in Western Germany," in Wallace Oates, ed., *The Political Economy of Fiscal Federalism,* 75–92.

118   Coordination between the federal government and the provinces is an important part of the strategy for the new Liberal government in Canada to address its massive budget deficit. See Edward Greenspon, "Finance Ministers Emerge Optimistic on Major Changes," *The Globe and Mail,* 2 December, 1993.

119   This is a frame budget so that the ceiling is only for the total by each organization or program, rather than a detailed allocation of funds.

120   Alberta M. Sbragia, *Law, Markets and the Public Investment Game* (Pittsburgh: University of Pittsburgh Press, forthcoming).

121   This effect has been the subject of countless debates among economists and between ideologues, with strong evidence on both sides. Although money allocated to the public capital budget is not burned, it may not have the accelerator effects of private investments.

122   Gunnar Eliasson and Bengt-Christer Ysander, "Picking Winners or Bailing Out Losers," *IUI Working Paper* No. 37 (Stockholm: Industriens Utredningsinstitut, 1981).

123   On Britain, see Brian W. Hogwood, *Trends in British Public Policy* (Buckingham: Open University Press, 1992), 181–2.

124   The British government in late 1993 considered it a major innovation when it moved decisions about revenue and expenditure to the same time.

125   A. G. Cuzan, "Political Profit: Taxing and Spending in the Hierarchical State," *American Journal of Economics and Sociology,* 40 (1981), 265–75.

126   The tendency toward deficits has increased under the pressures of German unification and an economic slowdown. See Gordon Smith *et al., Developments in German Politics* (London: Macmillan, 1992).

127   For a somewhat hyperbolic statement of the problem of off-budget spending, see James T. Bennett and Thomas J. DiLorenzo, *Underground Government: The Off-Budget Public Sector* (Washington, DC: Cato, 1983).

128   By "off budget" I mean funds that are accounted for separately and which do not appear to the public as components of public expenditures, and/or public debt.

129   Eric M. Patashnik, *Putting Trust in the US Government* (Cambridge: Cambridge University Press, 2000).

130   Allen Schick, "Controlling Non-Conventional Expenditures: Tax Expenditures and Loans," *Public Budgeting and Finance,* 6 (1986), 3–19; Dennis S. Ippolito, *Hidden Spending: The Politics of Federal Credit Programs* (Chapel Hill: University of North Carolina Press, 1986).

131   Stanley S. Surrey and Paul R. McDaniel, *Tax Expenditures* (Cambridge, MA: Harvard University Press, 1985); Organization for Economic Cooperation and Development, *The Personal Income Tax Base* (Paris: OECD, 1990).

132   See Aaron Wildavsky, "Keeping Kosher: The Epistemology of Tax Expenditures," *Journal of Public Policy,* 5 (1985), 413–31.

133   Donald F. Kettl, *Deficit Politics* (New York: Macmillan, 1992). In the United States, for example, major expenditures such as the "bail out" of the savings and loan industry are not included as a part of the budget deficit calculations.

Chapter 8

The politics of administrative accountability

We have documented the growth of public administration and the increasing influence of administrative agencies on public policy. These developments make the perennial political problem of the control of administration more important than ever. This problem may be phrased in terms such as "control," "accountability," or "responsibility," but the basic problem is the same: how do political leaders and the general public persuade, cajole, or force administrative agencies, and individual administrators, to do their bidding? This problem is as old as government itself, but the increased prominence of organizations implementing policies has made these questions more central.

There is the even more fundamental problem of whether public administrators always *should* follow the wishes of the public, when those wishes may be inimical to the long-range interests of the society or violate the civil liberties of some individuals in the society. On the one hand, political leaders expect their civil servants to follow the orders given to them and to exercise little discretion. On the other hand, civil servants are expected to make their own ethical and constitutional judgments and to resist following any directions that are inappropriate.[1] These are difficult judgments for the ordinary civil servants and involves their taking risks if they should choose to oppose the directions of their superiors.

There have been two broad schools of thought in political science regarding accountability. The first has assumed that control was attainable through "an inward sense of personal obligation"; the second school assumed that personal obligation was not enough, and some external forces must be employed in order to enforce responsible behavior.[2] The first approach to the problem assumes that civil servants have ethical values and professional standards that will guide them in the performance of their tasks. The second view assumes that these values are not sufficient, that there must be a means of identifying punishing behavior not in accordance with stated law and legislative intent. There should probably also be ways of rewarding very meritorious behavior by a civil servant.

Basic concepts

This chapter is entitled "accountability" but this is only one of several important concepts that come into play in the control of the public sector. There are three fundamental aspects of the process of regulating the behavior of the public service.[3] These three terms are often used interchangeably, but have rather different meanings. Indeed, the three terms are, in some instances, contradictory, so that doing well on one dimension may mean doing poorly on another.

Accountability

Accountability is used as the title of this chapter and is perhaps the most commonly used term.[4] In its simplest form accountability means the requirement of a public organization (or perhaps an individual) to render an account to some other organization and to explain its actions. This can be as uncomplicated as having to present an annual report, or it may be as politically charged as a minister fighting for his or her political life in Question Time in Parliament. Further, the accounting may be financial or administrative, or about the policy decisions that were made. Accountability, therefore, depends upon some external organization, usually one with political legitimacy, to assess what the bureaucracy has done and to evaluate it.

Responsibility is a rather different concept. As well as having to account to outsiders, bureaucracies also have to follow their own internal compasses based on ethical standards and their training as part of the public service.[5] In addition, civil servants must be obedient to the law, both to general laws about how to administer public policies and more specific laws defining their programs. The civil servants must then make some decisions of their own about the legality and the appropriateness of their behavior. These decisions may, in turn, bring them into conflict with their nominal political masters and result in resignations or perhaps "whistle-blowing."[6]

The third concept that constitutes a dimension of this broad discussion of controlling bureaucratic discretion is "responsiveness." The idea of responsiveness is that government, and individual civil servants, should respond to the needs and demands of the public – especially the clients of programs. Responsiveness is therefore a clearly democratic ideal, but also presents some problems for administrators. One problem is that, by responding to the demands of clients, individual administrators may, in fact, be expected to act against not only the wishes of their political masters, but also his or her own conscience. Further, identifying the clientele of a program is not always uncomplicated, and the interests of the more amorphous public in their role as taxpayer and voter may be ignored by concentrating attention on the immediate clientele of the program. Again, maximizing performance on one dimension of control may harm attaining other means of controlling discretion.

Ethics and control

This chapter dwells heavily on methods of enforcing accountability and responsibility, largely because governments spend so much energy implementing those methods. However, throughout the discussion it must be remembered that civil servants are probably no better or worse ethically than individuals working in the private sector. The major difference is that civil servants work for government, and in democratic governments it is assumed that they work at least indirectly for all citizens. Even in liberal democracies the state has a number of presumptive claims on individuals (such as arrest, taxation and conscription) that threaten abuse by the agents of the state. Thus, accountability questions are more acute in public agencies. This is not because of the individuals employed and their lack of responsibility, but because of the nature of the jobs, the nature of the tasks performed by government and the legitimate authority that is exercised by government.

Another factor that produces problems of control and responsibility is the vast growth of administrative involvement in governing. Not only do public administrators execute the laws, but they consciously also make laws and even adjudicate laws. Much of the legislation currently coming out of legislatures of political systems is actually enabling legislation for the bureaucracy. This legislation establishes broad outlines of policy but requires the bureaucracy to issue regulations to fill in the details.[7] As Eisner wrote about economic policy making in the United States:

> As the frontiers of state regulation have expanded elected officials have accepted the responsibility for making policy in a host of highly complex issue areas. Legislators lack the expertise necessary to make the reasoned and technically competent judgments regarding the details of policy, nor can they anticipate the problems that emerge during implementation.[8]

If it were not for this passing on of responsibility, legislatures would be even more overburdened than they already are.

In the same way, more adjudication is carried on in administrative tribunals than in the regular courts in many countries.[9] Although conducted by administrators, and often conducted informally, these adjudications have the same impact on the individuals as if heard in a regular court.[10] Thus the problems of controlling administration have grown from controlling the execution of policy to the more complex tasks of also controlling policy formulation and adjudication. It is, however, difficult if not impossible to separate these portions of administrative activity, since, to a degree, implementation and adjudication define policy.

Dimensions of responsibility

In a discussion of controlling the discretion of bureaucracy, the basic dualism with which the person in the street – not to mention politicians and academic commentators – regards bureaucracy is apparent.[11] On the one hand, bureaucracy is characterized as a leviathan, a monolithic and virtually uncontrollable force eating away at personal liberties and economic resources. On the other hand, bureaucracy is a fool: a fragmented set of individuals so bound with red tape and rule books that they do not know what they are doing at any one time, sending television sets to people who lack electricity and doing research on the optimal shape of toilet seats. These extremely contradictory viewpoints about bureaucracy co-exist in the thoughts and writings of the same commentators. Leaving those inconsistencies aside, it is also important to note the extent to which these two perspectives on the problem of bureaucracy in modern government point to different problems and different requirements for accountability and control.

On a more personal level, there is also a dualism in reactions to bureaucracy, although this is rarely expressed by the same individuals. On the one hand, there are frequent complaints about bureaucracy and bureaucrats operating *ultra vires,* beyond the scope of their authority. Complaints about police brutality, the behavior of the Bureau of Alcohol, Tobacco and Firearms in the disaster at the Branch Davidian complex in Texas, Swedish tax collectors breaking into homes, and Danish welfare workers removing children from their parents are all complaints about bureaucracy operating in an apparently illegal or arbitrary manner.[12]

In this view, bureaucrats go beyond the scope of their prescribed authority and act on the basis of personal values and "initiative."

On the other hand, we frequently hear complaints from clients of public agencies concerning excessive adherence to rules and procedures by public employees. In these cases the clients – most commonly clients of social service agencies – believe that they are denied the type of assistance they need, or indeed deserve, because of strict adherence to procedures.[13] This is the case of adherence to rules with a vengeance, so much so that the initial intention of the program may be lost. These two forms of maladministration are reflected in one British minister's list of bureaucratic errors: "… bias, neglect, inattention, delay, incompetence, ineptitude, perversity, turpitude, arbitrariness and so on."[14] Similarly, Gerald Caiden developed a list of over 150 terms used to describe the failures of administration – bureaupathologies – that are all too familiar to students of government as well as to ordinary citizens.[15]

The first two types of perceived problems with bureaucracy, the leviathan and the fool, are essentially institutional problems, describing the activities of the bureaucracy as an entity. The second set of problems is more commonly associated with the behavior of individuals occupying positions within the hierarchy – usually at the bottom rungs.[16] These problems involve the use of excessive power or the evasion of legal constraints or, conversely, the failure to go outside normal channels in seeking information, advice, or coordination. Four types of perceived problems of administrative accountability can be conceptualized as the product of the interaction of two dimensions of control. One is the personal or institutional level at which the problem occurs, and the second is the degree of activity of the administrator in question (overactive or underactive). These two dimensions and the resulting four types of problems are shown in Figure 8.1.

Other than being an intellectual exercise, the cross-classification of these two dimensions of administrative complaints enables us to conceptualize better the politics of administrative accountability. On one dimension – the institutional–individual – the politics are those of the institutional conflict of the bureaucracy with other political institutions such as the legislature or the executive, as opposed to the politics of influencing the behavior of individual administrators who interact with clients. Institutional control may involve large-scale political conflict, often quite intense, while individual control may involve only altering the attitudes or

		Actor	
		Institution	Individual
Action	Excessive	CIA Surveillance	Police Brutality
	Too Little	Red Tape	"Buck-passing"

Figure 8.1 Typology of perceived difficulties with bureaucracy

behavior of one individual. Obviously, different solutions are needed for the two problems. However, individual problems have the capacity of escalating to institutional crises, as illustrated by the relationship between the actions of individual policemen and major urban unrest in the United States and other countries.[17]

On the other dimension of accountability, the difference in politics appears to be the difference between institutionalizing and enforcing controls versus the politics of relaxing existing regulations. These actions are again somewhat contradictory but both involve getting administrators to do what the public, the clients and the political leaders want them to do. The former involves political action in writing legislation and, perhaps more importantly, political will in enforcing existing regulations. It also involves the willingness by individual citizens to invest time and possibly money to combat what they consider to be injustices resulting from the administrative process.

Loosening institutional rules or procedures that control the behavior of civil servants is a more difficult process. To some degree this control involves the legislation of broad discretionary powers for administrators, an action that clashes with a prevailing concern for accountability and control. It also clashes with constitutional doctrines about the responsibility of political actors for government policy. The need for greater flexibility is now evident in a number of policy areas. One proposed solution to "regulatory unreasonableness" is to permit greater latitude for individual inspectors to make decisions.[18] Countries that permit discretion have been more successful in obtaining compliance with environmental policy than have those such as the United States that limit discretion.[19] Likewise, the problems of the homeless in the United States (and to some degree in other countries) result in part from arcane and contradictory rules controlling decisions of welfare bureaucracies.[20] While many analysts consider greater flexibility and discretion a solution to many administrative problems, this solution encounters strong political opposition from those who want more control over the bureaucracy.

Another dimension of loosening the bonds of red tape is more personal and involves training administrators to better understand their clients. Some change may come within the individual administrator – and within the agency's culture. This involves an increased willingness to take personal responsibility for actions and a willingness to use rules for the benefit of the client rather than the protection of the civil servant. Each of these changes, especially the latter, is more easily said than done. The rules and procedures of an organization provide a great deal of security to its members, and those civil servants may be reluctant to abandon that security. This is especially the case when the general governmental climate in many countries is skeptical of the bureaucracy and eager to seize on evidence of its incompetence and wrongdoing. The movement to make government more friendly to its "customers" may help improve treatment of clients, but there is often a long way to go to improve the opinion that many clients have of the agencies that presumably exist to serve them.[21]

Another factor that must be taken into account in this prologue to the study of administrative accountability is that much of the problem is a function of that often mentioned desire to separate administration from politics.[22] In this case it is especially important that most Western societies, and nations following their examples, have sought to separate the tenure of most administrators from political control. When there was a spoils system – not necessarily the "good old days" – many of the problems of administrative accountability we encounter today simply did not arise. The administrator was in office at the pleasure of a political official, and if the public servant did not do what was expected, he or she was out of the job. This system did not ensure any more accountability to the public, and its difficulties have been well documented by reformers.[23]

Few people would seriously advocate returning to a patronage system of allocating public jobs, but it is important to remember that the choice of a merit system for public management has a number of latent consequences for administrative accountability. The most important of these is job security, and to some degree a resultant unresponsiveness, of public employees. The goods and services produced by public service are not marketed, or if they are it is often as monopolies. Failure to make a profit or break even is not associated with the termination of public employment, so there is little to make the civil servant responsive to the wishes of markets, politicians, or the public.

The above discussion should not be taken to imply that public employees are inferior ethically, or that they have chosen their jobs only to make a secure living. Rather, it is to imply that the structure of incentives within most civil service systems places greater emphasis on job security than on performance or on public responsiveness.[24] Thus, in insulating civil servants from political pressures, reforms in the public service have gone in the direction of insulating the civil service from virtually *all* pressures, and generate significant problems of accountability and control. These problems may be greater now that reforms (see Chapter 8) have eliminated many other mechanisms of control over public management.[25]

There is, of course, a great deal of variation in the ability of political leaders to influence appointments of officials under them. In the United States there is a relatively large, and growing number of appointees who come and go with changes in administrations and who help make the executive departments more politically accountable.[26] Likewise in Sweden and Germany, political leaders have considerable discretion in selecting their own senior civil servants, and may be able to dismiss sitting civil servants.[27] Political leaders in France, Spain and Belgium can exert some control over appointments to top civil service posts in their ministries, and they also appoint *cabinets* of politically loyal individuals to assist in managing the ministry.

These countries may be contrasted with the United Kingdom where, until very recently, political leaders exercised little choice over the civil servants who served them. Mrs Thatcher chose to be more active in the selection of senior officials and, in general, sought to mold the civil service to match her image of what government should be, a tendency continued and perhaps even accentuated by the Labour government.[28] The changes in the United Kingdom mirror general tendencies in developed countries for the civil service to be viewed more politically.[29] This development may be, in many ways, a positive one in that it may make the lines of responsibility and accountability in government clearer than in the past.

Developing countries tend to rely more on patronage appointments than

THE POLITICS OF BUREAUCRACY

do most governments in the industrialized democracies. There are fewer good jobs in the private economy for people with education than there are in the industrialized democracies so government positions are more important economically, and are also more important in creating patrimonial political loyalties.[30] In addition, many of these regimes are not competitive democracies so that political reliability is more important, and the concept of civil service neutrality is not well institutionalized. This politicized pattern of employment is often called "corrupt" by Western analysts but generally is not regarded so negatively within the countries, and may be important for the preservation of regimes.

With some idea of the dimensions of administrative accountability and control now in mind, we should examine the instruments through which accountability is enforced. The instruments available to each actor seeking to exercise control over the bureaucracy will be described and an attempt made to evaluate the relative effectiveness of these instruments within different national and organizational contexts. These instruments and their effectiveness will be linked back to the basic dimensions of accountability and the particular types of control over the problems already outlined.

Instruments of accountability

The list of procedures, institutions and actors that have been devised to attempt to control administration is by now extremely long, and equally varied. We cannot hope to discuss each method in this chapter, not even in a single book. Therefore, we shall concentrate on those instruments that appear to promise the greatest effectiveness, either to us as administrative analysts or to significant portions of public opinion. The one common thread that binds these solutions is that they depend upon implementation by someone, and this is the weak link in the chain of control. Most of the methods to be discussed could be effective, but all rely on human implementation. This runs the risk of creating an infinite regress of control. If we establish an institution or individual responsible for overseeing operations in the public bureaucracy, who will, in turn, oversee the operations of that oversight body? This is phrased more elegantly in the Latin aphorism: *Quis custodies ipsos custodients?*[31] It is important, therefore, to seek out mechanisms of control that depend less upon the good will or skills of those implementing them.

This point is linked with William Gormley's characterization of "muscles and prayers" as the means of enforcing bureaucratic accountability.[32] He argued that there were two basic strategies for accountability. "Muscles" involves the use of power of some sort, power meaning here the use of legal and political means to attempt to force proper conduct, and/or to punish malfeasance. "Prayers," on the other hand, involve developing either instruments for moral suasion of public servants, or sets of positive incentives for them to behave properly. Gormely tends to believe that prayers ultimately will be more effective, given that they depend more upon reinforcing the generally ethical and public interest values of most people in the public sector.

Organizational methods

The simplest means of policing public administration is to allow civil servants to police themselves. One way of doing this is that suggested by Friedrich – relying on the internalized values of the civil servants – and we shall return to that option later.[33] Here we are interested in the use of collegial or legal sanctions within the organization to gain compliance. Thus, while each individual in the organization may not accept the ethical standards proposed by Friedrich, are there still means by which the organization itself can control them? Although ostensibly the simplest method of control, this method may, in fact, involve the highest political costs simply because of the internal strife that it may create in organizations. Also, it may open up the agency to further attacks from other political institutions. An organization that publicly airs its own internal problems makes it that much easier for legislatures or the political executive to reduce its budget or impose other sanctions.

Publicity. Although it may be considered a method in itself, publicity is one organizational means of controlling the bureaucracy. It tends to be particularly useful in dealing with individual actions, both those going beyond and excessively adhering to rules. The characterization of this method as organizational may strike the reader as a bit odd, but the point is that publicity itself carries little or no direct sanction. Rather, the mechanism depends largely upon the organization to correct any errors brought to light. It may do so either in order to do its public duty or merely to avoid further embarrassment. In either case, the effect will be to improve performance. If the organization itself does not respond to a problem once it is openly identified, then executive, legislative or legal methods can come into play. However, it is easier, cheaper and quicker for the organization to respond. Doing so reduces the external control on the organization and may preserve some autonomy for future action. If an organization establishes the reputation of dealing with its own problems, it is much more capable of resisting external political or legal pressures.

Perhaps the administrative system most notable for using publicity as a control device is Sweden. Swedish public officials have been described as working within a "goldfish bowl," in that their actions are almost entirely open to public inspection.[34] Whenever an official reaches a decision, this decision must be justified in writing, and the written justification is recorded as a part of the file made available to the citizen(s) upon request. In addition, many forms collected by the government that in most societies would be regarded as confidential – such as income tax returns – are public in Sweden.[35] This system is intended to make the administrative system and the political system as a whole more responsive to the people for the simple reason that if people know what decisions have been reached and why, they are better able to understand and contest them.

In addition, openness to the press enables even greater dissemination of information. This openness also must have a deterrent effect on administrators; they will not do anything that cannot be well justified. Of course, there are means of circumventing this publicity. An officer in each ministry decides which materials are private or confidential, and although there is an appeal to the decision, in most cases it is final. Likewise, sensitive information may be sent through private communication rather than through public channels. Finally, the press is frequently criticized for being insufficiently interested in pursuing matters that appear in the files; the overload of information actually may make it less utilized.[36] Despite these problems, the system appears to be a step in the right direction for advocates of more public control over the public bureaucracy.

Sweden is the most publicized of several systems relying upon information for control, but some steps have been taken in other political systems to use information as a mechanism of control. Norway has adopted a system of publicity quite similar to that in Sweden. In the United States the excesses of Watergate and an increasing distrust of government have led to the passage of the Freedom of Information Act at the federal level, along with similar acts in most states.[37] There are also a number of "sunshine laws" at state and local government levels allowing public access to records and to meetings of administrative bodies, especially those functioning in a quasi-legislative or quasi-judicial manner.[38] Canadian administrative procedures have also been modified to allow greater publicity of decisions and information.[39]

Even in Great Britain, where the national government is an extreme example of closed government (see below), local governments have adopted policies of openness, and court decisions have begun to open central government. While Prime Minister John Major made several pledges to make the central government more open and responsive to the public, and the Blair government made the same pledges, central government remains relatively closed.[40] British local governments have already encountered some of the problems of indifference and information overload that have reduced the effectiveness of policies of open government in other countries.[41] It is probably fair to say that a general increase in distrust of government and in political awareness of populations has been associated with increased pressure on government to open its proceedings to the people and the press.

Open government is usually discussed in terms of citizens' access to information after decisions are reached. This is important as a means of knowing what was decided, by whom and why, but it can do little about altering the manner in which policy is actually made. Another aspect of open government is opening up the decision-making process to citizens while the decisions are being made. This can be done in a number of ways. A very basic mechanism is the public hearing. A number of federal programs in the United States, for example, require public hearings before government can take action.[42] This requirement is present for many environmental programs, some urban programs and the decennial review of the Social Security Program. In addition, state and local governments require hearings on a number of issues, most commonly local zoning changes. Similar local government controls over zoning and land use exist in most industrialized societies. One tenet of open government is that decisions that affect citizens in very identifiable ways, such as those on land use, should be subject to some comment by the public prior to action.

In addition to direct contact between citizens and government in a public hearing, there are other means of allowing citizen participation in administrative decisions. This possibility is exemplified in the Administrative Procedures Act of

1946 and the procedures it stipulates for writing regulations in the federal bureaucracy.[43] Before a federal agency in the United States can issue a regulation (secondary legislation), it must publish in the *Federal Register* a statement of its intent to do so, and a draft regulation, and then allow several months for interested citizens and groups to comment on the proposal. The comments received become a part of the record, and the decision finally reached about the regulation should bear some resemblance to the comments received by the agency. Some programs have even more stringent requirements for formal meetings analogous to court proceedings.[44] This openness to citizens makes the process of issuing secondary legislation through the bureaucracy in many ways more democratic than the writing of primary legislation by Congress.

Although largely associated with political theory rather than more practical administration, the ideas of deliberative democracy reflect the drive for more open government. Open hearings and most other conventional devices for involving the public tend to be "one-off" events in which the public responds to a predetermined agenda. Deliberative democracy, on the other hand, attempts to involve the public on a more continuous basis, and to permit the public to have some say in the issues to be discussed. Given a lack of a need to run for office and to represent constituencies, the bureaucracy may be a more desirable locus for these types of activities than would be legislatures.[45]

The government of the day can also use information to hold its bureaucracy accountable for performance, as well as for malfeasance. Governments now increasingly require schools systems and hospitals and other parts of the system that have large numbers of relatively autonomous organizations to publish "league tables" to show the public the relative performance of those organizations. If parents see that their children's school is one of the poorly performing ones, they are likely to put pressure on the teachers and administration to bring it up to standards. This method of accountability implies an aware and active group of "consumers" of the service, and hence may be useful for some population groups but not for others.

Publicity and open government, like many other aspects of administrative responsibility and accountability, are not wholly positive values. While public access to relevant information about administration is certainly important, working in a goldfish bowl can rarely be as efficient as working in private. Further, such openness tends to expose the activities of administrators to political pressures that might not be felt directly in a more closed system. The contrast with Great Britain comes to mind almost immediately. The tradition of British administration has been that of almost total secrecy and privacy for administrators.[46] Although the press is placing pressure on this secrecy, as far as most of the public know – especially for policy decisions and advice – bureaucrats are "faceless." Secrecy has been adopted quite simply to ensure that administrators as public servants will be isolated from short-term political pressures and be free to make decisions in what they consider to be the "public interest."[47] Court decisions concerning the publication of several diaries and other similar memoirs, the institutionalization of a parliamentary ombudsman (see below), the select committee system, leaks from individual civil servants, and continuing public pressure have opened even this closed system, but it remains more private than most. Certain values can be maximized by a closed system of administration, just as certain benefits can be gained in a very open system. It is simply a matter of choice for the public and for political elites of what type of system they want, and what form of administrative system will conform best to the political culture and other institutions in government.

Internal discipline. Internal discipline within public organizations is another potentially effective means of controlling administration without resorting to the imposition of external political control. It is therefore a relatively "cheap" means of control in terms of time and institutional energy. On the other hand, it assumes that there is someone in a responsible position within the hierarchy who has values closer to those assumed to be held by the public than the values of erring subordinates, or even erring superiors. Given our conception of the average public administrator as probably no better or no worse than the average citizen, the probabilities of finding such a person in the hierarchy are good. However, there are a number of impediments to any person within an organization exercising authority over subordinates guilty of anything other than the most obvious malfeasance in office.

First, the punishments available within conventional civil service systems are not particularly strong, especially if the person involved is not a "climber" seeking advancement.[48] The problems of using internal sanctions are especially apparent when the individual whom the superior would like to censure is guilty only of being overzealous in applying the rules rather than of circumventing rules. Further, application of existing organizational control mechanisms requires long and often complex administrative hearings, with the scales often weighted in favor of the civil servant.[49] Police review boards, for example, generally include mostly other police officers who, despite their intentions of maintaining the integrity of the force, also well understand the problems of the individual police officer faced with a dangerous or compromising situation. Unionization of public employees – both industrial and non-industrial – adds to the difficulties of implementing internal controls.[50] Civil service systems themselves require complex procedures to impose the sanctions that do exist; one official in the Carter Administration, for example, abandoned attempting to discipline an employee because it would have taken up the rest of his time in office.[51] Thus, sanctions that can be readily employed tend to be rather weak, and those with teeth are difficult to implement.

There are powerful organizational reasons for not enforcing censures against employees. As noted earlier, bureaucratic politics play a major role for many public administrators and their agencies.[52] They must compete for money, employees and legislative time with other agencies, and there is no quicker way to reduce their potential success in this conflict over resources than to have a scandal. Although the agency can attempt to make the best of it by saying they were "cleaning their own house," the scandal may still create considerable difficulty for the agency at the next budget time.[53] In a period of tight public funds, firing an employee may mean that a replacement cannot be hired and the organization loses the position. Further, administrators (one hopes) want to get things done and, consequently, do not want to employ excessive amounts of time and energy in prosecuting their own colleagues. Also, senior officials are usually rated on their ability to reach goals rather than on internal discipline in their organization. Of course, legal and moral constraints must be taken into account, but success in program management is generally more important than most other facets of the job – at least in an era of managerialism in the public sector.

Another factor favoring non-enforcement of administrative regulations within an agency is that it is frequently necessary to circumvent regulations in order to achieve the stated goals of the organization. In countries that have had major political scandals, this reasoning may sound dubious to many readers, but there are situations in which administrative rules and regulations are impediments to providing a service or getting a job done. Blau provides a now classic example of FBI agents who had to engage in an explicit violation of the rules requiring reporting an attempted bribe in order to perform their jobs well.[54] Air traffic controllers regularly handle more airplanes per hour than they are supposed to by contract – if they did not, air travel would be even more awkward than it now is. Many rules associated with granting of social services make it more difficult for the clients of public agencies to receive aid, and regulations must frequently be ignored by agency employees attempting to assist a client.[55] The difficulty with this justification is, however, that it requires each employee to decide what the *real* goals of the organization are. This practice is at best suspect, and it may become quite dangerous in a democratic regime.

Finally, we must remember that the civil service constitutes a career, just as does working in any other organization or profession. Therefore, there is a certain amount of camaraderie and *esprit de corps*, which makes strict adherence to internal discipline more difficult. Despite formal lines of authority, informal organizations link individuals who are formally superior and subordinate as equals, thus making imposing discipline difficult. Where the civil service is regarded as highly differentiated from the rest of society (France or Japan perhaps), or within segments of the public bureaucracy that are themselves internally integrated (the police or the military), there is an unwillingness to bring discredit upon the service, so many internal indiscretions may not be exposed.[56] Even in less differentiated positions there may be a feeling that one should not criticize one's fellow civil servants unduly, if for no other reason than the tables may be turned in the future.

Whistle blowing is a special case of internal controls on bureaucratic abuse.[57] This term refers to individuals exposing what they consider wrong-doing in their own agency, especially when that wrong-doing is by their superiors. One early and famous case of whistle blowing was the accountant in the Department of Defense who exposed massive cost over-runs on the C-5A airplane. This led to a great deal of embarrassment for the Department of Defense and the firing of the accountant.[58] Since then greater protection for whistle blowers has been built into the American federal bureaucracy, including inspectors general who serve as officials in each department to whom such abuses can be reported with little fear of reprisal.[59] Further, the federal False Claims Act[60] provides individual whistle blowers with a strong financial incentive (up to one-quarter of recovered funds from fraud) to report wrong-doers to the Justice Department.

The United States is not the only country that has begun to support whistle blowers. For example, the general openness of Swedish government to publicity means that whistle blowers are not going outside the bounds of normal behavior to the extent that they might in other systems.[61] Most other countries, however, are less supportive of whistle blowers and some, such as the United Kingdom, have often dismissed and prosecuted officials who take it upon themselves to expose what they consider to be improper actions in government, largely because those actions violate the strong norms of confidentiality.[62] The British system is becoming more open but still has a long way to go to support whistle blowing. More ideological or authoritarian regimes certainly do not provide support for any civil servant exposing malfeasance by the regime.

Internal administrative controls over bureaucracy depend not only on institutions and procedures, but also on the willingness of senior officials to employ those procedures. For internal discipline within an organization, both procedures and the willingness to use them may be absent. The absence of will is rarely a function of collusion or rampant immorality, but commonly is due to the politics of bureaucratic agencies and their need to survive in a potentially hostile political environment. Likewise, the methods available for internal discipline are at best awkward and cumbersome, and at worst unworkable. There are an increasing number of ways of using carrots for motivation – merit pay, for example – but the few sticks available are difficult to employ.

The market and other external controls

Changes in the public sector and the increasing influence of private sector mechanisms have introduced another means for controlling administration. For example, rather than using accounting or budgetary controls to influence spending for a service, government can put the service out for competitive bids to limit the amount spent. Even without a formal market, quasi-markets can be created within the public service to provide some market testing and contestability.[63] For example, the National Health Service in Britain, and health services in other countries, have separated purchasing services through Regional Health Councils and budget-holding general practitioners from service provision through hospitals.[64]

One virtue of market controls of bureaucracy is that they function relatively automatically. There is no need for another public institution to determine the propriety of decisions: if decision makers will follow proper economic logic they will find a way to provide services at the least possible cost. If this means of control is effective, then there is less need to worry about legal standards and organizational interests of persons exercising oversight on the public bureaucracy. The exercise becomes a relatively automatic process of feedback through market signals. The problem with this approach, on the other hand, is that it tends to be effective only for monitoring efficiency. Efficiency is certainly an important value but it is by no means the only one. Further, if a service maximizes economic efficiency, it may minimize other important values such as service to clients and thoroughness in investigating complaints. Controlling the public sector is generally a matter of balancing numerous values, but relying on the market permits attention to only a single, rather limited, set of signals about government performance.

Group and public pressures

Another means of exercising control over administration without resorting to formal conflicts between institutions is through pressure group activity and public opinion. We have already discussed some aspects of the relationship between pressure groups and the bureaucracy, with the conclusion that pressure groups may frequently be the source of administrative failure to operate in the "public interest."[65] Can these same pressure groups also function as a check on administration? First, although pressure groups may not, in fact, serve the public interest broadly defined, they do certainly serve their clientele, and it is frequently that clientele that is most affected by agency activities. Thus, by informing their members of the activities of the agency, they can exercise some effective popular control. Of course, the end result of this process is frequently legislation or administrative action favoring the special interest, but even this constitutes *some* responsiveness by the agency.

Second, one important political development in recent years has been the organization of so-called public interest pressure groups, organized and functioning much as any other pressure group but ostensibly representing no special interest. In the United States this movement first manifested itself through Common Cause and the consumer movement.[66] Publicity and publication of complaints against government are the weapons most frequently employed by these organizations, but they have lobbied both legislators and administrative agencies.[67] Finally, in the American context these organizations have been reasonably successful in court, while in the European nations the creation of a number of ministries and boards for consumer affairs has tended to absorb many complaints without resort to judicial means.

Third, closely related to the development of consumer groups has been the formation of so-called "action groups" or *Burgerinitiateven* in continental European countries.[68] These are typically single-issue groups that develop to protest a single decision or policy and then dissolve after their success or their frustration by government. These groups are commonly oriented toward decisions taken by political officials but also concern themselves with bureaucratic decisions. Action groups have become increasingly institutionalized as the change of enviromental groups into Green political parties in a number of European countries indicates.[69] Although most of these groups have been on the "libertarian left" – ecology, antinuclear, peace, etc. – there also are a number on the right, e.g. taxpayers' organizations.[70]

Another especially interesting aspect of using interest groups as a check on the public bureaucracy has been government's fostering organizations, almost to the point of creating their own opposition. During the War on Poverty in the United States, the doctrine of "maximum feasible participation" was meant to allow community residents affected by these social programs to have some input into making and implementing the policies.[71] The idea of this and subsequent participatory initiatives has been to allow residents to gain political skills and, simultaneously, to prevent programs from becoming excessively bureaucratized and bound in red tape.[72] In Britain one reorganization of the National Health Service included development of Community Health Councils designed to prevent domination of the service by specialist physicians, and to permit greater consideration of community wishes.[73] These and their successors were strong opponents to the Conservative's cuts in the National Health Service and have pressed the Labour government for expansion.[74] In many Third World countries undergoing political mobilization and social change, village councils and other local organizations have been developed, again with the intention of providing local input and checking bureaucratic excesses.[75] In all these cases, governments have actively fostered organizations that serve as oppositions to the bureaucracy, an interesting if not always entirely successful approach to administrative accountability.

Another development facilitating interest group control over administration has been the growth of client organizations for public services that previously have been more autonomous, e.g. the Welfare Rights Organization in the United States. These groups have existed for some time for middle- and upper-class services such as education, but a more interesting development is growth of organizations of lower-status recipients of social benefits. These clients had once been regarded by the community, and even by themselves, as having the right to express nothing but gratitude for benefits. Now they are increasingly vocal in their demands for improved benefits and improved treatment by administrators. The increasing political mobilization of the elderly – "gray power" – has become effective in pressuring government for increased pensions and improved administration of pension programs. These organizations clearly do not represent the broader public interest, but can be effective in placing pressure for improving social administration. At the extreme, groups of social service clients may even assume the management of the social service. Self-management has, for example, become important in public housing projects. This pattern of involving clients is especially apparent in Northern European countries with their strong participatory cultures and with less stigma about being in public programs.[76] Involvement in self-management projects has, in turn, become the basis for developing other social service projects, the privatization of some services to be owned and run by their recipients, and general "empowerment" of groups who had been excluded from effective participation in the political process.[77]

A variant of empowering client groups for self-management is developing parental management in education. For example, in Chicago dissatisfaction with local schools produced a movement to permit parent committees to control the schools.[78] Also, in the United Kingdom, the Education Reform Act of 1988 permits schools to opt out of local education authority control in favor of management by parents. Again, Northern Europe and especially Denmark give parents a great deal of power over local schools. Similarly creation of "trust hospitals" allows greater control by employees and management committees and minimizes the constraints imposed by the hierarchical structure of the National Health Service.[79] A modified version of this management style is being attempted in social welfare services.[80]

Despite the obvious success of some groups it is difficult to be very sanguine about their utility as a general solution to problems of administrative control. Their effectiveness is limited by the same factors that limit the effectiveness of pressure groups more generally, mainly that they must function through second and third parties to have their demands realized. Further, despite short-term successes, social groups that could benefit most by client organizations of this type have few of the political and organizational skills required for continued success. Finally, consumer groups may, in the long run, prove to be little different from other types of pressure groups. They may represent a special interest or, more appropriately, a particular approach to consumer problems, perhaps requiring yet another set of controls to control the controllers.

Political methods of control

If the methods of publicity, organization and internal discipline within the organization do not prove effective in controlling administration – as, indeed, they may not – then a second level of control will be required. This control is through political institutions. The logic is that political institutions rightly regard themselves as the representatives of the people, even when not directly elected. They rightly regard themselves as the source of the delegated powers that the bureaucracy currently exercises and as having the right to withdraw those powers if they are abused. The conflict between political institutions and the bureaucracy over policy has already been discussed.[81] Many points made there apply here as well. Rather than arguing over the ability of the two sets of institutions to control policy in a broad sense, here we examine their respective abilities to control decisions in specific cases, even if only *ex post factor*. Many powers of the several institutions are similar, but it is necessary to examine the ways in which those powers can be brought to bear on specific cases of administration or maladministration.

The legislature. Legislative institutions have, in recent years, come more to the forefront of the battle over administrative control. This is true in part because the growing concern among voters has been translated into action by their elected representatives. Further, the sheer volume of administrative work now being performed has meant that there is more need for the legislature to exercise oversight. This is especially true of the increasing volume of administrative rulings having the force of law and issued by powers delegated from the legislature. The legislature must attempt to keep track of these rulings, even if it is not always possible to control their content. Finally, executive dominance in policy making has left harassing administration one of the few remaining ways in which individual legislators can acquire wide publicity and national stature.[82]

    1. Ministerial responsibility. The most fundamental mechanism through which legislatures exercise control over the bureaucracy in parliamentary governments is through the doctrine of ministerial responsibility.[83] In parliamentary regimes the conventions are typically that a minister is responsible to parliament for what occurs within his or her ministry.[84] Thus, in principle, he or she is required to answer for the behavior of the public servants within the ministry whether or not that public servant was following ministerial orders or simply exercising legitimate discretion. Some of the mechanisms of legislative control discussed below, e.g. question time, help to implement this concept of responsibility,

315

but in parliamentary governments accountability should be understood within this fundamental constitutional context.

Ministerial responsibility has increasingly become a convenient myth.[85] Ministers are increasingly reluctant to have their political futures jeopardized by the mistakes of lower-echelon civil servants. They therefore must answer parliamentary questions about problems that are identified but have become more than willing to deflect public attention onto the civil servants thought to be culpable. The traditional principle (especially in Westminster systems) that civil servants would remain anonymous while the minister would take public responsibility for errors has become honored more in the breach than in the observance.

The notion of parliamentary responsibility has relatively little meaning in presidential regimes such as the United States.[86] In these systems, found mostly in Latin American and African regimes, ministers or their equivalents are not answerable in the legislature as they would be in a parliamentary regime. The fusion of powers in a parliamentary regime means that embarrassment in the legislative arena may also mean the end of the minister's effectiveness and hold on office. There are still a number of means by which the legislature can exercise its oversight but the separation of powers inherent in a presidential regime does make that sort of control more difficult. Further, the institutional competition found in a presidential regime tends to make the exercise of legislative control an even more contentious issue.

2. Funding. Funding is a principal means through which the legislature can exert control over administration. Some problems of exercising policy control through funding have already been discussed at length. However, although the power of the purse may be a blunt instrument in exercising policy control, it may be successful in dealing with a recalcitrant administrator or agency. Although we might hope that legislatures had something better to do with their collective time, the instances of committees and even whole legislatures spending substantial amounts of time on small problems of individual agencies, and even individual administrators, are legion. This "law of triviality" holds that legislators deal with small portions of the budget because they can understand those parts, but allow huge expenditures to be passed with only cursory examination.[87] Further, it is often the trivial details that excite constituents, and legislators focusing on those details are seen to be doing something for their voters.

Legislative involvement in the budget, sometimes discussed as "meddling," are especially important in the United States. Few other political systems permit their legislature the freedom in budgeting to enable them to delve into the financial and administrative details of agencies. At the sub-national level, again within the United States, legislative involvement in administration via the budget is more evident, to the point of removing people from office simply by refusing to appropriate money for the positions they occupy. The punishment for (real or perceived) improper administration is rarely so direct, but it does frequently occur by reducing the appropriations for the whole agency. These powers over budgeting give the American Congress and state legislatures significant controls over agencies that have been largely forfeited in parliamentary systems with stronger party discipline.[88]

Even in parliamentary regimes, however, legislatures do attempt to exercise some control over the budget and thereby over the executive branch and its bureaucracy. In many cases this control is reduced to reviewing what has happened rather than any active involvement in the formulation of spending priorities.[89] In others, however, the controls are more real and prospective. More importantly, legislatures appear to be attempting to reassert their historical powers over the public purse strings and have been developing the analytical capabilities which are central to any attempt at real influence.[90] The fiscal crises which many governments faced during the 1990s made that oversight all the more important, and also more possible.[91] Another aspect of the power of the purse in checking administration, the ability to pass private legislation to compensate individuals for administrative actions, is much blunter. Most political systems provide means of passing "private bills" to afford such compensation, but these stipulate no penalties for offending civil servants and require political leverage for citizens who want a grievance redressed. Further, this power can be abused and become a personal political resource for powerful legislators.

The control of legislatures over administration through funding is potentially a vital and powerful force, but as with many legislative weapons, it is difficult to employ effectively. By their very nature, legislative bodies are cumbersome, and detailed consideration of administrative actions occurs primarily in sensational or highly politicized cases. This is true even in systems such as the United States, that pride themselves on the ability to use the budget for control. Also, the increasing importance of macro-economic policy means that substantial budget control has passed from legislatures to executives and central banks.[92] Budgets have become too important (economically and politically) to allow legislatures to use them to punish the wicked and reward the just.

3. Investigation. Probably the most frequently cited power of the legislature to control administration is their power to conduct investigations. Investigations range from simple questions in legislative sessions to full-scale committee investigations to the institutionalization of an officer to investigate for the legislature. All these devices rely, in part, upon publicity to right a wrong, but they can also be useful in writing new legislation and correcting defects in old legislation.

The simplest form of legislative investigation is the parliamentary question period. In virtually all parliamentary systems there is some means for legislators to ask questions of government ministers. While these may be about policy decisions made by the minister, they may also pertain to administration within the ministry. This is especially true of Westminster systems in which the minister is considered responsible politically (at least by convention) for all that goes on within the ministry, even down to the behavior of lowly clerks. Question time can extract information, embarrass the government and alert an "attentive public" to current administrative problems. Other than producing broader political debate on the topic, however, it rarely goes further. While in rare instances issues raised in question time can produce moves to dismiss a member of the government, or perhaps even the entire government, this is rare. Rather, parliamentary questions depend upon the government actions, the administrators themselves, and perhaps the public, to produce real change.

Within the American context, the most common form of legislative investigation is through congressional committees, generally operating through hearings.[93] The functional specialization of congressional committees and the further specialization into sub-committees, special committees and select committees provide an extensive and well-qualified array of investigative bodies. This investigative role in Congress came into greatest prominence during the McCarthy period in the early 1950s, and more recently was prominent in investigations over the "arms for hostages" deal with Iran, the activities of the Food and Drug Administration and various scandals within the Clinton administration.[94] While these hearings made headlines, they are overshadowed in volume by a large number of ongoing investigations into virtually every policy area of the federal government. The ostensible purpose of these investigations is legislation, but in practice both airing information and close examination of their conduct affect the behavior of the public bureaucracy.

Although the committee system of Congress and its investigations in the United States are the extreme example, similar methods exist in other political systems. Germany has an extensive array of legislative committees specialized along functional lines and exercising oversight of the administration.[95] There is also a functionally specialized committee system in the *Riksdag* in Sweden, including the unusual right of the committee on the constitution to review minutes of cabinet meetings.[96] The United Kingdom has instituted a series of select committees of Parliament, which roughly mirror the organization of the executive branch and are the closest things to legislative oversight that this system of government possesses.[97] The mere existence of legislative committees does not, however, mean that they will be effective in oversight. There is a well-developed committee system in the *Storting* in Norway, but the low prestige of the oversight committees and the relative lack of interest in their work make them largely ineffective.[98] Further, parliamentary committees that exist without staff or other supports for their work, as they do in some countries, are not likely to be able to invade the complex policy-making world of the public bureaucracy.

We could go on enumerating slight differences in committee and investigatory arrangements in parliaments,[99] but the basic point is that legislatures investigate, they tend to do so through committees and the investigations are generally related to exercising oversight within a specific policy field. These committees and their investigations generally comprise a most effective legislative means of influencing the conduct of administration. The relationship between the committee and the administrative agency tends to be ongoing, so the agency has a great deal to gain in the long run by cooperation. Further, the committees tend to be expert, especially where members can and often do remain on the same committee for a long time. Nevertheless, there is a danger of the committee and the agency becoming too friendly, much in the way described in the relationship between agencies and pressure groups.[100]

The final method of legislative investigation might be discussed as a separate topic, given the interest expressed in it. This is the institution of the ombudsman or its equivalent.[101] Although often presented as a magical cure for what ails administration and society, this method of control generally relies upon the legislature for implementation. Although there are variations among countries, the powers of the ombudsman generally do not include the ability to issue binding judgments on administrators or to effect restitution for an aggrieved citizen. In general, the ombudsman can investigate, negotiate with civil servants, report to the legislature, or perhaps introduce legislation. The legislature is then expected to carry the case onward if a reason for further action is found. Most commonly, this will involve simply providing some redress for the citizen, but several systems allow the ombudsman to introduce more general suggestions for procedures to prevent future problems.[102]

The ombudsman system is most commonly associated with the Scandinavian countries, but some version of the system has been adopted in (among other countries) the United Kingdom, New Zealand, Israel, Japan, Yugoslavia, India, Ghana and in modified forms in Poland and the former Soviet Union.[103] Germany and Sweden have a specialized ombudsman to deal with military affairs, commonly complaints of enlisted personnel against officers. Canada has gone even further with a number of "specialized ombudsmen" – Prison Ombudsman, a Transportation Ombudsman, a Commissioner of Official Languages, a Human Rights Commissioner, and a Privacy Commissioner.[104] A number of countries have also institutionalized officers to protect citizens against centralized data collection.[105] In addition, many US states, provinces in Canada, states in Australia and sub-national governments in numerous other countries have adopted some form or another of the ombudsmen.[106] Even France, with a tradition of a powerful and autonomous civil service, institutionalized the office of "mediator" in 1972 to help protect citizens from that powerful bureaucracy.[107]

The systems may all be referred to as "ombudsmen," but variations among the role of that official are substantial. One major difference is the ability to act independently or not, with some officers such as the Parliamentary Commissioner in the United Kingdom requiring a request from a Member of Parliament before initiating action.[108] Another variation is the ability of the officer to initiate legislation or not, with the Finnish ombudsman among others having the ability to introduce legislation as a matter of right.[109] There is also the question of the coverage of policies; some countries extend the system to cover prisoners and soldiers, and others confine it to civil administration.[110]

The ombudsman system is difficult to evaluate. On the one hand, it provides a tribune for citizens, with the advantage of being both inside and outside government. Being inside, or more properly being an officially sanctioned gadfly, allows the ombudsman access and requires that his or her findings be taken seriously. On the other hand, being outside government makes the office appear to most people as one in which they have an advocate free of most bureaucratic connections who will, therefore, freely speak for the "people." At the same time that the office is symbolically well placed, its success requires a number of steps to be completed. Citizens who may be most in need of help are most unlikely to be aware of the office. Success also depends upon the willingness of the legislature to follow through on the ombudsman's suggestions. This willingness is, in part, dependent upon the stature of the individual holding the office, the degree of institutionalization of the office and legislative procedures in handling suggestions from the ombudsman.[111] It may also depend upon the type of results sought, whether compensation for individuals or punishment for administrators. The former may be easy to obtain, since sums of money sought are frequently small or the privileges rather minor. Actions against individual administrators may be more difficult, may have destructive effects on civil service morale and may, in fact, accentuate problems of rigidity within the bureaucracy. Thus this system may be useful in redressing personal grievances but less successful as a means of producing significant procedural or policy changes.

4. Constituency service. The fourth major means through which the legislature can influence conduct of the civil service is what Americans call "constituency service." In Ireland the same behavior has been referred to as "going around persecuting civil servants."[112] The idea is that the average citizen often feels powerless in the face of bureaucracy and looks for some means of influencing that bureaucracy. One handy device is the elected representative; citizens put this person in office, and citizens should therefore be able to get some assistance from their representative. Thus, many legislators are expected to spend significant portions of their time solving problems that their constituents encounter with the civil service. Perhaps the constituent did not get a pension check on time, or a grant for a local government project is not paid. The legislator can become directly involved in attempting to find out what has happened, to get the problem corrected as quickly as possible.

In addition to providing service to individual constituents, legislators can also provide services to the geographical area they represent, and often become ambassadors for sub-national governments as much as they are national law makers. This role is very evident in the United States but is common elsewhere as well.[113] Thus in France and Belgium the *cumul des mandats* has produced national politicians who remain elected local officials.[114] Their national office allows them to exert pressure on the public bureaucracy to provide benefits for their own locality and enables them to short-circuit much of the Parisian or Brussels bureaucracy.[115]

In practice, many legislators find constituency service to be a significant portion of their workload, and an activity that is highly visible to constituents and is very favorably regarded by those constituents.[116] This activity may be a useful means of control, but it is often also inefficient. It concentrates on particular cases, and the legislature may not have time to develop legislation covering more general problems of malfeasance by civil servants or poorly-designed programs. It also exhausts much of the credit that legislators may have with bureaucrats, by "persecuting" them over relatively petty issues. It is generally highly regarded as a method of control by recipients of its benefits but it may, in the long run, perpetuate problems of control rather than solve them.

5. Reviewing secondary legislation. In addition to exercising general oversight over bureaucracy, legislatures may also review secondary legislation – "regulations" in the language of American government, or "statutory instruments" in Britain – issued by the bureaucracy.[117] In all democratic countries, the bureaucracy (acting in the name of the minister) is given substantial power to issue binding rules, provided those rules conform to the will of the legislature as expressed in law. The problem for the legislature is to monitor the huge amount of secondary legislation made by the bureaucracy, and to nullify decisions they believe subvert the intentions of the legislature.[118]

One means of ensuring legislative knowledge of the rule-making activities of the bureaucracy is to require reporting of especially sensitive regulations to the legislature. The US Congress, for example, instituted a "legislative veto" which required reporting to Congress, and an opportunity for a veto by Congress, of certain regulations. This procedure was declared unconstitutional, but it was one mechanism of ensuring legislative monitoring and control of secondary legislation.[119] To be effective, however, it required a substantial staff even to review the regulations that were reported.

Even though few countries have gone to the lengths of the United States in ensuring legislative control, most do have review mechanisms. This is done typically through parliamentary committees – for example, a standing committee on statutory instruments in the British House of Commons. Of course, merely reviewing what the bureaucracy has done is not sufficient for real control. That, however, requires the involvement of the government of the day, and that government may have been responsible for issuing regulations that some in the parliament find objectionable. The control of secondary legislation then becomes a more strictly political issue rather than a question of preserving the prerogatives of the legislature and the integrity of the law.

6. Post-audit. The final legislative power over administration to be discussed here is the post-audit of government accounts.[120] The legislature have powers in the appropriations process and may also exercise an oversight function after the funds have been spent. In virtually all political systems the post-audit function is a legislative function. In the United States the General Accounting Office is a creature of the Congress, responsible for reporting to the Congress on the improper expenditure of public money by administrative agencies.[121] The vast majority of auditing agencies, such as the *Bundesrechnungshof* in Germany and the Italian *Corte di Conti*, report to the legislature. The *Cour des Comptes* in France is a major exception to this generalization, linked to the civil service through recruitment and staffing, and to the President of the Republic by its formal organization.[122] The post-audit function in the United Kingdom was becoming increasingly dominated by the Treasury rather than by Parliament but the creation of the National Audit Office in 1983, and the more vigorous role of select committees, have to some extent returned the function to Parliament.[123] In addition, the Audit Commission was established to audit the accounts of local authorities in England and Wales.

The concept of the post-audit is quite simple. The legislature appropriates money for specific purposes, and it must therefore be certain that the executive spends the money as appropriated. In some political systems this function is justified by the concept of the separation of powers, while in others it is simply to ensure that the public treasury is protected from undue demands. In either case, actual spending is compared with authorized expenditure, and any discrepancies are noted. Depending on the system in question, individual ministers or civil servants can be held personally responsible for any differences.

The post-audit system for legislative control of public spending through the bureaucracy made a great deal of sense when bookkeeping in government was a bit like your grandfather's old ledger in the desk upstairs. It is still a valuable means of checking on what has happened, but less so as the finances of

government become more complex, both in terms of the variety of items purchased and the complexity of financial arrangements. Government programs can
no longer be readily calculated on the basis of annual appropriations; building a
dam or an aircraft carrier simply takes much too long, so funds appropriated in
any one year may be kept "in the pipeline" and quite legally spent some years
later. Also, the exact purposes for which the funds were originally allocated may
have become obsolete or the cost of performing a function become (remarkably)
cheaper, so that some of the funds in the pipeline may become discretionary. The
Pentagon once calculated that, even if Congress were to cut off funds for the
Vietnam War, it had sufficient funds authorized in that pipeline to keep the conflict going for some months.

In addition to money that may be remaining in the budget pipeline, there is
a great deal of public money flowing through private pipelines as well, and with
the increase in third-party government, there have come substantial increases in
problems of financial accountability. Some of these problems involve simply the
ability to track the flow of funds through complex routes to their final destination.
Also, to attempt to provide public institutions greater flexibility a number of
funding schemes – trust funds, public corporations, trading funds and the like –
have been developed by governments. The flexibility created makes tracking and
controlling the funds that much more difficult.

Some of the problems may be more conceptual, involving differences in
accounting and in accountability standards in the public and private sectors. That
is, as the public sector becomes more dominated by private sector management
ideas then the somewhat less accountable standards of the private sector may
penetrate the public sector.

An even grayer area of control is the increasing interest in efficiency, or
"value for money" auditing.[124] Instead of being concerned solely with the legality
of expenditures, auditing organizations such as the General Accounting Office
have become increasingly interested in the efficiency with which outputs are produced.[125] Similarly, the new National Audit Office in Britain is exploring the possibilities of "value for money" auditing in addition to traditional financial
accounting.[126] This trend has developed most significantly in Sweden, where not
only do several organizations monitor efficiency, but new organizations have been
created to develop procedures for more efficient government.[127] However, as well
intentioned as these efforts are, the fundamental problems of defining outputs –
and even inputs – make the measurement of efficiency in government a very difficult problem.

The shift from input budgeting to output budgeting, through bulk and frame
budgeting, also exacerbated problems of enforcing fiscal accountability. Money is
no longer doled out with pre-defined spending purposes, so that determining if
the money was spent appropriately depends upon being able to discern if the
outputs promised were actually delivered. Modern government finance makes the
job of the auditor difficult, and makes the legislative job in understanding the findings of the auditor equally difficult. Except in cases of *clear* misappropriation, the
legislature must deal with a number of gray areas of law and policy, making
control that much more difficult.

7. Summary. The instruments of administrative control available to legis-

latures, while important, suffer from many of the difficulties mentioned in our discussion of the relative strengths of legislatures and bureaucracies in making public policy. These powers depend upon the concerted action of the legislature, which is not always forthcoming. Further, even if there is that action, it is more likely to be removed in time from the actual commission or omission of the offending administrative action. Likewise, it is increasingly difficult for legislatures to keep pace with the quantity of work required of modern governments, and so delegated legislative powers of the administrative agencies are even more crucial to effective government. Finally, the political power base of legislators is not generally enhanced by performing the time-consuming, painstaking, and generally dull job of keeping track of agencies and their actions. The influence of partisan loyalty on decisions might prevent full exercise of oversight. Except for the occasional case that generates publicity and political hay, much of this oversight work is unlikely to aid a legislator's career either with constituents or his or her own party.

There are, however, two major sources of legislative strength in exercising control. First, the major source is the value structures of legislatures – possessed to some degree by certain committees in the American Congress and the German *Bundestag* – which value highly keeping track of the bureaucracy.[128] These norms are difficult to enforce and do little for the legislator who is standing for re-election, but they are crucial to effective control. Second, as policy-making powers pass to bureaucrats and to the political executive, the legislature's role may become increasingly that of watchdog. More time and energy may be available for the job of pursuing problems and persecuting the perpetrators. In fact, given the increasing technical complexity of policy in industrialized countries, this may be the most efficient means of the legislature's having an effective voice in public policy.

The executive. An examination of the organization chart of government would make one believe that the political executive is in the best position to control the performance of the public bureaucracy. The lines of authority and control are all right there on the organizational chart; all that is required is the willingness to exercise that authority. Or so it appears if we look solely at the formal structures. In practice, enforcing executive authority over the bureaucracy is substantially more difficult. Civil service systems and other aspects of public personnel management frequently prevent political executives from obtaining the service and advice of the administrators that they might most like to employ. This problem is confounded by the feeling of many legislative bodies – perhaps quite accurate – that the best way of controlling an executive is to control executive latitude in leading the bureaucracy. Thus, the ability of the executive to control the bureaucracy – which frequently operates as a separate branch of government – is seriously curtailed. Further, just as managers of an organization may not want to expose any problems within their own organization, political executives may be loathe to correct – and thereby expose – malfeasance in their government. In cabinet governments the political executive is, in theory, responsible for everything that happens in a department, so politically it may not be advisable to raise questions of possible wrong-doing.[129]

In the absence of the ability of the executive to hire, promote, move and fire whomever he or she wants, a number of less overt controls come into play. Some of those controls operating through the budgetary process have already been mentioned, although more drastic executive fiscal powers such as impoundment may be used to place controls on the bureaucracy. These controls in many ways may constitute a set of blunt instruments when the precision of a scalpel is needed, and consequently cannot be readily employed. They offer little if any means of dealing with recalcitrant individuals or just plain rigidity in administration.

1. Personnel powers. Powers of the executive in dealing with the bureaucracy vary across political systems. The major variations appear in the ability to appoint and remove officials, the ability to move employees between agencies and on and off personal staffs, and the ability to use executive authority to reorganize government. Some variations have already been noted in the ability to appoint. The ability of an American President to appoint about 3,000 people in the executive branch, to remove most of them without Senate approval, and to appoint his own personal staff, are important powers even if restrained by customs and procedural checks.[130] It becomes especially significant when compared with the British Prime Minister, who has relatively few appointment powers and whose ministers have limited powers over the permanent secretary and other civil servants who serve them. Although the Thatcher government went to some lengths to increase its appointment powers, they remain meager when contrasted with the ability of the French, Belgian and German ministers to select their own *chef du direction* or its equivalent.[131] Attempts have been made, however, to politicize more fully appointments in British government.[132] Likewise, many less developed countries – especially in Latin America – have the form without the substance of civil service arrangements, so that a new government has a wide choice of senior civil servants and advisors.[133] Totalitarian or authoritarian systems have more extensive controls over personnel; those who may be considered politically unreliable can be easily removed, demoted, or reappointed.[134]

2. Investigation. The executive also has the ability to conduct investigations of administrative activities. These investigations may be initiated by legislative action, as when a question in Parliament is sufficiently embarrassing to provoke an executive response. Investigations are commonly done internally, and in fact many executive departments have their own divisions associated with continuous inspection and review. The military is perhaps most notable in this regard, with institutions such as inspectors general serving as an internal check on the administration and efficiency of the services. The civilian government of the United States has now adopted the concept of the inspector general as an internal watchdog on the management of the executive branch.[135] Likewise, the use of inspectorates is a quite common feature of the administrative system of France and of administrative systems derivative from the French tradition.[136] These inspectorates have been largely financial, but more recently have been expanded to other areas such as social services to emphasize their importance.

In other countries inspectorates may be established for some especially significant functions, such as H.M. Inspectors of Schools in the United Kingdom. Indeed, one response to administrative reform in the United Kingdom has been to create a number of new inspectorates to monitor the actions of government and to recommend means of correcting both particular and general wrongs.[137] While the work of public sector inspectorates is not entirely investigative, it certainly does involve substantial snooping into proper administration of the laws, especially financial laws.

Finally, many political executives, meaning here mainly ministers in parliamentary systems, may initiate their own investigations of problems and procedures simply because they are concerned about the functioning of their department. However, just as was true for agencies, there are strong incentives for a "spending minister" to keep irregularities in administration very quiet indeed. Investigations of administration may also be initiated by higher executives, such as presidents and prime ministers, and frequently involve broad examinations of administration. In the United States, the Brownlow Commission and the two Hoover Commissions were examples of executive initiatives directed at thorough reviews of the structures and procedures of administration.[138] In the United Kingdom, commissions such as Fulton and Plowden also involved extensive investigations of basic structures and procedures of administration, and advocated sweeping reforms,[139] as did the Glasco Commission, the Lambert Commission and, more recently, the Macdonald Commission in Canada and the series of commissions on the reform of the Australian civil service.[140] Other investigative initiatives by the executive branch into the work of public administration may be less general and sweeping and tend to be initiated by scandal or crisis. Even in societies with long histories of respect for the bureaucracy and of good administration, major scandals frequently generate large-scale investigations of administration.

3. Reorganization. One important power granted to executives is the power to reorganize government. This power is not totally executive; legislatures many times have equal or coordinate powers. While the legislature may help to change the shape of the organization chart and then go away to see what happens, the executive gets the opportunity to work with the new structure. Thus an activist executive such as Franklin Roosevelt was able to effect extensive reorganizations and use those reorganizations for his own purposes.[141] At other times, governments cannot adequately anticipate the results of reorganization efforts, as was the case for the numerous reorganizations of the British government in the 1960s and 1970s, and may well be true of the more radical reforms of the 1980s.[142] However, the executive still gets the opportunity to try to make the reforms work.

Reorganization can be used to place a mortmain on the activities of future executives and can, therefore, control administration for some time in the future. Reorganizations – if that is not too weak a word – such as nationalization of industry make it difficult for any future executives to reverse the economic policies of an earlier administration. It is simply too difficult to nationalize and reprivatize industry after every election, so once done, nationalization tends to persist. Likewise, when activities of government are "hived off" and depoliticized, by being placed into quasi-autonomous bodies such as "quangos," it becomes difficult for subsequent executives to alter their structure without appearing excessively partisan in handling public policy.[143] Although such depoliticized bodies are much less accountable to the people than are organizations within government, many citizens appear to like them. The depoliticized bodies may give the appearance of businesslike efficiency and of being above the political fray in government, and thus give an appearance of better management. With this public appeal of the organizational form, "hiving off" may actually be "blanketing in."

Reorganization may also be important for establishing executive control. Many sub-national governments, and some national governments, have gone to great lengths to depoliticize, hive off and judicialize important political decisions. The existence of numerous appointive commissions, boards, institutes and other groups, many of which are self-perpetuating or have sufficiently long tenures of office to prevent a political executive from having much real control over their composition, severely dilutes the ability of an executive to exert control. He or she becomes, much as Neustadt's president, a bargainer but not a commander.[144] The justifications for independent bodies are well known, but the latent consequences must also be considered. As executives have come to be blamed, if not praised, for virtually everything that occurs within their governments, they want to be able to control what actually does happen and, consequently, would want to bring as many functions as possible under their purview. Doing this does not ensure their success in exercising control, but it does give them a structural base with which to try. Even when agencies are controlled by the executive, reorganization can be used to make them conform more with the executive's program, as moving of the functions of the previously independent Office of Economic Opportunity under more conventional departments illustrates.[145] Again, there is no guarantee of success, but only of an improved opportunity to influence agency behavior.

Although there may be many good practical reasons for reorganizing, we must remember that this activity is also symbolic.[146] There may be instances where, because of the power of client groups or the legislature, effective control over an agency in government is not possible. Reorganization in that case may demonstrate the power of the chief executive and his or her political supporters, and perhaps gain greater compliance. Further, by altering authority patterns and communication flows, reorganization may change the direction of policy, even if it does not improve the efficiency of the organizations delivering the policy.[147]

4. Fiscal powers. The executive may seek to control administration through its fiscal powers. In most political systems the budget is an executive function and an executive document. Legislatures are certainly involved in the final determination, but in a parliamentary system this role is frequently little more than a rubber stamp. Legislature often lack the staff and the time to review the budget thoroughly, as well as the power to alter individual items. Thus, the executive has the opportunity to reward friends and punish enemies in a tangible fashion. This power may be exercised through government grants to the constituencies of friendly politicians, or tax concessions to friendly interest groups.

The actual impact of many fiscal powers of the executive may be more limited. First, these powers are not often sensitive or flexible. It is difficult to punish one administrator, or at times even one agency, through the budget. Doing so might involve reduction or elimination of appropriations of a larger administrative unit, which may be exactly the policy area in which the executive wanted more, rather than less, activity. Further, even if the fiscal powers of executives were more sensitive, the political base of an agency may be such that an executive could not realistically afford to cut appropriations. Powers such as the line-item veto, given to the governors of many American states and proposed for the President, would help strengthen the fiscal powers of the executive.[148] With that power, the selection of cuts can be much more precise and some real impact on specific policies and administrators can be obtained.

An executive is also limited in the ability to control many actors in the budgetary process. A Prime Minister in Britain, for example, may find it somewhat difficult to control the actions of the Treasury, just as it is difficult for other executives to control the actions of economic and fiscal planners or central banks.[149] In general, ministers of finance and their counterparts have gained substantial institutional powers over the budget, so it may be difficult or impossible for a chief executive to intervene in the process personally, especially when intervention is seen to be politically motivated. In Germany, for example, a special majority of the Cabinet is required to over-ride a decision of the Minister of Finance.[150] Further, the expertise of financial ministries may make political involvement unwise. The chief executive may certainly have political influence over the actions of the finance minister, but frequently that cannot be translated into control of the budget, so the ability of a chief executive to use the fiscal powers will depend upon his or her ability to command the loyalty and obedience of the financial officer.

One fiscal power given to the President of the United States, but only implied in most other political systems, is impoundment. Under the Congressional Budget and Impoundment Control Act of 1974 a President's power to reduce the appropriations of Congress is limited. If the President wishes to cancel an appropriation – a recision – he must obtain agreement of both houses of Congress within 45 days or the appropriation is continued. However, if the President only wants to delay an expenditure – a deferral – then unless one house of Congress disapproved, the wishes of the President would be implemented. These powers over expenditures, even with the possibility of congressional veto, give the President substantial independent control over expenditures and over the priorities of government. These powers are somewhat irrelevant in a parliamentary regime in which the executive is derived from the legislature and where there is party discipline within the parliament. Even there, however, an executive might wish to be sure of the ability to control the execution of the budget.

5. Ministerial advisors and cabinets. In some political systems ministers appear very lonely when they must deal with their civil servants. In some countries, especially Britain and the systems derivative of the Westminster tradition, ministers have little help in office. Even in a large department of government there may be only five or six political appointees (a Minister, several junior ministers and a Parliamentary Private Secretary).[151] Likewise in Germany, the creation of the post of Parliamentary State Secretary as a kind of junior minister generated a significant political debate as to why the minister would need someone like this when he or she had a competent and loyal civil service.[152] Other political systems allow ministers to appoint groups of advisors – called *cabinets* in France and some other countries – and to put these officials on the public payroll. Even in Westminster systems there is a growing use of, or interest in, personal advisors and the functional equivalents of *cabinets* to assist ministers.[153]

No matter how competent and loyal a civil service may be, a minister may still feel that he or she needs help of the sort that a civil servant cannot, and perhaps should not, give. The minister may want this advice in part to have an independent source of policy advice in a system that relies heavily on the civil service for such input.[154] This is a control over the input side of the civil service's role in a modern democracy, and it is an important one. Policy making in modern democracies tends to be driven out of executive departments, whether directly through issuing secondary legislation or through writing the primary legislation for parliaments. Therefore it is helpful for a minister to have advisors that he or she can count on for advice that is of the same stripe politically, and which will have political as well as technical dimensions.

The use of ministerial cabinets is also useful on the output side of government. A limited number of ministers are not able to control the widespread implementation activities occurring within a department. A ministerial cabinet of a dozen or so members certainly cannot monitor and control all activities within a department either, but they have a better chance than the few ministers. Further, if the people recruited to a cabinet are selected for their skills and training, e.g. in management or finance, rather than just for political reliability, then political leaders have the opportunity to enhance their chances to make the department work as they want it to.

Chief executives are a special case of the need to provide some additional advice and support for political executives.[155] They often require assistance not only in controlling the bureaucracy but in controlling and coordinating the rest of their own government. As a part of the process of controlling the bureaucracy, chief executives have created their own bureaucracies that mirror and monitor the rest of government. The members of organizations are generally personally loyal to the executive so that they will supply the advice and the help in implementation that the chief executive needs.

6. Summary. The executive powers in dealing with the bureaucracy, despite the formal position in government, are somewhat constrained. Just as with internal discipline within administration, many tactics that would be useful in enforcing accountability would involve some political risk to the executive. Further, many reforms in the nineteenth and twentieth centuries removed many of the options available to executives in controlling their organizations. Thus the executive is left with a number of powers, but these are blunted by difficulty in distinguishing between whole agencies, individual administrators and even effects on clients. Executives remain in a strong position to negotiate with the bureaucracy for compliance on policy and on procedure but rarely are in a position to command obedience.

The judiciary. The final institutional checks on the power of the public bureaucracy are through the legal system. We have already noted that the bureaucracy is a major formulator of policy and a major adjudicator of claims against government. It is crucial, therefore, that there are some legal restraints on the exercise of those powers. Virtually all political systems provide a means of citizens' challenging the administrative actions as well as policy choices made by government through administration. Even the European Community, often criticized as having a remote and uncontrolled bureaucracy, can be made to answer in the courts.[156]

There are, however, important variations in the extent and nature of judicial powers over bureaucracy, which become important for an understanding of judicial control of administration.

The first major difference among Western and Western-derivative systems of law is between those systems having a separate system of administrative courts and those relying on the regular courts to process administrative cases. This difference is not entirely clear-cut, however. Even legal systems using regular courts for administrative matters (such as the United States, the United Kingdom and many former British colonies) have numerous administrative hearings conducted in separate administrative tribunals within administrative organizations themselves.[157] These, in volume terms at least, greatly surpass the number of cases in the regular courts. Further, these systems tend to have separate bodies of administrative law, dealing with such matters as proper administrative procedure, the rights and duties of administrators, and the like, even if the cases are adjudicated in the regular courts. Finally, even in countries using the regular courts, there may be some special courts that handle purely administrative matters, especially taxation. These three caveats aside, there is a difference between countries such as the United Kingdom, Denmark and Norway, which use regular courts, and France, Germany and Sweden (among others), which use administrative courts to handle administrative matters. To reach the regular courts, a case must generally have some relevance as a matter of general law – in the United States it may frequently involve a constitutional question or denial of guaranteed rights such as due process or equal protection. This limitation simply makes it more difficult to bring administrative cases than would be true in systems that are more used to dealing with strictly administrative malfeasance.

The general format of administrative courts is illustrated by France, with a series of administrative courts roughly paralleling the organization of the regular courts. These end in the *sections de contineaux* of the Conseil d'Etat.[158] The individuals serving as judges in these courts are generally former administrators or at least trained as administrators at ENA. As such, they bring special knowledge to their roles as adjudicators, which raises the problem of their being potentially partial to an administrator involved in a conflict. These courts have the right both to quash administrative actions and to provide redress for individuals harmed by administrative actions – this redress may at times be recovered from the offending administrator. They can also punish the offending civil servant, even to the point of having the individual dismissed from service.

While legal protections available in administrative law are certainly important, they also present significant difficulties for the average citizen seeking relief from what he or she considers an improper administrative act. The proceedings are legal, even in systems having separate administrative courts, and therefore involve specialized knowledge of procedure and form, which only a lawyer can provide. Thus the expense of acquiring a lawyer – even if compensated later, as it is in some systems if the citizen wins the case – can be an impediment to the citizen. Likewise, the need to have a justifiable complaint against the administrator, as opposed to simply a complaint about rudeness or delay that did not produce economic or personal harm, limits the law as a device for control of mundane but still irritating aspects of maladministration.

Finally, administrative law operates as a check largely after the fact. It can generally only redress harm or quash actions; only rarely can it command the administrators, or their organizations, to perform actions. As a result, it remains a negative check on bureaucracy. Thus, despite the general importance of the existence of administrative law as a control on administration, the check is limited by the complexity of most procedures, the slowness of proceedings (the Conseil d'Etat currently has a backlog of several years) and the negative nature of the remedies available.

Normative restraints

The final means of enforcing administrative accountability – that advocated by Friedrich – is normative control.[159] By this we mean the development of mechanisms within the bureaucracy and within individual bureaucrats that serve to shape administration "in the public interest." This is certainly the cheapest form of control obtainable, and in the end the most efficient in that it can *prevent* grievances rather than merely correcting them *ex post facto*. Even if the institutional mechanisms for control outlined were more effective than we tend to think they are, the lack of commitment to public service – or, more properly, an active commitment to private service – could prevent them from working just through the sheer magnitude of the problem. And if such a commitment to the public service were generally held – as indeed we believe it is – the need to employ institutional mechanisms would be rather slight, and any of them could do the job.

The current state of administrative practice would appear to approximate more closely the latter situation than the former one of rampant bureaucratic malfeasance, even given the number of complaints that arise against bureaucracy. If we examine the volume of complaints relative to the number of decisions and actions taken, it seems that, on average, most civil service systems do a decent job. The major complaints about illegal or immoral activity in government are laid at the feet of the *political officials*, not the career civil servants, although we still need institutional mechanisms for the deviant cases.

It should be pointed out that all administrative systems need not have – nor do they have – the same values about accountability of public officials. Ilchman speaks of the need for role congruence between the expectations of the population and the behavior of administrators.[160] Some empirical studies have investigated the degree of value congruence, with varying findings. The variance appears greatest in developing countries, where the civil servants may have accepted Western ideas of responsibility but many of the population perceive the world of government very differently.[161] The ideas of universalism and equality, prized so highly in Western societies and forming the basis of many complaints against bureaucracy, find few supporters in non-Western countries. In fact, an administrator employing those values in decision making would encounter some of the same difficulties as would an administrator in Western countries making decisions primarily on the basis of clan membership or race. In other words, the problems of accountability vary, as do the cultures of administration, the basic consideration being that administrators do what is expected of them by citizens.

Other than singing songs of praise to good administrative values, what can be done to promote accountability through normative constraints? In the short run, perhaps very little. As noted, most political systems have a well-established conception of bureaucracy, and in most systems this conception is not generally positive.[162] It is perhaps becoming less favorable because of increases in the size and cost of the public bureaucracy. Thus, the projection of good administrative values usually cannot come from the larger society, so it must be generated internally. This is relatively easy to do among the elite branches of the civil service, those which have strong *esprit de corps*, a feeling of responsibility for the guidance of society, and favored positions within that society.[163] It is considerably more difficult among ordinary public employees, who have little to distinguish themselves from private employees upon whom demands of public service and loyalty are not made. Again, we do not think that those who opt for public service are any better or worse than those who opt for private employment; the major differences are the demands and expectations of the job. If an employee of a private firm does not give the customer satisfaction, there is recourse to future consumer behavior. If a public employee fails to provide satisfaction, it may literally become a federal case.

The vast improvements in public salaries and benefits, condemned on many accounts, may also serve a useful function in terms of internalized controls in bureaucracy. The higher salary levels make the public service a safe and rewarding place of employment, and they also provide some tangible reward for the demands of the office. Higher salaries may also recruit more people of great talent to the public service, people who would have been deterred previously by the relatively low compensation. As the trend toward higher civil service salaries was reversed in many countries during the 1980s and into the 1990s, and probably beyond, so too has the apparent quality of the personnel attracted and retained in the public sector.[164] We have yet to see what effect this will have on the behavior of civil servants in office, although the general lowering of morale appears to indicate that the effects will be far from positive.[165]

The causal factor in some increases in public sector salaries – unionization of public employees – may play a valuable role in raising morale and standards in the public service. Unions can make the job of the civil servant more of a profession, just as higher salaries attract more qualified people. This is especially important in societies such as the United States or Australia, where the civil service has not been highly regarded and has not enjoyed the high status it commands in Western Europe or Canada. One possible side effect, however, is to make the public service too much of a profession and thereby further isolate it from society at large. Again, however, there are some contrary trends. Both the increased politicization of the public service, and opening civil service jobs in more countries to outsiders to ensure political commitment, will tend to make the public service more closely linked to the society. The public service may more closely reflect value changes in the mass public as winners in elections are able to bring more of their supporters into government.

Normative control, then, is the ultimate control on bureaucracy. It is inexpensive, is reliable and operates before the grievance rather than simply providing punishment or compensation afterward. Most societies are indeed fortunate that they have such high levels of this form of control already in operation, so that the institutional mechanisms outlined above have to be employed relatively infrequently. Even with the number of control institutions that have been developed, it would probably be impossible to have control without the internalized values of most public employees.

The limits of control

Aside from the average, garden-variety problems of administrative accountability and control, there are a number of more specialized problems and considerations that also deserve attention. In these cases, the conventional mechanisms for public control and accountability are strained to their limits and are often exceeded. As significant as these problems are, they are no longer unusual and, hence, require some extensive thought and even reconceptualization if the organizations involved are to be brought into conformity with conventional thinking about responsible bureaucracy. The numerous innovations that governments and their employees have undertaken to cope with changing economic and political demands have generated a new and difficult set of control problems.

The professions

One commonly mentioned problem straining administrative control is the existence of professional employees within the public bureaucracy. Almost by definition, a professional has the type of internalized value structure that was advocated earlier as the ultimate control on civil servants. These professional value structures, which are promulgated, inculcated and policed by the profession itself, place the interest of the client above that of the practitioner, and prescribe strict propriety in dealing with the interests and privacy of the client.[166] The problem is that these values often conflict with the values of the organization for which the professionals work. A common case is the scientist who works for a government research office. One norm of the scientific profession is free flow of information and ideas.[167] That free flow of ideas, if doing work for the government on secret materials, just would not be tolerated. In the same manner, a physician employed by a public agency continues to believe in his or her primary responsibility to the patient, a belief that conflicts with record-keeping demands or requirements of standard treatment in a public organization.[168] The list of similar conflicts could be extended, but the basic point is made. Professionals may have values that conflict fundamentally with the requirements of their public jobs. The public sector needs to employ professionals, so some accommodation of values must be made, perhaps on both sides. This is, however, one instance in which normal procedures of control and accountability may simply not be applicable.

A special case of the problem of controlling professionals arises when the public service itself is conceptualized as a profession. As more and more schools of public service emerge in the United States, there is a tendency for the graduates of those schools to think of themselves as professionals, much as would graduates in law or social work, and to have internalized value systems that are like those of the other professionals.[169] In other countries, as in France with its ENA, this professionalism is of longer standing. The difficulty this presents from a control perspective is that the professional self-concept may make civil servants even more resistant to control by the "amateurs" in political office. By training and by concern for the client or the "public interest," the civil servant may believe that he or she knows best.[170]

Autonomous and semi-autonomous agencies

Governments now use a wide variety of autonomous and quasi-autonomous organizations to deliver public services. We pointed out above that the creation of agencies, quangos and a host of other such organizations has been justified on the basis of economic efficiency. As was true for public corporations in the past, the dominant assumption is that these less-directly controlled organizations will be able to make decisions on the basis of economic and performance criteria, rather than on the basis of political considerations. These organizations, on the other hand, present new problems of accountability.[171]

Public corporations appear to present fewest problems of control: after all, they have a statement of profit or loss (usually the latter), so that one can see at a glance just how well they are managed. In practice it is not that easy. First, making a profit is only one goal, and perhaps not a very important goal, for a public corporation. If the activity is profitable and profit is all we care about, the industry should be private. In the case of public transportation, the goals of providing cheap and rapid transportation, reducing the numbers of automobiles on the roads, spreading out peak hours of traffic, redevelopment of declining areas and so on, may conflict with the profit goal. Thus, evaluating management of a public corporation may involve considerably more than simply looking at the balance sheet at the end of the year.

There is almost invariably a difficulty in controlling public organizations that have been "hived off" from direct political control.[172] One common governance arrangement for such organizations is to have an independent or semi-independent board of directors, thus removing them from direct lines of executive authority.[173] While conventional lines of authority are no panacea for the problems of control, they at least provide a connection with political authority. An agency or public corporation is meant to be independent of such control, presumably so that it can make more independent, managerial judgments about its direction. This leaves the organization in the position of being a political entity with only limited connection with political leadership and guidance.[174] It is perhaps as awkward a position for the managers as it is for the public. It is also an awkward position for political leaders who may be held accountable for actions over which they have little or no control.

This problem of the accountability of public corporations is an especially important one for developing countries, where those organizations are central to the strategy of economic development. They may also offer many of the best positions for public employees in these relatively poor countries. This, then, presents political leaders with the need to balance political and technical criteria in the appointment of officials.[175] There have been some major successes for national-ized industries in Latin America (PEMEX in Mexico and Petroles de Venezuela, S.A. in Venezuela) and many in the Newly Industrializing Countries of Asia, but in general there has been too much emphasis on political rather than economic cri-teria in the management of these countries. This pattern helps create political coalitions but may not help generate greater socio-economic development.[176]

Contracts and third-party government

The difficulties encountered with nationalized industries, both economically and managerially, have encouraged many countries to privatize many of those indus-tries.[177] In general, nationalized industries and direct service provision have been replaced with a variety of contractual and third-party mechanisms that involve an interaction of the public and private sectors.[178] Those changes in delivery mechan-isms may be desirable from an economic perspective, but they present their own administrative challenges. These challenges are especially evident for control and accountability, and require some substantial rethinking of the instruments through which government delivers its services.

Government by contract often presents a difficult control problem for politi-cal officials.[179] So long as the personnel implementing a program are within the public sector, a certain amount of hierarchical control can be exercised over them. Likewise, the values of public sector employees are likely to be more consonant with the "public interest" than are those of private sector employees, especially ones working for a "for profit" organization.[180] Further, implementation through the public sector may ultimately be more direct than the development of a complex contractual or partnership arrangement. It therefore, everything else being equal, will be easier to monitor.

The difficulties in monitoring government contracts appear especially prevalent in the procurement of goods and services from the private sector – particularly in defense procurement.[181] The numerous horror stories of defense procurement in the United States can be matched in other countries, although the scale of the defense establishment in the US may make the scale of apparent mis-management appear extreme. Defense procurement is difficult because it is largely prospective, asking contractors to develop new weapons systems. In addi-tion, there are a limited number of possible suppliers for large systems such as airplanes. Government also has an interest in keeping those few large contractors in business so that it will have the weapons it needs in the future, and spare parts for existing weapons, so that many of the bargains that are struck are "sweetheart deals." The above are not excuses for the "fraud waste and abuse" that sometimes occurs in defense contracting but they do point to reasons for difficulties in exer-cising tight control.

It should also be pointed out that most of the problems that arise in govern-ment contracting arise from unethical behavior in the private sector rather than from corruption in the public sector.[182] Certainly government agencies contracting with the private sector should monitor their contracts as well as they can to ensure that the public gets value for money, but that would not be quite the problem that it is if the private sector were living as fastidiously as we expect the public sector to. There is evidence of occasional incompetence on the part of public contract monitors, but generally not of corruption or malfeasance.

Unions

In addition to the positive benefits that unions of public employees can have for the public service, some problems of control are also created. In addition to the protection afforded public employees by civil service regulations, many are now provided additional protection through unions. Likewise, many industrial employees who were minimally protected by civil service procedures are more fully protected by unions. While these patterns are rather common in modern societies, where individual rights are a central concern in management and in government, they make the job of the public manager much more difficult. There is the procedural problem of conforming to both civil service and union regulations on hiring, firing and transferring employees. It is simply that much more difficult to manipulate staff the way the manager might like. In addition, employees must now be dealt with as a bloc, with threats of strikes even against vital services such as police, fire fighting and sanitation. Unlike the situation with most industrial firms, when there is a strike there is no way of doing without those services for more than a short period of time, so public managers and political officials are under pressure to find a settlement to the dispute – and frequently must accede to the demands of the unions. Although some jobs may have a very low status, e.g. sanitation workers, their importance to the community may be such that they will be in a bargaining position comparable to that of physicians in the public service. Therefore, with unionization, the political system risks losing control over its budget as well as of its personnel policies.[183]

Political structure

The political structure of the country can also present significant difficulties for controlling public administration. Federalism is perhaps the most obvious structural factor inhibiting control of administration. The arrangements of federalism need not be as extreme as those found in Germany or the European Community, which has most programs of the central government administered by the constituent *Lander* or member states, but even the less extreme versions of the structure require some program implementation by administrators not directly responsible to the policy makers.[184] For example, in the United States, most federal social-welfare law is executed by employees of state and local governments, as is most federal education law. This means simply that the control of the federal government is reduced; this level is left primarily with the rather blunt power of withdrawing federal money from the program. Control was weakened more by Reagan's "New Federalism," in which previous categorical programs were converted into block grants, with increased difficulty in monitoring the use of federal money. With money being provided in a block, it is difficult to monitor what proportion is used for which services, and the states are therefore able to impose some of their own priorities in the federal program. While this relocation of priority setting is one intention of the program, and it may make political sense, it poses difficulties in financial accountability and control.

A variant of structure that also inhibits control of administration is the separation of policy-making and implementing agencies, as has existed in Sweden for a number of years and is being copied by numerous other countries such as Britain, the Netherlands and New Zealand.[185] In this scheme ministries are held responsible for formulating policy, while boards are responsible for executing those policies. Again, there is a separation that can only make it more difficult to control what actually happens with a policy rather than simply what the policy is on paper.

A variant of separating policy and administration is the increasing dependence of government on non-governmental actors to deliver public services. An increasing share of public programs are implemented by individuals not directly in government, or certainly not employees of the level of government that funds the program.[186] We have noted the financial problems that the flow of funds among levels of government poses. These problems are even greater when something less tangible than money, like authority or responsibility, must be audited. They increase further when the actors involved are not sub-national governments but not-for-profit institutions, businesses, or interest groups. Unfortunately for those interested in applying objective controls to government, such methods of service delivery appear more common every day.

Culture

We have already outlined variations in culture affecting the success or failure of bureaucratic means of policy execution.[187] We should perhaps remember those variations now in regard to control of administration. The basic point is that some political systems and cultures lack normative commitment to public morality and proper administration so important for controlling administration. Many, in fact, regard the Western model of bureaucracy alien and almost immoral. Having a bureaucrat's job may not be evidence of a public trust or responsibility, but rather an opportunity for the individual and the family. It is the individual who fails to provide handsomely for the family, rather than the individual who does, who will be regarded as immoral in such cultural settings. While Western (or non-traditional) values have certainly spread, they are still not universal, so we must be cognizant when speaking of administrative control of the very different cultural settings in which the problem may occur.

Even within Western countries, there are important cultural changes that can influence the manner in which administration is conducted and resultant problems of administrative control. At least since the 1960s, a more individualist, less hierarchical, political culture has been emerging. This developing culture represents a problem for many conventional methods of control, since it makes accepting hierarchy, and presumably of authoritative commands within the organization, less certain. On the other hand, there has been some reassertion of traditional ethical values that may make normative controls which are, as we have already argued, central to effective enforcement of responsibility, all the more influential in decisions made by individual public servants.

Non-administration

Non-administration, just like non-policy, is difficult to control.[188] It is more difficult to control something that does not happen than to compensate for tasks that have been done improperly or unfairly. In other words, it is much harder to get the bureaucracy to do something that it should than it is to stop it doing something it should not. There are few positive checks to force individuals or agencies to make decisions, while there are numerous procedures for stopping them, or for obtaining compensation for improper decisions. Even the political executive, who is presumed to be able to command action from the bureaucracy, may not be able to command in practice, but may only bargain with the myriad of actors, all of whom are somewhat involved in executing policy. Even a President, concerned about the presence of missiles in Cuba or urban problems in Oakland, or a minister of education concerned about educational reform, cannot command action.[189] The bureaucracy apparently has its own ways of doing things, which means that things will not necessarily be done when government executives want them done. If presidents and prime ministers have these problems, what about the average citizens? The answer is that, first, we must rely on general acceptance of the ideas of "good government" by most people in the public service, and second, we must be willing to go to the trouble of using the available political methods when those internal norms do not work.

Summary

The basic conclusions of this chapter are actually summed up in the preceding sentence. Control of public administration, even in the currently enlarged state of government and bureaucracy, seems to depend on two rather personal characteristics of people. The first is civil servants' internalized sense of their proper role. This sense of civic responsibility, duty, or even honor may vary across cultures, even within the narrow range of Western governments, but basic ideas of responsiveness to demands, responsibility to political leaders and accountability are found in virtually all systems. They may not always be put into effect, but the values are generally understood. Most civil servants appear to accept these values and generally try to put them into operation. If it were not for this widespread acceptance of values, all the institutional mechanisms of control outlined here would be buried in the sheer volume of maladministration.

The second component of a properly functioning system of administrative accountability is the population served by the civil service. Most methods of accountability depend upon individuals or groups pressing demands before the mechanism goes into operation. Thus, responsibility and accountability imply a pair of actors – there must be someone to be responsible to. Even institutional mechanism such as legislatures are ineffective if politicians find that the public does not care. There is little or no incentive to expend energy and time and there is no means of ensuring proper administration for an apathetic, cynical population.

If we return to the several dimensions of accountability and control at the beginning of this discussion, we can see that the two are well covered by the accountability mechanisms we have outlined. First, there are a number of checks on bureaucratic institutions but rather fewer checks on individuals, in large part because of their insulation by the organization. It is often difficult for political institutions to deal with individuals without dealing with an entire organization. Thus, in order for the wheels of government to continue turning, many personal actions may yet go unpunished. Likewise, there are any number of procedures for dealing with sins of commission but relatively few for dealing with sins of omission, or simply excessive rigidity. In many cases "non-administrators" are technically correct in terms of the rule book but manage to undermine the intent of programs by their adherence to the letter of the law.

It is clear from earlier chapters that the role of public bureaucracy in making public policy is increasing. Therefore questions of accountability and control become more crucial. Social and political trends appear to make control both easier and more difficult for future generations of citizens and politicians. On the one hand, the spread of mass education and the mass media makes it easier for the population to become informed about the actions of bureaucracy. Legal changes in the requirements for publicity in several countries are making information more widely available. Mass education may also mean that the public bureaucracy will be drawn from a broader spectrum of the population and therefore have both greater empathy with the problems of citizens and a better understanding of the public's conception of bureaucracy. Finally, recent events in a number of countries – Belgium, Japan, Germany and Italy are examples – have led their populations to be concerned about government and to be more willing to question the activities of public officials. If such healthy skepticism does not develop into cynicism and a rejection of the political system as immoral and essentially unjust, then it can help to promote effective popular control over bureaucratic behavior.

At the same time, there are several developments promoting greater administrative insulation from control. In addition to the increasing size of bureaucracy and the complexity of the tasks it undertakes, a number of public programs, such as social security in the United States and many other countries, have become "sacred cows" that few politicians have the fortitude to attack. As popular programs age and their clientele and their procedures become institutionalized, they may become at once inefficient and unassailable. In addition, a number of personnel practices in the public service tend to insulate the bureaucracy further. In particular, the growth of public employee unions may limit the ability of managers to control personnel. Finally, there appears to be a tendency to "hive off" and depoliticize public services. This is in part a reaction to the popular revulsion over politics already mentioned, due to both the increasing involvement in services with some market characteristics, and as a means of cutting costs. In any case, depoliticization is, in most instances, simply a formula for bureaucratic power.

In sum, the pressures for greater accountability appear stronger than those for greater insulation. We may expect more public concern and involvement in public affairs. How effective this will be will ultimately depend upon the willingness of the population to persist in pressing its demands and using the mechanisms available to it. There is the danger that short-term failures may produce enduring cynicism and a long-term "tuning out" of the population from the affairs of government. The numerous institutional mechanisms discussed here are available to aid in the search for responsibility, but, in the long term responsibility in government can come only from the interplay of responsible officials and citizens.

Notes

1   See Richard A. Chapman, ed., *Pubic Sector Ethics in the New Millennium* (Aldershot: Ashgate, 2000); see also, Report of Deputy Ministers' Task Force on Ethics (Ottawa: Privy Council Office, 1998).
2   · Carl J. Friedrich, "Public Policy and the Nature of Administrative Responsibility," in *Public Policy,* Friedrich and A. T. Mason, eds (Cambridge, MA: Harvard University Press, 1940); Herbert Finer, "Administrative Responsibility in Democratic Government," *Public Administration Review,* 1 (1941), 335–50. See Judith Gruber, *Controlling Bureaucracies: Dilemmas in Democratic Governance* (Berkeley: University of California Press, 1987).
3   On the regulation of the public sector, see Christopher Hood *et al., Regulating Inside Government* (Oxford: Oxford University Press, 2000).
4   See, for example, Patricia Day and Rudolf Klein, *Accountabilities: Five Public Services* (London: Tavistock, 1987).
5   See, for example, Deputy Minister's Task Force, *op. cit.*
6   The Rodney King case in Los Angeles is perhaps the most obvious example. See Lou Cannon, *Official Negligence* (New York: Times Books, 1997).
7   Gary C. Bryner, *Bureaucratic Discretion* (New York: Pergamon, 1987); C. Harlow and R. Rawlings, *Law and Administration* (London: Weidenfeld and Nicolson, 1984).
8   Marc Allen Eisner, *Antitrust and the Triumph of Economics* (Chapel Hill: University of North Carolina Press, 1991), p. 6.
9   In the United Kingdom administrative tribunals handle several hundred thousand cases each year. See Brian W. Hogwood, *From Crisis to Complacency: Shaping Public Policy in Britain* (Oxford: Oxford University Press, 1987), p. 217. For the United States, see Jerry Mashaw, *Bureaucratic Justice* (New Haven: Yale University Press, 1983).
10 Christopher F. Edley, *Administrative Law: Rethinking Judicial Control of Bureaucracy* (New Haven: Yale University Press, 1990); Yves Meny, *Government and Politics in Western Europe,* 2nd edn (Oxford: Oxford University Press, 1993), pp. 333–8.
11 Anthony Downs, *Inside Bureaucracy* (Boston: Little, Brown, 1967), pp. 132–3.
12 See Kenneth O'Reilly, "Bureaucracy and Civil Liberties: The FBI Story," in Ronald M. Glassman, William H. Swatos Jr and Paul L. Rosen, eds, *Bureaucracy Against Democracy and Socialism* (New York: Greenwood Press, 1987).
13 See Michael Hill, ed., *New Agendas in the Study of the Policy Process* (New York: Harvester, 1993).
14 Richard Crossman, *H.C. Debates,* 18 October 1966, v. 734, 55, col. 51.
15 Gerald E. Caiden, *Administrative Reform Comes of Age* (Berlin: de Gruyter, 1991), p. 127.
16 The contemporary movement toward empowerment of the lower echelons of the bureaucracy may exacerbate this problem. The benefits that this movement gains from enhanced involvement of the workers may be lost through the potential alienation of clients.
17 For one somewhat contrary view see Frank Anechiarico and James B. Jacobs, *The Pursuit of Absolute Integrity: How Corruption Control Makes Government Ineffective* (Chicago: University of Chicago Press, 1996).
18 Eugene Bardach and Robert A. Kagan, *Going by the Book: The Problem of Regulatory Unreasonableness* (Philadelphia: Temple University Press, 1982).
19 David Vogel, *National Styles of Regulation: Environmental Policy in Great Britain and the*

United States (Ithaca: Cornell University Press, 1986); Lennart Lundqvist, *The Hare and the Tortoise: Clean Air Policies in the United States and Sweden* (Ann Arbor: University of Michigan Press, 1980).

20   For example, it may be necessary to have a mailing address in order to qualify for assistance but the homeless, almost by definition, do not have a stable mailing address and cannot get one without assistance. Joseph Heller wrote about similar problems with the military bureaucracy in *Catch-22*.

21   See Old Borre and Elinor Scaborough, *The Scope of Government* (Oxford: Oxford University Press, 1995).

22   Colin Campbell and B. Guy Peters, "The Politics/Administration: Death or Merely Change?," *Governance,* 1 (1988), 79–100.

23   Ari Hoogenboom, *Outlawing the Spoils* (Urbana, Ill: University of Illinois Press, 1968); Henry Parris, *Constitutional Bureaucracy* (London: Allen & Unwin, 1968).

24   As noted in Chapter 3, the evidence concerning the structure of incentives in the public sector is that relatively few people are attracted because of their ability to do something for or to society, but rather because of social and financial rewards.

25   See B. Guy Peters, *The Future of Governing,* 2nd edn (Lawrence, KS: University Press of Kansas, 2001).

26   G. Calvin Mackenzie, *The In and Outers: Presidential Appointees and Transient Government in Washington* (Baltimore: Johns Hopkins University Press, 1986).

27   Hans-Ulrich Derlien, "Repercussions of Government Change on the Career Civil Service of West Germany," *Governance,* 1 (1988), 50–78; Kurt Holmgren, "Suede," in Francois Meyers, ed., *La politisation de l'administration* (Brussels: Institut Internationale des sciences administratives, 1985).

28   Peter Hennessy, *Whitehall,* rev. edn (London: Collins, 1990), pp. 635–40.

29   Francois Meyers, *La politisation de l'administration* (Brussels: Institut International des Sciences Administratives, 1985); Hans-Ulrich Derlien, *op. cit.*

30   Oscar Ozelak, "Public Policies and Political Regimes in Latin America," *International Social Science Journal,* 38 (1986), 219–36.

31   "Who will be the guardian of our guardians?" See Martin Shapiro, *Who Guards the Guardians?* (Athens, GA: University of Georgia Press, 1988).

32   William T. Gormley, *Taming the Bureaucracy: Muscles, Prayers and Other Strategies* (Princeton: Princeton University Press, 1989).

33   John Rohr, "Ethics in Public Administration," in Naomi Lynn and Aaron Wildavsky, eds, *Public Administration: The State of the Art* (Chatham, NJ: Chatham House, 1989).

34   H. Stromberg, "The Press Law in Sweden," in P. Lahav, ed., *Press Laws in Modern Democracies* (New York: Longmans, 1984).

35   Stanley V. Anderson, "Public Access to Government Files in Sweden," *American Journal of Comparative Law,* 3 (1973), 419–73.

36   Roger Choate, "The Public's Right to Know," *Current Sweden,* 93 (Stockholm: Swedish Institute, 1975), p. 4.

37   B. Guy Peters, "Regulation of Administrative Data Collection in the United States," *Journal of Behavioral and Social Sciences,* 29 (1989), 1–15.

38   Bernard Rosen, *Holding Government Bureaucracies Accountable,* 2nd edn (New York: Praeger, 1989), pp. 138–9.

39   Gregory Albo, David Langille and Leo Panitch, *A Different Kind of State?* (Toronto: Oxford University Press, 1993).

40   See Peter Hennessy, "The Blair Style of Government," *Government and Opposition,* 33 (1998), 3–20.

41   The Local Government (Access to Information) Act of 1985 is the relevant legislation. See Bob Franklin, "Public Relations, the Local Press and the Coverage of Local Governments," *Local Government Studies,* 12 (1986), 21–33.

42   Barry Checkoway, "The Politics of Public Hearings," *Journal of Applied Behavioral Science,* 17 (1981), 566–82.

43 James O. Freedman, *Crisis and Legitimacy* (Cambridge: Cambridge University Press, 1978); Philip J. Cooper, *Public Law and Public Administration,* 2nd edn (Englewood Cliffs, NJ: Prentice Hall, 1988), pp. 111–80.

44 So called formal rule making takes place in agencies such as the Food and Drug Administration and generally involves right to counsel and other legal protections. See Glen O. Robinson, *American Bureaucracy: Public Choice and Public Law* (Ann Arbor: University of Michigan Press, 1991).

45 Christian Hunold and B. Guy Peters, "Deliberative Democracy and Bureaucracy," in Matti Malkia, ed., *Citizen Involvement and Bureaucracy,* forthcoming.

46 P. Birkinshaw, *Freedom of Information: The Law, The Practice and the Ideal* (London: Weidenfeld and Nicolson, 1988).

47 For a contrary view, see Clive Ponting, *The Right to Know: The Inside Story of the Belgrano Affair* (London: Sphere, 1985).

48 The term "climber" comes from Anthony Downs, *Inside Bureaucracy* (Boston: Little, Brown, 1967).

49 These protections are most well developed in political systems with separate administrative courts. In addition, the general opening of government to citizen complaints during the 1980s has generated greater ability of a citizen to gain redress. See Marie-Christine Henry-Meininger and Anne Gazier, "Fonction Publique: stabilite juridique et effets des changements sociaux," *L'Annee administrative,* 88 (Paris: Institut Internationale d'Administration Publique, 1988).

50 See p. 335.

51 Leonard Reed, "Firing a Federal Employee: The Impossible Dream," *Washington Monthly,* 9 (July, 1977), 14–25. Federal personnel regulations have been relaxed somewhat but the basic difficulties remain.

52 See Chapters 5 and 6.

53 As Wildavsky argued many times, trust is a central element in the budgetary process. See Aaron Wildavsky, *The New Politics of the Budgetary Process,* 2nd edn (New York: Harper Collins, 1992), pp. 111–13.

54 Peter Blau, *The Dynamics of Bureaucracy,* 2nd edn (Chicago: University of Chicago Press, 1963), 137–93.

55 Alex Bryson and John Jason, *Policing the Workshy: Benefit Controls, the Labour Market and the Unemployed* (Avebury: Aldershot, 1992).

56 See Ezra Suleiman, *Elites in French Society: The Politics of Survival* (Princeton: Princeton University Press, 1978), pp. 140–4. The attempts at cover-ups of the "Tail Hook" scandal in the US Navy is one recent and extreme example of this phenomenon.

57 Myron Peretz Glazer and Penina Migdal Glazer, *The Whistle-Blowers* (New York: Basic Books, 1989).

58 Edward Weisband and Thomas M. Franck, *Resignation in Protest* (New York: Viking, 1975).

59 Paul C. Light, *Monitoring Government: Inspectors General and the Search for Accountability* (Washington, DC: The Brookings Institution, 1993).

60 This is also known as the "Lincoln Law" because it was first advocated by Abraham Lincoln to help recover money from defense contractors in the Civil War.

61 Lennart Lundquist, "Freedom of Information and the Swedish Bureaucrat," in Richard A. Chapman, ed., *Ethics in the Public Service* (Edinburgh: University of Edinburgh Press, 1993), pp. 81–3.

62 Richard A. Chapman, "Reasons of State and the Public Interest: A British Variation on the Problem of Dirty Hands," in Chapman, ed., *Ethics in the Public Service* (Edinburgh: University of Edinburgh Press, 1993).

63 M. Jerome-Forget, J. White and J. M. Wiener, *Health Care Reform Through Internal Markets* (Montreal: Institute for Research on Public Policy, 1995).

64 John Appleby, "The Use of Markets in the Health Service: The NHS Reforms and Managed Competition," *Public Money and Management,* 10 (1990), 27–33.

65 Theodore J. Lowi, *The End of Liberalism,* 2nd edn (New York: Norton, 1979); Jeremy J. Richardson and A. Grant Jordan, *Governing Under Pressure* (Oxford: Martin Robertson, 1982).

66   Lawrence S. Rothenberg, *Linking Citizens to Government* (Cambridge: Cambridge University Press, 1992).

67   For a novelist's account of the role of these groups in Britain, see Michael Frayn, *Now You Know* (London: Viking, 1992).

68   David P. Conradt, *Germany's New Politics* (Tempe, AZ: Arizona State University Press, 1995).

69   Herbert Kitschelt, *The Logic of Party Formation* (Ithaca, NY: Cornell University Press, 1989); Thomas Poguntke, "Unconventional Participation in Party Politics: The Experience of the German Greens," *Political Studies,* 40 (1992), 239–54.

70   Paul A Taggart, "The New Populism and the New Politics: Transformation of the Swedish Party System in Comparative Context," Unpublished Ph.D. Dissertation, Department of Political Science, University of Pittsburgh, 1993.

71   For one of many negative evaluations, see Daniel Patrick Moynihan, *Maximum Feasible Misunderstanding.* (New York: Free Press, 1969).

72   See Jack DeSario and Stuart Langton, *Citizen Participation in Public Decision Making* (New York: Greenwood Press, 1987).

73   Rudolf Klein, *The Politics of the National Health Service* (London: Longman, 1983), pp. 95–8.

74   See "Health Critics Attack Moore from all Sides," *Financial Times,* 20 January, 1988; Fedelma Winkler, "Consumerism in Health Care," *Policy and Politics,* 15 (1987), 1–8.

75   R. B. Jain, *The Panchayati Raj* (New Delhi: Indian Institute of Public Administration, 1989).

76   E. Sorenson, "Democracy and Empowerment," *Public Administration,* 75 (1997), 553–67.

77   Thomas A. Laveist, "Segregation, Poverty and Empowerment: Health Consequences for African Americans," *Milbank Quarterly,* 7 (1993), 41–64; Don Tomlin, "A Professional's Reflection," *Journal of Housing,* 49 (1992), 216–18.

78   Robert Guskind, "Rethinking Reform," *National Journal,* 25 May 1991, 1235–9.

79   Department of Health and Social Security, *Caring for Patients* (London: DHSS, 1989).

80   Gerard Wistow and Marian Barnes, "User Involvement in Community Care: Origins, Purposes and Applications," *Public Administration,* 71 (1993), 279–99.

81   See Chapter 6.

82   This appears to be particularly well developed in Ireland.

83   For a general discussion, see Geoffrey Marshall, *Ministerial Responsibility* (Oxford: Oxford University Press, 1989).

84   Parliamentary regimes are by no means uniform in the meaning of ministerial responsibility in their constitutional documents and doctrines. In general the tradition of Westminster systems has been somewhat more demanding on ministers than has that in other traditions.

85   Sharon L. Sutherland, "The Al-Mashat Affair: Administrative Accountability in Parliamentary Institutions," *Canadian Public Administration,* 34 (1991), 573–603; "Responsible Government and Ministerial Responsibility," *Canadian Journal of Political Science,* 24 (1991), 91–120.

86   There is a modified version in the "semi-presidentialist" system of Fifth Republic France. See Maurice Duverger, "A New Political System Model: Semi-Presidential Government," *European Journal of Political Research,* 8 (1980), 165–87.

87   Hans Klausen Korft, "Planning and Budgeting in the Federal Republic of Germany," *Public Budgeting and Finance,* 3 (1984), 57–80.

88   Party government is, however, far from perfect, and there are options for legislatures to act. See Richard S. Katz, "Party Government: A Rationalistic Concept," in Francis G. Castles and Rudolf Wildenmann, eds, *Visions and Realities of Party Government* (Berlin: de Gruyter, 1986); see also Special Issue of *European Journal of Political Research* on party government, 24, 1 (July, 1993).

89   See, for example, Donald J. Savoie, *The Politics of Public Spending in Canada* (Toronto: University of Toronto Press, 1980), pp. 26–37.

90   Allen Schick, *Congress and Money* (Washington, DC: Urban Institute Press, 1980); John R. Nethercote, *Parliament and Bureaucracy* (Sydney: Hale and Iremonger, 1982); Anne Robinson, "The Financial Work of the New Select Committees," in Gavin Drewry, ed., *The New Select Committees* (Oxford: Oxford University Press, 1985).

91 At the extreme, the Maastrict agreement in the European Union, requiring that countries lower drastically their debt and deficit levels as a condition of entering the Economic and Monetary System, provided a means of strengthening the Italian and Belgian governments against the claims of special interests.

92 John B. Goodman, *Monetary Sovereignty* (Ithaca, NY: Cornell University Press, 1992).

93 See Joel D. Aberbach, *Keeping a Watchful Eye: The Politics of Congressional Oversight* (Washington, DC: The Brookings Institution, 1990).

94 Aberbach, *Keeping a Watchful Eye,* pp. 52–5.

95 Thomas Saalfeld, "The West German Bundestag After 40 Years: The Role of Parliament in a Party Democracy," *West European Politics,* 13 (1990), 81–3.

96 Torbjorn Larsson, *Att vara riksdagsledamot* (Stockholm: SOU 27, 1985).

97 Gavin Drewry, ed., *The New Select Committees,* 2nd edn (Oxford: Oxford University Press, 1989).

98 Toril Skard, *Utvalgt til Stortinget* (Oslo: Gyldendal, 1980).

99 See Christian Hunold and B. Guy Peters, *European Politics Reconsidered,* 2nd edn (New York: Holmes and Meier, 1998), Chapter 4.

100 See Chapter 6.

101 Donald C. Rowat, *The Ombudsman Plan: The Worldwide Spread of an Idea,* 2nd edn (Lanham, MD: University Press of America, 1985).

102 These prospective powers are better developed in the Scandinavian countries with their longer experience with the institution than in the countries that have copied it later. The major exception is New Zealand where there is a clear right for the ombudsman to suggest procedural remedies.

103 "Poland's Ombudsman Swamped with Complaints," *Financial Times,* 1 March, 1988; Victor Ayeni, "State Complaints Officer in Nigeria – Coping with a Federalised Ombudsman System in the Third World," *Indian Journal of Public Administration,* 28 (1992), 153–68.

104 V. Seymour Wilson, *Canadian Public Policy and Administration* (Toronto: McGraw-Hill Ryerson, 1981), pp. 252–4.

105 Colin J. Bennett, *Regulating Privacy* (Ithaca, NY: Cornell University Press, 1992).

106 Robert D. Lee, Jr, "The Ombudsman in a Political Context: The Commonwealth and Victoria Ombudsman in Australia," *International Review of Administrative Sciences,* 57 (1991), 441–64.

107 Jean-Claude Masclet, *Nouveaux Droits d'administres,* Documents d'Etudes 4.03 (Paris: La Documentation Francaise, December, 1986).

108 D. Clark, "The Ombudsman in Britain and France," *West European Politics,* 7 (1984), 64–90; Roy Gregory and Jane Pearson, "The Parliamentary Commissioner After Twenty-Five Years," *Public Administration,* 70 (1992), 469–98.

109 Paavo Kastavi, "Finland's Guardians of law," in Rowat, pp. 58–74.

110 Germany, for example, has only a military ombudsman, while Sweden and Norway have a separate military ombudsman. The Danish and Finnish ombudsmen also receive complaints on military affairs. The ombudsman in almost all countries can receive complaints from prisoners, although few are received except in the Scandinavian countries.

111 Donald Rowat, *The Ombudsman Plan*; Frank Stacey, *The Ombudsman Compared* (Oxford: Clarendon Press, 1978).

112 Basil Chubb, "Going Around Persecuting Civil Servants: The Role of the Irish Parliamentary Representative," *Political Studies,* 11 (1963), 272–86; *The Government and Population of Ireland,* 3rd edn (London: Longman, 1992), pp. 143–6.

113 Philip Norton and D. Wood, "MP's Constituency Service and the Personal Vote," *Parliamentary Affairs,* 43 (1990), 196–208.

114 Reforms in France are beginning to limit this practice.

115 Andrew Knapp, "The Cumul des Mandats, Local Power and Political Parties in France," *West European Politics,* 14 (1991), pp. 18–40.

116 For example, Morris Fiorina, *Congress, Keystone of the Washington Establishment,* 2nd edn (New Haven, CT: Yale University Press, 1988).

117 Robert Baldwin, *Rules and Government* (Oxford: Clarendon Press, 1995).

118 For a very negative view of secondary legislation, see David Schoenbrod, *Power Without Responsibility: How Congress Abuses the People Through Discretion* (New Haven: Yale University Press, 1993).

119 See I.N.S. v. Chadha 462 US 919 (1983); Barbara Hickson Craig, *The Legislative Veto* (Boulder, CO: Westview Press, 1983).

120 Ray C. Rist, "Management Accountability: Signals Sent by Auditing and Evaluation," *Journal of Public Policy,* 9 (1989), 355–69.

121 Frederick D. Mosher, *The GAO: The Quest for Accountability in American Government* (Boulder, CO: Westview Press, 1979).

122 *La Cour de Comptes* (Paris: La Documentation Francaise, 1998).

123 Sir Gordon Downey, "National Audit Reports," *Public Money,* 4, 3 (1984), 10–11; Anthony Harrison, "Auditing the Public Sector," *Public Money* 4, 1 (1984), 31–5.

124 M. Henkel, "The New 'Evaluative' State," *Public Administration,* 69 (1991), 121–36.

125 Andrew Gray, Bill Jenkins and Bob Segsworth, *Budgeting, Auditing and Evaluation* (New Brunswick, NJ: Transaction, 1993).

126 Downey, "National Audit Reports"; Harrison, "Auditing the Public Sector."

127 Rune Premfors, "Sweden," in *Efficiency and Effectiveness in the Civil Service* (House of Commons, Treasury and Civil Service Committee, 8 March, 1982).

128 Thomas Ellwein and Joachim Jens Hesse, *Das Regierungssystem der Bundesrepublik Deutschland,* 6th edn (Opladen: Westdeutscher Verlag, 1987), pp. 266ff.

129 Geoffrey Marshall, *Constitutional Conventions: Rules and Forms of Political Accountability* (Oxford: Clarendon Press, 1984).

130 Mackenzie, *The In and Outers;* Robert Moranto, *Politics and Bureaucracy in the Modern Presidency: Careerists and Appointees in the Reagan Administration* (Westport, CT: Greenwood Press, 1993).

131 See, for example, Hans-Ulrich Derlien and Renate Mayntz, "Party Patrongage and Politicization of the West German Administrative Elite 1970–1987," *Governance,* 2 (1989), 384–404; Leo Moulin, "Politicization of Belgian Administration," in Mattei Dogan, ed., *The Mandarins of Western Europe* (New York: Halstad, 1973).

132 Sir John Hoskyns, "Whitehall and Westminster: An Outsider's View," *Fiscal Studies,* 3 (1982), 162–72; David Dillman, "Personnel Management and Productivity Reform: Taming the Civil Service in Great Britain and the United States," *International Journal of Public Administration,* 8 (1986), 345–67.

133 See John W. Sloan, *Public Policy in Latin America* (Pittsburgh: University of Pittsburgh Press, 1984) pp. 136–48; Ben Ross Schneider, *Politics Within the State: Elite Bureaucrats and Industrial Policy in Authoritarian Brazil* (Pittsburgh: University of Pittsburgh Press, 1991), pp. 70–92.

134 For the impact of this pattern on the democratization of the former communist states, see Hans-Ulrich Derlien and George J. Szablowski, eds, *Regime Transitions, Elites and Bureaucracies in Eastern Europe,* Special Issue of *Governance,* 6 (1993).

135 Paul Light, *op. cit.*

136 See, for example, Pierre Lalumiere, *L'inspection des finances* (Paris: Presses universitaires francaises, 1959).

137 Christopher Hood *et al., Regulating Inside Government* (Oxford: Oxford University Press, 2000).

138 Peri E. Arnold, *Making the Managerial Presidency: Comprehensive Reorganization Planning 1905–1980* (Princeton: Princeton University Press, 1986).

139 Geoffrey K. Fry, *Reforming the Civil Service: The Fulton Committee on the British Home Civil Service 1966–1968* (Edinburgh: University of Edinburgh Press, 1993).

140 Michael Atkinson, "Academics and Public Policy: The Royal Commission on the Economic Union and Development Prospects for Canada," *Governance,* 1 (1988), 205–9; *Reforming the Australian Public Service* (Canberra: Australian Government Publishing Service, December, 1983); Peter Wilenski, "Administrative Reform: General Principles and the Australian Experience," *Public Administration,* 64 (1986), 257–76.

141 See Arthur M. Schlesinger, *The Coming of the New Deal* (Boston: Houghton Mifflin, 1959), pp. 521–7.

142 Richard A. Chapman and J. R. Greenway, *The Dynamics of Administrative Reform* (London: Croom Helm, 1980).

143 Christopher Hood, "The Politics of Quangocide," *Policy and Politics,* 12 (1980), 247–66.

144 Richard Neustadt, *Presidential Power* (New York: John Wiley, 1960). For an updated discussion, see Matthew Robert Kerbel, *Beyond Persuasion: Organizational Efficiency and Presidential Power* (Albany: SUNY Press, 1993).

145 "Who is Responsible for Caring for the Poor?," *Congressional Digest,* 52 (August, 1973), 195–224.

146 See B. Guy Peters, "Government Reorganization: A Theoretical Analysis," *International Political Science Review* 13 (1992), 199–217.

147 See Lester M. Salamon, "The Question of Goals," in Peter Szanton, ed., *Federal Reorganization* (Chatham, NJ: Chatham House, 1981).

148 See *Prospects for the Line-Item Veto at the Federal Level: Lessons from the States* (Washington, DC: National Academy of Public Administration, 1988).

149 Sir Leo Pliatzky, *Getting and Spending* (Oxford: Basil Blackwell, 1982).

150 Nevil Johnson, *State and Government in the Federal Republic of Germany: The Executive at Work* (Oxford: Pergamon Press, 1983), p. 113.

151 See, for example, Kevin Theakston, *Junior Ministers in British Government* (Oxford: Basil Blackwell, 1987).

152 Hans-Ulrich Derlien, "Piecemeal Reforms in Germany: The Intelligence of Bureaucracy in a Decentralized Polity," in Johan P. Olsen and P. Guy Peters, eds, *Learning from Experience: The Lessons of Administrative Reform* (Pittsburgh: University of Pittsburgh Press, 1994).

153 William Plowden, "Providing Countervailing Analysis and Advice in a Career-Dominated Bureaucratic System: The British Experience, 1916–1988," in Colin Campbell and Margaret Jane Wyszomirski, eds, *Executive Leadership in Anglo-American Systems* (Pittsburgh: University of Pittsburgh Press, 1991).

154 B. Guy Peters and Anthony Barker, *Advising West European Government: Inquiries, Expertise and Public Policy* (Pittsburgh: University of Pittsburgh Press, 1993), especially articles by Bulmer, Muerswick and Mills.

155 See B. G. Peters, R. A. W. Rhodes and Vincent Wright, eds, *Administering the Summit* (London: Macmillan, 2000).

156 Andrew Hill, "When Bureaucrats are Brought to Book," *Financial Times,* March 2, 1992.

157 Patrick Birkinshaw, *Grievances, Remedies and the State* (London: Weidenfeld and Nicolson, 1986).

158 See Francoise Dreyfus and Francois d'Arcy, *Les institutions politiques et administratives de la France* (Paris: Economica, 1987).

159 Carl Friedrich, "Public Policy and the Nature of Administrative Responsibility"; Lennart Lundquist, *Byrakratisk etik* (Lund: Studentlitteratur, 1988).

160 Warren F. Ilchman, *Comparative Public Administration and the "Conventional Wisdom"* (Beverly Hills: Sage, 1971), pp. 35–8.

161 Samuel J. Eldersveld, V. Jagannadham and A. P. Barnabas, *The Citizen and Administrator in a Developing Democracy* (Glenview, IL: Scott, Foresman, 1968); Akira Nakamura and Osamu Koike, "Responsible Governance and Problems of Administrative Reform: Experiences of Developing Countries of Asia," *Governance,* 5 (1992), 484–92.

162 One interesting counter-attack on this view is Charles T. Goodsell, Jr, *The Case for Bureaucracy* (Chatham, NJ: Chatham House, 1994).

163 The obvious examples are the *grands corps* in France and the senior civil service in Japan. See, for example, Yves Meny, "A la jonction du politique et de l'administratif: Les hauts fonctionnaires," *Pouvoirs,* 40 (1987), 5–24.

164 See Nicholas Holgate, "Commission Fails to Find Recruits in FDA Grades," *FDA News* (May 1986), 4–5; Charles H. Levine and Rosslyn S. Kleeman, "The Quiet Crisis in the

American Public Service," in Patricia W. Ingraham and Donald F. Kettl, eds, *Agenda for Excellence: Public Service in America* (Chatham, NJ: Chatham House, 1992).

165   B. Guy Peters, "Morale in the Public Service: A Comparative Inquiry," *International Review of Administrative Sciences,* 57 (1991), 421–40.

166   Andrew Abbott, *The System of the Professions* (Chicago: University of Chicago Press, 1988).

167   J. W. Grove, *In Defense of Science: Science, Technology and Politics in Modern Society* (Toronto: University of Toronto Press, 1989); Malcolm Goggin, *Governing Science and Technology in a Democracy* (Knoxville, TN: University of Tennessee Press, 1986).

168   James W. Bjorkman, "Professionals in the Welfare State: Sociological Saviours or Political Pariahs?," *European Journal of Political Research,* 10 (1982), 407–28.

169   See Kenneth Kernaghan and O. P. Dwivedi, eds, *Ethics in the Public Service: Comparative Perspectives* (Brussels: International Institute of Administrative Sciences, 1983).

170   See, for example, Harry Smart, *Criticism and Public Rationality: Professional Rigidity and the Search for a Caring Government* (London: Routledge, 1991).

171   For a discussion of the differences from conventional accountability, see Patricia Day and Rudolf Klein, *Accountabilities* (London: Tavistock, 1987).

172   Raymond Vernon, "Linking Managers with Ministers: Dilemmas of State-Owned Enterprise," *Journal of Policy Analysis and Management,* 4 (1984), 39–55.

173   See G. Bouckaert, D. Ormond and B. Guy Peters, *Restructuring Central Government: The International Dimension* (Helsinki: Ministry of Finance, February, 2000).

174   Harvey Feigenbaum points out that French public corporations have, at times, engaged in policies very much at odds with the goals of the government as a whole. See his *The Politics of Public Enterprise: French Oil and the State* (Princeton: Princeton University Press, 1985).

175   Ben Ross Schneider, *Politics Within the State: Elite Bureaucrats and Industrial Policy in Brazil* (Pittsburgh: University of Pittsburgh Press, 1991).

176   John W. Sloan, *Public Policy in Latin America* (Pittsburgh: University of Pittsburgh Press, 1984), pp. 136–9.

177   V. V. Ramandham, *Privatization: A Global Perspective* (London: Routledge, 1993); Ralph M. Kramer, *Privatization in Four European Countries: A Comparative Study* (Armonk, NY: M. E. Sharpe, 1993).

178   Lester M. Salamon, *Beyond Privatization: The Tools of Government Action* (Washington, DC: Urban Institute Press, 1989).

179   For an excellent review, see H. Brinton Milward, "Nonprofit Contracting and the Hollow State," *Public Administration Review,* 54 (1994), 73–7; see also John Stewart, "The Limitation of Government By Contract," *Public Money and Management,* 13, 3 (1993), 7–12.

180   See p. 91.

181   Catie Meyer and Mitchell Norton, "Government Contract Fraud," *American Criminal Law Review,* 29 (1992), 429–84.

182   Robert Pear, "Federal Audit for Clinton Finds That Billions Are Being Wasted," *New York Times,* 8 January, 1993.

183   See Sar A. Levitan and Alexandra B. Noden, *Working for the Sovereign* (Baltimore: Johns Hopkins University Press, 1983).

184   For a negative view of the consequences of administrative federalism in Germany (and the European Community), see Fritz W. Scharpf, "The Joint Decision Trap: Lessons from German Federalism and European Integration," *Public Administration,* 66 (1988), 239–68.

185   See, for example, Brian W. Hogwood, "Restructuring Central Government: The 'Next Steps' Initiative in Britain," in Kjell Eliasson and Jan Kooiman, eds, *Managing Public Organizations,* 2nd edn (London: Sage, 1993).

186   Christopher Hood and Gunnar-Folke Schuppert, *Delivering Public Services in Western Europe* (London: Sage, 1988);

187   See pp. 39–42.

188   Peter Bachrach and M. Baratz, "The Two Faces of Power," *American Political Science Review,* 56 (1962), 947.

189   Graham T. Allison, *The Essence of Decision* (Boston: Little, Brown, 1971); Jeffrey L. Pressman and Aaron Wildavsky, *Implementation* (Berkeley: University of California Press, 1974).

Administrative reform

One of the many paradoxes in public administration is that, during an era in which much of the public considers government irrelevant and almost inherently ineffi- cient (see Chapter 2) their elective leaders have been spending an immense amount of time and energy reforming public administration. For the most part the goals of these reforms are the same as those expressed in the Gore Report (National Performance Review) in the United States: to make government work better and cost less.[1] The definition of "working better" may differ across govern- ments, and even across components of the same government. The basic point, however, is that if government is to be able to overcome the discontent and dis- trust of its citizens, it must find ways to become more efficient and effective in the processes of making and implementing policy. At the same time, however, there are also pressures for government to become more responsive to the public and to be more transparent in the way in which it makes decisions.

The goals of making government more efficient and effective are worthy in this period or any other, and there have been many attempts to achieve them. Some reforms have been sweeping changes, such as those implemented in the post-communist systems in Eastern Europe, as well as in many democra- tizing countries in the Third World.[2] Other reforms have been more incremen- tal, with many governments in the First World making relatively minor changes in the way they administer policies.[3] It is almost impossible, however, to find a political system that has not seriously examined its public administration and imposed some manner of change.[4] There are differences in the extent of change, and in the style of change being adopted, but there almost certainly has been change.

This chapter will consider the reform of public bureaucracies in a compara- tive perspective. We will do this by first discussing the *ideas* that have motivated reform during the past several decades, rather than by taking the question on a country by country, or even a policy area by area, basis. We will also look at the diffusion of relatively common ideas about change, and discuss what factors cause many countries to adopt reforms that appear, at least on the surface, to be of little relevance to the objective political and economic conditions being addressed. Indeed, we will question the efficacy of reform in many settings, and point to alternative strategies.

Ideas for reform

To some extent the word "reform" itself has a positive connotation so that simply promising to reform may be sufficient politically to motivate change. What distin- guished reform in the 1980s and 1990s, and reform going forward in the first decade of the twenty-first century, is that there are concepts and ideas that have informed and justified the changes. In some cases these ideas are used very explicitly to guide the reform, as when Margaret Thatcher used the ideas of the economist William Niskanen to justify her campaign for reform of the British civil service.[5] In most cases, however, the ideas are more implicit, although they can often be discerned through anything more than a cursory reading of reform docu- ments.

As well as being a set of ideas guiding reform, these ideas are not necessarily compatible, so that embarking on reforms motivated by one set of ideas may mean that adopting other types of changes, appealing though the other set of reforms may appear, will be counterproductive. Thus, the would-be reformer must be very careful about the intellectual provenance of any reforms adopted, as well as about their compatibility with the political and administrative institutions being reformed. A wide range of political and administrative leaders appear to favor change in the public sector, and to be interested in promoting administrative reform, but in practice it is more difficult than simply developing a political consensus for change. In this instance we should perhaps reverse the old adage and ask: "That is fine in practice but will it work in theory?"

NPM – *The market*

The dominant idea for changes adopted during the past two decades has been the market. The assumption is that the public sector would be more efficient and effective if it were more like the private sector. William Niskanen, the economist whose ideas were so favored by Mrs Thatcher, argued famously that bureau managers within government were aggressive entrepreneurs who attempt to maximize their own utilities.[6] Those bureau chiefs pursue their personal goals in the public sector by increasing the size of their agency and its budget. The monopoly character of those bureaus, and the asymmetry of information in favor of the bureaucracy, has enabled bureaus to disguise the true costs of production for their goods and services. This control of information enabled them to extract larger than necessary budgets from their "sponsors," the legislature.

The dominant diagnosis of what is wrong with government in the market approach is that most government services are monopolies, hence their managers have few incentives to become more efficient or to reveal its costs of production. Those monopolies range from services that are clearly public and perhaps never will be subject to real competition – defense and provision of benefits for the population – through services such as the post office that historically have been public but could easily be subjected to private competition. At the other extreme are services that, in many societies, are in the private sector but in the public sector in other countries – for example, airlines or telecommunications. Most government services fall between those two extremes, with some potential for being subjected to competition but also with some characteristics that argue for their remaining in the public sector and provided as a public monopoly. For example, postal service has long been a public sector activity but its traditional monopoly is now eroded by courier companies, private messengers, not to mention electronic communications.

In the extreme cases, introducing market-based reforms has meant privatizing activities that had been under the direct ownership and control of the public sector. In the former communist states of Eastern and Central Europe, privatization has meant a massive sell-off of industries, although in many cases finding buyers for the outmoded industrial plants left from the Soviet era has proved quite difficult.[7] A similar level of selling-off of public assets has occurred in some Third

World countries, as they encounter pressures from international organizations to adjust their economies to greater market involvement.[8] Most West European countries have also implemented extensive sell-offs of public enterprises, although the manner in which those privatizations have been implemented have varied substantially.[9] Somewhat paradoxically, privatizations in Western Europe have often involved less complete divestment than those in the former communist systems. In many cases governments have maintained some level of involvement in their former enterprises, if only a "golden share" that gives them some voting rights on the management board.

In addition to selling-off publicly-owned corporations and returning those industries to the control of private sector managers, governments have also sought to implement market ideals by separating the implementation of policy from its formulation. Also, the implementation structures are being broken down so that, when possible, each organization becomes responsible for implementing only a single program. The logic of this disaggregation of responsibility for implementation is that the presence of a number of functions within a single organization results in those activities cross-subsidizing each other. If the activities are separated, sponsors can tell more easily the costs of each and make better decisions about their funding and better assess their efficiency.

In addition to the structural changes in the public sector, the introduction of market reforms has meant using market ideas to change the operations of government itself. This can be seen perhaps most clearly in the management of public sector personnel.[10] We have discussed the nature of civil service systems in an earlier chapter, but although these personnel systems represent the triumph of one style of good government, they also remove the employees from the same pressures and incentives found for employees in the private sector. So, for example, the traditional pay system based upon grading of positions and seniority is being replaced with "pay for performance" and other private sector techniques.[11] Similarly, public sector positions are no longer the preserve of career public service but rather are now open to more overt competition, and positions in government are advertised much as private jobs would be.[12]

Even when governments cannot divest themselves of firms and services, they have been finding ways of introducing market thinking into policy making. The market has been introduced in part through the concept of internal markets, or attempting to make people within the public sector act as if they actually were in a competitive situation. For example, the National Health Service in the United Kingdom, and health programs in some other countries as well, have made a split between "purchasers" and "providers."[13] For example, in health care, a regional health authority may be the purchaser and hospitals the providers. Hospitals may then prepare bids for the "business" of the health authority in a number of different areas, e.g. varieties of surgery. This may be only a facsimile of a market, given that there is a limited opportunity to enter and all the money involved is tax money. This arrangement, however, may still be able to instill some sense of competition into making policy.

As well as making policy through internal markets, the market model also advocates allowing the public to make more of their own choices about public policy. Given the basic indictment of public monopolies inherent in the market model, policies that permit individual citizens to decide what services they want from government are logically central to the market reforms.[14] One standard policy remedy depending upon the market is the voucher.[15] The concept of the voucher is that, instead of providing a public service such as education as a monopoly, government may decide to provide consumers of those services with a voucher which they can use to choose among a number of alternative providers. For example, government may continue to provide education but parents would be able to choose to use their vouchers for their local public school, another public school, or for a variety of private sector providers. Thus, the citizen becomes a real consumer making choices, providing, of course, that these private opportunities actually exist.

The voucher also has obvious disadvantages for the public bureaucracy. The shift to private sector provision of services means that there is less need for public employees. It is not surprising, therefore, that public sector unions tend to oppose this reform, often disguising self-interest in terms of the interests of the clients. Further, there may be some potential problems for clients and even for the private sector if the voucher becomes a standard means of delivering public services. For the clients, there are major information demands – knowing what the options are and evaluating them is not easy for most citizens. Likewise, the citizen in the role of taxpayer may find that he or she is paying for two school systems or for two housing sectors, both operating at a sub-optimal level.[16]

The market also offers a somewhat different answer to the classic administrative problem of accountability than does the conventional pattern of operation in this field (see Chapter 8). As well as Niskanen's ideas about monopoly and maximization, another strand of academic thinking in the market approach to reform is the principal-agent model.[17] In this view organizations can be seen as a series of relationships between principals and agents, the latter assumed to be acting on the commands of the former. The difference between this view and conventional thinking about hierarchy is that agents are assumed to be self-interested and will attempt to "shirk" – get paid for compliance while simultaneously pursuing their own goals. Therefore, contracts can be seen as a means of attempting to control shirking, and as the principal means of ensuring the accountability of public organizations.

The idea of using the market and competition is the most successful in the current round of reforms, but they are certainly not universally accepted and there are numerous strong critiques of its dominance.[18] Perhaps the most important critique of the market model is normative, arguing that government is *not* the same as the private sector, so that any attempt to substitute competition and to permit (or encourage) different outcomes for citizens, threatens the values of equality that have been central to the public sector. Further, services such as health care may be too important to tamper with and create artificial markets that often appear to replace medical personnel with accountants to manage the complex interactions within them.

Even if the delivery of services is not the same as in the public sector, might not management be the same? Empirically it is not clear that market incentives always work in the public sector, and civil servants may be interested in promoting values other than money in their jobs, something that is not recognized readily by the market model.[19] Further, normatively it is not clear that the public is best served by public employees who are motivated primarily by financial rewards. Many public programs may actually serve the public better if they are inefficient and if they absorb a great deal of personnel time and energy. Further, the old-fashioned values of service and commitment to the public interest may well produce a better set of public programs than a commitment to personal profit.

Participation – Participative

The market model is obviously based on economic perspectives. The second model of reform – participation – is a much more political model. The diagnosis of the problems of the public sector here is that government is excessively hierarchical. It is thought that there is a need for participation, in the first instance, within the organizations themselves. The assumption of the participatory reformers is that government organizations would work better if the members of those structures were provided the opportunity to be intimately involved with the decisions of their organizations. Further, advocates of the participatory model would also provide these employees with more opportunities to make decisions on their own.

Like the market, the participatory model is actually an old management idea, going back at least to the "human relations" approach to organizations.[20] These ideas of participation are, in turn, based on even more basic assumptions about human nature. In particular, the participatory model assumes that individuals are interested in their jobs and, given the opportunity, will do the best job possible. Although employees certainly want to be paid a decent wage, money is not the only means of motivating people to do their job well – involvement and having an interesting job are potentially even more important. The creation of values and commitment among employees is particularly important in the public sector, and public employees (especially at the top of the organizational pyramids) are often strongly motivated by sincere commitments to the programs they are implementing, as well as to the general concept of public service. Many senior civil servants may, in fact, be insulted that their political masters assume that they are interested primarily in the financial rewards of the job.

As well as fostering the involvement of public employees, the participatory approach to reforming the public sector also emphasizes greater involvement of clients, and of the public more generally, in the design and implementation of the programs. The assumption of these reforms is that the public is also interested in exerting some control over the public sector and are willing to invest time and energy in doing so. It is difficult for the public to have such influence in the conventional bureaucratic structures of government so that reforms are then required to produce those opportunities for participation. These can range from simple voting in referenda through public hearings and discussions to the actual management of public programs by their clients (see pp. 160–2).

One of the major recommendations that the participatory approach to reform makes about structure is to reduce the hierarchy within government organizations. For example, the National Performance Review (the Gore Commission) in the United States has attempted to reduce the number of hierarchical levels from top to bottom in federal agencies and in this process also to remove layers of control over lower-echelon workers.[21] Although justified by the ideology of participation and empowerment, this structural change is made possible in large part by the development of information technologies that enable senior managers to monitor and control those lower-echelon workers with much less immediate supervision.[22] While flattening organizations does not foster per se more internal participation, concepts such as "reinvention" and Total Quality Management do place a premium on the role of employees and their ideas about how to run the organizations.

The quality movement is but one of many attempts to use participative mechanisms as a way to involve workers, and also as a means for managing those same workers. On the one hand these devices can be a crucial means of both involving the workers and bringing forward their ideas to improve the performance of the organization. On the other hand, the mechanisms of the quality movement have the potential for manipulating those same workers. It may offer them only the semblance of participation in return for their acquiescence in, or active support for, the programs of the agency. Further, managers may not really understand the extent to which the participation they are offering is less than genuine and may believe that they are indeed being open and participatory.

Participation is being extended to making policy as well as implementation. Again, this participation is usually argued to include both the clients of the program as well as the program's employees. If lower echelons are "empowered"[23] to make more of their own decisions and can exercise greater discretion, then they clearly must become more important in making policy. In addition, mechanisms such as TQM and the reinvention process functioning as a central component of the National Performance Review in the United States, all assume that lower-level employees of the agency will be more closely involved in shaping policy than in the traditional government bureaucracy.[24]

Empowering clients is being achieved in a number of ways. The market model advocated choice for citizens and clients, and the participation model does the same, although the forms of choice are rather different. In the market model that choice is to be achieved through an economic mechanism, while in the participatory approach that choice is be achieved through more political means. For example in education, rather than relying on a voucher and the opportunity to purchase the service, the participation model assumes that the parents will have to participate in committees or boards that may manage the school directly. In Denmark, for example, most local schools are in essence managed by the parents and teachers, albeit within the guidelines of national educational authorities. This is a more time consuming approach to choice, and one that depends upon collective choice, not just an individual's decision about how to spend the voucher.

The idea of the "citizen's charter" is another way of permitting citizens, in their role as clients, to participate more in the delivery of services. This is basically a form of enforcing accountability, but enumerating a set of quality standards that a citizen has a right to expect, and then using those to empower the citizens against the bureaucracy. While the redress of grievances implied by the charters is only *ex post facto,* complaints can be used as a means of guiding managers in efforts to improve services, and in rewarding and punishing employees. This idea first came to wide-scale notice in the United Kingdom, but has now been spread to a large number of countries, including the United States, France, New Zealand and Argentina.

The market model has its problems, and the same is true for the participatory approach to reforming the public sector. We have already noted that participation may be inauthentic, with the result that clients or employees may believe they can shape policy when, in fact, they cannot. This may be true for legal as well as managerial reasons. In addition, attempts to empower both clients and lower-echelon employees may produce conflict between these groups that have, in many cases, contradictory interests in the program.[25] Further, the clients of the program and the general public may also have different interests, especially as clients tend to want programs expanded and the general public often wants to contain programs and the associated taxation.

Deregulation — *deregulated*

Another strand of thinking about the reform of the public sector argues that what is wrong with government is that the people in the public sector are constrained by rules and regulations that prevent them from doing their jobs efficiently and effectively. These rules represent the outcomes of previous rounds of reform, but now have (at least in the eyes of this school of reformers) become dysfunctional. For example, creating civil service systems in many countries was a long and arduous political process, requiring overcoming political leaders who wanted to continue to use public office as a means of rewarding their political allies. As important as the civil service has been in creating probity in public office, it is now felt by many reformers to be an impediment to good management.[26] A manager in the civil service system usually cannot hire, fire and compensate employees as he or she would like. Likewise, purchasing regulations were adopted in order to ensure that political and administrative officials did not use government contracts to enrich their friends and political supporters. These rules now appear to prevent government from getting the cheapest prices for goods, and may also slow the procurement process.[27]

The obvious solution for a problem of too many rules is to eliminate some of those rules, and this is indeed the course of the reforms being implemented in many countries. For example, in the United States the rules that had guided recruitment and retention of public employees through the civil service are now de-emphasized and organizations are allowed substantial freedom in the personnel process. Likewise, managers are now free to purchase goods and services up to a very high price without having to go through a competitive bidding process, providing they can justify the choices made.[28] The budget process is also being deregulated in many countries, with "bulk" or "frame" budgeting replacing traditional line-item budgeting (see pp. 280–1). This increase in managerial freedom is designed to "let the managers manage," one of the phrases often used as a justification for administrative reforms of this type.

Managers in this reforming view of government are also more than just managers; they are also, to some extent, policy makers. The assumption is that they know as much, and probably more, about what should be done in their policy area as politicians, and therefore should be permitted to function as policy entrepreneurs in their own right.[29] The hero in the deregulatory conception of reforming government is the public manager. He or she is presumed to be capable of managing well, and also should be an expert in the policy being administered. This is a substantial range of expectations for the manager, but perhaps little more than conventionally ministers have been expected to be able to do.[30] Indeed, the public manager has a distinct advantage in not having to run for office, and therefore not having that range of political responsibilities that can be extremely time consuming. Further, the manager is freed from having to think (at least very much) about the electoral consequences of decisions and, therefore, may be able to press for the technically correct, rather than the popular, decisions.

Given the emphasis on the role of the manager in deregulatory reforms, it should be no surprise that these officials should also be the central focus of accountability in this version of public sector reform. In a deregulated government, ministers might become less responsible for the day-to-day actions of their ministry than they have been, at least in the conventional Westminster model of ministerial responsibility.[31] Also, the focus of accountability might be expected to shift toward the average performance of a government organization rather than exceptional events that can be used to embarrass the minister and the government of the day. Thus, accountability itself becomes more managerial rather than political in the managerial model of governing that is emerging in some societies.

Flexible government

A final, and perhaps less fully developed, approach to administrative reform can be termed "flexible government."[32] The problem with government identified in this approach to reform is that their organizations are excessively stable so that they institutionalize patterns of governing that may have been functional at one time but which are not capable of responding to changes in the socio-economic environment. Further, the stable and rather tightly-defined tasks assigned to ministries in governments makes coordination of services around new problems more difficult than it might be in a less institutionalized system of governing.

Creating flexible government is an intriguing challenge for conventional government structures. The political and budgetary incentives of government have been for organizations to capture emerging problems and identify them as their own policy "property." Likewise, interest groups that may motivate the policy process also tend to have narrow definitions of issues and problems and may not like the flexibility implied by a more responsive and coordinated government. Politicians and citizens may also be skeptical about more adaptable government arrangements given that a flexible system may make monitoring and enforcing accountability in government even more difficult than in conventional structures where those tasks are already difficult enough.

Summary

Administrative reform is now informed by a number of ideas about how government should and could work, as well as about the failings of what had been the conventional model of government and administration. Each of the several models of change discussed above has a certain amount of validity, and has clear implications. The problem with implementing those ideas is that many implementers have been less clear about, and dedicated to, the concepts and their implications than have the academic and political advocates of change. That is, many implementers of reform have assumed that they could simply choose among a set of structural and procedural changes that appear to have worked elsewhere and then make them work in whatever combination they chose.

I would argue, however, that many of these ideas and programs are incompatible, and picking one reform may preclude implementing others effectively. This rather random borrowing of ideas and programs has been the pattern in the past, but it appears less viable with the current set of reforms. This difference from the past is, in large part, because of the stronger ideological and even intellectual[33] content of the contemporary reforms. For example, the underlying importance of individualism in the market model may be incompatible with the more collective view in the participatory model. Likewise, the market model is, to some extent, incompatible with the emphasis on management and activity in the deregulatory model of change.

Specific reforms

The above discussion contained some examples of change in government over the past several decades, but may have appeared rather abstract in places. We will now proceed to discuss some of the specific reform initiatives that have been implemented during that same time period. We do not have the space or time here to detail all the numerous types of reform and to assess their success in all the settings in which they have been implemented. Therefore, we will concentrate on some of the principal types of change, especially those that have been implemented in more than one country.

Agencies and deconcentration

One of the principal structural reforms that has been implemented has been to break up integrated ministerial departments of government, such as those that have characterized the United Kingdom. The ministerial structures made policy as well as implementing it, and had a relatively clear and common hierarchy from top to bottom. The model that has been widely favored to replace that style of organizing has been termed the "agency model," meaning that implementation activities were to be moved into relatively autonomous agencies while the policy-making activities remained within a small cabinet department. Further, the employees of the agencies may (albeit not necessarily) cease to be civil servants in the conventional sense, especially the employees toward the apex of the agencies.

The logic of the agency system is to deconcentrate the role of government as an implementer and to permit those agencies to do the job in a more business-like manner. The assumption is that if an agency has only the single function to perform, and is held closely accountable for performing that activity, it will do the job better than if the same activity is buried within a large multi-purpose organization. Further, separating some activities from the ministries may make those activities more subject to competition from private organizations or perhaps from other parts of the public sector. For example, some information technology agencies have been created with no stable budget; they are expected to earn their money from contracts with the other agencies. Those other agencies can, of course, take their business elsewhere (other agencies or the private sector) if the service is superior or the costs are lower.

The most famous example of using the agency model has been "Next Steps" in the United Kingdom.[34] Since this project was initiated more than a decade ago, approximately 75 percent of central government employment in the UK has been moved into agencies. These organizations are headed by chief executives on fixed-term contracts, rather than conventional career civil servants, and those executives are subject to being removed prior to the end of their contracts if their performance is not satisfactory. Although less extensive, this pattern has been tried in other countries. For example, Canada has created a limited number of "special operating agencies" and some of the Australian and New Zealand reforms have elements of the agency model. Japan now is adopting a limited form of the agency model.[35] In other cases the change went in something of the opposite direction, with formerly nationalized industries being converted into agency structures in Finland.

Interestingly, at the same time that many governments have been breaking up their integrated ministry structures and forming agencies, other governments have been creating some versions of those structures. This has been true of Sweden, among others, that had served as the principal prototype for the agency model adopted in the United Kingdom. Sweden is retaining the basic agency form that it has had for centuries but, at the same time, is attempting to tie those agencies more closely to the ministries and to more closely link their decision making and their patterns of policy to the priorities of the government.[36] Also, in Denmark some ministries (notably education) have gone back and forth between agencies and more centralized structures.[37]

Personnel management

As noted above, one of the major manifestions of reform has been in the area of managing public sector personnel. This is perhaps natural since personnel costs make up the bulk of the operating costs of government.[38] In addition, some reforms have had as central components attempts to address the complaints that personnel have about working in government. On the other hand, some reforms also address complaints that citizens have about the ways in which they are treated by government employees; as we have been stressing throughout this book, the public bureaucracy is the principal point of contact between government and its citizens so that, if this relationship can be improved the confidence and trust of the public may be enhanced.

Although there is no shortage of interest in reforming personnel management, there is certainly no common approach to achieving this end. As already noted, implementing programs of pay for performance and performance management more generally are crucial elements of the market approach to reform. Their assumption is that making rewards more competitive will make the employees perform better. The deregulators want to remove many of the controls now constraining top management, but appear less concerned with measuring and rewarding the performance of the lower echelons of government. The managerialist approach assumes that effective management will take care of any problems arising in that echelon of government structures. The participatory reformers have been more concerned with employees at the bottom of organizations, appearing to assume that if these employees become effectively involved in their organizations, then those public entities will themselves function more effectively.

Thus, public personnel are definitely important in the process of reforming government, but we need to be clear about which personnel are being considered, and what assumptions are being made about the nature of public employees and about how they relate to government. Indeed, some of the assumptions and recommendations about public employees are almost directly contradictory. For example, the market reforms tend to individualize the relationship of the employees to the organization, while the participatory reforms are attempting to build teams and enhance cooperation within those organizations. Unless a clear linkage is made between group performance and individual performance (and rewards) these strategies cannot be pursued simultaneously with any realistic expectation of success.[39]

The public sector will always have a significant number of employees. Technological change is reducing the need for employees to perform many of the routine tasks that have been the foundation of public sector employment, but there will still be thousands if not millions of people in government. Given this fact, deciding how best to manage these personnel is crucial for making government "work better and cost less." Personnel policies also point to some of the trade-offs that are embedded in reform. That is, placing pressures on the employees to perform through monetary incentives may *not*, in fact, create the caring and effective government that many other reforms demand. In this area, as in all others, there are important policy choices to be made, and choosing one horn of a dilemma may preclude other subsequent choices.

Consumerizing government

Another of the common strategies for change in the public sector is to attempt to make government more friendly to the "consumer" and to institutionalize ideas about "serving the customer" in public services. The consumer notion is perhaps strongest in the market interpretations of the problems of government. If possible, the market model would like to make citizens real consumers and provide them with real options about how to receive the services – education, health care, housing, etc. – that they demand from the public sector. For example, the idea of vouchers and providing citizens with genuine opportunities to choose among publicly and privately provided services is an important component of market thinking about the public sector.[40]

The advocates of a more participatory government also have an interest in serving the customer and creating greater choice for citizens in public policies. Not surprisingly, the interpretation of the concept of "serving the customer" in the participatory model differs from that of the market model. In particular, while the market model sees choice in terms of individual consumers making their choices of programs, the participatory model is more interested in how clients and consumers as a group can make choices about the nature of the services they are offered. Thus, consumerization here means the capacity for citizens to be involved directly in a political and administrative process that make decisions about the services. This notion of consumerization also involves their capacity to make decisions collectively about those services. In some ways the participatory version of the idea is not as clearly a case of consumerization as the market, given that the individual cannot make a choice without convincing others that this choice is the correct one.

One major example of these participatory reforms is found in a number of countries that have adopted changes in management of their educational system. There, changes permit parents and teachers together to decide on the nature of the education to be offered on a school-by-school basis, rather than depending on a more centralized school board to make those decisions.[41] Similar arrangements are being instituted in housing and other local government services.[42] These modes of participation have perhaps even more problems of equal capacity to be effective participants that all forms of participation beyond voting have. That is, getting what one wants in a political process involves the ability to speak effectively, organize and persuade others and, increasingly, also involves more technological skills such as the ability to use the Internet. These skills are not evenly spread across the population but tend to be concentrated in the more affluent and the better educated.[43]

These two rather antithetical versions of the meaning of consumer involvement in government do not by any means exhaust the range of possible interpretations of the term. For example, one analysis of the consumerization of public service produced some 16 alternative interpretations. These alternatives were a product of thinking about the level of activity expected of the participants, and the degree to which their participation could affect the nature of the policy in question. In this analysis market and participatory techniques tended to be intermixed, although in general the participatory mechanisms tended to have a somewhat more direct influence over policy than did market-based instruments.

When government attempts to apply the consumer idea to its programs, there is a basic question about who the customers are for a program. Identifying the client appears simple for a program such as education or social welfare, or even economic programs. The real client becomes more ambiguous for a program such as prisons. On the one hand the public is the client, expecting to be protected against the illegal activities of the incarcerated. On the other hand, the prisoners have the right to be treated properly and should have some ways to ensure that they are treated properly, even if they are being confined. Likewise, the public has the right to be treated well by tax officials but yet the ultimate clients may be the public as a whole.[44] Thus, any simple idea about serving the customer may not take into account the range of customers that must be served, and the possibly competing nature of the services that need to be provided.

Despite all the various meanings of consumerization, there is a central normative question that is almost certainly more important for the nature of the public service. This question is whether the public sector is better advised thinking about the public as consumers or as citizens. There are two elements to this question. The first is that thinking about the consumer may only be concerned with the economic and service recipient nature of the public's involvement with government, while that relationship is actually more complex and multi-dimensional. In addition, focussing on the consumer role tends to undervalue the role of the citizen with its political basis, and with the political and civil rights that citizenship implies. Thus, an emphasis on consumers may de-emphasize the essential public nature of the public sector and tends to assume that all that citizens want is to consume public services.

Accountability

Finally, all versions of reform are argued to be directed at enhancing the transparency and accountability of the public sector, although the meanings of these terms, and consequently the nature of the reforms themselves, are markedly different in each of the models. Indeed, it could be argued that the net effect of some of reforms is actually to reduce the level of accountability, at least as that term has been conventionally understood (see Chapter 8). Some of the very features of government that have been the targets of reform, for example the linkage of administration with political authority, have also been crucial to maintaining control over discretion in government.[45]

The reform ideologies discussed above have somewhat different conceptions of accountability than does the conventional political means of exercising control over the bureaucracy. The market model assumes that, very much as its advocates do for other problems in government, the creation of competition and the availability of alternatives to conventional monopoly services will be sufficient to control discretion. Further, positive incentives for outstanding performance and the ability to employ sanctions (e.g. dismissal) for poor performance will handle any problems with individual performance in the bureaucracy. In this conception of how to manage government, hierarchical controls and political supervision are more impediments to exercising control than they are necessary to it.

Another element of accountability built into the market perspective is the use of performance targets. The assumption of this approach to accountability is that the creation of measurable indicators and making managers responsible for achieving those targets will make government work better. In some ways this is a superior form of accountability to the "shame and blame" concept of traditional political accountability. The focus on performance is an attempt to measure average performance, rather than identify any embarrassing exceptions to what might be overall adequate or even exceptional realizations of goals.[46] On the other hand, however, this approach may make accountability too mechanical and not attuned to the political as well as the managerial dimensions of what government does. If goals are not reached, is it necessarily the fault of the manager, or is it inadequate funding, or unrealistic expectations?[47]

The participatory reforms, again as might be expected, tend to rely upon more populist mechanisms for accountability. In these reforms the dominant assumption is that clients and the public in general should be capable of signaling when they are not satisfied with the services being provided. Similarly, public employees themselves are expected to monitor the performance of their organizations and make recommendations about how to make those organizations perform better. While these ideas are commendable from a democratic perspective, they may also be somewhat naive. First, many clients of public organizations are often dependent upon the programs for their basic livelihood and may fear making any serious complaints. Further, many programs may not have clients that are so clearly identifiable (see above) so that there will not be the continuous monitoring assumed. Finally, too much reliance on the good intentions and professionalism of public employees may leave the public with few protections against malfeasance and incompetence.[48]

The deregulatory reformers emphasize the role of the public manager in ensuring accountability. For advocates of this approach, placing responsibility in the hands of capable managers and then assessing the performance of those managers is the most effective form of accountability. There is some of the same interest in establishing performance targets and using those as a surrogate for other forms of oversight of government. In this way deregulatory reforms are rather similar to some aspects of the market approach. The principal difference is that, rather than the emphasis being spread broadly throughout the public sector, it was focussed on the manager. In addition, management rather than competition and more decentralized mechanisms are thought to be the central element of achieving accountability.

The above discussion of accountability has been directed at issues common in the industrialized democracies. In other countries the accountability issues, and hence some of the motivations for reform, are quite different. In particular, the accountability issues in countries emerging from communist political systems, and most less-developed countries, are concerned with corruption and the improper use of public office for personal gain.[49] Corruption may be difficult to root out in these regimes given the limited respect for the public sector, the very low wages paid to employees in many governments and the dominance of familial and clientelistic ties in society.[50] There are strong international pressures for reforms of this type, coming from donor organizations (governmental and non-governmental) as well as coming internally from some new political leaders. Still there is a very long way to go before corruption can be eliminated.

Accountability is a central concern for public administration, no matter how it is structured. The conventional forms of accountability depend upon the use of political institutions or actors. The reformed versions of accountability discussed above rely more on setting performance targets or on the capability of holding managers to account for their actions and those of their organizations. These mechanisms may be effective, but they do tend to keep accountability within the bureaucracy rather than using external actors. Further, these forms of accountability do not depend upon the internalized values of civil servants, or on their acceptance of law.

The politics of administrative reform

One obvious question, after having been through all the ideas and all the types of reform, was why governments should invest all this time and energy in the pursuit of reform. After all, the previous history of reorganization and reform had not been such a success as to create great optimism for the would-be reformer.[51] Even when reforms were actually implemented there was little evidence of their producing genuine changes in the performance of government. Indeed, there is more than a little evidence that reforms can create outcomes quite contrary to those intended by their advocates.

Why reform?

Reforms have been justified on a number of grounds, ranging from economics and the costs of programs to partisan politics and a search for electoral advantage. Few reforms have a single cause and many represent the confluence of political opportunity, the spread of ideas about reform, and economic crises. Still, we can discuss some of the roots of reform and the ways in which they work through the political process.

Costs and efficiency. One of the principal justifications for adopting reforms is that government costs too much. This is true for government costs in general, and also true for efficiency, or the cost for producing each unit of output. For example, the large-scale reform process in New Zealand was prompted in part by the country "hitting the wall" in international economics and were faced with finding some means of addressing that problem.[52] Likewise, the large-scale reforms in many of the post-communist systems have been prompted by the need to rebuild their economies and make them competitive in the international market. Going along with the overall economic problems are particular problems of the economics of the public sector and the costs that taxes and public debt place on the economy.

The above having been said, there are cases in which real economic problems have produced little or no administrative response – Germany in the 1990s was argued to be a case in point for this type, although that characterization is also disputed.[53] There are also cases in which (relative) economic success stories and governments that are already very low cost in comparative terms have been associated with very high levels of reform – Australia appears to be a clear case here.[54] Thus, as noted above, economic conditions have to be perceived as important, and must be seen in conjunction with a set of ideas that can promise to produce the positive changes desired.

Quality. As well as being expensive, government services are often perceived to be of poor quality. This may be a function of the same lack of competition that Niskanen argued was associated with excessive costs.[55] Lacking any incentives to improve the programs they deliver, government organizations may simply continue to deliver services in any way they want. The public often believe that they are poorly treated by public servants and that the programs delivering their services are themselves poorly designed. In some cases those concerns are well justified, and the quality of programs has been allowed to deteriorate. In these cases the costs of public programs may have been the dominant concern, lending to a quality decline.[56]

We have already noted that performance measurement and the use of targets is one of the dominant features of contemporary reforms. The focus on performance is not an entirely new set of ideas; the program budgeting ideas of the 1960s and 1970s also relied on quantifiable measures and linking those indicators with the budgetary process.[57] Although not new ideas, the ideas are now being implemented in a more aggressive manner than in the past, and there is greater emphasis on the quality being delivered to clients. In addition, the customer focus featuring in contemporary reforms does tend to emphasize that measure of quality and performance as much as more objective forms.

The employees. The employees of the public sector also constitute a major reason for reform. This basis of reform may, however, mean different things to different people. One reason for reform is that the employees of the public sector do not have sufficient power and influence over policy, and are demotivated by traditional patterns of management in the public sector. As noted above, the participatory reforms provide those employees with more control over their own jobs, as well as a greater role in making decisions about the policies of the organization. The assumption is that these reforms should make public sector jobs more attractive to prospective employees, as well as making their organizations more effective.

Other critics of the existing role of the public bureaucracy argue that career public employees have excessive influence over policy and that political leaders elected to determine policies are often thwarted by their own bureaucrats. Thus, another approach to reforming the public sector has been to reduce the power of senior public services and to place politicians more clearly in charge of policy. For example, some of the reforms initiated by the Thatcher government in the United Kingdom were designed to reduce the power of the "Sir Humphrey's" in the public sector and put politicians more clearly in charge.[58]

Structure. One of the most common reasons for reform in the past, and a continuing source of contemporary changes, is the desire to get the structure of government "right" – this has most commonly been referred to as reorganization. At one time there was an assumption that there was one best way to organize, both individual organizations and the public sector as a whole.[59] That certainty about the scientific basis of organizational structure has largely vanished, but the desire to change structure to make government perform better remains alive and actively pursued by political and administrative leaders.

One of the common patterns of reorganization has been to put similar organizations and activities together. This is a logical approach to thinking about organizing government, permitting some synergy among related activities and perhaps also reducing total administrative costs. The problem is that relatively few government programs have only a single activity or a single purpose. Therefore, most organizations could be allied with several other groups of organizations. For example, the United States Coast Guard has at various times been in the Department of the Treasury, the Department of Defense, and currently is in the Department of Transportation.

Another reason for reforming the structure of government is to improve coordination of the numerous activities of the public sector. Government generally works reasonably well vertically, linking interests in society with the agencies and ministries that serve and protect those interests; ministries of agriculture are linked with interest groups and also perhaps with relevant committees in the legislature. Government is not nearly so good at structuring interactions across policy areas, or at producing coherent goals and programs; those same ministries of agriculture are rarely made to confront the interests of environmentalists. Therefore, reorganization is sometimes used as a means of attempting to improve coordination and coherence.

Changing policy. Lester Salamon has argued that using reorganization as a means of changing policy is more likely to be successful than is using it in an attempt to produce efficiency.[60] Salamon's assumption was that by changing the patterns of communication and interaction experienced by an organization, there could be changes in public policy, while any efficiency gains from reform were likely to be short-lived. For example, if we continue the example developed above, moving the Coast Guard from Treasury to Transportation means that the commandant is likely to receive more memos about marine safety and fewer about interdicting smugglers, although his or her organization will continue to perform both functions. The priorities of the organization would be expected to be changed in response to this change in location within government.

The market reformers may have even more fundamental policy goals when pursuing reform. They will want to change as many policies as possible into market-based policies, meaning that the programs will be faced with competition and the participants will have some choices among alternative providers of the service. Likewise, the market reformers may want to institute some form of price mechanism where possible as a means of both reducing the tax price of the program and of revealing the real level of public demand for the service. Thus, in the 1980s and 1990s a number of programs that had been "free"[61] began to charge fees to cover all or part of their costs.

Transparency and accountability. As we have already mentioned several times, one of several reasons for pressing for reform is a desire to enhance the transparency and accountability of the public sector. These terms are important in managing government and defining its relationship to the remainder of the public sector, but their meaning can be elusive and can also be simply a component of political rhetoric associated with different views of the public sector. The assumption of many advocates of reform, while expressing a variety of different ideas about reform, is that the traditional instruments of accountability in the public sector were no longer functioning as they should.

Interestingly, one common response to the reform process has been to reassert the importance of older styles of accountability and to attempt to revive those forms of control. This has been especially true in some Westminster governments in which the theory of accountability has virtual constitutional status. It has also been true for some legalistic administrative systems in which it has been felt to be crucial to return to a stricter form of legal accountability and constraint on the actions of civil servants. These conservative reactions to problems of accountability have, however, been largely overwhelmed by the desire to create new and more popular forms of imposing the will of the public on the bureaucracy.

Politics.   Finally, in the process of administrative reform, politics is trumps. Although there may be any number of good objective reasons for reforming, unless there is the political will to change the administrative system there probably will be little change. We have already demonstrated that the public sector is often considered a problem by much of the population. Therefore, it is good politics to assail the bureaucracy in electoral campaigns and to make some attempt to demonstrate that something is being done to control and to devalue the bureaucracy once elected to office.

While there is some political gain to be had from castigating the bureaucracy, ironically there may be little to be gained politically from actually investing substantial political capital in changing public administration. Even the large-scale reforms implemented during the past several decades appear to have been little noticed by the public and, hence, may not have created any substantial electoral advantage for the politicians that pushed for them.[62] The public in many countries appears likely to assume that any changes in the bureaucracy are largely cosmetic, rather than more genuine transformations of the manner in which public services will be delivered. Therefore, politicians often have a short attention span when it comes to reforming the bureaucracy and initial enthusiasm may be followed, once in office, by apparent loss of interest in change.

Not all politics is partisan, electoral politics. In any government there is also a good deal of organizational politics involved in administrative reform. On the one hand central agencies[63] are often crucial for promoting reform and encouraging (or coercing) other components of the public sector to reform. On the other hand, those organizations are themselves often the most unreformed parts of government. Thus, there is often a good deal of jostling over just what are the meanings of certain reforms, and how they should be implemented. In all this bureaucratic politics, one of the apparent outcomes has been that power over programs has become more centralized in the hands of central agencies during a period in which decentralization is thought to be a dominant value. This is but one of many paradoxical outcomes in the process of reforming the public sector.[64]

Conclusion

Administrative reform has been a central activity of governments during the past several decades. It is not, however, an undifferentiated activity, and has assumed several different forms in the different political settings in which it has occurred. Those differences are in some ways related to the different intellectual roots of the reforms. The differences in interpretations may also be related to differences in the political and administrative traditions of the countries within which they are being implemented. Thus, the meanings of reforms are constructed politically and culturally and the same nominal changes in the public sector may in actual practice mean very different things. These differences are especially pronounced between the industrialized countries and the emerging democracies of Central and Eastern Europe, and then again with the Third World countries. While some of the same reforms being adopted in the wealthier countries are also being implemented in the less-developed, their meaning may be different and they may be avoiding, or even exacerbating, problems of accountability and control in these systems.

While there are crucial differences in the interpretations of reform ideas in these administrative systems, there are (as we have already noted) also some remarkable similarities in the reforms themselves. Many of the same changes are being implemented in almost all these countries, albeit in different manners and at different speeds, and even for different reasons. The importance for comparative research is that we can use the different outcomes of these common stimuli as means of looking at how different political and administrative systems respond to demands change, and respond to the need to interpret a set of policy and management ideas.

The good news is that reforms have been creating a whole new laboratory for understanding public administration around the world. One useful way of understanding political and administrative processes comparatively is to observe the ways in which various countries respond to the common stimuli for change. There have been such common stimuli in the reform process of the past several decades, as ideas about what constitutes good public management have been spread around the world both autonomously and through the action of agents such as international organizations and consultants. These ideas have been understood differently, and implemented differently, when they have come into contact with the different administrative cultures, so that a common language of change masks much greater complexity and variation.

Notes

1   National Performance Review, *Creating a Government That Works Better and Costs Less* (The Gore Report) (Washington, DC: Government Printing Office, March, 1993).

2   See Tony Verhiejen and D. Coombes, eds, *Innovations in Public Management* (Cheltenham: Edward Elgar).

3   It is often argued, for example, that Germany and other administrative systems sharing the German *Rechtstaat* approach to administration have changed relatively little in response to the spate of reform in the rest of the world. It does appear true that there have not been the sweeping reform programs found in many countries. On the other hand, however,

there has been a succession of smaller reforms that have amounted to significant changes in the system. See E. Schroter and H. Wollmann, "Public Sector Reforms in Germany: Whence and Where," *Haillonen Tutmikus,* 3 (1997), 184–200.

4   See, for example, M. M. Khan, *Administrative Reform in Bangladesh* (New Delhi: South Asian Publishers, 1999).

5   See Peter Hennessy, *Whitehall* (New York: The Free Press, 1987).

6   William Niskanen, *Bureaucracy and Representative Government* (Chicago: Aldine/Atherton, 1971).

7   Atilla Agh, "Paradoxes of Reform in Eastern and Central Europe," in J. J. Hesse, C. Hood and B. G. Peters, *Paradoxes of Administrative Reform* (Berlin: Nomos, 2000).

8   E. F. Rosenbaum, Frank Bonker and Hans-Jurgen Wagener, *Privatization and the Emergence of Markets* (New York: St. Martin's Press, 2000).

9   See Vincent Wright, *Privatization in Western Europe*; L. Parotti and V. Wright, *Privatization Policies* (Cheltenham: Edward Elgar, 2000).

10 S. Horton and D. Farnham, eds, *Human Resource Flexibilities in the Public Service: International Comparisons* (London: Macmillan, 1999).

11 See Organization for Economic Cooperation and Development, *Private Pay for Public Work: Pay-for-Performance for Public Sector Managers* (Paris: OECD, 1993).

12 In some systems this has been true for some time, but even in those that have had a closed career structure, there is now competition for a range of posts.

13 M. Jerome-Forget, J. White and J. M. Wiener, *Health Care Reform Through Internal Markets* (Montreal: Institute for Research on Public Policy, 1995).

14 Of course, the advocates of these reforms assume that choice is enhanced if there are both public and private sector alternatives from which to choose.

15 E. Steurle, "Vouchers," in L. M. Salamon, ed., *Handbook of Policy Instruments* (New York: Oxford University Press, 2000).

16 See E. Steurle, "Vouchers," in Lester M. Salamon, ed., *Handbook of Policy Instruments* (New York: Oxford University Press, 2001).

17 See Murray Horn, *The Political Economy of Public Administration* (Cambridge: Cambridge University Press, 1995); J. Brehm and S. Gates, *Working, Shirking and Sabotage: Bureaucratic Response to a Democratic Public* (Ann Arbor: University of Michigan Press, 1999).

18 Peter Self, *Government by the Market?* (Boulder, CO: Westview, 1995); James G. March and Johan P. Olsen, *Democratic Governance* (New York: Free Press, 1995).

19 See Patrician W. Ingraham, "Of Pigs and Pokes and Policy Diffusion," *Public Administration Review.*

20 Rensis Likert, *The Human Organization: Its Management and Value* (New York: McGraw-Hill, 1967; Chris Argyris, *Increasing Leadership Effectiveness* (New York: Wiley, 1976).

21 Most of the positions lost in federal organizations have been middle managers whose jobs were to look over the shoulders of the "street level bureaucrats" who actually do the work of government.

22 On empowerment, see B. Guy Peters and Jon Pierre, "Citizens Versus the New Public Manager: The Problem of Mutual Empowerment," *Administration and Society*, 22 (2000), 9–28.

23 Empowerment is one of the central battle cries of the advocates of participation. The problem is that, by extending empowerment in so many directions, they may engender conflict as well as participation.

24 The mechanisms for creating this involvement in making policy often are not so well-developed as are those for implementation. If anything, "democratic" means such public hearings may give more of a role to the general public than to the members of an organization.

25 Peters and Pierre, "Citizens Versus the New Public Manager," *op. cit.*

26 See Constance Horner, "Deregulating the Federal Service: Is the Time Right?, in J. J. DiIulio, ed., *Deregulating the Public Service* (Washington, DC: The Brookings Institution, 1994).

27 See Steven Kelman, "Deregulating Federal Procurement: Nothing to Fear But Discretion

Itself?," in J. J. DiIulio, ed., *Deregulating the Public Service: Can Government Be Improved?* (Washington, DC: The Brookings Institution, 1994).

28 *ibid.*

29 R. Raamamurti, "Public Entrepreneurs: Who They Are and How They Operate," *California Management Review*, 28, 142–58.

30 See Richard Rose, *The Problem of Party Government* (London: Macmillan, 1974).

31 See Peter Aucoin and Ralph Heintzmann, "New Dimensions of Public Accountability," in B. Guy Peters and Donald J. Savoie, eds, *Governance in the 21st Century* (Montreal: McGill/Queens University Press, 2000).

32 S. E. Bleecker, "The Virtual Organization," *The Futurist*, 28 (1994), 9–12; D. Chisholm, *Coordination Without Hierarchy* (Berkeley: University of California Press, 1988).

33 As noted, these models and especially the market conception do have a clear connection to the academic literature on government and administration.

34 Chancellor of the Duchy of Lancaster, *Next Steps: Agencies in Government,* 1997 Report (London: HMSO, 1998).

35 Jong S. Jun and Hiromi Muto, "The Politics of Administrative Reform in Japan: More Strategies, Less Progress, *International Review of Administrative Sciences*, 64 (1998), 195–202.

36 S. Wilks, "Sweden," in N. Flynn and F. Strehl, eds, *Public Sector Management in Europe* (London: Prentice-Hall, 1996).

37 A.-S. Krarup, "Administrative Reform in Danish Central Government," Paper prepared for Administrative Reform Seminar, University of Aarhus, Aarhus, Denmark, Fall, 1999.

38 That is, the costs of operating government itself as opposed to the money that may be distributed to citizens through programs.

39 Linking individual and organizational performance is another of the philosopher's stones in public (and private) management.

40 Steurle, *op. cit.*

41 M. Vander Weele, *Reclaiming Our Schools: The Battle Over Chicago School Reform* (Chicago: Loyola University Press, 1994).

42 E. Sorenson, "Democracy and Empowerment," *Public Administration*, 75 (1997), 553–67.

43 J. Hoff, "Medbergskab, brugerrolle og makt," in J. Andersen, ed., *Medbergsmakt* (Kobenhavn: Sistema, 1993), pp. 75–106.

44 The treatment of the public by tax officials has been a concern of reforms of the Internal Revenue Service in the United States.

45 See P. Aucoin and R. Heintzman, *op. cit.*

46 See B. Guy Peters, *The Future of Governing*, 2nd edn (Lawrence, KS: University Press of Kansas, 2001).

47 For an interesting exposition of these difficulties in light of the National Health Service in Britain, see Melanie Phillips, "Think the NHS is Sick? They'll Make it Sicker," *The Sunday Times,* 17 October, 1999.

48 The ancient adage of "qui custodiet ipsos custodes" applies very easily here.

49 Of course, there is also a good deal of corruption in the developed democracies. See D. Della Porta and Yves Meny, *Democracy and Corruption in Europe* (London: Pinter, 1997).

50 Vito Tanzi, *Policies, Institutions and the Dark Side of Economics* (Cheltenham: Edward Elgar, 2000).

51 Per Laegreid and Paul G. Roness, "Administrative Reforms as Organized Attention," in M. Egeberg and P. Laegreid, eds, *Organizing Political Institutions: Essays for Johan P. Olsen* (Oslo: Scandinavian University Press, 1999).

52 J. Boston, "The Theoretical Underpinnings of State Restructuring in New Zealand," in J. Boston *et al.*, eds, *Reshaping the State* (Auckland: Oxford University Press, 1991).

53 But see Eckhard Schroter, "Bureaucrats and Politicians in Germany," in J. Pierre and B. Guy Peters, eds, *Bureaucrats and Politicians in Administrative Reform* (London: Routledge, 2001).

54 John Halligan, "Australia and New Zealand," in J. J. Hesse, C. Hood and B. G. Peters, eds, *Paradoxes of Public Reform* (Berlin: Decker and Humblot, 2001).

55   William Niskanen, *Bureaucracy and Representative Government* (Chicago: Aldine/Atherton, 1971).

56   One example might be the National Health Service in the United Kingdom. Health costs as a percentage of GDP are the lowest among the developed countries, but health outcomes, e.g. survival rates for cancer victims, are also much poorer than in other countries.

57   See Chapter 7.

58   See Christopher Hood, "De-Sir Humphreying the." The reference is to the character in the BBC television series, *Yes, Minister*.

59   For the classic critique see Herbert A. Simon, *Administrative Behavior* (New York: Free Press, 1947).

60   Lester Salamon, "Rethinking Public Management: Third Party Government and the Changing Forms of Government Action," *Public Policy*, 29 (1981), 255–75.

61   There had always been a cost but it had been borne by taxpayers not the consumer.

62   The possible exception to this generalization is Mrs Thatcher in the United Kingdom. See Christopher Hood, "Of Shocks and Long-Tenure," in J. P. Olsen and B. G. Peters, eds, *Lessons from Experience: Learning About Administrative Reform* (Oslo: Scandinavian University Press, 1996).

63   Central agencies are organizations that control other organizations in government, and generally are closely related to the chief executive. See Colin Campbell and George Szablowski, *Superbureaucrats: Central Agencies in Comparative Perspective* (Toronto: Macmillan of Canada, 1974).

64   For a discussion of a range of paradoxes, see J. J. Hesse, C. Hood and B. G. Peters, eds, *The Paradoxes of Administrative Reform* (Berlin: Decker and Humblot).

Chapter 10

Public administration in the twenty-first century

Administering public programs has never been an easy task. The very nature of government programs – their diffuse goals, their unmeasurable or even unidentifiable benefits and their political nature – make effective administration difficult. But the administration of public programs became even more difficult during the 1990s, and problems continue to mount as we move into the twenty-first century. This increasing difficulty of effective public management is a function of several different aspects of the economic, social and political environments within which administration is being conducted. In addition, changes in managerial ideas and ideologies have generated serious challenges for public managers accustomed to hierarchical management, a Weberian-style bureaucracy and political forms of accountability.

Perhaps the most important factor affecting administration is the real – or perceived – scarcity of resources available to the public sector. The "go-go" days of the 1960s economy are now long past, and even the confused economic picture of the 1970s may now appear more hospitable to political leaders having to make decisions about revenues and expenditures at the beginning of the new century. What is most disconcerting about the economic problems of the 1980s is that, unlike the case in other recessions during the post-war period, there was apparent agreement that there was no short-term solution and there was likely to be an extended period of slow or non-existent economic growth. Despite periodic ups and downs, this period of uncertainty has already extended a decade and a half, and there is no end in sight.

The absolute (low) level of growth is not the only economic problem impacting administration in the twenty-first century. Even if growth returns to levels achieved earlier, it appears certain that levels of employment growth will not move in parallel with growth of productivity. This has been particularly the case for blue-collar occupations but is increasingly true for white-collar jobs as well. This means that a large portion of the workforce in industrialized countries will have to rethink their economic futures and be prepared to adjust rapidly if they want to continue employment. It also means that the public sector will have to become more involved in adult education, job training, etc., and also have to rethink social programs such as social security premised upon stable employment. For the less-developed countries there will be renewed competition from the industrialized countries which may become willing to reduce salaries and benefits in their economies in order to compete with lower wage countries.

It is not just the state of the economy that makes administration difficult. Citizens have become increasingly wary of the power of the "bureaucracy" over their lives, and even in countries with histories of strong and relatively benevolent government (Sweden, the United Kingdom) there has been some reaction against bureaucracy and administration. In other, very heavily bureaucratized systems (Cuba, the People's Republic of China), desire for more rapid economic progress has dictated some substantial debureaucratization.[1] This popular resistance to public organizations is, at least in part, a function of the failures of past policies and programs, which in turn produce skepticism about the efficacy of any "new" programs. The weakness of economic management is chief among these failures, but it is also found in a number of social and education programs that have been deemed to be failures.[2]

Third, the increasingly centrifugal nature of government and its growing complexity make administration more difficult. Public organizations are tied directly to private sector organizations, so citizens may wonder whether the public sector is indeed acting in the "public interest." Furthermore, within the public sector itself, there are so many organizations that affect the administration of a single program that inter-organizational politics complicate the administration of what is apparently a simple program.[3] Further, there is an increasing dependence upon private actors to deliver public services, and this has accentuated the centrifugal forces already in existence.

Finally, just as organizations within government are beset by strong pressures from the private sector, so too are national governments beset by international forces.[4] Governments, that at one time could exert substantial control over their domestic economic and social systems, find that their control in the 1990s is limited by a more pervasive international environment. This situation will call for the development of organizations and policy instruments that are more flexible and adaptive than those usually encountered in the public sector. In addition, the targets of policies may have to change in order to match the increasing mobility of the factors of production, especially capital, in a globalized economy. Thus, if government wants to affect the location of a business, the appropriate target may be the citizens of the community rather than the company itself.

Scarcity and public administration

For most of the countries in the world, scarcity is a basic and continuing fact of life, while for the majority of Western countries it is a more recent phenomenon. The long-term scarcity facing almost all Third World countries creates massive problems for public program administrators in those countries. The uncertainty of the budgeting and planning process, combined with the simple fact that there are not enough resources to meet legitimate needs of the population, makes trying to manage these economies and societies very difficult for even the most capable administrator.[5]

For the Western world the economic constraints were imposed after several decades of rapid and sustained economic growth.[6] This environmental change has required an adjustment in policies and policy-making styles premised on that economic growth continuing. For political leaders, scarcity has meant that instead of only distributing good news, they must take at least a part of the blame for the poor shape of economies. For public administrators, scarcity has meant adjusting the internal functioning of their organization, their relationships with their program's clients and their expectations about the future of their programs. Administrators who once would make a name for themselves by expanding their programs now have to try to protect their images (and careers) by restricting growth or even by careful pruning.

One fundamental factor that has changed is that economic growth cannot be relied upon to fund ever-increasing salaries for civil servants. Money may not be the only – or even the best – means of motivating civil servants, but it certainly does not hurt.[7] When the real incomes of civil servants begin to decline – as they have done in many countries – then it is likely that morale will also decline.[8] The

psycho factor

decline in morale may be even more pronounced when the civil servants must also deliver programs providing reduced real benefits to clients. It is quite probable that a feeling of failure and alienation from the program, and even from the political system more broadly, will be generated by such a combination of reductions. Those workers will have been denied both the direct rewards of their salary and the indirect rewards of providing services to clients in ways that they and the clients would both prefer. Consequently, the (very difficult) task of administrative leaders is to provide alternative sources of satisfaction for workers. As we will discuss below, this to some extent has been attempted through changes in the management practices of programs.

The denial of some of the satisfactions of employment is not made any easier by the threats of cutbacks and terminations of organizations that became more common during the 1990s than perhaps even during the 1980s. It was conventional to assume that government organizations were immortal, but the events of the 1980s do not support such a contention.[9] The fundamental cultural change that has occurred in most industrialized countries, as well as many others, has made the activities of the public sector more suspect. In the United States the Reagan administration had discussed the termination of the newly-created Departments of Education and Energy, as well as a number of lesser agencies. In the United Kingdom, a round of "quango bashing" has resulted in the elimination of several hundred small quasi-governmental bodies.[10] Even in Sweden, the paragon of the welfare state and Big Government, organizations have been terminated and cut back severely. In virtually all countries one of the reactions of government to increasing demands for expenditures and decreasing real revenues has been to reduce the number of employees or eliminate whole organizations. The difficult task for managers, therefore, is to manage these cutbacks in manners that produce minimal disruption for remaining organizations, workers and clients. This is especially important given that government experiences functional termination much less frequently than program or organizational termination. That is, even though some employees and organizations may be dispensed with, government will continue to provide some of the same types of services, and mechanisms must be found for consolidating or reorganizing the implementation of the programs without completely upsetting the routines of government. As noted above, one of the most important methods for achieving these ends is "privatizing" public programs and using a variety of alternative service delivery mechanisms to achieve public ends.

Charles Levine offered some guidance for "cutback management" in the public sector.[11] A first decision that any manager must make is whether to resist cutbacks or only to smooth the transition from the more affluent to the less affluent mode of service delivery. These strategies may be quite different, for the rigidity that may be generated in a pitched battle against retrenchment may make any subsequent cutbacks more difficult or may lead to the total elimination of the program rather than just a cutback. Likewise, a manager must decide what the sources of his or her difficulties are. Strategies will be very thorny if the source of the difficulties is entirely economic, as compared with problems that stem from changes in the demand for the service being rendered, or in the political support available to the organization. In the case of economic decline, it may be more productive to attempt to resist the change and displace greater cuts onto other organizations, whereas when there is a decline in support more may be gained by making the transition as painless as possible. Neither of these options may be palatable for managers bred on years of growth and expansion, but they may be the only options open.

Thus during the 1980s and 1990s management became, and will continue to be, the task of attempting to produce positive results with meager resources. Doing this requires extremely capable managers, but dwindling resources and the declining competitive position of public sector salaries may keep those managers from being attracted to government. Government appears to be in a double bind – those who believe that it is inefficient may limit its ability to gain greater efficiency. For example, the attacks of the Reagan administration on the federal bureaucracy in the United States has been argued to make government less efficient despite the pleas for efficiency.[12]

Increasing challenges to government and administration

Not only does the economic environment generate difficulties for administrators, but citizens themselves do not represent the pliant population for their governors that they once did. This increasing difficulty experienced by administrators appears related to a number of factors. When faced with those factors, they have the options of "exit, voice, or loyalty."[13] That is, they can attempt to escape from the impact of government, they can express their disapproval of action, or they may merely accept what is happening to them.

One factor that causes citizens to consider these three options is the magnitude of contemporary government. Some citizens feel themselves disadvantaged by the growth of government and, consequently, do not feel like accepting the dictates of that government. Such a reaction may be specific, as individuals refuse to honor certain types of laws and regulations, such as tax laws; or it may be more general, as some citizens attempt to withdraw from the monetized, regulated economy to a simpler life.[14] Even in the absence of these extreme reactions, citizens may simply be less willing to accept laws and regulations without question, and may try to avoid rather than evade taxation and other laws perceived to be intrusive.

Associated with the size of government is its increasing complexity and the interactions of many laws and regulations. An individual in a modern society is affected by a range of policies, some of which may be contradictory or mutually cancelling. The number of individual bureaucracies making rules about any industry or any type of behavior may be so large and so effectively uncoordinated that the individual feels that, if government does not know what it wants, then why should the citizen attempt to figure it out for them? This is often seen most clearly for social policies and their relationship with tax policies in which these policies may be uncoordinated and self-defeating.[15]

Also, citizens have seen it all before. An administrator attempting to implement a "new" program may find that, in fact, it is really a program that has been tried previously – and often failed previously. Frequently governments appear to rediscover solutions that they have previously rejected, especially when there are changes in governments and the institutional memory is at least partially lost.[16] Even when there is not a return to a rejected solution, a number of changes in a policy area may generate cynicism and an unwillingness to accept any programmatic changes. This problem has been especially pronounced in social policy, where change after change has been advertised as *the* solution to the problems of the less fortunate, but where each program is actually just another milepost in a long journey attempting to solve those problems.

Finally, many policies simply have not worked or have not produced the intended effects.[17] Further, many that have worked may appear inefficient and excessively clumsy. In fairness, government is often called upon to solve the problems for which the private sector has already been proven inadequate, but there are still a number of manifest failures and inefficiencies. Many of the complaints directed against regulations as mechanisms for producing certain desired benefits of the society have been that direct prohibition of activities may not be as efficient as incentives or tax-based mechanisms. Consequently, several alternatives to direct public intervention have been proposed for government intervention.

One of the most commonly mentioned alternatives to direct intervention is replacement with tax incentives, especially in the area of environmental regulation. Instead of prohibiting pollution or setting maximum allowable levels, firms would be taxed according to the amount of pollution that they emitted. This threat of taxation would provide the firms with an incentive to clean up their plants. Further, given that more efficient firms could better afford to pay the effluent taxation, they could become more profitable relative to less efficient firms, and the utilization of resources in the economy as a whole would be improved.

A more extreme approach to the problem of perceived governmental inefficiency and clumsiness would be to reprivatize the public activities in question.[18] That is, instead of having government administer the program at all, it could be returned to the private sector, albeit with some public control and regulation. In principle, almost all public sector programs could be provided through the private sector, and some reprivatization is already well under way in the United States and other countries. Even some traditional defining functions of government, such as fire and police protection, could be – and have been – provided by the private sector.[19] Some extreme positions hold that even items such as public streets should be sold off to private firms. In practice, an increasing number of local governments are requiring private property developers to install all infrastructure (roads, water, sewers, etc.) for their new projects rather than depending upon government provision. There is no guarantee, however, that this system would satisfy more than the ideological preferences of such advocates. As many public services involve the granting of monopoly rights – for example, a street – there would be no more competition than there was when the service was in the public sector. Further, many of the inefficiencies found in the delivery of government services may be functions of large-scale organization per se as much as functions of large-scale organization in the public sector.

But it is not just the preferences of citizens that have changed over the decades. The attitudes of employees – again whether working in the public or the private sector – are different than they were prior to the 1980s. Large organizations have traditionally depended upon the willingness of employees to accept the authority of their organizational superiors, and to accept the correctness of the rules and procedures of the organization. Most workers are no longer willing to accept this degree of control in an unquestioning fashion. Rules and orders now require explanation, and workers expect to be involved in the making of policy that affects their work. This involvement, or "empowerment," of workers may produce improved performance in the long run, since it provides employees with more of a commitment to the goals and procedures within the organization. This has been especially true in Japanese organizations, and to a somewhat lesser extent in Scandinavian organizations. But the process of adjustment for managers who have not been accustomed to dealing with employees in this manner may be difficult. Management has ceased to be conducted by authority and is increasingly a process of explanation and discussion. Interestingly, this is true even in public sector organizations that have been most oriented by authority, such as the military.

Complexity in administration

The point above concerning privatization of public functions relates to another salient feature of administration in the 1980s that makes the job of the public sector manager more difficult. This is the increasing complexity of the "implementation structures" within which those managers manage. One of the aspects of that complexity is the increasing degree of fusion between the public and private sectors. Another aspect is the degree of complexity that exists within the public sector itself. Traditional liberal social thought has made the distinction between state and society, with the former serving as the embodiment of the legitimate authority of the latter, so long as basic contractual or natural rights were fulfilled.[20] In the 1980s, the arbitrary distinction between state and society does not have much validity in the majority of industrialized societies. Similarly, extensive differentiation of state institutions may not have occurred in most less-industrialized societies[21] and certainly is not true of the few remaining socialist governments.

In the first place, the public sector is making increasing use of the resources and capabilities of the private sector. A large number of public programs are implemented by private organizations. These range from the announcements made by cabin personnel in airplanes requiring passengers to buckle their seat belts to professional organizations deciding who should and should not be given the right to practice the profession. A more complex pattern of private enforcement of public policies is the wide-scale utilization of agricultural organizations to implement public agricultural policy.[22] The implementation of these laws typically involves a local organization dividing among its members an acreage allocation determined centrally. Finally, private organizations are used to provide services that might otherwise be directly provided by public employees. For example, in the United Kingdom the government contracts with the Law Society to provide legal services to the population. Governments contract to obtain a variety of goods and services, but contracts such as the above are significantly different. They enable – and require – an organization to act in the name of government in order to implement a law. Government by contract is government at one remove, and the problems of accountability and control central to the understanding of public administration become even more pronounced (see Chapter 8). Similar problems of accountability arise when government must depend upon partnership arrangements with the private sector to provide important public services. For example, economic development is increasingly undertaken by joint arrangements between government and private actors, with potential repercussions for the resultant direction of development.

Second, not only does government adopt private methods for the achievement of its purposes, but the private sector has become quite adept at utilizing the public sector for its purposes. We have already discussed some of the means by which this occurs. In general, the division of government into a number of "sub-governments," a feature of almost all developed societies, means that it is difficult for elected leaders to exercise coordination and control over policy as a whole. The expertise located within each of these segments of government, combined with the strong political linkages between organizations in the private sector and those in the public sector, makes the exercise of coordination and control even more difficult. Government in a bureaucratic age has become government pursuing a number of ends – some of them contradictory – rather than government that speaks with a unified voice attempting to achieve only a limited range of objectives.[23]

Finally, government itself has become increasingly complex. Some of this complexity stems from the fact that government is doing so many more things than it was doing even at the end of World War II. And even when an organization is created in an area that government has allegedly not been involved in previously, it will likely have some relationships with existing organizations. And given the political environment in which public organizations are created, there is an even greater probability of overlap and duplication. Dozens of federal organizations are involved to some degree in health policy in the United States, and there is not any political system that has been capable of resolving problems of duplication and overlapping jurisdictions. Public administration has never been the simple command system assumed by some traditional treatments of the problem – for example, that of Woodrow Wilson – but the level of complexity has been increasing significantly. The "implementation structures" that a public organization now faces include a number of central agencies, other line agencies providing complementary (or perhaps competing) services and private organizations. As the complexity and the size of the public sector have increased, central organizations such as those concerned with budgeting, personnel and other areas have, in turn, attempted to impose greater central control. Likewise, as scarcity has become a more important feature of contemporary administration, other organizations are more prone to compete for resources. This all amounts to a much more complex system of administration and of policy making than would have been found even in the 1970s.

Managing in the new millennium

Management in the public sector has never been easy, but it became even more difficult in the 1990s. Scarcity, changing social and cultural values, and increasing organizational and interorganizational complexity have all made it more difficult than previously to accomplish assigned tasks through the public sector. Paradoxically, however, it becomes even more important for those in government to manage their operations effectively. Scarcity, as well as imposing constraints on managers, makes their skills more valuable. There is the simple need to get the most out of each dollar, pound, or rupee of public money. Some of the managerial changes of the 1980s and 1990s were designed to allow managers to manage, but even those changes may not value sufficiently the skills and dedication that public managers bring to their jobs.

As has been noted, one of the many responses to the demands for greater efficiency and effectiveness in government has been the attempt to reprivatize many public services. However, in the long run this may have the effect of reducing the effectiveness of government, with little short-term economic savings. As government loses control over functions considered to be public, it may lose the ability to effectively direct the society; it may lose the steering ability that constitutes the root of the word government. Short-term cost effectiveness may be limited, for many of the monopoly characteristics of public provision may be present in private provision, and this limited saving may be purchased at the expense of long-term alienation and ineffectiveness. Government may lose the ability simply to govern by authority and may have to resort to intervention by more obtrusive and more expensive mechanisms.

The "market model" of governance implied in the above paragraph is but one of several contending models of running government that were being advocated in the mid-1990s. It is the most commonly advocated alternative to the status quo, but by no means the only alternative available.[24] For example, an alternative that is ideologically at odds with the market model, but also contains some similar specific elements, could be labelled the "participatory model."[25] Rather than having administrative decisions and structures dominated by economic considerations, this perspective on good management emphasizes the involvement of the lower echelons of organizations and perhaps of the clients of the organization. While both this model and the market model are at odds with traditional hierarchical management, the former decentralizes to enforce competition while the latter decentralizes to maximize participation and involvement of those who are ordinarily disenfranchised in large, complex organizations.

A third alternative to the status quo in managing public organizations is to focus on the possibilities of creating more flexible organizations and a more flexible workforce. Hiring people permanently through civil service systems, and making government organizations virtually permanent through law and budgets, builds in a number of potential diseconomies. These might be remedied by creating temporary and more informal organizations and relying more upon part-time and temporary public employees. This is certainly the trend in the private sector and there may be some reasons for government to follow suit. This model of reorganization may be at once more efficient and more responsive to changing public needs than the existing more or less permanent structures. There will, of course, be problems in following this model of management, such as motivating temporary employees, but there are advantages that may offset the disadvantages.

A final alternative model might be called "deregulating government." The principal idea here is that many of the dysfunctions we have identified in public organizations are a function of the rules and regulations imposed upon them by other actors, usually political institutions. For example, much of the reason that public personnel systems are difficult to manage is that legislatures have added layer after layer of protections and rules. In part, the dysfunctions of public administration have become a self-fulfilling prophecy in which the perceived need to control inefficient and ineffective organizations actually contributes to their inefficiency. If that diagnosis is correct then government can be improved by trusting in the good sense and appropriate values of public employees and let them get on with their tasks. This has some inklings of the "let the managers manage" approach of the market model but rather than assuming that the private sector is the source of good management this model assumes that public employees have the capacity and the dedication to do the job properly.

Summary

Public administration faces a huge array of challenges in the new century. In addition to coping with scarcity, managers will have to confront the declining morale of workers and perhaps of their clients. Arguably, changes in organizational formats and managerial styles have not kept pace with changes in society. Employment in large-scale organizations is more common in the economy but is less satisfying for many – if not most – workers. Managers may therefore be in the position of trying to obtain improved performance from disaffected workers in order to provide reduced services to disgruntled clients. Organizational forms that involve, or "empower" workers and clients to a greater extent have been experimented with but continue to be experimental, and there remain a number of organizational problems simply in motivating and rewarding employees adequately. Public management in the new century, in almost any country one would want to consider, may require extraordinary patience and skills. And, more important, it may require an extraordinary conviction that the quality of life can be enhanced by collective action. It will further require the conviction that administration is not the "mere application of the law'" but rather is a vital component of the governmental process with a tremendous – and often untapped – potential for assisting in the creation of a better economy and society.

Notes

1   There is also a desire for increased human rights in these regimes but these pressures have not be as important as economic pressures in producing liberalization.
2   To some extent the degree of failure is a product of ideology and social construction as well as of real failure. Given the measurement problems encountered in government programs it is difficult to say when and why programs do fail. See Martin Cave, Maurice Kogan and Robert Smith, *Output and Performance Measurement in Government* (London: Jessica Kingsley, 1990).

3   Benny Hjern and David O. Porter, "Implementation Structures: A New Unit of Administrative Analysis," *Organisation Studies*, 3 (1981), 211–24.

4   See Donald J. Savoie, "Globalization and Governance," in D. Savoie and B. Guy Peters, *Governance in a Changing Environment* (Montreal: McGill/Queens University Press, 1995).

5   Naomi Caiden and Aaron Wildavsky, *Planning and Budgeting in Poor Countries* (New York: John Wiley & Sons, 1974).

6   See Richard Rose and B. Guy Peters, *Can Government Go Bankrupt?* (New York: Basic Books, 1978).

7   See Chapter 4.

8   Christopher Hood and B. Guy Peters, eds, *The Rewards of High Public Office* (London: Sage, 1994).

9   Herbert Kaufman, *Are Government Organizations Immortal?* (Washington, DC: The Brookings Institution, 1974).

10   Christopher Hood, "Axeperson, Spare that Quango...," in C. Hood and Maurice Wright, *Big Government in Hard Times* (Oxford: Martin Robertson, 1981).

11   Charles H. Levine, "Organizational Decline and Cutback Management," *Public Administration Review*, 38 (1978), 316–25; Andrew Dunsire and Christopher Hood, *Cutback Management in Public Bureaucracies* (Cambridge: Cambridge University Press, 1989).

12   Robert F. Durant, *The Administrative Presidency Revisited* (Albany: State University of New York Press, 1992).

13   Albert O. Hirschman, *Exit, Voice and Loyalty* (Cambridge: Harvard University Press, 1970).

14   B. Guy Peters, *The Politics of Taxation* (Oxford: Basil Blackwell, 1992), pp. 135–47.

15   Hermione Parker, *Instead of the Dole: An Enquiry into the Integration of the Tax and Benefit System* (London: Routledge, 1989).

16   Brian W. Hogwood and B. Guy Peters, *Policy Dynamics* (Brighton: Wheatsheaf, 1983), pp. 261–4. On the importance of institutional memory, see Johan P. Olsen and B. Guy Peters, *Learning from Experience* (1996).

17   Sam D. Sieber, *Fatal Remedies: The Ironies of Social Intervention* (New York: Plenum, 1981); Brian W. Hogwood and B. Guy Peters, *The Pathology of Public Policy* (Oxford: Oxford University Press, 1985).

18   E. S. Savas, *Privatization: Key to Better Government* (Chatham, NJ: Chatham House, 1987).

19   Richard Rose, "On the Priorities of Government," *European Journal of Political Research*, 4 (1976), 247–89.

20   P. E. Kraemer, *The Societal State* (Meppel, The Netherlands: J. A. Boom, 1966);

21   To the extent that the institutions have differentiated, the societal interests may remain dominant. See Joel S. Migdal, *Strong Societies and Weak States* (Princeton: Princeton University Press, 1988).

22   John T. S. Keeler, "Corporatism and Official Union Hegemony: The Case of French Agricultural Syndicalism," in *Organizing Interests in Western Europe*, ed. Suzanne D. Berger (Cambridge: Cambridge University Press, 1981); Clemens Pedersen and P. H. Knudsen, "Landbrugets organisationen andelsbevaegelsen," in Landsbrugsradet, *Landbruget i Danmark* (Copenhagen: Landsbrugsradet, 1977), pp. 99–139.

23   B. Guy Peters, "Public Bureaucracy and Public Policy," in Douglas E. Ashford, ed., *History and Context in Comparative Public Policy* (Pittsburgh: University of Pittsburgh Press, 1992).

24   On the *status quo*, or the *status quo ante*, see John Stewart and Kieron Walsh, "Change in the Management of Public Services," *Public Administration*, 70 (1992), 499–518.

25   For a general discussion of these models, see B. Guy Peters, *Models for Governing in the 1990s* (Ottawa: Canadian Centre for Management Development, 1994).

Index

Printed in the United States
207179BV00003B/1-46/A

9 780415 194778